THE EIGHTEENTH-CENTURY
REVOLUTION IN SPAIN

The
Eighteenth-Century
Revolution in
Spain

By RICHARD HERR

PRINCETON, NEW JERSEY
PRINCETON UNIVERSITY PRESS

To Louis Gottschalk

PREFACE

THE story of this book begins with a conversation with Professor Louis Gottschalk in the spring of 1950. I was eager to start my dissertation; and if my own inclination had prevailed, the topic would have been some aspect of French history bearing on the Revolution. Mr. Gottschalk turned my gaze instead toward the fields across the Pyrenees, far greener for the historian of this period than the close-cropped ones in France. The resistance to Napoleon was perhaps the only event in Spanish history I could then have called to mind between the last of the Habsburgs and the Spanish-American War, but with his encouragement I undertook to investigate the beginnings of Spanish liberalism.

Only work in Spain could make the study profitable, and only financial generosity could get me to Spain. The University of Chicago's Catherine Cleveland Fellowship, together with a few remaining months of eligibility under the seldom sufficiently appreciated "G.I. Bill," enabled me to spend an academic year in Madrid and Paris. When this year proved more easily exhausted than the materials for research, a second grant from Chicago—the Cleo Hearon Fellowship—and help from my father kept me in the libraries and archives of Madrid for another winter.

No cooperation could be more cordial than that given me by the directors of those institutions: the Biblioteca Nacional, the Ateneo de Madrid, the Academia de la Historia, the Biblioteca Municipal, the Hemeroteca Municipal, the Servicio Histórico Militar, and the Archivo Histórico Nacional. Without hesitation they opened their collections to me, and with spontaneous good will their staffs helped beyond the call of their regulations in producing the books, pamphlets, and manuscripts that I desired. Don Luis Morales Oliver, director of the Biblioteca Nacional, consented to my investigating the welter of uncatalogued pamphlets (normally closed to the public) in the Sala de Varios. Here many afternoons were spent with the assistance of the attendant in opening creaking cupboard doors, dusting and going through

vii

Preface

bundles of broadsides and pamphlets labelled simply "Fernando VII" and "Carlos IV." All these men were worthy artisans of good will for their country, for they made those years of research a time for later nostalgia. The kind ladies who helped me in the Archives des Affaires étrangères similarly strengthened my affection for France.

I remember believing at the outset that liberalism had come to Spain in the baggage wagons of Napoleon. It did not take long to learn that there were roots deep in the years before 1808 for the beliefs of the men who supported the "intruder king," Joseph Bonaparte, as well as of the deputies to the Cortes of Cadiz who rejected the siren song of the French emperor. An introductory survey of the reign of Carlos IV, after 1788, became imperative. This survey gradually took on the air of a major project, and then a glance at the Enlightenment seemed necessary. In the end these introductions acquired a unity of their own and became the present book. The notes taken on the Napoleonic period still lie by, awaiting their breath of life.

The dissertation was completed in 1954 with the typically cumbrous title, "The Enlightenment and Revolutionary Spirit in Eighteenth-Century Spain (to 1795)." Soon thereafter M. Jean Sarrailh published his *L'Espagne éclairée de la seconde moitié du XVIIIᵉ siècle*. I could only applaud this fundamental study of the thought and activities of enlightened Spaniards; nevertheless I felt that my picture had not been superseded, for it dealt more directly with the changing effects on Spain of foreign enlightenment and the French Revolution. Encouraged at this point by M. Jacques Godechot and Professor Robert R. Palmer, I undertook to eliminate unnecessary duplication and develop the distinctive aspects of my study. The account was extended to the end of the century, when a clear turning point occurred in the reign of Carlos IV. Professor Beatrice F. Hyslop enabled me to improve the chapter on French Revolutionary propaganda by generously letting me consult the notes she took in the archives of Perpignan. A suggestion of Professor Franklin L. Baumer led to the addition of the chapters on economic and social con-

Preface

ditions. The maps were a by-product of the writing of these chapters. Their appearance owes much to the advice and skill of Mr. Robert L. Williams and Mr. John A. Bogan.

The completion of this book, like its start, was made possible by the generosity of others. My mother paid for the final typing of the manuscript, and the Princeton University Press has borne the entire costs of publication.

My thanks go to all who have helped me and made my work easier and better. Above all, they go to Professor Gottschalk, who directed the dissertation and has since read most of my revisions. Few besides his other students will realize how much time, care, and insight he gives to such a task.

The book remains that of an autodidact in Spanish history. It cannot but suffer from this weakness, but it can claim at least that it was written with a fresh mind.

R.H.

Madison, Connecticut
January 1958

CONTENTS

xi

Contents

MAPS

PART I

THE ENLIGHTENMENT

CHAPTER I

THE TIME OF ENLIGHTENMENT

AFTER the culture of the Middle Ages passed its zenith, there began a gradual development in the intellectual spirit of Europe that was to culminate in the eighteenth century. Religion, which was the medieval basis for men's thinking on the problems of life, was slowly driven from its prominent position by knowledge of a more secular kind. At the same time, freedom to express unorthodox ideas advanced.

The humanism of the Renaissance marked the first big step along the path. The Reformation brought the next, although its leaders had not intended to do anything but strengthen the religious spirit of Christianity. By the middle of the seventeenth century the Christian church had lost the supreme social authority which it had always asserted. The Reformation had destroyed its unity, and out of the ensuing chaos came the reality, soon justified by the theory, of religious toleration. At the same time in many lands the church fell under state control. Even the most powerful of the various churches that now were claiming to be the sole interpreters of the teachings of Jesus no longer had its former political influence. The Peace of Westphalia of 1648 was made against the wishes of the head of the Roman Catholic Church and accepted despite his condemnation. This flouting of the pope was symbolic of the determination—and ability—of Catholic princes in the future to be princes first and Catholics second.

By this date a new spirit of independence from traditional religion and theology was invading all fields of thought. Because of the stricter control of thought in Catholic countries, Protestant lands were in general the first scene of the new development. In England, Francis Bacon opened the seventeenth century by dismissing Aristotle, the authority on whom medieval Christian scientific and philosophic thought had rested, in favor of the direct observation of nature as the source of knowledge; and

3

Isaac Newton closed it by publishing his profoundly influential discovery of the law of gravitation. Henceforth, the universe and man as part of it were looked upon more and more as subject to rational laws, laws which God meant for man to discover by reasoning upon facts observed directly in nature rather than by the study of revelation and ancient authorities. Political science felt the same emancipation. Hugo Grotius, in the Netherlands, writing on international law, gave currency to a new meaning for the time honored concept of the law of nature. Instead of being synonymous with Christian political doctrines derived from the commandments of the Bible, the term now meant a universally valid law for human society based on reason and the nature of man. John Locke followed at the end of the century by stating that men have natural rights, such as personal freedom and the possession of property, which they did not give up when they formed an agreement to enter into society, abandoning the state of nature in which Locke supposed they had originally existed. René Descartes, writing like other Frenchmen in the safety of voluntary exile, had in the meantime given metaphysics its freedom from scholastic theology. Descartes demonstrated the fallibility of all accepted sources of knowledge, including Christian philosophy, and then relied on his reason alone to prove the existence of God and the immortality of the soul. Locke thereupon laid the foundation for modern epistemology by destroying the belief, still accepted even by Descartes, that God placed certain basic ideas in the minds of men at birth. He asserted instead that man's information comes only from his sense perceptions. Finally the Christian religion itself was openly attacked. Benedict Spinoza, like Descartes consulting his reason alone, substituted for the anthropomorphic Judeo-Christian God, who created the universe, an impersonal, all-embracing concept of God that seemed to make him identical with the universe. In England, meanwhile, from an observation of the new multiplicity of the Christian sects and the newly discovered religions of other lands, a group known as deists evolved the idea of a natural religion, the true primitive religion, from which, they said, all others had departed. These men held that to worship God no instituted church was necessary; certainly no church was justified in receiving state support and persecuting dissenters.

Spinoza and the deists, it is true, were honored more by being detested than by being read, and it was Grotius, Descartes, Locke, and Newton who inspired their contemporaries. By the end of the seventeenth century, nevertheless, the basis for a lay, or at least a religiously unorthodox, outlook on life had been established in Protestant lands. The next hundred years was to see its penetration into Catholic countries and wide diffusion throughout Europe, a movement which has been called the Enlightenment. Early in the century, Voltaire brought back to France from England an admiration for the science of Newton and the philosophy of Locke. The French mind had already been prepared by Descartes, and Voltaire's enthusiasm was soon shared by a group of men who were referred to derisively as *philosophes.* Motivated by a deep faith in the ability of the human mind to learn the truths of nature through observation and reason, these men questioned all accepted beliefs. Locke's sensationalist theory of epistemology was carried to an extreme form by Étienne Bonnot de Condillac and Claude Adrien Helvétius. The concept of natural religion became common, and even the need for the existence of God to explain natural phenomena was denied by materialist writers such as the Baron d'Holbach. The *philosophes* introduced their sensationalist and empirical spirit into a gigantic venture undertaken to gather all knowledge into one work of reference. This was the *Encyclopédie,* edited by Denis Diderot and Jean le Rond d'Alembert, which became famous as much for its iconoclastic approach to knowledge as for its useful collection of information.

Once the *philosophes* had made good their rupture with Catholic tradition, they turned their attention to the improvement of man's earthly lot. They refused to believe that because of an original fall man was doomed to depravity. They had a faith of their own in the natural goodness of man and his ability to perfect himself. Jean-Jacques Rousseau, not in complete agreement with the optimistic view of the encyclopedists, said that it was society that had corrupted man's goodness. This goodness he still felt could be maintained, however, by the right kind of education, which would keep children away from the evil influences of society and develop their intellect by observation and experience. This was the theme of his *Émile*. The book was an attack on the system of instruction by rote practiced in contemporary church schools, which had a near monopoly of education. Rousseau added insult to injury in the training he prescribed for Émile by postponing religious education to the age of adolescence and then recommending a form of natural religion.

Another group of persons that was equally effectively destroying the traditional Christian outlook was the physical and natural scientists, who were making astounding advances. Their achievements became the fascination of cultured circles. Men came to accept as true the proposition which the church had made Galileo Galilei recant in 1633, that the earth revolves about the sun, and the one that the Comte de Buffon had been forced to retract in 1751, that the earth had existed for many more epochs than the Bible said. The accomplishments of the men who, following Bacon's advice, chose to observe the facts thus further weakened the prestige of scholastic reasoning. By the end of the eighteenth century experimental science had largely replaced theology in the minds of educated men as the queen of sciences.

From France the Enlightenment spread through Europe. Its exportation was facilitated by the intellectual pre-eminence which the French language and literature had acquired under Louis XIV, because of both the political hegemony of the nation and the superiority of its writers. Its "culture rayonnante" was the pabulum of those in Germany, Italy, Russia, and elsewhere who made a pretense of being educated. Everywhere French writing made known the names of Voltaire, Rousseau, Buffon, Locke, and Newton.

The great enemy the *philosophes* and scientists faced, especially in their early years, was the Catholic Church. Their proposal to re-examine all knowledge clashed with the assertion of the church that, as a divinely instituted body, it was the guardian of the truth that God had given through revelation. The Catholic Church had not abandoned its medieval claim to teach the only true religion. It called upon the temporal monarchs to aid in suppressing other religious beliefs and in silencing writers who questioned its truths. In France works of the *philosophes* were prohibited by the government, and in Rome they were put on the Index, a formal list of books whose reading was forbidden to Catholics on pain of excommunication. Writers in the ranks of the church meanwhile mobilized to refute the *philosophes* and to sustain the faith of Catholics in their religion. To do so successfully, however, they were forced to adopt much of the new way of thinking about man's place in creation. Their very writing was eloquent testimony of the evolution in thought since the Middle Ages.

Another historical phenomenon that coincided with this development of thought was the growth of the middle class. This social group too had its origins in medieval Europe, and it had multiplied prodigiously since then. Its members were the craftsmen and merchants who had transformed the medieval agrarian society into a thriving economy of expanding urban centers, international commercial exchange, and handicraft manufacture. In their business ventures they had had to slight the views of the church on the wickedness of usury and the blessedness of poverty. Theirs was a worldly spirit, and it was their rise that to a great extent explains the triumph of secularism. Where they were strongest, in the Netherlands, England, and France, the new intellectual spirit had made the most progress.

A third development which paralleled both of these was the growth in the power of the state. The eclipse of the Christian church as a rival governing power and the expansion of the economy beyond the control of local institutions had combined with other factors to give kings more direct control over the lives of their subjects than they had ever had before. With control came enlarged responsibility for the welfare of their subjects. By what was perhaps more than coincidence, a number of rulers

7

appeared in the eighteenth century who were able to take advantage of their new role. Frederick II in Prussia, Catherine II in Russia, Joseph II in Austria, and a series of less important princes in Germany and Italy were capable monarchs who were inspired to make use of their personal power to reform their countries. Like the *philosophes*, they had assimilated the spirit of experimental rationalism and optimism in the future of man. They supported scientific research for the improvement of the agriculture and manufacture of their states. They simplified the complicated agencies of government they had inherited, reformed the administration of justice, and, in accordance with the economic doctrine known as mercantilism, adopted legislation that would further the commercial economy so that it would enrich their states. In these and other projects their aim was to make their people more prosperous and happy because they believed that the king should be the first servant of the state and that the prosperity of the state rested on that of its subjects. These rulers are known as the enlightened despots, and they were as typical of the latter half of the eighteenth century as were the *philosophes* and the scientists.

Like the last two, in Catholic lands the enlightened despots clashed with the church. Economic reforms could not be carried out without disturbing the tithes of the clergy or the extensive ecclesiastical property in mortmain. The apparent uselessness of many monastic orders conflicted with the desire of these rulers to see their subjects profitably employed. The monarchs wished to have progressive scientific knowledge given to the people, but the church had a near monopoly of instruction and imparted an increasingly discredited classical and scholastic education. Finally, when all the activity of the state was being drawn under their control, these princes objected to the allegiance and monetary payments given to the papacy by the branches of the Catholic church in their lands. More and more they interfered with the power of the pope to direct the local churches in temporal matters and limited the money that could be sent to Rome. Like the middle class, the enlightened despots embodied the new outlook that rejected the authority of revealed religion and the Christian church in the affairs of life on this earth.

In this conflict of ideas the role of the nobility was less well defined. Although the nobles enjoyed a privileged position inherited from the Middle Ages, as a class they did not take a firm stand against the Enlightenment. Many welcomed its ideas and patronized its partisans in France and their own countries. But they did not thereby give up their former social and political pretensions. In France they still claimed the right to voice the will of the people and approve the acts of the king. Their case was stated eloquently by the Baron de Montesquieu in *De l'esprit des lois*, one of the most widely known works of the century. The nobility was singing no swan song. Throughout Europe it was strengthening its control over the land and profiting at the expense of the peasantry. Capitalism could be applied to agriculture as well as to commerce, and the aristocracy had come to know the power of money. Even enlightened despots were in no position to challenge them. For all her fine words, Catherine gave free rein to the growing tyranny of Russian nobles over the serfs; Frederick chatted with Voltaire but remained convinced that the authority of his Junkers over their peasants contributed to the military strength of Prussia; Joseph tried seriously to free his serfs from their obligations to their masters, and his infuriated nobles forced his successors to destroy his work. Although aristocrats might appear enlightened, nowhere in Europe could kings and bourgeoisie in hatching their schemes overlook the power and pretensions of this traditionally minded class.

In the eighteenth century France did not have a king who could rank with the best enlightened despots, but it did have a powerful middle class, and it was the center for the radiation of the Enlightenment. Immediately to the south was Spain. By its proximity Spain was amply suited to receive the lay outlook on life, but it was the land that had for centuries most strongly maintained the Catholic religion at home and supported it abroad with its wealth and blood. Its commercial and manufacturing class had declined since the sixteenth century, while its nobility,

The Enlightenment

one of the proudest in Europe, had lost none of its land. Despite its nearness, Spain did not seem to present fertile ground for the Enlightenment. There remained, however, the possibility that it might be granted an enlightened despot who would favor the new spirit.

CHAPTER II

REGALISM AND JANSENISM IN SPAIN

WITH the advent of Philippe de Bourbon, grandson of Louis XIV of France, to the Spanish throne in 1700, Spain experienced more than the turn of a century. The power and prestige of the nation that had reconquered its home from the Moors, had colonized America, and had held European hegemony, was frittered away by the last of the Spanish Habsburgs through exhaustive foreign wars and domestic misgovernment. The Bourbons brought to Spain what it possibly needed most, personal attention. The three kings who ruled in the next eighty-eight years, Philippe, who ascended the Spanish throne as Felipe V, and his two sons, Fernando VI and Carlos III, were moved by a sincere desire to improve their country. Under them it made remarkable moral and material progress. Its population increased, it again showed signs of prosperity, its colonial empire received much needed reform, and before the end of the century it once more had weight in international affairs.

In order to promote the welfare of the country, and in the tradition of European monarchs in general and their forbear Louis XIV in particular, these kings strove to enhance the royal power. Supported by a series of capable and devoted councilors, they attacked the few checks on the regal prerogative that had been inherited from the Habsburgs. Castile had, since Fernando and Isabel, fallen beneath royal absolutism, but the *reynos* of the crown of Aragon still held on to some of their medieval political and economic privileges. Now these were largely destroyed by Felipe V in retaliation for the support given the Habsburg pretender by the lands of Aragon in the War of the Spanish Succession at the beginning of his reign. Felipe soon ceased to convoke their parliament or Cortes and instead invited various cities of the *reynos* of Aragon to send deputies to the Cortes de Castilla, which in effect, but not in name, now became the Cortes of Spain. They were called in the eighteenth century only to swear allegiance to the heirs to the throne and ratify important decrees. The Consejo de Aragón, in existence since 1494, was also abolished, and its affairs were taken over by the Consejo de Castilla, henceforth the supreme executive, legislative, and judicial body for all Spain. In the north the Basque provinces and the *reyno* of Navarre still preserved considerable autonomy; otherwise the political centralization of Spain, never achieved by the Habsburgs, was now an accomplished fact.

In the interest of efficiency, the Bourbons also introduced new royal officials patterned on those of Louis XIV. Felipe created five ministers (called "secretaries of state") responsible for specific branches of the administration, who shared authority with the Consejo de Castilla. Fernando VI in 1749 divided most of Spain into provinces and gave the royal governor (*corregidor* or *asistente*) of the leading city of each province the added title of "intendant" and full responsibility for fiscal matters in the province. The intendants quietly and efficiently organized royal finances until their new provinces became by the end of the century the most important territorial divisions of Spain.[1]

In the eighteenth century only one organized body remained that still had the vitality to be a serious threat to royal absolutism. Largely because it was part of an international institution, the Catholic Church in Spain had grown rather than declined in power in the last hundred years. The extent of its landed property had increased, and its right of mortmain meant that any real property it acquired could thereafter not be alienated. The Santo Oficio de la Inquisición, the ecclesiastical tribunal and police force established in 1478 to maintain the purity of the Catholic religion in the realms of the Spanish kings, had cemented its control over public and private expression. The papacy had at the same time gained a strong influence over the Spanish church, which it had not had in the sixteenth century.

Fernando and Isabel, Carlos V, and Felipe II had all asserted

---

[1] Rafael Altamira y Crevea, *Historia de España y de la civilización española*, IV (Barcelona, 1911), 145-47, 153-66; G. Desdevises du Dezert, *L'Espagne de l'Ancien Régime*, Vol. II, *Les institutions* (Paris, 1899), pp. 23, 59-60, 134-37, 406-7.

the royal will over temporal affairs of the church in their realms and had obtained papal recognition of their claims. The later Habsburgs had continued the policy, except for the last hapless scion, Carlos II. It was not until the reign of the immediate predecessor of the Bourbons that the pope had been able to extend his influence over the Spanish branch of his universal church. The Bourbon kings of Spain thus had strong precedents for enforcing the authority of the crown over the church. In the Spanish colonies, moreover, the kings had never lost the privilege acquired by Fernando and Isabel of absolute control over the church in all save spiritual questions, a subordination of the church to its temporal lord that was unique in the world. Finally the Spanish Bourbons had the example of Louis XIV, who had made the church in France to a large extent a handmaiden of royal absolutism.

The eighteenth century witnessed a war of skirmishes between the Spanish court and Rome. At the beginning of Felipe V's reign, two thirds of the appointments to Spanish church offices were made in Rome, and the pope enjoyed a large income from vacant Spanish sees and benefices and from the fees charged Spaniards in ecclesiastical courts. The pope's support of the Habsburg pretender during the War of the Spanish Succession gave Felipe an excuse to break off relations with the Holy See. After the war was concluded in 1713, a complicated series of negotiations between Madrid and Rome ensued that finally was sealed under Fernando VI with the Concordat of 1753. By this agreement the king and the pope virtually exchanged their positions in relation to the temporal affairs of the Spanish church, the king assuming the rights of appointment and income held previously by the pope. The pope also renounced the privilege of exemption from taxation for church lands in Spain.

Insofar as the position of the crown of Spain vis-à-vis the papal court was concerned, this concordat achieved most of the goals of royal absolutism. Opposition to royal control of the church was by no means limited to Rome, however; it was found strongly entrenched in the clergy of Spain. Two bodies in particular resisted extension of the king's authority, and they were, naturally, those that had a strong position of their own to defend. They were the Company of Jesus and the Inquisición. During the first two thirds of the eighteenth century these two institutions represented, practically speaking, one force, because the Jesuits had dominated the Santo Oficio since the days of Carlos II.[2]

For a moment during the early years of his reign Felipe V gave promise of asserting his authority over the Inquisición. In 1714, during Felipe's negotiations with the pope, the Inquisición condemned as heretical the memoir drawn up presenting the royal position by the king's minister Melchor de Macanaz. The first reaction of the king was to dismiss the inquisitor-general and to order the condemnation retracted; but then Felipe, who had a pliant will and a Jesuit confessor, changed his mind. The verdict of the Santo Oficio was upheld. Macanaz, in Paris at the time, chose to remain in exile rather than stand trial, but he had his possessions confiscated.[3] Thereafter the first two Bourbons limited their efforts in ecclesiastical matters to reaching an agreement with Rome. The problem posed by the Jesuits and the Inquisición was still pending when Carlos III ascended the throne in 1759, giving up to his third son the crown of the Two Sicilies, which he had worn for twenty-four years.

2

Meanwhile there had emerged within the church of Spain itself a group that was willing to lend support to a strong royal policy. The members of this group were known as "Jansenists," a name applied to them by their enemies, primarily the Jesuits. To explain the significance of the term "Jansenist" as used within the Spanish church, one must look back briefly at developments with-

[2] Memoir of Pedro Rodríguez de Campomanes and Josef Moñino, May 3, 1768, quoted in Juan Antonio Llorente, *Historia crítica de la Inquisicion de España* (10 vols.; Madrid, 1822), v, 234-38.

[3] Marcelino Menéndez Pelayo, *Historia de los heterodoxos españoles*, ed. E. Sánchez Reyes ("Edición nacional de las obras completas de Menéndez Pelayo," Vols. xxxv-xlii) (Santander, 1947-48), v, 55-62; Altamira, iv, 212-14; G. Desdevises du Dezert, *L'Espagne de l'Ancien Régime*, Vol. i, *La société* (Paris, 1897), pp. 104-6.

in the Catholic Church during the previous century. The Jansenist movement, properly so-called, owed its origin to the followers of the seventeenth-century Flemish Catholic theologian, Cornelius Jansen. Jansen's work *Augustinus*, published posthumously in 1640, gave an interpretation of the writings of Saint Augustine that stressed the theory of predestination to the detriment of man's free will. A sect grew up in France, especially at the monastery of Port Royal, which accepted his views. It upheld an exacting, puritanical moral code. The Sorbonne on the other hand condemned Jansen's position, and the Jesuit order came to the defense of the doctrine of free will. Eventually Louis XIV and the papacy both attempted to stamp out the heresy; Jansenism nevertheless continued to smolder in France in the eighteenth century.

The so-called Spanish Jansenists were not direct heirs of the French sect. No trace has been found in Spain of the propositions attributed to the Jansenists and condemned by the popes.[4] It is to ramifications of the original controversy and to related developments within the Catholic Church that one must look for the origins of the Spanish movement. The Jansenists in their controversy with the Jesuits had particularly accused the doctrines of the Spanish Jesuit Luis Molina of subverting true morality. The extremists of the Jesuits, eager to defend Molina's position, included in their attacks on the Jansenists, who cited Augustine as their authority, other theologians who upheld the writings of this church Father. One such person at the end of the seventeenth century was Enrico Noris, of the Augustinian order. In 1673, with approval of the papal Inquisition, Noris published a work entitled *Historia pelagiana*, in which in passing he defended Augustine's teachings against the writings of Molina. Jesuit leaders attempted to have the work put on the Index of Rome as Jansenistic, but successive popes steadfastly supported its orthodoxy. In France, however, the Jesuits succeeded in preventing its pub-

4 This conclusion is admitted by the authority on Spanish heterodoxy, Marcelino Menéndez Pelayo (p. 132), and accepted after an exhaustive investigation of the writings of the period by Jean Sarrailh in *L'Espagne éclairée de la seconde moitié du XVIIIᵉ siècle* (Paris, 1954), pp. 702-4.

lication. In the first third of the eighteenth century they introduced the controversy into Spain. Here Jesuit authors wrote against Noris, and their company got the Spanish Inquisición to silence his defenders in the Augustinian order.

The controversy was embittered by the publication of a new edition of the Spanish Index in 1747. This was a list of works which were prohibited or required expurgation that was drawn up by the Inquisición for the realms of Spain. It was not identical with the Roman Index in every case. Because of the influence of the Jesuits, the new Spanish Index carried as an appendix a list of works said to be Jansenistic. Their titles were taken from a book that had been published in Brussels by a member of the Company of Jesus.[5] Contrary to regulations, the Inquisición had not reviewed all the works in the list prior to publishing their prohibition. Among them were publications of Dominican authors and the *Historia pelagiana*. The Augustinians complained to Rome, and the pope ordered the Spanish inquisitor-general to remove the name of Noris from the Spanish Index, since his works had been thrice examined in Rome and found orthodox. Protected by Fernando VI, who was deftly managed by his Jesuit confessor, the Inquisición successfully refused obedience to Rome. The inquisitor-general replied to the Holy See that the regalian rights over the Inquisición did not permit him to obey the pope in this instance. Not until the advent of a new inquisitor-general and a new royal confessor in 1757 did the pope have his wish fulfilled to see Noris removed from the Spanish Index.[6]

The religious orders that felt injured in this affair were naturally not well disposed toward the Company of Jesus. With gross lack of foresight the Spanish Jesuits continued to stir the fire. One of their number, José Francisco de Isla, in 1758 published a novel, *La historia del famoso predicador Fray Gerun-*

[5] "Cathalogo de los libros jansenistas que en Idioma Francès han llegado à nuestra noticia . . . ," *Index librorum prohibitorum ac expurgandorum novissimus* (2 vols.; Madrid, 1747), II, 1097-1112.

[6] *Dictionnaire de théologie catholique*, s.v., Henri Noris; Manuel F[raile y] Miguélez, *Jansenismo y regalismo en España* (Valladolid, 1895), pp. 44-132, 237. The latter work gives full details of the dispute.

dio de Campazas, in which he satirized the religious preaching of his day. Within twenty-four hours all copies had been sold. Even though the Inquisición promptly banned the book, the other orders felt wounded by the satire.[7] Another sore spot was the universities. Disputes between the various schools of theology within their walls had long been frequent and acute, while at times student rivalry went beyond mere name calling to the use of sticks and stones.[8] The Jesuits seemed determined to increase the tension. After 1760 they still permitted attacks on Noris in public functions at the university of Salamanca.[9] To the enemies of Molina's doctrine on grace and free will they steadfastly aplied the epithet Jansenist.[10]

The first implication of the term "Jansenist" as it appeared in Spain therefore was opposition to the theological and moral teachings of the Jesuit order. A second implication arose indirectly from the traditional mission of the Company of Jesus to be the right arm of the papacy, a tradition that had been weakened in the past hundred years by quarrels between the company and the Holy See such as that over Noris but had not been destroyed. Since the end of the seventeenth century the Jesuits had been fighting a tendency within the church itself to limit the authority of the pope. In 1682 the bishops of France proclaimed what became known as the Gallican principles, namely that the secular power was independent of the church and that declarations of the pope in matters of faith could be refused assent by bishops until a general church council confirmed them as infallible. Gallicanism, like the Enlightenment but somewhat earlier, spread from France to other Catholic countries. Early in the eighteenth century, at the university of Louvain, Zeger Bernhard van Espen

---

[7] Juan Sempere y Guarinos, *Ensayo de una biblioteca española de los mejores escritores del reinado de Carlos III* (6 vols.; Madrid, 1785-89), III, 128; Fraile y Miguélez, pp. 271-74.

[8] Llorente, VIII, 216; Gerónimo Borao, *Historia de la Universidad de Zaragoza* (Saragossa, 1869), p. 97.

[9] Fraile y Miguélez, pp. 306-12.

[10] Llorente, VIII, 216; Joaquín Lorenzo Villanueva, *Vida literaria . . . o memoria de sus escritos y sus opiniones eclesiasticas y politicas, y algunos sucesos notables de su tiempo* (2 vols.; London, 1825), I, 17.

wrote a notable work on canon law in which he exalted the authority of the bishops against that of the pope. In 1763 the bishop of Trier, Johann Nikolaus von Hontheim, writing under the name of Justinius Febronius, denounced as illegal the growth since the Middle Ages of the ecclesiastical authority of the papacy, or, as such writers preferred to say, of the "Roman curia." Infallibility and supreme authority rested only with an ecumenical council, Febronius maintained. Although promptly condemned in Rome, his work had a wide appeal among both churchmen and lay rulers. A Portuguese contemporary, Antonio Pereira, justified the policy of the king of Portugal, who broke relations with the papacy in 1760, and held that under the circumstances the bishops of Portugal could exercise those legal powers by custom vested in the papal curia. He based his argument on the belief that the bishops held final authority in the church. All these writers were opposed by the papacy and the Jesuits. The latter applied to them the name they used for their other enemies, "Jansenist."[11]

3

A similar spirit of regalism in church matters existed in Spain. In 1765 the Imprenta Real or royal printing office published an anonymous work, *Tratado de la regalía de amortización*, "in which is demonstrated throughout the various ages since the birth of the church in all centuries and Catholic countries the constant practice by the civil authority of impeding unlimited alienation of landed property to churches, religious communities, and other mortmains." It was an open secret that the author was Pedro Rodríguez de Campomanes, a *fiscal* of the Consejo de Castilla, one of the lawyers whose duty it was to draw up recommendations for approval by this highest official Spanish body.[12] His work aimed at disproving the claim of the church to the un-

[11] Villanueva, I, 4-6; *Catholic Encyclopedia, s.v.*, Espen; Fredrik Nielsen, *The History of the Papacy in the XIXth Century*, trans. A. J. Mason (London, 1906), I, 125-30; Menéndez Pelayo, v, 135-45.

[12] Augustin-Jean-Charles Clément, *Journal de correspondances et de voyages d'Italie et d'Espagne pour la paix de l'église en 1758, 1768 et 1769* (3 vols.; Paris, 1802), II, 127.

limited right to amass real property. Despite its thesis, the book was approved for publication by an Augustinian member of the Consejo de Castilla, a Benedictine professor of theology at Salamanca, and the provincial of the Dominicans of Castile. Its fame spread outside the country and several Italian editions of it were made in the next decades.[13]

Campomanes was not a churchman but a rising lawyer of low birth. His treatise was written to support the policy of his master, Carlos III. Carlos, who was more intelligent and persistent than his predecessors, was determined to complete the subordination of the church to the throne which the Concordat of 1753 had left unfinished. He did not have to wait long after his accession for an incident to touch off the conflict. In 1761 the pope sent to his nuncio in Spain a breve condemning a catechism by the French Abbé François-Philippe Mésenguy because, in typical "Jansenist" fashion, it denied papal infallibility and opposed the Jesuit order. Contrary to custom and to what the nuncio and inquisitor-general believed to be legal, Carlos prohibited the publication of its condemnation in Spain. The inquisitor-general proceeded to make public the prohibition of the catechism anyway, and as a consequence he was banished from Madrid to a monastery, where he was kept until he begged pardon of the king. Carlos declared that henceforth royal permission, known as the *exequatur*, must be given to papal bulls or breves before they could be accepted in Spain. Carlos' extremely Catholic conscience shortly led him to revoke this measure, but in 1768 the *exequatur* was revived as a result of another conflict with the pope.[14]

Carlos had reasons to believe that the Company of Jesus had been responsible for the trouble over Mésenguy's catechism. He

[13] Menéndez Pelayo, v, 163.
[14] Decree of Nov. 27, 1761, quoted in Edward Clarke, *Letters Concerning the Spanish Nation Written at Madrid during the Years 1760 and 1761* (London, 1763), pp. 37-40; *real pragmática*, June 16, 1768, *Novísima recopilacion de las leyes de España* (Madrid, 1805), libro II, titulo iii, ley 9 (hereafter cited as *"Nov. rec.*, II, iii, 9"). See Antonio Ferrer del Rio, *Historia del reinado de Carlos III en España* (Madrid, 1856), I, 384-98, II, 229-30; Menéndez Pelayo, v, 158-60; Fraile y Miguélez, pp. 285-89; Vicente Rodríguez Casado, "Iglesia y estado en el reinado de Carlos III," *Estudios americanos*, I (1948), 31-33.

also blamed the Jesuits for the growing division within the Spanish church brought about by the Noris affair. He and his government had other causes for disliking the company. The Jesuits thwarted his efforts to get canonized the seventeeth-century Mexican bishop Juan de Palafox y Mendoza, who had been the enemy of their order.[15] Their loyalty and obedience to the crown in the American colonies were questioned. In Spain their company was using its control of the institutions of higher education to maintain an alliance with the aristocracy by favoring students of noble lineage. Finally, although the Jesuits had at times defended Spanish regalism, they could not rid themselves of their reputation of being the soldiers of the pope. If the royal victory over the papacy was to be meaningful, their strength must be broken.

The conclusion of the struggle between the crown and Jesuits was brought on by an unexpected domestic crisis. Since Carlos' arrival in Spain many of his subjects had resented his penchant for appointing foreigners to high offices. The most prominent of these were the Italians Marchese di Squillace (called by Spaniards the Marqués de Esquilache), who was made secretary of state for war and finances, and the Marqués de Grimaldi, an old servant of Felipe V, raised to secretary of state for foreign affairs during the negotiations of 1761 that led up to the alliance with France known as the Pacte de Famille. Spain's ensuing participation in the Seven Years' War was inglorious, Florida was lost to Britain in 1763, and the Italian ministers bore much blame in Spanish eyes. The following years increased their unpopularity. The arrival from America of specie that had accumulated during the war set off a sudden inflation and three successive years of bad harvests, 1763 to 1765, caused food prices to spiral higher, particularly in central Spain.[16] The winter of 1765-66 was severe, and the lower classes in the cities suffered marked privation. They saw the cause for their plight in the grain policies of Squillace, who had already acquired a reputation for squeezing taxpayers to

[15] Rodríguez Casado, *loc.cit.*, p. 31.

[16] Earl J. Hamilton, *War and Prices in Spain, 1651-1800* (Cambridge, Mass., 1947), p. 158 and tables on pp. 254-55. The price of wheat almost doubled in New Castile, 1760 to 1765.

pay for innovations like better highways and street lamps in Madrid. Rumors not surprisingly were rife of his peculations and the immorality of his household.

Under the circumstances, his decision was injudicious to repeat on March 10, 1766 an old and forgotten law that forbade men to wear in Madrid their common broad brimmed slouch hats and long capes, on the ground that these articles made it easy for criminals to hide their faces and escape arrest.[17] Strong-armed attempts to force popular swaggerers to give their hats the required three cornered shape by turning up the brims eventually provoked a violent riot on Palm Sunday, March 23. Mobs of common people sacked the house of Squillace, stoned that of Grimaldi, and destroyed the street lamps. On the twenty-fourth Carlos had to accept the terms of the representative of an uncontrollable crowd screaming outside his palace: exile of Squillace, revocation of the order changing the dress of Madrileños, a lowering of the price of foodstuffs, and other points of less moment. After another day Madrid grew calm; but the disturbances were imitated in April by two dozen provincial cities and towns, mostly in central Spain. Here the demand was more frankly for cheaper bread. The man of the hour turned out to be a leading *grande* of Aragon and an experienced general, the Conde de Aranda, whom Carlos made president of the Consejo de Castilla immediately after the departure of Squillace. Aranda's diplomatic tactics pacified the country, and within a year he revoked most of Carlos' concessions of March 24. An excellent harvest aided him by bringing down prices. Nevertheless, the "Mutiny of Esquilache" was the worst internal disturbance since the War of the Spanish Succession, and Carlos' even temper had for once been shaken.[18]

Reports were soon current that the riots had been planned in advance by secret groups of nobles or clergy who wished to get rid of Squillace and discourage Carlos from further reforms.

---

[17] *Bando* of Mar. 10, 1766, *Nov. rec.*, III, xix, 13.

[18] Hamilton, pp. 158-59; Altamira, IV, 53-57; Ferrer del Rio, I, 288-89, II, 6-116. Most histories of Carlos III deal at length with the Motín de Esquilache.

Historians are still arguing the truth of these reports,[19] but the government was ready to give them credence. The Jesuits were singled out to be the scapegoat. A royal commission, which included four bishops and an archbishop, found them guilty of using their influence to incite the riots. How just this verdict was has remained a strongly debated mystery, for the major portion of the documents of the commission has disappeared. In any case, because of this verdict or the other causes for displeasure that he had, Carlos felt that his duty as king was to order the expulsion of the Company of Jesus from his realms.[20] The idea was not original; Portugal and France had already expelled their Jesuits in 1759 and 1764. The decree of Carlos was efficiently carried out by the Conde de Aranda in April 1767 without a semblance of public disturbance or of opposition from the individual Jesuits.

Eventually the Spanish Jesuits settled in papal lands. Carlos was not happy, however, until, cooperating with the court of France, he got the pope to abolish everywhere the Company of Jesus in 1773. Carlos rewarded Joseph Moñino, the second *fiscal* of the Consejo de Castilla, who had gone to Rome and successfully elicited this act from the pope, with the title of Conde de Floridablanca.[21] In 1776 Floridablanca replaced Grimaldi as secretary of state for foreign affairs. Ten years after the Mutiny of Esquilache, Carlos got rid of his last prominent foreign adviser; in seventeen years since his accession he had become thoroughly Hispaniolized.

Because of the growth of so-called Jansenism among its members, the Spanish church hierarchy was divided in its views on the expulsion of the Jesuits. The episcopate on the whole sup-

[19] See Vicente Rodríguez Casado, *Política interior de Carlos III* (Valladolid, 1950), pp. 24-29, who believes the riots were instigated. He attacks P. Eguia, *Los Jesuitas y el Motín de Esquilache* (Madrid, 1947), who concludes they were spontaneous.

[20] Carlos José Guttiérez de los Rios, Conde de Fernán-Núñez, *Vida de Carlos III*, ed. A. Morel-Fatio and A. Paz y Melia (Madrid, 1898), I, 211.

[21] The negotiations are dealt with best by François Rousseau, *Règne de Charles III d'Espagne (1759-1788)* (Paris, 1907), I, 176-417.

ported the measure. When the pope in 1769 asked the Spanish bishops for their opinion on the expulsion, the large majority gave evidence that they approved the king's act.[22] Various bishops, including the Augustinian Padre Francisco Armañá y Font of Lugo, publicly defended the expulsion, terming the Jesuit order a "rotten tree," "teachers of perverse morality and deceitful maxims," and their colleges "chairs of pestilence." The Augustinian order, which had been most directly in conflict with the Jesuits, also strongly welcomed their departure. One of its monks actually echoed the accusation of contemporary French Jansenists that the Jesuits had sown the seeds of natural religion and of the impieties of Voltaire and Rousseau.[23] The general of the Augustinians, the Peruvian Francisco Xavier Vázquez, who had been outraged by the attacks on Noris, cooperated closely with the representatives of Carlos in Rome in procuring the final abolition of the Company of Jesus.[24]

To help in healing the breach within the clergy, the royal order expelling the Jesuits imposed public silence on the affair. In the succeeding decades the royal government took pains to enforce the prohibition by issuing specific orders against the circulation of works published abroad in defense of the Company of Jesus.[25] On the other hand, although it was also illegal, expression of the point of view of the company's enemies was at first tolerated, especially at court; but, within two years, an incident in Barcelona led to an absolute prohibition of satires of

[22] Forty-two approved, 6 opposed, and 8 gave no opinion. The bishops named before Carlos III's reign were as strongly in favor of the measure as those whom he nominated (Rodríguez Casado, "Iglesia y estado," *loc.cit.*, pp. 50-51). Menéndez Pelayo gives slightly different figures (v, 188), as does Melchor Fernández Almagro, *Orígenes del régimen constitucional en España* ("Colección Labor") (Barcelona, 1928), p. 27.

[23] [Padre Flórez], *Delacion de la doctrina de los intitulados jesuitas sobre el dogma y la moral* (Madrid, 1768), quoted in Fraile y Miguélez, pp. 323-24.

[24] Menéndez Pelayo, v, 118; Fraile y Miguélez, pp. 321-22, 340-48; Sarrailh, pp. 130-32, 664, 667; *Enciclopedia universal ilustrada europeo-americana* ("Espasa-Calpe"), *s.v.* Vázquez, F. J.

[25] *Nov. rec.*, VIII, xviii, 6, 7, 8. Probably the *Puntos de disciplina eclesiastica propuestos a los señores sacerdotes* (Valencia, 1770) and *La verdad desnuda* ([Madrid, 1772?]), surreptitiously published and immediately prohibited by the Consejo de Castilla, were also Jesuit apologies (*ibid.*, ley 9 and notas 9, 10).

the Jesuits.[26] The Inquisición, whose members on the whole remained sympathetic to the company, lent its support to this part of the royal policy by prosecuting clergymen who used the pulpit to denounce the Jesuits and the supposedly lax morality they had introduced.[27]

4

The expulsion of the Jesuits led to extensive changes in the field of higher education, in which their influence had been powerful. The colleges and universities of Spain had heretofore been relatively free from royal interference and subject only to local religious prelates or the monastic orders that furnished their faculties.[28] The government, eager to extend its authority to all spheres, now took upon itself the task of reorganizing these institutions. The king kept on in Madrid the five bishops who had been members of the commission to judge the Jesuits and put them in charge of disposing of the property that had belonged to the exiled order, including the buildings that had housed their schools. The Jansenists hoped that the opportunity would be seized to have Jesuit doctrines banished from Spanish education. Fortunately for them, the royal government was equally determined to root out what it considered a source of division within the church and universities. In the following years the university chairs devoted to giving instruction in the Jesuit school of theology were abolished and the use of Jesuit works in the study of theology and morality was prohibited.[29] The crown nailed down its new authority over the universities by ordering all recipients of degrees and faculty members to swear not to uphold or teach any ultramontane beliefs opposed to its regalian rights over the church.

[26] *Resolución*, Aug. 22, 1769, *Nov. rec.*, VIII, xviii, 5.
[27] On these incidents see Clément, II, 16-17, 29-31, Ferrer del Río, II, 195; Sarrailh, p. 706; Llorente, V, 165 (cases of Francisco Balza and Manuel Berrocosa).
[28] G. Desdevises du Dezert, *L'Espagne de l'Ancien Régime*, Vol. III, *La richesse et la civilisation* (Paris, 1904), p. 188.
[29] *Cédulas*, July 1 and Aug. 12, 1768, July 29, 1769, *Nov. rec.*, VIII, iv, 4. See Luis Sánchez Agesta, *El pensamiento político del despotismo ilustrado* (Madrid, 1953), pp. 110-13.

Royal censors were established at the universities to insure observance of this regulation.[30]

The most effective means the Jesuits had employed to dominate the universities was their control of the colegios mayores. These were institutions which had been founded in the fifteenth and sixteenth centuries in the major university towns, four in Salamanca and one each at Valladolid and Alcalá de Henares, with the charitable purpose of giving lodging and support to poor students. Time and private interest had corrupted them, however, so that by the middle of the eighteenth century they were monopolized by second sons of wealthy landholding families, who had usurped the funds intended for the maintenance of indigent scholars. These *colegiales*, after a few years in the colegios mayores, devoted more to pleasure than to study, would spring to high posts in the church or government. Thus after graduating the *colegiales* formed an aristocracy in the clergy and royal administration which loyally protected the status of the colegios and saw to it that new graduates were given preference for important vacancies. The faculties of the colegios had fallen under the dominance of the Jesuits, who worked closely with the *colegiales* to maintain the position of the colegios and to extend their own influence within the church and government of Spain. Meanwhile students of the lower nobility, now scornfully excluded from these institutions, struggled to maintain themselves by other means and were known disdainfully as *manteistas* from the long capes they were required to wear.

Within the government of Carlos III, however, important enemies of ultramontanism, including the *fiscales* Campomanes and Moñino, had been *manteistas*. After the expulsion of the Jesuits a return of the colegios mayores to their original purpose as homes for poor students was suggested to the king and was put into effect by decrees signed in February 1771. Not without

---

[30] *Real provisión*, Sept. 6, 1770, *Nov. rec.*, VIII, v, 3. See Clément, II, 14-15, 124; Ferrer del Rio, III, 186; Villanueva, I, 24-25. Clément, a French churchman who visited Spain to encourage Spanish regalism, provides a good picture of these religious disputes. Sarrailh gives an excellently documented account of the role of the Jesuits in Spanish education and the reforms brought on by their expulsion (pp. 185-201).

a struggle did the *colegiales* abandon their *almae matres* to poor hidalgos and commoners. Carlos was long subjected to pleas from many sides, but he remained firm.[31] Unfortunately, as it turned out, the measure did not have the desired effect of reviving the ancient purpose of the colegios, for these rapidly declined, until in 1798 the government decided to take over their income for its own needs.[32] Nevertheless the reform of the colegios mayores did have the effect of freeing the universities from their suffocating control. The action was a significant victory for regalism over ultramontanism and also for the commoners and lower nobility over the landed aristocracy.[33]

Regalist, Gallican, or "Jansenist" precepts known abroad thus had the way opened for them. The book of Febronius circulated and was becoming popular.[34] University professors who opposed the power of the Roman curia began to spread their beliefs to their students. The university of Saragossa officially introduced the text on canon law of the Louvain professor Van Espen in 1775, and the university of Valencia followed suit a dozen years later.[35] The faculty of Valladolid was split on the question. One professor of theology was ultramontane while others favored Gallicanism, and their students were going home with new views on the limitations of the authority of the pope.[36] Where such instruction was not officially sanctioned, Jansenist works were being read by the students, often through the recommendation of their professors. Students at the university of Valencia since the

[31] *Reales decretos*, Feb. 15 and 22, 1771, Feb. 21, 1777, *Nov. rec.*, VIII, iii, 6, 7, 8.

[32] Ferrer del Rio, III, 193-210; Desdevises, III, 197-98. Ferrer used the papers of Francisco Pérez Bayer, the moving spirit of the reform. See also Pio Zabala y Lera, *Tesis doctoral: las universidades y colegios mayores en tiempo de Carlos III* (Madrid, 1906), pp. 18-34; J. M. Sánchez de la Campa, *Historia filosófica de la instrucción pública de España* (Burgos, 1871-74), I, 386-87.

[33] Llorente, IX, 21; Villanueva, I, 10-11. See Antonio Domínguez Ortiz, *La sociedad española en el siglo XVIII* (Madrid, 1955), pp. 102, 179; Vicente Rodríguez Casado, "La revolución burguesa del XVIII español," *Arbor*, XVIII (1951), 5-29.

[34] Clément, II, 31.

[35] Borao, pp. 42-43; Menéndez Pelayo, V, 196.

[36] Juan Antonio Posse, "Documentos de historia española moderna, memorias de don Juan Antonio Posse," *La lectura*, XVI[1] (1916), 20-22, 116.

middle of the century had been familiar with the writings of the French Gallicans Bishop Jacques Bossuet and the church historian Claude Fleury.[37] Van Espen and Fleury were read by the poet Juan Meléndez Valdés at the university of Salamanca in 1777 in preparation for a degree of canon law.[38] By the time of Carlos' death in 1788, the partisans of regalism or Jansenism in the faculties of theology and canon law were growing in numbers and influence, while the defenders of ultramontanism, though still influential, were more and more on the defensive.[39]

5

Ultramontanism in Spain had not been eliminated by the expulsion of the Jesuits. While its partisans in the universities fought a stubborn rear-guard action, it found support in the Inquisición. The Jesuits continued to have friends in the Santo Oficio, which they had so long controlled, who were ready still to accuse their enemies of Jansenism. The Inquisición investigated charges of Jansenism brought against the archbishop and four bishops who had been members of the royal commission to try the Jesuits and also against the bishop of Barcelona, suspected of praising the Jansenist church of Utrecht. It eventually dropped their cases for lack of explicit evidence of heresy.[40]

The royal government was well aware of the attitude of the Inquisición. Campomanes and Moñino, as *fiscales* of the Consejo de Castilla, wrote a memorandum dated May 3, 1768, pointing out the ultramontanism of the Santo Oficio while it was in the

[37] Clément, II, 29-31.

[38] Meléndez Valdés to G. M. Jovellanos, Oct. 6, 1777, quoted in M. Serrano y Sanz (ed.), "Poesías y cartas inéditas de D. Juan Meléndez Valdés," *Revue hispanique*, IV (1897), 309-10; Meléndez Valdés to Jovellanos, July 11, 1778, in "Cartas inéditas de Meléndez Valdés á Jovellanos," *Poetas líricos del siglo XVIII*, ed. L. A. de Cueto, Vol. II ("Biblioteca de autores españoles desde la formación del lenguage hasta nuestros días" [Madrid, 1846-80] [hereafter cited as "B.A.E."], Vol. LXIII), p. 80.

[39] See, e.g., Juan Ortega Rubio, "Consulta que hizo Carlos IV en nombre de los católicos de Inglaterra á la Universidad de Valladolid," *Revista contemporánea*, CXXV (1902), 385-90; Enrique Esperabé Arteaga, *Historia pragmática e interna de la Universidad de Salamanca* (Salamanca, 1914-17), II, 63.

[40] Llorente, V, 118-19, 123-24; Villanueva, I, 21.

hands of the Jesuits. They concluded, "The tribunals of the Inquisición today compose the most fanatic body in the state and the one most attached to the Jesuits, who have been expelled from the kingdom; the inquisitors profess exactly the same maxims and doctrines; in fine, it is necessary to carry out a reform of the Inquisición."[41] The Inquisición had justified its opposition to the pope in the case of the Index of 1747 by insisting on its responsibility to the king. The government turned the same argument against the ultramontane point of view now put forward that the Inquisición received its power in delegation from the pope and could not be reformed without his consent. The Consejo de Castilla gave expression to the regalist concept of the relation of the Santo Oficio to the king:

> The king, as patron, founder, and endower of the Inquisicón, possesses over it rights inherent in all royal patronage. . . . As father and protector of his vassals, he can and ought to prevent the commission of violence and extortion on their persons, property, and reputation, indicating to ecclesiastical judges, even in their exercise of spiritual jurisdiction, the path pointed out by the canons so that these may be observed.[42]

Using the prerogative so plainly asserted. Carlos proceeded to enforce his authority over the Inquisición. In 1768 he established the procedure it was to follow in censoring books in order to prevent unjust prohibition of the works of Catholic authors. Two years later the inquisitors were told to concern themselves only with crimes of heresy and apostasy and to avoid imprisoning a person until his guilt was convincingly established,[43] and in 1784 Carlos ordered that the proceedings of all cases involving *grandes de España* and royal ministers and servants be submitted

---

[41] Quoted in Llorente, v, 234-38.

[42] *Consulta*, Nov. 30, 1768, quoted in Henry Charles Lea, *A History of the Inquisition of Spain* (New York, 1922), IV, 389-90.

[43] *Cédula del Consejo*, June 16, 1768, *Nov. rec.*, VIII, xviii, 3; *real cédula*, Feb. 5, 1770, *ibid.*, II, vii, nota 13. See William Coxe, *Memoirs of the Kings of Spain of the House of Bourbon . . . 1700 to 1788* (2d ed.; London, 1815), IV, 407; and Ferrer del Rio, II, 516-17.

to him for examination.[44] He moreover appointed inquisitors-general who were beginning to feel the spell of the opinion common in more enlightened countries that condemned the use of physical violence to attain religious unity. As a consequence, the local officials of the Inquisición, already tending to negligence because of their small pay, did not carry through their investigations with the zeal they would have shown in previous centuries.[45] Tortures and public burnings of relapsed heretics on the whole became things of the past. Further than this even the new president of the Consejo de Castilla, the Conde de Aranda, who was a notorious enemy of ultramontanism, felt it would be dangerous to go, since the public believed that all religion depended on the Santo Oficio.[46] Carlos was of the same opinion now that the claws of the institution had been drawn. He is reported to have replied to the suggestion that he imitate his son, the king of the Two Sicilies, who had abolished the Inquisition in his lands, "The Spaniards want it and it does not bother me."[47]

6

Other features of the Spanish church remained that troubled the royal government. One was the great number of the clergy. In 1788 Spain had some 2,000 convents and monasteries for men and over 1,000 for women, containing 68,000 monks and 33,000 nuns. There were moreover 88,000 secular clergy and several thousand other religious officers. This made a total of close to 200,000 ecclesiastics in a population of 10,000,000.[48] At this time

---

[44] So according to Coxe, v, 205. The law is not in *Nov. rec.*

[45] [Jean François Bourgoing], *Nouveau voyage en Espagne, ou tableau de l'état actuel de cette monarchie* (3 vols.; Paris, 1789) (hereafter cited as "Bourgoing [1789]"), 1, 354-55; Llorente, IX, 1-2; Lea, IV, 388-89.

[46] So he stated to Clément (Clément, II, 124). The story that Aranda planned to abolish the Inquisición after the expulsion of the Jesuits but had his secret revealed by Voltaire or was checked by intrigues of the Inquisición around Carlos (see Coxe, IV, 408 n.; Segismundo Moret y Prendergast, *El Conde de Aranda* [Madrid, 1878], pp. 158-60; and Jefferson Rea Spell, *Rousseau in the Spanish World before 1833* [Austin, 1938], p. 51) seems unfounded in view of this conversation.

[47] Villanueva, I, 28-29.

[48] Tomás Mauricio López, *Geografía moderna* (Madrid, 1796), pp. 254-59;

France, with a population perhaps two and a half times that of Spain, had but an equal number of clergymen.[49] The percentage of the population of Spain that belonged to the clergy had declined in the eighteenth century, but even so at the end of the century in no country in Europe except Portugal did the churchmen form so large a sector of society.[50]

The opulence of the church was another disturbing feature. Monasteries and convents were proportionally more numerous than clergy, for many had but a handful of inmates. Yet they possessed extensive lands. In the contemporary Spanish scene the edifices of the church presented an unwelcome contrast to their secular surroundings. A German traveller remarked this situation in Old Castile in 1797:

> Uniform plains, few houses, stony and almost barren fields, with a few vineyards here and there, numerous flocks of sheep, few horned cattle, no meadows, no forests, no gardens nor country houses, and in general a dreary and monotonous scene. Even the few villages we meet with but show the misery of the inhabitants. The houses are of mud and half ruined, the roofs, which let in the light, loaded with stones in order to resist the wind, but the churches, chapels, and monasteries [are] massive and magnificent.[51]

This disparity between the poverty of the mass of population and the riches of the church in income, lands, and precious objects was particularly striking in Old and New Castile. For over two hundred years the plateau lands had suffered soil exhaustion from sheepgrazing, economic ruin from overtaxation to support foreign wars, and a consequent loss of population. The humid northern

José Canga Argüelles, *Diccionario de hacienda* (London, 1826-27), *s.v.* "Población de España"; A. Moreau de Jonnès, *Statistique de l'Espagne* (n.p., 1834), pp. 32-33, 71-72.

[49] R. R. Palmer, *Catholics & Unbelievers in Eighteenth Century France* (Princeton, 1939), p. 13 n. 6.

[50] Moreau de Jonnès, p. 70.

[51] Frederick Augustus Fischer, *Travels in Spain in 1797 and 1798* (London, 1802), pp. 186-87.

provinces and the *reynos* of Aragon had been hurt less. Still, Gaspar Melchor de Jovellanos, one of the younger and most capable of Carlos III's officials, could lament a general decline of Spanish wealth in recent centuries, during which, he pointed out, only the church prospered. "What is left of that former glory except the skeletons of its cities, once populous and full of factories and workshops, of stores and shops, and now only peopled by churches, convents, and hospitals, which survive amidst the poverty that they have caused?"[52]

Jovellanos and the other royal advisers who worried about Spain's sad economy objected not only to the large share of the national resources controlled by the church but to the, in their eyes, misguided employment of this share. The church's right of mortmain kept lands waste that many thought could benefit from private ownership, and its very practice of charity, on which it spent a great part of its income, was an encouragement to idleness. It is true that the church maintained orphanages, hospitals, and retreats for the invalid; but it had also for centuries made a virtue of giving food and alms indiscriminately to all who begged at its doors. Throngs of mendicants gathered as a result around monasteries and cathedrals, subsisting on their free pittance and spending their lives in rags and idleness. The bishop of Granada, for instance, by actual count gave daily bread to some two thousand men and from three to four thousand women. When Joseph Townsend, an Anglican minister travelling in Spain, asked the bishop of Oviedo in Asturias if he did not think that the practice was harmful, he got the disarming answer: "Most undoubtedly, but then it is the part of the magistrate to clear the street of beggars; it is my duty to give alms to all who ask."[53]

[52] Gaspar Melchor de Jovellanos, *Informe de la Sociedad Económica de esta Corte al . . . Consejo de Castilla en el expediente de ley agraria* (Madrid, 1795), p. 56.

[53] Joseph Townsend, *A Journey Through Spain in the Years 1786 and 1787; With Particular Attention to the Agriculture, Manufactures, Commerce, Population, Taxes, and Revenue of That Country* (3 vols.; London, 1791), II, 9 and III, 57-58 (Granada). The author repeatedly remarks the church's custom of almsgiving.

While the prelates and convents were so lavish in their charities, the simple monks and priests of Spain were remarkable for their backwardness and ignorance. Many peasants' and artisans' sons were accused of entering the church only to gain the social prestige of being a *fraile* or *cura*.[54] After taking their vows, these youths of low origin were given little education, and what they received was mainly limited to worn-out scholastic theology. True spiritual direction of others was frequently the least of their concerns, as Padre Isla's satire, *Fray Gerundio*, pointed out. Many priests hurried through their masses unaware of the meaning of the various parts of the service.[55] Priests often suffered economic misery, especially in the countryside, while monks and canons regularly basked in leisure and abundance. As a result, despite the number of Spaniards wearing the cassock, two thousand parishes were without priests.[56]

The general ignorance of the clergy had the effect of fostering superstitions within the religion of the still more ignorant people. Unnecessarily frequent crossing of oneself, preference of some images of the Virgin to others without reason, prayers to the images of saints to perform miracles, and self-flagellation in the churches were symptoms of the distorted beliefs of the Spaniards. In some towns the congregations extended their arms at the end of mass to receive the blessing of the priest, which they thought would otherwise be lost.[57] Charlatans were not missing to take advantage of the public credulity. One young woman, known as the *beata* of Cuenca, with the help of several priests and monks, had the local citizens believing her flesh had been converted into the body and blood of Christ and was carried in procession surrounded by tapers and burning incense. Another *beata* in Madrid, in connivance with her confessor, feigned paralysis

[54] *El duende de Madrid*, No. 2 (1787), p. 48; *Semanario erudito y curioso de Salamanca*, May 6, 1794.

[55] Villanueva, I, 37. *Fray Gerundio* is directed at the ignorance, vanity, and cupidity of the *frailes* (see Sarrailh, pp. 631-33).

[56] Sarrailh, pp. 83, 646; Desdevises, I, xvi-xvii, 82; Domínguez Ortiz, pp. 142-45.

[57] *El censor*, Discurso 41, p. 731; *El corresponsal del censor*, Cartas 41, 42, II, 669-95; Jean François Bourgoing, *Tableau de l'Espagne moderne* (3 vols.; Paris, 1797) (hereafter cited as "Bourgoing [1797]"), II, 279-95.

and pretended that her only nourishment was the host she consumed in a daily mass said in her bedroom. Among her devotees were members of the aristocracy, who contributed with donations to her well organized imposture. The Inquisición inflicted punishment in both cases on the culprits, but the basic cause of the frauds was the unquestioning reverence of the people for anyone wearing the cassock.[58] Devotion to the Catholic religion, carried frequently to superstitious exaggeration, was probably the strongest force in Spanish society at the end of the eighteenth century.

All of these abuses were the objects of royal concern. Throughout Carlos' reign measures were taken to reform the church. Over a dozen royal regulations were issued strengthening the discipline of the religious orders, reducing the number of their monks, and abolishing one order completely.[59] The king used his power of appointment to raise the quality of the Spanish episcopate. Whereas the lower clergy remained on the whole notorious for its ignorance and lax morals; by the end of the reign the bishops of Spain were recognized to be outstanding in their austerity and attention to their duties.[60] Under the leadership of the Conde de Floridablanca, who headed the royal government after 1776, and with the advice of Campomanes, the government attacked the problem of mendicity. It sponsored vocational schools and work-houses for the truly needy children and

---

[58] Bourgoing (1797), II, 290-92; Villanueva, I, 91-94; Menéndez Pelayo, V, 471-72.

[59] *Auto de consejo*, Feb. 14, 1762; *real decreto*, May 31, 1762; *real orden*, Oct. 27, 1762; *reales cédulas*, Sept. 11 and Nov. 25, 1764, Aug. 1, 1767, Oct. 22, 1772; and *real provisión*, Feb. 11, 1787, restricting the activities and places of abode of monks and nuns; *real cédula*, Sept. 6, 1774, reducing the number of Calced Mercedarians (Severo Aguirre, *Prontuario alfabético, y cronológico por orden de materias de las instrucciones, ordenanzas . . . y demas reales resoluciones, expedidas hasta . . . 1792* [Madrid, 1793], pp. 351-54); *real cédula*, Sept. 26, 1769, and *real provisión*, Feb. 4, 1772, reducing the number of Trinitarians and Carmelites (Severo Aguirre, *Continuacion y suplemento al prontuario . . . 1793* [Madrid, 1794], pp. 120-22); *real cédula*, July 28, 1774, reducing the number of Discalced Mercedarians (Severo Aguirre, *Segunda continuacion y suplemento al prontuario . . . 1794* [Madrid, 1794], p. 59); *real orden*, Mar. 12, 1788, extinguishing the order of San Antonio Abad in Spain (*Nov. rec.*, I, xxvi, nota 14).

[60] Bourgoing (1797), I, 334; Townsend, II, 150-51, III, 275.

adults, meanwhile ordering royal officials to prevent the able-bodied from begging. The bishops were encouraged to help provide useful work for the poor.[61] Beggary was too widespread and inveterate, and able officials too scarce, for the government to achieve great success, but even in the realm of charity the church was feeling the hand of the king.

To the royal government these measures represented only a beginning. In 1787 Carlos and Floridablanca drew up a program of action for the newly established Junta de Estado, an institution that was to initiate regular joint meetings of all the royal ministers. In the ecclesiastical sphere the king and his first secretary recommended that the bishoprics be divided into smaller territories which could be more thoroughly administered; that the enlightenment of the clergy be promoted by education in mathematics, economics, public law, and the sciences, so that they could instruct the people; that educated inquisitors be found who would extirpate rather than foment superstitions; and that the religious orders be brought back to their pristine forms.[62]

7

Already the government had accomplished much. The subordination of the church to the state in temporal matters, which the Concordat of 1753 had left unfinished, was definitely accomplished during Carlos III's reign. The expulsion of the Jesuits got rid of the most determined ultramontane group in the church, and this measure had been followed by others aimed at assuring the loyalty of the institutions in which ultramontanism had flourished, largely through the influence of the Jesuits. In every case the crown acted on its own authority, but it had the invaluable moral support of an influential segment of the clergy.

[61] Modesto Lafuente y Zamolloa, *Historia general de España* (Barcelona, 1922), xv, 18-27; Sarrailh, pp. 534-35. On the problem of the Spanish clergy, see Sarrailh, pp. 631-47.

[62] Carlos III, "Instrucción reservada que la Junta de Estado, creada formalmente por mi decreto de . . . 8 de julio de 1787, deberá observar . . . ," in *Obras originales del Conde de Floridablanca* . . . , ed. Antonio Ferrer del Rio (B.A.E., Vol. LIX), arts. 38, 39, 26-28, 32-34, 15, pp. 215-19.

Those groups in particular which had welcomed the expulsion of the Jesuits were in sympathy with the royal reforms. They believed that the Jesuits upheld lax moral standards, and they were ready to see their church cleansed of many practices which they felt were extravagant, superstitious, and un-Christian. They accused those who resisted their reforms of hiding behind a screen of ultramontanism and were led themselves to support canonical doctrines that denied supreme authority to the pope and Roman curia. Since they saw the only hope of reform in the activity of Carlos III's government, they supported its regalism.[63] The king responded by using his authority of appointment, won in the Concordat of 1753, to advance those members of the clergy who sympathized with his activity. In the minds of persons inside and outside the church, reform had come to be associated with regalism, and regalism in ecclesiastical matters was looked upon as a means to reform.

To their contemporaries, the reformers within the clergy were known as "Jansenists," rather than as "regalists." They had been given the name because of their views on the limited authority of the papacy and not for accepting the heretical beliefs of the French Jansenists. Yet, since the reforms they advocated involved a stricter discipline of clergy and laity and a reduction in the wealth and ostentation of the church, there was a certain justification, which their contemporaries at times sensed, in applying to them the name of the French sect that had been convicted of trying to make Catholicism too austere and repellent.

Although they reached prominent positions, the Jansenists were a minority of the clergy. Their cause had an intellectual appeal to which the majority of the Spaniards who had taken religious vows were perforce impervious. The mass of the clergy had, moreover, a vested interest in the status quo. Nevertheless, out of tradition and also out of self-interest, they stilled their complaints and remained attached to the throne. Floridablanca told the king that the Spanish church was the most loyal and devoted in the world, and for this reason he recommended that

[63] See Llorente, IX, 21.

its legitimate privileges "be maintained and protected from the odious discussions and degrading measures that have been employed in other lands."[64] Floridablanca's words were unnecessary. Carlos' personal piety and devotion to the church were notorious. His instructions to the new Junta de Estado opened with the words, "The first of my obligations and of all my successors is to protect the Catholic religion in all the dominions of this vast monarchy." The leading ministers, even the strongest regalists, were attached to the Catholic faith.[65] A falling out between the royal government and the body of the clergy was hardly conceivable.

Carlos had shown, however, that his piety did not lead him to approve of everything that was done in the name of religion. He conceived that his duty as king required him to control and reform the church in his lands. It was his tact and his unimpeachable moral and spiritual character more than the tenor of his projects that saved him from arousing concerted opposition in the ranks of the church. He avoided the mistake of contemporary enlightened despots, like Joseph II of Austria, whose impetuosity stirred up a spirit of revolt within their clergy that led to the ruin of their reforms.

Throughout Europe the Catholic Church was the most determined opponent of certain aspects of the Enlightenment, and Spain had always been one of the strongholds of the church. But the regalist policy of the Spanish Bourbons and the rise of men of Jansenist views to leading posts in the hierarchy after the middle of the eighteenth century destroyed the independence and authority of the Spanish church. The most immediate effect of Spanish regalism and Jansenism was to establish in Spain a royal absolutism equal to that of Louis XIV. In so doing, however, they also breached the thickest wall that stood between Spain and the Enlightenment.

[64] Memorial to Carlos III, Oct. 10, 1788, quoted in Hermann Baumgarten, *Geschichte Spanien's zur Zeit der französischen Revolution, mit einer Einleitung über die innere Entwicklung Spanien's im achtzehnten Jahrhundert* (Berlin, 1861), p. 147.

[65] Rodríguez Casado, "Iglesia y estado," *loc.cit.*, pp. 21-24.

CHAPTER III

THE ENLIGHTENMENT ENTERS SPAIN

SINCE the sixteenth century, there had been Spaniards who felt that, though God was, of course, in his heaven, all was not right with the world, at least not their corner of it. Criticisms of the government, the economic policies, the haughtiness of the aristocracy, had been penned if not always published; but similar complaints must have been heard everywhere since men began to live in society. They did not, as a rule, suggest that what Spain needed was to become aware of what men were doing and thinking abroad.

Early in the reign of the Bourbon kings, isolated Spaniards began to point out that it was precisely attention to foreign achievements that their country most needed. Of these it was a Benedictine monk, a professor in the out-of-the-way university of Oviedo, who almost single-handed kindled the flame that was to arouse Spain from the intellectual slumber into which it had fallen at the end of the seventeenth century. In his childhood, during these dismal years, Benito Gerónimo Feyjóo y Montenegro began to show a critical spirit that was to make him the outstanding figure of the reigns of Felipe V and Fernando VI.

When I was a boy, everyone said that it was very dangerous to eat anything right after the [morning] hot chocolate. My mind, for some reason which I could not then perhaps have explained very well, was so skeptical of this common apprehension that I decided to make the experiment. . . . Immediately after my chocolate, I ate a large quantity of fried salt pork, and I felt fine that day and for a long time thereafter, wherefore I had the satisfaction of laughing at those who were possessed by this fear.[1]

[1] B. G. Feyjóo, *Teatro crítico universal*, Vol. v, No. 5, quoted in G. Delpy, *L'Espagne et l'esprit européen, l'oeuvre de Feijóo (1725-1760)* (Paris, 1936), p. 345.

The Enlightenment

Although he was the first born son of a modest provincial nobleman, Feyjóo chose to become a monk. He studied in Galicia and Asturias and at Salamanca, and at thirty-three he became a professor of theology. During these years his remarkable intellectual curiosity had led him to read foreign books whose existence was scarcely known in Spain. Passionately he learned what was being said beyond the Pyrenees and realized the intellectual backwardness of his country. He remained, however, an unknown member of a provincial university in northwest Spain until in 1726, at the age of fifty, he began to publish his wealth of accumulated information in a series of essays to which he gave the impressive title of *Teatro critico universal*. Henceforth his peaceful life of study was transformed into the agitated one of an active writer and controversialist. Nine volumes of the *Teatro critico* were published by 1739, and they were followed by five others with the name *Cartas eruditas*. Feyjóo did not lay down his pen until 1759. Five years later he died, at the age of eighty-eight.

Feyjóo's subject matter was, as his first title said, universal. Literature, art, philosophy, theology, natural science, mathematics, geography, and history were among his topics. Toward all of them his approach was critical, in the sense that modern European learning was critical of the learning that had been handed down from the Middle Ages. Spain, he said, had no need for more works on theology, of which it already had the best in the world. Nor did it lack religious unity. What it needed was progress in science. Modern science did not necessarily clash with religion, Feyjóo maintained, asserting that the sway of Aristotle in Spanish education could be broken without harm to the Catholic faith. He described to his countrymen the scientific discoveries of Descartes and Newton, but his real hero was Francis Bacon, the great enemy of Aristotelianism, who had hitherto been dismissed in Spain as a heretic. Against the Spanish scholastics, Feyjóo courageously upheld the experimental method of the English Protestant. Revealing the progress of science was but one of the ways in which the Benedictine monk chose to enlighten his fellow citizens. He showed the fallibility of contemporary doctors, denounced exaggerated devotion to the saints and false religious miracles, and he especially belabored superstitions. He culled his information from the best sources he could find; his essays referred to over two hundred French works and sixty-four of other foreign origin.[2] At the same time, Feyjóo never questioned the greatness of Spain's former intellectual figures or expressed a view that he believed was the least opposed to the Catholic religion. He united a strong devotion to his faith with a sincere desire to see his country enter the world stream of thought.

Feyjóo's writing marked the beginning of a new era in Spanish intellectual life. His ideas were not new, but many of them had not been heard in Spain, and their spirit of skepticism was especially fresh in his land. But their tremendous influence was due to the extent to which they were read and discussed. His articles, many of which attacked beliefs that established institutions had a vital interest in seeing maintained, roused violent controversy. One bibliographer has found thirty-seven publications that stemmed from an attack he made on the practices of the medical profession alone. He lists seventy-four more on other subjects treated by Feyjóo.[3] Almost all of these were published before 1750, for in that year Feyjóo achieved the unique honor of having Fernando VI issue a royal order prohibiting the publication of refutations or replies to his writings, because his works were declared to enjoy royal favor ("eran del real agrado")[4] His fame had also brought him a tremendous correspondence, so great that he was not able to answer it all personally. Many of his later essays became a kind of editor's replies to his public. "All desire to know something, and many of them with inquietude, with anxiety, with a strange im-

[2] A list of Feyjóo's sources is given in *ibid.*, pp. 334-41. Delpy's book is an excellent study of Feyjóo's writing and of contemporary Spanish intellectual life. Sánchez Agesta discusses his political philosophy, pp. 35-84.

[3] [Agustín Millares], "Apéndice," in Benito Jerónimo Feijóo [sic], *Teatro crítico universal*, Vol. i ("Clásicos castellanos," Vol. xlviii) (Madrid, 1941), pp. 55-78.

[4] *Real orden*, June 23, 1750, cited in *ibid.*, i, 35, n. 2, and Menéndez Pelayo, v, 87.

patience."[5] The number of editions of his works testifies to their popularity. Within six years, the first volume of his *Teatro critico* had been reprinted four times. The first editions of the fifth and sixth volumes were of three thousand copies, a tremendous issue for Spain at this time. Fifteen editions of the *Teatro critico* and the *Cartas eruditas* were made before 1786, in a period when it was unusual for a book to be reprinted at all. Only one work rivalled Feyjóo's in popularity, and that was the ever-loved *Don Quixote*.[6]

By the end of the century Feyjóo's name had become a national by-word. In Galicia a candidate for a curacy used the Benedictine monk as an authority for his assertion that fathers should not force their sons to follow their own professions;[7] while in Seville a future apostate priest received his first urge to knowledge from the clandestine reading of his aunt's copy of the *Teatro critico*.[8] "Thanks to the immortal Feyjóo," one admirer wrote, "spirits no longer trouble our houses, witches have fled our towns, the evil eye does not plague the tender child, and an eclipse does not dismay us."[9] Campomanes took time from his official duties to write an enthusiastic prologue for a new edition of his works;[10] and Juan Sempere y Guarinos, one contemporary who bothered to analyze and appreciate Spanish writers of his time, summed up the nation's debt to Feyjóo: "The works of this man produced a useful fermentation, they made us begin to doubt, they made known

[5] Prologue to *Cartas eruditas*, Vol. III, quoted in Delpy, p. 348 (see *ibid.*, p. 22).

[6] *Ibid.*, pp. 335-36; Sempere, III, 25. Twenty editions of *Don Quixote* are known to have been printed in Spain between 1725 and 1785, but many appear to have been of limited numbers (J. D. M. Ford and Ruth Lansing, *Cervantes, A Tentative Bibliography of His Works* . . . [Cambridge, Mass., 1931]).

[7] Posse, *loc.cit.*, XVI[2] (1916), 2. See *ibid.*, XVI[1] (1916), 116, for a dispute over Feyjóo.

[8] José María Blanco y Crespo [Blanco White], *The Life of the Rev. Joseph Blanco White, Written by Himself*, ed. John H. Thom (London, 1845), I, 14; J. M. Blanco y Crespo [pseud. Don Leucadio Doblado], *Letters from Spain* (London, 1822), pp. 97-100.

[9] Antonio Marqués y Espejo, *Diccionario Feyjoniano* . . . (2 vols.; Madrid, 1802), Vol. I, "Prólogo del redactor."

[10] "Noticia de la vida y obras de . . . Fr. Benito Gerónimo Feyjó . . . ," in Benito Gerónimo Feyjó y Montenegro, *Teatro critico universal* (Madrid, 1778), I, i-xlvi. The author is identified in Gaspar Melchor de Jovellanos, *Diarios (memorias íntimas) 1790-1801* (Madrid, 1915), p. 224, May 14, 1795.

other books very different from those there were in the country, they aroused curiosity, and they opened to reason the door which had been closed by indolence and false knowledge . . . for they are in the hands of everyone."[11]

It was not entirely true that Feyjóo had expelled superstition from Spain. Small ivory or glass fists were still hung around children's wrists in Valencia to protect them from the evil eye, and witches, ghosts, and the devil pervaded his native Galicia long after his death;[12] but contemporaries were not mistaken in believing that his writing marked the beginning of a new intellectual ferment in Spain. Hardly a facet of new Spanish thought in the rest of the century was not to be in some way indebted to him.

2

Experiment in sciences and skepticism of authority were the lessons which Feyjóo preached most strongly to his countrymen. Of the modern sciences, the one that he particularly encouraged was medicine. He had the satisfaction before his death of finding his attitude adopted by some advanced doctors in Spain. From their own reading in recent foreign medical treatises, fortunately still written in Latin, these men began to question Hippocrates and Galen and to seek new cures by experimentation. Many of their ideas have since been shown to be crudely mistaken, but their daring brought fresh life to Spanish science. Of these men the most capable was Andrés Piquer, who taught at the university of Valencia in the middle of the century, became familiar with the recent discoveries of the leading Dutch doctors, and produced an original *Tratado de calenturas* [*fevers*] in 1751, which was later translated into French. His interests had already led him to transcribe for Spanish readers the philosophy of Descartes in a work entitled *Logica moderna*. Like Feyjóo, Piquer upheld controlled experiment and observation as the basis for the improvement of the medical science.[13] In his own day Piquer was a pioneer, but

[11] Sempere, III, 24.
[12] Chrétien-Auguste Fischer, *Tableau de Valence* (Paris, 1804), p. 196; Townsend, III, 165-66; Posse, *loc.cit.*, XVI[1], 9.
[13] Sarrailh, pp. 411-33.

a generation later, at the end of the reign of Carlos III, the majority of Spanish doctors were disciples of Piquer, having studied while his fame was at its height. Younger men had meanwhile moved on to more recent techniques.[14]

At the zenith of the activity of Feyjóo and Piquer, the imagination of Spaniards began to be excited by the discoveries being made abroad in other sciences. Works of popularizers, addressed to readers who lacked scientific training, came forth to whet the interest of the Spanish public. Of these, the Abbé Noël Antoine Pluche's *Spectacle de la nature* of 1732 had become one of the best read books in France. By spreading knowledge of the latest scientific advances in easily digested form, Pluche sought to inspire reverence for God and his marvelous works. A few years later another abbé, Jean-Antoine Nollet, attracted large crowds in Paris to his lessons on physics and in 1746 published an *Essai sur l'électricité des corps*. The writings of these two men appeared in Spanish translation in the following decade. Pluche achieved definite success, for the *Espectaculo de la naturaleza* was reprinted twice before 1785, despite its sixteen volumes.[15]

Twenty years later Spanish readers were ready for more solid fare. A Frenchman, the Comte de Buffon, and a Swede, Karl Linnaeus, were rivals in the middle of the century for international recognition as the greatest natural scientist of the age, Linnaeus being known for his classification of plants and Buffon for his *Histoire naturelle,* a work that presented the findings of extensive research in an unusually artistic literary style. In the

[14] Townsend, III, 281-82.

[15] Noël Antoine Pluche, *Espectaculo de la naturaleza, o conversaciones acerca de las particularidades de la historia natural, que han parecido mas a proposito para excitar una curiosidad util, y formarles la razon à los jovenes lectores. Escrito en el idioma frances por el Abad M. Pluche, y traducido al castellano por el P. Estevan de Terreros y Pando . . .* (16 vols.; Madrid, 1753-55). Reprinted in Madrid, 1757-58 and 1771-85 (?) according to the catalogue of the Biblioteca Nacional. *Historia del cielo, obra del Abad de Pluche.* Traducida por el P. M. Fr. Pedro Rodríguez Morzo (2 vols.) was advertized in *Gazeta de Madrid* (hereafter cited as "*Gazeta*"), Jan. 1, 1805 (date of publication not given). Rodríguez Morzo published translations of Claude Marie Guyon and Claude François Nonnotte in 1769-70 and 1771. For Nollet see Sarrailh, pp. 457-58.

1770's extracts or résumés of the works of both men appeared in Spain, and more extensive translations followed in the eighties.[16] The writings of individual scientists were insufficient, however, to bring Spaniards abreast of the myriad foreign advances in science and technique. A work which might have done so was the French *Encyclopédie*, but it was prohibited by the Inquisición in 1759.[17] Public organizations in Barcelona, Madrid, and the Basque provinces managed, nevertheless, to acquire its volumes, the latter two bodies with permission from high ecclesiastical authorities.[18] In 1775 Campomanes recommended that articles of the *Encyclopédie* on arts and crafts be translated, with careful censorship to remove the irreverent passages for which it had become notorious. This was not done, but in the same year a Spanish translation was published of a less suspect history of scientific progress of the Frenchman Alexandre Savérien.[19] After 1780 the royal government gave hesitant permission for the circulation of a second French encyclopedia, the *Encyclopédie méthodique* of the Paris publisher, C.-J. Panckoucke, and also allowed a Spanish editor to undertake a translation of it.[20]

Ever since Fernando VI had bestowed special protection on Feyjóo, the government had been supporting the progress of

[16] G. L. Leclerc, Comte de Buffon, *Historia natural del hombre*. Escrita en frances por el Conde de Buffon. Y traducida al castellano por don Alonso Ruiz de Piña (Madrid, 1773); and *Historia natural, general y particular*, escrita en francés por el Conde de Buffon, . . . y traducida por D. Joseph Clavijo y Faxardo . . . (20 vols., Madrid, 1785-1805). The early volumes of Clavijo's translation were reprinted in 1791. Antonio Palaú y Verdera, *Explicacion de la filosofia, y fundamentos botanicos de Linneo* (Madrid, 1778). Karl Linnaeus, *Parte práctica de botánica del Caballero Cárlos Linneo, que comprehende las clases, órdenes, géneros, especies y variedades de las plantas* . . . . Traducida del latin al castellano é ilustrada por don Antonio Palaú y Verdera . . . (9 vols.; Madrid, 1784-88).

[17] *Indice ultimo de los libros prohibidos y mandados expurgar: para todos los reynos y señorios del Catolico Rey de las Españas, el señor don Carlos IV* (Madrid, 1790), p. 88.

[18] Sarrailh, pp. 269-70, and see below, p. 161.

[19] [Pedro Rodríguez de Campomanes], *Apéndice a la educacion popular* (4 vols.; Madrid, 1775-76), II, ccxiii. Alexandre Savérien, *Historia de los progresos del entendimiento humano en las ciencias exactas y en las artes que dependen de ellas*. . . . Compuesta en francés por Monsieur Savérien y traducida al castellano por don Manuel Rubin de Celis (Madrid, 1775).

[20] See below, p. 220.

science. In 1751, a favorite student of Linnaeus was brought to Spain to improve its botanical studies. Thereafter other foreigners were invited to direct various scientific projects, royal support was given to Spanish specialists in physics and the natural sciences (some of whom achieved well deserved international reputations), promising youths studied abroad often with government support, and foreign and Spanish scientists went to the New World at royal expense to carry on research in natural history and astronomy. Three observatories were erected in Spain by Fernando VI and Carlos III. A botanical garden was created in Madrid in 1755 and soon given an imposing site by Carlos. Later four others were established in major provincial cities. A museum of natural history (Gabinete de Historia Natural) was instituted by Carlos and enriched with the purchase of a private collection owned in Paris by a Spanish-American. Lectures by professors of physics, chemistry, and mineralogy were opened to the public in Madrid, although they were apparently not greatly frequented.[21] The improvement of the medical profession also received official support. Besides founding new schools of medicine and improving old ones, Carlos began a campaign to make common in Spain the recently discovered inoculation against smallpox; but the masses, conservative clergymen, and even at times members of the royal family did not readily receive this boon to society.[22]

Nevertheless, a literate and well-to-do minority were by the 1780's becoming scientific amateurs in the manner of the cultured groups of more enlightened countries. The periodical press of the time, whose multiplication was itself a recent phenomenon south of the Pyrenees, mirrored the new popular interest in the attention it paid to science. Two examples can show the trend. In January and February 1789, which were average months, the *Diario*

---

[21] Fernán-Núñez, II, 26-27; Townsend, II, 154, 252; *Gazeta*, Mar. 17, 1789. See Ferrer del Rio, IV, 484-500; Desdevises, III, 252-60; and, for an excellent discussion of the progress of botany and chemistry in Spain, Sarraïlh, pp. 441-61.

[22] Fernán-Núñez, II, 35-36; Ferrer del Rio, IV, 504-9; Lafuente, XV, 132; Desdevises, III, 261-64; Serapio Mugica, "Un caso curioso de viruelas," *Revue internationale des études basques*, XVI (1925), 306-20; Julio de Urquijo, "Los Amigos del País y la vacuna," *ibid.*, pp. 321-22.

de Madrid had eleven articles on scientific and technical advances. The semiweekly *Correo de Madrid*, devoted to light noncontroversial subject matter, carried twenty-six articles on "Física" in the year from October 1787 to October 1788. On April 18, 1787, it contained a "Rasgo filosofico-moral. Reflexiones sobre el espectaculo de la naturaleza" that reads as if it were taken from Pluche.

Special periodicals meanwhile were devoted to the progress of foreign knowledge, in which science was very prominent. In 1780-81 and 1786-87 the Imprenta Real published a weekly *Correo literario de la Europa*, "which gives notice of the new books, inventions, and progress made in France and other foreign kingdoms pertaining to sciences, agriculture, commerce, arts, and trades."[23] This journal was succeeded in July 1787 by the privately edited *Espiritu de los mejores diarios literatos que se publican en Europa*. Its aim was also to make known in Spain the state of sciences, arts, literature, and commerce of the century, which was "the most scientific of all that compose the lengthy epoch of seven thousand years."[24]

Typical of the articles on practical science of the last journal were several letters of "Mr. Franklin" on naval science and his stove that would not smoke.[25] The name was not new to the public. Benjamin Franklin, famous in French society as a natural philosopher, was looked upon in the Spanish press as one of the leading scientists of his time. One periodical, *El censor*, grouped him with Pluche, Descartes, and Newton; the *Correo de Madrid* gave a brief biography of him in an article on natural science; and the *Espiritu de los mejores diarios* translated a French epigram, "Franklin snatched the spark from the heavens and the scepter from the tyrants."[26] In Spain it was as the inventor of

---

[23] Listed in *Biblioteca periodica anual para utilidad de los libreros y literatos. Contiene un índice general de los libros y papeles que se imprimen, y publican en Madrid y las provincias de España* (3 Nos.; [Madrid, 1785-87]), No. 3, 1786.

[24] *Espiritu de los mejores diarios literatos que se publican en Europa*, prospectus.

[25] *Ibid.*, July 9, Dec. 10 and 13, 1787.

[26] *El censor*, Discurso 165, p. 633 n.; *El correo de Madrid*, Apr. 17, 1790; *Espiritu de los mejores diarios*, Jan. 12, 1789.

the lightning rod that he was known rather than as a father of
American independence, thanks to the spreading knowledge of
scientific progress.

There was one aspect of foreign science that did not triumph
in Spain. Buffon, like others, had run into trouble because his
writings contradicted the account of the creation given in the
Bible. In 1751 the faculty of theology of the Sorbonne forced
him to proclaim that he submitted to the teachings of the sacred
scriptures, calling his propositions mere philosophical supposi-
tions. His work continued to circulate freely in France, however,
and few scientists bothered about the theological implications of
their discoveries. This was not yet the case in Spain. In his prologue to the Spanish edition of Buffon's *Histoire naturelle*, the
translator, Joseph Clavijo y Faxardo, repeated the author's submission to revealed truths. At the same time Clavijo admitted
that Buffon's hypotheses explained more natural phenomena
than all previous "systems." Clavijo urged that, just as the hypoth-
esis of the earth's movement around the sun was tolerated in
Spain, although there was nothing "more opposed to a multitude
of texts of the sacred scriptures," so too should Buffon's theory
be tolerated. "Let us take from it that which is of use to our
teaching, and let us never forget that when God speaks all men
and all creatures should be silent."[27] This readiness to use the
most recent foreign knowledge without contesting the authority
of church dogma was revealed repeatedly by Spanish scientists
from the time of Feyjóo. It had the support of the government,
interested both in scientific progress and in maintaining the
purity of the Catholic religion. Soon after publishing the first
volume of his translation, Clavijo was made assistant director
of the Real Gabinete de Historia Natural.[28]

[27] Clavijo, "Prólogo del traductor," in Buffon, *Historia natural, general y
particular*, I, lxiii-lxv.

[28] This title is applied to him in *ibid.*, Vol. II, title page. On the submission of
Spanish science to dogma, see Sarrailh, pp. 497-503.

3

Although royal ministers, like others, were probably fascinated by scientific discoveries for their own sake, the government policy of encouraging the spread of scientific knowledge was justified primarily as a way to improve in quality and quantity the manufactured and agricultural products of the country. In this policy the kings' councilors were following the teachings of contemporary Spanish economic thought, which in turn was reflecting ideas that had developed in the rest of Europe. The mercantilist theory of economics had long maintained that a nation's wealth was measured by the quantity of precious metals that it possessed. Spanish kings had acted on this theory in the sixteenth and seventeenth centuries, attempting vainly to keep from flowing abroad the large quantities of silver and gold that Spain was receiving from its American colonies. Their projects went little farther than direct prohibitions of the exportation of specie and an attempt to limit purchases abroad. Contemporary economists, beginning with Sancho de Moncada in 1619 and going through Fray Francisco Martínez de la Mata in 1678, lamented the royal mismanagement and recommended government action to encourage agriculture, industry, and commerce. They went unheeded.[29] It was left to other countries, especially the France of Louis XIV under the minister Jean-Baptiste Colbert, to develop mercantilism into an elaborate policy of economic warfare of the state against all other states for conquest of the supply of precious metals in the world. The measures Colbert proposed involved the creation of a prosperous and self-sufficient national economy under the watchful and controlling eye of the monarch. Agriculture should feed the country and supply all possible raw materials. These materials should not be exported to benefit foreign industries but be kept at home and elaborated in domestic factories, if necessary with government subsidies, so that the state would produce its own manufactures and have a surplus for

[29] See Earl J. Hamilton, "Spanish Mercantilism before 1700," *Facts and Factors in Economic History* (Cambridge, Mass., 1932), pp. 214-39.

export. In the interest of the whole, private initiative should be left free to seek profits but only insofar as it would not conflict with state policy. Colbert did not achieve all his plans, but they long remained a theoretical objective and characterized the economic measures of the enlightened despots a hundred years later.

It was Colbert's version of mercantilism which first stirred Spanish economic thought to renewed activity in the eighteenth century. A series of writers made it familiar during the same years that Spain was being introduced to foreign science. The first work of note was Gerónimo de Uztáriz's *Theórica y práctica de comercio y de marina*, published for private circulation in 1724 and republished under government auspices in 1742. Uztáriz's lessons, well developed and explained, were essentially those of Colbert.[30] Two other writers, Bernardo de Ulloa and the minister of finance José del Campillo y Cossio, joined Uztáriz about 1740, urging the need to increase Spain's manufactures, commerce, and population.[31]

Under Carlos III the writers became almost legion who abandoned the former Spanish faith in its American gold and silver to plead for an active agricultural and industrial economy under royal direction. The ideal of the progressive minds of the day has been characterized by the most profound student of their thought as a "culture utilitaire et culture dirigée," two concepts which form the core of Colbert's system.[32] These Spanish economists all had pet ideas of their own to champion. Miguel Antonio de la Gandara in 1762 urged the government to encourage a growth in population and build factories so that it could end

[30] Earl J. Hamilton, "The Mercantilism of Gerónimo de Uztáriz: A Reexamination (1670-1732)," *Economics, Sociology and the Modern World* (Cambridge, Mass., 1935), pp. 111-29.

[31] Henri Bérindoague, *Le mercantilisme en Espagne* (Paris, 1929), pp. 176-77, 177 n. 1; José del Campillo y Cossio, *Lo que hay de más y de menos en España, para que sea lo que debe ser y no lo que es* (Madrid, 1898). Bérindoague gives a list of eighteenth-century Spanish works on economics, but it contains some errors (pp. 220-31).

[32] Sarrailh, p. 165. Sarrailh, like others, views the Spanish economists of the eighteenth century as physiocratic. I am indebted to Professor Earl J. Hamilton for first pointing out to me the basically mercantilist nature of their thought.

the trade of foreign merchants with its colonies.[33] A few years later a writer who used the pseudonym Antonio Muñoz attacked the policy of Felipe III that had brought about a decline in Spain's population by expelling the Moriscos, who were good farmers and artisans. He wanted to see industry revived with government support; but, echoing perhaps the contemporary French physiocratic doctrine, he held agriculture to be the basis for all wealth, since on it depended the prosperity of manufacturing and commerce.[34] Nicolás de Arriquibar, on the contrary, in reply to the physiocrats wrote a series of letters between 1764 and 1769 which admitted the benefits of agricultural improvement but insisted that the country's prime need was to revive the industry that Felipe II's false taxation policy had ruined. The country then would no longer be forced to buy half its manufactured goods abroad.[35]

The basic beliefs of these writers had permeated the royal government. Perhaps they were never better expressed than by Bernardo Ward, an Irishman who settled in Spain and became a royal official under Fernando VI. He was sent by this king on a tour of Europe and of Spain to observe foreign economic progress and recommend domestic improvements. After his

[33] Gandara's work must have circulated in manuscript. With the title, "Apuntes sobre el bien y el mal de España, escritos de órden del rey. Por D. M. A. de la G.," it appeared twice in 1804 as the first and only work of a collection planned under the title *Almacen de frutos literarios inéditos de los mejores autores* ([Madrid, 1804?] and Leon de Francia [*sic*], 1804). The copy in the Biblioteca Nacional of the first edition has the title page missing, but a MS note on the flyleaf indicates that it bore the publication data, "Madrid, 1804." Another MS note at the end says, "Suspendiose la publicacion de esta obra por orden del gobierno en 30 de Nŏvbre de 1804." The edition attributed to Lyon looks suspiciously as though it were also published in Spain after this prohibition.

[34] *Discurso sobre economía política por D. Antonio Muñoz* (Madrid, 1769), pp. xlii-lii, 83-88. A MS note dated 1823 in the Biblioteca Nacional copy identifies the author as "Enrique Ramos, Capitan de Reales Guardias de Infant[a] y Academico de la Española." This identification has been generally accepted. In 1764 Ramos translated a French work urging free commerce in grain (Sarrailh, p. 552).

[35] Nicolás de Arriquibar, *Recreacion política. Reflexiones sobre el Amigo de los Hombres en su tratado de poblacion, considerado con respecto á nuestros intereses* (Vitoria, 1779). The "Amigo de los Hombres" is the Marquis de Mirabeau, author of *L'ami des hommes* and an early physiocrat.

return, he was made minister of commerce. Ward wrote down his recommendations in 1762 in a work entitled by him *Proyecto económico*. He died before his manuscript was published, and it did not see the light until 1779.[36] Carlos III's famous *fiscales,* Moñino and Campomanes, took up the plans where Ward had left them. In 1770 the future Conde de Floridablanca submitted an official report on sheep raising in Extremadura that rang with concern for the growth of Spanish factories. He almost sounded like Colbert when he said, "Greed and interest are the main incentives for all human toil, and they should only be checked in public matters when they are prejudicial to other persons or to the state."[37] Campomanes, in various writings that often drew on Ward, pointed out ways to improve agriculture, foster manufactures, and increase population. In 1774 the Consejo de Castilla published his *Discurso sobre el fomento de la industria popular.* Campomanes in it showed how to put to work all the idle classes of the nation in both agriculture and industry. He urged the cultivation of domestic crafts that would not take people from the small towns and farms, and hence he preferred the manufacture of common products to that of fineries. The reason for the reputation of Spaniards for being lazy, he asserted, lay not in the people but in the "political constitution" of Spain, which kept the land in the hands of a few while "popular industry" was lacking. He wanted widespread education in the arts and crafts and the familiarization of Spain with advances in all fields. "A large population, all usefully employed, and an industry incessantly encouraged in all ways . . . are the two certain bases for the expansion of a nation."[38] This discourse was, with royal

[36] Bernardo Ward, *Proyecto economico, en que se proponen varias providencias, dirigidas á promover los intereses de España, con los medios y fondos necesarios para su plantificacion* (2d ed., Madrid, 1779). Besides his own observations, Ward made use of a manuscript left by Campillo (see Hamilton, "Gerónimo de Uztáriz," *loc.cit.,* p. 112 n. and Sánchez Agesta, pp. 308-9). Sarrailh goes deeply into Ward's work (*passim*).

[37] [José Moñino], *Respuesta fiscal en el expediente de la provincia de Extremadura, contra los ganaderos transhumantes,* quoted in Sempere, IV, 87-89.

[38] [Pedro Rodríguez de Campomanes], *Discurso sobre el fomento de la industria popular* (Madrid, 1774), p. clxxxv.

approval, sent by the council to all the local governing officials and bodies of Spain as well as to the bishops for distribution to the parish priests and the religious orders.[39] In the following year Campomanes supplemented it with a *Discurso sobre la educacion popular de los artesanos y su fomento*, stressing especially the need for agencies to spread knowledge of the latest technological advances.[40]

After 1780 the amount of literature on economics circulating in Spain swelled rapidly. Translations were published of works by several eighteenth-century mercantilists, including François Melon, one of the leading French writers in the field, and two prominent Italian economists, Gaetano Filangieri and Antonio Genovesi.[41]

At the same time, various aspects of recent mercantilist thought continued to be recommended in the works of the Spanish authors. A lawyer in Seville, Antonio Xavier Pérez y López, defended the right of manufacturers, merchants, and artisans to be considered honorable classes and held them therefore qualified to be chosen for those public offices which only persons with "honor" were legally entitled to hold. He was following Campomanes, who had already urged recognition of this right in his

[39] Sempere, II, 79.

[40] [Pedro Rodríguez de Campomanes], *Discurso sobre la educacion popular de los artesanos y su fomento* (Madrid, 1775).

[41] Lorenzo Normante y Carcavilla, *Espiritu del señor Melon en su ensayo sobre el comercio* . . . (Saragossa, 1786), a summary of Melon's *Essais politiques sur le commerce* (1731); Gaetano Filangieri, *Reflexiones sobre la libertad del comercio de frutos* (Madrid, 1784) (listed in *Biblioteca periodica anual*, 1784); Antonio Genovesi, *Lecciones de comercio o bien de economia civil del Abate Antonio Genovesi, catedratico de Napoles*, trans. Victorian de Villalva y Aybar (listed in Félix de Latassa y Ortín, *Biblioteca nueva de escritores aragoneses, que florecieron desde . . . 1500 . . . hasta 1802* [6 vols.; Pamplona, 1798-1802], VI, 249-50). Other translations published were Giovanni Rinaldo, conte Carli, *Carta del Conde Carli al Marques Maffei sobre el empleo del dinero y discurso del mismo sobre los balances económicos de las naciones*. . . . Traducido del italiano . . . por D. Victorian de Villavay [*sic*] Aybar (Madrid, 1788); and Mathon de la Cour, *Discurso sobre los mejores medios de excitar y fomentar el patriotismo en una monarquia*. . . . Traducido al castellano por don Juan Picornell y Gomila (Madrid, 1790). The last is in Biblioteca Nacional, Madrid, Sala de Varios (hereafter cited as "Varios"), Carlos IV, legajo 24, 4°.

The Enlightenment

Discurso sobre el fomento de la industria popular.[42] Juan Sempere y Guarinos wrote a history of luxury in Spain in which he approached the problem from the point of view of a contemporary mercantilist. Sempere condemned the extravagance of luxury as a vice but found it inevitable in a society that encouraged inequality by permitting inheritance and that admired a man more for his ostentation of wealth than for his virtue and moderation. In such a society, he said, needless consumption was actually a necessity, for it alone kept industry, and hence the state, thriving. The economic ruin of Spain under the Habsburgs came from failing to realize this truth and applying sumptuary laws. The government should not try to check extravagance but see to it that luxury goods are supplied by domestic rather than foreign producers. The main authority Sempere acknowledged was the seventeenth-century Spaniard, Martínez de la Mata, since, he said, one need not appeal to foreigners like Montesquieu, Hume, or Melon, "whose doctrine is suspect in many points for not having taken care always to associate religion and politics."[43]

While Spain was busy assimilating foreign mercantilism, elsewhere in Europe since the middle of the century the sway of the mercantilist economic theory was being destroyed by new beliefs. The first of these was that put forward by the group of French writers known as physiocrats. These men proclaimed that human economy is governed by natural law, the law of nature dear to the Enlightenment. According to them princes could not control the economy of their states by legislation, they could only harm the natural order of society by interference. "Laissez faire," they urged the governments, let natural laws function freely. Men should be allowed to engage in the economic activities they prefer and to dispose of the products of their land without trammels. The last point was important, for the physiocrats felt that the products of the land were the only source of wealth. Somewhat

[42] Antonio Xavier Pérez y López, *Discurso sobre la honra y deshonra legal* . . . (Madrid, 1781); Rodríguez de Campomanes, *Discurso sobre el fomento de la industria popular,* p. cxix. Sánchez Agesta discusses this topic, pp. 139-57.
[43] Juan Sempere y Guarinos, *Historia del luxo, y de las leyes suntuarias de España* (2 vols.; Madrid, 1788), II, 210. See I, 7-24, II, 198-218.

later a Scot, Adam Smith, wrote *An Inquiry into the Nature and Causes of the Wealth of Nations*, which was destined to have much more permanent influence than the works of the physiocrats. Like the latter, with which he was familiar, Smith preached the existence of a natural economic order that appeared when men were left alone to follow their private interests. Whereas the physiocrats were the prophets of an agrarian economy, however, Smith, by insisting on the contribution to wealth made by capital and labor as well as land, prepared a theory which suited the industrial revolution that was beginning in England and France. Meanwhile other writers—the English philosopher David Hume; an English merchant living in Paris, Philip Cantillon; and the *philosophe* Condillac—while not following either of these leading theories, also helped destroy the mercantilist monopoly by insisting on the need for economic freedom.

Of these writers Hume, Condillac, and the physiocrat Marquis de Mirabeau were the only ones whose economic treatises appear to have been given to the Spanish public at this time.[44] Spaniards felt not only their ideas but also those of other recent economists whose works had not been translated. Bernardo Joaquín Danvila y Villarrasa, professor at the Real Seminario de Nobles in Madrid, wrote a textbook on "economia civil" that included a markedly economic interpretation of history. He saw civil society as the outgrowth of four successive economic stages, beginning with a society of hunters. In the third or agrarian stage, when all land is appropriated, laws and property appear as a means to establish social stability. At this stage, society is divided into two groups, "landowners and the others who live at their expense."[45] Except

---

[44] *Discursos politicos del señor David Hume, caballero escoces* (Madrid, 1789) (listed in *Memorial literario, instructivo y curioso de la corte de Madrid*, Sept. 1789, p. 101), which includes his essays "Of Refinement in the Arts" (as "Luxo"), "Of Commerce," "Of Money," "Of Interest," "Of the Balance of Trade," "Of the Balance of Power," "Of Taxes," and "Of Public Credit." Jovellanos mentions a translation of extracts of Mirabeau's *L'ami des hommes* (1780) (Sarrailh, p. 240 and n. 2). On the translation of Condillac and of other economists see Robert S. Smith, "The *Wealth of Nations* in Spain and Hispanic America, 1780-1830," *Journal of Political Economy*, LXV (1957), 104.

[45] Bernardo Joaquín Danvila y Villarrasa, *Lecciones de economia civil, ó de el comerico, escritas para el uso de los caballeros del Real Seminario de Nobles* (Madrid, 1779), pp. 13-17, 31-34.

for including the landless peasants in the nonproductive group, Danvila sounded physiocratic. The fourth, or commercial, stage arises from the division of nonproductive groups into various classes. Danvila next discussed value and price, drawing explicitly on Condillac and Cantillon. Before he finished treating all sides of economy, he cited also Melon and Hume, as well as Uztáriz.[46] Francisco Cabarrús, the leading financial adviser of Carlos III, urged the right of property, a laissez-faire policy with industry, and a reduction of tariffs and internal trade barriers.[47] The editor of the periodical *El censor* boldly asserted, "The nation that has the most gold is the poorest, not the wealthiest, as Spain has shown." He compared meddlesome economic policies to the measures of a doctor who does not let nature cure his patient. "Absolute liberty" he called "the mother of abundance."[48] Vicente Alcalá Galiano, an enthusiastic devotee of political economy in the small city of Segovia, was one of the first men in Spain to have read the *Wealth of Nations*. In a work he published in 1788 he called its author enthusiastically "el profundo Político Smith." He denounced the mercantilist belief that economic growth of one nation is incompatible with that of its rivals and also the physiocratic one that a country's wealth lies in its soil. Wealth is the product of the labor of the country's individuals. It requires the "sacred right of property" and the accumulation of capital unhampered by the state. The rights of citizens must be protected by the courts.[49] After all these fancy phrases, however, Alcalá Galiano proceeded to make many recommendations that Spanish mercantilists had long urged.

[46] *Ibid.*, pp. 43-49, 114-15, 119.

[47] Francisco Cabarrús, *Cartas sobre los obstáculos que la naturaleza, la opinión y las leyes oponen á la felicidad pública* (Vitoria, 1808), "Memorial al rey nuestro señor Carlos III para la extinción de la deuda nacional y arreglo de contribuciones en 1783," nota tercera; Francisco Cabarrús, *Elogio del . . . Conde de Gausa . . .* (Madrid, 1786), pp. 89-90, n. xxvii; Francisco Cabarrús, *Elogio de Carlos III. rey de España y de las Indias* (Madrid, 1789), pp. 12, 17-18, 30.

[48] *El censor*, Discursos 70, 156.

[49] Vicente Alcalá Galiano, *Sobre la necesidad y justicia de los tributos, fondos donde deben sacarse, y medios de recaudarlos* (n.p., n.d.), pp. 2-4, 8-12, 62 (signed, Madrid, Mar. 18, 1788). See Antonio Alcalá Galiano, *Memorias* (Madrid, 1886), I, 4-5.

Other writers who did not mention Smith's name seem also to have felt his influence. Joseph Isidoro Morales, a priest, in a discussion of education, held that a growth of population depended on the ability of the working men to earn a living. The productive classes create a fund of wealth out of which are paid the unproductive classes, the clergy, the militia, and the government servants. The latter are useful classes nonetheless, for they are the "deposit of the nation's lights" and direct its forces. Although Morales does not say so, he is very evidently drawing on Book II of the *Wealth of Nations*. Morales does cite the French translation of Hume's essay on commerce.[50] In 1791 a naval lieutenant, Martín Fernández Navarrete, also divided society into a producing class, which should be encouraged, and a nonproducing class of owners and government employees.[51] Valentín de Foronda was another who approached the Scotch economist. He attacked at length the belief in selling abroad without buying in return. It is the buyers who gain, "for they receive useful things in payment for something that is of no use to them." He objected to what he called the Spanish tendency to close their eyes and be guided by Colbert and the English. "The English are men, and God did not bestow on them the gift of infallibility as he did on the church."[52] Foronda was referring to the English mercantilists, for, although he gave no credit to others for the ideas he voiced, he was close to Smith. He denounced the physiocrats—Mirabeau, "Quesnai" (François Quesnay), and "La Rivier" (Pierre Mercier de la Rivière)—for calling artisans and merchants a sterile class. On the positive side he recommended a policy of laissez-faire toward the crafts, the

[50] Joseph Isidoro Morales, *Discurso sobre la educacion, leido en la Real Sociedad Patriótica de Sevilla* . . . (Madrid, 1789), in Servicio Histórico Militar, Madrid, Colección documental del fraile (hereafter cited as "Fraile"), Vol. 146, fol. 32.

[51] Martín Fernández Navarrete, *Discurso sobre los progresos que puede adquirir la economia politica con la aplicacion de las ciencias exactas y naturales. . . . Pronunciado en la Real Sociedad Matritense* . . . (Madrid, 1791), pp. 18-19.

[52] Valentín de Foronda, in two of a series of "Cartas . . . sobre materias politico-economicas y otros asuntos de importancia," *Espiritu de los mejores diarios*, Jan. 5, Aug. 10, 1789.

merchandizing of grain, and commerce, including free foreign trade.[53]

It was not the general fashion to fail, as these men did, to acknowledge foreign sources. Most Spanish economists had few ideas of their own or even a determined conviction in favor of one school of thought. They were eclectics and as often were pleased to cite their authorities, old or recent, as to feign originality. The extreme of the tendency was reached by Francisco Xavier Peñaranda y Castañeda, a barrister in the royal councils. In the introduction to a proposal for a "supreme economic council" to coordinate the efforts toward Spanish economic progress, he claimed to draw upon many Spanish authors and Bacon, Locke, Newton, Hume, Montesquieu, Condillac, Filangieri, Colbert, and so many others that one wonders how he found time to do any writing.[54]

At the end of the 1780's interest in political economy had in fact become so strong that it was a subject for polite conversations. A contributor of an article on economy to the *Espiritu de los mejores diarios* in 1789 claimed to have been at a *tertulia* or evening social gathering at the home of the "Marqués de N" where there occurred what he evidently presents as a typical Spanish discussion of economics. The names of Ulloa, Uztáriz, Campomanes, and other Spanish economists were bandied about with those of the French mercantilists Colbert, the Marquis de Vauban, and "Neker" (Jacques Necker), the physiocrats Mirabeau and "La Rivere," and the enemies of both groups, the Abbé Raynal and Simon Linguet.[55]

It can be said that what was true of this *tertulia* was in general true also of those writers who show the influence of recent economic thought. They do not give the impression that they knew exactly where they were going. Most still seem to have held as their objective the strong, independent national economy of the

[53] *Ibid.*, Jan. 19, 26, Sept. 7, 1789 (p. 4 n. 11), and Apr. 19, 1790.
[54] Francisco Xavier Peñaranda y Castañeda, *Resolucion universal sobre el sistema económico y político mas conveniente á España* (Madrid, 1789), pp. 6-8.
[55] "Discurso económico-político sobre los medios de restaurar la industria, agricultura y poblacion de España," *Espiritu de los mejores diarios*, Mar. 2, 1789.

mercantilists. Yet Spanish economic thought, which at the beginning of Carlos III's reign still looked upon Colbertism as an innovation, was, by the time of his death, becoming familiar with the latest foreign beliefs.

On one thing many Spanish thinkers had come to agree, and in this they were not behind European thought. Political economy was the long-sought natural science of society, whose laws showed the way for man to live and prosper according to the dictates of reason. "Behold the true philosopher's stone with which all nations can become happy," wrote a newly appointed professor of political economy at Saragossa.[56] "The beneficent science that proposes to maintain societies," Foronda called it.[57] The young royal councilor Gaspar Jovellanos pronounced a eulogy of Carlos III shortly before the king's death that sounded as much like a panegyric of political economy as of the Spanish monarch. After praising Carlos for furthering the study of exact sciences in Spain, he added: "But another science is still necessary to make profitable the application of these. . . . This is the true science of the state, the science of the public magistracy, Carlos turns his gaze upon it, and civil economy appears once again in his dominions."[58] To Spanish enthusiasts, economics was already the unchallenged arbiter of social relations and justice that it was to become in the nineteenth-century industrial states.

4

Although enlightened Spaniards tended to look upon political economy as the panacea for their nation's ills, they did not neglect new foreign ideas in the less novel field of political philosophy. The best known work of the century on the subject was Montesquieu's *De l'esprit des lois*, published in 1748. Unlike John Locke,

[56] Lorenzo Normante y Carcavilla, *Discurso sobre la utilidad de los conocimientos económico-políticos y la necesidad de su estudio metodico* (Saragossa, [1784]), p. 11.

[57] *Espiritu de los mejores diarios*, July 6, 1789.

[58] Gaspar Melchor de Jovellanos, "Elogio de Carlos III, leido en la Real Sociedad Económica de Madrid el día 8 de Noviembre de 1788," B.A.E., XLVI, 314.

whose fame as a political philosopher had not yet been made, and the later *philosophes,* Montesquieu sought to understand the proper working of government from a historical study of actual societies and not from abstract considerations of a natural law identical for all men. He concluded that the character of a people depends on climate and physical environment, and their institutions must vary accordingly. In a good monarchy, he held, the basic social motivation is a desire for honor—an aristocratic trait—in a republic it is virtue—love of country and of equality. His ideal of political liberty he found guaranteed in a moderate monarchy like the English; and he favored a similar constitution for his own France, where aristocratic bodies should be entrusted with the protection of the fundamental laws of the kingdom.

Book XXV of *De l'esprit des lois* contained a "remonstrance to the inquisitors of Spain and Portugal" in the form of an imaginary plea for religious tolerance by a ten-year-old Jewish girl about to be burned in a Portuguese *auto-da-fé.* The reaction of the Inquisición was to prohibit the work in 1756,[59] and no Spanish translation of it or any other of Montesquieu's writings appears to have been published before 1820. His renown penetrated Spain just the same in the time of Carlos III. A Spanish mercantilist writing in 1769 demonstrated acquaintance with his work and called him the man who had founded the science of government, "one of the greatest statesmen of our century."[60] José Cadalso, a popular writer of this period, who had travelled in England, France, and Italy, was especially impressed by Montesquieu and helped spread his fame. In a satire of Spanish scientific amateurs, Cadalso portrayed a discussion between a sensible Spanish father and his foppish son concerning Montesquieu's uncalled for insults to Spain in his *Lettres persanes.* Despite the Frenchman's injustices to their country, the father called him a great man with "very great authority in other matters." The *Biblioteca española de los mejores escritores del reinado de Cárlos*

[59] *Indice ultimo,* p. 95. Henceforth, unless otherwise indicated, the source for prohibitions by the Inquisición is this *Indice,* which lists the works alphabetically.
[60] *Discurso sobre economía política por D. Antonio Muñoz,* p. xxi.

III of Sempere y Guarinos reproduced the passage in full.[61] Cadalso later chose to imitate the *Lettres persanes* in a criticism of Spanish society which he entitled *Cartas marruecas*. They were first published posthumously in the *Correo de Madrid* in 1789.[62] Other Spaniards knew of Montesquieu's existence. Jovellanos, addressing the Real Academia de la Historia in 1780, cited his authority on a point of early Spanish constitutional history, and a few months later the periodical *El censor* voiced theories from the *Esprit des lois* and mentioned the work by name. A lecturer in these same years before the locally supported Sociedad Bascongada de Amigos del País gave a detailed summary of Montesquieu's analysis of the various types of government; while a professor at the university of Seville used his name to uphold the statement that monarchy is based on honor.[63] By the 1780's his identity and significance were probably known at least by hearsay to most educated Spaniards.

The work of another eighteenth-century political scientist, now long forgotten, had more immediate success in Spain. Jacob Friedrich, Baron von Bielefeld, one time councilor of Frederick the Great, published under the title *Institutions politiques* a treatise on political philosophy, government, and international relations, with a survey of the geography, economy, and government of the European nations. Five volumes of a Spanish translation appeared between 1767 and 1781, with a sixth to follow in 1801.[64] The economist Valentín de Foronda began another

[61] [José Cadalso], *Los eruditos a la violeta o curso completo de todas las ciencias dividido en siete lecciones . . . por Don Joseph Vazquez* (2d ed.; Madrid, 1781 [1st ed., 1772]), pp. 125-30; Sempere, *Biblioteca*, ii, 23-26.

[62] *Correo de Madrid*, Feb. 14 to July 29, 1789, Nos. 233-80.

[63] Gaspar Melchor de Jovellanos, "Discurso leido por el autor en su recepción á la Real Academia de la Historia, sobre la necesidad de unir al estudio de la legislación el de nuestra historia y antigüedades," B.A.E., xlvi, 291; *El censor*, Discurso 31; *Discursos que D. J. A. Ibáñez de la Rentería presentó a la Real Sociedad Bascongada de los Amigos del País en sus juntas generales de . . . 1780, 1781 y 1783* (Madrid, 1790), cited by Sarrailh, pp. 239-40, 576; Antonio Xavier Pérez y López, *Principios del orden esencial de la naturaleza, establecidos por fundamento de la moral y politica, y por prueba de la religion . . .* (Madrid, 1785), chap. xxv.

[64] Jacob Friedrich, Baron von Bielefeld, *Instituciones politicas. Obra en que se trata de la sociedad civil, de las leyes, de la policía, de la real hacienda . . .*

translation of the work but published only the chapters on Spain and Portugal in Bordeaux in 1781.[65]

The contemporary field of legal and political theory was dominated by two outstanding Italians, and both had their works accepted in Spain. The Marchese de Beccaria's *Dei delitti e delle pene*, which stressed the need to reform penal laws, was given to the Spanish public in translation in 1774.[66] The Consejo de Castilla was not yet sure how such a work would be received, so it issued a warning inserted after the title page that the book was to be considered as intended for public instruction only, it was not a recommendation to violate the laws of the kingdom. The translator's prologue made the same point and was followed by a "protest," that if anything in the work opposed the opinions of the church or the regalias of the king, "of course with complete submission and respect we detest it."

The other renowned Italian jurist was Gaetano Filangieri. A translation of his *La scienza della legislazione*, of 1780, was published in Madrid between 1787 and 1789.[67] By now the Consejo did not insert a note of warning, nor was the translator so cautious. He said that the political and moral revolution caused by new interests and "holy and pure religion" have rendered Plato and Cicero out of date as writers on law. Montesquieu and Filangieri have taken their place, the first as a philosopher, the second as a writer on practical legislation, whose maxims are simpler and less open to error than the Frenchman's. Filangieri's

---

y en general, de todo quanto pertenece al gobierno. Escrita en idioma francés por el baron de Bielfeld, y traducida al castellano por D. Domingo de la Torre y Mollinedo (6 vols.; Madrid, 1767-1801).

[65] Jacob Friedrich, Baron von Bielefeld, *Instituciones politicas. Obra en que se trata de los reynos de Portugal, y España. . . .* Escrita en idioma frances por el varon de Bielefeld y traducida al castellano aumentada con muchas notas por don Valentin de Foronda (Bordeaux, 1781). See Valentín de Foronda, *Miscelánea ó coleccion de varios discursos . . .* (Madrid, 1787), "prólogo."

[66] [Cesare Bonesana, marchese de Beccaria], *Tratado de los delitos y de las penas.* Traducido del italiano por D. Juan Antonio de las Casas (Madrid, 1774).

[67] Gaetano Filangieri, *Ciencia de la legislacion,* escrita en italiano por el caballero Cayetano Filangieri. Traducida al castellano por don Jayme Rubio (5 vols.; Madrid, 1787-89).

work roused immediate interest in Spain. The semi-official *Memorial literario* and the *Espiritu de los mejores diarios* both compared him favorably to Montesquieu.[68] "He enlightens the public conscience on the laws of nature. . . . In our opinion Filangieri has found better than the author of *The Spirit of the Laws* the true road to philosophy," said the latter. In 1788 Foronda, in a contribution to the same paper, cited Filangieri in the original Italian, and another periodical also quoted him in an article that stressed that crime is the result more frequently of necessity than of malice.[69] Several years earlier some Spanish monks had been moved to write a refutation of the Italian author.[70]

The fact was that a public had been prepared in Spain for the *Ciencia de la legislacion*. Spanish penal legislation was in a state of veritable chaos. Legal reform was a subject of discussion and was under consideration by the government.[71] In 1770 Alfonso de Azevedo had published a work in Latin attacking the use of torture. A canon of Seville, Pedro de Castro, replied in 1778 defending the practice.[72] Meanwhile, after the publication in Spain of Beccaria's treatise, the Consejo de Castilla, carrying out a royal order, commissioned its member Manuel de Lardizabal to form an extract of the Spanish penal laws. Lardizabal, as a consequence, published a *Discurso sobre las penas contraido a las leyes criminales de España, para facilitar su reforma*. In it he discussed the philosophy of criminal legislation from a modern point of view. Castro, the defender of torture,

---

[68] *Memorial literario*, Oct. 1787, pp. 342-43; and review of the French translation in *Espiritu de los mejores diarios*, July 5, 1787 (a favorable review of Vols. III-V appeared in *ibid.*, June 27, 1789).

[69] *Espiritu de los mejores diarios*, Nov. 17, 1788; *Conversaciones de Perico y Marica* (1788), "Conversacion tercera," p. 165.

[70] Félix Torres Amat, *Vida del Ilmo. señor don Felix Amat, arzobispo de Palmyra* . . . (Madrid, 1835), pp. 42-43.

[71] See the list of Spanish legal treatises in Manuel Danvilla y Collado, *Reinado de Carlos III* (Madrid, n.d.), VI, 117-23; and Sempere, *Biblioteca*, I, 84-92, III, 167-72, 218-19; Desdevises, II, 151.

[72] Sempere, *Biblioteca*, I, 78-79, III, 176; Danvila y Collado, VI, 123.

would not be silenced and, unable to get a license to publish his views, upheld them in a clandestine publication. He drew down upon himself the wrath of his progressive contemporaries. Sempere y Guarinos denounced him and pointed out that the civil courts of Madrid no longer employed torture.[73] An address read in the Real Academia de Derecho Español y Publico was directed against the practice.[74] The outspoken editor of *El censor,* Luis Cañuelo, said that its theory was in contradiction with the original agreement men made when they entered society, and the *Espiritu de los mejores diarios* published two letters by Foronda stating that punishments should be aimed at correcting the criminal, not at taking vengeance on him.[75]

Both Foronda and the speaker at the royal academy cited as one of their authorities the contemporary French partisan of legal reform, Jacques-Pierre Brissot de Warville. Brissot had come to the attention of the Spanish public in an exchange of views with Pedro de Castro, whom Brissot had called typical of the unenlightened Spanish jurists.[76] Castro inserted a rebuttal, defending torture, in a French periodical. Thereupon Brissot let his pen run freely, and the *Espiritu de los mejores diarios* published his reply in full. He termed Castro's medieval authorities "the jumble that preceded the century of philosophy." "To organize society few laws are needed; once their mother, reason, is perfected, what need is there to recur to remote ages?" No more than there is now of monks, who once too were useful, said Brissot in one of the rare irreverences published in Spain. "I confess that neither *The Spirit of the Laws* nor the *Social Contract* is worth anything beside the *Summa*; but can I help it if our taste has been corrupted and Rousseau is read while the existence of the *Summa* is forgotten?"[77]

[73] Sempere, *Biblioteca,* III, 172-79, I, 84-85.

[74] Ramón Santurio García on Oct. 24. 1788, published in *Espiritu de los mejores diarios,* Feb. 2, 9, 16, 23, 1789.

[75] *El censor,* Discurso 64; *Espiritu de los mejores diarios,* Jan. 12, 1789, Nov. 1, 1790. On the movement to reform criminal justice, see Sarrailh, pp. 535-41.

[76] Quoted in Sempere, *Biblioteca,* I, 84-85.

[77] *Espiritu de los mejores diarios,* Sept. 24, 1787.

5

Brissot was thinking of France, of course; nevertheless his remark applied almost as well to Spain. The fortune of Jean-Jacques Rousseau's writings in Spain has been studied in detail, and it is seen to be exceptional.[78] Probably no other foreign author was so well or so widely received south of the Pyrenees in the second half of the century. Feyjóo first introduced his name in 1752 when he refuted the *Discours sur les sciences et les arts*, which had brought Rousseau to the public eye. Jean-Jacques asserted that the arts and sciences had corrupted men's customs, a point of view which Feyjóo, as a devotee of modern science, could not stomach. The controversy which Rousseau's discourse aroused in France was also given publicity in 1755 and 1756 by the Madrid journal *Discursos mercuriales*. The future scientist Clavijo y Faxardo, while publishing a periodical in the early 1760's entitled *El pensador*, further contributed to the fame of the Genevan, drawing particularly on Rousseau's novel that was a treatise on education, *L'Émile*.

In April 1764 Rousseau's name was put on the Spanish Index as a heretical philosopher and all his works were forbidden. Before a Sunday high mass in the church of the Dominicans in Madrid in 1765 a large quarto volume was solemnly burned. It was proclaimed to be Rousseau's *Émile*, although at least one acute witness smiled who knew that no edition of this had been printed in larger format than octavo. Conservative circles soon looked on the Genevan as one of the most dangerous writers of their time; but neither this reputation nor the Santo Oficio's anathema served to prevent enlightened Spaniards from becoming his partisans. The press of the 1780's, periodical and otherwise, while being cautious enough seldom to mention his name, gave unmistakable signs of the high appreciation in which he was held. The *Correo de los ciegos de Madrid* even quoted in French from "J.J.R. Orig. de l'ineg. parmi les hom." Before

---

[78] By J. R. Spell in his *Rousseau in the Spanish World*. Unless otherwise noted, the following information on Rousseau comes from Spell.

1789 a royal official in Valladolid had read with particular attention and accepted the arguments of the *Contrat social*, Rousseau's
major treatise on political philosophy.[79]

It was this author's ideas on education that particularly appealed
to progressive Spaniards, who had since the days of Feyjóo
become convinced of the need to reform their educational institutions. An article on raising children in the *Espíritu de los mejores
diarios* began with a quotation from "Emilio" in favor of exposing babies to fresh air.[80] In 1788 Valentín de Foronda preceded
the series of letters on political economy which he published in
the same journal with the introductory remark that many would
probably think his ideas as chimerical as "the *Republic* of Plato"
or "the *Education* of Rousseau."[81] One year later in a eulogy of
Carlos III, Cabarrús, a native Frenchman, lamented the in-
adequacy of the education given to future kings. "Let us be
happy if . . . this education is negative and if their position,
which keeps them from the principal and most important truths,
keeps away also the vain and impertinent doctrines which
corrupt the rightness of reason that men receive generally from
nature." There is little doubt that the author of these words
was familiar with the "negative education" given Émile.[82] Even
more obvious enthusiasm was expressed by Cañuelo in a number
of *El censor* entitled "Reflexiones sobre la educacion de los niños."
He established the principle that the punishment of children
should be done for their own good, not in a spirit of vengeance.
This he called "a maxim of a very famous writer, who has treated
this matter with more reflection and judgment than any other,
and from whom is taken the basis for some of the observations
that I shall make in this discourse." The argument Cañuelo used

[79] Antonio Alcalá Galiano, *Máximas y principios de la legislacion universal*
(Madrid, 1813), "prólogo."

[80] Guyena, "Del modo de criar los hijos, articulo dedicado a las buenas
madres," *Espiritu de los mejores diarios,* Nov. 30, 1789.

[81] Preface to Valentín de Foronda's "Cartas . . . sobre materias politico-
economicas y otros asuntos de importancia," *ibid.,* Nov. 10, 1788.

[82] Cabarrús, *Elogio de Carlos III,* pp. 5-6. "La première éducation doit donc
être purement négative. Elle consiste, non point à enseigner la vertu ni la vérité,
mais à garantir le coeur du vice et l'esprit de l'erreur" (*Émile,* Livre II).

to support this maxim indicates that he was referring to a proposition in the second book of *Émile*, "a fundamental maxim of education, a general rule to which I know of no exception or limitation whatever."[83] Despite its public burning in 1765, *Émile* was one of the literary products of the French Enlightenment which were most highly appreciated in Spain.

Rousseau's innocuous operetta for one actor, *Pygmalion*, was rendered into Spanish by several authors and presented on the stage in the 1780's. Otherwise none of his works appeared in translation at this time, but a Spanish work of fiction that swept the reading public in the late 1780's and 1790's was vibrant with Rousseau's ideas on education. This was *Eusebio*, a four-volume novel published in Madrid between 1784 and 1788 and written by a secularized Jesuit in Italy, Pedro Montengón. In it a noble Spanish boy, Eusebio, is orphaned in a shipwreck off the coast of Pennsylvania and is rescued and educated by a sympathetic Quaker couple. They find for him an enlightened Catholic tutor, who follows the maxims of *Émile*. Eusebio is taught a craft, basket weaving, and such are his later adventures that at one point only by turning to this craft is he able to support his wife and baby. Montengón managed also to have Eusebio exposed while travelling through France to Montesquieu's theory of the influence of climate, "the spirit of the laws," and religion on a people's character; while the Jesuit author's description of Philadelphia is reminiscent of the flattering pictures of the American states that circulated in France at this time. All in all, the novel was capable of revealing important features of the foreign Enlightenment to the many readers who turned to it seeking entertainment.[84]

Some of these readers were shocked to see that Eusebio, like Émile, was not taught religion until he reached early manhood.[85] In 1790 the novel was denounced to the Inquisición for breathing

---

[83] *El censor,* Discurso 28, p. 436. Spell notes other references to *Émile* in the Spanish press (pp. 68-69).

[84] Pedro Montengón, *Eusebio* (2 vols.; Madrid, 1836), esp. I, 12, 167, II, 6-7, 394-404. See Spell, pp. 72-74.

[85] Sempere, *Biblioteca,* IV, 75.

"Quakerismo, tolerantismo, etcetera." Proceedings began that led to its condemnation in 1799, but by then Eusebio had achieved an amazing success. Montengón, in a legal action which he won against his publisher for defrauding him of his just returns, claimed that three editions had been issued and sixty thousand copies sold. Montengón felt that his story was such a good source of income that he spent eight exasperating years after 1799 revising it to meet the views of the Inquisición's censors.[86]

6

When Rousseau wrote his early works, he was in close relations with Diderot and the *philosophes*. Although he broke with them before writing *Émile* and the *Contrat social*, his name nevertheless remained linked with theirs in the popular imagination. Those persons in Spain who admired Rousseau might have been expected also to read and appreciate Voltaire and the other *philosophes*. But did they?

In 1734 Leonardo de Uría y Orueta, "licenciado en sagrada teologia," published the *Historia de Carlos XII rey de Suecia, traducida del idioma frances al español*. The title page did not give the author's name, but the text was preceded by the opinions of church officials who had examined it, one of whom remarked that it had been "admirably written in French by Monsieur de Voltaire" and that "this history has deserved the ultimate glories of applause in all France."[87] Another edition, corrected and annotated, appeared in 1740.[88] Obviously Voltaire had not yet achieved his reputation for impiety.

By 1747 the Inquisición found that the book had to be expurgated, and on August 18, 1762, it issued a blanket condem-

---

[86] Archivo Histórico Nacional, Madrid, Papeles de Inquisición (hereafter cited as "A.H.N., Inq."), legajo 4460, No. 7; and Ángel González Palencia, "Pedro Montengón y su novela 'El Eusebio,'" *Revista de biblioteca, archivo y museo*, III (1926), 355.

[87] [F.-M. Arouet de Voltaire], *Historia de Carlos XII rey de Suecia*, traducida del idioma frances al español por don Leonardo de Uria y Orueta (2 vols.; Madrid, 1734), quotations from pp. vii, xi.

[88] 2 vols.; Madrid, 1740.

nation of all Voltaire's works.[89] Yet new editions of the *Historia de Carlos XII* were issued in 1763 and 1771, and it was still on sale in 1793. The edition of 1763, which had received a license from the Consejo de Castilla dated a month after the Inquisición's decree of 1762, was not even expurgated according to the Index of 1747.[90] The Consejo, not the Inquisición, issued licenses to publish books, and it could hardly have more glaringly ignored the opinions of the Santo Oficio.

The tolerance of the royal government extended to the plays of Voltaire as well, so long as their author's name was not made obvious. In 1765 his *Tancrède* was put on at a function given by the French ambassador in honor of the marriage of the Principe de Asturias, heir to the throne. The text of the play was included in the published account of the festivities, but its author's name was kept silent. Seven other of his plays were also published in translation before 1788 without stating the playwright's name.[91] The only one that achieved any popularity with Spanish audiences was his *Zaïre*, probably because in it Voltaire seemed to be inspired by the medieval Christian spirit of the Crusades. Three translations of it reached print in this period, one of which had two editions. As for the rest, their appearance does not demonstrate any wide appreciation of his plays in Spain. They were the result of official support given by men like Aranda, who had met Voltaire during a mission in France in the 1750's and had become an admirer of the *philosophe*. Voltaire's plays indulged the neoclassic taste of a group of Spanish writers who also translated other French plays, and they were staged as experimental pieces, usually in the private homes of aristocrats or in the royal court.[92] In any case the criticism of the church or other existing institu-

---

[89] *Index librorum prohibitorum*, ii, 812; *Indice ultimo*, p. 279.

[90] 2 vols.; Madrid, 1763; 2 vols.; Madrid, 1771. Advertised in *Gazeta*, June 7, 1793.

[91] Gerhard Moldenhauer, "Voltaire und die spanische Bühne im 18. Jahrhundert," *Philologisch-philosophische Studien; Festschrift für Eduard Wechssler zum 19. Oktober 1929* (Jena, 1929), pp. 115-31.

[92] *Ibid.*, pp. 130-31; and Luis Coloma, *Retratos de antaño* (Madrid, 1895), pp. 268-69, where the home of Pablo Olavide, recently returned from Paris, appears to be the center for such efforts in 1767. See Danvila y Collado, iv, 8.

tions that they embodied was presented much too subtly to become apparent to the average spectator or reader.

Although Voltaire's less tendentious writings could evidently be published with impunity if their author's name was kept silent, these plays and his *Historia de Carlos XII* appear to be his only works printed in Spanish before 1788. None of his other histories, much less his irreverent satiric tales, reached the reading public in the Spanish language.

But what of those educated Spaniards who could read his works in their original language? To do so, they would have to violate the edicts of the Inquisición, but this tribunal had given evidence of its laxity in persecuting Voltaire's writings, and, because of the decline in its efficiency, the misdemeanor of reading forbidden books no longer involved the risk it once did. Jovellanos in 1778 wrote a judgment of the "lights and shadows of the author of the *Henriade*," and sent it to Fray Diego González, an enlightened monk and poet. González liked Jovellanos' criticism because it admitted Voltaire's poetic ability. "The sons of light," González said, should admire the gifts of God, even when they find them in "the sons of darkness."[93] Both poets had evidently read Voltaire's epic and liked it, but otherwise they saw in him a "son of darkness." Were there other enlightened spirits in Spain who gained a more favorable impression of the *philosophe* from their clandestine reading? If there were, signs of it might reasonably be expected to appear in contemporary writings and publications, the official limitations on whose contents, as has been seen, was relatively lenient. Such signs are extremely scarce. In a note to the text of a speech made in 1785, Francisco Cabarrús, of known predilections for French culture, referred to "el célebre Voltaire," "that man whose errors in religion are the more worthy of pity because he alone was enough to educate a century by the universality of his genius."[94] There is no reason to suspect that his lament of Voltaire's impiety was all artificial. Three years later

[93] González to Jovellanos, Apr. 7, 1778, quoted in Leopoldo Augusto de Cueto, "Bosquejo histórico-crítico de la poesía castellana en el siglo XVIII," B.A.E., LXI, cci n. 2.

[94] Cabarrús, *Elogio del Conde de Gausa*, p. 95 n. 36.

the *Espiritu de los mejores diarios* published an anecdote involving Voltaire, the style of which indicated it was taken from a foreign journal. In 1789 a book review in the same paper praised the author for having "the clarity and precision of Voltaire," but the review was translated from a Dutch source. A Spanish contributor in the same year attacked Rousseau's and Voltaire's ideas of religious tolerance and cited Feyjóo against them.[95] Another periodical in an article taken from a French publication quoted the *"Siglo de Luis XIV"* without naming the author.[96] In sum the references to Voltaire found in a search of the most likely part of the press, periodical and otherwise, at the end of the reign of Carlos III indicate that, although his name was generally known, his prose writings had made practically no mark on the Spanish mind.

Voltaire's case was not true for all the *philosophes*. At least one could be grouped with Rousseau as making a definite imprint on the Spanish Enlightenment. This was Étienne Bonnot de Condillac, famous for pushing John Locke's epistemology to the extreme of believing that all knowledge, judgments, and passions are but various forms of sensation. A Spanish translation was published in 1784 of his *La logique ou les premiers developpements de l'art de penser*, not one of his most famous works but one that summarized his philosophy.[97] Within two years a portion of his *Cours d'études pour l'instruction du Prince de Parme* devoted to his epistemology also appeared in translation. In the same volume was included Pierre Louis Moreau de Maupertuis's *Essai de philosophie morale*, which gives a version of the theory, common among the *philosophes*, that morality is based on the natural desire to seek pleasure and avoid pain.[98]

[95] *Espiritu de los mejores diarios,* Apr. 23, 1788, Jan. 12, 1789 (review of the second [French] edition of *"Historia filosófica y política de los establecimientos . . . de los Europeos en las dos Indias,* por Guillermo Tomas Raynal"), Apr. 6, 1789.

[96] "Pierre Bayle," in *Correo de Madrid,* Nov. 18, 1789.

[97] Étienne Bonnot de Condillac, *La logica, o los primeros elementos del arte de pensar.* . . . Escrita en frances por el Abad de Condillac. Y traducida por D. Bernardo María de Calzada (Madrid, 1784).

[98] Étienne Bonnot de Condillac and Pierre Louis Moreau de Maupertuis,

Condillac rapidly achieved a certain popularity. A professor at the university of Seville cited him favorably in 1785 in a work on political philosophy.[99] In 1790 the author of a letter to the editor of the *Correo de Madrid* asked where he could get the *Lecciones preliminares de Condillac*, which had been recommended to him, and a treatise on education in the same periodical recommended for the study of logic "el tratado de los conocimientos humanos de Condillac" together with "Loke," Descartes, "Wolfio" (the German philosopher Johann Christian von Wolf), and Descartes's follower Malebranche, but not Aristotle.[100] Another periodical grouped Condillac with Newton, Descartes, Franklin, and others as a producer of useful knowledge.[101] Condillac was evidently being looked upon in Spain as the heir to Descartes and Locke rather than as a friend of the Encyclopedists. Since Locke was not published in Spanish at this time, what Spaniards learned of sensationalism was Condillac's severe version.

A professor of philosophy at the Seminario de Murcia, Ramón Campos, published a treatise in 1791 entitled *Sistema de logica*. It gave a crude explanation of sensationalist epistemology, discussed the importance of the invention of language for the advancement of man's knowledge, and ended with a defense of the experimental scientific method.[102] Campos called it an original work, but his contemporaries should have seen that he was mainly drawing on Condillac's *Logique*. The episode indicates that in the mind of at least one Spanish professor the reputation of the French philosopher had risen to the point where he was worth plagiarizing.

A lesser *philosophe* whose work was little designed to please the Spanish government was the Abbé Guillaume Raynal. His

---

Las lecciones *freliminares* [*sic* by mistake] *del curso de estudios* que escribió en frances el Abad de Condillac . . . *y el ensayo de filosofía moral* que escribió en frances Mr. de Maupertuis traducido al castellano por don Lope Nuñez de Peralveja (Madrid, 1786).

[99] Pérez y López, *Principios del orden esencial de la naturaleza*, p. 160.
[100] *Correo de Madrid*, June 23, July 14, 1790.
[101] *El censor*, Discurso 165, p. 633 n.
[102] Ramón Campos, *Sistema de logica* (Madrid, 1791).

Histoire philosophique et politique des établissements et du commerce des Européens dans les deux Indes, first published in 1770, frankly criticized the work of the European conquerors and the Catholic Church in colonizing America and the Far East. The Inquisición banned it in 1779. Nevertheless in 1784 the Duque de Almodóvar, recently returned from abroad, began to publish a free version of it. The translator's identity was disguised under an anagram in the title page, yet he made no attempt to hide his responsibility for its appearance. He even gave a copy to Carlos III.[103] Raynal's name was nowhere mentioned in the translation, but Almodóvar admitted in the prologue that the work had been written by a foreign pen, "a pen that, dipped many times in venomous blood, is a mortal poison."

> My labor has not been short to purify it of its noxious effusions and to correct it of that pride and elation which are inseparable from the thoughts of a man who calls himself the *defender of humanity, of truth, and of liberty*. Those who are cultured know full well what that vain attribute means nowadays.

Almodóvar had undertaken this task because the European colonies were upsetting the politics of Europe—witness the foundation in 1783 of "the republic of the thirteen united provinces," whose ultimate strength, he said, could not be guessed—and this work was the best on the subject. By 1790 Almodóvar had published five volumes covering the European conquests in Asia. The last one was the first to deal with Spanish colonization. For reasons never made clear, but which one may conjecture, no further volumes appeared.

Raynal's fame was boosted by the *Espiritu de los mejores diarios*. It quoted a French author's praise of his history and gave the second edition a long and very favorable review.[104] In this review, although Raynal's "fanaticism" and "cynicism" are con-

---

103 [Guillaume T. F. Raynal], *Historia política de los establecimientos ultramarinos de las naciones europeas por Eduardo Malo de Luque* (5 vols.; Madrid, 1784-90). See Llorente, v, 293-94, Villanueva, I, 16.

104 *Espiritu de los mejores diarios*, Oct. 18, 1787, Jan. 5, 12, 19, 1789.

demned, he is called an "anathematized Socrates." The review quotes his eloquent praise of the United States, "a place where reviled humanity has raised its head, where the harvests belong to the people."

To complete the picture of the works of the foreign Enlightenment that appeared in Spain, one must mention a translation of *Entretiens de Phocion, sur le rapport de la morale avec la politique, traduits du grec de Nicoclès* given to the public in 1788. Its author, Gabriel Bonnot de Mably, was the brother of Condillac, but he was a strong adversary of the *philosophes*. The theme of this work, which echoed the spirit of Rousseau's later writing, was an attack on the belief of the *philosophes* that society progresses as a result of the self seeking of its individual members. Mably upheld the ideal of communism. The translator praised the author for seeking to make society happy by means of religion, temperance, love of one's country, and of work, glory, and humanity.[105] Mably's *De la législation ou principes des lois* was also known in Spain, at least to Sempere y Guarinos.[106]

Beyond these writers very little of the tendentious literature of the French Enlightenment penetrated into Spain. Two of Diderot's *comédies larmoyantes* were translated and published before 1788, but passion and intrigue were their substance, not philosophic reason.[107] As was seen, the *Encyclopédie* was, except for a few copies, successfully kept out of Spain. A military engineer in a published account of an examination of students of mathematics in Saragossa in 1788 praised highly D'Alembert, co-editor of the *Encyclopédie*, as a scientist and mathematician;[108] but such appreciation was exceptional. The French extremists, such

---

[105] Gabriel Bonnot de Mably, *Entretenimientos de Phocion sobre la relación que tiene la moral con la política*. Traducidos del griego de Nicoclés con algunas notas por el Sr. Abate Mably y del idioma frances al castellano por D. Juan Francisco Xavier Somoza i Ulloa (Santiago, 1788), "Dedicación del traductor."

[106] Sempere, *Biblioteca*, i, 36.

[107] Denis Diderot, *El padre de familias,* comedia en prosa por Monsieur Diderot, y en verso por don Lorenzo María de Villarroél, Marqués de Palacios (Madrid, 1785), and *El hijo natural ó pruebas de la virtud*. Comedia en prosa de Diderot. Puesta en verso por don Bernardo Maria de Calzada (Madrid, 1787).

[108] Sarrailh, p. 270.

as Helvétius, Holbach, and La Mettrie, were all but unknown south of the Pyrenees. Not once in the literature examined were these men found referred to favorably by Spanish writers.

7

The most famous role of the *philosophes* was as critics of contemporary social, political, and especially religious institutions and practices. They upheld freedom of thought and action against the oppressive forces of church and legal privilege. Did the failure of the Spanish press of the 1780's to echo their message testify to lack of interest among Spaniards in this side of the Enlightenment, or did Spaniards have other reasons for not parading an appreciation of such writings?

One reason for their silence might have been that Spaniards, living under royal and inquisitorial censorship, never had the opportunity to learn about these men. The interest in Montesquieu and Rousseau, both also under the ban, has already provided evidence to suggest that this is not the real explanation. There were ways to circumvent the censors. An obvious one was to go across the Pyrenees, and as was only natural, some Spaniards did enjoy this privilege. A number of well-born youths were sent to France to study. Eighty-six students from Spain were enrolled in the military college at Sorèze between 1761 and 1790. They came from all parts of the country, only a few being from Madrid.[109] Many aristocratic Spanish boys and girls were sent to convents and other institutions in Pau and other cities near the Spanish frontier during this period.[110] Others crossed the Pyrenees to study in Jesuit schools until this religious order was expelled from France in 1764. Some noble families sent their sons on private tours abroad,[111] while those who were residing in foreign cities nat-

[109] Alfred Morel-Fatio, *La satire de Jovellanos contre la mauvaise éducation de la noblesse (1787)* (Bordeaux, 1899), pp. 47-48.

[110] Ferdinand Brunot, *Histoire de la langue française des origines à 1900*, Vol. VIII, *Le français hors de France au XVIIIᵉ siècle* (Paris, 1934), p. 54.

[111] Julio de Urquijo saw the class notes and text books of some Basque students (*Los Amigos del País (según cartas y otros documentos inéditos del XVIII)*) [San Sebastián, 1929], p. 18). The Conde de Peñaflorida studied in Toulouse and sent

urally educated their children near them. These latter sometimes brought tutors from Spain, thereby giving a chance for educated Spanish adults to travel.[112] The government of Carlos III sent promising youths to Paris to study the natural, medical, and engineering sciences and the arts of manufacture.[113] Nevertheless, given the type of education these various young persons were sent abroad to receive, few of them could have absorbed much of the iconoclastic spirit of the *Encyclopédie*. Other aristocratic sons indulged in gadding about foreign lands, but all they apparently gained were a few silly fashions and the scorn of their more tradition-minded countrymen, who, mimicking their propensity for employing Gallicisms in their speech, termed them "petimetres" (petits maîtres).[114]

A few Spaniards abroad came into personal contact with the *philosophes*. One was Joseph Clavijo y Faxardo, the Spanish journalist and future translator of Buffon.[115] Pablo Antonio de Olavide, who was later to support the presentation of Voltaire's plays in Madrid, visited Paris, entered the fashionable salons, and became a friend of Diderot, Holbach, and D'Alembert. He also went to Ferney to make Voltaire's acquaintance.[116] The Spaniard

---

his son there and then to Paris, the Low Countries, Scandinavia, Germany, and Italy, gathering scientific information (Sempere, *Biblioteca española*, v, 175; Urquijo, *Los Amigos del País*, pp. 42-90). José Cadalso went to England, France, and Italy (Juan Tamayo y Rubio, "Prólogo" to José Cadalso, *Cartas marruecas* ["Clásicos castellanos," Vol. CXII] [Madrid, 1950], pp. xii-xiii). See also Martín Fernández Navarrete, "Elogio del Conde de Peñaflorida," in *Colección de opúsculos* (Madrid, 1848), II, 348-49; Eustaquio Fernández de Navarrete's biography of Samaniego in Félix María de Samaniego, *Obras inéditas ó poco conocidas* (Vitoria, 1866), pp. 11-12; and Nicolás Rodríguez Laso, *Elogio histórico del excelentísimo señor Duque de Almodóvar* (Madrid, 1795), pp. 1-7 (in "Varios," Carlos IV, leg. 36. 4º).

[112] A. Morel-Fatio, *Études sur l'Espagne, deuxième série* (Paris, 1890), pp. 187-98. In this way the future noted botanist Antonio Cabanilles was able to study in Paris.

[113] Sarrailh, pp. 348-49; Emilio Cotarelo y Mori, *Iriarte y su época* (Madrid, 1897), p. 323. On foreign travel as a source of enlightenment, see Sarrailh, pp. 337-72.

[114] See Cadalso's satire in *Los eruditos a la violeta*, pp. 55-60, and Morel-Fatio, *La satire de Jovellanos*, p. 13.

[115] Llorente, v, 181-83.

[116] Danvila y Collado, IV, 7-8.

whose relations with the whole sect of *philosophes* became most notorious was the Conde de Aranda, the president of the Consejo de Castilla who in 1767 took charge of the expulsion of the Jesuits. In the 1750's he was in Paris and became acquainted with Voltaire, Diderot, and D'Alembert. He saw them again during a visit in 1760. From 1773 to 1787 he was Spanish ambassador to Versailles, once more close to his philosopher friends. Voltaire and Aranda admired each other strongly. The Aragonese *grande* sent wines, silks, and porcelains to the patriarch of Ferney, who replied with odes in honor of the Spanish "scourge of the Jesuits" and (as Voltaire mistakenly anticipated) "vanquisher of the Inquisition."[117] Jean-Jacques Rousseau also had his Spanish friends. None other than the Duque de Alba, royal ambassador in France from 1746 to 1749, was one of the Spaniards abroad who became an admirer of the wandering citizen of Geneva. After his return to Spain, Alba wrote Rousseau in 1773 to send him a set of his works regardless of the price.[118]

Of all the Spaniards who knew the *philosophes*, Alba was probably in the best position to mold the course of Spanish letters. For over twenty years until his death in 1776 he was director of the Real Academia Española. Aranda, too, was able to make his influence felt while he was president of the Consejo de Castilla, from 1766 to 1773. After his retirement and return to Madrid in 1787, he was also surrounded by a group of admirers; but these were mainly military men and aristocrats and hardly furnished fertile ground for philosophic ideas.[119] Less conspicuous individuals who had studied or lived abroad also came home with the impression that achievements were being made with which Spain should catch up, and some of these were to be found after their return helping to infuse the new spirit into their country. On the whole, however, those few Spaniards who had the advantage of foreign travel seldom returned enlightened. Any share they had

[117] Menéndez Pelayo, v, 235-40; Jacobo de la Pezuela, "El Conde de Aranda," *Revista de España*, xxv (1872), 36, 43-44, 349-51; Morel-Fatio, *Études*, p. 243.

[118] Spell, pp. 15-18, quoting Rousseau about two Spaniards he met in Venice, and pp. 57-58, on the Duque de Alba.

[119] See Ferrer del Rio, iv, 216-17, 226-28, 244-49.

in determining what *philosophes* were read in Spain was definitely limited.

Of course, it was not necessary to travel in order to become acquainted with the progress of the Enlightenment. One needed only to procure foreign books and be able to read them. So far as the difference in language was concerned, it became steadily a less formidable barrier as the century advanced. Almost the last of Feyjóo's recommendations was that Spaniards should prefer the study of French to that of Greek after they had acquired Latin.[120] Feyjóo was only expressing explicitly one of the morals of all his writing. By 1785 Sempere y Guarinos observed that the Benedictine's words and example had had their effect. "Although at first many scorned it [the French language] . . . later, little by little, it came to be liked until it became fashionable and was made part of the education of the nobility." Sempere approved of its spread because, as he said, French had become a language of culture throughout Europe, just as Spanish had been in the sixteenth century.[121] In the next year Juan Pablo Forner published in Madrid a discourse that had been pronounced in French in Berlin in defense of Spanish culture against French attacks. In his preface Forner, who was a violent Francophobe, explained that he had not translated this discourse because it was written in a language generally understood.[122] Between 1786 and 1789 five private schools to teach French were opened in Madrid, so much in fashion was the language by then.[123]

French was the only foreign tongue to achieve such popularity. The edition of the Spanish Index of 1790 is crowded with titles of works in French condemned since 1750. There are a few in Italian, a language that educated Spaniards, who had a knowledge

[120] Delpy, p. 333.

[121] Sempere, *Biblioteca,* I, 17-19.

[122] "Réponse à la question, que doit-on à l'Espagne? Discours lu à l'Académie de Berlin . . . par Mr. l'Abbé Denina," p. ii, in Juan Pablo Forner, *Oracion apologética por la España y su mérito literario, para que sirva de exórnacion al discurso leido por el Abate Denina* . . . (Madrid, 1786).

[123] Angel González Palencia, "Notas sobre la enseñanza del francés a fines del siglo XVIII y principios del XIX," *Eruditos y libreros del siglo XVIII* (Madrid, 1948), pp. 419-24.

of Latin, could almost read at sight, but almost none in any other living language. On the other hand, the Index includes the titles, "Algernon Sidney. *Discours sur le Gouvernement,* traduits de l'Anglois," *"Le Spectateur,* ou *le Socrate moderne," "La Vie et les Avantures de Robinson Crusoe,"* and other books translated from English, and the *"Code Frederich, ou Corps de Droit pour les Etats de Sa Majeste le Roy de Prusse.* Traduit de l'Allemand." Since the Inquisición condemned a work only after the work had been denounced and a copy of it reviewed by officials of the Inquisición, it is evident that French books, and a few Italian ones, were practically the only writings in modern foreign languages circulating in Spain. Spanish translators also regularly used French editions of contemporary works, even those by English authors. Before 1788 the person who could read English was a rarity in Spain, but the Enlightenment was accessible to a significant minority in the form and colors given it by its French advocates.

It was accessible, that is, provided these men were able to get books prohibited by the Inquisición and were willing to read them. That they could and did is suggested by the admiration bestowed on Montesquieu and Rousseau, and other evidence bears out this conclusion. A journalist who opposed the Enlightenment wrote in 1763, "Through the effect of many pernicious books that have become the fashion, such as those of Voltaire, Rousseau, and Helvétius, much coolness of faith has been felt in this country."[124] In 1769 the translator of a French Catholic apologist said that despite the prohibitions of the Inquisición the works of Voltaire and Rousseau "are not invisible." "Whatever care is taken to maintain the cordon against contraband, there are clandestine importations of some books capable of perverting and corrupting."[125]

Such importation was indeed going on. The future Venezuelan liberator, Francisco de Miranda, acquired copies of Raynal's his-

[124] Francisco Mariano Nipho in his *Diario extrangero,* quoted in Spell, p. 36.
[125] [Claude Marie Guyon], *El oraculo de los nuevos philosofos, M. Voltaire, impugnado, y descubierto en sus errores por sus mesmas obras. . . .* Escritos en francés por un anonymo y traducidos al español por el R. P. Mro. Fr. Pedro Rodriguez Morzo . . . (2 vols.; Madrid, 1769-70), i, iv-v.

tory and Rousseau's works while in Spain in the 1770's.[126] Cases before the Inquisición also confirm the circulation of prohibited books. Pablo Olavide, who had met Voltaire, was condemned by the Inquisición in 1778, among other reasons for corresponding with Voltaire and Rousseau and holding philosophic opinions. A royal councilor who witnessed the reading of Olavide's sentence was so impressed by the ceremony that he confessed to the Inquisición to having read Voltaire, Rousseau, Hobbes, Spinoza, D'Alembert, Diderot, and other prohibited authors. Forced, in order to obtain absolution, to name all other persons whom he knew also to be reading such works, he gave a detailed list that included Aranda, Campomanes, Floridablanca, Almodóvar, and other government officials too prominent for the Inquisición to risk troubling.[127] Other aristocrats were accused of reading forbidden books, the Marqués de Aviles in Saragossa and the Marqués de Narros in Vitoria.[128]

Although aristocrats and important members of the government would have no difficulty in making arrangements to receive foreign books, the ordinary Spaniard was forbidden by law to import them unless they had been approved by the Consejo de Castilla.[129] The law was not always closely enforced, but few would know how to go about circumventing it. A group that did have the opportunity and the motivation to bring in books from abroad was the large foreign population in Spain. Ever since the seventeenth century the depopulated and depressed condition of the country had attracted enterprising men from abroad. The French came in the largest numbers and they installed themselves both as laborers and entrepreneurs in Spain.[130]

---

[126] Spell, p. 131.   [127] Llorente, v, 316-18; Villanueva, 1, 20-21.

[128] Llorente, ix, 19, 27-29. Julio de Urquijo doubts the truth of Llorente's report of the trial of Narros; but he seems to believe it would have had to occur before 1780, whereas Llorente's facts indicate it was between 1789 and 1791 (Julio de Urquijo, *Menéndez y Pelayo y los caballeritos de Azcoitia* [San Sebastian, 1925], pp. 41-55).

[129] See below, p. 201.

[130] Alexander and Eugen Kulischer, *Kriegs- und Wanderzüge: Weltgeschichte als Volkerbewegung* (Berlin, 1932), pp. 113-14; Ludwig Pfandl, *Cultura y costumbres del pueblo español de los siglos XVI y XVII* (2d ed.; Barcelona, 1929), pp. 108-9.

All important cities had their foreign colonies, which were continually being renewed by fresh arrivals. The number of French workers in Madrid in 1750 caused concern to their consul,[181] and higher up in the social scale in the capital were Italian restaurateurs, who had branches in Cadiz and Barcelona, and French dressmakers, hairdressers, cooks, clockmakers, and manufacturers of cutlery, buckles, silks and carriages.[182] Four hundred and ninety-five heads of French families were gainfully employed in Seville in 1773, including over 150 keepers of taverns and restaurants and their employees.[183] The colonial commerce of Cadiz attracted an important group of foreign merchants, and after 1760 French craftsmen and laborers went to Barcelona to earn the high wages being paid there.[134] In 1771 the king encouraged new immigrants by promising them exemptions from taxation and military service.[135] A census of foreigners in Spain made twenty years later was to reveal over 27,000 resident heads of families and 6,500 transients. Frenchmen were in the majority, with Italians second in numbers.[136] Not until after 1789, when the government began to investigate their activity more closely, is there clear evidence of foreign entrepreneurs serving as agents for disseminating prohibited foreign literature; but in 1787 a French bookseller in Seville was found by the Inquisición to be selling Condillac's *Cours d'études*, a work not yet on the Index.[137] Since foreign businessmen belonged to the class most interested in the Enlightenment, had relations both abroad and with Spaniards, and enjoyed royal favor, one can conjecture that in the time of Carlos III they also imported books and were willing to circulate them to Spanish acquaintances with scant attention to the edicts of the Santo Oficio.

---

[181] Desdevises, III, 75.   [182] Sarrailh, pp. 331-32.

[183] *Lista de todos los individuos franceses establecidos y residentes en Sevilla . . .* ([Seville, 1773]) in "Fraile," Vol. 792, fol. 99.

[134] Desdevises, III, 145; Pierre Vilar, "Dans Barcelone, au XVIIIᵉ siècle: transformations économiques, élan urbain et mouvement des salaires dans le bâtiment," Colegio Notarial de Barcelona, *Estudios históricos y documentos de los Archivos de Protocolos*, II (Barcelona, 1950), 47-48.

[135] Sarrailh, p. 330 and n. 2.

[136] See below, p. 257.

[137] Sarrailh, p. 297.

It seems clear that those persons who ignored the prohibitions of the Inquisición could obtain the French books they wanted with little worry if they did not talk much about them. The majority of literate Spaniards, however, could still not read French, and devout or timorous persons still obeyed the Santo Oficio. Even so, there was no reason for these people to be ignorant of the more radical *philosophes*. Books were printed in Spain and circulated without opposition that painted a wide picture of contemporary French thought.

After three years in Paris as secretary to the Spanish embassy, Ignacio de Luzán published a collection of essays in 1751 entitled *Memorias literarias de Paris*. He gave a thorough report of intellectual life in the French capital: of its schools and libraries, its passion for sciences, and the state of its letters and theater. He praised Voltaire's tragedies and *Henriade* and his recently published tale, *Zadig*.[138]

Two other works published in the 1780's were able to complete a Spaniard's knowledge of the Enlightenment abroad. Both were devoted to the history of literature. The author of the first was Raynal's translator, the Duque de Almodóvar, who as a boy had travelled in Italy, Prussia, England, and France, and had later been successively Spanish ambassador to Russia, Portugal, and England.[139] In 1781 he published under a pseudonym a series of ten letters said to be written from Paris on the present state of French literature, *Decada epistolar sobre el estado de las letras en Francia*. Paris had been the center for good letters for a hundred years, he said, and knowledge of its activity would give Spaniards a chance to improve their own literature. He saw the French scene divided between the "filósofos," who "adopt and gild the paradoxes of some impious persons of the last centuries," and their adversaries, who "maintain religion in proper reverence, keep their impartial public which does not want to be deluded,

---

[138] Quoted in Marcelino Menéndez Pelayo, *Historia de las ideas estéticas en España* ("Edición nacional de las obras completas de Menéndez Pelayo," Vols. I-V) (Madrid, 1946-47), III, 239-40.

[139] Fernán-Núñez, I, 323, 326; Rodríguez Laso.

and attack the harm of the philosophers who flatter human passions and have on their side the weakness of the passions."[140]

Almodóvar admitted that his book did not cost him the effort it might have because what he had done was to extract and paraphrase the work of the Abbé Sabatier, *Les trois siècles de la littérature françoise*. The second letter of the *Decada*, forty-three pages long, consisted of a translation of Sabatier's account of Voltaire's writings. The French abbé took a moderate Catholic position. "Great talents and the abuse of them to the ultimate excesses, passages worthy of admiration and a monstrous liberty, lights capable of honoring his century and errors that are its disgrace, . . . philosophy and absurdity," Sabatier said of Voltaire.[141] Almodóvar added:

> The praise, the statues, the madness with which a Voltaire is adulated here deserve much thought. I have never been able to admire him. Several of his things have amused me, others I have liked, and some have given me reason to form an idea of his great genius; but many have exasperated me. I note that many persons of good judgment are in the same position.[142]

The next letter gave Sabatier's account of Rousseau, which was hardly flattering. Expressing his own view, Almodóvar said that Rousseau's political system—which Almodóvar maintained could be reduced to two points: equality and religious and civil liberty—was opposed to nature and impossible of achievement; but he nevertheless preferred the Genevan as a writer to "his enemy" Voltaire. Rousseau was more moderate, a better logician, more consistent, and "more dangerous, especially for persons with a cultivated talent."[143] The remaining letters described the other *philosophes* and their Catholic enemies, as well as contemporary scientists, critics, and the like. La Mettrie was anathematized, but the philosophies of both Maupertuis and Condillac received high praise.

[140] [Pedro de Luxán, Duque de Almodóvar], *Decada epistolar sobre el estado de las letras en Francia. . . . Por D. Francisco Maria de Silva* (Madrid, 1781), pp. 3-4. The author is identified by Rodríguez Laso and Sempere (*Biblioteca*, IV, 5-6).
[141] Almodóvar, p. 7.   [142] *Ibid.*, pp. 4-5.   [143] *Ibid.*, pp. 5, 66-69.

The Enlightenment

The other author to inform Spain about the French writers of the Enlightenment was a Spanish ex-Jesuit in exile in Italy, Juan Andrés. He wrote in Italian a history of literature that was translated into Spanish by his brother. It was published in Madrid in ten volumes between 1784 and 1806 with the title *Origen, progresos y estado actual de toda la literatura.* Andrés discussed the *philosophes'* writings, including Voltaire's *Candide*, under several headings. In the fifth volume, which appeared in 1789, he criticized Voltaire's style. Voltaire's pen made difficult subjects pleasant reading, "all the thorns are removed, and the flowers alone remain." Those who seek in him instruction rather than amusement, however, "cannot endure to see how truth, religion, decency, and justice are abandoned."[144] As for Rousseau, Andrés admitted the ability of his passages to convince even in "those matters that one does not believe and that reason does not admit." "One cannot take up his writings without feeling one's breast inflamed, one's heart wounded, one's mind overcome, and all one's senses upset."[145] On the other hand Andrés praised without reserve the progress made in human knowledge by Descartes, Locke, Montesquieu, Condillac, and D'Alembert. The ex-Jesuit was an admirer of the Enlightenment, but he felt called upon to denounce those writers who had attacked the Catholic Church. "I venerate religion profoundly, and this respect creates in my mind such an aversion for the harmful writings that contradict it that I cannot look without indignation upon the presumptuous wretches who, lacking talent and erudition, boast of being philosophers." "But," he added, "considering religion and letters as two entirely different things, . . . I do not understand why one cannot, or rather, why one should not prefer the fine taste of Voltaire, the eloquence of Rousseau . . . to the mediocre talents of the majority of their adversaries."[146]

With the works of Luzán, Almodóvar, and Andrés in open

[144] Juan Andrés, *Origen, progresos y estado actual de toda la literatura.* Obra escrita en italiano por el abate D. Juan Andres, . . . y traducida al castellano por D. Carlos Andres . . . (10 vols.; Madrid, 1784-1806), v, 254-55.
[145] *Ibid.*, v, 252.   [146] *Ibid.*, II (1784), 352-54.

circulation, no one in Spain needed to make excuses for knowing who Voltaire or the other *philosophes* were. It is true that those *philosophes* whom they praised were often those whose works were translated and read in Spanish, like Condillac and Maupertuis. But Rousseau was not recommended and D'Alembert was, yet Rousseau's impact in Spain was probably unequalled, while D'Alembert was hardly mentioned in the press. The fear of censorship in part may explain the failure of Spanish writers to speak glowingly of the irreligious *philosophes*, but the case of Rousseau shows how easily the danger could be circumvented by indirect references, and the royal censors have been seen to set little stock by the inquisitorial fulminations. An incident involving the *Espiritu de los mejores diarios* in 1789 gives a strong insight into the attitude of contemporary writers and editors. The periodical published a translation of a vigorous French attack on a Catholic opponent of sensationalist epistemology which read in part:

> I invoked the names of Condillac, Locke, Hume, Helvétius, Buffon, Diderot, because they are competent judges in the matters in which we disagree, because philosophy is entirely distinct from theology, and because these questions can very well be aired without recurring to the Bible. Philosophy wants peremptory proofs . . . not mysteries that do not admit discussion.

The Spanish editor added the note: "The eulogies lavished on Condillac in this and previous issues are to be understood as applying to the philosophical part of his works, which is not yet prohibited, as is the historical part."[147] The Inquisición had banned the last six volumes of Condillac's *Cours d'études* on the day before this article appeared,[148] and this fact accounts for the editor's sudden discretion. He made no apology for the French author's reference to Diderot and Helvétius, both of whom had works on the Spanish Index.

147 *Espiritu de los mejores diarios*, May 11, 1789, pp. 20-32.
148 Edict of May 10, 1789, *Indice ultimo*, p. 61.

Fear of censorship, then, can be eliminated along with other objective factors as the cause for the failure of Spanish writers to lavish indirect praise on the anti-Catholic *philosophes*. One must conclude that it was by their own preference that Spaniards paid scant attention to this side of the Enlightenment. The Spanish public read Condillac's and Montesquieu's philosophy because it was not aware that this philosophy might be dangerous to religious faith, and Raynal's history was presented to it with the sting removed. Rousseau was admired for the works, particularly the *Émile*, which he wrote after he broke with the *philosophes*. His popularity was not due to his anti-Catholic position but to the strong moral and religious appeal of his later writing. Voltaire's poetry was admired in some circles, but his attacks on the institutions that opposed human liberty, especially in religion and expression, and his friends' demonstrations of inconsistencies in the sacred dogmas were not read or appreciated. Those government officials or noblemen whom the Inquisición discovered to be reading the dangerous *philosophes* were not necessarily exceptions to the rule. The men brought before the Inquisición, even when they admitted reading forbidden books, protested their continued attachment to the Catholic faith. Made under such circumstances, their claims may be discounted; but Campomanes and Floridablanca, who doubtless had read the *philosophes*, and Aranda and Almodóvar, who are known to have read them, all did remain faithful, if open-minded, Catholics.

If one had asked the partisans of enlightenment what they were trying to introduce into Spain, their answer would have been "las luces," translating the French "lumières," but they probably would have added "filosofía." To some *filosofía* meant political philosophy. "Filangieri . . . has found . . . the true road to philosophy."[149] Political economy was *filosofía* to others. "Philosophy is correcting men's way of thinking," said the economist Alcalá Galiano.[150] "Philosophy has assigned the esteem they deserve to the labor of the farmer and the complicated tasks

[149] *Espiritu de los mejores diarios*, July 5, 1787.
[150] V. Alcalá Galiano, p. 2.

of the craftsman," added Fernández Navarrete.[151] Juan Andrés urged abomination of "the desire of so many presumptuous persons to appear to be philosophers while despising the authority of our elders and destroying the most sacred mysteries of religion." Yet he too saw the eighteenth century as having "that philosophic spirit which deserves praise" because it had destroyed scholasticism, furthered experiment, and seen the flowering of Feyjóo, Hume, Buffon, and Franklin.[152] The terms *filosofía* and *luces* were not applied to the irreligious writings of the *philosophes* mainly because no one was interested in these writings. Progressive Spaniards were by no means pleased with everything they saw in their church—they agreed with the government and Jansenists that reforms were necessary—but their remedy was not foreign materialism, deism, or even religious tolerance.

One of Spain's best journalists and most astute observers, Luis Cañuelo, complained of the large number of preachers who were denouncing the incredulity and atheism of the "philosophers of the times." So far he had been able to find no more unbelievers than he had ghosts. All he had observed was "some fool, some fop, who, because of his senseless vanity and in order to make others believe he has read books that they have not . . . speaks ignorantly about things of which he has not the slightest idea. . . . And this I judge to be the only effect that has been produced by these worthless books that have been introduced surreptitiously into the nation."[153] Cañuelo was right and not the preachers. Scarcely differing in spirit from Feyjóo, the enlightened Spaniards who mourned the death of Carlos III in 1788 were partisans of new ideas concerning scientific progress, educational reforms, economic prosperity, and social justice—all of which could be described as *luces*—but one would have had to search hard among their growing numbers to uncover the inevitable few who questioned their Catholic faith.

151 Fernández Navarrete, *Discurso sobre los progresos*, p. 27.
152 Andrés, II, 358-66.
153 *El censor*, Discurso 46 (1781), pp. 731-32.

CHAPTER IV

LAND BOOM AND LAND HUNGER

A MEANINGFUL picture of the *luces* in Spain must show not only what part of the European Enlightenment was entering the country but also how widely this part was disseminated among the people and what opposition it aroused. Since acceptance of the *luces* meant not only adopting new ideas about the universe but also championing changes in the structure of Spanish society, reaction to the Enlightenment depended largely on the individual's position in society and his goals in life. At the same time, his social position, by determining the extent of his education and the circles in which he moved, was likely also to decide how much he would learn of the *luces* in the first place.

Two fundamental developments underlay the social and economic history of Spain in the eighteenth century—a steadily increasing population and an upward trend in prices. The best estimates, which are little better than guesses before a census taken in 1768, indicate that the population reached its lowest point in modern times between 1650 and 1680 and then began slowly to climb: in 1650 it was perhaps under 4.5 million; by 1723 it had passed 6 million; in 1747 it was about 7.4 million. In 1768, it reached 9.3 million; in 1787, 10.4 million.[1]

One of the causes for the decline of population under the Habsburg kings was that many of the artisans and peasants of the central plateau of Spain were driven away by the excessive royal taxes levied on Castile and by a desire of landowners to transform farm lands into pastures for sheep. A profound inequality of population density had resulted in the seventeenth century between the heartland and the peripheral regions of Spain. The new growth of population did nothing to overcome this lack of balance. The kingdom of Valencia was growing

[1] Albert Girard, "Le chiffre de la population de l'Espagne dans les temps modernes," *Revue d'histoire modern*, III (1928), 420-36; IV (1929), 3-17.

fastest, followed by the northern coastal areas and Andalusia. Although the central plateau was also becoming more populous, it remained an area of vast tracts of vacant land by comparison with the rest of the country. Of 932 deserted towns (*despoblados*) listed in the census of 1797, 739 were in the two Castiles and León. Near Badajoz in Extremadura there was an area where pasture land extended unbroken by permanent habitation for eighty miles in one direction and forty miles in another. This was an extreme case but not the only one. The *reyno* of Aragon was also deserted, except for its fertile river valleys and the slopes of the Pyrenees. It had 61 *despoblados*.[2] The same phenomenon appeared in urban growth: except for Madrid the large cities were near the sea. Barcelona, Valencia, metropolitan Cadiz (including Isla de León and Puerto de Santa María) all rose in the eighteenth century to 100,000 or more. Seville and Granada had 80,000, Cartagena 60,000, Málaga perhaps 50,000. Saragossa, capital of Aragon, had 40,000. But no city in the two Castiles or León had over 25,000 except Madrid. As the seat of government since the sixteenth century, Madrid had always attracted people, and by 1787 it was by far the largest city in Spain, with over 150,000 inhabitants.[3]

Prices were also rising. During the wars of Louis XIV economic instability and an absurd manipulation of the currency had produced violent rises and falls of prices in Spain. In the second decade of the eighteenth century Spanish prices dropped rapidly and thereafter remained relatively stable until 1750. Then a moderate rise began that was to continue steadily, despite short term declines, until 1790. By this time prices were some 35 per cent higher than in the middle of the century. Yet, gentle inflation was an economic blessing by comparison with the disastrous fluctuations of prices during the previous century.[4]

2 Canga Argüelles, *s.v.* "Despoblados"; Desdevises, III, 8, 17, 20-21.

3 Fischer, *Travels in Spain*, pp. 133, 279, 293, 311, 330, 357; Townsend, I, 135, II, 288, 344, III, 122; Albert Girard, "La répartition de la population en Espagne dans les temps modernes, XVI° XVII°, XVIII°, siècles," *Revue d'histoire économique et sociale*, XVII (1929), 347-62; Domínguez Ortiz, pp. 69-75.

4 Hamilton, *War and Prices*, pp. 54-55, 155-56.

The Enlightenment

Rising prices and growing population were both typical of eighteenth-century Europe. England, France, and Holland experienced an inflation that paralleled closely that of Spain. A major cause of this movement was an increased world production of precious metals after 1750, particularly from Mexican silver mines. Another factor in Europe that pushed up prices was its rising population, which naturally increased the demand, especially for agricultural products. The average annual rate of growth of population for the continent between 1770 and 1800 has been estimated as 6.8 per thousand.[5] The Spanish censuses for 1768 and 1787 show an annual growth of 6.3 per thousand. Clearly, the demographic and price trends in Spain were part of a greater European whole. In both respects Spain had been sadly out of tune with its neighbors in the seventeenth century, but under the Bourbons it again was participating in the economic development of western Europe. The more closely one looks at Spanish society, the more evident this truth becomes.

2

As was true of all Europe, Spain's agriculture was still the basis for the livelihood of the vast majority of the population. The hopes and drives of the millions of persons that made up this majority were largely molded by their relation to the land and to each other. A thorough investigation of these relationships has not yet been made, but from contemporary accounts and statistics and some later studies a picture can be drawn of the general nature of land tenure and the changes taking place in the eighteenth century.[6]

[5] *Ibid.*, pp. 55-56, 66-67; A. M. Carr-Saunders, *World Population: Past Growth and Present Trends* (Oxford, 1936), p. 22.

[6] The major secondary sources for the rest of this chapter are Fermín Caballero, *Fomento de la población rural* (3d ed.; Madrid, 1864), pp. 25-69; Francisco de Cárdenas [y Espejo], *Ensayo sobre la historia de la propiedad territorial en España* (2 vols.; Madrid, 1873-75), II, 124-46, 181-83, 334-46; Joaquín Costa, *Colectivismo agrario en España* (Madrid, 1898), pp. 118-43, 264-389; *Desdevises*, I, 52, 121-41, II, 166-96, 372-82; III, 18-23; Rudolf Leonhard, *Agrarpolitik und Agrarreform in Spanien unter Carl III.* (Munich and Berlin, 1909), pp. 179-252; and Sarrailh, pp. 9-14, 562-68. Other secondary sources cited below give additional information on specific points. This chapter was written before I saw the ex-

Land Boom and Land Hunger

The land was divided between five different kinds of owners: the crown; the church; the cities, towns, and villages; private owners whose lands were in entail; and private owners whose lands were without entail. Of these the royal domain (*patrimonio real*) was the least significant. Much of it consisted of barren mountains or poor plains, like the neglected expanse of "ruined cottages and half-naked peasants" that the English traveller Joseph Townsend saw between Écija and Seville in 1787.[7] The royal lands in Aragon were more productive and so too were the farms of Granada that had been confiscated from the Moriscos after they rebelled in 1568 and were now let out to farmers under hereditary leases.[8]

Of greater importance than the royal domain were the lands controlled by ecclesiastical institutions. How extensive they were is far from clear. The census of 1797 showed 2,592 cities, towns, and villages under the jurisdiction of the church (*señorío eclesiástico*) exclusive of Aragon.[9] Of these, 1,423 were in Galicia and 61 in La Mancha, the only provinces where the church controlled more than half the towns. Elsewhere only one locality in twelve on the average was under *señorío eclesiástico*. *Señorío* did not give the church outright ownership of all the lands in these towns but only certain extensive lord's rights over them. The bishop of Tortosa, for example, exercised temporal domain over a large area of northern Valencia, "appointing the magistrates and receiving three thirty-sevenths of their wheat, barley,

---

cellent section of Domínguez Ortiz on "Las clases rurales" (pp. 255-97), and Marcelin Defourneaux, "Le problème de la terre en Andalousie au XVIIIᵉ siècle et les projets réforme agraire," *Revue historique*, ccxvii (1957), 42-57. Domínguez Ortiz deals primarily with Andalusia and Castile. Our information differs considerably, but many of our conclusions on the social and economic evolution of the agricultural classes agree. Defourneaux looks closely at conditions and proposed reforms in Andalusia and draws a parallel with reforms since 1931.

[7] Townsend, ii, 285.

[8] Costa, pp. 286-90; Jaime Carrera Pujal, *Historia de la economía española* (5 vols.; Barcelona, 1943-47), iv, 313-14.

[9] Total of the various provincial statistics given in Canga Argüelles under the names of the different provinces. In 1787 there were 3,148 for all Spain according to Desdevises, i, 48.

and oil, with three-fortieths of their wine."[10] Of course, the church also owned lands and buildings outright both here and in localities that were under royal or noble jurisdiction. A government survey carried out in the 1760's showed one sixth of the lands of the Castiles and León to be owned by various religious institutions.[11] Royal and canon law both recognized that these lands could never be alienated. They were in mortmain (*de manos muertas*). The clergy that controlled them enjoyed the further valuable privilege of being able to sell their crops without paying the *alcabala*, a tax collected in Castile on most sales.

The properties of the cities, towns, and villages, the *tierras comunes* or *tierras concejiles*, were more extensive than either of the above types. During the Reconquista the rulers of Spain had granted extensive lands to towns and villages. These common lands usually consisted of tracts of woodland and waste (*montes y baldíos*) lying beyond the privately owned lands that immediately surrounded a municipality. They supplied pasture for the animals of the townspeople and fuel for heating and cooking, permitting the peasants to devote their own lands entirely to agriculture. Since most towns had more land than they needed for communal purposes, a custom grew up of using part of the commons to supply income to meet the expenses of the town. In some areas, particularly in northern Spain, tracts of town land were cultivated in common and their products sold for the benefit of the town. More widely, tracts that were suitable for farming were rented to private users. The income from these lands, together with other less important revenues of a fixed nature, was known as the town *propios*. By the eighteenth century the *propios* were lumped together with the revenue from local direct taxes (*arbitrios*), and the two were the basis for the town and city budgets of Spain.

Both law and tradition forbade the alienation of town lands. At various times in the late Middle Ages and the sixteenth

---

[10] Townsend, III, 300.

[11] Carrera Pujal, IV, 316. Domínguez Ortiz, p. 128, says one seventh in area, one fourth in rent collected.

century municipalities had been forced by the crown to sell *tierras de propios* to private owners in order to meet exceptional royal imposts. When Felipe II asked the Cortes de Castilla to grant a new tax on items of common use known as the *millones,* the Cortes obtained in return a guarantee that the king would not permit town lands to be sold in the future. Later Cortes zealously enforced this promise. The town lands, both lands used in common (*tierras de aprovechamiento común*) and *tierras de propios,* thus formed perhaps the most important section of Spanish land whose ownership could not change hands.

Town lands were rivalled in extent only by private lands in entail, known as *mayorazgos.* The practice of entailing lands began with the decline of feudalism in order to protect the holdings of a noble family from being squandered by a reckless heir. At first only the king could give a license to set up a *mayorazgo,* but in 1505 the Cortes de Castilla decreed that henceforth anyone could create a *mayorazgo* out of as much of his property as the law of Castile permitted him to bequeath to his oldest son (usually about one half). After 1505 royal permission was needed only to dispossess his other heirs and include a larger proportion of his property in the new *mayorazgo.* The law permitted commoners as well as nobles to entail their land. As a result in the next centuries many small *mayorazgos* were created, especially by commoners who wished to become gentlemen and perpetuate their family names. Once a *mayorazgo* was established, future acquisitions of property by marriage or purchase were joined to it and became inalienable. After entailing his land, the next step of the rising commoner was to buy a title of nobility from the crown, easily enough done under Felipe II and his successors, or simply to wash his hands of his former productive calling and to pass himself off as an hidalgo, living as best he could on the income of the family *mayorazgo.*[12] The economists of the seventeenth century strongly denounced

---

[12] Altamira, III (Barcelona, 1906), 193-94, 422-33; Leonhard, pp. 76-80; Cárdenas, II, 134-43.

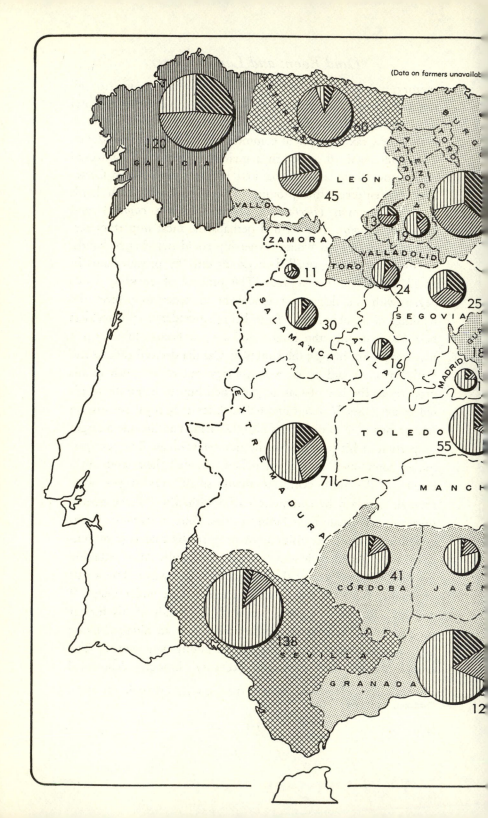

(Data on farmers unavailab

MAP I

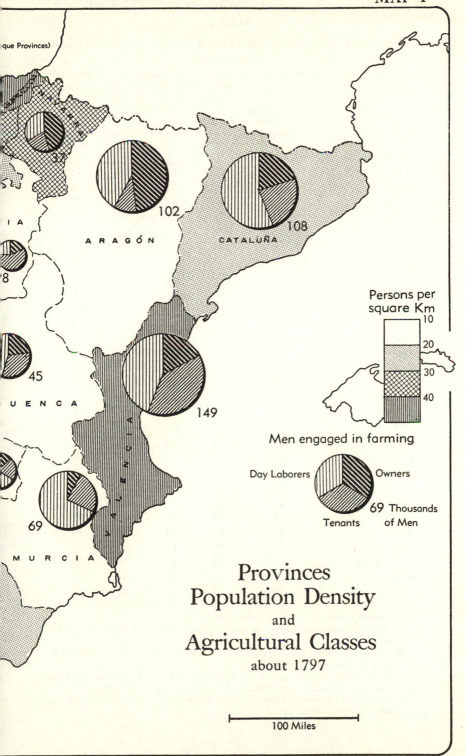

que Provinces)

ARAGÓN 102

CATALUÑA 108

I A

8

45

U E N C A 149

69

V A L E N C I A

M U R C I A

Persons per
square Km
10
20
30
40

Men engaged in farming

Day Laborers   Owners

Tenants   69   Thousands
of Men

Provinces
Population Density
and
Agricultural Classes
about 1797

100 Miles

MAP I

Provinces of Spain, Population Density, and Agricultural Classes
about 1797

Province	Population Density per Square Km	MEN ENGAGED IN AGRICULTURE			
		Total in Thousands	Percent		Day
			Owners	Tenants	Laborers
Álava	—†	—	—	—	—
Aragon	18	102	48	10	42
Asturias	39	60	6	89	5
Ávila	18	16	11	42	47
Burgos	24	83	36	35	29
Catalonia	28	108	20	24	56
Córdoba	24	41	5	14	81
Cuenca	10	45	23	32	45
Extremadura	12	71	13	33	54
Galicia	62	120	26	48	26
Granada	28	121	16	16	68
Guadalajara	25	18	13	49	38
Guipúzcoa	67	—	—	—	—
Jaén	26	32	3	17	80
León	16	45	21	51	28
Madrid	18*	17	13	11	76
Mancha	11	31	13	21	66
Murcia	19	69	8	24	68
Navarre	36	37	46	20	34
Palencia	27	19	13	29	58
Salamanca	15	30	9	50	41
Segovia	19	25	30	36	34
Seville	33	138	4	10	86
Soria	19	28	18	57	25
Toledo	17	55	20	13	67
Toro	20	13	24	52	24
Valencia	43	149	17	39	44
Valladolid	23	24	13	39	48
Vizcaya	35	—	—	—	—
Zamora	18	11	25	43	32

† Population density of Álava is estimated on map.

* Madrid city is omitted from the calculation of population density of Madrid province.

Map copied from P. Lapié (1814) based on López and Tofiño (1800). Some provincial enclaves are omitted.

Statistics from Spanish census of 1797 as recorded in Canga Argüelles, *Diccionario de hacienda*, s. vv., "Población de España" and "Labradores."

[Later calculation indicates the above population densities are about 3 per cent too high.—Author's note, 1969.]

this practice of entail, for it was creating a large idle class and taking Spain's land out of circulation. Furthermore it was debasing the privilege of nobility. By the end of the eighteenth century nearly half a million Spaniards claimed to be nobles—more than in France, which had over double the population of Spain.[13]

Distinct from the *mayorazgos*, which were family estates, were *señoríos legos*, lands over which the crown had granted laymen the rights of lords. Some *señoríos* had come down from the Middle Ages, but the majority in existence in the eighteenth century had been sold to the nobility or to wealthy commoners by the needy Habsburg kings. As lord of the *señorío*, the señor had jurisdiction over it, with the right to name the judges and local officials. In Valencia, for instance, Townsend found that the prosperous city of Elche, of 17,300 souls, belonged to the Conde de Altamira and was governed by his *corregidor* and *regidores*.[14] Altogether seventeen cities and one third of the towns and villages of Spain belonged to *señoríos legos*. The proportion was highest in the Castiles, Extremadura, western Andalusia, and Valencia, which were areas where over half the towns owed allegiance to señores.[15]

The *señoríos* were a major source of noble income, since Spaniards who lived on them had to pay dues to their lords. Many señores enforced medieval rights—such as a monopoly of hunting and fishing, of operating mills and ovens—and also received a share of the crops and livestock. Others took money payments instead. In the latter case the dues differed little from payments of rent, and by the eighteenth century these *señoríos* were hard to distinguish from *mayorazgos*, where the noble owned the land

[13] According to the census of 1787, there were 480,589 hidalgos and nobles. In the census of 1797, when a closer check was made, only 402,059 claimed nobility (Canga Argüelles, *s.v.* Población de España). According to Georges Lefebvre, *The Coming of the French Revolution*, trans. R. R. Palmer (Princeton, 1947), p. 7, France had no more than 400,000 nobles just before the Revolution.

[14] Townsend, III, 162-63. See III, 229-30 (the Marqués de Dos Aguas is señor of Fuente de Higueras in Valencia).

[15] 5,300 localities belonged to *señoríos legos* outside of Aragon according to the provincial statistics in Canga Argüelles. Desdevises, I, 130, gives a higher figure.

outright. Although a lord's *señorío* was usually more extensive than his *mayorazgo*, contemporaries seem often to have confused *señoríos legos* with *mayorazgos*. A similar confusion occurred between *señoríos eclesiásticos* and lands of *manos muertas*.[16]

Socially, however, there was a big difference between a señor and an hidalgo with a small *mayorazgo*. The señores were the real aristocracy of Spain, for they alone had the income to support extravagant living. Highest among the señores were the titled nobility, the *grandes de España* and *títulos de Castilla*. Kings had been lavish in granting new titles, so that the original 25 *grandes* of 1520 had been increased to 119 by 1787 and by that date there were 535 *títulos* besides. In the hands of this group were the truly large *señoríos* and *mayorazgos*. Townsend reported: "Three great lords, the dukes of Osuna, Alba, and Medina Coeli, cover almost the whole province of Andalusia [an exaggeration]; and the last of these, claims by inheritance, the greatest part of Catalonia." Medinaceli employed "thirty accomptants in Madrid, besides vast establishments on his estates" to keep track of his affairs.[17]

Below the *grandes* and *títulos*, but on a par with most señores, were the caballeros. These were lucky hidalgos named by the king to life membership in one of the four military orders of Spain: Santiago, Alcántara, Calatrava, and Montesa. They shared the income from the extensive holdings given to the orders during the Reconquista (three cities and 783 other places, largely in Extremadura and La Mancha). Besides the crusading orders, Carlos V had brought from Burgundy the Order of the Golden Fleece and Carlos III founded the Order of Carlos III. Membership in either one was considered a high honor and carried a large pension.

By comparison with the señores and caballeros, most hidalgos and other owners of modest *mayorazgos* hardly cut a figure at

---

[16] See, for instance, Jovellanos, *Informe de ley agraria*, p. 52 n. 1. The best discussion of the señorío in this period is Domínguez Ortiz, pp. 299-342. He does not treat *mayorazgos*.

[17] Townsend, II, 228-29, 157.

all. Legally the hidalgos enjoyed a few privileges which set them off from the common Spaniard: they could not be arrested for debts or forced to quarter soldiers, and they had the right to display their coats of arms and be addressed as "Don." But unlike the French nobility, they did not enjoy valuable fiscal advantages. The only tax levied exclusively on commoners was a property tax known as the *servicio ordinario y extraordinario y su quince al millar*. It was collected only in the lands of the former crown of Castile and produced a bare two and one half per cent of the royal income from that area.[18] Most hidalgos lived in the north, especially in Asturias, the Basque provinces, and Navarre, and in their way of life they were hardly distinguishable from commoners. In Old Castile they could be found working as cowherds, masons, and weavers. Large numbers of them were pitifully poor. Pablo Olavide, intendant of the province of Seville, reported about 1768 that owners of small *mayorazgos*, which abounded in Andalusia, could be seen daily begging in the public streets, "with their permits in their pockets."[19] A royal ordinance of 1770 gave inadvertent testimony of the sad plight of these hidalgos. In 1682 nobles had been permitted to own factories, provided they did no manual labor. Now Carlos III abolished this limitation, which had fallen into neglect: "I order that nothing stand in the way of hidalgos supporting their families by engaging in a craft, in order to avoid the disadvantage of their living idle or badly occupied and becoming a charge on society."[20] As for the title "Don," Cadalso humorously claimed that it had been so debased that to address a man simply as "Don Juan" or "Don Pedro" was to treat him as a servant.[21] In the new outlook of the eighteenth century, a man's income, not his nobility, determined his social position. Only legal recognition of class status and legal

[18] Desdevises, ii, 379-80; Townsend, ii, 179; Bourgoing (1789), i, 120.

[19] Quoted in Leonhard, p. 228. For the occupations of hidalgos, see M. Lasso de la Vega, Marqués del Saltillo, "La nobleza española en el siglo XVIII," *Revista de archivos, bibliotecas y museos*, lx (1954), 417-49, and for their geographical distribution, Domínguez Ortiz, p. 78 and map, p. 80.

[20] Quoted in Carrera Pujal, iv, 116. Carrera Pujal gives the date as 1773, but it is clearly the *ordenanza* of Nov. 3, 1770, referred to in *Nov. rec.*, viii, xxiii, 8.

[21] Cadalso, *Caltas Marruecas*, pp. 264-69, Carta 80.

prohibition to sell *mayorazgo* lands kept the ancient *hidalguía* alive.

Another type of landed property was that which could be bought and sold by private individuals. Contemporary economists lamented that the growth of *mayorazgos* and the possessions of *manos muertas* had taken too much land out of circulation, but a surprising amount could still change hands. An unreliable tabulation made in Cadiz during the Napoleonic invasion concluded that three tenths of the "cultivated land" of Spain was not entailed. More trustworthy figures provided by the official census of 1797 show that there were then 364,000 peasant proprietors (*labradores propietarios*), 22 per cent of all men engaged in farming. In Aragon, Navarre, Vizcaya, and Galicia about half the men who worked on the land owned their farms. In Andalusia the ratio was low—from 3 to 7 per cent; but in most other parts the proportion was between 10 and 25 per cent.[22] At times these figures are deceiving. In Extremadura 14 per cent of the farmers were landowners, but mostly they owned only a house and small lot.[23] Furthermore, many *labradores propietarios* lived in a *señorío* and owed dues to their noble or clerical lord.

3

As the population increased and the value of agricultural products rose in the eighteenth century, the demand for farm land grew correspondingly. A struggle developed everywhere to see who would pocket the profits accruing from the new situation— whether the man who worked the land or someone else who owned or controlled it. The decision was bound to be affected by the different types of legal status described above, but another factor appears to have been as important in determining the victor in the struggle. This was the geography of the country, and especially the supply of water.

Spain can be roughly divided into a rainy and an arid region.

[22] Canga Argüelles, *s.vv.* "Tierras cultivadas" and "Labradores." See map 1.
[23] Leonhard, p. 252.

The former is the smaller. It includes the northwestern and northern coastal regions: Galicia, Asturias, and the Basque provinces; and the southern slopes of the Pyrenees in Navarre, Aragon, and Catalonia. Most of the rain coming toward the central part of the peninsula from the Atlantic is dropped over Portugal so that only a small area of northern Extremadura and southern León is humid. The rest of Spain is dry, verging on desert in central Aragon, La Mancha, southern Andalusia, and the southeastern coast.[24] Here, however, since Moorish times, certain areas like the cultivated *huertas* or *vegas* of Valencia, Alicante, Murcia, and Granada made up for lack of rain by irrigation.

The pluviose region of northern Spain was also the land that had first been reconquered from the Moors. Climate and history appear to have combined to produce customs which guaranteed the peasantry against the sudden greed of large landlords. A contemporary wrote of the Basques: "The majority of the houses and land attached to them are lived in and tilled by the owners themselves."[25] Here every peasant claimed he was an hidalgo. In Navarre, Rioja, and northern Aragon the ratio of landowning peasants was also high. In these areas, furthermore, tenant farmers held their land under favorable conditions. They could pass it on from generation to generation within the same family and their payments of rent were fixed by custom or in writing.

Most of the land in Catalonia belonged to *señoríos legos* and *eclesiásticos* (742 and 319 localities respectively with only 404 directly under the crown). Here the *señorío* was treated as the private property of the lord,[26] and since the Middle Ages señores let out much of their land to peasants by special long term contracts (*enfiteusis*) that were written to last for several lives or indefinitely (or in the case of vineyards for the life of the vines). The peasant paid a moderate quitrent or *censo* and other dues to the señor. The peasant was free to improve, inherit, and

[24] Margaret Reid Shackleton, *Europe, A Regional Geography* (New York, 1934), pp. 77-78.
[25] Guillermo Bowles, quoted in Sarrailh, p. 563.
[26] See, e.g., the statement of the audiencia of Barcelona of 1770 cited in Carrera Pujal, v, 282.

mortgage or sell the land, but special fees had to be paid to the lord on such occasions. So well protected was the Catalan peasant that he virtually was the owner of his farm. Reforming ministers in the eighteenth century recommended an extension of the *censo enfitéutico* to the other tenant farmers of Spain.[27] The only recourse of the Catalan señor who wished to profit from the rise in prices was to let out new land for a money rent or a share of the crops. Since such land had previously been used as pasture, in 1770 the sheepowners of Catalonia complained to the local royal tribunal or audiencia. The audiencia held that it was the right of a señor to dispose of his land in this way.[28]

A comparable situation existed in Asturias and Galicia. Here *manos muertas* and *mayorazgos* virtually monopolized the land. The peasants held their farms under hereditary leases known as *foros* that were binding for three generations. At the end of the lease the lands returned to the owner with all the improvements made on them, and he was free to offer it at a higher rent. In this way the owners (*foreros*) had been able periodically to increase the income from their lands in keeping with rising prices. At various times in the seventeenth century representatives of the Galician tenants (*foristas*) had asked the crown to freeze the rents at their existing level. Nothing was done until the middle of the eighteenth century when certain *foreros*, urged on by rising prices, again began to raise the rents. Complaints were brought by *foristas* to the local audiencia until in 1763 the Consejo de Castilla determined that for the time being rents could not be raised in Galicia or Asturias nor could *foristas* be evicted unless they fell behind in their rent or did not till their land. Despite negotiations in the next decades, the measure was not abrogated and remained in force for over a century. Monasteries, churches, and owners of large *mayorazgos* could afford to see their income frozen, but the law applied also to small private owners who

---

[27] Townsend, III, 328-33, who cites Campomanes. See Jovellanos, *Informe de ley agraria*, pp. 12-17.

[28] Arthur Young, *Travels during the Years 1787, 1788 and 1789 . . . of the kingdom of France, to which is added, the register of a tour into Spain* (2 vols.; Dublin, 1793), I, 640-41, 645; Townsend, III, 332; Carrera Pujal, V, 282-84.

rented their lands and would be caught in the pinch of price inflation.

This was not the only evil to arise from the royal act. The *foristas*, assured of their holdings at a low rent, were free to sublet them at a profit. The temptation to sublet was especially strong in Galicia because it was the most densely populated province of Spain. The practice had already been known, but now it became general. The *forista* became in turn a virtual landlord. Since the *subforo* also was perpetual, the process was repeated and the lands were sublet again and again until the actual tiller found himself owing rent not to one man but to a series of three or four, to all of whom he was forced to pay directly. In the process of subleasing, or simply through inheritance, the original lots were also divided until they became minute plots.[29] By the death of Carlos III the land of Galicia and part of Asturias was becoming so divided and the income from it taken by so many hands who did no farm work that the lot of the peasant was critical. Young Gallegos and Asturians were driven to seek a living outside their provinces. They became the typical porters and water carriers of Madrid, and Gallegos travelled to Andalusia or Portugal at harvest time to seek seasonal employment.[30] Under the pressure of circumstance Gallegos also became noted for their domestic manufactures, particularly their linens.[31] The growth of population and the vicious system of *subforos* meant that few in Galicia or much of Asturias, least of all the husbandman, benefited from the rise in the price of land and crops. The area differed markedly in this regard from the rest of northern Spain, where rainfall and hereditary leases produced a comfortable peasantry.

Although they lacked rainfall, the farmers of the irrigated lands of the east and south belonged to the category that enjoyed a sufficient water supply. They too were generally well off. In

[29] On Galicia see Townsend, II, 50-51; Caballero, pp. 41-42; Cárdenas, II, 339-40; Carrera Pujal, IV, 179; Desdevises, III, 22-23; Leonhard, pp. 247-48.

[30] Charles E. Kany, *Life and Manners in Madrid, 1750-1800* (Berkeley, 1932), pp. 263-64; Altamira, IV, 130; Leonhard, p. 199.

[31] Rodríguez de Campomanes, *Fomento de la industria popular*, pp. lxxiii-lxxiv.

some towns of Valencia the peasants owned the land; elsewhere the *huerta* was divided between small landowners and tenants who enjoyed a fixed *censo* somewhat higher than that of Catalonia. The families lived in whitewashed houses with straw roofs and exhibited an air of prosperity and satisfaction. According to Townsend, the *huerta* of Alicante, thirty thousand acres in extent, was made up of small private farms, a "delightful vale" which gave employment and well-being to twenty thousand persons.[32] In the *vega* of Granada royal ownership, hereditary leases, and small holdings also provided the basis for a prosperous agriculture.

In all the regions observed so far, the peasant was protected from the greed of a landowner. He benefited also from another circumstance, his nearness to the sea. The northern and eastern coasts of Spain carried on an extensive export trade in wines and fruits, olive oil, rice and nuts, silk, wool, rush, and potash. Because they dealt with a European market, the peasants stood to gain from the general increase in prices of agricultural products. They had to beware of middlemen, but their greatest plague was their own fecundity, which led in Galicia and Asturias to excessive division of the profits from the land.

4

The fortunate lot of the husbandman who was not at the mercy of a landlord was much less general in the dry, grain growing areas of central Spain. Nevertheless, everywhere, except in Andalusia, a significant number of peasants owned their fields and also, of course, enjoyed the use of the town common lands. Specific evidence suggests that private ownership tended to exist in out-of-the-way hilly districts. Thus Townsend found that the peasants owned their land in the village of Pinilla, situated in rich grain hills above Cartagena.[33] Such towns must have been scattered about most of Spain. Their biggest concentration was in the rough wheat land of the Alcarria, northeast of Madrid.

[32] Townsend, III, 194-97.
[33] *Ibid.*, p. 119.

In this district, a contemporary observed, "rare are those who do not possess the land they till and some head of livestock, which save them from great need." Legal equality had long prevailed. Over a local town hall an old inscription read, "Our laws permit no hidalgos or friars or steers."[34]

Many of the beneficial effects of private ownership were also present in towns that, following an immemorial practice, divided their common lands into fields for distribution to all households for their own use. The practice was general where most or all land belonged to the community. It required a democratic town government and a strong communal spirit, yet it could be found scattered widely south of the ranges that separated dry Spain from the rainy north. In the valleys of the Pyrenees of Aragon and Catalonia and on the slopes of the Cantabrian Mountains, devoted primarily to sheepraising, the peasants often owned only their houses and gardens. The pastures belonged to the town and were subdivided and redistributed annually by a drawing of lots for private use during the summer. The rest of the year the pastures were used in common. Where the main livelihood was farming, the inhabitants paid a modest and equal amount to the town *propios* for fields they received. The fields were redistributed by lot at intervals of two years or longer. Here too the only private property usually consisted of the houses and vegetable plots. Fifty-six towns of this type existed around Bermillo de Sayago west of Zamora and others could be found in the provinces of Salamanca, Burgos, Navarre, Aragon, and very widely in León. The institution also functioned in the hills of Galicia and Asturias. Here lands belonged to *señoríos*, but the peasants used them in common and the town paid the dues owed the lord. Examples of this use of lands of *señorío* were also present in the provinces of León and Valladolid.

Such a communal system was productive of a democratic feeling of equality and common well-being, but it had its drawbacks. The town council controlled the use of the land, every peasant being

[34] Antonio Ponz, *Viaje de España* (1772), and Tomás de Iriarte (1781), quoted in Sarrailh, pp. 563, 387.

required to cultivate his fields according to a common plan. The individual farmer merely attempted to get what he could out of a piece of land while it was his, so that the system precluded permanent improvements or experimentation with new crops. Furthermore, the ideal of equality broke down in practice. Only peasants who had tools and animals and capital to buy seed could use their fields. The others would most often rent their lots to the well-to-do peasants and work for them as hired labor. Communal life had had to come to terms with a money economy and was on the defensive. Rising prices let the better-off peasants pull ahead of their neighbors.

Although the towns and villages where land was privately owned or used in common were often isolated and relatively self-sufficient, their inhabitants were the fortunate farmers of dry Spain. The fate was very different of the majority of men who lived from agriculture from Andalusia, Extremadura, and La Mancha across the Castiles and southern León to the uplands of southern Aragon and Valencia. They had to make their living from land belonging to *mayorazgos, manos muertas*, and municipalities in whose government they had no say. They were usually tenant farmers or day laborers.

The south was the region where agriculture had most definitely produced a proletariat. Whereas in most parts of Spain, only between one quarter and one half of the men engaged in agriculture were hired laborers, the census of 1797 showed that from Madrid south through La Mancha to Granada and Murcia, the ratio was two thirds or more. It was highest in heavily populated Andalusia: four out of every five men living from farming in the provinces of Jaén and Córdoba were landless laborers, five out of six were in Seville. Here there were extensive *mayorazgos* and *manos muertas*, whose owners often left them in the care of an overseer. The vast tracts east of Córdoba belonging to the Duquesa de Alba were administered for her by an efficient *corregidor*, who saw to it that hired hands kept the plantations of olive trees in prime condition. The Condesa de Peñafiel had similar olive groves near

Bailén that were less well tended.[35] On some *mayorazgos* in Seville province hired laborers plowed and sowed wheat and made a poor job of it because of their ignorance and apathy. Other estates were used as pasture for sheep. In this category were the holdings of the Carthusian monasteries of Jerez and Seville, whose monks accompanied their own sheep and hogs to market.

Throughout this part of Spain the towns and cities had always been far apart. Special settlements therefore existed on the estates to feed and perhaps house the laborers during the periods of work. These agricultural units, called *cortijos*, in off-seasons were inhabited only by a few caretakers and possibly an overseer. Olavide, the intendant of Seville, described the miserable life of the men who went to work at the *cortijos*:

> They are the most unfortunate men I know in Europe. They work in the *cortijos* and olive groves when the overseers summon them. . . . Then, although nearly naked and with only the ground for a bed, they at least live on the bread and soup they are given; but when bad weather stops work, . . . starving, homeless, and hopeless, they are forced to beg. . . . Half the year these men are laborers and the other half beggars.[36]

Campomanes filled in the picture:

> Their wives and children are without work, and all, piled together in the cities or large towns, live at the expense of charity . . . in terrible want that is out of keeping with the fertility of the soil and is not the effect of the laziness of the people but of the political constitution.[37]

Except for these estates tilled with hired hands, most of the owners of large holdings in arid Spain preferred to let out their land in small farms on short-term leases, either for payment in money or in kind. An example was the town of La Guardia in

---

[35] Townsend, II, 273-78.

[36] Pablo de Olavide, "Informe de Olavide sobre la ley agraria," ed. R. Carande, *Boletín de la Real Academia de la Historia*, CXXXIX (1956), 386-87. See Leonhard, pp. 206-15.

[37] Rodríguez de Campomanes, *Fomento de la industria popular*, p. lxxiii (quoted in Desdevises, III, 25).

La Mancha through which Townsend passed: "Their land is divided into small allotments, but their chief proprietor is Don Diego de Plata. The rents are paid in corn."[38] Legally the owner of a *mayorazgo* could not lease his land beyond his own lifetime, and the average term of the leases, even on church lands, was only six years. Since the first half of the seventeenth century, however, in many regions the contracts had been regularly renewed without change until the peasants felt confident that the leases were hereditary and the rents fixed.

After 1750 inflation and growing population brought tension to central and southern Spain. Landowners suddenly decided to break the custom and ask higher rent of their tenants or offer the farms to the highest bidders. They did not hesitate even to break leases before their expiration date. A tenant of the cathedral chapter of Salamanca, for instance, complained to the government of Carlos III that his rent had more than doubled in twelve years, and similar complaints came from Zamora and Ávila, Burgos and Soria. Contemporaries who visited Valladolid, Rioja, Aragon, and the dry hills of northern Valencia have left pictures that reveal religious institutions and landowners also leasing to the highest bidder and peasants weighed down by their rents and taxes.

In this way the peasant was driven to pay more for the land than it was worth. According to Olavide, in Andalusia:

At each expiration of the lease the owner demands rent in advance from the tenant and threatens to lease to another if he meets with refusal, knowing full well that with the lack of farm land and the excess of farmers he can always find someone ready to rent. The tenant, who has sunk his supply of tools, animals, feed, and other provisions into the farm and stands to lose everything if he loses his lease, finds himself in the sad necessity of signing the terms that the tyranny of the owner has set for him, and every year the owner raises the prices until they become intolerable.[39]

[38] Townsend, II, 258.   [39] Olavide, *loc.cit.*, p. 374.

An unlucky tenant might mortgage his tools, lose them in a year of drought, fail to pay his taxes, and be driven off the land into the city as a beggar or the hills as a brigand. He could not afford to improve land which he feared to lose, and he did not dare to try new crops. He got all he could out of the farm while it was his, and the landowner, whose income was rising, took little interest in the plight of his tenants or in improving the productivity of the land.

Because of the rising value of the land the practice of subleasing (*subarriendo*) developed in the large estates of Andalusia and La Mancha. Few wealthy nobles cared to bother with the details of renting their *mayorazgos*. When they did not employ an administrator to run their estates, they often leased their lands to men of means who could afford to rent extensive tracts, merchants or well-to-do peasants who sought investments and social prestige. These large tenants often succeeded in leasing more than one *cortijo*. Sometimes they farmed the land with hired labor, but more often they divided it and sublet fields to tenant farmers. They became familiar figures, dominating the local scene, cowing town officials, sloughing off the taxes on the poor, and monopolizing the pastures. They were already being called *caciques*, after the native chiefs of the Indian villages of the Spanish empire, a name that was to become odious in the nineteenth century. As prices rose, subleasing became so profitable that at times several men stood between the peasant and the real owner, much as in Galicia, except that everyone involved knew their lease could expire momentarily and grabbed all the profit they could. Complaints of the evils of *subarriendo* came from the intendants of La Mancha, Jaén, Córdoba, and Seville.[40]

Private individuals were not alone in practicing *subarriendo*. Repeatedly the intendants pointed out to the government that among the most greedy dealers in land were the religious institu-

[40] Domínguez Ortiz believes that a "rural bourgeoisie" was arising rapidly out of the better off peasantry, but he provides few details to show the economic basis of this new class (pp. 281-82, 295). Since he does not discuss *subarriendo*, perhaps the *subarrendadores* were the group he is accounting for.

tions. Not only did they charge excessive rents for their own land, but they made a regular business of leasing *mayorazgo* lands cheaply to put to their own use. They failed to pay the *alcabala* on their produce, although the privilege applied legally only to church lands. The *procurador síndico personero* of Seville, whose office had just been created by Carlos III to defend the common people, reported to the crown:

> A town over which a wealthy religious corporation or one of those *caciques* had gained control falls in a few years into the deepest misery. For, more influential than all their townsmen, they buy up today the fields, tomorrow the vineyards, later the houses and finally all real property, until they have forced once useful subjects down to the miserable level of beggars.[41]

The strength of this rising oligarchy was nowhere revealed more clearly than in their control and use of the municipal lands of southern and western Spain. These lands were very important. Two thirds of the province of Seville belonged to its towns and cities. In the Middle Ages the distribution of common lands to townsmen to farm on the pattern of Old Castile and León had been instituted widely in Extremadura, parts of New Castile, and over the Sierra Morena into Andalusia. In some areas, particularly along the Portuguese frontier of Extremadura and in the hilly country of Los Pedroches north of Córdoba, the institution worked as well as in older Spain.

The spirit of communal property ownership was rapidly disappearing in most other parts of Extremadura and Andalusia. Towns and cities here were larger and much more widely separated than in northern Spain, so that an intimate peasant community and familiarity with the town lands were lacking. Local city democracy with election of officials had disappeared since the time of Isabel, and instead the Habsburg rulers had

---

[41] Quoted in Leonhard, p. 193. An anonymous pamphlet of this time defending the Mesta also referred to "caciques poderosos, dueños de hierba y granjeros" (Carrera Pujal, iv, 71). On the *procurador síndico personero* see below p. 113.

sold off the offices of *regidores* in Castile to local hidalgos. By the eighteenth century city ayuntamientos and the smaller town consejos had become the stronghold of the local wealthy families, who inherited their offices by right and governed the cities and towns in their own interest, virtually independently of the royal government.[42]

In Extremadura and western Andalusia they had used this control to assure themselves of the best and largest shares in the distribution of the extensive *tierras de propios*, both for farming and grazing. The poor peasants were left with the most distant, sterile, and hilly tracts, while the periodical redistribution of these lands had been allowed to lapse. The practice was also growing of putting up the *tierras de propios* for auction. The wealthy took the best, only to fail later to pay the stipulated price. In complete violation of the communal system, outsiders who desired to profit from the rising value of land and crops were known to bid for the *tierras de propios* and get them. This procedure was reported as far north as Sayago, the heart of true communal use of the land. Wealthy Spaniards and religious institutions used this means to obtain land to farm, and the members of the ayuntamientos were not above making this addition to the *propios* disappear into their own pockets. Not infrequently the town oligarchies determined to put more common waste land (*baldíos*) under the plow and arranged to assign most of the new fields to themselves. The other townsmen, deprived of an equitable share of the *tierras de propios*, were driven to work as laborers for the wealthy on the unjustly appropriated common lands. As the century progressed, the men and institutions who controlled these lands began to subdivide them and rent small tracts at a profit to their poorer fellow citizens. By such subterfuges the extensive tracts of city and town land of western Castile and Andalusia had been made economically indistinguishable from the private lands of the wealthy nobles who controlled

---

[42] Desdevises, II, 166-68; Koenraad Wolter Swart, *Sale of Offices in the Seventeenth Century* ('S-Gravenhage, 1949), p. 26. Costa, p. 325, cites Olavide to the effect that two thirds of the province of Seville was municipal land. Defourneaux, *loc.cit.*, p. 45, suggests a smaller proportion.

the town and city councils or the lands of church institutions.

The local oligarchy also arranged to have the poor pay more than their share of the important tax known as the *millones*. This was a direct levy on meat, wine, olive oil, vinegar, soap, and candles first voted by the Cortes under Felipe II and collected only in Castile. By an arrangement called *encabezamiento* most towns paid the crown a fixed sum and collected the tax themselves. In each town an official store sold these items at retail, levying the *millones* on them. The wealthy could avoid the tax simply by buying the same goods wholesale. Since the clergy also was exempted from paying the full amount of the *millones*, it weighted most heavily upon the lower classes of Castile and so was the tax most bitterly resented by them.[43]

Clearly in dry Spain the profit from the rush for land and the rise of prices was going to the owners of large *mayorazgos* and ecclesiastical *manos muertas*, and to those who acted as intermediaries, leasing cheaply the lands of *mayorazgos* and *propios* and farming them with starved hired hands or subletting them to exploited peasants. Here Spanish agriculture had become thoroughly capitalistic, and an oligarchy was waxing fat and strong—an oligarchy of señores, hereditary municipal *regidores*, *cacique* capitalists, and, not least, religious orders and cathedral chapters.

5

Yet throughout southern and central Spain there were vast tracts of untilled land. According to Olavide the towns of Andalusia often had three to four times as much *baldío* as land under the plow. "One sees barely more land cultivated than one or two leagues right around the towns. The rest is waste. One can go six or seven leagues at a stretch without seeing a sign of human industry."[44] A major reason why this land was not rapidly given over to farming was that it had first to be taken from its present users, the owners of livestock. Every town had its flocks of sheep, goats, pigs, and possibly oxen which lived on the commons.

[43] Bourgoing (1789), II, 18-19.   [44] Olavide, *loc.cit.*, p. 436.

These did not create such a problem, however, as did the famous Spanish flocks of migrant merino sheep.

Since medieval times one of Castile's major economic activities was the raising of merino sheep for their wool. Vast herds passed the summer in the hills of León, Soria, Segovia, and Cuenca, and were driven south and west to winter in Andalusia and Extremadura. On their return in the spring they were shorn in large assembly areas, the greatest being at Segovia. The better grades of wool were exported to northern Europe via Bilbao, and the coarse wool remained in Spain for local weavers.[45]

The owners of migrant sheep had been organized into an official association known as the Mesta. In the eighteenth century its members included monasteries and great nobles who owned flocks as large as twenty-five thousand or more, and also about forty thousand *serranos* who had smaller flocks, some of as few as fifty sheep. On paper the Mesta was organized democratically, but by the eighteenth century, characteristically, the wealthy members had acquired control of its government. One of its tasks was to arrange for renting winter pastures. The small shepherds accused the owners of large herds of getting more pasture than they needed and subletting the excess at high prices to their lesser brothers. The story has a familiar ring.

Since Fernando and Isabel the Mesta had been strongly favored by royal legislation. It had acquired the right of *posesión*, which guaranteed it the use in perpetuity and at fixed rents of any land that it had once used as pasture. Although the Mesta only rented the land, *posesión* gave it a virtual entail of its pastures. Furthermore its own officials were judges in any disputes. Not only had the Mesta rented extensive pastures from *mayorazgos* and *manos muertas*, especially of the military orders, which had extensive holdings in the border lands between Extremadura, La Mancha, and Andalusia, but it had also acquired the use of many of the municipal *baldíos*. Farther north, in southern León and Old Castile it violated the spirit of the law of *posesión* by using pastures to raise sedentary hogs and cattle, and it had

---

[45] Townsend, II, 61-64; Bourgoing (1789), I, 55-58.

expanded beyond the routes assigned the sheep for their migrations until its flocks, in passing, overran pastures needed by local livestock. Before towns could put more *baldíos* under the plow, they had to get back the lands monopolized by the Mesta, to farm or to use as pasture for their own, non-migrant sheep and cattle.[46]

The demand for farm land in the eighteenth century led to encroachments on pastures, including those of the Mesta despite its privileges. After 1712 Felipe V began to give permission to towns in Castile and Andalusia to enclose part of their common pastures and sell lots for farming, under the watchful eye of commissioners, who were to protect the needs of the grazing interests. The motivation was partly fiscal, since the crown took the proceeds of the sales. Lands of the order of Alcántara in eastern Extremadura were sold. In 1738 authorization to sell *baldíos* was extended to all the town of the kingdom.[47] By 1747, 173 towns in Castile alone had received permits to enclose common pastures, and others had done so without royal supervision. The Mesta took alarm, and the permanent deputies of the cities with a vote in the Cortes joined it in interceding with the king to end the practice. In 1748 Fernando VI ended the permission to bring new land under the plow, ordered all land taken from pasturage in the last twenty years restored to the shepherds, and reconfirmed the Mesta's right of *posesión*.[48] In return, higher export duties were levied on wool. After a moment of weakness, the first two Bourbon kings remained loyal to the Mesta, whose taxes were looked upon as a valuable source of royal income.

6

Almost immediately after Carlos III came to the throne in 1759 the government began to intervene actively in agriculture.

[46] On the Mesta in the eighteenth century see Leonhard, pp. 258-80; Julius Klein, *The Mesta, A Study in Spanish Economic History, 1273-1836* (Cambridge, Mass., 1920), pp. 61-62, 133-34, 291-94, 322-46.

[47] Canga Argüelles, *s.vv.* "Venta de baldíos" and "Venta de bienes eclesiásticos"; Klein, pp. 343-45.

[48] Edict of Nov. 30, 1748, quoted in Leonhard, p. 265 n. 1.

Land Boom and Land Hunger

The king's mercantilist advisers were convinced that a prosperous peasantry would increase the wealth and population of the state. In the struggle in progress they took the side of the small farmer and tenant against those who exploited the land without working. They also favored grain growing over sheepraising. During the reign of Carlos the crown labored hard to achieve its objectives.

The initial step was to deprive the rural oligarchy of some of its freedom. In 1760 Carlos decreed that a special committee of the Consejo de Castilla, known as the Contaduría General de Propios y Arbitrios, with the help of the intendants, would thenceforth supervise municipal finances. Local *regidores* would be accountable to crown officials for their use of town moneys and lands, and they were ordered to put up all *tierras de propios* to auction regularly. Carlos followed this act in 1766 with another which erected two new sets of officials in each municipal council who were to be elected by all local taxpayers. Known as *procuradores síndicos personeros del público* and *diputados del común,* they were to intervene in the supply of food for the cities and towns and to sit in on all discussions touching municipal finances. Like Roman tribunes, they were intended to be a popular check on the local families that ruled the ayuntamientos by hereditary right.[49] Carlos also attacked the irresponsible authority of nobles over their *señoríos*. The king could not afford to buy back the privileges of jurisdiction that his predecessors had sold, but he required judges appointed by señores to be approved by the Consejo de Castilla, and he reserved for himself the naming of the *procurador síndico*, a kind of public attorney, in each town of *señorío*.

More drastic action took place after the serious riots of the spring of 1766, with their demand for cheap bread, awakened Carlos to the need to encourage wheat growing in Spain so that a repetition of famine prices could be avoided. Complaints of the need for more farm land had already been made in 1764 by the permanent deputy of the cities of Extremadura, who blamed

---

[49] *Real decreto*, July 30, 1760, *Nov. rec.*, VII, xvi, 12 and 13; *resolución*, May 5, 1766, *ibid.*, xviii, 1.

the shortage on the Mesta. In April 1766 the intendant of Badajoz brought the reluctant ayuntamiento to distribute *tierras de propios* at a low fixed rent to local citizens, beginning with the most needy. The Consejo de Castilla, now headed by Aranda and advised by Campomanes, approved his action and ordered the other towns of Extremadura "to divide among all citizens of the town their *baldíos* and *tierras concejiles*, by the right that each has to rent them, with the preference dictated by equity in favor of laborers and farmers who lack their own lands."[50] In 1767 similar instructions were sent to Andalusia, in 1768 to La Mancha. Two years later all Spanish localities were ordered to enclose and allot their *tierras de propios* not at present cultivated. By now experience had revealed the folly of favoring the very poor, for beggars could not take over and till unplowed land without tools or seed. After 1770 preference was to be given to peasants who owned animals but no land.[51]

On the whole the well-intentioned legislation went awry. Not only was it utopian to expect paupers to become prosperous farmers by simply handing them pieces of barren land, but, worse, the local oligarchies vitiated the laws in practice. *Regidores* of most ayuntamientos chose to ignore decrees that would deprive them of cheap labor and needy tenants, while others saw in the order to distribute town *baldíos* an excellent opportunity to extend their own possessions. The lower classes took little interest in voting for the new popular deputies, and once elected most of these preferred joining the local oligarchies to fighting them.[52] A witness later wrote: "In the few places where an attempt was made to put the *baldíos* under cultivation, the greatest injustice in their division has been committed, so that the poor peasant has been the least cared for and the last to enjoy these benefits, because first attention was paid to the members of the ayuntamiento and the important and wealthy people of the town."[53]

[50] Quoted in Costa, p. 120
[51] *Provisión*, May 26, 1770, *Nov. rec.*, VII, xxv, 17.
[52] Domínguez Ortiz, pp. 359-60.
[53] Pedro Franco Salazar, *Restauración política, económica y militar de España* (Madrid, 1812), quoted in Costa, p. 130; and in Leonhard, pp. 194-95.

Catalonia and Asturias, where no such oligarchy existed, seem to have been the only places where division of the *tierras de propios* for farming was successful. In Catalonia towns divided land to rich and poor alike, in Asturias to all but the most wealthy, subject to rent in kind. When Arthur Young visited Catalonia in 1787 he noted that such plots, often high on hillsides, were the best cultivated of all.[54]

The crisis of 1766 also led the government to order all its intendants in the Castiles, León, and Andalusia to report the exact situation of agriculture in their provinces. The answers soon came in, setting forth the situation described above and denouncing a regime that put tenants and laborers at the mercy of landlords. Recommendations for improvement were made galore. The *fiscales* of the Consejo de Castilla, Campomanes and Moñino, undertook to organize this material. Their reports as well as those of the intendants were published in 1771. The *fiscales* defended the measures taken so far and proposed, if necessary, to distribute private pastures too, in the interest of "the public good." The owners would be allowed a moderate rent.[55] In 1781 the intendant of Salamanca obtained an order from the Consejo de Castilla to carry out the peopling of two hundred *despoblados* on private lands. The owners were to be given a fixed rent, but their permission and approval were not required. The undertaking ran into difficulties, but it was still being pursued actively in 1791.[56] Otherwise little came of the recommendation to distribute private waste lands.

The objective of these reforms had been to repopulate the vast tracts of pasture and waste land with the laborers and

[54] Young, I, 660-61; Carrera Pujal, IV, 279-82 (Catalonia); Costa, pp. 297-301 (Asturias).

[55] *Memorial ajustado . . . sobre que se pongan en practica los 17 capitulos . . . de las ciudades y provincia de Extremadura para fomentar en ella la agricultura y cria de ganados . . .* (Madrid, 1771), quoted and cited at length in Costa, pp. 140-50, and Leonhard, pp. 176-230. The quotation is from Campomanes (Costa, p. 148).

[56] Costa, pp. 304-6.

tenants who were suffering exploitation under the system of extensive and inalienable land holdings. A beginning was also made at peopling uninhabited areas with foreign colonists brought in for the purpose. German states had used this expedient for a century, and a Prussian entrepreneur proposed to the Consejo de Castilla to bring German Catholics to Spain for the same purpose. In 1767 a royal cedula drawn up by Campomanes gave instructions for the creation of colonies in deserted regions of *patrimonio real* along the main highway from Madrid to Seville and Cadiz, in the Sierra Morena and between Córdoba and Seville. Land, houses, tools, and livestock were to be given to the colonists in return for rent in kind to the crown. To avoid the growth of large landholdings, the new owners were prevented from alienating, mortgaging, dividing, or increasing their properties. The practices of pasturing animals on common lands and tilling certain lands in common to pay town expenses were followed. Except for parish churches all religious institutions were prohibited, and the Mesta was kept out. The colonies embodied the ideals of Carlos III's reformers. Pablo Olavide was given charge of the project, which, after a few years of discouraging hardships, was able to boast forty-four villages and eleven flourishing towns of German and French immigrants spread over more than one thousand square miles. In 1776 Olavide was imprisoned by the Inquisición. The prosperity of the colonies of Sierra Morena and Andalusia declined as a result, nevertheless their towns still appeared like oases in the Spanish countryside.[57] Without question they represented the most successful venture of the government into the morass of Spanish agriculture. Plans were hatched to establish similar colonies in Extremadura,[58] but they never matured.

The government never forgot the husbandman, however. In the 1780's Floridablanca attacked the problem posed by the lack of capital under which the average peasant labored. Public credit

---

[57] Townsend, ii, 265-73, 281; Fischer, *Travels in Spain*, p. 319; Bourgoing (1797), iii, 180-81; Danvila y Collado, iv, 5-71; Costa, pp. 118-19.
[58] Costa, pp. 119, 295-97.

agencies known as montes píos were established in Valencia and Málaga to lend money to farmers to buy seed. The funds were furnished by the income paid to the crown from vacant bishoprics and benefices. Just before Carlos' death, Floridablanca proposed an ambitious project involving the creation of a nationwide fund to lend money to farmers to build houses, extend irrigation, buy tools and livestock, and try new crops, but the project never came to fruition.[59]

The original complaint of the cities of Extremadura had been levelled at the Mesta. Under the prompting of the reports of its intendants, the royal government finally abandoned the centuries-old protection of the migrant sheep industry. For a mercantilist economy the Mesta was falling in importance. Spain was losing its monopoly of merino sheep, which were successfully introduced with the cooperation of the Spanish kings into Sweden, Saxony, Prussia, and France during the century.[60] The price of wool in the international market was not keeping pace with that of grains, and Spain's practice of exporting wool to northern Europe and importing wheat from France, Italy, and Africa was providing a continually less favorable balance of trade.[61] The royal councilors, with Campomanes taking the lead, had become confirmed partisans of agricultural interests against sheepowners. In 1779 Campomanes was appointed president of the Mesta, and during the rest of Carlos' reign he used his authority to weaken the institution. He promptly issued instructions to the judges of the Mesta to recognize the precedence of local interests over sheepowners'. In 1786 the privilege of *posesión* was abolished, and in 1788 landowners were given the right to enclose their lands and plant whatever they wanted.[62] These measures were successful, because for once the objectives of the crown coincided with the desire of landowners to get more farm land under their control. When Carlos died, the Mesta still

[59] Townsend, III, 253-54; Canga Argüelles, *s.v.* "Monte pío"; Costa, p. 143.
[60] Leonhard, p. 283; Carrera Pujal, IV, 84.
[61] Hamilton, *War and Prices*, p. 185.
[62] *Cédula*, June 15, 1788, *Nov. rec.*, VII, xxiv, 19.

existed, but its prestige and authority were gone. At the height of the attack on it, in 1780, Pedro Rodríguez de Campomanes, who had been born of an obscure provincial hidalgo family, was honored by Carlos with a *título de Castilla* as the Conde de Campomanes.[63] More than any other person, he had been responsible for the royal legislation to meet the agricultural crisis.

7

The plans and legislation of Carlos' zealous councilors on the whole failed to change the course of Spanish agriculture. Where climate and institutions guaranteed the farmer against exploitation—in the fertile crescent from Galicia across northern Spain to Catalonia and down through the irrigated districts of the east—he was relatively prosperous and had little need of government actions. The crown's major decision in this area, to perpetuate the *foros* of Galicia and Asturias, did not check the impoverishment of local peasants, brought on by the rapid rise in population. In arid central and southern Spain, irregularity of harvests heightened the insecurity of the majority of small farmers, who had never achieved long-term leases or private property and had been defrauded of their just share of common lands. Here too inflation was making farming more profitable and land was being cultivated that had lain fallow for a century or more, but, despite the efforts of the government to create a prosperous peasantry, the profit was going to a rising oligarchy.

This oligarchy of *regidores* and other owners of large *mayorazgos*—that part of the old *hidalguía* that had known how to profit from changing circumstances—was running the countryside in alliance with the monasteries and cathedral chapters and the new *caciques*, while the titled nobility and great señores lived in Madrid and the large cities on the income their overseers, large *cacique* tenants, or dues-paying peasants provided them. All the practices that were increasing the economic power of this group were still flourishing at the death of Carlos III. Laws had been

[63] Vicente González Arnao, "Elogio del excelentísimo señor Conde de Campomanes . . . 27 de mayo de 1803," *Memorias de la Real Academia de la Historia,* v (Madrid, 1817), p. 34 n. 42.

issued to restrict them, but sufficient energetic officials to enforce the laws were lacking. The passive resistance of these men was more than the royal government could overcome. Nevertheless, the landowners and large tenants naturally resented the attitude of the government. Even if they had enjoyed sufficient education to appreciate the new official economic ideas or the other aspects of the Enlightenment that the government encouraged,[64] they could hardly be expected to favor them. Here was a powerful group that out of self-interest would not welcome the *luces*.

Logically the peasants and agricultural laborers might take the opposite attitude. Partisans of reform might find support in this important section of society, but to do so they would have to impart their message to it. The prospects were not bright, for the peasants were illiterate and ignorant of most events outside their vicinity. Their world outlook was a crude Christianity, full of miracles and demons, which they learned from their local priests or monks, men who were hardly more educated than they and who came from their own ranks. As has been noted, the church enjoyed the unquestioned loyalty of the mass of Spaniards. The peasant felt the scorn with which the other classes looked upon his calling, and his highest ambition, as enlightened contemporaries lamented, was to see his son enter the church. The smallest city in Andalusia had its *estudios de gramática*, where a young peasant, with the self-sacrifice of his parents, could achieve minor orders and become the pride of his family and an idle member of society.[65] Culturally the lower classes of the countryside were in the hands of the most backward part of the Spanish church. Throughout central Spain in their daily life they also had to seek favor with wealthy men who opposed the government. Even if an appeal could be made to the peasants' self-interest, to arouse support for new doctrines among them would be a Herculean task.

[64] One Englishman who visited Spain in 1809 considered the intolerably bad education and illiteracy of the upper classes one of Spain's worst evils (William Jacob, *Travels in the South of Spain* [London, 1811], p. 111). See also Morel-Fatio, *La satire de Jovellanos contre la mauvaise éducation de la noblesse (1787).*

[65] Leonhard, pp. 198 and 241, quoting Junta General de Comercio in *Memorial ajustado en el expediente para una ley agraria* (1784) and *Informe de la Sociedad Económica de Tarazona sobre la agricultura* (1794). See above, p. 32.

CHAPTER V

INDUSTRIAL RENAISSANCE AND
STAGNATION

HOWEVER much the planners in Madrid thought about the plight of Spanish agriculture, their prime concern, as good mercantilists, was with colonial commerce and domestic manufacture. The situation that faced Felipe V after he had made his throne secure was indeed sad. The trade of the Spanish colonies was in the hands of the English, French, and Dutch. The manufacturers and shippers of these countries had their agents in Cadiz, who arranged to forward goods from their home countries to Spanish America and send back specie and colonial wares, or they traded directly and illicitly with the Spanish colonies and avoided Spanish taxes and freight charges. Spain did not even supply its own needs in fineries, cloths, and other goods demanded by the well-to-do. The road to economic self-sufficiency and equality with the north European powers was clearly long and hard, but along this road the Bourbon ministers optimistically determined to lead Spain.

The task of reviving Spain's commerce was given to the Junta de Comercio, which had been created in 1679 with full jurisdiction in questions involving trade. The Bourbon kings increased its authority to include mining, manufacturing, and minting (after 1730 it was officially the Junta de Comercio y Moneda).[1] Most of the economic legislation of the century was hammered out in this committee. In the economic sphere its authority came to rival seriously that of the Consejo de Castilla, and jurisdictional disputes inevitably arose between the two. Carlos III managed to evade further difficulties by appointing the *fiscal* of the Consejo, Campomanes, to the Junta.

One of the most important changes in commercial policy made by the Bourbons was to end the monopoly of trade with the

[1] Desdevises, III, 109-10; Hamilton, *War and Prices*, p. 52.

colonies that had been given to Seville and Cadiz. The system of convoyed fleets sailing from here to America had collapsed under the last Habsburgs, and all efforts in the eighteenth century to revive regular sailings eventually were abandoned. Even while the convoys continued, the crown decided to open up direct trade between northern Spain and America by establishing monopolistic trading companies on the model of those created in the seventeenth century by the Netherlands, England, and France. In 1728 the Real Compañía Guipuzcoana de Caracas was founded. It gave shippers of San Sebastián a monopoly of trade with Venezuela, a neglected part of the empire whose commerce had hitherto been almost entirely in the hands of Dutch smugglers. Cacao began to be brought into Spain in Spanish rather than Dutch bottoms and the price fell as a result. Cotton, indigo, and tobacco were introduced into Venezuela. The company flourished until the last years of Carlos III.[2]

In 1755, after much urging by Barcelona merchants and Catalan missionaries in the West Indies, Fernando VI gave a Catalan company the right to trade with Puerto Rico, Santo Domingo, La Margarita, and Honduras. Its main achievements were to bring American cotton to Barcelona and Negro slaves to Puerto Rico. It paid no dividend until the 1770's, when its monopoly had already been destroyed by Carlos III. It never enjoyed the prosperity of the Guipuzcoa company, but it gave Catalonia its first sweet taste of direct trade with America.[3]

Under Carlos III a more far reaching change in colonial commercial policy was introduced. Tired of the stifling effects of the Cadiz monopoly, which chartered companies had only mitigated, and evidently eyeing the success of internal free trade within the British empire, the royal government gradually ended the restrictions on trade between Spain and the colonies. In 1765 it threw open trade with the Spanish West Indies to Barce-

[2] C. H. Haring, *The Spanish Empire in America* (New York, 1947), pp. 337-39; Ronald Dennis Hussey, *The Caracas Company, 1728-1784* (Cambridge Mass., 1934); Carrera Pujal, III, 53-54, 139-41, v, 37.

[3] Hussey, pp. 217-220; Carrera Pujal, v, 158-70.

lona, Alicante, Cartagena, and Málaga on the Mediterranean, and La Coruña, Gijón, and Santander in northern Spain. No licenses were needed to ship from these ports to the Caribbean. A year earlier regular mail packet service had been established from La Coruña to Havana every month and to Buenos Aires twice a month. Each ship was allowed to carry half a load of merchandise each way. So successful did this partial relaxation of the Seville-Cadiz monopoly prove in encouraging Spanish trade that in 1778 a famous *reglamento* permitted Spanish ports to trade with all parts of America except Mexico and Venezuela, where Cadiz and San Sebastián temporarily maintained insecure monopolies. The only major ports now excluded from direct trade with the empire were Valencia, Bilbao, and San Sebastián (whose Compañía de Caracas could trade only with Venezuela). The first lacked a harbor suitable for ocean-going ships. After much labor 1791 the port of El Grao was completed on the Guadalaviar River below Valencia for American trade. The *reglamento* did not open San Sebastián and Bilbao to direct traffic with America because the Basque provinces refused to surrender in return a long-standing privilege of importing goods from abroad for their own use duty free. Nevertheless, San Sebastián was added to the list of authorized ports in 1788, although Bilbao was not.[4]

The few remaining restrictions on trade between authorized Spanish ports and America were eliminated after 1780. The Compañía de Caracas lost its monopoly in 1781, although it was not abolished. It had suffered financially during the War of American Independence, however, and was unable to compete successfully in open trade. In 1785 its stockholders accepted a royal proposal to dissolve the Compañía de Caracas and invest their capital in a new company with a monopoly of trade with the Philippines. The Compañía de Filipinas, like its predecessor, succeeded in increasing trade between Spain and a hitherto

[4] Bourgoing (1789), II, 182-86; Desdevises, III, 147-48; Hussey, pp. 226-31; Carrera Pujal, v, 517.

dormant possession.[5] Cadiz's grip on the Mexican trade was also rapidly relaxed after 1778. Other Spanish ports were allowed to ship a limited number of tons to Vera Cruz, and after 1789 Mexico was opened on the same terms as the other American colonies.[6] Mexico and the Philippines were the last exceptions to the *reglamento* of 1778. Elsewhere within the empire during the 1780's free trade existed for the subjects of the king of Spain.

2

The evolution of royal policy toward manufacturing followed a pattern very similar to that toward colonial commerce. The first move was to create a number of government supported factories, each with a monopoly in its field, that would produce the luxury goods then being imported from other European countries. The influence of Colbert is clear. The first factory was of fine woolens in the Dutch style, built at Guadalajara in 1718. It soon had a branch at San Fernando (in 1768 moved to Brihuega). In the next decades factories were established at Madrid for tapestries, at Felipe V's summer residence of San Ildefonso for mirrors and fine glass, at Talavera de la Reina for silks. When Carlos III came from Naples, he brought with him Italian artisans for a factory of porcelains that he set up at the Buen Retiro outside Madrid. He also established a second manufacture of fine woolens at Segovia. Other royal factories were scattered throughout Spain for paper and pottery, swords and stockings.[7]

On the technical level these factories were successful. Skilled foreigners were imported to teach Spaniards their arts, and they produced splendid mirrors, porcelains closely imitating those of Sèvres and Wedgwood, and the tapestries for which Francisco de Goya painted the designs in the days of Carlos. The greatest efforts were devoted to the cloth factory at Guadalajara. Its

---

[5] Townsend, II, 377-78; Desdevises, III, 161; Hussey, pp. 265-300.
[6] Haring, p. 341.
[7] List in Townsend, II, 231. See Desdevises, III, 72-74; Carrera Pujal, IV, 148-69; and Map III.

success, the government thought, would end Spain's shameful dependence on England for cloths woven from Spanish wool. Despite a brief period of prosperity after 1740, when a trained Englishman ran it with many English weavers, it was not thriving when Carlos became king. He gave it enthusiastic support and turned it over to be run by the Junta de Comercio in 1760.[8] In the next decades it grew enormously. It wove the best merino wool and also made a specialty of vicuña wool of South America. According to the French traveller Bourgoing, the products were as good as Julienne woolens and cheaper. Guadalajara presented an unusual aspect of prosperity, for beggars, apparently ubiquitous elsewhere in Castile, were absent. In the 1780's the city boasted nearly eight hundred modern looms and employed almost four thousand weavers, while Brihuega had one hundred more looms for the finest cloth. The royal factory was one of the largest in Europe. Forty thousand spinners were kept active by it as far away as Madrid and La Mancha.[9]

Royal companies of this type were common in Europe in the eighteenth century. Nowhere were they financially successful,[10] so that the failure of Guadalajara or the other Spanish royal factories to make money is not surprising. Poor management was not their only weakness. Guadalajara, far from the main shearing points of the Mesta and from any large market except Madrid, had to face excessive costs of transportation.[11] Yet the government continued to support it financially in the hope that the importation of English woolens—calculated at two hundred million reales' worth annually in 1783 according to Bourgoing—could be stopped.[12]

The everyday manufacture of Spain had meanwhile long been in the hands of the craft guilds. Just as in France under Colbert,

[8] Carrera Pujal, IV, 101.
[9] Both Bourgoing (1789), I, 49-50, and Townsend, I, 239-40 give these figures, which were probably "official."
[10] Herbert Heaton, *Economic History of Europe* (Rev. ed.; New York, 1948), p. 366.
[11] Carrera Pujal, IV, 148.
[12] Bourgoing (1789), I, 50 n. (One pound sterling equals approximately 100 reales [see Townsend, II, 355-56].)

the seventeenth century saw in Spain the culmination of the guild system. The guilds, or gremios, were multiplied and subdivided until every craft or industrial activity was monopolized by local chartered groups which labored under government enforced regulations that specified minutely the nature of the processes and products. Gremios became closed monopolies of the master craftsmen, exploiting their *aprendices* and *mancebos*. Inevitably they hampered the introduction of new methods and the rise of self-made men.

Felipe V kept to this Colbertist love of guilds and extended them to include all merchants. Under Carlos III the official attitude changed, just as in colonial commerce. Campomanes, in the fashion of advanced mercantilists, denounced the drawbacks he saw in the gremios in the *Apéndice* to his *Discurso sobre la educacion popular* and demanded their suppression in the interest of Spanish production.[13] No such radical step was taken, but the Junta de Comercio and the Consejo de Castilla were already engaged in removing the restrictive aspects of guild regulations. For example, in 1762 government control of the price of books was abolished except for those of "prime necessity," such as elementary text books and books of religious worship, "for liberty of all trade being the mother of abundance, it will be for that of books too."[14] To meet French competition, the silk manufacturers of Valencia had obtained permission in the 1750's to imitate Lyon silks. After piecemeal extension, this freedom to imitate foreign products was granted to silk manufacturers throughout Spain in 1778 and was extended to makers of linens and canvas in 1784 and of woolens in 1786.[15] In 1787 cloth manufacturers were allowed to have as many looms as they wanted, notwithstanding any official regulations to the contrary.[16] These edicts put an end to the guild restrictions on the manufacture of cloth in Spain.

[13] Rodríguez de Campomanes, *Apéndice a la educacion popular*, iii, iii-cclxx; Desdevises, iii, 49-67.

[14] *Real orden*, Nov. 14, 1762, *Nov. rec.*, viii, xvi, 23.

[15] *Cédulas*, Mar. 8, 1778, Dec. 14, 1784, and *Real decreto*, Oct. 25, 1786, *Nov. rec.*, viii, xxiv, 5, 7, and nota 8; Carrera Pujal, iv, 118, 128-30.

[16] *Cédula*, June 27, 1787, *Nov. rec.*, viii, xxiv, 9.

At the same time the exclusiveness of all gremios was steadily weakened by royal fiat in the hope of creating a more prosperous artisan class. Instructions were issued for children in asylums to be taught crafts profitable to the state,[17] and no one was to be prevented thenceforth from exercising a trade because of illegitimate birth.[18] Provision was made for the establishment of schools for spinning in the towns where they would be most profitable,[19] and women were authorized to work at all jobs suited to the strength and modesty of their sex despite any contrary regulations of the guilds.[20] In 1777 all gremios were ordered to admit to their ranks craftsmen from other parts of Spain and even Catholic foreigners, provided they could demonstrate the necessary skills or had documentary proof of their having passed the proper examinations elsewhere.[21] By these means the pretension of the masters of the gremios to monopolize local production was done away with.

An attempt was also made, in accordance with a recommendation of Campomanes, to remove any social stigma from manual labor. The permission given to hidalgos in 1773 to engage in crafts has already been mentioned. Ten years later the occupations of tanner, smith, tailor, shoemaker, carpenter, "and others of this kind" were specifically declared honorable and compatible with the rank of nobility, and those who followed them were declared eligible for municipal offices.[22] If craftsmen were deprived of their exclusive privileges, they had the satisfaction of being told by the king (if not by hidalgos) that they were more valuable citizens than idle nobles.

The customs policy of the Bourbons also aimed at encouraging domestic production. The importation of foreign products that competed with Spanish ones was either taxed or prohibited. A

---

[17] *Real resolución*, July 21, 1780, *ibid.*, VII, xxxviii, 5 and 6.
[18] *Real cédula*, Sept. 2, 1784, *ibid.*, VIII, xxiii, 9.
[19] *Real cédula*, May 22, 1786, *ibid.*, xxiv, 8.
[20] *Cédulas*, Jan. 12, 1779, Sept. 2, 1784, *ibid.*, xxiii, 14, 15.
[21] *Cédula*, Mar. 24, 1777, *ibid.*, 7.
[22] *Cédula*, Mar. 18, 1783, *ibid.*, 8. See Desdevises, III, 68, 77; Carrera Pujal, IV, 117-30.

clear example was that of foreign cotton cloths, first prohibited in 1718. Their full story belongs below, with that of the growth of the Spanish cotton industry. The same policy was applied to other articles, especially under Carlos III. In 1775 the importation of foreign hardware was banned in order to favor the growing Basque iron industry. Three years later many small cloth articles, such as gloves, caps, and stockings, were kept out so that domestic crafts employing women might prosper. Foreign furniture was also prohibited, and in 1788 all cloths and other products of linen, wool, and cotton.[23]

Another aspect of mercantilism was evident in the government's policy of restricting the export of raw materials produced in Spain so that domestic manufacturers would not have to compete in the European market for their supplies. The interests of agriculture were disregarded in favor of manufacture. For example, in 1783 the export of coarse wool and esparto was stopped, although fine wool was too valuable an export to be treated this way.[24] Valencian peasants produced the finest silk in Europe and profited greatly from their foreign sales, yet the government collected heavy export duties on silk and from time to time forbade all shipments of it abroad. The purpose was to increase silk manufacture not only in Valencia but in Catalonia and Andalusia.[25] The policy was carried to absurd lengths in 1787 with the prohibition to export bulk cork. The restriction was ended only when the desperate cork growers demonstrated that domestic cork manufacturers used only a tenth of their product.[26]

Without an efficient customs service, these regulations only invited fraud and smuggling. French silk stockings came into Spain, were stamped with the marks of Spanish manufacturers, and were reexported to America. Valencian silk was smuggled out to France and Portugal via Barcelona and Seville. The government itself frequently vitiated its own laws by granting export and import

[23] Carrera Pujal, IV, 119, V, 27; royal decrees cited in Danvila y Collado, VI, 406-7.
[24] Carrera Pujal, IV, 125.
[25] Bourgoing (1789), III, 75-77.
[26] Carrera Pujal, IV, 131.

licenses to individuals. Nevertheless Spanish manufacturers felt that some benefit accrued to them in their competition with French and English factories, for they did not cease to clamor for such legislation.[27]

3

The Bourbon policies of opening all major ports to colonial trade and protecting Spanish manufacturers from foreign competition tended to unite Spain into a single commercial and industrial area. Two factors, however, continued to divide the country's industrial potential into two distinct regions. One was physical, the difference between areas with easy and difficult access to the sea. The other was the product of Spain's history, the difference in internal tax structures between the kingdoms of Castile and the other political divisions of Spain. True to their general policy, the Bourbons strove to reduce or overcome these differences and make all Spain equally industrious.

The kingdoms of Castile paid heavier taxes than the kingdoms of the former crown of Aragon, the kingdom of Navarre, or the Basque provinces. These local Castilian taxes, known collectively as the *rentas provinciales*, either had come down from the Middle Ages, before Spain was united politically, or had been initiated by the Habsburg rulers after the Cortes de Castilla had lost their ability to resist the demands of the crown. The most famous of these taxes was the *alcabala*, a tax dating from the fourteenth century that was assessed on all products and real property each time they were sold, whether wholesale or retail. As Jovellanos described it: "The tax surprises its prey, the product of the soil, at its birth and pursues and nips it as it circulates, never losing sight of it or letting it escape, until the moment of its consumption."[28] In the seventeenth century the *alcabala* had been raised

---

[27] See Bourgoing (1789), III, 76-78; Townsend, III, 257; Desdevises, III, 81; Carrera Pujal, IV, 160; and for large contraband shipments into Spain across the Pyrenees in 1782, Albert Girard, "Une negotiation commerciale entre l'Espagne et la France," *Revue historique,* CXI (1912), 301-4.

[28] Jovellanos, *Informe de ley agraria,* pp. 103-4.

from its previous 10 per cent to 14 per cent (becoming the *alcabala y [cuatro] cientos*). The two other major taxes levied exclusively on Castile have been referred to in the last chapter—the *millones*, another direct tax on articles of daily consumption, and the *servicio ordinario y extraordinario*, a property tax levied on commoners. A bevy of minor taxes on individual articles like silk, soda, and ice completed the *rentas provinciales*.[29]

The *reynos* of Aragon and Navarre and the Basque provinces had successfully defended themselves from paying as much as Castile. In 1610, according to the French ambassador, Aragon paid only one fiftieth the taxes of Castile.[30] When Felipe V destroyed the political privileges of Aragon and brought it under Castilian institutions, he determined to end this inequality. His ministers were too mindful of efficiency, however, to impose on it the Castilian tax system and established a single tax in its place. In the *reynos* of Aragon and Valencia it took the form of a tax on the heads of families, called the *equivalente*. In Catalonia it was an income tax, the *catastro*: 10 per cent on revenue from land and 8 per cent on profits from industry and commerce and on wages. Heads of Catalan families also paid a tax. Nevertheless, in the end these provinces continued to be less burdened than Castile. One author has calculated that for every fourteen reales paid to the crown by a Castilian an Aragonese paid nine.[31] In Catalonia, according to Bourgoing, the income from land was taxed at only one eighth its real amount, while industry was similarly favored.[32]

Navarre and the Basque provinces were even more privileged. Here alone the Spanish medieval ideal of no taxation without expressed consent remained alive. The local governing bodies had to consent to the requests of the king for money and paid the sums directly to the crown. The collection and spending of public moneys was in their hands.[33]

These areas also enjoyed more favorable tariff regulations than

---

[29] Desdevises, II, 374-83. [30] Baumgarten, pp. 13-14.
[31] Desdevises, II, 395-96. [32] Bourgoing (1789), II, 23.
[33] Desdevises, II, 396-99.

Castile. Goods entering the Basque provinces from abroad paid no duties unless they were shipped on to other parts of Spain, when the duties were collected at the inland borders.[34] In Catalonia, according to Bourgoing, the import and export tariffs levied were 4 per cent rather than the 15 per cent that was standard for Spain.[35]

Clearly, the economy of Castile suffered fiscal burdens that would discourage entrepreneurs from founding industries in this part of Spain. Townsend, who had an acute eye in economic matters, saw in their freedom from *alcabalas, cientos,* and *millones* a major factor in the prosperous condition of Valencia and Catalonia. "Their industry is free, whilst that of less favored provinces, harassed incessantly by the collectors of the revenue, is crippled in all its operations."[36]

The government was not unaware of this factor. During the century the *alcabala* had been reduced or eliminated on the sales of certain favored factories or towns.[37] In the 1770's the crown was ready to sacrifice extensively this source of income in order to foster Castilian manufactures. In 1779 the *alcabala* was abolished on wholesale dealings in domestic woolens, including shipments to America, and it was reduced to 2 per cent on retail sales. Foreign woolens continued to pay a 10 per cent *alcabala*. In 1785 the *alcabala* was reduced on all objects between 2 and 8 per cent, and next year all *alcabalas* were ended on domestic linen and hemp cloth sold in Spain.[38] Castile was still not as free from taxes as the rest of Spain, but its manufacturers were henceforth on a reasonable level of equality fiscally. They still had to face the problem of their distance from the sea and lack of good communications.

"Since the roads are so bad in the majority of provinces of your country, it is not surprising that carriages frequently break down, that mules stumble and travellers lose days," Cadalso's

---

[34] Bourgoing (1789), I, 10-12, II, 183.
[35] *Ibid.,* II, 7.
[36] Townsend, III, 326-27. See *ibid.,* III, 286-87.
[37] Bourgoing (1789), II, 20.
[38] Carrera Pujal, IV, 120, 129; Desdevises, II, 376.

fictitious Moroccan wrote to his Spanish friend.[39] All travellers voiced the same complaint: the roads of Spain, and especially of Castile, were hardly fit for wheeled vehicles. The elevation and numerous mountain ranges of Castile have always hindered communications and road building, yet some wagon traffic had existed in the Middle Ages. Fernando and Isabel had striven to improve Spain's roads, but their successors failed to maintain the network they inherited. The Bourbons returned to the task. Felipe V, in the interest of the national economy, began a star of wagon roads that radiated from Madrid to the Basque lands, the Mediterranean ports, and Cadiz. The pattern reflected the political centralization of Spain; never before had all roads led to Madrid.[40] Carlos III also worried about the condition of the roads. Excellent highways were built in his reign, but the best were in the Basque lands and along the Mediterranean coast from Valencia to the French border.[41] Stagecoaches were initiated from Madrid to Pamplona, Barcelona, Cartagena, Cadiz, and Lisbon; and Floridablanca in the 1780's attempted to improve the filthy roadside inns. He succeeded only partially. Arthur Young north of Barcelona found "an inn no better than in the mountains, yet we are now on the high road from Paris to Madrid; a stinking dirty dreadful hole, without anything to eat or drink, but for muleteers."[42]

These improvements barely alleviated the problem of freight shipments. Bourgoing noted that the interior commerce of Spain consisted mainly of wine, oil, grain, wool, and supplies for factories, all shipped "by the same slow and consequently expensive conveyance," the mule or ass.[43] Occasionally on passable roads oxcarts supplemented pack animals; thus on the road to Cartagena Townsend "met nine wagons, and a long drove of asses, loaded with flax, going to Granada."[44] Muleback was still

[39] Cadalso, *Cartas marruecas*, p. 233, Carta 69.
[40] Gonzalo Menéndez Pidal, *Los caminos en la historia de España* (Madrid, 1951), pp. 71-72, 83-84, 122.
[41] Bourgoing (1789), I, 6-7; Townsend, III, 296, 316-17.
[42] Young, I, 645; Bourgoing (1789), I, 3-4; Menéndez Pidal, p. 125.
[43] Bourgoing (1789), II, 155-56.   [44] Townsend, III, 104.

the only way to get from Castile to Asturias or Galicia or most places in Extremadura.[45] To the novice entering Spain Townsend recommended in hilly country "to go by the common carrier, in which case he will be mounted on a good mule, and take the place, which would have been occupied by some bale of goods."[46] Fear of bandits also slowed up travel in the hills and mountains; for travellers and muleteers instinctively banded together and made "a tacit agreement to support each other, or at least, by their numbers, to intimidate the thieves."[47]

The resulting cost of freight prejudiced Castilian commerce. Except for the merino wool exported via Bilbao, Castile sold few of its products outside its own borders. The Basques bought their grain from France, for, "although it is cheaper in Castile, they do not bring it in because of the distance and bad roads."[48] Central Spain was a grain-growing area; yet Andalusia and the Mediterranean coasts also imported wheat, from France, Italy, and Africa.[49] Toledo revived its silk industry between 1715 and 1738, but by the end of the century Seville and Valencia had ruined its business. It could not compete after paying the expense of bringing raw silk from Valencia and sending goods destined for America to Seville.[50]

The only hope for a flowering of the industry of central Spain was cheaper transport. Like the statesmen of other European countries, Carlos' councilors saw the answer in a series of canals that would tie these regions to the sea. They were not discouraged by the obvious physical difficulties. One canal, already conceived by Carlos V, was to run beside the Ebro from Tudela to the Mediterranean Sea and give new life to Navarre and Aragon. A second was planned from Segovia along the river beds of Old Castile, past Valladolid and Reynosa, to enter the Bay of Biscay

---

[45] Alexandre de Laborde, *Itinéraire descriptif de l'Espagne* . . . (5 vols.; Paris, 1808), I, 376-77 (Extremadura); Desdevises, III, 13, 134; Menéndez Pidal, pp. 126-27.

[46] Townsend, I, 2-3.

[47] *Ibid.*, II, 279-80.

[48] Joaquín de Ordóñiz (died 1769) quoted in Carrera Pujal, v, 44.

[49] See map II and Desdevises, III, 13.

[50] Desdevises, III, 99.

near Santander. Late in Carlos' reign a French engineer proposed to build a third canal from the Escorial and Madrid south to the Atlantic, crossing New Castile and La Mancha by the best river valleys and entering the Guadalquivir above Córdoba.

Only the third canal failed to go beyond the planning stage. It was approved by Floridablanca and money had been subscribed when construction was postponed by the death of the engineer.[51] Everyone meanwhile was encouraged by the progress of the other two. Thanks to the energy of a canon of Saragossa cathedral, Ramón Pignatelli, to whom supervision of the canal of Aragon was entrusted, barges were floating in the 1780's from Tudela to Saragossa, crossing the deep valley of the Jalón high on an aqueduct nearly a mile long. Subsidiary irrigation canals were giving fertility and prosperity to the valley of the upper Ebro.[52] New loans were raised in 1785 and 1788 to drive the main canal on to the sea.[53] Spirits were also animated by the canal of Old Castile, although it was not so far advanced. Townsend found Medina del Rio Seco being stirred from its misery by "the influence of the canal" that had attracted new cloth factories and commercial houses. Zamora and Segovia were still slumbering, but "when the communication shall be opened by the canal, for the transport of its productions, [Zamora] will daily grow in wealth," and so too might Segovia.[54] With such signs of government activity in their interest, hope sprang anew among Castilians for a future as prosperous as that past of which everywhere ruined buildings were mute reminders.

4

Until this future date, Castile appeared doomed to watch other parts of Spain take the lead in manufacture. Three areas in particular were the scenes of new industrial activity: Valencia,

[51] Bourgoing (1789), I, 266.
[52] *Ibid.*, I, 20-22; Hispano [*sic*], "Colonización y aprovechamiento de aguas en el reinado de Carlos III," *Madrid científico*, xx (1913), 669-70.
[53] Hamilton, *War and Prices*, p. 81.
[54] Townsend, I, 372-73, II, 70-71, 118.

Catalonia, and the Basque provinces. These regions were already favored by an active foreign commerce in the products of their soil, but as the century advanced their manufactures became an even greater source of prosperity.

Valencia was noted for its linens and tiles, both of which it produced in important quantities. In the eighteenth century, however, it was the weaving of silk that turned it into an industrial center. The kingdom already grew the best silk in Europe, which it had been used to sell abroad. Now, aided by government restrictions on the export of raw silk, the domestic silk weaving industry grew steadily during the century. Townsend was able to obtain the following figures for the number of silk looms in the city of Valencia: 800 in 1718, 3,195 in 1769 including 107 stocking frames, and 5,000 in 1787 including 300 stocking frames; and "the trade is still increasing."[55] The last figure is probably high; other contemporaries reported from 3,500 to 4,000 looms.[56] By comparison Lyon had 11,000 silk looms in 1769 but only 7,500 in 1789.[57] The French industry was probably still larger than the Spanish, but it was in decline after 1770 while the Spanish was experiencing a marked boom. As the Spanish lands had been one of France's main customers, Spain's gain may account in part for France's loss.

The control of the industry in Valencia was in the hands of the merchants of the city, who had organized it on a putting-out basis. The operations were done in separate workshops, and the silk was provided by the merchants. According to Bourgoing, some furnished silk for only four or five weavers, while others had several hundred at their orders. Spinning was done in outlying towns, mostly by the traditional system used in Spain, but in the 1780's the improved silk spinning machines of the

[55] *Ibid.*, III, 254-55.

[56] Bourgoing (1789) says 4,000 looms (III, 77); Cabanilles says 3,247 looms for velvets, 278 for ribbons, and an unstated number of stocking frames (cited by Carrera Pujal, V, 516). On the other hand Peyron, *Nouveau voyage en Espagne*, 1777-78, says 5,000 looms for cloth, 500 for ribbons, 200 to 300 for stockings (cited *ibid.*).

[57] Henri Sée, *L'évolution commerciale et industrielle de la France sous l'Ancien Régime* (Paris, 1925), p. 301.

French inventor Jacques de Vaucanson were being introduced.[58]

The government took an active interest in the progress of the industry, which it hoped would supply the silk needs of Spanish America. Silk weaving was encouraged in Catalonia, Andalusia, and the royal factory at Talavera de la Reina. In Valencia the government had given the task of supervising the industry and improving its methods to a remarkable Spanish entrepreneur, Joaquín Manuel Fos. Early in life, although he was already a rich silk manufacturer, Fos determined to study in person the better production methods used abroad. Instead of taking his family into his confidence, he departed without a word, leaving behind in a field some bloody clothes that convinced everyone he had been murdered. He went to France and England, worked in silk factories there, and brought back trade secrets to his native city and his overjoyed family. His findings were published by the government in a handsome illustrated volume that was dedicated to Carlos III.[59] Bourgoing had to admit that Fos was able to produce *moirés* as good as the best in France, but on the whole the quality of Spanish silks was still not equal to that of French.[60] Their quantity on the other hand had turned Valencia into a flourishing city which foreigners readily admired.

Like Valencia, the Basque provinces were known primarily for one product; theirs was ironware. Economically they had benefited from being the main transit area between central Spain and northern Europe. Bilbao, and to a lesser extent Santander, were visited by English, Dutch, and French ships that discharged wheat, woolens, and manufactured goods, and took on Castilian wool, Basque chestnuts, and crude iron. Bilbao iron, exported unworked, had a longstanding reputation. As the eighteenth century advanced, local forges and factories produced more and more finished goods. Hardware, firearms, and anchors became specialties, above all the last, of which many were exported to the northern maritime powers.[61] Here too merchants dominated

58 Bourgoing (1789), III, 79, 82-88.
59 *Ibid.*, p. 79; Sarrailh, pp. 347-48.
60 Bourgoing (1789), III, 90-91; Townsend, III, 258.
61 Bourgoing (1789), II, 168.

the industry. They advanced money to foundries against future deliveries and got their iron about 5 per cent cheaper as a result. The merchants got rich while the ironmasters were pinched, according to a contemporary Jesuit who opposed usury.[62]

A law of 1775, already mentioned, which prohibited the importation of foreign hardware into Spain or the colonies gave a strong impetus to the industry. In 1777 the consulado or chamber of commerce of Bilbao calculated the total crude iron production at seven thousand tons.[63] In 1790 almost four thousand tons of finished Spanish iron products were exported to America and more were consumed within Spain.[64] Every valley town in Vizcaya and Guipúzcoa and around Santander seemed to have its forge, foundry, or factory, turning out nails, ship fittings, and ornamental hardware. Since smelting was done with charcoal, local forests were being rapidly exhausted by the end of the century.[65] The Basques also produced much copperware and had the major shipyards of Spain, building transatlantic packet boats and ships for the royal navy.[66] As the provinces also had a flourishing agriculture and kept alive their self-government, they were among the most highly favored and most valuable regions of the peninsula.

Only in Catalonia was manufacturing more advanced. The War of the Spanish Succession and the bitter siege of Barcelona that lasted from July 1713 to September 1714 were harmful to the local economy.[67] Nevertheless the province had as early as 1720 the basis for industrial growth. Barcelona, Vich, Olot, and Reus produced woolens and silks; Barcelona also made cutlery; and Mataró, Ripoll, and Solsona made firearms and cannon. All of these industries grew during the century, encouraged by the royal ordinances permitting more and more direct trade with

[62] Carrera Pujal, v, 67, citing Padre Calatayud.
[63] *Ibid.*, p. 27: 140,000 *quintales*. One *quintal* equals approximately 100 English pounds.
[64] *Ibid.*, pp. 28-29. See pp. 19-26.
[65] Laborde, ii, 138.
[66] Carrera Pujal, v, 20-21, 79.
[67] Though perhaps not as harmful as Hamilton asserts (*War and Prices*, p. 145).

America. The woolen industry took on the characteristics of early capitalism, abandoning the guild system in favor of wage work. Since the seventeenth century wool-dressers (*pelaires*) had become entrepreneurs, hiring weavers who did not belong to guilds. Here, rather than in Guadalajara, lay the answer to the importation of English woolens. The government long failed to realize the fact, but the royal edicts of the 1780's permitting factory owners to have as many looms as they wanted and freeing them from official specifications indicate that Madrid had at last awakened to the possibilities of a capitalistic woolen industry. The decrees brought on the triumph of the factory system and large scale production.[68]

Two relatively new industries became important in the eighteenth century, not only in Catalonia but in western Europe: paper making and cotton weaving. The rapid growth of publications brought an increased demand for paper everywhere. In Spain it was met primarily by mills established in Catalonia, where official statistics showed 109 paper mills in existence in 1775 though 23 were not active. Valencia and the Basque provinces also furnished paper for Spain. Barcelona and Bilbao entered the field of wallpaper, for which they found a market in the colonies.[69]

More than paper making, the spinning and weaving of cotton represented the new industrial trend of the century. The cotton industry had the advantage of never having been organized into guilds with government-enforced specifications. The famous English inventions that announced the early stages of the eighteenth-century "industrial revolution" were mostly made in this field. The history of cotton manufacture in Catalonia began a half century after that of England with an official prohibition to import Asian cloths in 1718.[70] The measure was intended partly to prevent the export of specie and partly to help domestic woolens and linens, but by cutting off Indian calicoes it encouraged

[68] Carrera Pujal, v, 150-51, 312-13.
[69] *Ibid.*, iv, 107, 123, v, 350; Sarrailh, pp. 556-57.
[70] *Real decreto*, Sept. 17, 1718, *Nov. rec.*, ix, xii, 17.

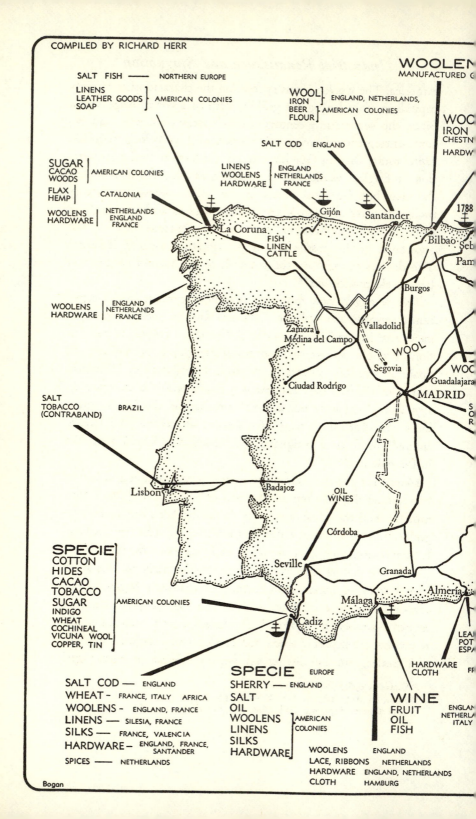

COMPILED BY RICHARD HERR

SALT FISH —— NORTHERN EUROPE

LINENS
LEATHER GOODS } AMERICAN COLONIES
SOAP

WOOLEN
MANUFACTURED G

WOOL
IRON } ENGLAND, NETHERLANDS,
BEER } AMERICAN COLONIES
FLOUR

WOC
IRON
CHESTN
HARDW

SALT COD   ENGLAND

SUGAR
CACAO } AMERICAN COLONIES
WOODS

FLAX
HEMP |

WOOLENS } NETHERLANDS
HARDWARE ENGLAND
FRANCE

LINENS } ENGLAND
WOOLENS NETHERLANDS
HARDWARE FRANCE

1788

La Coruña

Gijón

Santander

Bilbao   Seb

Pam

FISH
LINEN
CATTLE

WOOLENS } ENGLAND
HARDWARE NETHERLANDS
FRANCE

Burgos

Valladolid

Zamora
Médina del Campo

WOOL

WOC

Segovia

WO

Guadalajara

SALT
TOBACCO
(CONTRABAND)

BRAZIL

Ciudad Rodrígo

MADRID
S
O
R

Lisbon

Badajoz

OIL
WINES

Córdoba

SPECIE
COTTON
HIDES
CACAO
TOBACCO
SUGAR
INDIGO } AMERICAN COLONIES
WHEAT
COCHINEAL
VICUNA WOOL
COPPER, TIN

Seville

Granada

Almería

Málaga

Cadiz

LEA
POT
ESPA

HARDWARE
CLOTH

FF

SALT COD —— ENGLAND
WHEAT – FRANCE, ITALY AFRICA
WOOLENS – ENGLAND, FRANCE
LINENS —— SILESIA, FRANCE
SILKS —— FRANCE, VALENCIA
HARDWARE – ENGLAND, FRANCE,
              SANTANDER
SPICES —— NETHERLANDS

SPECIE   EUROPE
SHERRY —— ENGLAND
SALT
OIL
WOOLENS } AMERICAN
LINENS COLONIES
SILKS
HARDWARE

WOOLENS   ENGLAND
LACE, RIBBONS NETHERLANDS
HARDWARE ENGLAND, NETHERLANDS
CLOTH   HAMBURG

WINE
FRUIT
OIL
FISH

ENGLAN
NETHERLA
ITALY

Bogan

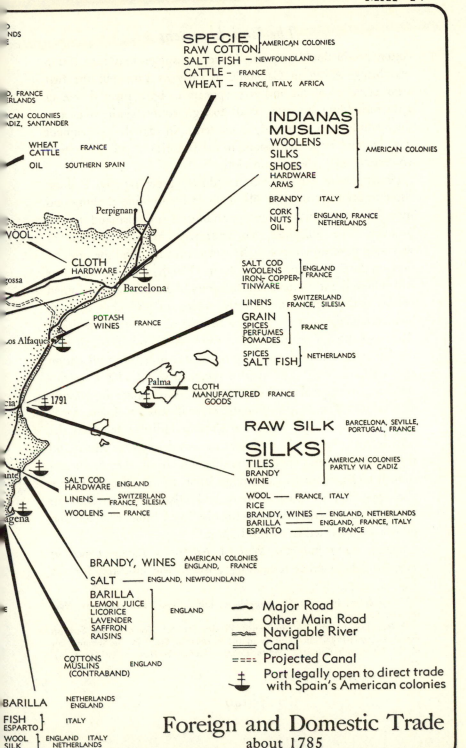

MAP IV

SPECIE] AMERICAN COLONIES
RAW COTTON]
SALT FISH — NEWFOUNDLAND
CATTLE — FRANCE
WHEAT — FRANCE, ITALY, AFRICA

...NDS

..., FRANCE
...RLANDS

...CAN COLONIES
...DIZ, SANTANDER

INDIANAS]
MUSLINS]
WOOLENS
SILKS   AMERICAN COLONIES
SHOES
HARDWARE
ARMS

BRANDY   ITALY

WHEAT
CATTLE   FRANCE

OIL   SOUTHERN SPAIN

CORK]
NUTS] ENGLAND, FRANCE
OIL]   NETHERLANDS

Perpignan

...OOL

CLOTH
HARDWARE

SALT COD]
WOOLENS] ENGLAND
IRON- COPPER-] FRANCE
TINWARE]

...ossa

Barcelona

LINENS   SWITZERLAND
FRANCE, SILESIA

POTASH]
WINES] FRANCE

GRAIN
SPICES]
PERFUMES] FRANCE
POMADES]

...os Alfaques

SPICES] NETHERLANDS
SALT FISH]

Palma

CLOTH
MANUFACTURED FRANCE
GOODS

...ia   ‡ 1791

RAW SILK   BARCELONA, SEVILLE,
PORTUGAL, FRANCE

SILKS]
TILES]   AMERICAN COLONIES
BRANDY]   PARTLY VIA CADIZ
WINE]

SALT COD]
HARDWARE] ENGLAND

WOOL — FRANCE, ITALY
RICE
BRANDY, WINES — ENGLAND, NETHERLANDS
BARILLA — ENGLAND, FRANCE, ITALY
ESPARTO — FRANCE

LINENS — SWITZERLAND
FRANCE, SILESIA

WOOLENS — FRANCE

...ante

...agena

BRANDY, WINES AMERICAN COLONIES
ENGLAND, FRANCE

SALT — ENGLAND, NEWFOUNDLAND

BARILLA]
LEMON JUICE]
LICORICE]
LAVENDER] ENGLAND
SAFFRON]
RAISINS]

COTTONS]
MUSLINS] ENGLAND
(CONTRABAND)]

Major Road
Other Main Road
Navigable River
Canal
Projected Canal
‡ Port legally open to direct trade
with Spain's American colonies

BARILLA   NETHERLANDS
ENGLAND

FISH]
ESPARTO] ITALY

WOOL] ENGLAND ITALY
SILK] NETHERLANDS

Foreign and Domestic Trade
about 1785

cotton production in Spain. There are suggestions that cotton was being woven in Catalonia as early as 1715, but the first clear evidence of the industry appears to be a royal decree of 1730 forbidding imports of all foreign cotton cloth to protect the Spanish factories already in existence. In 1741 the government gave tax and tariff concessions to the factories of printed cottons (*indianas*) and other cotton cloths.[71]

Under Carlos III the cotton industry grew rapidly. Fashion chose to favor cotton over silk or linen for the fine clothing and mantillas of Spanish ladies, providing a sure demand for its products. The difficulties that arose were mainly the result of wavering government policy. In 1760 Carlos III lifted the prohibition on foreign cotton cloths. Even though a heavy duty was still collected, the cotton manufacturers of Barcelona complained of the change often and bitterly, saying in 1768 that of 1,111 looms available 393 were stopped because of foreign competition. That year foreign printed cottons were again prohibited; in 1770 the ban was extended to all muslins and in 1771 to all cotton cloths whatsoever.[72] The British merchants at Cadiz were dismayed, but their ambassador was powerless to change the decision of Carlos.[73] The king's strength of will was rewarded, for a decade of rapid growth of the Catalan industry followed the edict of 1768. Craftsmen were sent to copy foreign machines, and the manufacturers obtained permission from the municipal council of Barcelona to use foreign labor. By now factories were also appearing in Mataró, Reus, and Olot. With government encouragement cotton from the Spanish West Indies replaced that previously imported from the Levant.[74]

Spain's entry into the War of American Independence in 1779 brought another temporary crisis to the industry, for the

[71] Carrera Pujal, v, 327-29.

[72] *Real orden*, July 8, 1768, *pragmáticas*, July 4, 1770, Nov. 14, 1771, *Nov. rec.*, IX, xii, 19-21.

[73] Vera Lee Brown, "Anglo-French Rivalry for the Trade of the Spanish Peninsula, 1763-1783," in "Studies in the History of Spain in the Second Half of the Eighteenth Century," *Smith College Studies in History*, xv (1929-30), 57-58.

[74] Sarrailh, pp. 350-51, 556.

British navy cut off the supply of American cotton. Most manufacturers of Barcelona organized themselves into a Compañía de Fabricantes de Hilados and weathered the war years by obtaining permission to import cotton from Malta and the Levant.

The decade after the peace of 1783 saw the industry at its zenith. The Compañía de Fabricantes de Hilados by now included sixty factories with 2,162 looms, and at least twenty other factories with 350 looms had refused to join it.[75] The Compañía complained of the spread of unaffiliated workshops turning out cheap products:

> The factories that do not adopt the royal ordinances have multiplied to such an extent that the street or alley of this city and its environs is rare that does not have signs of a factory of printed cottons. The first, second, third, and fourth floors of tiny houses that barely hold one or two printing tables have been made into shops of this noble and important industry, and the scorn of it has gone so far that tables for printing can be found side by side with the casks of tavern keepers and the filthy yards of the market gardeners.[76]

In 1792 the Catalan cotton industry was reported to employ eighty thousand workers and to export two hundred million reales' worth of *indianas* to America.[77] No region in France yet had an industry that could match it,[78] so that Catalonia ranked second only to the English midlands in production of cotton cloth at this time.

The industry of Barcelona was growing so rapidly that labor became scarce. Since 1770 the wages paid in the city had been rising noticeably, and after 1785 the rise became steep. A common laborer who earned 7 sols per day in 1760 earned 8¾ in 1781 and 12⅙ in 1790 (two sols were a little over one real). This rise did not keep pace with prices, but nowhere else in Spain or most of Europe did wages show such gains, and the workers of

[75] Carrera Pujal, IV, 105-12, V, 331-37.
[76] Quoted in *ibid.*, pp. 339-40.   [77] Desdevises, II, 97-98.
[78] See Sée, pp. 286-87.

Barcelona won the further advantage of a seven-hour day.[79] In 1780 a witness wrote: "Today not only in Barcelona but in all Catalonia laborers for farms and other callings are hard to find even at very high wages. Maids are just as scarce. They say the cause is the many factories."[80] The situation resembled closely that of the English midlands, where wages were also soaring and employers like Josiah Wedgwood complained of lack of workers.[81]

Joseph Townsend, just arrived from England, was favorably impressed by everything he saw in Barcelona:

> The industry which every where appears in Catalonia seems to act with concentrated energy in Barcelona. Early and late, not only is the hammer heard upon the anvil, but every artist is seen busily employed, each in his several way adding to the general stock.

Townsend spent nearly a month in 1786 studying the institutions and economy of the city. Among its important industries he placed those that supplied the Spanish armies—the crafts of tailor and shoemaker, of which Catalonia made a specialty, and the manufacture of firearms. "It is impossible anywhere to see either finer metal, or work executed in a neater and more perfect manner" than in the cannon produced by the royal foundry of Barcelona.

The manufacturers of silk, cotton, and wool, however, impressed him most deeply by their advanced technology. He saw the spinning of American cotton done by a chartered company which employed "fourteen of the Manchester machines" and others built on a French model that resembled the water powered spinning frame patented by Richard Arkwright in 1771. The company also employed a machine invented locally for cleaning the raw American cotton, which arrived full of sand and dirt. On the other hand he found the printing of cotton cloth still

---

[79] Vilar, *loc.cit.*, pp. 28-43; Townsend, I, 144.

[80] Caresmar, "Carta en la cual se prueba ser Cataluña en lo antiguo más poblada," quoted in Vilar, *loc.cit.*, p. 50.

[81] Earl J. Hamilton, "Profit Inflation and the Industrial Revolution," *Quarterly Journal of Economics*, LVI (1941-42), 256-73.

being done with stamps and consequently more slowly than by the latest English method, which used cylinders.

The woolen industry was also progressive in his eyes:

> The manufacture which gave me the greatest pleasure was one of woollen, carried on by Don Vincente Vernis. He employs three hundred and fifty persons in making cloth for Spanish America, which indeed takes most of the Barcelona goods, except for some silk smuggled with their brandy through Guernsey into England. He has a very compact and elegant machine for winding and twisting worsted, in which fourscore reels are managed by one little girl, whilst another gives motion to the whole, and at the same time employs herself at knitting. . . . When one of the girls is weary the other takes her place.

When Townsend finished also observing the techniques of the skilled craftsmen, especially those who worked wood and metal, he concluded that inventive genius was no monopoly of his native England. "In every country a traveller can pass through, he will find some mechanical contrivances, some modes of expediting work, which are of late invention, or at least new to him; and I am inclined to think, that no country, if thoroughly examined, would furnish more than Spain."[82]

The more famous traveller Arthur Young corroborated Townsend's impression of Catalan industry. "There is every appearance as you walk the streets [in Barcelona] of great and active industry. You move nowhere without hearing the creak of stocking engines." He also pointed out the active maritime commerce of the city. As he travelled north along the coast, he remarked the lace and stocking production in Mataró and the shipbuilding in Arenys and Canet. "All these towns are well built; the houses white, clean, and very good, with an equal appearance of general industry, and its right concomitant, private comfort."[83]

As soon as the traveller left the northern and eastern coasts of

82 Townsend, I, 138-46.
83 Young, I, 635, 644-45.

Spain, he left the land of industrial activity. Most of the manufacture of central Spain—Aragon, the Castiles, and Andalusia—was conducted on a small scale to supply local wants and was marked by little excitement. Traditional woolen, pottery, leather goods, and other common necessities were the products. The few factories of note were mainly those which the crown had set up and subsidized so that they could overcome the disadvantages of their geographic location. Exceptions could be made for Madrid, where there was a local market for luxury goods, and Seville, which could ship by water to Cadiz. But even in Seville, the largest enterprises were the royal tobacco and cannon factories.

Yet initiative was not lacking and a few central cities witnessed valiant attempts to revive industry. One attempt that failed was Toledo's to animate its silk production. Another that deserved note was Segovia's drive to become a woolen center. Its location was logical: it was the major shearing point of the Mesta. The royal factory established in 1763 with a local monopoly of weaving fine woolens was finally closed in 1779 as a failure. Private individuals bought the factory and soon had 63 large looms at work and were giving employment to nearly 3,000 persons, including spinners. At the same time the right to weave fine woolens had been extended to all weavers of Segovia. In 1779 these weavers included 58 "manufacturers" (*fabricantes*) with 228 looms.[84] The true capitalists of Segovia, however, were the merchants who handled the wool of the Mesta. They advanced money to the smaller sheepgrowers and provided wool for the less important *fabricantes* and got the major profit of both enterprises. Besides selling abroad the fine merino wool, they cooperated with foreign buyers to export the common wools, despite the prohibition on such exports. "The result is that the shepherds are regularly poor and the buyers or merchants rich,

[84] Bourgoing (1789), I, 53-54; Carrera Pujal, IV, 159-60, citing Eugenio Larruga, *Memorias políticas y económicas sobre los frutos, comercio, fabricas y minas de España* (45 vols.; Madrid, 1787-1800).

without other labor than buying and selling."[85] The putting-out system of Segovia was a small image of that of silk in Valencia, but it was virtually unique in Old Castile, and under existing conditions it could not be expected to grow fast.

5

The economy of western Europe as a whole was quickening more rapidly in the second half of the eighteenth century than before. The so-called "industrial revolution" was in its early stages. It is another indication that Spain under the Bourbons formed part of the western European economy that its industry and commerce were also swelling apace. Yet much credit must go to the decisions of the government, guided primarily by Campomanes, to free Spanish entrepreneurs from guild restrictions, to facilitate direct traffic between Spanish ports and the colonies, and to override the objections of foreign countries and prohibit their products. The hope of Spanish industry was to supply Spain and its empire. Spanish industrial goods could not yet compete in the world market, but under its own flag Spain had one of the richest sectors of this market. By its dependence on English cloths and hardware, Spain had for over a century been "the darling—the silver mine of England";[86] and English, French, and other merchants had at the same time supplied the bulk of goods for the Spanish colonies by licit trade through Cadiz and illicit smuggling. If Spain could take over this trade, it had need of no other to rival the industry of any country.

The favorable effects of Carlos' legislation were becoming apparent when Spain entered the War of American Independence against Britain in 1779 to strike a blow at its major rival for American empire and trade. Contact between Spain and the colonies was severed by the enemy, the Catalan cotton industry suffered, the Compañía de Caracas was ruined, and the government was unable to receive its income from the colonies. But all

---

[85] Larruga, quoted in Carrera Pujal, IV, 158-59.
[86] Anon., *A Proposal for Humbling Spain* (London, 1711), quoted in Brown, *loc.cit.*, pp. 43-44.

the effects were not black. The war encouraged the expansion of the metallurgical and shipfitting industries of Catalonia and the Basque provinces. Bilbao merchants took vengeance on the British by turning to privateering and made up for their loss of trade by the capture of English ships.[87] At the conclusion of peace in January 1783 Spain received Menorca and Florida from Britain. Spain's colonial empire had never been more extensive or better protected. Only Gibraltar, on which an attack had failed, and Jamaica remained *irredenti*.

The temporary loss of American treasure was meanwhile turned to account by Francisco Cabarrús, a French-born financier. When an increase in taxes by one third and loans from the merchant guilds of Madrid and the bishops failed to supply enough money for the war,[88] Cabarrús won official adoption of a project to issue interest-bearing royal bonds, known as *vales reales*, which would circulate as legal tender. Repeated issues finally forced them off par, and in October 1782 they were being discounted at 22 per cent. In part to meet this threat to royal credit, Cabarrús was authorized in June 1782 to found the first national bank of Spain, the Banco de San Carlos, with the task of redeeming the *vales*. To assure its financial strength, the bank was given a monopoly of issuing contracts to supply the army and navy and of exporting specie, and was to receive a commission for its services in both cases.[89] After the signing of peace, the pent-up treasure came in from America, and the bank began to retire the *vales*. These not only recovered their value but circulated at 1 to 2 per cent above par in the years 1786 to 1792.[90] The credit of the king of Spain for once was as good as his Mexican silver and gold.

The last years of Carlos' reign saw the Spanish economy

[87] Carrera Pujal, v, 77.

[88] *Ibid.*, IV, 326 (taxes); Rodríguez Casado, *Política interior*, p. 57 n. (guilds); Carlos III, "Instrucción reservada," *loc.cit.*, p. 216, art. 25 (bishops).

[89] *Real cédula*, June 2, 1782, *Nov. rec.*, IX, iii, 6; Earl J. Hamilton, "The Foundation of the Bank of Spain," *Journal of Political Economy*, LIII (1945), 97-114.

[90] On the *vales* see Townsend, II, 196-205; Hamilton, *War and Prices*, pp. 78-82.

flourish in a way that had been unknown for centuries. The directors of the Banco de San Carlos in 1785 gloated over "the progress of our industry, the multiplicity of modern factories in Catalonia, the extension of those in Valencia, the growth of agriculture, and the increase in demand for its products."[91] Spanish wool, silk, cork, wines, brandies, nuts, and dried fruits were eagerly sought by north European merchants; and post-war consumer demand in Spain and the colonies spurred on factory owners. At the end of the seventeenth century only about one eighth of the goods shipped from Spain to America had been of Spanish origin.[92] In 1784, a year of heavy trade following the war, Spanish products already accounted for 45 per cent of the value of all goods (about 435 million reales) shipped from Spanish ports to America. The Spanish share continued to mount and in 1788 it was 53 per cent of 300 million reales, in 1789 about 50 per cent of 370 million reales.[93] After the *reglamento* of 1778 and the end of the war, foreign contraband sales to Spanish colonies also became less lucrative.[94] Exporters of northwestern Europe, brought up in the firm belief that Spain maintained its empire for the profit of others, were faced with the prospect of a Spanish America for Spain. In 1792 the English historian William Robertson expressed their uneasiness when he observed that Spain's progress "must appear considerable, and is sufficient to alarm the jealousy, and call for the most vigorous efforts, of the nations now in possession of the lucrative trade which the Spaniards aim at wresting from them."[95]

[91] Quoted in Hamilton, *War and Prices,* p. 221.

[92] This is my calculation from the rough figures in a contemporary document cited by Enrique Sée [*sic*], "Notas sobre el comercio francés en Cádiz y particularmente sobre el comercio de las telas bretonas en el siglo XVIII," *Anuario de historia del derecho español,* II (1925), 179-95, which does not break down clearly what share of the trade to Cadiz was for the domestic Spanish market and what for the colonial.

[93] Tables in Townsend, II, 387, using £1 = 100 reales (1784), and in Laborde, IV, 377 (see Desdevises, III, 147-48) (1788); report of Pedro de Lerena, secretario de hacienda, cited in Carrera Pujal, IV, 568 (1789).

[94] Haring, p. 343.

[95] Quoted in Hamilton, *War and Prices,* p. 222.

6

This economic expansion was giving rise to a strong middle class. The retail trade of Madrid was dominated by the Cinco Gremios Mayores, the five merchant guilds for the sale of cloths of silk, gold, and silver; woolens; linens; spices and drugs; and jewelry. They had been given a privileged position among Madrid guilds in 1686, and their members formed the élite of local merchants. In 1777 there were 375 members, each with his prosperous shop that enjoyed a monopoly in its neighborhood and would be inherited by his widow or son. The new spirit had taken hold of them. In 1763 Carlos III established a privileged company to which only members of the Cinco Gremios could belong. It owned ships and brought spices and drugs from the colonies. It farmed royal revenues. At one time or another it ran royal silk factories in Valencia, Talavera, and Murcia and royal woolen factories at Cuenca and Ezcaray and sold their products. In 1785 it was entrusted with the completion of the canal of Aragon. It was in charge of the food supply of Madrid, and until the Banco de San Carlos was founded, it had a monopoly of furnishing food and clothing for the army. The Cinco Gremios Mayores were a powerful group. At the start of the War of American Independence they lent thirty million reales to the crown.[96]

Barcelona had its strong bourgeoisie too, engaged in manufacture and export. In 1776 a company of maritime insurance was founded in the city and in 1779 a life insurance association. A bank to handle foreign exchange was planned, but the crown refused it a license. Citizens of Barcelona who had been enriched by cotton manufacture or American trade began to move into new resplendent houses in the nearby towns of Sarriá, Gracia, and Sant Gervasi.[97]

Leading merchants of Spain's major commercial centers were members of officially sponsored consulados, which acted both as

[96] Desdevises, III, 137-39; Hussey, p. 224; Carrera Pujal, IV, 166-70, 551-52.
[97] Carrera Pujal, V, 173, 272; Vilar, *loc.cit.*, p. 32.

chambers of commerce and as fiscal police. There were twelve consulados in the peninsula at the end of the century—at Madrid, Burgos, Bilbao, Seville, and most of the ports open to colonial trade.[98] But the bourgeoisie had expanded beyond the narrow limits of officially privileged organizations. Every center of trade or manufacture had its exporters and importers, its merchant entrepreneurs who advanced money to farmers or shepherds or smiths against future deliveries or provided wool or silk for spinners and weavers, or its factory owners who hired labor to run their machines.

In the midst of this Spanish bourgeoisie was a large group of foreign merchants also interested in the trade of Spain and its colonies. In 1772 Cadiz had seventy-nine French wholesale houses.[99] The export of Málaga wines was done by fourteen foreign houses (including that of Joseph Martinis) which profited from making advances to poor farmers. Townsend found a John Murphy here engaged in developing new wines and a Thomas Vague in control of the wine export of Sagunto.[100] Under Carlos III the French became the most prominent foreign colony. French manufacturers were attracted by the possibilities of the silk and potash industries in Valencia and the cotton industry in Barcelona. A Frenchman established a hat factory at La Coruña and others became wealthy entrepreneurs in Talavera, Saragossa, and Madrid.[101] Englishmen had been more numerous before the Seven Years' War, when they were forced to leave. After the war English exports to Spain revived, but Spanish merchants largely took over the distribution of the goods.[102]

Spanish merchants and entrepreneurs thus had to compete with foreigners, and many of them were doing so successfully.

[98] Desdevises, III, 111. In his fine discussion of the middle classes, Domínguez Ortiz underrates the importance of this new bourgeoisie (pp. 182-200).

[99] Desdevises, III, 145. Bourgoing (1797), III, 129-31, lists fifty large French commercial houses and thirty shops in 1790.

[100] Townsend, III, 29-30, 292; Carrera Pujal, IV, 90; Desdevises, III, 34.

[101] Sarrailh, pp. 331-34.

[102] Brown, *loc.cit.*, p. 47.

Some had been abroad to travel or study foreign techniques or were sending their sons abroad for these purposes, and the crown and local organizations gave them support.[103] Catalans spread throughout Spain as much as Frenchmen, selling the products of their native province. They became so important in Madrid that in 1783 the Junta de Comercio restricted the monopoly of the Cinco Gremios Mayores by permitting representatives of national factories to sell their products at retail in the capital. The Cinco Gremios were ordered to give membership to Catalan merchants in Madrid who wished to join.[104]

Though the new bourgeois descended from old families of local merchants and guild masters, their spirit was a far cry from that of their great-grandparents. Expansion and profit were their objectives, not stability and security. They were prospering members of a cosmopolitan world of business venture. They had every reason to be satisfied with the policies of the royal government, which were aimed at giving them the fullest possible protection and encouragement. Here was one section of society that had cause to welcome the *luces*. Among them, as among the middle class of France, the Enlightenment should find supporters.

Beneath them was the great majority of the city dwellers—the working classes. They did not benefit from Spain's prosperity. Their wages hardly rose in the century and did not keep up at all with the cost of living. Even in Barcelona though money wages were rising real wages seem to have been falling, and elsewhere the proletariat was much worse off.[105] "In traversing the city [of Valencia], to view whatever was most worthy of attention; considering its flourishing condition, and the opulence of the citizens, whether merchants, manufacturers, ecclesiastics, the military, or gentlemen of landed property, I was struck with the sight of poverty, of wretchedness, and of rags, in every street," Townsend wrote.[106] The lag of wages behind prices

[103] Sarrailh, pp. 346-51.   [104] Carrera Pujal, IV, 100, 262-63.
[105] Hamilton, *War and Prices,* pp. 214-16; Vilar, *loc.cit.,* pp. 47-48.
[106] Townsend, III, 251.

directly increased the profits of manufacturers and helped make possible the rapid industrialization of Spain, as of France and England, in the second half of the century.[107] Campomanes' *Discurso sobre la educacion popular de los artesanos y su fomento* and the legislation of the 1770's envisaged creating a prosperous artisan class by weakening the gremios. No such class appeared, and in the 1780's full support was switched to large industry. No laws protected the workers from the new *fabricantes*, for the prosperity of the state, not the happiness of the individual, was the pole star of the official economists.

The laborers were consequently in a poor position to hear of the *luces* or to appreciate them. They remained loyal to traditional Spanish customs and amusements. A worker would pawn his shirt to go to a bull fight, to the distress of his enlightened superiors.[108] In Madrid the idols of the lower classes were the *majos*, pompous young bullies who ostentatiously wore the long national capes, long hair, and broad-brimmed hats and smoked black cigars instead of donning the French three-cornered hat, full skirted coat, and wig, and taking snuff in the manner of the elegant classes. It was the edict of Squillace in 1766 forbidding further use of long capes and broad hats that touched off the popular insurrection of Madrid. The fashionable *petimetre* trembled for his safety when his mistress persuaded him to take her to a popular dance of *majos* and *majas*, for among these people all men and all things French were despised.[109]

Devotion to the church marked the lower classes in the city as much as in the country. The processions of Easter Week in Barcelona brought out over one hundred thousand spectators from the city and the surroundings, according to Townsend, "hurrying from church to church to express the warmth of their zeal, and the fervor of their devotion, by bowing themselves in each, and kissing the feet of the most revered image."[110] In Madrid crowds of artisans and workers poured into the streets to watch

---

[107] Hamilton, "Profit Inflation and the Price Revolution," *loc.cit.*
[108] Sarrailh, pp. 62-63.   [109] Kany, pp. 220-23, 279.
[110] Townsend, I, 107.

Carlos III descend from his carriage and walk beside it so that a priest carrying the holy sacrament might ride. The king was applauded for his religious devotion.[111] Innumerable other instances of the habitual religious fervor of the city proletariat could be drawn from contemporary accounts. The grotesque nature of many of their practices, verging on superstition, were the despair of those who wished to see the church of Spain made more strict and austere.

The city proletariat could not be expected, any more than the peasantry, to formulate programs in its own interest or to follow any in a disciplined manner. The lower classes could only be led by others. The direction of Spanish society would come from two main groups, those who were getting wealthy from capitalistic agriculture and those who were getting wealthy from capitalistic industry and commerce. One group was a new bourgeoisie. The other was largely, but not entirely, made up of nobles and churchmen.

Very much the same situation existed in France, where on the eve of the French Revolution a middle class, enriched by banking, manufacture, and colonial trade, disputed control of the state with a nobility that was also increasing in strength largely by reviving the collection of neglected lords' dues, taking over part of the common lands, and making greater use of an agricultural proletariat. Socially as well as economically Spain had become much like France in the eighteenth century.

The parallel should not be overdrawn, however. French peasants were to a great extent protected from the greed of their lords by institutions that resembled more closely those of Catalonia than those of arid Spain; consequently the French nobility sought to assure its supremacy by getting control of the royal government, not, as the Spanish oligarchy did, by ignoring it. In the drive of the French nobles to control the government, they had barred the French bourgeoisie from avenues to social and political advancement that had been open to it under Louis XIV.

---

[111] Kany, pp. 359-62. See Sarrailh, pp. 653-61, and Kany, pp. 356-96, for other examples of religious enthusiasm.

Legal class privileges had thus become a major source of contention in France; they were not so in Spain. In Spain, furthermore, one could almost draw a geographic line dividing the north and east, where industry was flourishing and peasants were well-to-do, from the center and south, where industry was backward, peasants and agricultural laborers were exploited, and a rural oligarchy ruled.

CHAPTER VI

THE CHANNELS OF ENLIGHTENMENT

MOST Spanish writers who applauded the material advances they saw taking place in their country were ready to give credit for this progress to the enlightened policies of their king Carlos III. None of his measures aimed directly at creating national prosperity were so much admired, however, as the encouragement his government gave to institutions that would spread the *luces* to the people. Three of these were especially important: the periodical press, the universities, and the societies of Amigos del País.

Of these three the societies of Amigos del País were the most directly concerned with improving the economy of the country. They owed their origin to the private initiative of a Basque nobleman who had studied in France in his youth. Javier María Munive e Idiáquez, conde de Peñaflorida, returned from France in 1746 with the desire to see Spain imitate the academies and societies of learning that were having such success in other countries. He consulted his former Jesuit teachers at Toulouse in 1753 and soon organized an informal salon or *tertulia* in his home, at which were discussed mathematics, physics, history, and current events.[1] A leading figure in this group was a man who had known Rousseau personally.[2] In 1764 Peñaflorida and fifteen other Basque noblemen requested a license from the royal government permitting them to establish an official organization. The license was granted in 1765.

Thus began the Sociedad Bascongada de los Amigos del País. The stated purpose of these Basque "friends of the country" was to encourage agriculture, industry, commerce, and the arts and sciences. They soon got royal permission to establish instruction

---

[1] Fernández Navarrete, "Elogio del Conde de Peñaflorida," *loc.cit.*, II, 348-49; Urquijo, *Menéndez y Pelayo y los caballeritos*, p. 63; Nicolás de Soráluce y Zubizarreta, *La Real Sociedad Bascongada de los Amigos del País, sus antecedentes y otros sucesos con ella relacionados* (San Sebastián, 1880), pp. 101-7.

[2] Manuel Ignacio Altuna (Spell, pp. 15-16).

of pupils in Latin, French, geography, Spanish history, and experimental physics. To further the local economy, they ordered linen seed from Riga, supported a knife factory, offered one thousand reales for a memoir on the best kind of blacksmith's bellows, and built up a library at Vergara of Spanish and foreign works of a practical nature. Their first public meeting consisted of a reading of papers and the oral examination of five students. In 1768 the society published a collection of the memoirs it had produced, containing useful suggestions on agriculture, commerce, and industry.[3] Three years later the royal government showed its continued interest in the group. The king became its patron and the society added "Real" to its title.[4]

Campomanes, who was responsible for many of the crown's economic measures, became an enthusiastic supporter of the new institution. His *Discurso sobre el fomento de la industria popular*, devoted to the problem of establishing local industries, recommended as most suitable to undertake this task "patriotic bodies, erected in imitation of the Sociedad Bascongada de los Amigos del País." The provincial nobility, "which commonly lives in idleness," should be the prime movers of these societies, both by their personal activity and with their fortunes. "Without any expenditure by the state, the nobles will be the promoters of industry and the permanent support of their fellow citizens."[5] Only such societies, Campomanes felt, could find out the true condition of their own provinces and the industry suitable to each. Their job would be to encourage agriculture, commerce, and industry, become acquainted with economic treatises, translate and publish foreign works, and supervise instruction in mathematics and the vocations. Moreover, individuals of all classes should be admitted to the societies, and the only difference in rank at their

---

[3] *Ensayo de la Sociedad Bascongada de los Amigos del Pais. Año de 1766. Dedicado al rey N. señor* (Vitoria, 1768). The book begins with an "Historia de la Sociedad," probably by Peñaflorida, from which the above facts are taken. See also Sarrailh, pp. 234-35.

[4] Soráluce, p. 24.

[5] Rodríguez de Campomanes, *Fomento de la industria popular*, pp. lix-lxi.

meeting should be between the members and elected officers. There should be no distinction based on social class.

Campomanes' discourse was distributed to government officials and the clergy by the Consejo de Castilla. The wishes of the government for the establishment of more groups of "friends of the country" was clear, but the initiative was left to local individuals. The response was all that could be desired. In June 1775 a license was granted for a society in Madrid, to be known as the Real Sociedad Económica de Madrid. At the request of its proponents, Campomanes helped found it. By September it had eighty-seven members. In the next decade it doubled the number and membership became a highly-prized honor. Its statutes called for it actively to further industry and agriculture, to offer prizes for memoirs on agriculture, and to maintain industrial and vocational schools. Its expenses were to come out of the dues of the members, but the king demonstrated his support by endowing it with three thousand reales yearly for prizes.[6] The charter of the society of Madrid served as a model for economic societies that sprang up in cities throughout Spain. Valencia's in 1776 was the eleventh to be approved, Segovia's twenty-fourth in 1780. By 1789 fifty-six had been founded.[7]

Barcelona never established one. The city government, none too friendly toward Campomanes because of his known opposition to guilds, which were still influential in Barcelona, decided not to create a society of Amigos del País. It could point out that since 1758 the city had its own Junta de Comercio busy furthering local economic growth. The Junta encouraged the cotton industry and the expansion of the port, supported a successful nautical

[6] [Real Sociedad Económica de Madrid], *Memorias de la Sociedad Economica* (5 vols.; Madrid, 1780-95), Vols. III and IV (1787), list 165 members divided into three classes: "Agricultura," 45; "Industria," 77; and "Artes y oficios," 43. Sempere, *Biblioteca*, V, 137, 178-88 publishes its statutes. José Lesén y Moreno, *Historia de la Sociedad Económica de Amigos del País de Madrid* (Madrid, 1863) gives full information on its early years. The work was left incomplete.

[7] Sempere, *Biblioteca*, V, 224, VI, 1-3, 21-22. *Kalendario manual y guia de forasteros en Madrid para el año de 1789* (Madrid, 1789), pp. 136-43, lists them in chronological order of foundation. On the Amigos del País see the excellent chapters in Sarrailh, pp. 223-85.

school and a school of fine arts, and its members were the major stockholders of the new company of marine insurance. The Junta and the hidebound gremios had clashed more than once. The gremios and the city government saw no need for another local body to second the Junta's activity.[8]

Not all societies of Amigos del País lived up to expectations, but many did become highly active. The Sociedad Bascongada led the way in the support of education. In 1776 its school at Vergara was granted the title Real Seminario Patriótico Bascongado, with permission to give instruction in primary letters, religion, humanities, mathematics, and the physical sciences. The king soon endowed it with chairs of chemistry and mineralogy. It established a free school of design in 1777. The later societies followed its example, particularly in the field of vocational education for the idle poor. Madrid's set up four schools for spinning for girls aged five to sixteen with prizes for the most proficient students; Seville's had thirteen schools for weaving, mathematics and mechanics, to whose students it awarded gold medals; Mallorca's established elementary schools, supported by the bishop, and others for mathematics and drawing; Lugo's had three "escuelas patrióticas" and gave the students 1,560 reales in prizes in 1789; Zamora's had a spinning school for thirty girls and a night school of design for an equal number of poor artisans; Valencia's offered prizes to its elementary students and Cuenca's to its students of design and spelling. The Sociedad Aragonesa at Saragossa, besides keeping public schools for girls, set up chairs of law, moral philosophy and civil economy and commerce. Lorenzo Normante y Carcavilla, whose enthusiasm for economics has been noted, was given the last position in 1784.[9] Within two

---

[8] Sarrailh, pp. 87, 250, 262-64; Carrera Pujal, v, 173.

[9] *Gazeta*, Apr. 4 (Madrid), June 26 (Lugo), Dec. 11 (Seville), 1789, Apr. 23 (Saragossa), Sept. 3 appendix (Cuenca), 1790; Sempere, *Biblioteca*, v, 206-12 (Madrid), 218-28 (Valencia), vi 23 (Seville), 27-30 (Mallorca); *Memorias de la Sociedad Economica*, iii, 309 (Madrid); Soráluce, pp. 35, 45 (Basque); Miguel [de los] S[antos] Oliver [y Tolra], *Mallorca durante la primera revolución (1808 á 1814)* (Palma, 1901), pp. 46-52; Cesaro Fernández Duro, *Memorias históricas de la ciudad de Zamora, su provincia y obispado* (Madrid, 1883), iii, 183-86; Latassa y Ortín, vi, 174-75; Villanueva, i, 32-34; Borao, pp. 188-89 (last three Saragossa).

years he gave a public examination of two of his students.[10]

Another outstanding service of these societies was the encouragement they offered to the production of works on theoretical and practical economics. Several of the economic works written by Spaniards at this time were first presented at their meetings. The society of Madrid at a public function presided over by Floridablanca in 1789 gave honorable mention to two papers on "what should be the true spirit of legislation."[11] By then it had already published four volumes containing almost two hundred memoirs printed in full or in résumé on agriculture, industry, and the arts and crafts. Besides the Basque society, those of Segovia, Seville, and Mallorca had also published volumes of memoirs by 1790.[12] The society of Saragossa offered prizes both for memoirs and practical achievements in the fields of agriculture, arts, commerce, and natural history, and those of small cities like Oviedo, Santiago, Segovia, Jerez, Tudela, and Tarragona did likewise.[13]

In their quest for their country's well-being, the societies often showed individual initiative. The Amigos del País de Mallorca published a periodical paper listing the local market prices. The society at Valencia encouraged new methods of silk weaving and set up a commercial company to sell the products; while that of Segovia got the bishop to reduce the number of religious festivals so that artisans could work more days;[14] Valladolid's undertook experiments in raising saffron.[15] At Madrid the society opened its doors to women in 1786. A heated debate over the advisability

[10] His *Espíritu del señor Melon* was prepared for their instruction, and they were examined on it.

[11] *Gazeta*, Apr. 14, 1789.

[12] Sempere, *Biblioteca*, v, 188-205, vi, 1-20, 22-23, 27-30, gives an account of these. See also n. 6 above (Madrid); *Correo de Madrid*, Dec. 24, 31, 1788 and *Espíritu de los mejores diarios*, Jan. 18, 1790 for other papers presented at the society of Seville; and *Espíritu de los mejores diarios*, Sept. 22, 29, Oct. 6, 13, 20, 1788 for a paper read at the Madrid society.

[13] *Gazeta*, Nov. 27 (Jerez), Dec. 18, 22 (Oviedo), 29 (Santiago), 1789, Apr. 23, 26, 30 (Saragossa), May 11 (Segovia), Dec. 10 (Tarragona), 1790; *Espíritu de los mejores diarios*, July 26, 1790 (Santiago); Sarrailh, pp. 261-62 (Tudela).

[14] Sempere, *Biblioteca*, v, 218-28, vi, 4.　　[15] Sarrailh, p. 259.

of this act developed, in which Jovellanos and Cabarrús took leading parts. Carlos III ended it by asserting that it was his royal
pleasure for women to be included. The ladies were given charge
of the girls' schools.[16] The Basque and Aragonese societies also
decided to admit women.[17]

Besides the sixteen institutions so far mentioned, at least an-
another eight had enough life in 1789 publicly to express their sor-
row at the death of Carlos III.[18] These societies were a minority
of the fifty-six that had been founded. Concerning the others,
the historian of contemporary Spanish letters, Sempere y Guarinos,
lamented, "Many have given scarcely more signs of existence than
to have announced their foundation in the *Gazeta* and to keep
their name and those of their directors and secretaries in the *Guia
de forasteros* [the guidebook of Spanish officialdom]." Sempere
explained that the evident favor with which their establishment
was regarded by the government caused many to be founded in
towns that did not have the necessary resources to support them,
and the early desire to see one's name in the papers was followed
by lack of interest, scantily attended meetings, and a shortage of
funds.[19] Such an outcome is hardly surprising. Their failure did
not detract from the over-all achievements of the new economic
societies. It indicated rather that Spain was not yet ready to maintain such societies outside the larger cities. The Amigos del País
were engaged in a struggle to reform the practices of the vast
majority of the common people of Spain. Their task was overwhelmingly difficult. Public meetings in the cities and printed
memoirs could not have an immediate influence on more than a
small minority. Actual examples of the benefits derived from the

---

[16] Sempere, *Biblioteca*, III, 137-38, V, 212-18. *Memorial literario* printed the
speech of Cabarrús objecting to their entry (May 1786, p. 74) and of Jovellanos
in their favor (Apr. 1786, pp. 475-78), the royal order of Aug. 27, 1787 (Oct.
1787, pp. 208-9), and the speech of the first woman member (Mar. 1786, pp.
357-61).

[17] *Memorial literario*, Apr. 1786, p. 474; Sempere, *Biblioteca*, III, 137-38.

[18] *Gazeta*, Mar. 6 (Jaca), Mar. 31 (Tárrega), Apr. 3 (Talavera), May 5 (Gran
Canaria), July 7 (Córdoba), July 10 (Málaga), Sept. 8, 1789 (Tenerife), Jan. 5,
1790 (Jaén).

[19] Sempere, *Biblioteca*, V, 148.

use of new tools and agricultural methods were displayed and were more convincing, but few peasants could invest in new tools or risk experimenting with new crops and techniques, and most landlords showed little enthusiasm for improved agricultural methods.[20] It required groups of determined men not to succumb to the apathy that greeted their efforts.

The full explanation of their failure involved more than the lethargy of the masses and a shortage of enlightened persons, how-ever. The institutions also had to face the active opposition of conservative groups. In 1786 a royal order spoke of the king's "vanishing expectations" and instructed all societies to submit a report on the causes of their decadence. The order identified one such cause as "the parties that have been created harmful to the harmony and cooperation [*correspondencia*] that should exist between fellow citizens."[21] According to Sempere many local tribunals and ayuntamientos looked upon the societies as danger-ous rivals for royal favor and became their enemies.[22] One can sense behind the royal order and Sempere's comment the opposi-tion of Spain's rural oligarchies, none too pleased at seeing out-siders joining the government in working to upset their happy state of affairs.

Part of the church was also hostile to the economic societies. Clergymen frequently refused to reply to their requests for help and information.[23] The Sociedad Aragonesa incurred the op-position of the faculty of the university of Saragossa because it had set up what the faculty considered to be rival chairs of law and moral philosophy. Normante, the professor of economics of the society, had to face a violent storm stirred up by local clergy-men, who attacked his activities from the pulpit in the "cause of God." They made use of a well-known Franciscan missionary of remarkable oratorical abilities, Fray Diego de Cádiz, who preached against the society and denounced to the Inquisición Normante's

---

[20] Sarrailh, pp. 25-34.
[21] *Real orden*, July 28, 1786, and *circular del Consejo de Castilla*, July 14, 1786, *Nov. rec.*, VIII, xxi, 2 and nota 4.
[22] Sempere, *Biblioteca*, v, 148-51.
[23] *Ibid.*

economic doctrines of the usefulness of luxury and the inconveniences of monasticism. For the society's activities to be investigated by the Santo Oficio threatened its honor, but it was vindicated by the support of the Consejo de Castilla.[24] The Sociedad Aragonesa sent the other Amigos del País a report on the affair, and fourteen societies wrote back to assure their injured sister of their sympathy and confidence. Of these, five were not among those whose activity was otherwise noted above.[25]

The attacks on the orthodoxy of the economic societies were not justified. Attachment to religion was one of their strongest features. Their elementary schools regularly gave instruction in the catechism.[26] The teacher of design of the Sociedad de Amigos del País de Mallorca was an agent (*familiar*) of the Inquisición. The Sociedad Bascongada began every meeting with a mass, and high church officials recognized its orthodoxy. In 1770 it received permission to use the *Encyclopédie* by nothing less than a papal breve. It later acquired 166 volumes of the *Encyclopédie méthodique* without asking the approval of the church, but in 1793, when the tribunal of the Inquisición at Logroño confiscated them, the inquisitor-general ordered the volumes returned to the society. In 1776 the society of Madrid was given permission by the inquisitor-general to read prohibited works on economics.[27]

In fact, instead of opposing the societies, the more enlightened members of the clergy gave them their active support. Between 1770 and 1786 the Sociedad Bascongada had ninety-six ecclesiastical members, nine of whom belonged to the Inquisición.[28] Five

[24] Borao, pp. 188-89; Villanueva, I, 32-34. On Fray Diego's oratory see Townsend, III, 147, and Menéndez Pelayo, *Heterodoxos*, v, 414. A MS "Resumen de la vida del V. P. Fr. Diego José de Cádiz, religioso capuchino de la provincia de Andalucía . . ." is Vol. 554 of "Fraile."

[25] Sarrailh, p. 276 and n. 4. The new societies were Baza, Ciudad Rodrigo, Granada, Murcia, and León.

[26] See, e.g., the *reglamento* of the Sociedad Bascongada (Urquijo, *Menéndez y Pelayo y los caballeritos*, p. 74), of Cuenca (*Gazeta*, Sept. 3, 1790, appendix), and of Seville (*Gazeta*, Dec. 11, 1789).

[27] Oliver, p. 46 (Mallorca); Urquijo, *Menéndez y Pelayo y los caballeritos*, pp. 118-21 (Bascongada); Sarrailh, p. 270 (Madrid).

[28] Urquijo, *Menéndez y Pelayo y los caballeritos*, pp. 96-99, 102-3.

bishops and a monk were directors of societies in 1789.[29] One of
these was the Augustinian enemy of the Jesuits, Francisco Armañá y Font, now archbishop of Tarragona. He had one of his
canons draw up the statutes for his society.[30] The bishop of Oviedo
established prizes to be given by the society of Benavente,[31] and
the founder and guiding light of the highly active Sociedad Aragonesa was the canon of the cathedral of Saragossa famous for
his encouragement of the economy of Aragon, Ramón Pignatelli.[32] The divided attitude of churchmen toward the new institutions was reminiscent of the division within the Spanish
church between those sympathetic toward reform—the Jansenists
—and the conservative ultramontanes.

Campomanes' discurso had pointed to the nobility as the logical
patrons of the Amigos del País. Although the example had been
set by the Conde de Peñaflorida, who had pioneered the movement, only in a minority of cases did the aristocrats of Spain respond to the call. Aranda, in Paris at the time, offered to endow
three prizes for the society of Aragon, and the Marqués de Peñafiel founded the society of Benavente.[33] Most of the first women
members admitted to the Madrid society had titles of nobility.[34]
The Duque de Almodóvar, translator of Raynal, was director
of the Amigos of Segovia. In all, however, only eight directors and
four other officers of the societies were titled nobles in 1789.[35]

The activity of these progressive aristocrats and prelates was
not sufficient to account for the evident success of this economic
experiment. The names of the officers of the societies and of the
contributors of memoirs indicate that the main impetus came from
highly enthusiastic commoners. The outstanding figures in the list

[29] *Kalendario manual y guia de forasteros* . . . *1789*, pp. 136-43.
[30] Torres Amat, p. 39.
[31] Fernández Duro, III, 183-86.
[32] Conde de Sastago, *Elogio del mui ilustre señor D. Ramon Pignatelli* . . . *18 de marzo de 1796* (Saragossa, [1796]).
[33] Aranda to Pignatelli, Mar. 5, 1776, quoted in Ricardo del Arco, "Dos re-novadores de antaño: el Conde de Aranda y Pignatelli," *Nuestro tiempo*, XVIII[2] (1918), 134-35; Fernández Duro, III, 185-86.
[34] *Memorial literario*, Oct. 1787, pp. 203-9.
[35] *Kalendario manual y guia de forasteros* . . . *1789*, pp. 136-43.

of members of the society of Madrid in 1787 were Campomanes, Cabarrús, and Jovellanos—all closely involved in the economic planning of the government—Cristóbal Cladera, editor of the periodical *Espiritu de los mejores diarios,* and Sempere y Guarinos. Of the other hundred and sixty members only ten had titles of nobility and only one was a clergyman. Judging from the Amigos del País, both in Madrid and the provinces, it was the educated commoners and hidalgos with no titles to distinguish their names from those of commoners who most readily supported the efforts of Carlos to reanimate their country.

2

While the economic societies were engaged in furthering primary and vocational instruction for the lower classes, the government had undertaken to reform higher education in Spain. Before 1765 most of the education in the universities was limited to the reading of stale and mediocre texts. Feyjóo had lamented the situation, urging a revision of instruction in philosophy, physics, and medicine.[36] The question was brought to the fore after 1767, when the crown followed up the expulsion of the Jesuits by destroying their influence within the schools. The government took the opportunity to begin a general housecleaning of the institutions of higher learning.

In the capital the Company of Jesus had supplied the faculty of the Colegio Imperial de Madrid, founded in 1625. After their departure the "college" or preparatory school was completely reorganized and was reopened with solemn festivities on November 1, 1771 under the new title of Reales Estudios de San Isidro. The establishment was to include courses in experimental physics, the law of nature and of nations, and logic, the last to be taught "according to the *luces* given it by modern authorities and without scholastic disputes." The regular clergy was barred from its faculty, and laymen began to appear on its rostra. To the Estudios

---

[36] Millares, "Prólogo," in Feyjóo, *Teatro crítico* (1941 ed.), pp. 40 and 45; Desdevises, III, 189-97.

was attached a group of chaplains known as the canons of San Isidro, who were to become notorious before the end of the century for their Jansenist views on religious questions.[37] The tenor of its instruction can be judged from the fact that its professor of logic in the 1780's considered the certainty of the Copernican system to be a demonstrated fact.[38] In 1787 its professor of physics offered a course on "experimental philosophy" open to the public, and in January 1789 the Reales Estudios opened another public course on the history of literature, using the work of Juan Andrés for its text. In October 1790 the latter course had 168 steady attendants, including the Duque de Almodóvar.[39] At the capital and under the patronage of the king there thus was flourishing a preparatory school devoted to giving modern education, free from the religious quarrels of the regular orders.

Carlos' government also decided to modernize the universities. In 1769 Olavide, who was then royal governor (*asistente*) of Seville, was given the task of disposing of the buildings formerly occupied by the Jesuits in that city. He drew up a plan which recommended giving the buildings to the university of Seville and took the occasion also to propose a reorganization of the curriculum of the university. His report was preceded by an introduction praising Descartes for destroying scholasticism and reviving science in Europe. "This great revolution is owed to a single man who did nothing except to abandon the Aristotelian and scholastic method, substituting for it a geometric one. . . . Unfortunately for us not a single shaft of this light has entered the universities of Spain," he lamented.[40] Olavide proposed to reform the teaching of philosophy and introduce mathematics.

[37] "Filosofia. Noticia de los progresos que en esta ciencia se van haciendo en España," *Memorial literario*, June 1786, p. 229; Sempere, *Biblioteca*, IV, 9-10; and *Kalendario manual o guia de forasteros . . . 1780* (Madrid, 1780), which gives the names of the professors. See Ferrer del Rio, III, 210-12. The *real decreto*, Jan. 19, 1770, reestablishing the colegio is in *Nov.rec.*, VIII, ii, 3.

[38] Torres Amat, p. 28.

[39] Townsend, II, 154, 252; *Gazeta*, Feb. 20, May 15, 1789, Oct. 1, 1790; *Memorial literario*, Jan. 1791, pp. 39-51.

[40] Quoted in Antonio Gil de Zarate, *De la instrucción pública en España* (Madrid, 1855), I, 59-60. See *ibid.*, I, 55-63, III, 233-35; Ferrer del Rio, III, 188-89.

The interminable disputes between the various theological parties, Thomist, Scotist, and Suarist, were to be forbidden and the regular clergy was to be excluded from teaching or studying in the university. An effort was to be made to get good professors. The entire proposal received royal approval in August 1769.

Satisfied with this step, the Consejo de Castilla in 1770 ordered all universities to draw up new curricula in accord with modern needs and including chairs of moral philosophy, elementary mathematics, and experimental physics. The first reply, from the university of Salamanca, was hardly encouraging. Its faculty of arts did not see any advantage in changing the curriculum. "The principles of Newton, if indeed they dispose the student to be a perfect mathematician, teach nothing that will help him be a good logician and metaphysician; those of Gassendo and Cartesio do not resemble as much the revealed truths as do those of Aristotle"; "Obbés" is "very obscure" and "the Englishman Juan Lochio . . . besides being very obscure, should be read with much caution." The university ended recommending continued use of the current text on philosophy, that of Antoine Goudin, "because it is concise and has good Latin."[41] Despite the faculty's opinion, the Consejo made limited reforms in 1771, providing for enforcement of attendance at lectures and the study of anatomy and physics. In 1778 it ordered a change in Salamanca's philosophy courses to give impetus to the study of science and mathematics.[42] Nevertheless Spain's leading university on the whole continued in its stagnant routine.

Some of Spain's twenty-odd other universities were less recalcitrant. Alcalá de Henares replied to the Consejo that it favored teaching the physics of Peter van Musschenbroek (the Dutch admirer of Newton) and the purchase of scientific instruments. Although its philosophy was still to be limited to Aristotle, the text recommended was that in use at the Sorbonne, written by Pierre Leridant, a member of the Parlement de Paris and a con-

41 Quoted in Sempere, *Biblioteca*, IV, 211-12, and Sarrailh, pp. 91-92.
42 Universidad de Salamanca, *Informe* (n.p., [1814]), p. 20, in "Varios," Fernando VII, leg. 45 folio.

firmed enemy of Rome.[43] The university of Santiago underwent reform in 1772, that of Oviedo in 1774, of Saragossa in 1775, and of Granada in 1776. The universities of Santiago and Saragossa were to provide instruction in experimental physics and Granada's this subject and mathematics and natural law as well.[44] The university of Valencia responded ten years later. By 1784 its professor of theology, philosophy, and languages had introduced the study of Musschenbroek and Condillac in philosophy. A new rector, appointed in that year, proceeded to the most complete revision of all. In 1786 a new plan of studies for this university received governmental approval. It included moral philosophy, mathematics, and physics for those studying philosophy, and the law of nature and of nations for all students of civil or canon law.[45] Townsend was highly impressed by its new intellectual value. It was not only Spain's most progressive university, it was the largest, with some 2,400 students. Salamanca had 1,909 matriculated in 1785, while less important ones like Seville and Toledo had four to five hundred.[46]

Meanwhile the obstinacy of the faculty of Salamanca was fought intramurally. From 1771 to 1774 José Cadalso resided in its city. He became satisfied that the official curricula did not necessarily enslave the minds of professors. "There are many in Spain," he wrote in his *Cartas marruecas*, "who learn thoroughly by themselves the true positive sciences, study Newton in their rooms, and teach Aristotle from their chairs."[47] While at Sal-

[43] Sempere, *Biblioteca*, IV, 217-21; Sarrailh, pp. 135-36, 139 and n. 1.

[44] Paulino Pedret Casado, "Las cátedras de la Universidad de Santiago hasta el plan de estudios de 27 de enero de 1772," *Cuadernos de estudios gallegos*, II (1944), 242-44; Sarrailh, pp. 92-93; Fermín Canella Secades, *Historia de la Universidad de Oviedo y noticias de los establecimientos de su distrito* (2d ed.; Oviedo, 1903), pp. 94-95; Borao, pp. 42-43; Sempere, *Biblioteca*, IV, 225-32.

[45] *Plan de estudios aprobado por S. M. y mandado observar en la Universidad de Valencia* (Madrid, 1787) ("Fraile," Vol. 809, fol. 110), p. 12; Antonio Cabanilles, *Observaciones sobre el artículo España de la nueva Encyclopedia*. Escritas en frances por el doctor D. Antonio Cabanilles, presbítero. Y traducidas al castellano por don Mariano Rivera (Madrid, 1784), p. 47; Sempere, *Biblioteca*, IV, 238.

[46] Townsend, III, 243-51, II, 79, 304, I, 321.

[47] Cadalso, *Cartas marruecas*, p. 192, Carta 78.

amanca, Cadalso befriended a young student and poet, Juan
Meléndez Valdés. Without informing him that they were on
the Index, he set Meléndez to work reading the *Esprit des lois*
of Montesquieu and *Le droit des gens* of the Swiss jurist,
Emmerich de Vattel.[48] Three years later Jovellanos, who was
then in Seville, learned of Meléndez's ability as a poet and entered into correspondence with the young student. To his new
mentor, Meléndez Valdés confessed the character of his reading.
"Since I was a child I have had an excessive liking for this
[English] language, and one of the first books that was put in
my hands and that I learned by heart was of a most learned
Englishman. To the *Essay Concerning Human Understanding*
I owe and shall owe all my life the little I know about how to
reason," he wrote in one of his first letters.[49] In 1779 he admitted
having Locke's *Treatise on Education* and was soon expecting
Rousseau's *Émile*. In the meantime he had become familiar
with Voltaire's *Henriade*, Montesquieu's *Lettres persanes*, and
works of Leibnitz and Malebranche, Milton, Pope, and the recent English poet Edward Young. He obtained the *Cours d'études*
of Condillac and set about devouring it. He was asked by the
Sociedad Bascongada to write a defense of luxury, but he hesi-
tated because he did not have at hand the works of Hume and
Melon. He was an eclectic rather than a discerning reader, and
his poems usually echoed the latest ideas he had read, for he
apparently had few of his own. On the other hand, like most
Spaniards who felt the Enlightenment, he claimed never to
have been shaken in his religious faith.[50]

In 1778 Meléndez was named substitute for the temporarily
vacant chair of humanities of the university of Salamanca. Thanks
to the influence of Jovellanos, who was then a member of the

[48] Cadalso to Tomás de Iriarte, early 1773, quoted in Cotarelo y Mori, p. 132;
Meléndez to Jovellanos, July 11, 1778, B.A.E., LXIII, 80; Tamayo y Rubio,
loc.cit., pp. xxii-xxiv.

[49] Meléndez to Jovellanos, Aug. 3, 1776, B.A.E., LXIII, 73.

[50] See his correspondence with Jovellanos, 1776-80, in *ibid.*, pp. 73-85, and
Serrano y Sanz, *loc.cit.*, 307-10. See also E. Merimée, "Études sur la littérature
espagnole au XIX⁰ siècle: Meléndez Valdés," *Revue hispanique*, I (1894), 217-35.

Consejo Real de las Ordenes [militares] in Madrid, in 1781 he obtained full possession of the chair. Four years later his first volume of verses made him famous. Within the walls of the university his influence was being felt, not only by his students but by his fellow professors, who were deserting scholasticism for Locke and Montesquieu.[51] By then political economy was being taught in the faculty of law.[52] In 1787 a liberal rector of the university was proposed by the faculty and approved by the Consejo de Castilla, Diego Muñoz Torrero, who was later to be the leading author of the Spanish constitution of 1812. The progressives among the professors felt encouraged enough to complain of the self assumed predominance of the faculties of theology and jurisprudence. Meléndez Valdés proposed to defend in debate the equality of all sciences against all challengers, and the mathematician Juan Justo García upheld that advances in nonrevealed theology, medicine, and the other sciences depended on the advance of "filosofía." The university took under consideration the study of the law of nature and of nations, and it sent to the Consejo de Castilla a proposal for a new course of studies in philosophy.[53]

The reply of the Consejo was an order for the university to employ the text of François Jacquier in its philosophy courses. It was no mere whim of the council that dictated this decision. One of the means it had been using to renovate university education was to change the textbooks used. In philosophy courses it had here a particularly potent weapon, for the study of philosophy was the heart of the early years of the university curriculum. After the expulsion of the Jesuits, the "Suarist" influence was attacked by making general the use of the four-volume *Philoso-*

[51] Meléndez to Jovellanos, Nov. 3, 1778, B.A.E., LXIII, 83-84; Cotarelo y Mori, pp. 226-27; Manuel José Quintana, "Noticia histórica y literaria de Meléndez," B.A.E., XIX, 113; José María Blanco y Crespo [Blanco White] in *El Español*, II (1811), 460.

[52] Manuel Belgrano, *Autobiografía y memorias sobre la expedición al Paraguay y batalla de Tucumán* (Buenos Aires, 1942), p. 12; Emilio Alarcos, "El Abate Marchena en Salamanca," *Homenaje ofrecido a Menéndez Pidal* (Madrid, 1925), II, 462 n. 1.

[53] Esperabé Arteaga, II, 61-63.

phia Thomistica of Antoine Goudin, a French Dominican.[54] The work was virtually limited to teaching Aristotelian-scholastic philosophy. Within a few years it lost favor with the Consejo de Castilla. The new university plans of study, including the highly advanced Valencia plan of 1787, were abandoning this work in favor of the physics of Musschenbroek and the more modern philosophy text written by François Jacquier, who, although a monk, was a mathematician and teacher of experimental physics in Rome. Jacquier's *Institutiones philosophicae* still began with two volumes of logic and ontology that smacked of scholasticism, but Volumes III to VI freely dealt with arithmetic, algebra, geometry, physics, astronomy, geography, and moral philosophy. To meet the growing demand for this work, at least three editions were published in Spain before 1790 and another three in the next sixteen years. A Spanish translation was published in 1787-88.[55]

Meanwhile in 1774 the king ordered the university professors to prepare texts of their own. The Consejo de Castilla held a contest for the best philosophy text by a Spaniard that would include the theories of Descartes, Malebranche, and Leibnitz. In 1779 official approval was given to that written by the Capuchin friar Francisco Villalpando.[56] The Consejo ordered its adoption by all educational establishments that had not yet introduced the philosophy of Jacquier and the physics of Musschenbroek.

[54] Antoine Goudin, *Philosophia Thomistica, juxta inconcussa, tutissimaque Divi Thomae dogmata.* . . . Auctore P. Fr. Antonio Goudin . . . (4 vols.; Madrid, 1769). Sarrailh, p. 195.
[55] François Jacquier, *Institvtiones philosophicae ad stvdia theologica potissimvm accomodatae.* Avctore Francisco Jacqvier . . . (6 vols.; Valencia, 1782-94). Sarrailh, p. 154 n. 4. The Biblioteca Nacional has editions of Valencia, 1777-78, 1782-94, 1796-97, Alcalá de Henares ("Compluti"), 1786, 1794, and Saragossa, 1806. François Jacquier, *Instituciones filosoficas*, escritas en latin por el P. Fr. Francisco Jacquier. . . . Traducidas al castellano por don Santos Diez Gonzalez (6 vols.; Madrid, 1787-88).
[56] Francisco Villalpando, *Philosophia ad usum scholae FF. Minorum S. Francisci Capuccin.* . . . *in meliorem, concinnioremque formam redacta, antiquis, obsoletisque opinionibus libera, ac recentiorum inventis, tum pro ratione efformanda, tum pro rerum naturalium cognitione adipiscenda, aucta, & locupletata.* . . . Auctore R. P. Francisco a Villalpando . . . (3 vols.; Madrid, 1777-78). Desdevises, III, 203.

Such orders were not necessarily at once obeyed, but by 1786 Villalpando's book was in use by the universities of Cervera, Granada, and Baeza, and the university of Saragossa combined it with the physics of Musschenbroek.[57]

Villalpando claimed he presented a middle-of-the-road philosophy, keeping always in mind that men are born "non ad disputandum sed ad operandum."[58] Sensitive to modern trends, he preceded his logic with a discussion of the operations of the mind and devoted the second of his three volumes to physics, astronomy (including both the Ptolemaic and the Copernican systems), and human physiology. Although Volume III on ontology hardly seemed modern, Villalpando's text represented an advance over pure scholasticism, and students who used it were given the means to appreciate modern scientific and philosophic concepts.

Not only the universities but the religious orders were beginning to feel the impetus. All Capuchin convents adopted the text of Villalpando, and so did the college of Augustinians of La Coruña.[59] The Franciscans of the province of Granada, believing in the need for "filosofía moderna," switched to Jacquier in 1782. A year before, the general of the Spanish Discalced Carmelites, while still preferring Goudin as a text, urged all his teachers also to read Plato, Aristotle, Cicero, Bacon, Descartes, Newton, Leibnitz, Wolf, Locke, Condillac and other ancient and modern philosophers.[60] The provincial of the Discalced Trinitarians of Castile reformed the course of studies in his monasteries to avoid the abuses of scholastic disputes.[61] Under the bishop Rubín de Celis, the Seminario de San Fulgencio at Murcia was reformed in 1774 and later became famous for its modern instruction under progressive lay teachers;[62] while the bishop of Pamplona, in

---

[57] Manuel Serrano y Sanz, "El Consejo de Castilla y la censura de libros en siglo XVIII," *Revista de archivos, bibliotecas y museos*, xv (1906), 391-92; *Memorial literario*, June 1786, p. 230; Borao, pp. 188-89.

[58] Villalpando, "Proloquium," I, xvii-xviii.

[59] *Memorial literario*, June 1786, p. 250.

[60] Sempere, *Biblioteca*, IV, 245-51.   [61] Ferrer del Rio, IV, 297-98.

[62] Manuel Josef Narganes de Posada, *Tres cartas sobre los vicios de la instruccion publica en España* . . . (Madrid, 1809), p. 65 n.

establishing a seminary, ordered that the curriculum include ancient and modern philosophers.[63]

Among the religious orders, the Augustinians particularly were pushing the new learning in their seminaries. Their general Fray Francisco Xavier Vázquez, who had taken a leading part in procuring the abolition of the Jesuits, carried out a radical modification in the curriculum of his order. The new plan was written by an Augustinian professor at the university of Valencia and introduced "filosofía moderna" in place of scholasticism.[64] As a result, throughout Spain students at Augustinian schools in the 1780's discussed propositions of modern philosophers. In Santiago one brother upheld the concepts of the nature and origin of ideas of Saint Augustine and Malebranche. At La Coruña a penchant for Descartes and Malebranche was evident, while at Barcelona and Seville the "eclectic" method was preferred, that is, experimentalism and the rejection of systems. A provincial chapter meeting in the last city in 1786 fully examined Newtonian attraction and natural law, being careful, however, to refute Hobbes, Rousseau, and Milton. In their Colegio de la Incarnación of Madrid, the students held annual public contests (*oposiciones*) for teaching posts in which they demonstrated "a philosophic liberty restrained by Religion to the middle road between the two dangerous extremes into which rush pusillanimous and daring spirits." In 1785 the exercises included discussion of Descartes' and Helvétius' beliefs about the soul. Helvétius was, of course, impugned.[65]

This picture of the rapid growth of the new spirit of education must not be allowed to become misleading. It was still an exception in Spanish schools, especially where they were in the hands of the clergy. Despite the efforts of the Consejo de Castilla, Goudin continued popular as a text. Seven editions were published in Madrid from 1763 to 1779 and an equal number from

[63] Ferrer del Rio, IV, 297.

[64] Conrado Muiñoz Sáenz, "La Orden Agustiniana en la Guerra de la Independencia," *Ciudad de Dios*, LXXVI (1908), 14.

[65] *Memorial literario*, June 1784, p. 46, May 1785, pp. 85-93, June 1786, pp. 230-33 (quotation from pp. 231-32).

1782 to 1800.[66] The university of Oviedo was still employing it in 1792.[67] Although the Consejo de Castilla had ordered the university of Salamanca to substitute Jacquier in 1787, its faculty of law stubbornly continued to use Goudin at the end of 1788.[68] Members of its faculty had also attacked Villalpando's text. One Padre Ajofrín claimed that it placed Newton, Leibnitz, Galileo, and Bacon above Augustine and Aquinas.[69] Of all the religious orders, the Dominicans, who had fallen heirs to the Jesuits' role as champions of ultramontanism, remained most stubbornly conservative. They continued to employ Goudin and to teach their students how to construct syllogisms and to distinguish between material, formal, and final causes. When young José María Blanco in Seville cited Feyjóo against his Dominican teacher's Aristotelianism, the *fraile* and other students were horrified, and José María had to be taken out of the school.[70] Some French Dominicans who emigrated to Spain a few years later and were taken in by their Spanish brethren were amazed, as they put it, having left France at the end of the eighteenth century, to find themselves in Spain in the middle of the fourteenth.[71] A strong impetus had been given to educational reform, but much yet remained for it to become general in Spain. Among the clergy, it was usually those who were called Jansenists, such as the Augustinians, who favored educational reform. The conservative, in general ultramontane, majority of professors preferred to continue teaching scholasticism.

3

Although the tenor of philosophy courses was an index to the progress of higher education, this subject was not the only one to feel the breath of new air. Instruction in mathematics and

[66] These are the editions in the Biblioteca Nacional. There may have been more.

[67] Jovellanos to Antonio Carreño, Dec. 25, 1792, in Julio Somoza García Sala, *Documentos para escribir la biografía de Jovellanos* (Madrid, 1911), p. 150.

[68] *Correo de Madrid*, Jan. 7, 1789, pp. 1399-1400.

[69] Serrano y Sanz, "El Consejo de Castilla y la censura," *loc.cit.*, pp. 392-94.

[70] Blanco y Crespo, *Life*, I, 12-14.

[71] Servando Teresa de Mier, *Memorias* ("Biblioteca Ayacucho," Vol. XIX) (Madrid, n.d.), pp. 191-92. See also Posse, *loc.cit.*, XVI[1], 15-18.

medicine also advanced. More important for its contribution to the progress of Spanish thinking, however, was the introduction of the law of nature and of nations, which first appeared in Spain in the curriculum of the Reales Estudios de San Isidro in 1771. Carlos III encouraged its study by requiring attendance at this course for one year of all lawyers who desired a license to practice in Madrid. He offered life pensions to the students who most profited from this course.[72] José Cadalso gave the popularity of the new subject a boost in the next year in his *Eruditos a la violeta*, in which he recommended a superficial knowledge of it for garnering social prestige. By 1776 *derecho natural y de gentes* was being studied eagerly in private in the provinces.[73]

Before the death of Carlos, the universities were also showing interest in the subject. In 1785 a professor at the small university of Huesca publicly defended fifteen theses (*conclusiones*) of natural and civil law that read like a ragout of Cartesian, physiocratic, and *philosophique* beliefs on the nature of man and natural law.[74] The new plan of studies of the university of Valencia in 1786 made the study of *derecho natural y de gentes* obligatory for all students of civil and canon law. By 1791 it was being taught at the universities of Saragossa and Granada, and at the Real Seminario de Nobles in Madrid.[75] At other universities which had not specifically established chairs for the subject and had not included it in the official curricula, the law of nature and of nations was nevertheless being taught in other courses.[76] This practice had the evident favor of the royal government, for in 1787 Carlos and Floridablanca recommended that the law of nations be taught even to the clergy.[77]

[72] Sempere, *Biblioteca*, IV, 9-10.

[73] Joachín Marín [y Mendoza], *Historia del derecho natural y de gentes* (Madrid, 1776), pp. 58-59.

[74] Pedro María Ric y de Monserrat, June 18, 1785, reported in *Memorial literario*, June 1787, pp. 175-82.

[75] Borao, pp. 188-89; Sempere, *Biblioteca*, IV, 232; *Kalendario manual y guia de forasteros . . . 1789*, p. 105.

[76] *Real orden*, July 31, 1794, *Nov. rec.*, VIII, iv, 4.

[77] Carlos III, "Instrucción reservada . . . Junta de Estado," *loc.cit.*, p. 217, art. 27.

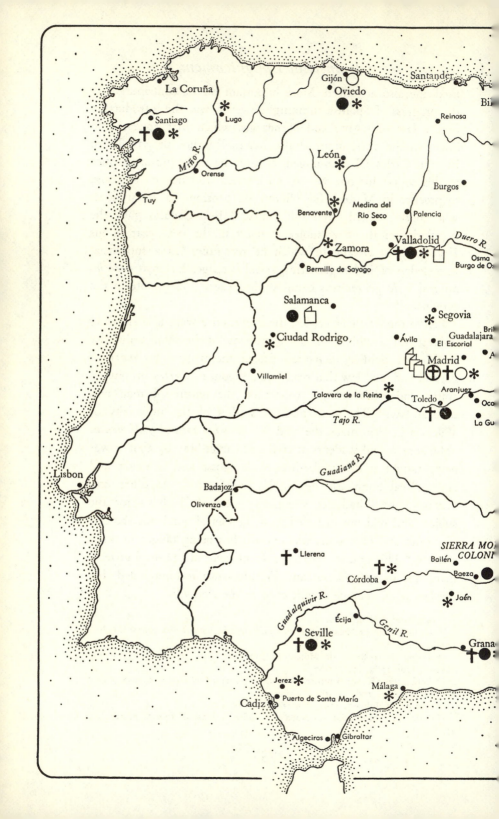

MAP V

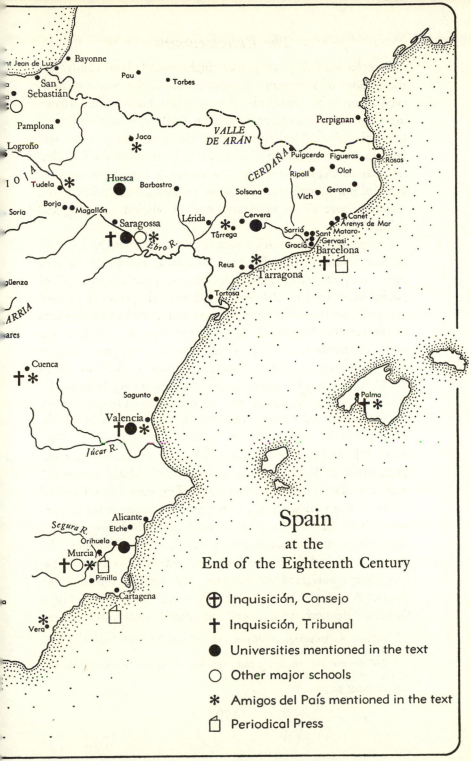

nt Jean de Luz • Bayonne

• Pau • Tarbes

San
Sebastián

Pamplona •

Logroño

*VALLE
DE ARÁN*

Perpignan •

CERDAÑA Puigcerda Figueras
Ripoll • Olot • Rosas

I O I A
Tudela * Huesca Barbastro

Soria Borja • Magallón

Solsona • Vich Gerona

güenza Saragossa *Ebro R.* Lérida Tárrega Cervera Sarriá Canet
Arenys de Mar
Sant Mataró
ARRIA Reus Gracià Gervasi
ares Tarragona Barcelona

Tortosa

† * Cuenca

Sagunto •

Valencia
† ● *

Júcar R.

Palma
† *

Spain
at the
End of the Eighteenth Century

Segura R. Alicante
Elche ●

Orihuela
Murcia ●
† ○ * □
• Pinilla

⊕ Inquisición, Consejo

† Inquisición, Tribunal

Cartagena

□

● Universities mentioned in the text

○ Other major schools

* Amigos del País mentioned in the text

□ Periodical Press

*
Vera •

Derecho natural y de gentes might sound dangerously like the theories of Rousseau's *Contrat social*. Carlos was not, however, a man to be hoist with his own petard. He was only following a general European movement in Catholic as well as Protestant universities. The term "law of nature and of nations" had been in common use in Europe for a hundred years.[78] Carlos' instructions were to teach the new course "subjecting always the lights of our human reason to those of the Catholic religion and showing above all the necessary union of religion, morality, and politics."[79]

The person whom Carlos named to the chair at the Estudios de San Isidro, Joachín Marín y Mendoza, proved to be well suited to putting the king's desires into practice. In 1776 he published an *Historia del derecho natural y de gentes* to be used as a guide for further reading by those who had the first elements of the subject. This work and the textbooks in use show the tenor of instruction being given. Natural law, according to Marín, who was merely repeating a concept at least as old as the Middle Ages, is a "collection of laws proceeding from God"; it is called natural because it was not made by man but was given by the Author of nature. The law of nations consists of the same principles applied to the relations between states. Here Marín followed Samuel Pufendorf, who had written one hundred years before.[80] Since both come from God, Marín continued, men have always had this science. In rudimentary form it existed in the ancient philosophers, but not until the seventeenth century was a body of doctrine firmly established which would have been "the most glorious monument to those who enlighten the human mind, had those who dedicated themselves to its investigation always navigated on the high seas without touching the shores." Among its greatest lights he listed "its founder" Hugo Grotius, Pufendorf, who, he said, introduced ethics to the subject,

[78] William A. Dunning, *A History of Political Theories from Luther to Montesquieu* (New York, 1943), p. 162 n. 1.

[79] *Real decreto*, Jan. 19, 1770, *Nov. rec.*, VIII, ii, 3. See Sempere, *Biblioteca*, IV, 9-10; Marin, 58.

[80] Dunning, p. 321.

and Montesquieu. On the other hand Marín said that Rousseau's *Contrat social* "has been justly scorned and proscribed on all sides."[81] Under the rubric "detestable modern writings" he grouped *Emilius, l'Esprit,* and the *Système de la nature.* He detected two major errors in these works: they abandon all authority of sacred and profane authors in favor of right reason, which then becomes a tyrant, and they declare that man's most sacred law is to seek his comfort and avoid harm, overlooking man's higher destiny. Such writings, he said, can be recognized because they find sovereignty in the will of the people and they place religion under the control of civil government. Clearly Marín was following the royal injunction to subject his teaching to religion and morality.

The text books employed by the various institutions followed the same pattern. For the use of his students Marín reedited, "with corrections according to the doctrine of the Catholics," what he considered to be the best compendium of the subject, the *Elementa juris naturae et gentium* of the German Protestant Johann Gottlieb Heineccius.[82] The university of Saragossa adopted this work, but the university of Valencia preferred the *Institutiones juris naturae et gentium,* whose author's name appeared in Latinized form as Johannes Baptista Almicus. Its title page indicated it too was "in accordance with Catholic principles."[83] The plan and chapter headings of both works are almost identical: a first book entitled "Jus naturae" and a second, "Jus gentium." "Jus naturae" deals with the origin and nature of man's actions; his duties to God, himself, and other men, and the nature of social relationships, including compacts or covenants (*pacta*). Under "Jus gentium" are discussed the different forms of society, from the state of nature, through domestic society to civil society. The crux of both Heineccius' and Almicus' work lies in the

---

[81] Marín, pp. 2-3, 18, 42-43.

[82] Johann Gottlieb Heineccius, *Elementa juris naturae et gentium castigationibus ex Catholicorum doctrina, et juris historia aucta.* Ab Joachimo Marin et Mendoza . . . (Madrid, 1776) (2d ed.; Madrid, 1789).

[83] Johannes Baptista Almicus, *Institutiones juris naturae et gentium secundum Catholica principia, Johannis Baptistae Almici* (Madrid, 1789).

chapter entitled "De societatis civilis origine, forma, et adfectionibus" (in Almicus ". . . origine, forma, & constitutione"), where the authors present the causes and manner of establishing civil society.

Heineccius admits that in the state of nature men are free and equal and that they could be happy in family society, but he observes that everywhere men live in civil society. The problem is to explain this phenomenon, and Heineccius does so by what he presents as a new view. The first form that society took was groups of wicked men united under an elected leader for the purpose of enslaving and despoiling other men. The only defense of the just was to organize in other societies strong enough to resist the bands of thieves. In all cases the purpose of the state was to secure the safety of the citizens against the violence of their neighbors. Since society cannot be formed without the express consent of those who are forming it, according to Heineccius the founding of the states involves a *pactum*, either voluntary or extorted by a conqueror. In the former case, those present who disagree are free to leave the new state. In the latter case the conquered are assumed to acquiesce in the *pactum* by the simple fact of preferring the terms of the conqueror to death. The *pactum* should specify the form of government of the new society, that is whether the people will henceforth submit to one person, several, or many: monarchy, aristocracy, or democracy. The *pactum* should also establish a "fundamental law" which will bind the rulers as well as the ruled "so that nothing is judged to be done justly if anything is done contrary to that primary law of the republic."[84] Heineccius does not indicate whether an act opposed to the fundamental law should be obeyed, but he implies that it should. Moreover, of the three forms of government, he clearly prefers monarchy, for the other two forms he believes easily degenerate. The power of the monarch, once established, is absolute, but its aim must be the welfare of the people. "Populi securitas et salus suprema monarchae lex

---

[84] Heineccius, p. 385, §cxii: adeo ut nihil auctum merito censeatur, si quid contra legem hanc reipubl. primariam . . . auctum sit.

esse. . . ."[85] Heineccius was voicing no new views. Practically the same theory of the basis of absolute monarchy in an original agreement of the people had been held by the sixteenth century Spanish theologian Francisco Suárez, Grotius, and Thomas Hobbes.[86]

Almicus on the whole differs little in this theory from Heineccius. Like the German jurist, he sees the origin of society in the desire to resist wicked men, and a *pactum* and fundamental law are at the basis of the state. Almicus, a Catholic, shows more liberal tendencies than the Protestant Heineccius, however. An act that violates the fundamental law he calls frankly null and void, but he too leaves moot the right to resist oppression.[87] More significantly he clearly prefers a "mixed government" to pure monarchy, citing a famous passage of Polybius on the Roman republic in its favor. Almicus continues, "Of this type the admirable English state gives an example, which, composed in a wondrous way, comprises in one body monarchy with a king, aristocracy with parliaments, democracy with the entire people, wherefore it endures so flourishing and so well constituted."[88] One could almost expect him to refer to Locke. He does not, but his footnotes, besides citing as might be expected Jean Bodin, Pufendorf, and Montesquieu, refer to the "auctor opusculi inscripti 'De inégalité parmi les hommes,'" and in another place more frankly to "Rousseau, De inaequalitate. . . ."[89]

Such were the texts employed in the official courses of *derecho natural y de gentes*. They contained explicitly the contract theory of the origin of society. Although they used the theory to justify absolute monarchy, they denied by implication the divine right of kings. Kings, however absolute they might be, were established by their peoples, the books said, and their acts could be judged unjust by reference to a "fundamental law" of society. The next

---

[85] *Ibid.*, pp. 374-96, Book II, chap. vi.
[86] Dunning, pp. 144, 180-81.
[87] Almicus, p. 271.
[88] *Ibid.*, pp. 275-76.
[89] *Ibid.*, p. 270, in support of his statement that those who do not accept the *pactum* remain outside society.

step to the theory of the inalienable sovereignty of the people and their right to resist a king who breaks the fundamental law was not a very great one, but it meant the difference between Suárez, Grotius, and Hobbes on the one hand and Locke and Rousseau on the other. Marín in his *Historia del derecho natural y de gentes* had warned against the danger, and well he might, for Rousseau, as has been seen, was becoming popular with advanced Spanish minds. It was not clandestine reading but the royal government itself, by its policy of promoting the study of natural law, that was encouraging the discussion in Spain of the origin and nature of society.

The discussion was not restricted to academic circles. It began to appear in public and in the press. The lawyers of Madrid, who were required to study the law of nature and nations, quite naturally ventilated the subject. In 1787 and 1788 in the Real Academia de Derecho Español y Público, papers were read on the question. The first speaker attacked the theories of Grotius, Hobbes, Bodin, Machiavelli, and other modern writers. He gave an analysis of Locke's *Treatise of Civil Government* and large parts of the *Contrat social*. Then, like the French bishop Bossuet attacking the Protestants, he asserted that the very variety of all these opinions "in a subject that should be considered of pure fact" showed that they were not correct.[90] The following year the speaker was Cristóbal Cladera, editor of the *Espíritu de los mejores diarios*. He attacked the theory of the "pact," which he said was based on two mistaken concepts: the belief of Hobbes and Heineccius that the state of nature is one of war and the idea that "societies began by the peoples' electing their sovereigns and drawing up certain conventions with them." As to this "contrato social" of a philosopher "whose pride made him scorn what he should most have honored," Cladera said he agreed with "a profound and thoughtful author" (Voltaire?) that it was a chimera, since no historian had ever recorded such a social

---

[90] Josef de Oromi, Feb. 1787, reviewed in *Memorial literario*, March 1787, pp. 303-6.

contract.[91] Both speakers were evidently familiar with the political theory of the Genevan philosopher and expected their audiences to be too.

The press reflected the current interest in the subject. An anonymous article in the *Correo de Madrid*, like the textbooks, saw the origin of society in a desire to avoid the injustice of the stronger over the weaker and echoed the dictum, "the safety of the people is the supreme law."[92] The *Espiritu de los mejores diarios* published an article by Valentín de Foronda which showed how easily the discussion might lead thinkers on to more advanced ideas. Foronda was writing to an imaginary friend who was establishing a government:

> I advise you first to concentrate all your attention on accepting the most important truth, which is that the rights of property, liberty, and security are the three wellsprings of the happiness of all states. . . . The Monarch of nature has inscribed these [principles] in man, in his organs and his understanding, and not in weak parchments that can be torn to bits by the fury of superstition or tyranny.[93]

In the following year the translator of a French work spoke of England as being the best governed European state, "where men are philosophers, who, looking on other men as their brothers, sacrifice their tranquility to preserve the inviolate rights of man."[94]

When statements such as this were being published, one can imagine what was being said in private. An inkling is given by a series of letters written between 1787 and 1789 and not made public until a century later. Their author is unidentified, but

[91] Quoted in *Espiritu de los mejores diarios*, June 2, 9, 1788. Cladera is identified in Eugenio Hartzenbusch [e Hiriart], *Apuntes para un catálogo de periódicos madrileños desde el año 1661 al 1870* (Madrid, 1894), p. 14.

[92] *Correo de Madrid*, Oct. 31, 1787, p. 168.

[93] In the first of his "Cartas político-económicas," *Espiritu de los mejores diarios*, Nov. 17, 1788.

[94] [De Sapt], *El amigo del príncipe y de la patria ó el buen ciudadano*, traducido del frances . . . por D. Jayme Albosía de la Vega (2 vols.; Madrid, 1788-89), Vol. 1, "prólogo del traductor."

their contents indicate that he had been high in the service of the royal finances. They were addressed to the Conde de Lerena, currently secretary of finance.[95] Their author sees three essential rights, property, equality and liberty. Laws should guarantee "the most sacred right of property," the "cement of all societies on earth."[96] Moreover, "laws, like gold, have a touchstone, and this is the equality of the citizens: they will be so much the more precious when they aim at establishing it."[97] But it is liberty especially that arouses his enthusiasm. "Liberty of thought, liberty of writing, liberty of speaking create even in the lowest class a spirit of confidence and mutual interest that we can scarcely understand." In their liberty he sees the strength of the English.[98] He admits that civil liberty is "a most delicate point to be discussed only with the greatest secrecy (*ocultísimamente*)." The basis for this discussion is the "social contract, that solemn contract" by which men sacrificed their natural liberty in order to achieve peace and security. "The social pact [the author employs the term of the texts as well as of Rousseau] is a mutual pact, and the rights that arise from it are equally sacrosanct on all sides." Kings are obliged to obey it; and, if society should see that the form of government is leading to its ruin, it has the authority by God's eternal law to remedy the situation.[99] The author continues by showing that in Spain he is content with enlightened despotism, but his thinking clearly establishes the basis for a popular revolt should the monarch cease to be enlightened.

[95] *Cartas político-económicas escritas por el Conde de Campomanes al Conde de Lerena,* ed. Antonio Rodríguez Villa (Madrid, 1878). The belief of the editor that the author was Campomanes has been generally discredited. For one thing, the prose style is too elaborate for Campomanes, and the ideas are hardly his. Cabarrús has been suggested, but the references in the letters to the Banco de San Carlos indicate the author was not its founder. G. Desdevises du Dezert gives a review of these letters, accepting the authorship of Campomanes without question ("Les lettres politico-économiques de Campomanes," *Revue hispanique,* IV [1897], 240-65). On the question see Sánchez Agesta, pp. 305-8.

[96] *Cartas político-económicas,* p. 79.

[97] *Ibid.,* pp. 210-11.

[98] *Ibid.,* p. 156.   [99] *Ibid.,* pp. 113-25.

The ideas of this anonymous author were the logical outcome of the courses in the law of nature and nations, leavened with some more dangerous reading. They showed to what lengths the educational reforms undertaken by the royal government might lead Spanish thinkers. The government, in the interest of enlightenment, had introduced into Spanish higher education new ideas on philosophy, science, and politics. For the present it could count on the support of those men who favored modern thought, but at the same time it was encouraging a spirit of free inquiry and progress that would demand in return a continuance of enlightened government. If the Spanish monarchy should react against its present policies, it could find that it had fostered a body of opinion which had become too strong for it henceforth to mold to its own desires.

4

A third institution besides the Spanish universities and societies of Amigos del País acted as a medium for the dissemination of contemporary thought. This was the periodical press. The frequent citations that have been made to contemporary Spanish papers have already given ample evidence of their importance; yet a picture of Spanish enlightenment would not be complete without an appreciation of the journals and newspapers that flourished in the last years of Carlos III.

Besides the official *Gazeta de Madrid*, privately sponsored journals had come and gone throughout the century without leaving many traces. The first years of Carlos' reign saw a flurry of periodical publications that collapsed for lack of interest. Most of these papers sought only to entertain or at most to criticize social fashions,[100] but one stood out for the daring and depth of its observations. *El pensador* was started in 1761 on the model of the *Spectator Papers* by Joseph Clavijo y Faxardo, the future translator of Buffon. Clavijo did not hesitate to stigmatize both the idle nobility and the ignorant clergy of Spain. In one number

---

[100] See Sempere, *Biblioteca*, IV, 178, 191.

he described how a modern Diogenes approaches with his lantern the guilded carriage of a wealthy aristocrat. What does he see inside? Certainly not a human being. "All the body of this animal is covered with gold paint. It speaks doubloons and spits forths *escudos*. It is working on a genealogy."[101] Elsewhere Clavijo damned those of his countrymen who defended their ignorance by accusing anyone with new ideas of being a heretic and an atheist. "They do not know with what care many Fathers worked to improve their intelligence by the study of profane sciences, and that in France, in Germany, and even in England there are Catholics as fervent as they are enlightened."[102] Several other issues were equally biting; but *El pensador* ceased publication in 1767, and not until more than a decade later did the periodical press assume a significant role in Spain.

In 1781 a new journal appeared reminiscent of *El pensador*. Its editor, Luis Cañuelo, a Madrid lawyer, boldly proclaimed, "All that departs in any way from reason hurts me." He promised to criticize everything he saw according to reason, "whenever decency, Religion, and political considerations do not stop me." He entitled his publication aptly *El censor*.[103] For several years it was issued irregularly in "discourses" of sixteen small pages each.

Cañuelo's censoring spirit early began to cut deep into the characteristics of Spanish society. His fourth discourse depicted the life of "Eusebio," a wealthy aristocrat. Eusebio never works but he pays all his debts. He scarcely sees his children but he goes to mass daily in his carriage and gives alms at the church door. He does not indulge in study, for this is the fount of atheism, and he lets his confessor run his affairs.

[101] *El pensador*, Pensamiento 7, quoted in Sarrailh, p. 523.

[102] *Espectador* [*sic, Pensador?*], II, 184-87, quoted in Sarrailh, p. 382. See also Sarrailh, p. 310 n., 329, 338-45, 399, 693. I have not seen *El pensador*.

[103] *El censor*, Discurso 1. The editor is identified in Sempere, *Biblioteca*, IV, 191-93. Antonio Alcalá Galiano, *Historia de España desde los tiempos primitivos hasta la mayoría de la reina doña Isabel II* (Madrid, 1845), V, 317-18, and Hartzenbusch, pp. 11-12, say Cañuelo was aided by a certain Luis Pereira and other persons.

Oh enviable fate, Eusebio's! At the cost of some such small efforts, of these light inconveniences, and of these well profited moments, he is fashioning himself a crown of immortal glory. How different it would be if he were a pauper forced to shoulder duties and maintain his life!

A man useless to his fellow men—how can he be a good Christian? . . . I cannot conceive this sublime morality that knows how to reconcile all this with the love of one's neighbor and to dispense us from the penance imposed on the sons of Adam to eat their bread by the sweat of their brows. . . . [If Eusebio's life brings salvation,] . . . don't we have high reason to cry out against the whole doctrine of the Evangile?

Ever since the days of Clavijo's *Pensador*, enlightened Spanish writers, such as Cadalso and Jovellanos, had been belaboring the theme of the idle rich.[104] Cañuelo was to be outdone by none of them. Five discourses later he again condemned the rich, this time on the basis of economics and political philosophy. So long as the wealthy merely exploit their land, he said, they are useless to their fellow citizens. Nature denies man the right to property which he did not earn but holds merely through inheritance, for nature did not make all things in common for past generations alone. Society is recreated at every instant through new births, and all men still have equal rights to nature's gifts. Unless living men have ceded their rights to him, no man can justly hold more than his share of land. Cañuelo calls this kind of cession significantly a "pacto social," and like the textbook legists he says that it can only have been made for the greater good of all parties. If the wealthy landowner does not fulfill his end of the contract, he owns his land unjustly. Human laws cannot dispense with his obligation, for they are the "declaration of these pacts."[105]

Cañuelo's pen did not scourge the wealthy señor alone. Spain's other privileged order, the clergy, was treated with equal frank-

---

[104] Sarrailh, pp. 518-26; Sánchez Agesta, pp. 22-26, 77-78.
[105] *El censor*, Discurso 9.

ness. Cañuelo began by satirizing the obscurantist spirit that typified many of its members, who, he said, sought impieties in every work of any merit, calling atheists such men as Descartes, who "labored so hard to prove the existence of God," and Newton, "whose philosophy, without belief in God, would be totally absurd."[106]

> Suppose that the wisest authors of modern times had been born in Spain, behold, infallibly and with no difference at all, so many impious heretics. Why? Because Dame Fortune had the whim to give us here a sense of smell so delicate that we smell these vices a hundred leagues away. . . . We discover impiety or heresy and catch it in the very place where the wisest and most pious men of other nations overlooked it.[107]

Cañuelo turned next to attack the wealth of the Spanish church. He denounced the excessive ornamentation of the churches and asked rhetorically if the gold and silver of America, "tainted with blood unjustly spilled," could be an offering pleasing to a God of mercy.[108] In his seventy-fifth discourse he described a utopia, the land of the Ayparchontes. Their clergy, whose organization coincidentally reflected that of the Catholic Church, had once abandoned the state of poverty and thereby lost popular veneration. Finally a wise monarch appeared who was able to see through their clamors against violating "the most sacred rights of religion." He deprived them of their wealth. Now, again poor, the clergy of the Ayparchontes is once more beloved, and it worships that king as its greatest benefactor. Cañuelo was echoing the arguments of the Jansenist clergy, who were friends of the Enlightenment and partisans of reform of the church by royal order.

Even if the royal government sympathized with Cañuelo's ideas, it had determined to put a stop to publicity of the Jansenist controversy, and it intended to prevent any stirring up of the conservative majority of the clergy. It ordered collected the seventy-ninth discourse of *El censor*, of November 17, 1785, which

[106] *Ibid.*, Discurso 23. [107] *Ibid.*, Discurso 44.
[108] *Ibid.*, Discurso 72.

was relatively innocuous, although it did cast some ridicule on the religious orders. At the same time a Comisión de Imprentas was created to try periodicals for libel. The new commission was to permit the satire of vices but to put an end to personal attacks in the press.[109]

El censor was soon appearing again, and its spirit was still untamed. Cañuelo published poems by Jovellanos and Meléndez Valdés criticizing Spanish society.[110] He advocated laissez-faire economics and civil liberties based on the social pact.[111] Combined with earlier praise of Locke, Rousseau, and enlightened despotism,[112] his later issues proved Cañuelo to be one of the intellectual lights of contemporary Spain. Nor was his boldness his only recommendation. One of Spain's best contemporary essayists, in his style and biting irony he was a worthy member of the age of Voltaire.

He could not go on for long, however. In 1787 *El censor* stopped publication again, this time for good. Next year Cañuelo was brought to trial by the Inquisición and sentenced to abjure as slightly suspect of heresy. He was ordered not to write anything related to dogma or accepted opinions on matters of piety and devotion.[113]

Four periodicals briefly echoed *El censor* in the years 1786-88. The first was *El apologista universal*, which appeared in 1786. Its author was Pedro Centeno, a learned and pious Augustinian monk. He ridiculed with stinging irony the religious literature of his day. Those who felt his barbs denounced him to the Inquisición for adopting various heresies, including atheism and Lutheranism. More to the point he was accused of "Jansenism" and disapproving of certain "pious practices." He was arrested

109 Sempere, *Biblioteca*, IV, 191-92.
110 *El censor*, Discursos 154, 99, 155. See Morel-Fatio, *La satire de Jovellanos*.
111 *El censor*, Discurso 156.
112 *Ibid.*, Discurso 36, 28, 31.
113 Llorente, V, 170-72; Villanueva, I, 27. The date of the trial is given in the French edition of Llorente (Juan Antonio Llorente, *Histoire critique de l'Inquisition d'Espagne* [2d ed.; Paris, 1818], IV, 338). A. Alcalá Galiano, *Historia de España*, V, 317-18, blames Floridablanca for stopping *El censor*.

and eventually convicted of being very strongly suspect of heresy. It was not his periodical but the belief he steadfastly maintained that the existence of Limbo was not an article of faith that led the Santo Oficio to decide against him. The shock of being forced to abjure beliefs that he was convinced were correct destroyed his reason, and soon he died in the convent to which he had been confined.[114]

The periodical most obviously inspired by Cañuelo's paper was entitled *El corresponsal del censor*. It pretended to be a series of biweekly letters addressed to *El censor*. At first it did not give promise of discussing controversial subjects even though it too criticized the idle nobility.[115] Yet after several months' existence letters began to appear opposing extravagant practices of the Spanish church, as, for instance, the dancing festivals given in convents to celebrate the taking of nun's vows by a young girl.[116] The periodical ceased publication after fifty-one issues; why is not apparent.

The other two periodicals of this type were very ephemeral. *El duende de Madrid,* which lasted for seven issues claimed to be the observations of a good spirit, "christiano católico." It showed mercantilist and Jansenist sympathies, attacking the scorn in which the Spanish upper classes held farmers and tradesmen and denouncing the ignorance of certain religious orders and the futility of the education they gave to the youth of Spain. Rousseau-like, the *Duende* rendered parents responsible for bringing up their children properly.[117] In 1788 appeared three numbers of *Conversaciones de Perico y Marica*, modelled, not unsuccessfully, on the Platonic dialogues. Perico asserted that men formed societies to achieve their greater good while preserving their natural rights and liberty. He went on to claim as a result that Spain's "wise" government desired liberty of thought and speech as the best

---

[114] Hartzenbusch, p. 13; Llorente, *Historia*, v, 176-80; Villanueva, i, 80-82.
[115] *El corresponsal del censor*, Carta 2.
[116] *Ibid.,* Carta 39. Cotarelo y Mori, p. 319 n. 2, identifies the author as Santos Manuel Rubín de Celis y Noriega, an Asturian.
[117] *El duende de Madrid. Discursos periodicos, que se repartiran al publico por mano de D. Benito,* Nos. 1-4.

way to enlighten the whole people. So far so good, but Perico weakened when he attempted to justify the control of the press by the Inquisición. "Too much light will blind the people," he said, implying that it was light that the Santo Oficio shut out.[118] Having said this much in his first dialogue, the author had exhausted his store of ideas. The next two conversations merely repeated his belief in the need for enlightenment.

These papers all consisted of essays on topics of general interest. New periodicals were also established in the 1780's which were devoted to disseminating news or current information. Unlike the former type, these were significant not because of the advanced tone of their writing but because of the material they made available to Spanish readers. Such a paper was *El correo de los ciegos de Madrid*, which began in October 1786, soon shortening its title to *El correo de Madrid*.[119] In general it devoted itself to light subjects, including popular science, and the publication of many letters addressed to it by private individuals. Occasionally it carried articles that dealt with the new intellectual spirit, not always favorably. In July 1788 it published an attack on Rousseau's first essay entitled "Origen de la desigualdad entre los hombres." Men are born unequal, physically and mentally, the author asserted, and on this natural inequality are based the order and authority that makes society possible. "Would that the desire for equality among men will not cause more harm than that already felt in this enlightened century," its author cried one year before the fall of the Bastille.[120] On the other hand articles also appeared defending science and the *luces*.[121]

The major contribution of the *Correo de Madrid* to the enlightenment of Spain was a series of "portraits" of leading modern philosophers carried between October 1789 and April 1790. They

---

[118] *Conversaciones de Perico y Marica. Obra periodica*, Conversacion I, pp. 48-60.

[119] *El correo de los ciegos de Madrid*, Oct. 10, 1786 to Mar. 30, 1787. *El correo de Madrid*, Apr. 18, 1787 to Feb. 24, 1791. The term "los ciegos" was probably a reference to the indigent blind who sold newspapers in Madrid.

[120] *Correo de Madrid*, July 23, 26, 30, 1788.

[121] See above, p. 45.

were drawn from the *Histoire des philosophes modernes* of Alexandre Savérien. Sketches of the lives and writings of leading thinkers in all fields were given "including some whose systems are erroneous and heretical in order to show the errors into which human understanding can fall."[122] The freedom of their tone is remarkable. Hobbes, though stated to be an atheist, received sympathetic treatment; and Descartes brought forth raptures for the way in which he "broke loose from all prejudices of antiquity and authority in order to seek the truth."[123] Such suspect figures as the French Jansenists Blaise Pascal and Pierre Nicole were praised for their ethics and defense of the Christian religion. Grotius and Pufendorf were approved, as were the scientists Copernicus, Galileo, and Newton. The series ends with "Filosofos chimicos" and "Filosofos naturalistas." One figure who was not among these described by Savérien was Rousseau. In the midst of the series, however, the *Correo* published a "Noticia critica de J. J. Rousseau" that was longer than most "portraits" and did him more justice than anyone else. All his works, even the *Contrat social*, were discussed critically but without excessive prejudice. A reference in the article to Rousseau's unpublished memoirs and their expectation by the public suggests that it was written by a Frenchman between Rousseau's death in 1778 and the publication of his memoirs in 1782. Where the editors of the *Correo* got the article is not said.[124]

Reference has already been made to two periodicals whose specific aim was to make known in Spain the progress of knowledge abroad.[125] The *Correo literario de la Europa*, of 1780-81 and 1786-87, was dedicated especially to spreading practical information. The *Espiritu de los mejores diarios literatos que se publican en Europa*, which followed it, took a much less restricted view of its task. It published reviews of foreign books and digests of articles appearing abroad. Here Spaniards read of Filangieri,

---

[122] "Idea del tomo sexto de la obra periodica Correo de Madrid," *Correo de Madrid*, Vol. v.

[123] *Ibid.*, Oct. 24, Dec. 30, 1789.

[124] *Ibid.*, Dec. 9, 1789. Spell, pp. 106-9, gives quotations from the article.

[125] See above, p. 45.

Brissot, Raynal, and Franklin, and got a taste of the French concern for *sensibilité* and *bienfaisance*.[126] Within a few years the *Espíritu* began to accept domestic contributions, such as a "Carta sobre las ventajas que resultarían á una monarquia de que la nobleza pobre se dedicase al comercio,"[127] and Foronda's "Cartas sobre los asuntos más exquisitos de la economia política," in which the Spanish economist presented the advanced beliefs in political philosophy and economics that have been noted.

There was one other periodical, unique among contemporary Spanish publications, whose contents made its appearance significant. This was the *Semanario erudito*, founded in 1787 by Antonio Valladares de Sotomayor.[128] Not from abroad but from Spain's own writings of past ages did Valladares intend to draw his material, "propagating the instruction that many wise Spaniards left us." In his prospectus he reminded his readers that Spain had once been Europe's intellectual leader, that Felipe IV had erected chairs of language, letters, and natural and sacred sciences, which, Valladares asserted, had been the models for Richelieu's academies. Later, Spain's predominance had been destroyed by incessant wars and Felipe's mistake of "entrusting so sacred a commission [as the new chairs] to the hands of the regular clergy, which always forms within the state another state apart governed for its own private interest." "The ills of the nation and their cures will be seen," he promised. "It will be seen that statesmen were never wanting who recognized these ills and had the courage to oppose them." Let not the "weak souls" who desire these defects to remain unknown read the *Semanario*, he warned, "because after turning a few pages of mere erudition, they will find others which will tell them hard but useful truths."

If Valladares' frank reference to the regular clergy in his

---

[126] "Rasgo de sensibilidad," *Espíritu de los mejores diarios*, July 14, 1787, "Rasgo de virtud," July 23, 1787, "Rasgo[s] de beneficencia," Aug. 2, 4, 9, 1787, "Carta sobre la sensibilidad," Jan. 14, 1788, and many others.

[127] *Ibid.*, Feb. 22, 1790.

[128] *Semanario erudito, que comprehende varias obras ineditas, criticas, morales, instructivas, politicas, historicas, satiricas, y jocosas, de nuestros mejores autores antiguos y modernos.* Dalas a luz don Antonio Valladares de Sotomayor.

prospectus had not made it plain that he included them in his category of "weak souls," the contents of his journal soon did. The actions of the Jesuits in particular were exposed in documents which were here published. The first volume of the *Semanario erudito* contained an attack on their writing. Volume VI carried the writings of their seventeenth-century enemy in Mexico, Juan de Palafox, and an editorial denouncing the Jesuits' hatred of this saintly man. Carlos III's request to the pope for Palafox's beatification was also inserted. Valladares did not limit himself to discussing the Jesuits, who were after all defenseless. He also published an account of the reform of the regular clergy by Fernando and Isabel, a memoir of Felipe V's minister Melchor de Macanaz revealing an abuse of ecclesiastical privileges by the theft of a load of fish in Granada by three clergymen, and a report to the same king on the abuses of the Roman court.[129] There were many similar documents, included evidently to appeal to those of Jansenist sympathies. On the other hand, Valladares inserted the writings of leading eighteenth-century Spanish regular clergymen, the Jesuit Andrés Marcos Burriel and the Benedictine Martín Sarmiento,[130] and published as a separate volume an apology of the Inquisición by Macanaz.[131]

The church was only one of the many topics that Valladares' periodical dealt with. Previously unpublished manuscripts on a variety of subjects appeared: discussions of Spain's colonies, of her economy and literature, biographies of leading Spaniards, and a variety of documents which were source material for Spanish history of the last three centuries. There were several contemporary descriptions of the sad state of Spain under Carlos II with suggested reforms[132] and reflections on Spain's ills by leading eighteenth-century figures.[133] What influence such writ-

---

[129] *Ibid.*, III, 102-10, IX, 3-142, 206-86.

[130] *Ibid.*, II, 1-128, Vol. XVI (Burriel), and Vols. XIX-XXI (Sarmiento).

[131] Melchor Rafael de Macanaz, *Defensa critica de la Inquisicion contra los principales enemigos que le han perseguido y persiguen injustamente* (Madrid, 1788). See *Semanario erudito*, VII, 8-9.

[132] *Semanario erudito*, II, 129-44, Vol. IV, XI, 225-71, XXX, 256-72.

[133] By Melchor de Macanaz, *ibid.*, V, 215-303, Antonio de Capmany, X, 172-224, Marqués de la Ensenada, XII, 260-82, Gregorio Mayans y Ciscar XXV, 20-288,

ings might have is indicated by the note ordered printed before many of them by the Consejo de Castilla: "This should be read with the precaution necessary in order not to attribute more confidence and credit than correspond to the matter and information that it contains." In all Valladares issued thirty-four three-hundred page volumes between 1787 and 1791.

Among the periodical publications which were important in disseminating a new spirit of curiosity in intellectual achievements and in Spain's own failings and accomplishments, several others deserve at least passing mention. In April 1784 the Imprenta Real began to publish a monthly *Memorial literario, instructivo y curioso de la corte de Madrid*, which gave reports of the activities of the Spanish academies, universities, religious bodies, and press. An earlier publication which had expired, the *Diario curioso, erudito, economico y comercial*, was revived with the approval of the Consejo de Castilla in 1786. Soon known as the *Diario de Madrid*, one of its purposes was to "vulgarize" modern *luces*. There were also other minor periodicals, but they did not concern themselves with serious subject matter.[134] Together all of these journals gave eloquent testimony of the intellectual atmosphere that was flourishing in the last years of Carlos III's reign.

The rest of the Spanish press was affected by the new spirit much less than were the periodicals. In 1784 and 1785 over one third of the books and pamphlets published in Spain (about 160 of some 460) were on religious subjects—collections of sermons, saints' lives, prayer books, works on theology, etc. Some 7 per cent were on the sciences and scarcely over 3 per cent on industry, the arts, and commerce. Medicine was a popular subject (9 per cent) but not a new one, although the works undoubtedly reflected medical advances. A bare 2 percent of the books appear to discuss philosophical questions (mostly morality) independ-

---

XXVI, 1-117. The contents of the *Semanario erudito* are catalogued in James L. Whitney, *Catalogue of the Spanish Library . . . bequeathed by George Ticknor to the Boston Public Library* (Boston, 1879), pp. 327-29.

134 See Hartzenbusch, pp. 11-14.

ently of religion.[135] The predominance of religious matter in non-periodical publications emphasizes the importance of the journals as a channel for spreading the *luces* in Spain.

Another feature of these journals stands out—they were all published in Madrid. Only two provincial periodicals existed that were felt to be worth mentioning by Sempere y Guarinos, who dealt at length with those of Madrid because he realized their importance for Spain. One was the *Semanario literario y curioso de la ciudad de Cartagena*, which gave local news and articles on science and agriculture. The other was the *Diario Pinciano, histórico, literario, legal, político y económico*, published in Valladolid in 1777-78. This paper was devoted primarily to news of local events, but its editor was an enlightened priest who did not fear at times to criticize the city's university or praise its Amigos del País.[136] Barcelona also had a *Diario curioso, histórico, erudito* in 1772-73 that Sempere overlooked, but its *luces* were limited to a few notes on popular science.

5

Despite the paucity of provincial periodicals, the interest in new ideas was not limited to the capital. It was also present, as has been seen, in the universities and economic societies. Some of the journals, through lists of subscribers they occasionally published, provide other evidence of the spread of the Enlightenment in Spain. The *Correo de Madrid* between 1787 and 1790

---

[135] These figures are the product of a tabulation of the books listed in the *Biblioteca periodica anual*. They can be only rough, for the *Biblioteca* was not complete and one cannot always tell the contents of a book from its title. Funeral orations and poems in honor of the royal family were also common (8 per cent), and so were history and biography, in large part of ancient times (7 per cent). Fiction was practically non-existent. This list can be compared with Américo Castro's analysis of Nicolás Antonio, *Biblioteca hispana* (1672), in *The Structure of Spanish History* (Princeton, 1954), p. 663 n. 75. Although the percentage of religious works declined in the intervening century, the similarity is striking.

[136] Sempere, *Biblioteca*, IV, 197-98. The *Diario Pinciano* was reproduced in the *Boletín de la Academia de Bellas Artes de Valladolid*, Nos. 8-15 (1933-36). I have not seen this. My information comes from Sarrailh, pp. 66-67, 178-79, 401-2, 466, 536, and *passim*.

oscillated between 216 and 305 subscriptions, of which about 46 per cent went outside Madrid.[137] The *Memorial literario* in June 1785 claimed about 715 subscribers, of whom 265 or 37 per cent were in the provinces.[138] It sent copies to at least eighty cities and towns, in the majority of which there was only one subscriber. Besides Madrid, Cadiz (with 42 subscribers listed), Valencia (17), Barcelona (17), Seville (15), and La Coruña (13)—all major ports—received the largest numbers. The *Semanario erudito* rose from 218 subscribers at its start to about 325 for most of its existence. Nearly one hundred duplicate copies were often also ordered. Over 40 per cent of its issues regularly went to the provinces. Here Cadiz had the largest number of subscribers (about 40), several taking duplicate copies possibly for forwarding to the Indies; but it was distributed throughout Spain, to Valencia (17 subscribers in 1789), Málaga (8), Valladolid (8), Barcelona (5), and many other places, most of which received only one or two copies apiece.[139] By far the most popular of the privately published periodicals was the *Espiritu de los mejores diarios*. In 1788 it had 765 subscribers, in 1789, 630.[140] On January 5, 1789 it announced a reissue of its first nine volumes to fill the demand for them. Of its subscribers in 1789, 36 per cent were in Madrid, 53 per cent in the Spanish provinces, and the rest in America. It even boasted readers in New York: "El Excmo. Sr. D. Juan Jay, Expresidente del Congreso Americano," and "El Dr. D. Benjamin Franklin." This journal, which was most active in spreading foreign *luces*, not only had more subscribers than the others, but got most of them from outside the capital. Because of the high rate of postage, subscriptions to all these journals cost one and one half to two times as much delivered in the provinces as in Madrid.[141] It is likely that many readers

137 Lists published in Vols. II, IV, VI, VII. Only Vol. IV states which subscribers were outside Madrid.
138 Lists published Jan. to June 1785. Since some of the names are repeated, an accurate count would be difficult.
139 Lists in Vols. III, VI, IX, XV, XVIII, XXIV, XXVII. Figures for Vol. XVIII.
140 Lists in issues of June 23, 1788 and Dec. 28, 1789.
141 In 1788 the *Espiritu de los mejores diarios* cost 5 reales per month in Madrid and 9 outside, postpaid; in 1791 a subscription to the *Semanario erudito*

in the countryside had their issues delivered in Madrid and forwarded to them by private means.[142] Madrid was the center of Spanish intellectual life, but the circulation of its journals shows that its light was reaching throughout the kingdom.

The composition of the group that bought the periodicals is also suggestive. Of the subscribers to the *Espíritu de los mejores diarios* about 6 per cent were clergymen or ecclesiastical institutions and 10 per cent were titled nobles. The *Correo de Madrid* had about 8 per cent of each class; the *Memorial literario* and the *Semanario erudito* both had some 8 per cent noble subscribers and 16 per cent clerical. Whereas the number of noble subscribers was regularly higher in Madrid than in the provinces, the opposite was true of the clergy. In about one third of the cases where a provincial town had only one subscriber to the *Semanario erudito* or the *Memorial literario*, he was a local priest or monk.

The percentages of subscribers who were nobles or churchmen are small, however. The overwhelming majority of the names on the lists belonged to members of neither class but to commoners or to untitled hidalgos. Some of the lists give clues to the make-up of this group. The *Memorial literario* and *Semanario erudito* took pains to identify their subscribers' official positions. A relatively large share were members of the royal government, from Jovellanos (an hidalgo) down to the "Administrador de la Real Lotería" in Cartagena.[143] Almost 30 per cent of all Madrid subscribers to the *Semanario erudito* and 20 per cent of its provincial subscribers fall in this category. Military officers were a smaller group (10 per cent of the provincial subscribers to the

---

for three months cost 45 and 72 reales respectively. An unskilled laborer in Madrid made about 5 reales per day in 1788 (or a little over 100 reales per month) (Hamilton, *War and Prices*, p. 270). Eight thousand reales per year was considered a high salary for a royal official in 1793 (see Manuel Godoy, *Memorias de don Manuel Godoy, Príncipe de la Paz* [6 vols.; Paris, 1839], ii, 65), although a councilor of the Consejo de Castilla made 55,000 and its *fiscales*, ₤6,000 (Desdevises, *L'Espagne*, ii, 62).

[142] The *Memorial literario* lists 11 per cent of its subscriptions as "Madrid para las provincias," with the ultimate destinations given after the subscribers' names.

[143] Jovellanos took the *Semanario erudito*, the *Espíritu*, and the *Correo de Madrid*. For the "Administrador," *Memorial literario*, Apr. 1785.

Memorial but only 4 per cent of the more profound *Semanario*), followed by doctors, lawyers, and professors. Local municipal officials appear occasionally: for instance the *regidores perpetuos* of Gerona, Almagro, and Soria who took the *Memorial* and the *alcalde mayor* of Lugo, who was also secretary of its Amigos del País and subscribed to the *Semanario*.

The lists of the other periodicals give only the names of their subscribers, but some information can be drawn from them. Institutions of higher learning and societies of Amigos del País are present, but less frequently than might have been imagined (only four of each subscribed to the *Espiritu de los mejores diarios*). Other institutions may have entered subscriptions under the names of individuals. Partnerships and companies occasionally are listed: Sres. Viuda de Santander e Hijos (Valladolid publishers) and Vázquez Hidalgo y Compañía, for instance.[144] (The *Semanario* identified as many as fourteen subscribers in Cadiz as "comerciantes.") Clearer evidence that the business world supported the periodicals is the relatively frequent appearance of names of foreign companies and of persons of foreign origin— Honorato Dalliot y Compañía of Valencia subscribed to the *Memorial*; Pedro Bellocq of Madrid and Sres. Gahn y Compañía outside Madrid both took the *Espiritu* and the *Correo de Madrid*. Mariano Power, Faustino Borgnis Desbordes, Juan Fohr, Miguel Dupuis, Pedro Davout, and similar names reveal the relative importance of foreigners or their descendants among those who were reading Spanish journals. After these identifications have been made, however, there still remain a majority of subscribers listed simply as "Señor Don," whose social position cannot be stated. Very likely many of them were well-to-do commoners without official positions—shopkeepers, merchants, entrepreneurs, professional men, and the like.

If the subscribers to the periodicals were representative of the Spaniards who were interested in the *luces*—and no better evidence of the composition of this group seems readily available— they indicate that some members of all literate and well-off

144 *Correo de Madrid.*

197

sections of Spanish society could be found in this category. Although titled nobles furnished a smaller number of subscriber than clergymen or commoners, proportionally they were far ahead. Ten per cent of all titled nobles in Spain subscribed to the *Espiritu de los mejores diarios*.[145] Perhaps some of them seldom read the journals they paid for, but the fact remains that a progressive minority existed in the aristocracy. A similar group was present in the clergy. Since the periodicals as a whole favored stricter practices in the church, most clergymen who paid for the papers probably had Jansenist leanings. Basically the journals preached the middle class ideals of hard work, frugality, intellectual curiosity, and economic innovation. One can guess that the reason that only a small fraction of the total Spanish bourgeoisie subscribed was less a lack of sympathy for the *luces* on their part than their constant concern for their own enterprises, which left them little time, energy, or means to take up the reading of periodicals.

Even if only a small fraction of the bourgeoisie took the journals, commoners still formed a substantial majority of the total number of subscribers. As was seen earlier, the middle class members of the Amigos del País also contributed most to the success of these societies. Judging from the subscription lists, these middle class supporters of enlightenment consisted largely of professional men, entrepreneurs, and members of the royal bureaucracy—men who had very likely broken with the guilds or had come out of the universities and Reales Estudios de San Isidro and had consequently profited from royal reforms. Even if active elements of both clergy and aristocracy joined in propagating the *luces*, without middle class support such vital features of the Spanish Enlightenment as the periodicals and economic societies would have foundered, and the government would have lacked encouragement to proceed with its projects for improving the country.

The men who welcomed the Enlightenment were a minority

---

[145] Sixty-six in 1788 (including those whose wives subscribed) out of 654 *grandes* and *títulos*.

of their own classes; they were perforce a much smaller proportion of all Spaniards—how small can again be guessed from the
lists of journal subscribers. Even to Spanish editors the circulation of their papers must have seemed poor. They looked longingly at London, "where twenty thousand copies of a discourse
of the English *Spectator* used to be sold in a day."[146] The figures
should be judged by the standards of their time, however. These
periodicals were a luxury item. They were printed on good paper
and were paginated to be bound into volumes, as most copies
were that have been preserved. Any one copy probably had many
readers, especially in the provinces. Because of the cost, few
individuals or institutions probably took more than one paper.
If one assumes, as is not unreasonable, that the other journals
had a circulation similar to those for which we have figures,[147]
one can estimate that there were several thousand persons and
institutions in Spain that subscribed to these periodicals, and
several tens of thousands of readers. Less than one per cent of the
population, this would mean, actively participated in this phase
of the Enlightenment.

In France, it has been estimated, the Enlightenment was being
actively spread in this same period by several tens of thousands
of persons, and it was reaching the hundreds of thousands of
members of the *moyenne bourgeoisie*.[148] Both sets of figures are,
of course, only guesses, but even so one can state that approximately ten times as many persons were affected by the Enlightenment in France as in Spain before 1788. Since the population
of France was about two and a half times that of Spain, it would
appear that the percentage of enlightened persons was roughly
four times larger in France than in Spain. If it were possible
to give a rating to the degree of enlightenment attained in the
two countries, the lead of France over Spain would appear even
greater. In France traditional religious beliefs had been widely

[146] *Conversaciones de Perico y Marica*, p. 99.
[147] *Conversaciones de Perico y Marica* had 300 for its first issue (*ibid.*).
[148] Daniel Mornet, *Les origines intellectuelles de la Révolution française*
(*1715-1787*) (4th ed.; Paris, 1947), p. 419.

called into question since the middle of the century, and since the American Revolution there had been active discussion of the political ills of the country. In Spain economic, political, and scientific theories were grist for the periodical press, lecture halls, and *tertulias*; but the significance of the American Revolution was virtually unnoticed, absolute monarchy was not questioned, and the Catholic religion was still sacrosanct. By the death of Carlos III the Enlightenment was rapidly spreading in Spain, but the country's *luces* were a far cry from the *lumières* of its neighbor to the north.

CHAPTER VII

THE CONSERVATIVE OPPOSITION

THAT some Spaniards were not pleased with, or even indifferent to, the spread of enlightenment was, of course, inevitable and has already become evident. The opponents of the *luces* held up the reforms of the universities and hampered the work of the Amigos del País, but they did not rely solely on passive resistance and tactics of obstruction. They could and did counterattack against the new spirit.

The royal government itself was the first to prevent the free circulation of all ideas. It continued to enforce a strict control of the press that had existed since Habsburg times. The regulations were restated in 1752. No publisher could print or reprint a work, however short, unless it was covered by a license from the Consejo de Castilla or certain specified royal officials, under pain of two thousand ducats' fine and six years' exile. Books must give the name of the author and publisher and the place and date of publication, under even stricter penalties for the publisher and lesser ones for binders or booksellers who handled them. Worst of all was declared to be the publishing or selling of books that were on the Index of the Inquisición or of books on religion that did not have a license; the penalty being death and loss of property, if willful propagation of heresy could be proved, or six years in a military prison (*presidio*) and two hundred ducats' fine, if such malice were not established.[1] Since 1502 the importation of books printed abroad also required prior authorization by the Consejo de Castilla. This regulation was not being strictly observed, however, and, as will be seen, had to be repeated in 1784 with details on its enforcement as a result of excitement caused by the importation of the *Encyclopédie méthodique*.[2]

The Consejo de Castilla took seriously its task of censoring works for publication in Spain. The manuscripts were sent by it

---

[1] *Resolución a consejo*, July 27, 1752, *Nov. rec.*, VIII, xvi, 22.
[2] *Pragmática*, July 8, 1502, *real orden*, June 21, 1784, *ibid.*, 1 and 31.

to qualified persons, whose opinions were used to guide its decisions.[3] It shared the task with a *superintendente general de imprentas* and a *juez de imprentas*. These three authorities alone could grant licenses for publication or importation. They were required to send works on religion to the bishops' courts for their opinion. After 1773, in line with the regalism of the government, bishops, in stating approval of works, were prohibited from using the formula "imprimatur" or any other that indicated authority to grant permission for publication. A monopoly of this authority belonged to the civil government.[4] In 1788, after temporary measures had been used to cope with the new phenomenon of the periodical press, a royal resolution issued special rules to apply to it. All manuscript for periodicals had to be submitted to the *juez de imprentas* prior to publication. The periodicals were forbidden to print satires or indecent and insulting remarks about individuals or groups and to discuss acts or decisions of the royal government without permission. They were also ordered to indicate the source of quotations taken from foreign authors or publications.[5] Most objectionable material that might appear in Spanish publications was thus stopped before it got to the press. What did appear can be assumed to have passed government censorship of some sort and was therefore given to the public with official blessing.

Only occasionally did the government issue public prohibitions of specified books already in circulation. One such ban was issued in 1778, condemning the French work *L'an 2440* because it "applauds with excessive praise the most impious and detestable writers who in recent times, under the title of free philosophers, have . . . declared bloody and obstinate war on religion" and because "it attacks sovereigns and excites spirits to independence and absolute liberty."[6] Other works were also specifically prohibited by Carlos, but they mainly were papal bulls or products of the argument over the justice of the expulsion of the Jesuits.

---

[3] See Serrano y Sanz, "El Consejo de Castilla y la censura," *loc.cit.*
[4] *Real cédula,* Apr. 20, 1773, Aguirre, *Prontuario . . . 1792,* pp. 211-12.
[5] *Real resolución,* Oct. 2, 1788, *Nov. rec.,* VIII, xvii, 3. See above, p. 187.
[6] *Real resolución,* Mar. 17, 1778, *ibid.,* xviii, 10.

L'an 2440 was the only philosophic work to rate this attention
and its prohibition the sole official expression of concern over
the new philosophy to be made before 1789. The royal government, although it did control the press, cannot be classed as an
enemy of the Enlightenment, since it approved all the publications
and institutions that were bringing new ideas to the people. It
opposed only those extreme writings which it felt to be dangerous
to monarchy and Catholic religion.

Another institution existed to stop the spread of dangerous
thinking. Whereas the government checked bad ideas before
they entered circulation, the Inquisición acted to suppress those
that had got abroad. As was noted in the second chapter, Carlos'
opposition to ultramontanism led him to curb the arbitrary
powers of the Santo Oficio, while his desire for reform within
the church caused him to appoint inquisitors-general who
preferred on the whole the use of persuasion to force in ensuring
religious uniformity. The objective, maintaining the purity of the
Catholic faith in Spain, remained unchanged and was strongly
supported by the king.

The Inquisición existed independently of the regular or secular
clergy of Spain. At its head was the inquisitor-general, usually
a leading Spanish prelate, who was named by the king. He
headed the Consejo de la Suprema Inquisición, which included
representatives of the Dominican order and the Consejo de Castilla.[7] Beneath the council were fourteen tribunals located in
leading Spanish cities. The number of their members was small,
often three persons per tribunal, usually regular clergymen. On
the lowest level there were individual agents of the Inquisición
scattered throughout the towns and cities. These were called
either *comisarios* or *familiares*. They had no jurisdiction of their
own but acted only as agents for transmitting information to
the tribunals and for carrying out interrogations and investigations. Most were subject to the tribunals, but some in larger
cities reported directly to the Consejo de la Inquisición. These
comisarios and *familiares* could be either laymen or clergymen,

---

[7] Desdevises, *L'Espagne*, ii, 119; Clarke, p. 37.

although the latter undoubtedly were in the majority. Their duties did not take their full time, and their identity was not always public knowledge. Another category of persons associated with the Inquisición was the *calificadores*, the men to whom books, manuscripts, or the records of the testimony of witnesses were submitted by the tribunals or the council for an opinion as to the orthodoxy and propriety of the book or person being investigated. This censoring process was known as "qualifying" (*calificar*). The *calificadores* were presumably chosen for their learning and could be either laymen or clergymen but most frequently were monks. Finally, of course, the Santo Oficio relied on the cooperation of all the clergy in Spain, who were expected to report any matter which might concern the Inquisición. All of its activities were shrouded in silence. Everyone who had any dealings with the Inquisición had to swear not to reveal what he knew about it.

One of the main tasks of the Inquisición was to censor the reading matter of Spanish subjects. Printed works or manuscripts which were received by the tribunals or the council from their agents or directly from zealous clergymen or private individuals, were submitted to their *calificadores*. If the work was found worth prohibiting or expurgating by a local tribunal, it was sent to the Consejo de la Inquisición together with the opinions of the *calificadores*. Here the case would be reviewed, possibly with a new censoring, and, if the council confirmed the finding of the tribunal, it passed a decree to the effect. Periodically the decrees were collected and published by the inquisitor-general in edicts that were posted in the churches. From time to time a complete "Index" of all prohibited works was issued. One Index appeared in 1747, another in 1790. In theory the Spanish Inquisición did not prohibit any work or an author except after judging the case itself, so that its Index did not agree in all cases with that issued by the papal Inquisition in Rome or contain all the works condemned by foreign bishops.[8]

[8] This description of the Inquisición is based primarily on the documents of the Inquisición from the period of Carlos III and Carlos IV which I have investigated in the Archivo Histórico Nacional, Madrid.

To own or read books which had been prohibited or had not been properly expurgated was a sin for which one could be excommunicated. Priests were required to ask all who confessed, especially during lent, if they had or knew of any one who had books on the Index and to advise those who had such books or knowledge of them to seek absolution from the inquisitors. Only the officials of the Inquisición could grant absolution from this sin, and they were empowered to impose personal and pecuniary penances. A person who failed to delate a violator, however closely related to him by ties of family or friendship, was considered to be as guilty as a violator.[9] A person who printed or sold prohibited books also came under the jurisdiction of the Santo Oficio. Publishers and booksellers incurred a heavy fine, suspension of their business, and exile from their city for two years for the first offense. For a second the penalty was at the discretion of the Inquisición.[10]

Few suspect works, foreign or domestic, which had found their way into Spain, escaped the Index. The edition of 1790 contained 305 quarto pages with double columns and small type. Even this description does not give a proper idea of its extent, since authors like Wyclif, Luther, Calvin, Erasmus, Voltaire, and many others were disposed of in a single line as "first class," all of whose writings were prohibited. Dante, Petrarch, Boccaccio, Machiavelli, Cervantes, all had works prohibited or ordered expurgated. Pierre Bayle's irreverent *Dictionnaire historique et critique* was prohibited in 1747; *Robinson Crusoe* in 1756; Montesquieu's *L'esprit des lois* at the same time, and many other works of the *philosophes* before 1789. The writings of the astronomers Tycho Brahe and Johannes Kepler could not be read, nor the major works of authors of the law of nature and of nations, Hugo Grotius, J. J. Burlamaqui (after 1756), and Samuel Pufendorf (after 1787). Even the Spanish translation of Beccaria's *Dei delitti e*

[9] Edict of Inquisitor-General Felipe Beltrán, May 7, 1782, quoted in *Suplemento al Indice expurgatorio del año 1790* . . . (Madrid, 1805), pp. 3-4; Llorente, *Historia*, II, 156-57.
[10] *Indice ultimo* (1790), pp. xxvi-xxvii.

delle pene was prohibited in 1777, three years after its appearance. Foreign historians were especially suspect. Many histories of Europe and of Spain published in French were listed in the Index, including the well known "[William] Robertson (Mr.). *La Histoire du Regne de l'Empereur Charles V.*" All prohibited works were not of this nature. Many were books by Catholic authors on Catholic doctrine; while all books on witchcraft and magic, pornographic books, and those that did not indicate the name of the author, publisher, place, and date, were also forbidden. The published edicts were required to give the reasons for which the works listed were condemned. As they were actually issued, such statements were meaningless; for instance, the prohibition of Rousseau's *Confessions* declared them to contain "propositions respectively erroneous, impious, scandalous, injurious to the Catholic religion, *sapientes haeresim*, and formally heretical."[11]

There was little limit to the authority of the Index. The regulations of the Inquisición permitted Catholic scholars to obtain licenses to read specific prohibited books for the purpose of attacking them.[12] According to Juan Antonio Llorente, the official of the Inquisición who was later to write its history, such licenses were granted by the inquisitor-general fairly sparingly, to persons of known orthodoxy, and were given only for works on specific branches of learning. Permission could also be bought from the papal court without investigation as to motives; but before the end of the century, the inquisitor-general refused to recognize papal licenses unless he had approved them, thus rendering them meaningless and giving evidence of the independence of the Santo Oficio from Rome.[13] Moreover, many works, including the most objection-

[11] Edict of the inquisitor-general, May 10, 1789, in "Fraile," Vol. 863, fol. 148.
[12] *Indice ultimo*, pp. xxiv-xxv.
[13] Llorente, *Historia*, III, 149-50. Pierre-Nicolas Chantreau, a Frenchman long resident in Spain, claimed that permissions could easily be bought from the Inquisición (in his *Lettres écrites de Barcelonne à un zélateur de la liberté, qui voyage en Allemagne* [Paris, 1792], pp. 209-10), but Llorente's account seems more trustworthy.

able ones of the *philosophes*, were declared to be forbidden even to those with permission to read prohibited books.

The government of Carlos III, in keeping with its regalistic attitude toward the church, in 1768 specified the procedure that the Inquisición was to follow henceforth in prohibiting books. Before the work of a Catholic author could be prohibited, he or his representative was to be given a hearing. Until a book was finally adjudged, its circulation was not to be hindered by the Inquisición, and owners of books ordered expurgated were to be permitted to carry out the expurgation themselves. Finally, before an edict prohibiting books could be published, it must be submitted for approval by the government. This rule applied also to prohibitions coming from the papal court.[14] The new regulation laid the way open for the transformation of the Inquisición into a purely state agency for censorship. Its later activity under Carlos III does not indicate that this was the purpose. Carlos wished only to curb its arbitrary power, which was believed to have been used by partisans of the recently exiled Jesuits to condemn works of their enemies within the church.[15] On the other hand, since all later edicts presumably underwent civil review, it is clear that the royal government was not averse to seeing works of the *philosophes* on these edicts.

Perhaps a more effective limit on the authority of the Index was a growing scorn of it among the enlightened public. Jovellanos, asked by the Consejo de Castilla to give an opinion of a translation of Voltaire's *Alzire*, replied that the Consejo could, if it wished, approve its publication after certain modifications had been made, thereby ignoring the Inquisición's condemnation of all Voltaire's work. It was due to this spirit, no doubt, that other translations of Voltaire's plays also appeared

[14] *Cédula del consejo*, June 16, 1768, *Nov. rec.*, VIII, xviii, 3.

[15] This is indicated by art. 3 of the cedula, which says prohibitions of books should aim at rooting out, among other dangerous teachings, "the lax opinions which pervert Christian morality," an evident reference to the teachings of the Jesuits.

at this time.[16] The attitude of Sempere y Guarinos was similar. In discussing in his *Biblioteca española de los mejores escritores del reinado de Carlos III* the famous satire of Spanish monks, Isla's *Fray Gerundio*, Sempere stated that, in the short time it was allowed to circulate before it was prohibited by the Inquisición, it had a very salutary effect, a judgment that hardly flattered the decision of the holy tribunal.[17] On the whole, as has been seen, enlightened Spaniards freely read and published those new ideas that they liked even if they were found in prohibited books. The inquisitor-general himself admitted in 1782 that the fear of ecclesiastical censure for reading prohibited books was "nearly extinct";[18] and, if we are to believe Llorente, the cause lay in the very verdicts of the Inquisición. No one was any longer imprisoned for having prohibited books, he says. The punishment was usually a money fine (called pecuniary penance) and the declaration of being slightly (*de levi*) suspect of heresy; but even this verdict was omitted if there was reason to believe that the person had been guilty only out of curiosity and not out of acceptance of bad doctrines.[19]

The threat of the Santo Oficio hung in abeyance, nevertheless, persistently and menacingly over the heads of those who carried their violations to the extreme of becoming suspect of real heresy. The Inquisición would shake off its lethargy, defy the spirit of the times, and exact exemplary punishment from some well chosen victim in order to intimidate others of his ilk. It considered bringing to trial Floridablanca, Campomanes, Aranda, and other leading ministers in retaliation for the part they took in the expulsion of the Jesuits and the reform of the Inquisición. It was unable, however, to find enough evidence to justify the charges brought against them of accept-

---

[16] Jovellanos' report is quoted in Serrano y Sanz, "El Consejo de Castilla y la censura," *loc.cit.*, p. 36. See above, p. 67.

[17] Sempere, *Biblioteca*, III, 128.

[18] Edict of the inquisitor-general, May 7, 1782, *loc.cit.*

[19] Llorente, *Historia*, III, 149-50. My own investigation of cases of this kind before the Inquisición under Carlos IV confirms Llorente's statement.

ing atheism, materialism, and modern philosophy; and there was danger in attacking men so patently in the royal favor.[20] But the Inquisición did find a suitable culprit in the prominent figure Pablo Olavide.

Olavide, it will be remembered, was a native of Peru who had visited France and frequented the salons of Paris, getting to know several *philosophes,* including Voltaire at Ferney. After his return to Spain his every action seemed to challenge conservative churchmen. In Madrid his house became a center for spreading French culture and translating French plays. In 1766 he was denounced to the Inquisición for having in his home pornographic paintings—probably importations from France in the contemporary style of Boucher and Fragonard. After serving the king in Madrid, in 1767 he was named intendant of the province of Seville and superintendent of the agricultural colonies of Sierra Morena. It was thanks to his activity that these colonies flourished. In Seville he kept an open salon in which literature, politics, and economics were discussed, and which aroused the opposition of some clergymen. His outspoken dislike of the landholding practices of the church did not add to his popularity in this quarter. In 1768 the charge of having pornographic paintings was repeated. This time the pictures were confiscated and Olavide's license to read prohibited books was revoked. His plan of studies for the university of Seville, which inspired Carlos' reforms in the other universities of Spain, was denounced in 1773. The final blow came from the colonies of Sierra Morena. A German Capucin monk who had come to the colony reported directly to Madrid in 1774 that the religious system established by Olavide in the colonies was opposed to the Catholic Church. A limitation on the activities of the clergy had been incorporated in their charter and had been supplemented by Olavide: begging for alms, masses on week days, and other religious activities had been forbidden.

In this manner originated the most famous inquisitorial trial of the century. The tribunal of Madrid had the evidence against

[20] *Ibid.,* v, 295, 298-301, 306-7, 314-15, IX, 5.

Olavide reviewed by its *calificadores* of best integrity. Before acting, the Consejo de la Inquisición reported the case to Carlos III, stating that eighty witnesses had been examined, over half laymen, and many points of the accusation had been proved.[21] The king's support was requested and evidently obtained, for Carlos was no friend of heterodoxy. In November 1776 Olavide was arrested. On October 13, 1778, he was sentenced behind closed doors in a ceremony known as an *autillo*. Seventy prominent persons were present: leading nobles, members of the five royal councils, and various prelates. Olavide appeared in the full regalia of a convicted heretic and was pronounced to be a "formal heretic" for many transgressions. Primarily he was declared to have been misled through his correspondence with Voltaire and Rousseau, but among many other charges was that of upholding the Copernican system. Olavide maintained to the end that he had not lost his faith. After hearing the verdict, he fainted and had to be revived. Finally he abjured his errors, was reconciled with the church, and was condemned to lose all his property, to banishment for life from Madrid, Seville, the Sierra Morena colonies, and Lima, and to be confined to a monastery for eight years, where he was to undergo religious education. So impressive was the ceremony that one of the observers confessed the next day to reading the *philosophes* and accused the highest royal officials of doing likewise. In 1780 Olavide, whose health was suffering, got permission to take baths in Catalonia. He used the opportunity to escape to France and then made his way to Paris, where he was given a hero's welcome by his philosophic friends. Carlos III requested his extradition, but the matter was dropped after Olavide fled momentarily to Geneva.[22]

The trial of Olavide caused a sensation among the literate classes of Spain. The terror of the Inquisición, which had largely faded since the advent of Carlos III, suddenly was revived.[23] The

[21] Oct. 29, 1776, Ferrer del Rio, III, 54 n. 1.

[22] The best account of this case is in Danvila y Collado, IV, 44-55, who used the official records of the case. See also Llorente, *Historia*, V, 308-13; Villanueva, I, 16-19; Antonio Puigblanch [pseud. Natanael Jomtob], *La Inquisicion sin mascara* (Cadiz, 1811), pp. 193-95.

[23] Bourgoing (1797), I, 348-60.

passage of time gradually caused the fear once more to subside, but the Inquisición always managed to keep the public aware of its power. Two brothers, Bernardo and Tomás de Iriarte, the second a well known playwright, were soon brought to task. The Inquisición had been observing them since 1771, when reports began to come in that they blamed the ignorance of Spain on the Santo Oficio and that Bernardo publicly cast doubts on the virginity of Mary, corresponded with Voltaire, and boasted indiscriminately of being a deist and a materialist. In 1779 Bernardo was convicted of making blasphemous, scandalous, and heretical statements, and sentenced to solitary confinement, loss of property, and seizure of his books and papers.[24] This contretemps did not prevent him from being a member of the Sociedad Económica de Madrid a few years later.[25] The turn of Tomás de Iriarte came in 1786. He was accused of harboring the errors of the "false philosophers" and required to abjure *de levi* behind closed doors. In the same year an aged professor of mathematics in Madrid, Benito Bails, whose writings were among the highest products of contemporary Spanish learning, was accused of atheism and materialism and imprisoned by the Inquisición. Bails admitted that he had doubted the existence of God but denied he had accepted atheism or materialism. He was released but forced to do pecuniary penance and ordered to confess three times a year to a specified priest.[26] The editor of *El censor*, Luis Cañuelo, was made to abjure *de levi* in 1788.[27]

Clearly, if the Inquisición did not act in more such cases, it was not for lack of power or because of new tolerance for religious aberrations but mainly because religious doubt had not yet noticeably penetrated Spanish society. Even Olavide insisted he never lost his faith. The strong attachment of enlightened

[24] Miguel de la Pinta Llorente, "El sentido de la cultura española en el siglo XVIII e intelectuales de la época," *Revista de estudios políticos*, No. 68 (Mar.-Apr. 1953), pp. 94-100.

[25] "Catálogo de los socios de la clase de oficios," *Memorias de la Sociedad Economica*, Vol. IV.

[26] Llorente, *Historia*, v, 192-93, 163-64; Villanueva, I, 26-28. The dates are given in Llorente, *Histoire*, IV, 338.

[27] See above, p. 187.

Spaniards to their religion made the task of the Inquisición easier, but at the same time the Inquisición served to keep the forbidden fruit from the mouths of the Spanish literate groups. Its prestige remained the greatest deterrent from reading the advanced works of the French Enlightenment and especially from spreading knowledge of them. Those people who had lost their faith either kept their secret to themselves or abjured their beliefs before the feared tribunal. The future apostate Blanco White was to insist that the end of burnings in Spain was due not to a growing leniency of the Santo Oficio but to the lack of will among those of heretical ideas to uphold them to the end. He cited as proof the burning at the stake in Seville in 1781 of a woman who claimed saintly powers. She had steadfastly refused to renounce her unorthodox beliefs, but she too relented at the last moment, in time to be strangled before the pyre was lit.[28]

The plight of those who knew that they held forbidden doctrines was expressed by a Frenchman long resident in Spain as a teacher. He was incensed at the statement of Bourgoing that the Inquisición was not to be feared by those who outwardly conformed to the Catholic religion.[29]

> Without doubt the author . . . has not lived under the yoke of the Inquisition and suffered as I have for fifteen years the frightful state of not daring to confide even in one's wife for fear that some insidious priest would make her an informer despite herself. I recall with sorrow . . . that for fifteen years, in order to avoid this misfortune and others still worse, I indulged in all the puerilities which, echoing their priests, good credulous Castilians call devotion.[30]

These lines were written in 1792 and were addressed to partisans of the French Revolution, probably being colored to suit their readers. Yet they convey the gnawing anxiety felt by unorthodox Spaniards under Carlos III. Had large numbers of progressive Spaniards broken with their faith, no doubt they could have

---

[28] *El Español*, III (1811), 37-40. See Menéndez Pelayo, *Heterodoxos*, v, 472-75.
[29] Bourgoing (1789), I, 354. Bourgoing nevertheless denounced its secrecy.
[30] Chantreau, p. 363.

circumvented the control of the Santo Oficio. But since they did not, that tribunal was a sword suspended over those persons who were led beyond enlightenment to heresy. They went their lonely way afraid to publicize their convictions.

2

The Spanish opponents of enlightenment were not content to let the Inquisición stifle discussion of dangerous doctrines. Several writers took the offensive. One method used was to translate the works of French Catholic apologists. These were finding their way into private Spanish libraries,[31] but so long as they remained in the foreign tongue, their audience was limited. In 1765 the *Mercurio histórico y político* of Madrid published a translation of Omer Joly de Fleury's attack on the writings of Rousseau, especially his *Émile*, for their "impious and abominable principles, directed against the Catholic religion and against J.C., its Author."[32] Between 1769 and 1771 one of the royal preachers, the Mercedarian monk Pedro Rodríguez Morzo translated two important French attacks on Voltaire: *El oraculo de los nuevos philosofos, M. Voltaire, impugnado y descubierto en sus errores por sus mesmas [sic] obras . . . por un anonymo . . .* (the author was Claude Marie Guyon) and *Los errores historicos y dogmaticos de Voltaire, impugnados en particular por Mr. el Abad Nonote* (Claude François Nonnotte).[33] Rodríguez Morzo saw in Voltaire and Rousseau, whom he called followers of Spinoza, "enemies *in primo capite* of society" and hoped that they would imitate Helvétius, La Mettrie, and Montesquieu in (as he said) being terrified by the approach of death into renouncing their irreligious doctrines.[34] In 1788 another work of Nonnotte appeared, this one an apology of the Catholic religion.[35] Next year saw a

31 *Ibid.*, pp. 209-10.
32 April 1765, quoted in Spell, p. 43.
33 2 vols.; Madrid, 1769-70, and 2 vols.; Madrid, 1771.
34 Guyon, "Prólogo del traductor" to Vols. I and II.
35 Claude François Nonnotte, *Defensa de los puntos mas interesantes de la religion acometidos por los incredulos.* Sacada de las celebres obras que escribio en frances el Sr. Abate Nonnotte. . . . Por D. Josef de Palacio y Viana . . . (Madrid, 1788).

Discurso que comprehende en compendio las pruebas naturales de la existencia de Dios e inmortalidad del alma, traducido del frances, a small pamphlet that claimed to prove the existence of God from the marvels of nature for the benefit of those who rejected sacred writings.[36] Most popular of all was the mediocre but prolific apologist Louis-Antoine Caraccioli. Numerous editions of his tracts, such as *La religion de l'honnête homme, Le langage de la raison*, and *Le langage de la religion*, poured forth in Spanish.[37] This list does not pretend to exhaust the translations of this type that were published in Spain, but it is sufficient to show that those who opposed the *luces* were no more reluctant than the partisans of enlightenment to turn to French sources for their ammunition.

More ambitious Spaniards employed their own faculties in combatting the *philosophes*. Feyjóo himself led the way in 1752 with a refutation of Rousseau's first discourse.[38] By far the most impressive endeavor of this kind under Carlos III was a six-volume work by the Hieronymite monk Fernando de Zevallos, *La falsa filosofia o el ateismo, deismo, materialismo y demas nuevas sectas convencidas de crimen de estado contra los soberanos*, which appeared in 1774-76.[39] It consists of a jumble of arguments that often reappear under different guises. Zevallos found progenitors for his eighteenth-century enemies in Biblical and classical figures. He established, or attempted to establish, that

[36] Traducido del frances al castellano P.D.F.A.D.A. (Madrid, 1789), "Varios," Carlos IV, leg. 1, 4°.

[37] Louis-Antoine Caraccioli, *La religion del hombre de bien, contra los nuevos sectarios de la incredulidad*. Por el Marques Caraciolo. . . . Traducido de frances en castellano por don Francisco Mariano Nifo (Madrid, 1775); *Idioma de la razon contra los falsos filosofos modernos*. Por el Marques Caraciolo. . . . Traducido de frances en castellano por don Francisco Mariano Nifo (Madrid, 1775); *El idioma de la religion contra los nuevos sectarios de la incredulidad*. Por el Marqués Caraciolo. Traducido del frances en español por D. Francisco Mariano Nipho (Madrid, 1776). All had four editions by 1779 and the last two a fifth in 1784. At least thirteen other works of Caraccioli appeared in Spanish, probably all before 1789 although of five the Biblioteca Nacional has only later editions.

[38] Spell, pp. 20-21.

[39] Madrid. The author's name is usually given in secondary works as Ceballos [y Mier], but the title page carries Zevallos.

"*Impios, Deistas, Filósofos, Libertinos, Indiferentes, Naturalistas, Reformadores son unos nombres sinónimos*,[40] an argument which appeared under a slightly different color in his proof that the *philosophes* were the offspring of the Reformers.[41] All have no other God than the pleasures of the senses, Zevallos maintained, echoing French apologists, while the false philosophers go from here to the political heresy of denying social distinction in order to establish an iniquitous equality among men.[42] Both they and the Protestants teach tyrannicide. As proof for this assertion Zevallos quoted Voltaire's sentence, "The princes are the ones who should be personally punished and not the troops who lay waste the fields."[43] Zevallos, in his enthusiasm, also denounced the new theorists of penal law, especially Beccaria, whose treatise had just appeared in Spanish. The monk defended the use of torture and the death penalty.[44] Interspersed in his six volumes was a lengthy apology of the Catholic religion and monarchic government. His arguments in favor of the former, as for instance that it alone assured eternal life and was established by miracles, had already been heard in France and were, anyway, useless against skeptics. Such a hodge-podge may have had readers among those who already accepted its beliefs; it is hard to imagine that it could have been widely read or influential among those whom it was intended to sway.[45]

According to two other Spanish writers who tackled the job of defending religion, it was Descartes, and not, as Zevallos held,

---

[40] *Ibid.*, I, 102-3 (italics in original).   [41] *Ibid.*, v, 65-97.

[42] *Ibid.*, Vol. I, dedication to Campomanes and p. 6, IV, 23-26. Cp. Palmer, pp. 184-88.

[43] Zevallos, VI, 12-26.

[44] *Ibid.*, v, 353-88.

[45] Menéndez Pelayo gives a glowing but not too clear account of this work (*Heterodoxos*, v, 370-82). He asserts that Zevallos' attack on Beccaria as well as what appeared to be a threat to royal *regalías* led to a refusal of a license to publish the further volumes he had planned. The only source Menéndez Pelayo cites, although apparently not the only one he draws on, sounds partisan and unreliable. Luis Vidart, *La filosofía española* (Madrid, 1866), pp. 100-101, gives the same story. He cites a biography of Zevallos by Juan José Buen in Zevallos, *La Sidonia Betica* (Seville, 1864), a book I have not been able to find. Neither explains why, if what they say is so, the Inquisición was able to prohibit the Spanish translation of Beccaria in 1777 (above, pp. 205-6).

the ancients or the Reformers, who was responsible for the rise of modern philosophy. This was the thesis of the first volume of Vicente Fernández Valcarce's *Desengaños filosoficos.*[46] Descartes, he asserted, destroyed the harmony that had long existed in European letters, a sort of *pax scholastica* which Fernández Valcarce looked back at longingly. Valcarce, a canon of the cathedral of Palencia, brought to his task a wide knowledge of recent letters, English as well as French. Malebranche, Locke, Leibnitz, Montesquieu, D'Alembert, Helvétius, and many now obscure writers were subjects for his pen. He complained most bitterly of the threat they were to religion, although he also demonstrated that the state was in danger. A member of the faculty of the university of Seville, Antonio Xavier Pérez y López, agreed with Valcarce that present day disbelief went back for its source to Descartes, whose doubt of everything except his own existence, when applied to truths beyond human understanding, said Pérez y López, leads to atheism, materialism, and deism. Against these dangers he recommended reading French apologetic works.[47]

Pérez y López also attacked the extravagances of natural law.

Hobbes makes man equal to the tigers in fierceness, establishing force as the origin of natural law, that is, of a phantom of justice . . . Rousseau on the contrary makes man gentle by nature, but so stupid that he was [*sic*] incapable of distinguishing the beauty of one woman from another, and so unsociable that not even with the woman whom by chance he enjoyed, nor with his children, did he have social relations. But nevertheless he calls him happy because his spirit is calm, like the stones and tree trunks, and, without other evidence than his own word, says that all evils came from society and that that [former] condition (which is more savage than that of the bears) is natural to man. . . .

What can be the political theory [*Política*] that gushes from these envenomed sources? false, erroneous, and prejudicial to man, to religion, and to the state.[48]

[46] Vicente Fernández Valcarce, *Desengaños filosoficos, que en obsequio de la verdad, de la religion, y de la patria da al publico* . . . (4 vols.; Madrid, 1787-97).
[47] Pérez y López, *Principios*, pp. vii-x.   [48] *Ibid.*, pp. x-xi.

Pérez y López provided a theory of his own, which he said bound together nature, morality, religion, and wholesome political thought. God gave man natural rights and the duty to respect the rights of others so that all might achieve their purpose on earth, the glorification of God. The sovereign must contribute to their purpose, and so must protect the true religion, the Catholic, provide scientific instruction to all regardless of class, and must break up large landholdings in the interest of all citizens. But above all he must procure the political liberty of all his subjects.[49] In fact, despite Pérez's assertion to the contrary, he differed little from natural rights thinkers elsewhere except in his fervent equation of natural justice with the Catholic religion. Enlightened Spaniards could find little in his theory that was not already commonplace for them.

The best known figure to attack the *philosophes* was the caustic young poet and writer Juan Pablo Forner. In 1787 he published a volume of *Discursos filosóficos sobre el hombre*, of which the major portion was a heavy didactic poem modeled on Alexander Pope's *Essay on Man*. A "preliminary discourse" set forth his ideas and reasons for writing:

A Juan Jacobo Rouseau . . . will show you mathematically that civil institutions have made men degenerate from the state of man [*sic*], that the progress of arts and sciences has driven virtue from the world, that the sovereigns of the world are an army of wolves introduced in it to establish universal slavery, that the Christian religion is contrary to the good constitution of a state. A Helvétius will announce to you . . . that God has left man under the sole direction of pain and delight, . . . that the desire for sensual love is the most fecund source of virtue. A Voltaire will tell you resolutely that it is crass ignorance to deny that the human soul can be material.[50]

Forner, in contrast, provided a system based on "the corruption of man, the weakness of his reason, the need for revelation, . . .

---

[49] *Ibid.*, pp. xx-xxxii.
[50] Juan Pablo Forner, *Discursos filosóficos sobre el hombre* (Madrid, 1787), pp. 3-4.

and the existence of God."[51] Unfortunately, his theory, which he believed followed strict logical reasoning, abounds in *non sequiturs* that should have cast shame on the teachers of scholastic philosophy under whom he had studied at Salamanca.

Zevallos, Fernández Valcarce, Pérez y López, and Forner were the leading opponents of the Enlightenment in Spain but far from the only ones. Attacks against the new philosophy of the age from Spanish pulpits were becoming commonplace after 1780, according to *El censor's* Cañuelo.[52] In this instance Cañuelo must have been exaggerating to make a point, for there is little evidence to support his sweeping statement. Even those preachers who did attack the new danger seldom could have known much about it except from unreliable hearsay. Such was the case of the author of a pamphlet in 1786, *España triunfante en el actual siglo filosófico*.[53] Although he saw as its apostles "Espinosa, Bayle, Volter, Ruso," he conceived "Filosofía" as existing in England, Prussia, Holland, and Geneva; not in Catholic France. Most preachers who discussed "Filosofía" probably felt they were fulfilling their duty if they condemned writings that had been placed on the Index even if they did not know clearly what they contained. As a professor of theology at the still unreformed university of Salamanca—who did at least know what Rousseau taught—said in a public discourse urging students to avoid dangerous books, "This doctrine is not taught at Salamanca, hence it is false, tumultuous, and unworthy of my replying to it."[54]

All Spanish apologists agreed that the new philosophers were dangerous to the throne and the altar. Their work was aimed at the edification of their fellow Spaniards, and this being the case, the objection of Cañuelo to their activity, that it was unnecessary, was made on sound grounds. Of persons in Spain who were attacking either the altar or the throne hardly a trace has been

[51] *Ibid.*, p. 29. For a biography of Forner see Luis Villanueva in Juan Pablo Forner, *Obras* (Madrid, 1843), I, ix-xxii.

[52] *El censor*, Discurso 46, pp. 727-28.

[53] *España triunfante en el actual siglo filosófico*. Su autor D.J.C. (Madrid, 1786).

[54] Joseph Marín, *La sabiduria del siglo convencida de necedad, ó elogio de un sabio en lo mismo que ignoró* (Salamanca, [1777]), p. 47 (a eulogy of a late professor).

found. Catholicism and enlightened despotism were the ideals of even the most progressive Spaniards. The writers who were denouncing atheism, deism, and materialism or were warning of a threat to monarchic institutions were fighting ugly shadows in Spain but little else.

They were to a large extent even in agreement on essential points with the progressives. Forner praised the practical results that the study of science was having on Spain's economy.[55] Pérez y López lauded those achievements of Carlos III which had the blessings of Spain's economists: the creation of the patriotic societies, the colonies of Sierra Morena, the freeing of commerce. Fernández Valcarce, while attacking Descartes and those men he named as that philosopher's spiritual heirs, classed as "Filósofos inocentes" those who had destroyed scholastic science without harmful effects on politics or religion: Robert Boyle, Newton, Musschenbroek, and their like. In its own field, experimental science, he believed, was of great value.[56] The arguments of Spanish partisans of modern science went no further. As was seen, these men were strongly in favor of keeping God in his heaven and even letting science help in his worship.[57] Zevallos hated Beccaria, and certainly there were persons who opposed Spanish progressives, but what most reactionaries feared—or pretended to fear—was a state of mind which was not present in their country. On the fundamental questions of the form of government and religion there was no cleavage of any depth in Spain before the outbreak of the French Revolution.

3

Such a cleavage was latent, however, and it existed for everyone to see on a less fundamental level. The struggle to introduce new subjects into the universities and to reform the practices of the Spanish church and clergy bore witness to this division, but much of the maneuvering in these cases was hidden from public

---

[55] In *Correo de Madrid*, Sept. 15, 1790.
[56] Fernández Valcarce, I, 2-3, 29, 354.
[57] See above, p. 46.

sight. Not so was a *cause célèbre* that shook the Spanish world of letters in the last years of Carlos III.

In the 1780's a Paris publisher, Charles Joseph Panckoucke, encouraged by the success of Diderot's *Encyclopédie,* determined to edit an even more extensive collection of human knowledge, and one that would incidentally avoid the dangerous tendentious spirit of its predecessor. Panckoucke issued a prospectus in Spanish for his *Encyclopédie méthodique* and sent an agent across the Pyrenees who soon had over three hundred subscribers.[58] The Spanish government blessed the undertaking tacitly and gave a leading Madrid publisher, Antonio de Sancha, permission to issue a translation of the new encyclopedia. Unfortunately for Panckoucke's venture, the *Encyclopédie méthodique* was not entirely free of a "philosophic" approach to knowledge. In 1783 the first volume devoted to geography appeared, containing the article "Espagne." The author of this article, Nicolas Masson de Morvilliers, had already published in 1776 an *Abrégé de la géographie de l'Espagne et du Portugal.* His approach to his subject echoed that of Montesquieu's *Esprit des lois* and Voltaire's *L'essai sur les mœurs*: Spain was the country that typified everything against which the *philosophes* were struggling. Masson's article in the *Encyclopédie méthodique* broke into puerile exclamations of horror at Spain's ignorance and sloth, unable to profit from its own natural wealth, at its futile government and bigoted clergy, and, above all, at its cruel and tyrannical Inquisición. "What do we owe to Spain?" Masson asked rhetorically. "What has it done for Europe in the last two centuries, in the last four, or ten?"[59]

The first copies of the volume to reach Madrid caused an official row. The king read the article and was incensed. Florida-

---

[58] Bourgoing (1797), I, 283-84; *Encyclopedia Britannica* (14th ed.), *s.v.* "Encyclopedia." The latter says 330 subscribers were obtained.

[59] Nicolas Masson de Morvilliers, "Espagne," in *Encyclopédie méthodique ou par ordre de matières,* Series "Géographie moderne," I, 554-68. See Luigi Sorrento, *Francia e Spagna nel settecento: battaglie e sorgenti di idee* ("Publicazioni della Università Cattolica del Sacro Cuore," Series IV, "Scienze filologische," Vol. VIII) (Milan, 1928), p. 90. This is a study of the Masson *affaire.*

blanca held up the importation of the *Encyclopédie* and ordered it henceforth to be censored before being delivered. He complained bitterly to the French *chargé* in Madrid that he himself had been responsible for the permission to introduce the *Encyclopédie méthodique* into Spain and that he regretted that through the fault of some French writers he would be forced to prohibit this source of *lumières*. The age-old law against importing foreign publications without a preliminary censorship by the royal government, which had been officially neglected in the present case, was restated and tightened.[60] Meanwhile in Paris, the Spanish ambassador, Conde de Aranda, although a personal friend of the *philosophes*, was moved to express strong complaints to the French government. Through him Carlos III demanded official apologies and action against the publisher, and so insistent were the importunities of the king to whom France was allied that his demands were granted.[61]

The ban on the importation of the *Encyclopédie méthodique* was later lifted but only on condition that in the future its text be purged and submitted to the Consejo de Castilla for approval. This was not the end of Panckoucke's troubles. In 1788 the inquisitor-general entered the arena and ordered all volumes collected for an expurgation. Floridablanca gave him royal support. In Madrid alone 1,681 volumes were seized, resulting in great losses for Panckoucke and the financial ruin of his Madrid agent.[62] The promised expurgation never took place, and the volumes were left in the archives of the Inquisición to be eaten by worms.[63] Copies in private hands were not all collected, either then or later. Several persons were known to own them, especially in the Basque provinces. They were later called "encyclopedistas" and suspected of dangerous ideas, but their main interest was probably only in up-to-date knowledge.[64]

[60] See above, p. 201.

[61] Sorrento, pp. 104-9, quoting the official French correspondence.

[62] *Indice ultimo*, p. 88; A.H.N., Inq., leg. 4481, No. 15; Bourgoing (1797), I, 286; Sarrailh, p. 301, citing A.H.N., Inq., leg. 4450.

[63] Blanco White found many in the palace of the Inquisición in Seville in 1809 (Blanco y Crespo, *Life*, I, 151-54). See Sarrailh, p. 301.

[64] See Miguel Manuel de Gamón (?), *comisario* of the Inquisición in San

The fate of Antonio de Sancha, who had early obtained permission to publish a translation of the *Encyclopédie méthodique,* was less severe. The furor over the article on Spain held up his progress, but by 1788 he was again receiving full official support. The first volume of his translation, devoted to natural history, which had eight hundred folio pages, was obligingly censored by six *calificadores* of the Inquisición in four days in order to help Sancha meet a publication deadline.[65] For this volume Sancha had 335 subscribers, including 50 in the Spanish colonies and 82 clergymen. His second volume, also on natural history, appeared in the same year and had 47 more subscribers.[66] The crown and the Inquisición were both still ready to help the publication of a work by a Spanish firm that would further the knowledge of science and could be prevented from containing the irreverences whose fear had caused the confiscation in that year of the French original.

In the meantime, the glove thrown down by an *Encyclopédie*—Spaniards hardly distinguished between Panckoucke's and Diderot's—was picked up by Spanish authors. Antonio Cabanilles, a young Spanish botanist then in Paris, was the first to issue a public reply to Masson's article "Espagne." He published his rebuttal in French. He accused Masson of ignoring the present state of Spain, Carlos III's projects in favor of agriculture, commerce, and the arts and sciences, of scarcely having heard of the societies of Amigos del País, and of making up for his ignorance with invective to please his readers. Cabanilles outlined what Spain had contributed to Europe in the last thousand years in art,

---

Sebastián, to inquisitor-general, Aug. 8, 1791, A.H.N., Inq., leg. 4430, No. 33; and Fermín de Lasala y Collado, *La separación de Guipúzcoa y la Paz de Basilea* (Madrid, 1895), pp. 139-41. Blanco White and Lasala y Collado refer to the "Enciclopedia," but in Spain few people realized the difference between Diderot's and Panckoucke's, and I feel reasonably certain that the "Enciclopedia" in question in both cases was the latter.

[65] A.H.N., Inq., leg. 4481, No. 15.

[66] *Encyclopedia metodica,* Vol. I, *Historia natural de los animales,* traducida del frances al castellano por D. Gregorio Manuel Sanz y Chanas, and Vol. II, *Historia natural de las aves,* traducida del frances al castellano por D. Joseph Mallent (Madrid, 1788).

science, theology, industry, and agriculture, but he especially stressed the achievements of Carlos III, which Masson had overlooked. Cabanilles was no jingoist. He favored modern learning and believed that in this field Spain deserved its share of respect. No sooner had his pamphlet appeared in France than it was translated and published by the Imprenta Real.[67]

Italy as well as Spain had felt the stinging scorn of the *philosophes* and its writers and editors were promptly moved to defend their kindred nation against Masson. An Italian churchman, Carlo Denina, read an apology of Spain in January 1786 at Frederick II's Academy of Berlin. Denina's discourse was translated and published in Cadiz and Valencia in 1786.[68]

The Spanish government encouraged replies to Masson among its own authors. The Academia Española offered a prize for the best "apology or defense of the nation limited to its progress in the arts and sciences" to be submitted to it.[69] In 1786 Floridablanca independently rewarded the best refutation of Masson with publication by the Imprenta Real at the cost of the government. As an appendix was added Denina's discourse in the original French. The Spanish author was given 6,000 reales and all the profits from the sale.[70] The person so favored was the already well-known figure, Juan Pablo Forner, whose defense of the Catholic religion was to appear in the following year. His apology was entitled *Oracion apologética por la España y su mérito literario.*

Forner saw in Masson merely the representation of eighteenth-century French thought, and he used his reply as a pretext for attacking the *philosophes* in general. He was especially incensed at the claim of such writers to be philosophic. True philosophers made use of their wisdom for the good of humanity—they pro-

[67] Cabanilles, *Observaciones sobre el artículo España de la nueva Encyclopedia* (1784).

[68] Carlo Denina, *Respuesta a la pregunta: Que se debe a la España?* Discurso leido en la Academia de Berlin, etc. por el Abate Denina (Cadiz and Valencia, 1786) (Sorrento, pp. 231, 254-60).

[69] *Gazeta,* Nov. 30, 1784, cited in *ibid.,* p. 129.

[70] Luis Villanueva in Forner, *Obras,* I, xiv; Cotarelo y Mori, p. 315.

duced practical results, not vain speculations—they were the legislators and social benefactors like Lycurgus, Pericles, and Socrates,
not idle thinkers like Plato with his ideas or Epicurus with his
atoms. Only two moderns fitted Forner's classification of beneficial philosophers who had produced useful knowledge, the
sixteenth-century Spaniard Luis Vives and Francis Bacon. They
would not have been dazzled by the eddies of Descartes, the
monads of Leibnitz, or even the famous law of gravity of Newton, Forner maintained. He lamented that, while Vives' works
on ethics were far more valuable than anything Descartes wrote,
yet Descartes was called the progenitor of European philosophy
and the country that produced Vives was considered rude and
barbarian. Spain had been learned in all ages. "We have not had
famous dreamers like Descartes and Newton, but we have had
the most just legislators and excellent practical philosophers."[71]
In a word, Forner held up to admiration two philosophers who
had abandoned scholasticism; while at the same time he rejected
the last century and a half of European thought devoted to the
destruction of vain rationalist systems, because he asserted that
such persons as Descartes, Voltaire, Rousseau, and even Newton
typified the useless thinking he condemned. Forner's writing was
often characterized by its heat. In the present case his anger at
the *philosophes'* scorn of Spain led him to condemn the modern
scientific advances whose application in Spain he too approved in
calmer moments.

Cañuelo was quick to catch up Forner's self contradiction.
The one hundred and thirteenth discourse of *El censor* replied
to the *Oracion apologética por la España,* to Denina, and in general to those who denounced modern learning. True science is
that which assures eternal life, he argued, mocking their stand.
Therefore those sciences are best which produce subjection,
ignominy, weakness, hunger, nakedness, and everything that is
poverty, the condition which most assures one of getting to heaven.
The sciences that produce wealth and knowledge are not true
sciences, they are false and futile. "Hence the true arts and sciences

---

[71] Forner, *Oracion apologética,* p. 12.

have flourished among us as in no other part of Europe." Despite
their natural resources so conducive to wealth imposed on the
Spanish for the sins of their fathers, they labored for predominance
in the true science until they reached a nearly perfect state of
poverty under Carlos II. Unfortunately, with the advent of French
princes in the eighteenth century, false lights led to a considerable growth of agriculture and commerce. "But let us console our-
selves, . . . we still have apologists to maintain our ignorance." To
Masson's question, "What do we owe to Spain?" *El censor* replied
that Spain had exploited America to enrich the rest of Europe
while impoverishing itself. Besides, "if we had furthered the other
arts and sciences, no one could now claim, obviously, that the
other nations had furthered them."[72]

Having begun with such *éclat,* the controversy continued fer-
vently in the Spanish press. Forner replied with a long-winded
"Contestacion al discourso CXIII del Censor" that at times
matched Cañuelo's satiric wit. He objected to the implication
that theology produced poverty and challenged *El censor* to
show how one should insert some observations on the multiplication of hens into a treatise on the Trinity.[73] An anonymous author
in Burgos, probably a clergyman, who signed himself "Patricio
Redondo," also took offense at *El censor's* scorn of Spanish theology and religious institutions.[74] Naturally the other side replied.
El censor devoted an issue to an "Oracion apologética por el Africa
y su mérito literario," which was a masterful parody of Forner's
original *Oracion apologética por la España y su mérito literario*
(Masson had likened Spain to Africa).[75] An anonymous author
published ten letters discussing Forner's *Oracion,* said to be
written by a Spaniard in Paris to his brother in Madrid. The
author accused Forner of replying to Masson only with insults
and of painting only the bad side of foreign thinkers. "Descartes

[72] *El censor*, Discurso 113, July 13, 1786.

[73] Juan Pablo Forner, "Contestacion al discurso CXIII del Censor," included
as the first appendix to the edition cited of Forner, *Oracion apologética.*

[74] *En boca cerrada no entra mosca. Carta al Corresponsal del Censor sobre el
dicurso CXIII. pag. 841 del mismo Censor* . . . , por D. Patricio Redondo,
ciudadano de Burgos . . . ([Madrid, 1786]).

[75] *El censor*, Discurso 165.

did not write only his system, nor Newton his attraction, nor Bayle, Voltaire, and Rousseau only against religion." As for progress in the natural and physical sciences, "any comparison [Forner] wishes to draw can only make us blush."[76]

The Masson *affaire* spread from pamphlets into the periodical press. The liberal journals backed up *El censor, El apologista universal* taking the field against Forner in two numbers,[77] and the *Conversaciones de Perico y Marica* agreeing with *El censor's* opinion of apologists. Rather than bragging about their good qualities, the Spanish should work to stamp out the errors that existed in their country, Perico said. "If we, so proud of being Catholics, do not extirpate known errors, . . . let us not complain that M. Masson calls Spain a superstitious nation, because this complaint will make our ignominy eternal."[78] A letter published in the *Correo de Madrid* called Forner's reply to *El censor* unintelligible and its attempt to ridicule the sciences absurd.[79] Three years later the same periodical carried a detailed rebuttal of the first of the letters against Forner said to have been written from Paris. The author was none other than Forner himself. This was merely the last of a series of publications by this testy gentleman directed against the journalists who were nettling him, and like most of them it was anonymous.[80] The semi-official *Memorial literario* supported Forner's struggle indirectly by carrying "defenses" of Barcelona and Cadiz against the inexact descriptions of these cities given in Masson's article.[81] The point was reached in 1787 when one could scarcely read a periodical without finding a reference to Masson or "apologists" used to clinch some argument or other.

[76] *Cartas de un Español residente en París á su hermano residente en Madrid, sobre la oracion apologética por la España y su mérito literario de don Juan Pablo Forner* (Madrid, 1788). Cotarelo y Mori says many believed the author to be Tomás de Iriarte (p. 321), and Menéndez Pelayo attributes them to him (Sorrento, p. 238). Forner said the author was Antonio Borrego, but he was evidently playing on the meanings of the word "borrego," although Cotarelo y Mori takes him seriously (p. 321).

[77] Nos. 13 and 14 (Cotarelo y Mori, p. 318-20).

[78] Conversación segunda, p. 102, Conversación tercera, pp. 181-82.

[79] *Correo de Madrid*, Aug. 8, 1787.   [80] Cotarelo y Mori, pp. 318-22.

[81] *Memorial literario*, June 1787, pp. 182-94, Dec. 1787, pp. 537-48, 625-37.

Fortunately the excitement over the Masson *affaire* produced more than vain polemics. Sempere y Guarinos attributed the writing of his *Ensayo de una biblioteca española de los mejores escritores del reinado de Carlos III*, the best contemporary account of Spain's intellectual activity under its enlightened king, to the realization, which he got from reading Masson's article, of the need to publicize Spain's recent accomplishments. He conceived it to be the best kind of apology of Spain, and he had the satisfaction of seeing his volumes reviewed in French, Italian, and Swedish journals.[82] Valladares similarly considered his *Semanario erudito*, which published little known works of Spanish thinkers, to be a practical reply to foreigners and Spaniards who scorned Spanish letters.[83] Floridablanca himself in ordering a census of Spain in 1786 said that one of its purposes was to show foreigners "that the kingdom is not so deserted as they and their writers believe." When the census appeared, it stressed the point that Spain's population had increased almost one and one half millions since the last census in 1768 while the number of priests, monks, and other privileged persons had declined.[84]

The heat of the argument caused by the article "Espagne" of the *Encyclopédie méthodique* tended to hide the true nature of the dispute. Few of those who attacked Forner and the other "apologists" proposed to defend Masson. The war of pens was waged between those who saw in Spain's past greatness, material, intellectual, and religious, a far more valuable achievement than the, in their eyes, destructive efforts of the popular French *philosophes*, and those who felt that Spain's past greatness, however laudable, was separated from the present by two centuries of degradation, and that Spain's present need was to catch up with the last century and a half of European progress in practical and theoretical science and philosophy. Forner, by implication, denied the value of Carlos III's accomplishments. His enemies

[82] Sempere, *Biblioteca*, I, 40-41, IV, i-iv.

[83] *Semanario erudito*, prospectus.

[84] Circular of Floridablanca, July 25, 1786, and *Censo español executado de orden del rey . . . en el año 1787* (Madrid, 1787), "advertencia," both quoted in Sorrento, p. 229.

supported the king's policy of enlightenment and attacked Forner not to defend Masson's scorn of their country but to defend the break with the past that was being made in Spain. When the dispute is analyzed in this fashion, it becomes evident that those apologists who replied to Masson by pointing out Spain's recent progress, such as Cabanilles, Sempere y Guarinos, and, despite his official backing of the *Oracion apologética por la España*, even Floridablanca, agreed basically not with Forner and "Patricio Redondo" but with *El censor* and the *Conversaciones de Perico y Marica*. The dispute was essentially the same as that which had torn the Spanish universities since 1770 and which had distinguished the more advanced religious orders, like the Augustinians, from those who still defended scholastic philosophy. It was the struggle between enlightenment and conservatism. The Masson *affaire* only provided a pretext for airing the controversy widely in the public press.

The stand taken by conservative Spaniards in the debate could have been anticipated. Since the Counterreformation it had become second nature for millions of Spaniards to feel that their Catholic country confronted a hostile outside world and physically or spiritually to take their country's side. Those who objected to the doctrines of the Enlightenment found a plea to preserve national norms and traditions both natural and logical. Conservative replies to Masson fell back on this ingrained xenophobia.

The reaction of progressive Spaniards to Masson's contemptuous statements was not so cut and dried. For half a century they had been trying to assimilate the foreign Enlightenment and spread it at home. They wanted to bring Spain up to the level of the rest of western Europe. As was the case with their counterparts elsewhere, their motives combined a conviction that all men should be brothers with a strong love of their own country. In founding the first society of Amigos del País in 1765 the Conde de Peñaflorida exhorted its members, "My friends, love your native land, love your common glory, love Man, and finally show yourselves worthy friends of the Country and worthy friends of Humanity."[85] Ten years later, almost in the terms with which Rousseau was then addressing the sorely afflicted Poles, Cadalso urged Spain to stimulate the patriotism of its youth by honoring in public the memory of its past heroes. "Don't you think that every individual ought to devote every care to contributing to the good of the *patria*?"[86] Cadalso, Peñaflorida, and the other bearers of enlightenment felt that the best way to demonstrate love of country was by becoming members in good standing of an international fraternity devoted to the good of humanity. They did not realize that for all the generous talk of their French masters about Man, the French had unconsciously inherited from Louis XIV a conviction of their own superiority over the other peoples of continental Europe. When, like France's Sun King, Masson compared Spain to Africa, he was only giving conspicuous expression to the real feelings of the champions of the *lumières*. The Spaniards who had thought they best served their country by paraphrasing French writers suddenly had to choose between the two objects of their enthusiasm. Without hesitation they came to the defense of their wronged country. The stand they took was not unique in Europe. A more famous member of the Enlightenment, Johann Gottfried von Herder, was at this very time trying to convince Germans they had within themselves powers which, if nurtured, would outshine any light they could produce by reflecting French civilization.

Similar reactions of enlightened Europeans to the superior attitude of the *philosophes* could be found in Italy and elsewhere. The development has been credited with sowing the seeds of modern nationalism and preparing the breakup of the one mankind of the Enlightenment.[87] Spain felt this enlightened or humanitarian nationalism just as it shared the other currents of the time. The result was not the origin of Spanish nationalism; this was old and its spirit was embodied in the writing of the

[85] Quoted in Sarrailh, p. 245 n. 2.

[86] Cadalso, *Cartas marruecas*, pp. 57-60, 175, Cartas 16, 70. On Spanish enlightened patriotism see Sarrailh's remarkable chapter, "Connaissance et amour de l'Espagne," pp. 373-407.

[87] By Paul Hazard in *La pensée européenne au XVIII° siècle, de Montesquieu à Lessing* (Paris, 1946), II, 220-63.

conservatives. But the enlightened patriotism of progressive Spaniards was new in that their continued attachment to the *luces* gave it a profoundly different cast from the reactionary chauvinism of their domestic opponents. At the same time, the sudden realization of their patriotism, brought on by Masson's article, tended to break the spell that French thinkers had woven over Spanish partisans of enlightenment. The Masson *affaire* not only aired the difference between progressive and conservative camps in Spain but drove a wedge between the progressive camps in Spain and France. It was the most pregnant incident in the history of the Enlightenment in Spain before 1789.

4

Behind the struggle of ideas going on in the Spanish press, hidden from the casual reader but not hard to detect with a little insight, lay the less idealistic economic and social motives that affected the proponents of the two sides. The majority of the men who favored enlightenment were royal officials, those persons who were prospering from commerce and industry, and those nobles and clergymen who by individual temperament believed with Cañuelo that it was "the penance imposed on the sons of Adam to eat their bread by the sweat of their brows." They welcomed the *luces* and the royal reforms that they felt were bringing prosperity to Spain, and they wanted to see broken the economic and social preeminence of those who owed their present wealth and power to privilege and inheritance. The bourgeois wanted Spain to become economically strong and progressive, consciously or subconsciously aware that they would benefit from the growth of manufactures and trade. Idealistic nobles and churchmen were ready if necessary to sacrifice the position and authority of their successors to the good of the whole country.

Conservative members of the religious orders, on the other hand, in general feared the breakup of the large landholdings held under their dead hand. They feared the loss of control over education. They must have perceived more or less clearly that if land and education and government were to fall to men interested in progress and science, their own hold on the minds and hearts of the people of Spain would be weakened. Others besides them stood to benefit by their stand. In speaking for themselves they were also protecting the señores, *caciques,* and *regidores*—the rural oligarchy of Spain. Churchmen almost alone took the lead in championing their position openly if indirectly. The rest of the oligarchy for the most part still relied on evasive noncompliance and silent opposition. Many, lulled by their growing wealth, probably failed to realize distinctly their own stake in the great debate in progress.

Below these social groups the lower classes so far still remained outside the fray. Although clergymen had occasionally denounced the lights of the century in their preaching, appeal had not yet been made to the common people in any systematic fashion, and there is no evidence that significant numbers of workers or peasants were consciously taking sides. The contest was between the two groups who were profiting from Spain's economic recovery, and the court before which they pleaded their case was the reading public—the members of their own groups who were not yet emotionally involved in the dispute. And in the end, the pleadings were directed at the crown and its ministers, whose right to decide the policies to be adopted in Spain was not openly questioned by either side.

As was said before, the controversy did not involve a dispute over fundamental forms of government or religion. Absolute monarchy was the ideal political constitution of all parties; the progressives cheered enlightened despotism, the conservatives cried that the throne was in danger; neither advocated a change from the present political system. And even among the most enlightened, hardly a trace has been found of a desire to free Spain from universal observance of the Catholic religion. Carlos and his advisers must have sensed the strength that this basic agreement gave to the fabric of the Spanish nation. Sure of it, they could, with a minimum of interference, permit controversy in the press which indirectly brought into question their most cherished policies.

More than accident accounted for the continuation of Spain's underlying spiritual unity. The economic growth that the country experienced, especially after 1766, tended to reduce tensions between the new middle class and the landed oligarchy. In France, by contrast, 1770 saw a change from a period of increasing prosperity to one of diminishing prosperity. The next two decades witnessed mounting ill will between French nobility and bourgeoisie, but during this period the two leading social groups in Spain were both profiting from good times. Here the critical looks of the individuals who formed each group were directed less at the others' pretensions than at the economic policies of the crown, which they felt could have a strong influence on their own position.

More important perhaps than the economic factor in preventing discord between the potentially rival forces in Spain was the nature of the government. For a whole generation, while businessmen and landholders were growing strong, while the *luces* provided the basis for disputes in universities and press, while the reform spirit of the Jansenists was mining a breach in the clergy, Spaniards had a king who won their love and admiration. When Carlos came from Italy in 1759, his subjects felt slight attachment to this stranger surrounded by foreign ministers. The riots of 1766 showed how little they yet liked his administration. Carlos learned thereafter to become more Spanish and to look to Spaniards for his councilors. The process that began with the departure of Squillace and the advent of Aranda was completed when Floridablanca replaced Grimaldi as secretary of state for foreign affairs in 1776. The war against England from 1779 to 1783 and the flowering of the country in the succeeding years hardened the loyalty of Spaniards to their king. The unaffected religious devotion of Carlos, which shone through all his conflicts with Rome and domestic ultramontanes, gave Spaniards confidence in the wisdom of his policies. They admired his loyalty to the memory of his wife, dead a year after they reached Madrid, and his chastity, so rare in kings. They respected his frugality, which abhorred public display and extravagance; and they condoned, as a foreigner like Townsend could not, the time and money he devoted to his second passion, the hunt.[88]

His first passion, as with all great rulers, was in furthering the welfare of his state. As soon as he reached Spain, he astonished his court and councilors by spending several hours a day at matters of administration.[89] After twenty-four years' experience as king of Naples, he knew how to recognize and appreciate wisdom in his subordinates. The changes he made in his government regularly brought in men of higher quality; for, unlike many more famous sovereigns, he did not grow jealous of the reputation of his ministers. In his last years Floridablanca shared the confidence of Carlos like a partner more than like a servant. Bourgoing could well observe:

> The stability of the ministers is one of the most remarkable features of the court of Spain. The monarch, who consults public opinion when he fills the highest posts, has until now had the rare good fortune of almost never having had his expectations belied by later events. And so his ministers, instead of abandoning themselves to the idleness that such security would be expected to produce, seek to justify his confidence, and do not lose precious time in spying out the workings of intrigue and foiling its plots. They have the courage to form vast projects because they know that only their death will stop the execution of their plans.[90]

By giving no chance for divisions to flourish at the core of the Spanish state, Carlos helped check the growth of divisions throughout Spanish society. His cherished plans could be put into effect with the least possible opposition. In 1789 the Spanish ambassador to France wrote to Floridablanca: "None of the

[88] Townsend, II, 123-26.
[89] Dispatch of D'Ossun, French ambassador to Madrid, quoted in Sarrailh, p. 582 (date not given).
[90] Bourgoing (1789), I, 131-32.

causes [for revolution] that could have been observed here for many years exist in our country, where one finds religion, love for the king, devotion to the law, moderation in the administration, scrupulous respect for the privileges of each province and individual, . . . and a thousand other things that the French lack."[91] Largely because a sincerely religious king had given Spain firm leadership during the Enlightenment, the basic unity of the nation had been maintained.

Contemporaries did not anticipate a change in the near future. No one in Spain in the 1780's could know that within a decade they would be involved, without any fault of their own, in the greatest upheaval in Europe between the sixteenth and twentieth centuries and that this upheaval would reveal the instability of the balance achieved by Carlos III among the different forces in Spanish society. Historians are guilty of the worst kind of hindsight who vituperate or eulogize Carlos and his ministers because the movements they furthered were to react differently than they anticipated under situations which no one could then foresee or conceive. An honest observer must agree with the judgment of Carlos' contemporaries, who saw only that he was leading the country in a cultural and economic revival and that the country was united in loyalty to the king.

When one looks at that decade [1781-90], one is struck by the growth of the *luces* and the energy with which were sprouting the seeds sown under Fernando VI and the first years of Carlos III. In the countless writings that were published each year, in the dissertations of the academies, in the memoirs of the societies, in the scientific establishments that were founded, in those of charity that were everywhere being erected and endowed, in the reforms of the universities, in the governmental regulations that were issued in agreement with good principles of administration, in the new aspect of the Spanish landscape, with the canals, roads, and public

[91] Conde de Fernán-Núñez to Floridablanca, Nov. 23, 1789, quoted in Albert Mousset, *Un témoin ignoré de la Révolution, le comte de Fernan Nuñez* (Paris, 1924), pp. 155-56.

buildings that were being built and opened, in everything, finally, one could see a fermentation which, if continued, promised immense progress in Spanish wealth and civilization. Perhaps there were too many literary wars, perhaps the different branches which create prosperity were not furthered and more care and zeal were spent on the decoration of the edifice than on its mortar; these failings take away none of the honor deserved by a period of so much life, so much energy, so much hard work, and whose products we still enjoy after thirty years during which we have been spending them without cessation and one can say without replacing them.[92]

Such was the vision of his youth recalled by the liberal leader Manuel José Quintana as he looked back from the period of the Restoration. His memory was substantially correct. Carlos III did more for Spain than any monarch since Isabel. Among the enlightened despots of his own day, none was a more successful ruler.

92 Quintana, *loc.cit.*, pp. 113-14.

PART II

THE REVOLUTION

CHAPTER VIII

FLORIDABLANCA'S GREAT FEAR

CARLOS III died on December 14, 1788. His son ascended the throne as Carlos IV. Although the new king was already forty years old and had been initiated by his father into some of the complexities of government, his political capacities were still unknown. As Principe de Asturias, he and his strong willed wife, María Luisa, had headed a circle of friends that avoided the stern presence of the old king. Carlos IV's first reaction upon becoming the new master of Spain was, nevertheless, to leave untouched the policy and ministers that he inherited. Reportedly obeying a last request of his father, he kept the Conde de Floridablanca as first secretary of state.[1] Not the advent of a new king but a factor outside the country was the first to disrupt the Spain of Carlos III. That factor was the French Revolution.

In 1788 Louis XVI was forced by a collapse of the royal finances to convoke the Estates General of France for the first time in nearly two centuries. Although the Estates were not to meet until May 1789, excitement was immediate. Soon the Spanish ambassador to Versailles, the Conde de Fernán-Núñez, was describing in his dispatches the heated state of France. He told of a serious shortage of grain, of riots in Paris, of the growing enthusiasm for the Third Estate, and of the alarming spread of "anglomania" and "republican doctrines."[2]

News closer to home soon bore out the seriousness of the times. Spain too was in the throes of a grain shortage. In 1787 and 1788 the government legislated vainly to keep Spanish wheat from being exported and grain prices stable.[3] A sudden rise in

[1] Andrés Muriel, *Historia de Carlos IV* ("Memorial histórico español: colección de documentos, opúsculos y antigüedades que publica la Real Academia de la Historia," Vols. XXIX-XXXIV) (Madrid, 1893-94), I, 5.

[2] Dispatches of July 18, Aug. 30, Sept. 1, Nov. 28, 1788, Apr. 27, 1789, quoted in Mousset, pp. 40-43.

[3] Hamilton, *War and Prices*, pp. 196-97.

the price of bread in Barcelona, which imported much wheat from abroad, caused riots on February 28 and the first days of March, 1789. Taken by surprise, the captain-general of Catalonia submitted to the demands of the city for price control. Although peace was thus restored, the Madrid government sent in troops, and a new captain-general deported ninety-five ringleaders and hanged seven others despite the strong remonstrances of the city.[4]

A difficulty like this in a province traditionally restive made news from France seem doubly alarming to the Spanish rulers. When the Estates General met at Versailles in May 1789, a majority of its members, after overcoming the opposition of many noble and ecclesiastical deputies, decided to call themselves the National Assembly and draw up a constitution for France. The people of Paris and the countryside thereupon resorted to violence to show their sympathy with reform. These developments revolted Floridablanca. As a practical man he feared the consequences for the Franco-Spanish alliance if the Assembly should get control of the army and navy, as the English Parliament had.[5] But his worries went deeper. However much he believed in enlightened progress, his concepts left no place for leadership and authority outside the hands of the king and his servants. He wrote to Fernán-Núñez: "It is said that this enlightened century has taught man his rights. But it has also taken away, besides his true happiness, peace and the security of his person and family. We want here neither so much light nor its effects: insolent acts, words, and writings against legitimate authority."[6] Months earlier he had taken the decision to keep Spaniards ignorant of events in France.

The creation of the Junta de Estado, or council of ministers, in 1787 had centralized the Spanish administration under this body, with Floridablanca at its head. He was therefore able to translate his desire to suppress news from France into the policy

[4] Baumgarten, p. 240; Miguel S. Oliver, "Notes històriques sobre Catalunya en temps de la Revolució francesa," *Institut d'Estudis Catalans, Anuari*, IV (1911-12), 190-98.

[5] Dispatch of Sandoz-Rollin, July 27, 1789, cited by Baumgarten, p. 234.

[6] Floridablanca to Fernán-Núñez, July 1789 (?), quoted in Mousset, p. 49.

of all the organs of government. The official *Gazeta de Madrid,* devoted to domestic and foreign affairs, did not even mention the convocation and assembly of the Estates General. While the Estates were debating in May and June whether to meet as one body or three, the only news that the *Gazeta* carried from Versailles was of the burial of the dauphin and the movement of the royal court to Marly and back.[7] Reports from Paris in July, the month that saw the capture of the Bastille, covered only a meeting of the council of war and the royal presentation of a cardinal's hat to a bishop.[8] The officially imposed silence was to continue for three years. What bits of news from France were to appear in the *Gazeta* did not concern politics. The *Mercurio de España,* a monthly review of news, also official, was equally reticent; and the other periodicals had never been authorized to publish reports of foreign political events.

Spaniards soon gave encouraging evidence that they were being successfully shielded from the new French light that Floridablanca dreaded. On September 21, 1789 eight days of festivity began in Madrid to celebrate the coronation of Carlos IV. Some sixty-five thousand persons poured into the city from the provinces for the occasion. Bull fights were held in the Plaza Mayor at which crowds of over forty thousand were accommodated. These assembled masses of people, different from their northern neighbors, observed an order and decorum, without the need of police supervision, that astounded the foreigners present. The minister from Prussia, David Alfons von Sandoz-Rollin, on this occasion sang the praises of the Spanish people, so pious, so submissive, so content, the most reliable pillar of the Spanish regime. "The Spanish people are good, noble, and peaceable," he wrote home.[9]

At the same time Carlos IV convoked the atrophied Spanish representative body, the Cortes de Castilla, to recognize his son Fernando as the heir to the throne and to take up other important questions. Deputies from thirty-seven cities of Spain met for

---

[7] *Gazeta,* July 3, 10, 1789. [8] *Ibid.,* Aug. 4, 11, 1789.
[9] Quoted in Baumgarten, p. 249.

nearly two months under the presidency of the Conde de Campomanes. Acting under an oath of secrecy, they approved a revision
of the law of succession to the throne. They discussed royal
proposals to limit the privilege of entail of the nobility and to
permit the enclosure of orchards. By their lack of enthusiasm
rather than by direct opposition, they caused both proposals to
be abandoned. They made minor petitions and were satisfied
with evasive replies. Nowhere was there a sign of questioning
the royal power. If there was any opposition, it was a passive
resistance to the ideas of reform of the royal ministers. In the
literature of the time these Cortes went unperceived, and indeed
they could give little inspiration to future Spanish constitutional-
ists. In 1809 one of these, in need of domestic precedents, cried,
"Illustrious representative of Burgos, in the last [Cortes] celebrated in 1789, your patriotic voice was the last gasp of liberty!"[10]
The deputy from Burgos, immediately after the Cortes had been
formally opened by the king and before the oath of secrecy, made
three requests in the name of all the members of the assembly:
requests which were all three of trifling character (one was for
the deputies to be assigned good seats at the forthcoming bull
fights).[11] This was the hero of liberty of the Cortes of 1789.
"What a contrast between these Cortes and the French National
Assembly!" Sandoz-Rollin wrote after their meeting was closed.
"All the members kneeled with uncovered, bowed heads as the
king appeared to dismiss them."[12]

2

Floridablanca was less reassured than the Prussian minister.
Despite the loyalty of the Cortes, his peace of mind continued to

[10] [José Canga Argüelles?], *Observaciones sobre las Cortes de España y su
organizacion* (Valencia, 1809), p. 12.

[11] *Colección de documentos inéditos para la historia de España,* ed. Miguel
Salvá and Pedro Sainz de Baranda, Vol. XVII (Madrid, 1850), pp. 62-64. The
official records of the Cortes of 1789 are published in pp. 5-541 of this volume.
They have been ably analyzed by Baumgarten, pp. 241-65.

[12] Dispatch of Nov. 8, 1789, quoted in Baumgarten, p. 265.

be disturbed by the specter of the Revolution. It was soon clear that censorship of the official news organs could not alone keep Spain ignorant of events in France. French newspapers and pamphlets entered the country freely during the summer of 1789. By July 27 the fall of the Bastille was known in Madrid and had caused excitement among the people.[13] Throughout Spain there were those who had learned by the end of the summer that France was in ferment and that the National Assembly had attempted to calm the nerves of the countryside by declaring the abolition of feudal privileges and issuing a "Declaration of the rights of man and the citizen." The government's control of the entry into Spain of foreign publications had not been geared to the problems presented by the proliferation of the Revolutionary press.

Not until the middle of September was any determined action taken to check this influx of news. On September 18 and October 1 royal orders, products of the zeal of Floridablanca, instructed the customs officers at the frontiers and maritime ports that "all prints, papers, printed matter, manuscripts, boxes, fans, and any other object alluding to the events in France" were to be remitted by them directly to the secretary of state.[14] At the same time Floridablanca also turned to the Inquisición for help. On September 21 he sent to the inquisitor-general, Agustín Rubín de Cevallos, a royal determination charging the Santo Oficio with collecting any published or manuscript matter "directly or indirectly opposed to the subordination, vassalage, obedience, and reverence owed to our venerated monarch and to the vicar of Jesus Christ because such ideas are anti-evangelical and expressly opposed to the doctrines of the holy apostles Peter and Paul."[15] Four days later Rubín de Cevallos sent out the order

---

[13] M. Geoffroy de Grandmaison, *L'ambassade française en Espagne pendant la Révolution (1789-1804)* (Paris, 1892), p. 5.

[14] *Nov. rec.* VIII, xviii, nota 15; and reference to it in *real cédula*, Aug. 22, 1792, "Fraile," Vol. 785, fol. 100.

[15] Referred to in Inquisición de Toledo to Consejo de la Inquisición, Oct. 3, 1789, A.H.N., Inq., leg. 4430, No. 1.

to the fourteen local tribunals of the Inquisición and to its *comisarios* in the major Spanish ports.[16]

The replies of these tribunals upon receipt of the order showed the progress that the dissemination of French publications had made. The maritime ports and frontier provinces had been the most affected. The important colony of French merchants in Cadiz greeted the news of the Revolution with great joy. They had a sort of club for reading and recreation, known as the Casa de la Camorra, in a former opera house to which they alone had keys. Here they now began to receive Revolutionary publications in great quantities. On one day alone the postage paid on them was five hundred reales. These Frenchmen spread the tidings everywhere by their conversations and by circulating books, papers, and manuscripts. Such was the report of the local *comisario* of the Inquisición.[17] In Barcelona the tribunal received from a *comisario* on August 20 a two volume *Recueil de pièces intéressantes pour servir à l'histoire de la révolution de 1789 en France*.[18] At the other end of the Pyrenees the *comisario* in San Sebastián reported: "The printed works and manuscripts that have been circulating here since July are those that are concerned with the present events of the revolutions in France and its general assembly. The city is flooded with this kind of paper, whose acquisition is made easy by its commerce, its situation near the frontier, and its population, composed in large part of members of that nation, who praise and proclaim these events in their conversations."[19] The Inquisición de Logroño, charged with watching the provinces bordering southwestern France, replied to the inquisitor-general that it had already received thirty-six items dealing with the Revolution from various centers in northern Castile and the Basque provinces. Most of these were

---

[16] *Ibid.*; P. Sánchez Manuel to Rubín de Cevallos, Oct. 20, 1789, *ibid.*, leg. 4429, No. 34; M. M. de Gamón (?) to Rubín de Cevallos, Oct. 2, 1789, *ibid.*, leg. 4430, No. 5.

[17] Sánchez Manuel to Rubín de Cevallos, June 29, 1790, *ibid.*, leg. 4429, No. 34; Rubín de Cevallos to Floridablanca, July 9, 1790, *ibid.*, leg. 4430, No. 12. Fischer, *Travels in Spain*, p. 308, gives a few details on the Camorra.

[18] A.H.N., Inq., leg. 4429, No. 4.

[19] Gamón (?) to Rubín de Cevallos, Oct. 2, 1789, *loc.cit.*

separate issues of Paris newspapers and of the *Journal de ce qui se passe de plus interessant aux États généraux ouverts à Versailles le 5 mai 1789*, published in Bayonne, but among them were also the *Cahier du tiers état de . . . Lyon* and a speech by the Protestant leader Jean-Paul Rabaut-Saint-Étienne. This tribunal had moreover discovered several Spanish translations of Revolutionary pieces circulating in manuscript: a "Discurso que hizo sobre los bienes de la clerecia Mr. Alexandro Lamet en la Asamblea nacional," another beginning "En la asamblea se ha disputado mucho sobre si el Rey debe dar sancion a las leyes . . . ," and a third that began "Articulos—los hombres nacen y permanecen libres . . ." (the rights of man!), and others.[20]

Farther inland Revolutionary literature was less prevalent, but it was already present. The Inquisición de Valladolid reported in October that it had collected the observations on religion by the French minister Jacques Necker, five other volumes printed in France dealing with the Revolution, and manuscript copies in French of five issues of the *Courrier patriotique*.[21] A few days later it reported a Spanish translation, found in Oviedo, dealing with the fall of the Bastille.[22] From elsewhere appeared a manuscript translation made in August headed "Revoluciones de Paris, Segda edicion, Diario del 12 al 17 de Julio de 1789" covering the events of these days, and another describing the taking of the Bastille and the famous session of the National Assembly of the night of August 4, that declared an end to feudal privileges.[23] Another manuscript in Spanish describing the taking of the Bastille was turned up south of Madrid in Ocaña.[24] Even more

[20] Inquisición de Logroño to Consejo de la Inquisición, Oct. 26, 1789, A.H.N., Inq., leg. 4430, No. 5.

[21] Inquisición de Valladolid to Consejo de la Inquisición, Oct. 24, 1789, *ibid.*, No. 3.

[22] "Discurso sobre la libertad francesa, pronunciado en el dia miercoles cinco de Agosto en la festividad consagrada a la memoria de los ciudadanos, que murieron en la toma de la Bastilla, por Monsiur el Abate Fauchet," Inquisición de Valladolid to Consejo de la Inquisición, Nov. 3, 1789, *ibid.*, leg. 4429, No. 32.

[23] *Ibid.*, leg. 4430, Nos. 8, 15. The provenance of these MSS is not indicated.

[24] "Extracto de carta de un diputado de los Estados Grales escrita a un negociante de Nantes desde Versailles con fecha de diez y ocho de Julio de 1789," report of *comisario* of Ocaña, Feb. 26, 1790, *ibid.*, leg. 4429, No. 29.

startling was the news that the bishop of Palencia had a work in French "which appears to contain the fundamental maxims and rules and the form of government of the French constitution"—again evidently the Declaration of the rights of man—and that he was permitting copies of it to be made and circulated. The Consejo de la Inquisición promised to deal with him directly.[25]

The Inquisición de Valladolid had also found two manuscript copies of a "Cathecismo frances para las gentes del campo," one in French and the other in Spanish. Logroño too had turned up such a manuscript. The tribunals of Santiago in northwest Spain and of Murcia in the southeast also reported it, all within the month of October and all in Spanish. Although this catechism was apparently directed only to the French people, all the agents of the Santo Oficio considered it dangerous; for it denied the king the power of legislation, saying it belonged to the people, and "vastly despises the clergy according to the suggestions of the philosophers of this unhappy century."[26] How rapidly and how far this pamphlet must already have circulated can be conjectured from its having been found in five widely scattered spots within a few weeks of the royal order of September 18 to collect such matter. According to a dispatch of Fernán-Núñez of this very date, a member of a Paris club had boasted that preachers of the doctrine of liberty had been sent into Spain and that revolutionary papers were being translated for wider distribution.[27] Perhaps there was a direct connection between this boast and the appearance of the "Cathecismo frances."

The Consejo de la Inquisición ordered all the papers that had been found sent to it in Madrid. After they had been "qualified," that is, censored, Rubín de Cevellos issued an edict on December 13, 1789: "Be it known [he said] that having learned that there

[25] Inquisición de Valladolid to Consejo, Nov. 3, 1789, *loc.cit.*, and marginal note of Consejo.

[26] Inquisición de Valladolid to Consejo, Oct. 24, 1789, *loc.cit.*; Inquisición de Logroño to Consejo, Oct. 26, 1789, *loc.cit.*; Inquisición de Santiago to Consejo, Oct. 16, 1789, *ibid.*, leg. 4430, No. 2; Inquisición de Murcia to Consejo, Oct. 3, 1789, *ibid.*, No. 4 (quotation from Inquisición de Santiago).

[27] Dispatch of Sept. 18, 1789, cited by Mousset, p. 153.

had been spread in these kingdoms various books and treatises and papers that without limiting themselves to a simple narration of events in their nature seditious and of the worst example, seem to form a theoretical-practical code of independence from legitimate powers," the Inquisición had had them examined and had found that they were written "in a style of pure anti-Christian naturalism" and were the "products of a new race of philosophers, men of corrupted minds." The edict continued with a list of forty-one titles that were prohibited, and the condemnation was extended to include all other papers that should appear in Spain containing the same perverse doctrines.[28]

The civil government also took warning from this invasion of dangerous literature. Floridablanca signed a royal resolution on December 29, 1789 directed to all Spanish post offices. They were ordered not to deliver any printed matter coming from abroad either unsealed, as was customary in order to enjoy a lower postage rate, or sealed in envelopes if the size and weight of these betrayed their contents. If they were claimed by the addressees, the papers were to be examined and delivered only if found harmless. The reason given for this resolution was that private persons and public officials had received, through the mail from abroad in plain wrappers that did not indicate who had sent them, publications that defamed the royal ministers and magistrates of Spain and the "most respectable tribunals of the monarchy."[29] One can guess that these tribunals included the Inquisición. On January 1, 1790 a royal order prohibited the introduction, printing, or circulation of books, papers, prints, boxes, fans, folders, and other objects referring to the revolutions in France. The order contained a warning that it was to be rigorously enforced.[30] At the same time Fernán-Núñez was instructed to ask all Spaniards in France not to write of what was happening to any one in

[28] A.H.N., Inq., leg. 4429, No. 2. Its publication in León is in "Fraile," Vol. 855, fol. 59. The list of works prohibited is in *Indice ultimo*, pp. 290-92.

[29] Quoted in *Gazette nationale ou le Moniteur universel* (hereafter cited as "*Moniteur*"), Feb. 10, 1790, and referred to in Sánchez Manuel to Rubín de Cevallos, June 29, 1790, *loc.cit.*

[30] Aguirre, *Prontuario . . . 1792*, pp. 216-17.

Spain.[31] In other words the government had determined to silence all public discussion of events north of the Pyrenees. Even the officers of the army received instructions from Floridablanca to "abstain from speaking of the present state of France."[32]

3

With the coming of 1790, the atmosphere in France seemed to cool off. The Assembly was proceeding with the task of drawing up a constitution that would reorganize French society according to the lay spirit of the Enlightenment, obeying the dictates of nature and not those of tradition, feudal parchments, or revealed truth. In the new lay state, all religions would be tolerated, and, according to the Civil Constitution of the Clergy enacted in 1790, the French branch of the Catholic Church was made almost independent of Rome. A constitutional monarchy was to replace royal absolutism. France was presented with its new constitution in 1791.

While Floridablanca warily observed these developments, various domestic troubles combined to keep his nerves on edge. Since the last years of Carlos III, a group of aristocratic and military malcontents had gathered around the figure of the Conde de Aranda, recently retired from his post as ambassador in Paris. Manuscript satires were circulated attacking the Conde de Floridablanca, whom the nobility hated for his power and his low origin. The favor of Carlos IV did not abandon the first secretary he had inherited, and those involved in spreading the satires were caught and exiled from Madrid, but the high nobles hiding behind them were not molested.[33]

On June 18, 1790 Floridablanca, walking alone in the royal

[31] Floridablanca to Fernán-Núñez, Dec. 21, 1789, cited by Mousset, p. 156.

[32] Dispatch of Zinoviev, Russian ambassador in Madrid, Dec. 1789, cited by Alexandre Tratchevsky, "L'Espagne à l'époque de la Révolution française," *Revue historique*, xxxi (1886), 29.

[33] Cayetano Alcázar, "España en 1792: Floridablanca, su derrumbamiento del gobierno y sus procesos de responsabilidad política," *Revista de estudios políticos*, No. 71 (Sept.-Oct. 1953), pp. 93-112; Coxe, v, 358-60; Ferrer del Rio, iv, 230-49; Baumgarten, pp. 198-201. All cite and quote relevant documents.

palace at Aranjuez, was stabbed in the back, fortunately not fatally, by a man who cried, "Muera este pícaro!" The culprit turned out to be a Frenchman long resident in Spain. Although his motive never became clear, he had probably been maddened by lack of money and the continual refusal of the Spanish government to listen to his solicitations. He had no accomplices. The immediate reaction at court, however, was to believe him an emissary of the French clubs and to fear a revolutionary outbreak in Spain. Despite Floridablanca's plea for mercy, the would-be assassin was executed in Madrid with full pomp.[34]

In the winter of 1790-91 a new tax levy brought a violent rising among the overburdened peasants of Galicia, reminiscent of that two years earlier in Barcelona. The bishop of Orense, in sympathy with the rising, wrote a remonstrance to the king denouncing the tax system and accusing the collectors of heartlessness. He hoped Carlos would take pity on his miserable subjects.[35] The government rapidly retracted its tax and sent military reinforcements, but the province set up a local police force and restored order by itself before it again submitted to royal control. The government then carried out numerous arrests that served only to keep peace from being fully reestablished until June 1791.[36] Such an incident, whose likes had not been seen in the last two decades of Carlos III, increased the government's jitters, but it was not a symptom of Revolutionary sympathy.

On the other hand, the Spanish authorities continued to discover the kind of papers that upset them. In Cadiz the *comisario* of the Inquisición complained that, although many of the works prohibited by the edict of December 1789 had been spread there, "not one has been turned in to me." They were being kept in the houses of the French and the Casa de la Camorra, which he was prohibited from searching by an order of 1778. So enthusiastic were these Frenchmen that they had collected a donation of

[34] Alcázar, *loc.cit.*, pp. 101-6; Baumgarten, pp. 300-301; Geoffroy de Grandmaison, p. 18 n. 1; Muriel, I, 135; *Moniteur*, July 4, 1790.

[35] Quoted in *Moniteur*, Jan. 27, 1791.

[36] *Ibid.*, Dec. 3, 31, 1790, Jan. 27, Feb. 3, July 13, 1791; Baumgarten, pp. 306-7.

27,000 pesos for the National Assembly. Civil agents confirmed his reports. Rubín de Cevallos recommended to Floridablanca that the Casa de la Camorra, which Spaniards were also frequenting, be temporarily closed and the French merchants subjected to control.[37]

The "infernal malice" of these French, the *comisario* of Cadiz complained, had discovered means to evade the censorship of the mails by bringing Revolutionary papers in personally or having them sent in bundles of merchandise. The Spanish representatives in France were able to tell how some of this propaganda was being slipped into the port. A Paris hatter, Fernán-Núñez learned, was inserting separate pages of pamphlets into the lining of hats he sent to Cadiz. Another house used Revolutionary papers, torn into narrow strips, as wrapping for the works of clocks being sent into Spain.[38] Fernán-Núñez's successor, Domingo de Iriarte, reported in November 1791 that French ships in Spanish ports handled Revolutionary literature like any other contraband, dropping it to the bottom of the sea in sealed metal boxes which accomplices from the shore could later pull up by means of a string left attached to a floating piece of cork.[39]

The situation in northern Spain appeared even more dangerous than that of Cadiz. Floridablanca believed that persons just across the frontier in Bayonne and Perpignan were translating Revolutionary tracts and slipping them across the Pyrenees; while Fernán-Núñez heard that a French bookseller somewhere near the border sent papers into Spain by night.[40] The government discovered that French scissors-grinders, tinkers, and other wander-

[37] Sánchez Manuel to Rubín de Cevallos, June 29, Aug. 27, 1790, A.H.N., Inq., leg. 4429, No. 34; Floridablanca to Rubín de Cevallos, July 1790, and Rubín de Cevallos to Floridablanca, July 9 and 24, 1790, *ibid.*, leg. 4430, No. 12. Desdevises, *L'Espagne*, III, 145, cites Archives du Consulat français de Cadix to the effect that 237 French merchants there contributed 334,600 reales (about 22,000 pesos) in *dons patriotiques* in 1790.

[38] Dispatch of Fernán-Núñez, Oct. 9, 1790, quoted in Mousset, p. 161.

[39] Dispatch of Iriarte, Nov. 15, 1791, cited by Jacqueline Chaumié, "La correspondance des agents diplomatiques de l'Espagne en France pendant la Révolution," *Bulletin hispanique*, XXXVII (1935), 374.

[40] Floridablanca to Iriarte, Oct. 20, 1791, cited *ibid.*, p. 361; dispatch of Fernán-Núñez, May 24, 1790, cited in Mousset, p. 160.

ing craftsmen, whose numbers, it seemed, had suddenly multiplied in the northern provinces, were circulating wild maxims with printed papers and manuscripts.[41] In August 1790 at an annual fair in Bilbao a Frenchman from Pau was found selling cheap paper fans with designs picturing the fall of the Bastille, Louis XVI "restorer of liberty," and General Lafayette. He also had a fan with a poem in favor of religious liberty that showed "Le Cardinal de Lorraine bénissant les assassins de St. Barthélémi."[42]

The Inquisición de Logroño had ample evidence of the prevalence of French literature in its territory. By the end of 1791, in the two years since its first report to the Consejo de la Inquisición, it had collected 429 pieces. The largest numbers came from Pamplona, Santander, and San Sebastián, the major cities under its jurisdiction, but its *comisarios* in almost every town had sent in some. Most of these were French publications, especially newspapers, of which the *Assemblée nationale, Le Bulletin et Journal des Journaux,* and *La Feuille villageoise* were most prominent. Seven manuscripts in Spanish also appeared, including translations of the rights of man and the constitution of 1791.[43]

The reports from Catalonia were hardly more encouraging. The local captain-general advised Floridablanca early in 1790 that, despite all the measures taken, papers on the events in France were still being sent to religious prelates and other clergymen there. Floridablanca communicated this information to Rubín de Cevallos, who immediately passed it on to the Inquisición de Barcelona with orders to redouble its zeal.[44] This tribunal had also continued to find French pamphlets, which were now coming in by other means than the mails.[45]

In the interior of the kingdom there continued to be fewer

[41] Ordinance of June 18, 1791, quoted in *Nouvelles extraordinaires de divers endroits* (Leyden), Aug. 9, 1791, supplement.

[42] Joaquín de Ampuero to Rubín de Cevallos, Aug. 16, Sept. 3, 1790, and fans included, A.H.N., Inq., leg. 4429, No. 6.

[43] Inquisición de Logroño to Consejo, Nov. 3, 1791, *ibid.,* No. 15.

[44] Floridablanca to Rubín de Cevallos, Feb. 2, 1790; Rubín de Cevallos to Floridablanca, Feb. 3, 1790, *ibid.,* leg. 4430, No. 10.

[45] *Ibid.,* No. 9.

Revolutionary tracts in circulation than near the ports and French border. Yet they were discovered. In 1791 a government agent found in Aragon that a Revolutionary paper entitled *Ça ira* had been spread successfully.[46] Here too in Borja a *fraile* turned up a manuscript in Spanish attacking the condemnation which the pope had issued of the Civil Constitution.[47] The Amigos del País of Saragossa were upset in October 1790 to learn that a clothier of the city had received a shipment of watch chains from Lyon that included one with the inscription, "Vive la liberté!"[48] A few months later a local count found in his mail *Le livre aux trois couleurs, ou manifeste de la Révolution, par deux philosophes modernes.* It discussed the aims and accomplishments of the Revolution, but the pages on the reform of the clergy had not been included. The count turned it over to the inquisitor-general. He had no idea who sent it, but the envelope indicated it came from Catalonia and the address appeared to be in a Spanish hand.[49]

Elsewhere in the interior the story was similar. The bishop of Tuy, in Galicia, sent in a manuscript in Spanish in June 1792.[50] In Burgo de Osma there came to light a pamphlet entitled *Grande révolution operée à Madrid, capitale de l'Espagne—: Flagellation générale des moines voués à toutes les horreurs de l'Inquisition—Droits seigneuriaux supprimés—Tribunal de l'Inquisition aboli—Lettre de l'Évêque d'Orence au Roy d'Espagne.* Expressing philosophic scorn for the forces of darkness, it described a revolution which was supposed to have occurred in Madrid as a result of the French example. Probably because the Paris *Moniteur* had published his recent letter complaining of the tax system in Galicia and certainly without any reference to his true character, the bishop of Orense was pictured as supporting the changes which the *sensible* Spanish king had put into effect.[51] From Jaén,

---

[46] Francisco Zamora to Floridablanca, Dec. 14, 1791, quoted in Lafuente, xv, 182-83.

[47] A.H.N., Inq., leg. 4429, No. 35.

[48] Sarrailh, p. 264.

[49] Conde de Sastago to Rubín de Cevallos, Feb. 4, 1792 [dated Jan. 4 by mistake], A.H.N., Inq., leg. 4430, No. 13.

[50] *Ibid.*, No. 21.

[51] *Ibid.*, leg. 4484, No. 10.

in Andalusia, in February 1792 came a Spanish manuscript translation of a "Carta pastoral del obispo de Oleron en el Reyno de Francia" defending the Civil Constitution. When the Inquisición investigated, it discovered that this copy had been given to a local silversmith by a French commercial agent. Other copies had been spread in the region by another French salesman. These persons had got it from a third Frenchman who had lived in Spain since he was eight and who had received the original printed French version through the mail without an indication of the identity of the sender.[52] In Madrid meanwhile the Constitution of 1791 was attracting attention by its circulation. The French embassy reported that three hundred manuscript copies were abroad, but it certainly had no way of checking such a statement.[53]

For every paper that the tribunals of the Inquisición collected, there must have been many which, in the hands of interested readers, were never unearthed by official agents. This would have been especially the case for manuscripts translated into Spanish. Those who went to the effort involved in producing them would be likely to take care that they did not fall into the wrong hands. Jean-François Bourgoing, who was French ambassador to Spain in 1792, testified that from the beginning of the Revolution the Spanish "were very eager to get our papers and procured them in spite of all prohibitions."[54]

Floridablanca and the Inquisición continued all the while their struggle to keep out information on the Revolution. The number of pieces unearthed is testimony to the efforts of the Santo Oficio. The bitterness of the first secretary also continued to grow. Speaking to the French *chargé d'affaires*, he called the French deputies *misérables* with whom one could not deal. "If I were to follow my own advice, I would put a cordon on the frontier as for a plague!"[55] If government action alone could stem ideas,

[52] *Ibid.*, leg. 4429, No. 12.
[53] *Moniteur*, Sept. 14, 1791; Durtubise to Montmorin, Sept. 22, 1791, cited by Geoffroy de Grandmaison, p. 51.
[54] Bourgoing (1797), I, 296-97.
[55] End of Aug. 1790, quoted in Geoffroy de Grandmaison, p. 28.

Floridablanca would have succeeded in keeping out the pestilence. In August 1790 a royal order was devoted to banning the entry of any cloths or goods "containing paintings or expressions relative to the disorders in France." The order was consequent on the arrest of a Frenchman who had been caught in the treacherous act of wearing a waistcoat on which was pictured a galloping horse with the word "Liberté."[56] Soon another royal order was issued condemning a *Manifiesto reservado para el Rey D. Cárlos IV y sus sublimes ministros*, which was declared to be offensive to the Spanish rulers.[57] Early in 1791 Floridablanca carried out his threat to place a cordon of troops on the French frontier, although the official explanation he gave was that it was there "to keep trouble makers and vagabonds from disturbing the friendship of the two countries."[58] Next he wrote to Fernán-Núñez to ask the French government to stop the evident attempts being made in France to introduce into Spain publications that contained calumnies of that country. After repeated complaints, the Spanish representative received as his sole reply in December 1791 the reminder that freedom of the press was a right recognized for Frenchmen. The Spanish government was invited to prosecute any libel in the French courts according to established laws and told that it was up to it to enforce its own prohibitions.[59]

Floridablanca had no need to receive admonitions from the French. On September 16, 1791 a royal order was published in the *Gazeta de Madrid* and posted throughout Spain which repeated the prohibition of January 1, 1790. "Having now well founded reports that there is an attempt to introduce and spread in this kingdom from France seditious papers," the king ordered all persons who possessed or should receive such papers to sur-

---

[56] *Real orden*, Aug. 6, 1790, *Nov. rec.*, VIII, xviii, nota 16.

[57] *Real orden*, Oct. 28, 1790, *ibid.*, nota 13.

[58] Puyabry to Montmorin, Mar. 19, 1791, cited by Geoffroy de Grandmaison, p. 38; Muriel, I, 146-47.

[59] Floridablanca (to Fernán-Núñez?), n. d., and De Lessart to Domingo de Iriarte, Dec. 22, 1791, quoted in Muriel, I, 168, 203-4, and cited by Chaumié, *loc.cit.*, p. 387.

render them to the law courts, telling from whom they got them. Whoever held or disseminated such papers was to be tried for treason. The civil officials were commanded to show activity and vigilance and the ecclesiastical prelates were asked to enforce the order among the clergy.[60] The publication of this order did not change the legal situation, but it served as a warning of the determined spirit of the government.

Even this order was not sufficient. The infernal French revolutionaries were soon discovered, as one outraged Spanish clergyman put it, "to have found a new way of introducing their venom, not as before in books that discuss religion, but in treatises that have no relation to it, such as those on physics."[61] The venom had been found in the *Journal de physique* of 1790. The entire journal was banned by royal order on December 9, 1791. Moreover, henceforth no work in French was to be admitted without an express royal license.[62] This had been the Spanish rule since the beginning of the sixteenth century and had been restated in 1784 on the occasion of the appearance of Masson's article in the *Encyclopédie méthodique*, but apparently a Spanish law that was not frequently restated soon fell into disuse.

Floridablanca did more than just issue decrees. He inspired zeal among the civil agents. Bourgoing claims that they were more active than the officials of the Inquisición.[63] A Frenchman who visited Spain at the end of 1791 was astounded by the customs inspection of his books. They were checked against the list of the Inquisición and another list, far more exact, said to have been drawn up for the first secretary by two French bishops. It contained anti-Revolutionary as well as Revolutionary writings, and the Frenchman claimed that, despite his protests, even a copy of Nonnotte's *Les erreurs de Voltaire* was confiscated because the *philosophe's* name appeared on the title page.[64]

[60] *Real orden*, Sept. 10, 1791, *Nov. rec.*, VIII, xviii, 11.

[61] [Riesco de Llerena], *Discurso histórico-legal sobre el origen, progresos, y utilidad del Santo Oficio de la Inquisicion de España* (Valladolid, 1802), pp. 279-80.

[62] *Nov. rec.*, VIII, xviii, 12; see *Moniteur*, Feb. 16, 1792.

[63] Bourgoing (1797), I, 370.   [64] Chantreau, pp. 221-23.

Time and again reports coming into Madrid had pointed to the Frenchmen residing in Spain as the most determined importers of French publications. What was worse, they were generally believed to be preaching revolt. Several high ranking Frenchmen spoke too freely in favor of the Revolution in Madrid social circles in 1790 and were arrested or ordered out of Spain. The same occurred in Barcelona.[65] Fernán-Núñez told of a French merchant in Madrid and another in Seville who he had reason to believe were active propagandists. The latter had recently been in Paris and had associated with members of the Jacobin Club.[66] Such an attitude on the part of the most numerous foreign element in Spain came to be viewed as a real danger to the Spanish regime.

Floridablanca determined to stop this source of French news, whatever the international or economic repercussions might be. On November 26, 1789 a proclamation was posted ordering all foreign and Spanish non-residents out of Madrid within two weeks' time, a limit that was subsequently extended. Probably some of the crowds that had come to the capital for the recent coronation were still loitering there, but foreign observers felt the proclamation was aimed primarily at a large number of talkative Frenchmen in the city.[67] This measure could not clean up the problem throughout Spain, however. The inquisitor-general, Rubín de Cevallos, suggested to Floridablanca that all foreigners resident in Spain for ten years be considered subjects of the king of Spain and treated as his vassals. He cited precedents for such a denial of the rights of foreign citizenship.[68] The idea matured in

---

[65] Geoffroy de Grandmaison, pp. 10-11, 37-38, 51; *Moniteur*, Mar. 4, 1791.

[66] Dispatches of Fernán-Núñez, end of Dec. 1790 and Apr. 18, 1791, quoted in Mousset, p. 162.

[67] *Nov. rec.*, III, xxii, 11-13 and nota 5; Baumgarten, p. 269 (even when Baumgarten does not cite specific dispatches of Sandoz-Rollin, the Prussian minister, it is evident that these are his source of information); Tratchevsky, *loc.cit.*, pp. 29-30 (Tratchevsky uses the dispatches of the Russian ambassadors in Madrid but much less skillfully than Baumgarten, and he seldom cites the dispatches by date).

[68] Rubín de Cevallos to Floridablanca, July 9, 1790, *loc.cit.*

the mind of the first secretary. On June 18, 1791 he ordered supervision of all wandering craftsmen.[69] A month later, July 20, a royal cedula was promulgated putting into effect the inquisitor's suggestion. All foreigners were to be registered by the local justices and divided into two classes, *avecinados* and *transeuntes*, that is residents and transients. The *avecinados* must swear to give up the protection of their consuls and accept the Catholic faith and the sovereignty of the Spanish king. The *transeuntes* were not permitted to remain in Spain without a license from the secretary of state, nor could they carry on any business, profession, or craft, including that of domestic servant. They were given two weeks to leave or to become *avecinados* and take the oath.[70]

The law was aimed especially at the French. To avoid a collapse of its foreign trade, the government soon agreed not to apply the terms of the law to English merchants.[71] The required registration of foreigners showed how numerous the French were: of 27,502 resident heads of families, 13,332 were French; of 6,512 transients, 4,435 were French.[72] In Barcelona and Cadiz, Seville and Madrid, everywhere there was excitement as large numbers of Frenchmen began to leave Spain. "Carried away by their holy enthusiasm, they prefer to sacrifice their hopes, their fortunes, and abandon everything rather than abjure their country," a friendly witness reported.[73] Twelve hundred were said to have left Madrid by October. The Limousins and Auvergnats who engaged in retail trade in Spanish towns were faced with ruin.[74]

Frenchmen who preferred to remain had to submit to the control of the Spanish government, even though they did not always have to take the hateful oath.[75] In Cadiz the Casa de la

[69] Ordinance of June 18, 1791, *loc.cit.*

[70] *Gazeta*, Aug. 2, 1791; *Nov. rec.*, VI, xi, 8.

[71] *Moniteur*, Aug. 15, Sept. 14, 1791; Baumgarten, pp. 324-25; Bourgoing (1797), III, 131-33; Godoy, I, 70 n. I.

[72] Godoy, I, 70 n. I; Lafuente xv, 184-85.

[73] *Nouvelles extraordinaires* (Leyden), Aug. 12, 1792.

[74] Dispatches of Durtubise, Aug. 25, 29, Sept. 22, Oct. 7, 1791, cited by Geoffroy de Grandmaison, pp. 53-54; *Moniteur*, Aug. 28, Sept. 4, 15, Oct. 7, 1791. (The *Moniteur's* stories appear to have come out of Durtubise's dispatches.)

[75] Godoy, I, 70 n. I.

Camorra was temporarily closed and was reopened only on the condition that a royal official be present at its meetings.[76] The Inquisición also felt free now to imprison a certain Michel Maffre des Rieux, a Marseillais who professed deism. The case ended tragically. Although Maffre reaffirmed his Catholic faith, he was brought to be sentenced at an *autillo* in Madrid before many Spanish ladies and gentlemen. Believing he had been promised secrecy, Maffre cried out during the ceremony at this lack of faith and denounced the Catholic religion. After he had been returned to his cell, he committed suicide, leaving a note to his deistic God.[77] Such an exhibition of the solidarity of minister and inquisitor offered ample warning to French residents henceforth to temper their demonstrations of Revolutionary sympathies.

5

During these years, when Floridablanca was attempting to play a successful Canute to the tide of Revolutionary publications, he was slowly led to reappraise the policy of the crown toward the *luces* in Spain. Unlike his ban on French news, his change of attitude toward domestic enlightenment came hesitantly and reluctantly.

In 1789 and 1790 the flourishing Spanish press continued unfettered to spread the spirit of the age. It was during these years that the *Correo de Madrid* carried its long series of sketches on the lives and works of modern philosophers, that Foronda's "Cartas sobre los asuntos mas exquisitos de la economia política" were published in the *Espiritu de los mejores diarios literatos*, and that similar articles appeared elsewhere in the periodical press. The *Gazeta de Madrid* in 1789 advertised translations of foreign scientific works[78] and treatises on economics by the Marchese di Belloni[79] and Jacques Necker.[80] In 1791 appeared

[76] Bourgoing (1797), III, 131-33.

[77] Llorente, *Historia*, II, 168, 174, 195-200. Llorente witnessed the case.

[78] See, e.g., *Gazeta*, Oct. 9, 1789, Apr. 23, Oct. 19, 1790. There were others.

[79] *Disertacion sobre la naturaleza y utilidades del comercio* (*ibid.*, May 22, 1789).

[80] *Memoria . . . sobre . . . rentas provinciales*, trans. Domingo de la Torre y Mollined (*ibid.*, Sept. 8, 1789).

Floridablanca's Great Fear

Fernández Navarrete's enthusiastic *Discurso sobre los progresos que puede adquirir la economia politica* and Ramon Campos' *Sistema de logica*, modelled on Condillac. Late in 1790 was founded the periodical *La espigadera*. It boasted among its three hundred subscribers the names of Floridablanca, Campomanes, and Jovellanos.[81] Its first issue carried a "Discurso imparcial y verdadero sobre el estado actual del teatro español," which proposed measures to improve the Spanish theater so that it could stand comparison with that of the rest of Europe "in a century that calls itself philosophic and in which the sciences and arts are cultivated with so much energy." In the third issue of 1791 an article defended recent royal decrees against bull fighting because the fights were not in keeping with enlightened times. Since all publications had to pass government censorship, the appearance as late as 1791 of works like these indicates that the government was not yet taking any general stand against the Enlightenment.

Yet a change in official sentiment had gradually become evident since the height of the excitement over Masson's article on Spain. Even before the news of the Bastille came to disturb Floridablanca's peace of mind, a limit was being drawn for the subject matter of the Spanish press. In 1788 the Inquisición had proceeded against Cañuelo and confiscated the *Encyclopédie méthodique*, and a royal resolution had regulated the language and subject matter of the periodical press. The reign of Carlos IV was inaugurated with a more ominous event. On February 28, 1789 the inquisitor-general issued a decree: "We make known that having seen and read with the most profound meditation many and various anonymous papers that have been published, in whose expressions is discovered a libertine language that, under the pretext of instructing the public, hides the design of corrupting customs, encouraging arrogance, weakening the respect for the superior powers, destroying religious piety, and advocating the

---

81 *La espigadera, obra periodica* (Madrid, 1790-91). Twelve issues appeared in 1790, five in 1791. The dates of issue were not given; possibly it appeared bi-monthly. List of subscribers given at the end of Vol. 1.

pernicious writings of the declared enemies of the sacred dogmas," he prohibited twenty-two discourses and part of another of *El censor*, two issues of the *Correo de Madrid*, and two of the *Diario de Madrid*. *El censor* especially aroused his ire. It was accused of propagating the errors of the materialists, and two discourses were forbidden even to those with a license to read prohibited books because they were said to contain doctrines of Wyclif, Luther, and Calvin. Most of Cañuelo's essays remarked earlier for their bold social and religious criticism suffered now the ignominy of the Index. Even though the edict was not strictly enforced, its new tone caused a stir of excitement in Madrid.[82]

Once the Revolution had roused his fears, Floridablanca soon revealed that he supported the new policy of the Santo Oficio. In the fall of 1789 the first volume was published of the *Historia de la vida del hombre*, a Spanish translation of a work written in Italian by the exiled Spanish ex-Jesuit Lorenzo Hervás y Panduro. The introduction to Volume I gave an outline of the entire work, which was to be a survey of all sides of man's life from gestation through his physical, mental, and social development to death. Here Hervás y Panduro sketched his concept of society. He was strictly Catholic in likening political society to the family, but he carried the analogy one step farther than usual. As there are only parents and children in a family, so in society there is only the prince and his subjects, "all equal by nature, but through legal constitution the subjects inferior to the prince, equal among themselves and unequal only in personal merit." Hereditary distinctions, vassalage, primogeniture, entail of property, are typical only of despotism, not of a true monarchy based on paternal authority and filial obedience, he said.[83] Such statements condemning hereditary nobility sounded too reminiscent of the recent August decrees in France for the first secretary. When he learned of them, he ordered the sale of the work suspended. Less than one hundred of the fifteen hundred copies of Volume I that had

---

[82] Publication of the decree in Seville, Mar. 26, 1789, "Fraile," Vol. 863, fol. 147; Baumgarten, p. 215.

[83] Lorenzo Hervás y Panduro, *Historia de la vida del hombre* (7 vols.; Madrid, 1789-99), I, xix-xx.

been printed had not yet been distributed and could be confiscated, but the entire edition of the second volume was confiscated and further publication stopped.[84]

During the next year, the new official outlook was reflected in changes in the personnel of the government. Besides Floridablanca and Aranda, the three men who best typified the enlightened despotism of Carlos III had been Campomanes, Cabarrús, and Jovellanos. Cabarrús was especially noted for his enlightened point of view. Although Carlos IV had given him the title Conde de Cabarrús in 1789, his enemies at court made use of his liberal leanings to denounce his *Elogio de Carlos III* to the Inquisición[85] and to help procure his arrest in June 1790 and subsequent incarceration in the distant port of La Coruña. At the same time several women who were associated with him were exiled from the court or told to watch their tongues.[86] Jovellanos, who was tied to Cabarrús by bonds of friendship, returned from a commission to Salamanca in August 1790 to intervene in his friend's favor. Four days later he was ordered to depart immediately for his native Asturias to draw up a report on its coal mines. The manner in which the order was extended made it clear to everyone that Jovellanos had fallen into royal disfavor and that his departure amounted to banishment from the court.[87] While in Madrid Jovellanos had appealed to Campomanes for help in saving Cabarrús, but Campomanes had replied that he was in no position to take the part of a hero in the affair.[88] Campomanes' pusillanimity, so unworthy of his glorious career, was not destined to stand him in good stead. In the spring of the following year he was deprived of the position Carlos III had given him of governor of the Consejo de Castilla.

---

[84] Angel González Palencia, "Nuevas noticias bibliográficas del abate Hervás y Panduro," *Eruditos y libreros del siglo XVIII*, pp. 196-97, citing A.H.N., Consejo de Castilla, Impresiones, leg. 5554, expediente 119.

[85] A.H.N., Inq., leg. 4474, No. 4. For Cabarrús' title, Muriel, IV, 94.

[86] Fernán-Núñez, II, 25; Baumgarten, pp. 302-5, citing especially Theremin's dispatch of Sept. 20, 1790; Geoffroy de Grandmaison, p. 51.

[87] The documents on this affair are published in Somoza García Sala, pp. 87-102.

[88] Ceán Bermúdez to Francisco de Paula de Jovellanos, n.d., *ibid.*, p. 102.

Although he remained a member of the Consejo, his influence was gone.[89] Within the space of a year three of Spain's outstanding leaders had been put aside. Soon after the demotion of Campomanes, who had inspired the organization of the societies of Amigos del País, the directors of these societies received instructions to slacken their activities and to permit no more discussion of questions of political economy.[90] No one had to be astute to sense a cooling of the government and court toward reform and progress.

Just before Campomanes' fall, Floridablanca had already made this coolness painfully evident by his sharpest stroke of all. On February 24, 1791 a royal resolution ordered all private Spanish periodicals suspended.[91] The order was immediately enforced; the periodicals that were in existence, even those recently founded, ceased to appear after February. The very able *Espíritu de los mejores diarios, Correo de Madrid,* and Valladares' *Semanario erudito* were killed. Only the *Diario de Madrid,* which had never been very profound and which served the useful purpose of publishing classified advertisements, was permitted to continue, "limiting itself to the facts, and without permitting verses or political subject matter of any kind whatever." The official *Gazeta de Madrid* and *Mercurio de España,* devoted to current news, also continued but with the silence on France already remarked. Thus at a blow Floridablanca slew the thriving intellectual movement represented by the journals founded at the end of Carlos III's reign. They had committed no crime except

[89] Baumgarten, pp. 315-16; González Arnao, *loc.cit.,* pp. 20, 34 n. 42 (who purposely remains vague on Campomanes' disgrace).

[90] Godoy, II, 124-25. In 1789 the *Gazeta* had reported the activity of twenty societies, although many had held meetings only to honor the memory of Carlos III. In 1790 only six were mentioned in the *Gazeta* (Madrid, Feb. 26, Mar. 5, Apr. 13, 23, Aug. 10; Saragossa, Mar. 23, 26, 30; Segovia, May 11; Valladolid, July 30; Bascongada, Oct. 5, 8; Tarragona, Dec. 10), but this did not indicate a really marked decline. In 1791 only three societies were mentioned, however (Granada, June 17; Bascongada, Oct. 18; Seville, Dec. 6).

[91] *Nov. rec.,* VIII, xvii, 5. The resulting *auto de consejo* is dated Apr. 12, 1791, but the *resolución* was put into immediate effect (see the notice of Feb. 28 given by the *Espíritu de los mejores diarios* to its subscribers after its last issue, Feb. 14, 1791).

to have encouraged the Spanish to think that their kingdom could benefit from suggestions for improvement. The stench blowing over the Pyrenees had contaminated all ideas on reform, both foreign and domestic, and rendered them nauseating to the Spanish rulers.

At this point, the Inquisición, which had recently been too busy with Revolutionary works to attend to domestic products, took over the attack on the Spanish press. On March 6, 1791 it extended its ban of Spanish journals to include three papers that had appeared in 1787 and 1788 in the wake of *El censor: El duende de Madrid, Corresponsal del censor,* and *El observador.*[92]

The Santo Oficio also chose to make an example of a man who had become well known as a translator of the works of the *philosophes.* Since 1784 Bernardo María de Calzada had translated and published *La logique* of Condillac, *Le fils naturel* of Diderot, Voltaire's *Alzire* disguised under the title *El triunfo de la moral christiana,* and the *Vie de Frédéric II.* He had also had the poor judgment to write a satire of his own that angered some of the less broad-minded *frailes.*[93] As a result, although he held the rank of lieutenant colonel in the queen's cavalry regiment and served in the ministry of war, he was now imprisoned by the Inquisición and condemned to abjure *de levi,* that is, as slightly suspect of heresy. This relatively light sentence was accompanied by banishment from Madrid, with consequent loss of his professional position and hardships for his numerous family.[94] His translation of Frederick II's biography had particularly angered the Santo Oficio because it was found to con-

---

[92] Edict of Mar. 6, 1791, "Fraile," Vol. 863, fol. 151. Hartzenbusch p. 14, notes that *El observador* was announced in the *Gazeta,* Dec. 21, 1787, as a "periodical work that will appear every Monday similar to the one that appears with the title of *Censor.*" Apparently he had not seen it, nor have I.

[93] *Nueva floresta o coleccion de chistes* (Madrid, 1790).

[94] Llorente, *Historia,* ix, 26-27. Llorente was present at his arrest as an official of the Inquisición; hence it took place between the publication of Calzada's latest book in 1790 and the time when Llorente left Madrid in 1791 (Juan Antonio Llorente, *Noticia biografica . . . o memorias para la historia de su vida escritas por él mismo* [Paris, 1818], pp. 49-50).

tain fragments of Voltaire's works verbatim and to "proclaim triumphantly religious freedom and tolerance," opening an easy path for "young and uncautious readers" to slip into "pure materialism." The work was placed on the Index on March 4, 1792.[95]

Spain held an even more rash spirit than Calzada's, however. At the end of 1791 Mariano Luis de Urquijo, a twenty-three year old former student of Meléndez Valdés at Salamanca, published *La muerte de Cesar. Tragedia francesa de Mr. de Voltaire.*[96] After the prohibition of the periodical press, when the persecution of French papers had reached its height and everyone could sense Spain's opposition to the mention of enlightenment, this young man not only translated Voltaire but dared to violate the convention established in freer days of omitting the author's name. He did more, he accompanied the translation with a long introductory discourse calling on the Spanish theater to imitate Voltaire's play, and for what reasons! "All in it is great, all is heroic. What sublimity of ideas! what elevation of thoughts! what excellence of portrayal! what depth of political thought! what truth! what force of reasoning!"

Had Urquijo acted consciously to the purpose, he (and whoever gave him a royal license for publication) could not have issued a more spectacular defiance of the Santo Oficio. The inquisitors did not let the challenge pass. Urquijo was promptly denounced and his imprisonment was under consideration, but before it could act, the Inquisición found its hands were no longer free. On February 28, 1792 Floridablanca was dismissed by Carlos IV and his place was taken by the Conde de Aranda. The new first secretary was not the person to see a young man imprisoned for translating the work of a former friend and admirer. Urquijo was given a position in Aranda's bureau and

[95] Edict of Mar. 4, 1792, "Fraile," Vol. 863, fol. 152.

[96] F.-M. Arouet de Voltaire, *La muerte de Cesar.* Tragedia francesa de Mr. de Voltaire. Traducida en verso castellano y acompañada de un discurso del traductor, sobre el estado actual de nuestros teatros, y necesidad de su reforma. Por don Mariano Luis de Urquijo (Madrid, 1791). It is advertised in *Gazeta*, Oct. 18, 1791.

a place on the Consejo de Estado. The Inquisición decided to force Urquijo only to abjure as suspect *de levi* and carry out his penance in secret.[97] *La muerte de Cesar* was finally prohibited in 1796, but the name of the translator, which had been given on the title page, was not mentioned in the decree.[98]

6

The dismissal of Floridablanca caught contemporary observers by surprise. They were not even able to agree on the causes for his fall. Some felt that the intrigues of the high nobles grouped around Aranda had finally borne fruit. Others saw behind the act the hatred of the queen, María Luisa, for Floridablanca, who was believed to have slighted her in the days of Carlos III and now to have urged that Carlos IV send away a handsome young guardsman named Manuel Godoy, suspected by many of intimate relations with the queen.[99] While these factors perhaps contributed to weakening Floridablanca's position, the last straw appears to have been a plea from Louis XVI brought by a special emissary, Jean-François Bourgoing, the former French agent in Spain, whose *Nouveau voyage en Espagne* had been published in 1789. The decision of certain foreign powers, including Spain, to consider Louis' oath to the French constitution as having been made under duress was endangering the safety of the French royal couple. Bourgoing arrived two days before the dismissal of Floridablanca, bearing an urgent request for Carlos to state publicly his approval of Louis' acceptance of the French constitution and to use his good offices at the courts of Vienna, Berlin, Stockholm, and Saint Petersburg to get them

---

[97] Llorente, *Historia*, ix, 31-42; Villanueva, i, 64-65; Antonio de Beraza, *Elogio de don Mariano Luis de Urquijo, ministro secretario de estado de España* (Paris, 1820). The last work, written after Urquijo's death but presumably from information supplied by him, says Floridablanca first defended Urquijo against the Inquisición. This account conflicts with the other two first hand reports and the date of the event.

[98] *Suplemento al Indice*, p. 37.

[99] Cayetano Alcázar discusses the evidence and accepts the queen's responsibility, *loc.cit.* I do not, see below n. 101.

to abandon their hostile attitude toward the Revolution.[100] Officially Bourgoing made no mention of Floridablanca, but the warm hearted Spanish king decided that for the sake of his French cousin his intransigent minister must go.[101] At first Floridablanca was allowed to return to his native Murcia, where a gala welcome awaited him; but in July his successor, Aranda, had him arrested and confined in the fortress of Pamplona while his papers were searched for an excuse to convict him of abuse of his powers.

The minister who fell had once been the leading adviser of Carlos III, but in spirit he was a vastly different man. Since the accession of Carlos IV, a growing horror of revolution had warped all his policies. It led him to antagonize foreigners, recently so welcome, to resuscitate the Inquisición, and to vent his wrath upon the cherished ministers and institutions of the late king. The irony of this *volte-face* in domestic affairs is that there is scant evidence that it was justified by any germination of a revolutionary spirit in Spain.

It is true—and hardly surprising—curiosity was aroused about French events. There was even a certain amount of admiration for the National Assembly, especially in government and court circles. After the felicitous conclusion of the French constitution in September 1791 became known, the Madrid correspondent

[100] Bourgoing saw the Spanish *chargé*, Iriarte, before he left Paris, and Iriarte reported Bourgoing's secret instructions to Floridablanca (dispatches of Feb. 6, 8, 1792, cited by Chaumié, *loc.cit.*, xxxviii [1936], 515-16).

[101] This was the explanation of the nuncio. Bourgoing denied his complicity in a dispatch to Paris sent with the courier of the English ambassador—as if he did not have his own courier (Alcázar, *loc.cit.*, p. 115). Before news of Floridablanca's fall reached Paris on March 10, Louis XVI and Marie Antoinette asked Iriarte to undertake an extremely secret mission to Carlos IV because they said they were unable to trust anyone else. As soon as the news came, Iriarte asked Aranda to ignore his request to return home. Apparently Floridablanca's dismissal had satisfied the French royal couple (various dispatches of Iriarte of Mar. 10 and Apr. 2, 9, 1792, in Chaumié, *loc.cit.*, xxxviii, 523, 529, 531). Contemporaries regularly attributed decisions of Carlos IV to the influence of María Luisa, eager to satisfy her immoderate passions. While María Luisa took an interest in affairs of state and undoubtedly was listened to by Carlos, more worthy reasons can usually be found for the king's decisions than a desire to satisfy the whims of a domineering wife. See above, n. 99.

of the *Moniteur* wrote: "All the moves made by Louis XVI in the last two months are known here, as are your festivals and illuminations. The reasonable persons (and there are more than one supposes) rejoice to think that you have come safely to port."[102] At the same time Rubín de Cevallos complained to Floridablanca that the body of Madrid lawyers had him worried by its attitude and there were even judges "who say that the experiences of France are not evils."[103] In 1792 the former royal advisor Cabarrús, while in prison, spoke of "that constituent assembly of France, perhaps the greatest and most famous collection of talents and wide experience which has honored humanity."[104] Two years later his friend Jovellanos, still in exile from the court, wrote to an English acquaintance that Spain should aspire to a government on the English model or, "for example, a constitution such as the one to which Louis XVI swore in 1791."[105] Obviously members of the governmental party who favored enlightened despotism—both Jovellanos and Cabarrús had given ample testimony that this was their ideal before 1789—had felt the attraction of the first French constitution. Floridablanca's actions without doubt encouraged this sympathy.

Some of the Spaniards who circulated French papers outside the capital must have had similar feelings. It would be a mistake, however, to exaggerate this spirit. The case of the town of Magallón in Aragon, where a French émigré priest found everyone—at least, everyone he talked to—completely ignorant of the French Revolution at the end of 1792,[106] could not have been uncommon even in northern Spain. Only the small minority of literate Spaniards could profit even from translated manuscripts, and of these only the more open-minded would care to disobey

---

[102] *Moniteur*, Nov. 17, 1791.

[103] Rubín de Cevallos to Floridablanca, Oct. 26, 1791, A.H.N., Inq., leg. 4430, No. 20.

[104] Cabarrús, *Cartas sobre los obstáculos*, p. 120.

[105] Jovellanos [to Alexander Jardine, May 24, 1794?], B.A.E., L, 367.

[106] "Journal de l'Abbé Artigues," cited by J. Delbrel, "Le clergé français réfugié en Espagne pendant la Révolution," *Études religieuses, philosophiques, historiques et littéraires*, LV (1891), 38.

the royal government and Inquisición. The threat of denuncia-
tion to these bodies by the very religious common people prevented their disseminating the information gleaned to any but
a few trusted friends of advanced ideas. The official prohibitions
against spreading Revolutionary news and papers thus helped
to keep the majority of Spaniards from learning many of the
details of events in France. It is doubtful, however, that a significantly greater amount of sympathy for the Revolution would
have been generated if news had circulated more freely. No
evidence suggests that even among those who read clandestine
papers more than a few rare individuals desired to imitate
Frenchmen and take over control of their destinies. Although
Floridablanca obviously did not believe so, when he retired the
throne was as safe as when Carlos IV ascended it.

CHAPTER IX

THE FRENCH PROPAGANDA CAMPAIGNS

AS SOON as he replaced Floridablanca, the Conde de Aranda set about reversing his predecessor's policies. At Aranda's special request, Carlos at once abolished the Junta Suprema de Estado, the council of ministers created by Carlos III and Floridablanca in 1787 that had given the first secretary direct supervision of the activities of the other ministers. In its place the king revived the Consejo de Estado, once the stronghold of the *grandes* but moribund since the reforms of Felipe V. The king was to be its president; Aranda was named its dean. When it was completed, the Consejo de Estado included the state secretaries and other individuals appointed to it by the king. Carlos used it to give the aristocracy once more a place in the government. Of its twenty-eight members in 1798, thirteen were nobles with old titles and three were church prelates. The new council met regularly in the presence of the king to discuss important matters of state. Ministers and others could vie in it for the approval of Carlos, but the word of the king was still final. Over half the members seldom came to meetings, however; and aristocratic influence in government became no greater than before.[1] Had Carlos III been alive, the change from the Junta de Estado would have made little difference; but now state policy would depend not as in the last four years on the firm guidance of a single minister but on the whim of an irresolute king; and the extensive Spanish realms were about to face the most severe test of their history.

Aranda also relaxed the official attitude toward the Revolution. He urged in the Consejo de Estado that the mutual distrust of France and Spain be eased, and he largely neglected the control of foreigners in Spain. Frenchmen who favored the Revolution

---

[1] *Real decreto*, Feb. 28, 1792, *Nov. rec.*, III, vii, 1; Muriel, I, 226-29; Desdevises, *L'Espagne*, II, 56-59.

were again allowed into the country, provided they did not attempt to trouble the public peace.[2] Similarly, without officially withdrawing Floridablanca's laws, he once more permitted the Spanish post office to deliver French newspapers. Only seditious libels were henceforth to be refused entry.[3]

In France, meanwhile, after two relatively calm years, the Revolution was taking a violent turn. Upon the instigation of the Girondists, the war party in the Legislative Assembly, France went to war with Austria and Prussia. On August 10, 1792 Louis XVI was deposed and in September a newly elected Convention declared France to be a Republic. The military strength of the Revolution, at first of doubtful character, led, after the meeting of the Convention, to surprising victories that took the French armies to the Alps and the Rhine.

The news of the imprisonment of the French royal family on August 10 forced Aranda to change his attitude, whatever his personal feelings might have been. To the Consejo de Estado he posed the question of declaring war on France, but no decision was taken.[4] He also revived the former orders to inspect all works in French entering Spain. Those which touched on the Revolution were to be sent to the ministry of state, but the rest that were harmless were permitted to be delivered.[5] On October 15 a royal resolution set up two inspectors of books at each customs office, one a royal agent and the other a *comisario* of the Inquisición. Besides confiscating prohibited and suspicious books, they were to dispatch the useful ones, especially those dealing with the sciences, as fast as possible.[6] Foreign diplomatic representatives were asked to cooperate by keeping to themselves any

[2] Aranda to Iriarte, Mar. 28, 1792, in Chaumié, *loc.cit.*, xxxviii, 527-28; Muriel, i, 236-38 (Muriel used Aranda's personal papers); *Moniteur*, Apr. 15, May 11, 1792.

[3] Dispatch of Sandoz, July 8, 1792, cited in Baumgarten, p. 391; *Moniteur*, July 10, 1792.

[4] Aug. 24, 1792, Muriel, i, 273-75.

[5] *Real cédula*, Aug. 22, 1792, "Fraile," Vol. 785, fol. 100, and *Nov. rec.*, viii, xviii, 13. The cedula was not published in Barcelona until Oct. 9. (*Diario de Barcelona*, Oct. 17-18, 1792).

[6] *Nov. rec.*, viii, xviii, 14.

papers they received containing principles contrary to the Spanish constitution and government.[7]

Aranda's brief period of relaxed controls had had its effect. French newspapers had entered more liberally. In November a man in Orense called the inquisitor-general's attention to the *Moniteur* and the *Chronique de Paris*, various issues of which he had seen and found dangerous.[8] The case of the Basque port of Bilbao was more eloquent. The Inquisición de Logroño wrote its *comisario* there in November 1792 that it had evidence that French newspapers were circulating in that area. The *comisario* replied that he had not acted earlier because the head of the local post office had received an order to permit the entry of foreign papers and had refused to give him a list of their subscribers. From one of the subscribers, nevertheless, the *comisario* had collected eight issues of the *Gazette nationale de France* and seven of the *Mercure universel* for September and October. The tribunal of Logroño, with the support of the Consejo de la Inquisición, told its *comisario* to command the head of the post office to obey the royal orders and to give him a list of the subscribers. These men were to be examined by the *comisario* for disobeying the edicts of the Inquisición and warned that if they continued to subscribe to the papers they would be "criminals of state and of our holy faith."

Despite all the royal orders and the edicts of the Santo Oficio, the tribunal of Logroño was ready to admit that it was helpless under present conditions. "The multitude of seditious papers that come from France does not permit us to take formal action against the subjects who introduce, keep, and divulge them," it complained to the Consejo de la Inquisición. The penury of theologians with a knowledge of French to examine the papers caused dangerous delays in prohibiting their circulation. It expressed the hope that the council would establish more appro-

[7] Duque de la Alcudia to foreign ambassadors, Nov. 26, 1792, quoted in *Moniteur*, Dec. 17, 1792.

[8] B. M. C. Sotelo de Noboa to inquisitor-general, Nov. 18, 1792, A.H.N., Inq., leg. 4429, No. 35.

priate provisions.[9] Against the tide of French publications all royal and inquisitorial edicts, inspired primarily by Floridablanca before his dismissal, had simply proved ineffectual.

2

French residents in Spain or Spaniards in commercial relations with France appear to have been primarily responsible for the influx of Revolutionary papers. Itinerant French peddlers and muleteers who crossed the Pyrenees and French publishers and booksellers who wished to supply their subscribers in Spain found ways to get papers past the customs. Probably Revolutionary clubs at times sent pamphlets through the mail. But until the fall of the French monarchy no one in France appears to have organized a propaganda campaign directed at Spain. The government, on the contrary, frowned on the spread of Revolutionary literature outside France. When the minister of foreign affairs, the Comte de Montmorin, resigned in October 1791, he complained in a report to the Legislative Assembly of the attempts of French clubs to seek correspondents abroad and of the export of papers insulting foreign sovereigns. They were inciting the hostility of foreign powers toward France.[10] During his ministry the national policy had been one of non-interference. The government had not encouraged the business, but, as has been seen, it refused on constitutional grounds to accede to Floridablanca's request to put a stop to such activity.

The war in 1792 changed this policy. Faced with the problem of justifying the occupation of new territory and of maintaining popular favor there, the Convention decreed on November 19 that the French nation "will accord fraternity and help to all

[9] Joaquín de Ampuero to Inquisición de Logroño, Nov. 3 and 6, Inquisición, de Logroño to Consejo de la Inquisición, Nov. 26, *auto* of the Inquisición de Logroño, Nov. 26, and of the Consejo, Dec. 3, 1792, *ibid.*, No. 13. The title *Mercure universel* is not listed in L. E. Hatin, *Bibliographie historique et critique de la presse périodique française* (Paris, 1866). Possibly it was the *Moniteur universel*.

[10] Frédéric Masson, *Le département des affaires étrangères pendant la Révolution, 1787-1804* (Paris, 1877), pp. 115-16.

peoples who shall desire to recover their liberty." On December 15 it further ordered French generals to destroy existing privileges and governments in occupied territories and to have new administrations elected by those citizens who swore to uphold liberty and equality. These decrees embodied an overt policy of revolutionary expansion. Their corollary was the participation of the national government in foreign propaganda.

Since Spain and France remained at peace in 1792, these measures were primarily directed at the eastern frontiers of France. The first known seeds of organized propaganda activity directed across the Pyrenees sprouted independently of any measures taken by the government. In February and March 1792 the Spanish representative in Paris, Domingo de Iriarte, reported on apparently good authority that the clubs of Amis de la Constitution—better known as Jacobins—of Montlouis and Barèges, near the Pyrenees, had asked the Jacobin Club of Paris for Revolutionary papers to send into Spain. The club of Montlouis, he stated a little later, had acknowledged receipt of the desired papers on March 2.[11] A few months later the Jacobins of Bayonne took over the lead in this propaganda activity. The appearance in their midst of a young Spanish refugee, José Marchena, seems to have provided their inspiration.

About May 1, 1792 Marchena left Spain, fleeing, he claimed, from the threat of imprisonment by the Inquisición.[12] He posed as the subject of six years of persecution in his native land. This was no doubt an exaggeration, but it is certain that he had reasons for fearing the Spanish authorities. Born in 1768 in Andalusia, he had been sent at the age of twelve to study in Madrid. He remained there for four years, devoting the last year to moral philosophy at the Reales Estudios de San Isidro. Thence he went

---

[11] Iriarte's dispatches of Feb. 13, Mar. 10, Apr. 3, 1792, in Chaumié, *loc.cit.*, xxxviii, 517-18, 523-24, 530.

[12] Marchena to Pierre Lebrun, Dec. 29, 1792, Archives des Affaires étrangères, Paris, Correspondance politique, Espagne (hereafter cited "A.A.E., Esp."), Vol. 634, pièce 163. The letter is quoted in A. Morel-Fatio, "José Marchena et la propagande révolutionnaire en Espagne en 1792 et 1793," *Revue historique*, xliv (1890), 73.

to the university of Salamanca, where Meléndez Valdés gave
him an oral entrance examination. He studied civil and canon
law and took a bachelor's degree in 1788. In the meantime he
had made use of a marvelous gift for languages to translate into
Spanish verse *De rerum natura* of the Roman naturalist poet
Lucretius and to read and admire the works of the *philosophes*.[13]

> Rousseau, de la edad nuestra eterna gloria,
> Y modelo de los siglos venideros,

he apostrophized his favorite philosopher.[14] In his poetry he
greeted with joy the outbreak of the Revolution. Almost unique
among his countrymen at this time, he desired Spain to follow
the French example.

> Excita al grande ejemplo
> Tu esfuerzo, Hesperia: rompe los pesados
> Grillos . . .[15]

He dreamed of founding a literary society that would include in
its aims the observation of the crimes of despotism and intolerance
and the study of the natural rights and duties of man.[16] A student
who was expressing such ideas in his writing would have been encouraged to abandon Spain for France even if he had not yet
suffered the persecution he bragged of.

Thus in the spring of 1792 Marchena appeared in Saint-Jean-
de-Luz, a French coastal town on the road to Bayonne. He was
promptly admitted "by acclamation and unanimously" to the
Club des Amis de la Constitution of Bayonne. He delivered a
brief speech on the occasion, said to be impromptu, in which he
cried, "I come from the land of slavery, the land of religious and

---

[13] Marcelino Menéndez Pelayo, *El Abate Marchena* ("Colleccion austral")
(Buenos Aires, 1946), pp. 18, 27; Alarcos, *loc.cit.*

[14] "Discursos en la abertura de una sociedad literaria," José Marchena, *Obras
literarias*, ed. M. Menéndez Pelayo (Seville, 1892-96), I, 44.

[15] "La Revolución francesa," *ibid.*, pp. 15-16.

[16] "Discursos en la apertura de una sociedad literaria," *ibid.*, pp. 43-46.
Menéndez Pelayo believed the society actually existed, but his only evidence is
the undated MS of this poem intended to be read at its opening (*Abate Marchena*,
pp. 31-33).

civil despotism. . . . I come to the country of Liberty. . . . *Oh! Messieurs, oh! mes frères* . . . I come to devote myself to you." The club was delighted and had the speech printed on a small sheet.[17] Soon it published another of his discourses, this one fourteen pages long.

Copies of the *In-promptu* found their way into Spain. One was received in a plain envelope on June 22 by the Consejo de Castilla, and another was discovered in the Basque town of Marquina in November.[18] Marchena and the Club des Amis soon had the idea of producing a propaganda sheet expressly for Spanish consumption. Marchena wrote the text and it was printed on four octavo pages with the heading *A la nacion española*. It was, so far as is known, the first piece printed by the French in Spanish for Spanish readers.[19] It pretended to be the address of a Frenchman to the Spanish nation:

The time has come to offer the truth to the people. . . . The sublime revolution which has solemnly proclaimed the eternal rights of humanity, which has driven superstition and tyranny from their golden throne in order to place on it equality and reason, will not limit its beneficial influences to the narrow limits of the French nation. What! Who can stop the progress of an immense bonfire surrounded by combustible matter?

[17] *In-promptu d'un Espagnol, admis par acclamation & à l'unanimité, au Club des Amis de la Constitution de Bayonne* (Bayonne, [1792]). There is a copy in A.H.N., Inq., leg. 4429, No. 27. A note in ink on it written by an agent of the Inquisición reads: "Se llama este Español Dⁿ Jph Marchena y los Judios le obsequian mucho y se dice hijo de un agente fiscal ó Relator, y que ha estudiado en Salamanca y hizo esta oracion en el pulpito del Clu luego que llegó y se imprim [*sic*] por qta [cuenta] de los concurrentes del Clu." See Menéndez Pelayo, *Abate Marchena*, pp. 37-38.

[18] A. Galbes López Salzes to Inquisición de Corte, June 22, 1792, A.H.N., Inq., leg. 4429, No. 27, and Inquisición de Logroño to Consejo, Nov. 26, 1792, *loc.cit.*

[19] [José Marchena], *A la nacion española* ([Bayonne, 1792]). Copies can be found in A.A.E., Esp., Vol. 634, pièces 113, 164, 199, and in A.H.N., Inq., leg. 4429, No. 14. The first is dated in ink November 1792, but it was probably published in October. I have not seen the *Manifiesto reservado para el rey D. Carlos IV* . . . banned in October 1790. It may not have been in Spanish, for royal orders sometimes referred to the titles of foreign works by their Spanish translation (*Nov. rec.*, VIII, xviii, nota 13).

Nature did not intend man to be the slave of man; superstition may put a people to sleep for an instant in the chains of slavery; but if reason awakens it, beware, hypocrites and oppressors.

The main theme of Marchena's tract was the need for Spain to achieve religious liberty by destroying the Inquisición, which he so cordially detested:

Here the Jew helps the Christian, the Protestant embraces the Catholic. . . . If the religion of Jesus is the system of universal peace and charity, who are the true Christians, we who bring help to all men, who look on them as our brothers, or you who persecute, who seize, who kill all who do not adopt your ideas?

Because the Inquisición has always persecuted men of talent, what writer can Spain offer to compare with "our sublime Rousseau," "the great Buffon," "the virtuous Mably," "the daring Raynal," and "our universal Voltaire"?

Is it not time for the nation to shake off the intolerable yoke of the oppression of thought? Is it not time for the government to suppress a tribunal of darkness that dishonors even despotism?

Equality, humanity, fraternity, tolerance—Spaniards, this is in four words the system of the philosophers whom some perverse persons make you look upon as monsters. . . .

Only one way remains open to you, Spaniards, to destroy religious despotism, *this is the convocation of your Cortes.* Do not lose a moment, let *Cortes, Cortes* be the universal cry. . . .

The French have made their constitution to be happy and not to make other men unhappy. They cannot be happy, nor can anyone, without acquiring liberty. . . . Hence they do not want to conquer anyone. . . . What they want is to destroy the Tyrants. . . .

Peace and war the French carry with them, peace toward men and war on the tyrant kings.

Thus Marchena and the club issued a clear call for the Spanish to undertake their own revolution. They appeared to promise armed help and seemed to consider war between the two countries inevitable.

The club is reported to have had five thousand copies of the address printed.[20] It took immediate steps to spread them into Spain. Bayonne was well situated for such an enterprise, for it was at the northern end of the main road from Spain into France and also carried on an active maritime trade with Spanish ports. Many Spaniards of the northern provinces visited it for business or for pleasure.[21] One such person was an illiterate known as "Piernas." When brought later before the Inquisición he said that he had been given two copies of the leaflet in Bayonne about the end of October 1792 by a man who he was sure was a Jew. He saw this man give copies to another Spaniard, telling them both to take them to Spain so the Spanish would have news of the assembly. Piernas obligingly gave both copies away in Spain, one of which went through three hands in Almunia de Doña Godina, 125 miles from the French border, before being turned in to the Inquisición.[22] Meanwhile the Bayonne club was also using the well-tried expedient of sending the sheets through the mail in plain envelopes. One was received in this manner by a citizen of Logroño on November 3.[23] Such were the means, not ineffective, employed by the Bayonne propagandizers.

3

Meanwhile, in Paris during the last months of 1792, the new Girondin foreign minister, Pierre Lebrun, began to toy with plans for Spanish propaganda. Using part of a "secret fund" that had been assigned to his ministry, he published a series of pam-

[20] This is the information received by the Inquisición de Logroño (Inquisición de Logroño to Consejo, Nov. 12, 1792, A.H.N., Inq., leg. 4429, No. 14).

[21] Antoine Richard, "Un homme d'affaires bayonnais dans la politique, Jean-Pierre Basterrèche (1762-1827)," *Annales historiques de la Révolution française,* I (1924), 427; Fischer, *Travels in Spain,* p. 50.

[22] Inquisición de Zaragoza, "Expediente formado . . . para averiguar el autor del Libelo Impreso con el titulo *A la Nacion Española,*" A.H.N., Inq., leg. 4429, No. 14.

[23] Inquisición de Logroño to Consejo, Nov. 12, 1792, *loc.cit.*

phlets addressed to foreign peoples and written by the *philosophe* and Girondin Antoine-Nicolas de Condorcet. Among them was an *Avis aux Espagnols*, which appeared in November. Three thousand copies of it were ordered printed.[24]

Condorcet's tract was not especially skillful. For one thing its length, twenty-three pages, made it difficult to slip into Spain. Furthermore, its argument could not appeal to Spanish readers. Spain had been ruined, Condorcet said, by the Austrian and Bourbon dynasties, who since the sixteenth century had run the country only in the interests of Austria and France. The establishment of the French Republic had at last made it possible for Spain to shake off this plague. "Why do not the two nations unite . . . to precipitate the house of Bourbon from a throne where it can disturb French liberty while at the same time oppressing that of Spain."[25] Since the imprisonment of Louis XVI, the danger of Spanish interference worried the French leaders, who believed that "our liberty will never be sure so long as a Bourbon remains on a throne."[26] It is all too evident from Condorcet's *Avis* that he was much more preoccupied by the threat the Spanish Bourbons presented for the Revolution than by their oppression of Spain. Spain need not abandon monarchy nor violate the clergy or nobility to achieve liberty, he advised; all that mattered was that it get rid of the Bourbons. He ended with the suggestion that Spaniards call their Cortes or a "national Convention" as the first step in that direction. The next years were to show that he had entirely mistaken the temper of the Spanish people.

The existence of this pamphlet was soon known in Spain, for on December 14 a royal order specifically prohibited its circulation.[27] To reach a wide Spanish audience, however, it needed

[24] Masson, pp. 269-70. It was commented on in *Chronique de Paris*, Nov. 22, Dec. 1, 1792 (information given me by Professor Beatrice F. Hyslop).

[25] Antoine-Nicolas de Condorcet, *Avis aux Espagnols par Condorcet* (Paris [1792]), pp. 9-10.

[26] Brissot de Warville, Nov. 26, 1792, quoted in A. Mathiez, *La Révolution française* (8th ed.; Paris, 1945), II, 166.

[27] *Nov. rec.*, VIII, xviii, nota 17.

to be published and disseminated in translation. Lebrun realized this and had two translations made, one in Paris and the other in Madrid. The former version, with the title *Aviso a los Españoles*, turned out to be almost unintelligible. Andrés María de Guzmán, a Spaniard who was becoming a Revolutionary leader in Paris, wrote Lebrun to say that "it is not at all written in Spanish," and advised him that Condorcet's ideas would not have appeal in Spain. The author should have stressed the evils of Spain's poverty and worked to unite the nobility with the people, Guzmán (who was a nobleman) believed.[28] His opinion was water off Lebrun's back, since the minister felt that Condorcet's tract "ne pourrait être trop à mon gré."[29]

The other version was made by a Spaniard rapidly and at great risk at the behest of the secretary of the French embassy in Madrid, N. Carles. It was a better translation than that made in Paris. Even the title, *Advertencia a los Españoles por Condorcet*, was an improvement.[30] In December Carles ordered six thousand copies of it printed in Bayonne, since he could find no one in the Spanish capital who would undertake so dangerous a job.[31] In January 1793 he went to Bayonne to take charge of distributing the pamphlet. He asked Lebrun for permission to visit the frontiers of Aragon and Catalonia to set up agents for spreading it into Spain. Lebrun sent him the necessary passport but ordered him not to enter Spain because of the risk involved.[32] Carles delayed his departure until after the middle of March waiting

28 J.-P. Basterrèche to Lebrun, Jan. 5, N. Carles to Lebrun, Feb. 13, and Guzmán to Lebrun, Mar. 4, 1793, A.A.E., Esp., Vol. 635, pièces 11, 124, 194. Guzmán's letter is quoted in A. Morel-Fatio, "Le Révolutionnaire espagnol don Andrés María de Guzmán dit 'Don Tocsinos,'" *Revue historique*, CXXII (1916), 54-55.

29 Lebrun to Carles, Dec. 25, 1792, A.A.E., Esp., Vol. 634, pièce 170.

30 Inquisición de Logroño, "Expediente formado . . . sobre recoger un papel impreso en Francia con el titulo de Advertencia a los Españoles por Condorcet," A.H.N., Inq., leg. 4429, No. 28.

31 Carles to Lebrun, Dec. 10, 1792, A.A.E., Esp., Vol. 634, pièce 132. See Beatrice F. Hyslop, "French Jacobin Nationalism and Spain," *Nationalism and Internationalism: Essays Inscribed to Carlton J. H. Hayes*, ed. E. M. Earle (New York, 1950), p. 206 n. 42.

32 Carles to Lebrun, Jan. 18, and Lebrun to Carles, Feb. 2, Mar. 5, 1793, A.A.E., Esp., Vol. 635, pièces 47, 86, 200.

for the printing of several thousand more copies. At the end of March he was in Bordeaux and in April he reached Tarbes, but by May he was back in Bayonne.[33] His mission does not appear to have been particularly successful.

Yet the pamphlet was entering Spain. The Inquisición collected five copies in Bilbao in February. One was received by a Spanish merchant in a bundle coming from Bayonne. The other four were turned in by a person who stated that they had been given him in Saint-Jean-de-Luz, the small town south of Bayonne. He had been made suspicious by the way he had been asked if he would be examined at the frontier. Two of the copies were addressed to the Seminario de Vergara and to its professor and poet Felix María de Samaniego. Evidently they were being addressed to well-known persons and institutions. The *comisario* of the Inquisición identified the sender, who had signed an enclosed note "Ducos," as a doctor in Saint-Jean-de-Luz. The impression made on the *comisario* by this new piece of propaganda would have warmed Lebrun's heart: "If the many papers the French introduced up to now have prepared the mine for insurrection in these kingdoms of Spain, these *Advertencias* bring up the fuse for its explosion."[34] The Inquisición de Logroño at once referred the case to Madrid and warned the *comisarios* of the ports and French frontier to be on the lookout for the paper.[35]

While Carles was busy, Lebrun had entrusted the distribution of the Paris translation of Condorcet's tract to the mayor of Bayonne, Jean-Pierre Basterrèche, a young merchant of Girondin sympathies who had entered his office on December 18, 1792.[36] Other duties of his already had aroused Basterrèche's interest in Spain. Through his hands passed the dispatches from the Madrid embassy, and he had to dispose of Spanish emigrants who were

[33] Carles to Lebrun, Mar. 11, 19, 29, Apr. 9, May 14, 1793, *ibid.*, pièces 225, 256, 308, Vol. 636, pièces 32, 95.

[34] Joaquín de Ampuero to Inquisición de Logroño, Mar. 2, 1793, A.H.N., Inq., leg. 4429, No. 28.

[35] Mar. 6 and 8, 1793, *ibid.*

[36] Basterrèche to Lebrun, Jan. 5, 1793, A.A.E., Esp., Vol. 635, pièce 11. On Basterrèche see Richard, *loc.cit.*

arriving in Bayonne ready to fight for the Revolution. Until these men could be used, he sent them for indoctrination in Revolutionary principles to a Spaniard living in Bayonne, N. Rubín de Celis.[37]

One of these refugees, who arrived in mid-January 1793, like Marchena full of tales of pursuit by the Inquisición and the Spanish government, impressed Basterrèche with his possibilities as a propagandist. This was Vicente María Santiváñez, a man of some prominence in Spain. Born in Madrid in 1759, he had studied in the university of Valencia and taught at the Seminario de Vergara from 1782 to 1785. Since then he had been in Madrid and Valladolid publishing translations of a French novel and Alexander Pope's poem "Eloisa to Abelard." To this last he added his own "Cartas de Abelardo á Heloisa," which, when published in 1796, were promptly put on the Index. Marchena had known and admired him. Basterrèche at once recommended him to Lebrun: "Widely known in the best society, thoroughly familiar with the whole machinery of the Spanish government, and especially with its members, he could be extremely useful."[38]

Basterrèche soon put Santiváñez to work preparing propaganda. The Spanish refugee translated a decree of the Legislative Assembly of August 3, 1792 offering deserters from enemy armies a fraternal welcome in the land of liberty and a pension for life. Early in March 1793 it was available in print. Basterrèche took charge of sending it into Spain and addressed some copies to the mayor of Perpignan, at the other end of the Pyrenees, for him to pass across his frontier.[39] Santiváñez also wrote a new

[37] Taschereau to Lebrun, Mar. 26, 1793, A.A.E., Esp., Vol. 635, pièce 297; Menéndez Pelayo, *Abate Marchena*, p. 56; Muriel, II, 201-2.

[38] Basterrèche to Lebrun, Jan. 20, 1793, A.A.E., Esp., Vol. 635, pièce 52. See M. Núñez de Arenas, "Don Vicente María Santiváñez: un madrileño en la Revolución francesa," *Revista de la biblioteca, archivo y museo*, II (1925), 372-94; Julio de Urquijo, "Santiváñez el afrancesado: ¿quién fué el autor del elogio del Conde de Peñaflorida?" *Revue internationale des études basques*, XVI (1925), 323-29; Morel-Fatio, "José Marchena," *loc.cit.*, p. 81; Menéndez Pelayo, *Abate Marchena*, pp. 53-54.

[39] Basterrèche to Lebrun, Mar. 6, 9, 1793, A.A.E., Esp., Vol. 635, pièces 207, 208, 221. Pièce 220 is a copy of the printed sheet: *Ley relativa a los sargentos, cabos y soldados que abandonen los exercitos enemigos, para venir à servir en el de la Republica francesa* (n.p., n.d.).

281

opuscule addressed to the Spanish people. Basterrèche felt that it was perfectly adapted to the purpose, but he soon stopped publication of it because he felt that this task should be left to a new organization that Lebrun was creating.[40]

In December 1792 José Marchena, in need of a source of income, applied to Brissot de Warville, who was now head of the diplomatic committee of the Convention, offering his services to establish liberty in his native country. He was referred to Lebrun, to whom he wrote, sending him a copy of his *A la nacion española* and a memoir on how a "Revolutionary committee established on the frontiers of Spain" should approach its task.[41] Another Spaniard, Joseph Hevia, former secretary of the Spanish embassy in Paris,[42] added similar reflections to those of Marchena and also asked to work on the project. In January Basterrèche urged Lebrun to give the Spanish refugees that were reaching Bayonne useful work so that their exaltation would not turn to discouragement.[43] These suggestions for an organization to direct propaganda into Spain that should receive its authority from the national government found the foreign minister in a receptive mood, but it was two months before he took action.

In January 1793 the Convention voted to execute Louis XVI. Carlos IV tried to intercede through his representative in France to save the life of his cousin. His attempt was vain, for Louis was guillotined on January 21, but the Convention took umbrage at the intervention of Carlos and for that reason among others on March 7, 1793 declared war on Spain.

This was the stimulus Lebrun needed to undertake the new propaganda project. On March 8 he wrote to Basterrèche that

[40] Basterrèche to Lebrun, Mar. 18, 26, *ibid.*, pièces 254, 290. Basterrèche says he is sending several copies of the work, but there are no printed copies of it in the A.A.E., files. It has been generally assumed that *ibid.*, pièce 311, a MS "Reflexiones imparciales de un Español a su nacion," is the writing in question, although this is unsigned and there is no indication of its origin. The MS is not unworthy of Santiváñez.

[41] Marchena to Lebrun, Dec. 29, 1792, and memoir dated Dec. 23, A.A.E., Esp., Vol. 634, pièces 163, 165. Both are quoted in Morel Fatio, "José Marchena," *loc.cit.*, pp. 73-79.

[42] See Iriarte to Floridablanca, Nov. 15, 1791, Chaumié, *loc.cit.*, xxxvii, 370.

[43] Jan. 20, 1793, *loc.cit.*

Bayonne would be the best location for a "Comité espagnol" to unite the Spanish patriots.[44] Four days later he outlined the project to the deputies of the departments bordering on Spain and asked for their support.[45] By March 19 his plan had acquired definite shape. There were to be two committees, at Bayonne and Perpignan. Lebrun intended that the Bayonne committee be composed of Basterrèche, Carles, another former member of the embassy in Madrid, and the Spaniards Santiváñez, Marchena, Hevia, and a fourth recently arrived expatriate.[46] In April the all-powerful Committee of Public Safety adopted Lebrun's plan and formally established the two groups at Bayonne and Perpignan. They were to be known as "Comités espagnols d'Instruction publique." Their task was to be to maintain correspondence with the neighboring Spanish provinces and to circulate publications which would make known "the true principles of the French Republic" while "humoring religious opinions as much as possible." They were to be under the direction of the commander of the army of the Pyrenees and the *commissaires* of the Provisional Executive Council, of which Lebrun, as minister of foreign affairs, was a member. Each committee was to include three French members besides the *commissaires* and could add those Spaniards of whom it approved. Their personnel was named on April 25.[47] The membership of the Bayonne committee was hardly what Lebrun had envisaged. Basterrèche was not included although Carles was. The other two Frenchmen were new. The Spaniards who had been in Bayonne never did join the committee. They were carried by the tide of events into other adventures; all being forced soon to spend more or less time in Revolutionary prisons, where Santiváñez was to die.[48]

---

[44] A.A.E., Esp., Vol. 635, pièce 219.

[45] Lebrun to deputies of departments of Hautes and Basses Pyrenées, Haute Garonne, Ariège, and Pyrénées orientales, Mar. 12, 1793, *ibid.*, pièce 233.

[46] Lebrun to Basterrèche, Mar. 19, 26, *ibid.*, pièces 259, 291.

[47] "Memoire pour servir d'instruction au Comité espagnol établi à (Bayonne) (Perpignan)," dated May 3, Lebrun to ministre de la marine, May 24, Lebrun to Carles, May 28, 1793, *ibid.*, Vol. 636, pièces 79, 103, 108.

[48] On Marchena and Hevia see Brissot to Lebrun, May 4, 1793 and Lebrun to Comité de Surveillance and to Comité de Salut publique, May 5, 26, *ibid.*,

As for the committee in Perpignan, the only member of it that Lebrun considered capable was a certain Jacques Revest. Revest had recently applied to Lebrun for employment, stating that he had lived twenty-three years in Spain. He had also sent the foreign minister an address to Spaniards that he claimed to have written but which differed only slightly from Marchena's *A la nacion española.*[49]

By the end of May 1793 the two Comités espagnols should have been ready to go to work; yet various factors combined to make Lebrun's project miscarry. The sentiment of the French rulers was no longer what it had been at the time of the November decree promising help to all peoples in search of their liberty. With France facing new enemies since the execution of the king, this policy began to appear unrealistic. "This decree seems to engage you to bring help to a few patriots who would make a revolution in China," Danton cried in the Convention on April 13, "Above all what is necessary is to think of our own body politic." The Convention thereupon decreed that France intended not to interfere with the governments of other nations but only to defend its own right to choose its form of government. The new policy implied a discontinuance of propaganda directed abroad. Soon the Girondist party, which had fathered the policy of militant revolutionary proselyting, was destroyed by an uprising of the Paris populace on June 2. The Jacobin party, with Danton and Robespierre as its leading figures, took over control of France for the next fourteen months, the period of the so-called "Terror." Lebrun was arrested on June 4 in his ministry, where he was allowed to continue at his post until replaced on June 21.[50]

---

pièces 80, 83, 107, all cited but somewhat misinterpreted in Morel-Fatio, "José Marchena," *loc.cit.*, pp. 84-87. The rest of Marchena's vivid career is told in Menéndez Pelayo, *Abate Marchena.* On Santiváñez see Núñez de Arenas, *loc.cit.*

[49] Revest to Lebrun, Feb. 15, 1793, A.A.E., Esp., Vol. 635, pièce 130. His MS was entitled "Aviso al pueblo español" (*ibid.*, pièce 128) and is so similar to Marchena's that it has been believed a different version of it, although the MS has clearly at the end "Par le C^en Jacques Revest." Menéndez Pelayo, *Abate Marchena,* pp. 41-44, prints it in full as the work of Marchena.

[50] Masson, p. 281.

With his departure, the Comités espagnols lost their driving force.

The momentum Lebrun had imparted to them kept them briefly in motion, nevertheless. He had sent to both 750 copies in Spanish of Danton's decree of April 13 and the Convention's subsequent manifesto of April 16 to all peoples denouncing the desire of all kings to destroy liberty everywhere.[51] The Bayonne committee took immediate steps to circulate these across the Pyrenees.[52] In June it was also sent Spanish translations of the second, recently adopted French constitution;[53] and some copies of this too reached their destination, for they were found in Barcelona by September.[54] Meanwhile the Perpignan committee was probably responsible for the "address to Spanish soldiers" in the June 1 issue of the local *Echo des Pyrénées*, urging them to break their chains and join their French brothers.[55]

The committees never got the opportunity to do more. The *commissaires* of the Executive Council, C. Comeyras and J.-B. Borrel, showed a marked lack of interest in them. They even delayed inexcusably in sending them the instructions for their organization and duties. François Deforgues, Lebrun's successor, had to order the *commissaires* in June and July to report to their committees. Meanwhile the Perpignan group announced that its efforts were becoming useless.[56] To the surprise of the Revolutionaries, after war was declared the Spanish army invaded Roussillon in April and since May stood before the gates of Perpignan. When the *commissaire* Comeyras finally arrived at that city, he decided on July 8 that so long as Spanish soldiers

---

[51] Comité at Perpignan to Lebrun, June 7, 1793, and Comité at Bayonne to Deforgues, June 29, 1793, A.A.E., Esp., Vol. 636, pièces 111, 122. The text of the manifesto is in *Moniteur*, Apr. 19, 1793.

[52] Comité at Bayonne to Deforgues, July 11, 1793, A.A.E., Esp., Vol. 636, pièce 130.

[53] Deforgues to Comité at Bayonne, July 17, 1793, *ibid.*, pièce 135.

[54] *Real orden*, Sept. 14, 1793, *Nov. rec.*, VIII, xviii, nota 21, so states and orders them collected. It says three thousand more were prepared in France.

[55] Miss Hyslop gave me this information.

[56] Comités at Bayonne and Perpignan to Lebrun, May 23, June 7, and Deforgues to Comeyras and Borrel, June 26, July 12, 1793, A.A.E., Esp., Vol. 636, pièces 101, 111, 117, 137.

were on French soil, the committee could not fulfil its purpose. Its members agreed to disband and devote themselves to providing supplies for the French army.[57] Deforgues accepted this decision and recommended that Borrel adopt it for the Bayonne committee. Borrel needed no further urging. On August 12 he ordered its three members to various cities to supervise military supplies.[58] Thus perished Lebrun's scheme; the disappearance of this Girondist personality deprived it of the support it needed.

4

During the rest of 1793 the French Army of the Eastern Pyrenees was busy holding back the Spanish invasion. Its only conquests were high in the mountains, where it managed to occupy Spanish Cerdaña and the Valle de Arán. The Committee of Public Safety believed that it was a geographical error for the Treaty of the Pyrenees of 1659 to have assigned these valleys to the Spanish side of the Pyrenees, and preliminary steps were taken to put into force there the legislation of the Revolution. In the towns of the Valle de Arán docile "assemblées primaires" met in June 1793 and voted to request annexation to the French Republic, while a new "municipalité" was named for Puigcerda in Cerdaña. The French forces gave less attention, however, to conducting reforms than to seizing for their own consumption the harvests and food stores of these valleys.[59]

Propaganda activity was practically at a standstill on the Roussillon front in the second half of 1793. Yet in its issues of October 30 and 31 the Perpignan *Echo des Pyrénées* followed a bulletin describing French successes by an "Avis au peuple espagnol" in French and Spanish by "le brave montagnard Revest, commissaire du comité d'instruction publique."[60] The

---

[57] Revest to an unnamed member of the ministère des affaires étrangères, July 9, 1793, and Comité at Perpignan to Deforgues, July 3, 1793, A.A.E., Esp., Vol. 636, pièces 129, 132.

[58] Deforgues to Borrel, July 19, and Borrel to Camille, Carles, and Bérenger, Aug. 12, 1793, *ibid.*, pièces 137, 157.

[59] Emili Vigo, *La política catalana del gran Comitè de Salut Pública* (Barcelona, 1956), pp. 63-65, 73-74.

[60] Miss Hyslop discovered this article (*loc.cit.*, p. 216).

"brave montagnard" was still using the address that he had plagiarized from Marchena and submitted to Lebrun in February; only now he added a warning to Spaniards that their tyrant was endangering their possessions in America by his recent alliance with "your natural enemy the Englishman." The standing offer of rewards to deserters was repeated at the end. Handbills bearing this "Aviso al pueblo español" were also printed for circulation in Spain.[61] Revest had kept the idea of propaganda alive in Perpignan through the summer.

The year 1794 saw a reversal of the military situation on this front. In January the Committee of Public Safety placed General Jacques Coquille-Dugommier, who had recently captured Toulon from the British, in command of the Army of the Eastern Pyrenees. The committee also appointed two energetic Jacobins of the Convention, Jean-Baptiste Milhaud and Pierre-Auguste de Soubrany, to be "deputies on mission" to the army, invested with supreme authority. The three men cooperated to create an effective French force. Their cause was helped in March by the death of the victorious Spanish general, Antonio Ricardos. In April the French attacked and rapidly drove the enemy out of Roussillon. Only slowly did the Republican army penetrate Catalonia, however, and not until late in the fall was any real progress made again on this front.[62]

Even before large advances were made into Spain, the question of French policy toward occupied Spanish territory, which had been dormant in 1793, again became acute. Milhaud, Soubrany, and Dugommier favored annexation of Catalonia to France. They wrote to the Committee of Public Safety early in May 1794 urging this course of action. "Catalonia is ripe for the Revolution," the deputies said. Dugommier was more specific. He pointed out the tempting wealth of the province in agriculture, mining, manufacture, maritime commerce, and industrious inhabitants. It would moreover provide "a new boulevard between

61 Angel Ossorio y Gallardo saw such a sheet and quotes it in *Historia del pensamiento político catalán durante la guerra de España con la República francesa (1793-1795)* (Madrid, 1913) pp. 14-15 n.

62 Vigo, pp. 25-28, 45-51; Baumgarten, pp. 507, 510-13, 523-27.

Spain and France, safer than the Pyrenees." The Catalans were "enemies of Spain," he assured the committee, and would welcome French liberty and equality.[63]

While they waited for a reply from Paris, the deputies revived plans for French propaganda. In Puigcerda local Frenchmen had founded a "Popular Society." With the cooperation of the French commander in the area, the society held a festival on May 7 in a building termed the "Temple of Reason" to commemorate the French victories in Roussillon. The rights of man were read publicly in Catalan, and the municipal officers had the "sweet joy" of setting fire to "the emblems of the tyrant of Castile and the emblems of fanaticism."[64] Milhaud and Soubrany wrote to this society on May 19 encouraging its "sans-culottes" in their project of instructing their nation in the "eternal truths of reason." They promised the society that "thousands of copies of the rights of man and the Republican constitution will be scattered on all roads, attached to all trees."[65] Three days later they requested the Committee of Public Safety to send them copies of the speeches of Robespierre, Barère, and other leaders, which they intended to publish in French, Spanish, and "the other language of the country," together with an address of their own to the French army and the inhabitants of Catalonia.[66]

Cerdaña was the only place in Catalonia to which the Army of the Eastern Pyrenees made a serious attempt to bring the blessings of the Revolution. A "Commission Civile et Surveillante," made up of local Frenchmen, was established here in May 1794. Acting as a local government, it took over as national property

---

[63] Milhaud and Soubrany to Committee of Public Safety, and Dugommier to committee of Public Safety, both 22 floréal ii (May 11, 1794), quoted by Vigo, pp. 31-32.

[64] Report of the society to the Avant Garde de l'Armée des Pyrénées orientales, 30 floréal ii (May 19, 1794), quoted by *ibid.*, pp. 67-68.

[65] Milhaud and Soubrany to the "Sans-culottes composant la Société républicaine de Puigcerda," 30 floréal ii (May 19, 1794), quoted in J. Delbrel, "L'Espagne et la Révolution française: le Comte de la Union," *Études religieuses, philosophiques, historiques et littéraires*, XLVIII (1889), 70 n. 1.

[66] 3 prairial ii (May 22, 1794), quoted in *ibid.*, p. 68 n. 1.

the lands of the church and of the inhabitants who had fled and put these lands up for lease. The personal belongings and live-stock of those who had emigrated were sold. Another blessing of the Revolution which the commission allowed Cerdaña to share was the feeding and support of the troops who were fighting the tyrant of Castile. In fact the commission's major activities that summer consisted in finding laborers willing to harvest the crops of grain for the army and in searching out hidden valuables of the churches. To make these requisitions more palatable to the inhabitants on August 2 Milhaud and Soubrany suggested to the Committee of Public Safety that the tithe and all feudal rights should be officially abolished in Cerdaña, since it was now to be a part of France. The Convention, upon the proposal of the committee, passed a decree to this effect on August 11.[67]

On the other hand, the Committee of Public Safety did not adopt the earlier recommendation of Milhaud and Soubrany that France annex Catalonia. The nature of the suggestion was abhorrent to Robespierre and the other members of the com-mittee. After the Jacobins seized control of the government in 1793, they had abandoned the Girondist plans for revolutionizing foreign countries, and the defense of France from invasion on all fronts had absorbed their thoughts for the rest of the year. Faced now with the victories of their army in the south, the Committee of Public Safety compromised between the two extreme courses of non-interference in neighboring countries and outright conquests by coming back to an idea originally put forward by the Girondists—that of creating "sister republics" on the frontiers of France. In a letter of May 26, 1794, Robes-pierre's supporter in the committee, Georges Couthon, informed the deputies that Catalonia would become an independent re-public under French protection, a decision he felt would be more welcome to the Catalans than annexation to France. The deputies were to inspire "republican pride" and "the genius of liberty" among the Catalans but to take care not to offend "the objects of the cult to which that people is attached." They were, however,

[67] Vigo, pp. 69-73.

to destroy all foundries and arsenals, which would be of use to the Spaniards if recaptured.[68]

Milhaud and Soubrany bowed to the committee. "By education and by bayonets we shall establish the Catalan Republic during this campaign," they wrote back.[69] Leaving the matter of bayonets to Dugommier, they turned their attention to education. According to their own word they had eighteen thousand copies printed of an address headed: "Proclamation. The Representatives of the French people with the Army of the Eastern Pyrenees to Catalonia and the Republican Army." It was published in French, Spanish, and Catalan in small eight-page pamphlets. The Catalan version, at least, was also printed in one large sheet for posting.[70] They also published a second address, this one apparently only in Catalan but again both as a large sheet for posting and a small pamphlet. It had the heading: "The republican Catalan to all his fellow citizens friends of liberty, of the good and prosperity of their country—greeting, fraternity, union, and strength."[71]

Both pamphlets developed ideas which seemed particularly fitting for their audience. The Spanish rulers were trying to make their people think they were fighting a war for religion,

[68] Couthon to Milhaud and Soubrany, 7 prairial II (May 26, 1794), quoted by Vigo, pp. 36-37, and in part by Mathiez, III, 191. For the policy of "republiques sœurs" see Jacques Godechot, *La grande nation* (Paris, 1956), I, 80-84.

[69] Milhaud and Sourbrany to Committee of Public Safety, 11 messidor II, (June 29, 1794), quoted by Vigo, p. 52.

[70] The headings are respectively *Proclamacion. Los Representantes del Pueblo Francés, Prop lo exercito dels Pyrénéos orientales, a la Catalunia, y al Exercito Republica* and *Proclamacio. Los Représentans del Poblé francés prop la Armada dels Pyrénées orientals, a la Catalunya y à la Armada republicana* (Perpignan, n.d.). The Spanish version is signed "Los Représentantes del Pueblo Francés, Milhaud & Soubrany," and the Catalan correspondingly. The eight-page Spanish and Catalan versions can be found in A.H.N., Inq., leg. 4429, Nos. 8, 9. Vigo saw the French version in Archives nationales, Paris, AF II 256, cahier 2175 (Vigo, p. 55 n. 38). Lluis Serra y Riera has published the catalan proclamation in full in "Une proclamation républicaine aux Catalans," *Revue hispanique*, xxv (1911), 345-49. The copy he had was a single sheet 15 by 17 inches. For the number of copies printed, Milhaud and Soubrany to Committee of Public Safety, 11 messidor II (June 29, 1794), quoted by Vigo, p. 55.

[71] *Lo Catala Republica, a tots sos Compatriotas amichs de la Llibertad, del bé y prosperitat de sa Patria, salut, germandat, unió y força* (n.p., n.d.), one large double folio sheet or sixteen-page pamphlet. Both styles are in A.H.N., Inq., leg. 4429, No. 9.

they said. "Are you fighting for the infernal Inquisición that did not exist in the time of the *buen señor sin calzones Jesu-Christo?* ... the infernal Inquisición that, using the name of a God of peace and goodness, brings desolation to your families and commands thought itself." We worship the same God you do, they insisted; how could France be victorious over all its enemies "if Providence did not cover it with its divine wings."[72] The resemblance to Marchena's tract is striking. Both new papers, especially the "Republican Catalan," also appealed to the particularist tradition of Catalonia. The grandson of Louis XIV, using French armies, destroyed the privileges of Catalonia. "France, then enslaved, lent its arms to subjugate you, but France, free today, offers you the same arms . . . to restore you to your liberty."[73] They could not escape the commonplaces of the Revolution. France is at war with the "tyrants enemies of humanity,"[74] to the peoples it brings liberation from slavery. "Sovereignty hence resides essentially in the peoples, and all kings who reign against their wishes are violators of their sovereignty and usurpers of their imprescriptible rights," whence it is evident that the present king in Catalonia has usurped its sovereignty, said the "Republican Catalan." He ended, "Viva la Llibertat, viva la Igualdat, viva la Germandat, vivan tots los Estats llibres, y vivan tots los bons patriots que prendran part à esta santa insurreccio."

On June 23, the commanding officers of all French companies were ordered to read the French version of the *Proclamation* to their troops and to find ingenious ways of distributing the other versions to the enemy.[75] Even though action during the month of July was limited to skirmishes and minor activity, the French succeeded in getting the leaflets across the lines. When they retreated, they would leave the leaflets behind for the advancing Spanish soldiers to pick up. During forays, they also scattered the pamphlets about, and at night they spread them by stealth near the Spanish camps, where they would be found in the morning. The Republican generals even instructed their

72 *Proclamacion*, pp. 4-6.
73 *Lo Catala Republica*, p. 3.
74 *Proclamacion*, p. 2.
75 Vigo, p. 56.

soldiers to fraternize with the Catalans so that they might encourage them by word of mouth to believe in the French promises of friendship and good treatment.[76]

The Consejo de la Inquisición, on learning of this new French activity, wrote to its tribunals along the northern frontier to redouble their zeal.[77] The Conde de la Union, a young and very devoted Catholic and monarchist, who had taken the place of Ricardos as commander of the Spanish army in the east, also strove to nullify the propaganda campaign. On July 17 he issued a general order to collect all incendiary sheets and to cross-examine all French deserters to be sure they were not secret emissaries sent to corrupt the local people. The order was repeated individually to the Spanish generals, stressing the need for their soldiers to turn in the propaganda. In September La Union charged his officers with showing the Catalan populace the falsity of the French maxims, "despite the agreeable colors in which the Revolutionaries know how to clothe them." Local inhabitants were forbidden to have communication with the French on pain of death. On one occasion Republican soldiers coming expressly to converse with the inhabitants of a town were ambushed and massacred, and the order was issued to meet all French soldiers except official emissaries and deserters with fire. Prisoners also proved a source of propaganda. La Union ordered them scattered throughout Catalonia away from the theater of war and sent them as far as Seville. They were to be permitted no intercourse with Spaniards.[78]

Despite these stringent measures, the literature began to filter into Spain. The commander of the fortress of Figueras discovered that his soldiers had been reading one pamphlet and that through them some copies had reached Valencia. The case could hardly

[76] Delbrel, "L'Espagne et la Révolution," *loc.cit.*, p. 69 n. 1 and pp. 72-77. Delbrel used the Archives de la préfecture des Pyrénées orientales and the "Dépôt de la Guerre de Madrid, Section de la Guerre contre la République française."

[77] *Auto* of Consejo de la Inquisición, Aug. 6, 1794, A.H.N., Inq., leg. 4429, No. 9.

[78] The orders and dispatches of La Union are quoted in Delbrel, "L'Espagne et la Révolution," *loc.cit.*, pp. 72-75, 83-84.

have been unique. On July 25 a French general reported that Spanish soldiers were reading the leaflets and that they had been introduced into Barcelona.[79] This was no idle boast. The bishop of Gerona sent copies that he had collected of these two "infernal papers" to the inquisitor-general on July 24, priding himself, however, that his diocesans did not listen to such statements. Within a month the Inquisición de Barcelona sent copies of them to the Consejo de la Inquisición.[80] La Union complained to his government, "The French are waging war on us with pen and money more than with fire and sword."[81] A copy in Castilian of the *Proclamacion* now in the archives of the Inquisición was turned up in November 1795 as far in the interior as Cuenca. It has signs of being much handled. The Consejo de la Inquisición had merely scribbled on it, "Noted, and put this paper in the archives with the others of the same nature."[82]

5

It was the deputies on mission Milhaud and Soubrany who were inspiring this campaign. They had been sent to the Pyrenees during the ascendancy of the Jacobins. In July 1794 Robespierre fell from power, and the Jacobin Terror came to an end. The new French regime replaced Milhaud and Soubrany at the end of August by deputies who were not suspect of Robespierrist sympathies.[83] Only one of the new deputies, Pierre Delbrel, became active, since his companion was sick. In December he was cooperating with a committee of five members that included Revest to have posters in French and Catalan printed at the recently captured town of Figueras.[84] Delbrel ordered the French

[79] *Ibid.*, pp. 75-77.   [80] A.H.N., Inq., leg. 4429, No. 9.
[81] La Union to Duque de la Alcudia, Sept. 11, 1794, quoted in Delbrel, "L'Espagne et la Révolution," *loc.cit.*, p. 74.
[82] A.H.N., Inq., leg. 4429, No. 8.
[83] Gustave Bord (ed.), "Notes du conventionnel Delbrel, sur l'Armée des Pyrénées-orientales," *Revue de la Révolution*, v (1885), "Documents inédits," 18.
[84] Letter of committee, 22 frimaire [III] (Dec. 12, 1794), and poster in Archives de la préfecture des Pyrénées orientales, liasse 1060 (note of Miss Hyslop).

generals to distribute them,[85] but his interest in propaganda seems to have been perfunctory. At the siege of Rosas in the winter of 1794-95, the French troops by tacit agreement with the Spanish went into the town to exchange provisions. Delbrel was present and tolerated this practice, but tried not at all to use the occasion to win over Spanish soldiers.[86] On the western front there may have been an attempt to spread French literature during this winter. A Spanish royal order was issued on February 21, 1795 to collect a book entitled *Almanake de Aristides* [*sic*] "which the French have introduced into the kingdom of Navarre and the Basque provinces with the perverse intention of insinuating the republican venom under the pretense of promoting moral virtues."[87] This description of the *Almanake* suggests that it was not written specifically for the Spanish people. One must conclude that once again a change in the ruling party in the Convention had put an end to a promising French propaganda campaign.

Except for the activity of Soubrany and Milhaud during the French invasion of Catalonia in the summer of 1794, none of the official French attempts to propagandize Spain were fruitful. The Jacobin club of Bayonne had some success acting on its own in the winter of 1792-93; but soon after the central government

[85] Dec. 9, 1794, cited in Delbrel, "L'Espagne et la Révolution," *loc.cit.*, p. 69 n. 1.

[86] Bord, *loc.cit.*, p. 110. This account of Delbrel's activity during this period, written later by himself from original documents, makes no mention of French propaganda. He hardly would have failed to mention this subject if he had taken a lively interest in it. J. Delbrel says that Spain was flooded with French literature at this time ("L'Espagne et la Révolution," *loc.cit.*, p. 68 n. 1), but his study ends with La Union's death on Nov. 24, 1794, and all the reports he cites of the Spanish generals finding French leaflets are dated prior to mid-August. The papers of the Inquisición confirm the dates July-August 1794 as the period when the leaflets were being spread and mention nothing later. Beatrice F. Hyslop states: "Among all the official dispatches, the papers of local authorities, and the military papers—which are voluminous—I have found only a dozen mentions of propaganda and revolutionary action. Before the invasion suggestions of what should be done can be found, but military demands prevail over propaganda" ("Problèmes historiques des relations franco-espagnoles pendant la Révolution française," *Bulletin de la Société d'Histoire moderne*, Année XLVI, 10ᵉ ser., No. 16 [May-July 1949], pp. 14-15).

[87] A.H.N., Inq., Inquisición de Toledo, leg. 15, No. 2.

took over direction of their efforts the outbreak of the war between France and Spain in March 1793 and the fall of the
Girondists three months later put a stop to the endeavor. The
war also saw the end of the importation of French papers by
the channels that had been so common in the years 1789 to 1792.
This at least is the conclusion one must draw from the evidence
in the extant archives of the Consejo de la Inquisición. They
reveal few incidents of Revolutionary literature circulating in
Spain, except for that spread by Soubrany and Milhaud, between
March 1793 and the conclusion of the war in July 1795. The
young successor to Aranda as first secretary, Manuel Godoy,
received anonymously through the mail in February 1794 a
French primer and prayer book that contained a statement of
the rights and duties of man.[88] In Murcia a silversmith at this
time received in the same manner from Catalonia a *Rapport
fait à la Convention nationale au nom du Comité de Salut publique, par le citoyen Robespierre . . . sur la situation de la République.*[89] By comparison with the reports of the tribunals of
the Inquisición in the years 1789 to 1792, the paucity of these
incidents indicates an almost total disappearance of new Revolutionary papers in Spain after 1793.

This was no coincidence. The private initiative of French
merchants and peddlers and the interest of Spanish readers had
accounted for the spread of propaganda in northern Spain,
Madrid, and the major ports before 1793 and the scattering of it
throughout the rest of the country in the face of the utmost efforts
of the Inquisición and royal government. By 1793 the French
residents had either left or been intimidated by the decrees
placing them under Spanish jurisdiction. Meanwhile news of the
execution of Louis XVI and the subsequent Terror, combined
with the bitterness caused by the war, roused the Spanish nation
against the Revolution. It was no longer patriotic to read French
tracts. This new spirit in Spain rendered the sporadic attempts

---

[88] Godoy to Manuel Abad y la Sierra, inquisitor-general, Feb. 1, 1794, *ibid.*,
leg. 4430, No. 14.

[89] *Ibid.*, No. 7.

of the French officials to reach Spaniards with their message almost useless and at the same time made unnecessary the heretofore unavailing efforts of the Spanish authorities to stop the invasion of Revolutionary literature. A look at this change in atmosphere will show more clearly why French propaganda disappeared in Spain after 1792.

CHAPTER X

SPAIN'S LEVÉE EN MASSE

THE Spanish people, by their attachment to the monarchy and the Catholic religion, were poorly prepared to approve of the events in France. Nevertheless, opposition to the Revolution did not become manifest for some time after 1789. As has been seen, the censorship set up by Floridablanca was not directed at Revolutionary propaganda alone but at every mention of the French Revolution. He felt it a much safer policy to keep the masses ignorant of the events than, by attempting to rouse them to opposition, inadvertently to disseminate the dread principles. Some French writers tried to make their countrymen believe that the Spanish court was spreading counter-revolutionary propaganda,[1] but their statements lack corroboration. So long as Floridablanca remained first secretary, his policy was one of strict silence.

This official silence did not mean that no anti-revolutionary writings circulated in Spain. The Santo Oficio found manuscripts entitled "Apologia de uno de los curas de Francia contra la nueva constituc^n de la Asamblea y sobre el juramento que exige esta a los obispos, y demas Eccos," and "Causas y agentes de las revoluciones de Francia."[2] Excerpts of Edmund Burke's famous *Reflections on the Revolution in France,* attacking its bases, were secretly translated by two priests in Tarragona soon after its appearance in November 1790. Several manuscript copies of this translation were made there and in Barcelona and some were sent to Madrid, where it was later published clandestinely.[3] Burke's work had a certain popularity. It was found in French by the Inquisición in October 1792, and three years later the royal servant Jovellanos was lending it to a friend in Oviedo.[4] In 1796

---

[1] Chantreau, p. 292; *Moniteur,* Nov. 17, 1791.

[2] A.H.N., Inq., leg. 4430, Nos. 17, 20. The date of receipt of the former is not given; of the latter it is Oct. 1791.

[3] Torres Amat, pp. 52-53.

[4] A.H.N., Inq., leg. 4429, No. 26; Jovellanos, *Diarios,* Nov. 21, 1795, p. 277.

the Inquisición prohibited the French translation of the *Reflections*.[5] Attacks on the Revolution were evidently present in Spain, but they had to circulate as surreptitiously as its praises, and their quantity was negligible.

Although the press was being muzzled, there was one source of news of happenings north of the Pyrenees that the government could not in conscience check. A stream of émigrés soon began to cross the frontier into Spain, and they were more than willing to tell of the horrors they had left behind. Even in their case, however, the government did what it could to avoid exposing its people to their stories. The royal cedula that determined the fate of the French residents in Spain appeared on July 20, 1791, just as the refugees began to become numerous. It established as strict control of persons seeking asylum as of foreigners resident in Spain. Émigrés were to be allowed into the country only at the regularly recognized points of entry, where they must present good reasons for being permitted to enter. Thence they were to be sent by specified routes to towns in the interior to await formal permission to remain. They were to swear to obey the king and laws of Spain and were threatened with the galleys or expulsion from the kingdom if they used other roads than those designated. The oath they were required to take also included a promise not to talk about political events in France.[6] The laymen were restricted to the provinces bordering the Pyrenees. They were not allowed to remain in Barcelona or to go to Madrid but were sent to drink wine, empty their purses, and dream of invading their homeland in the towns of the Catalan countryside. By the beginning of 1792 some two thousand of them had been so disposed of, while a lesser number were quartered around San Sebastián.[7] Only a few leading émigrés, such as the Duc d'Havré, who arrived in September 1791 to

---

[5] July 9, 1796, *Suplemento al Indice*, p. 7.

[6] *Nov. rec.*, VI, xi, 8, art. 3; Chantreau, p. 103; Geoffroy de Grandmaison, p. 89.

[7] Chantreau, pp. 98-100, 103-4, 131-32, and *passim*; Geoffroy de Grandmaison, p. 89. Chantreau, from the figures given him for the daily emigration by Spanish frontier officials, arrives at the same number as the French ambassador.

plead the royalist cause with Carlos IV, were permitted to reside in the capital.[8]

Floridablanca gave a sop to his king's Bourbon conscience by indulging these refugees in their plans for a counter-revolutionary army. Although he was sending large sums to the French émigré forces in Italy and the Rhineland, he gave only token financial support to those in Catalonia.[9] Privately he complained to the Russian and Prussian ambassadors that this was money thrown away, since the émigrés were fonder of words than deeds, a judgment with which a French agent sent to spy on them agreed.[10] The secretary of state prohibited enrolling them in the Spanish army, ostensibly out of fear of disguised Jacobin emissaries, but very likely also to keep the true émigrés away from Spanish troops.[11] When Aranda came to power in February 1792, he was less equivocal. He cut off their subsidy at once. In October he informed the French government that he had expelled a hundred of their number from Spain.[12]

The émigrés did not cease to be a nuisance with the beginning of the war between France and Spain. They had formed two regiments, and, in order to increase their number, they incorporated deserters and even prisoners from the Republican army. This was a dangerous practice and was taken advantage of by the Republican leaders to place their spies within the Spanish camp. In 1794 these regiments had to be reformed and many suspicious persons weeded out.[13]

The official coolness toward the war-minded lay émigrés was motivated in part by a desire to keep Spain's strained relations with France from erupting into an affair of arms. No such worry

[8] Baumgarten, p. 339; Geoffroy de Grandmaison, pp. 66, 72.

[9] Dispatches of Durtubise, Jan. 9, Mar. 26, 1792 and of Bourgoing, June 4, 1792, cited by Geoffroy de Grandmaison, pp. 88-89.

[10] Tratchevsky, *loc.cit.*, p. 32; dispatch of Sandoz, Dec. 18, 1791, cited by Baumgarten, p. 339 n.; Chantreau, pp. 235-39, 281, 289-93, and *passim*. Chantreau was in Catalonia for this purpose in February and March 1792.

[11] Chantreau, p. 94.

[12] *Ibid.*, pp. 137-38; Tratchevsky, *loc.cit.*, p. 35; dispatch of Bourgoing, Apr. 2, 1792, cited by Geoffroy de Grandmaison, p. 89; Aranda to José Ocáriz, Oct. 25, 1792, quoted in Muriel, II, 37.

[13] Delbrel "L'Espagne et la Révolution," *loc.cit.*, pp. 77-82.

should have clouded the reception of the clerical émigrés who
soon came to join them. In November 1790 the National Assembly decreed that all ecclesiastics must take an oath to accept the
Civil Constitution of the Clergy. Those who refused, the so-called
nonjuring or refractory clergy, were gradually driven into exile
by the partisans of the Revolution. Although the bishop of
Tarbes arrived in San Sebastián in December 1790,[14] ecclesiastical
émigrés did not really begin to reach Spain until the summer
of 1791, and then still only in small numbers.[15] The *Moniteur's*
correspondent in Madrid did not speak of their presence until
the end of October.[16] It was at this time that they were beginning
to be seen throughout the country, but the stream did not become
a flood until after the fall of the French monarchy. On August
26, 1792, the Legislative Assembly commanded all refractory
priests to leave France within two weeks or be deported to Guiana.
After this order they left for Spain in hordes, often forcibly
deported.

Most of the clerical refugees were in great physical and mental
distress on their arrival. Luckily they had come to the right place.
The Spanish people received them with open hearts and asked
only their blessing in return.[17] The welcome given by their
brethren in Spain was even more outstanding. The Spanish clergy

[14] Louis Dantin, *François de Gain-Montaignac, évêque de Tarbes (1782-1801)
et son diocèse pendant la Révolution* (Tarbes, 1908), pp. 56-57.

[15] Geoffroy de Grandmaison, p. 86; Victor Pierre, "Le clergé français en
Espagne, 1791-1802," *Revue des questions historiques*, N.S. xxxi [1904], 478-
80, 486. Sandoz'ᶜ statement that thousands were coming by June 1791 is
evidently an exaggeration (dispatch of June 12, 1791, cited by Baumgarten, p.
319). He later said that they began to come in masses in September 1792, which
is correct (*ibid.*, p. 403). The secondary sources on the French clerical émigrés
in Spain, on which the following paragraphs are largely based, are Dantin;
Pierre, *loc.cit.*; Delbrel, "Le clergé français refugié en Espagne," *loc.cit.*; Jean
Contrasty, *Le clergé français exilé en Espagne (1792-1802)* (Toulouse, 1910); M.
Geoffroy de Grandmaison, "Le clergé français en Espagne pendant la Révolution,"
Le correspondant, clxiv (1891), 938-59, 1128-44; Juan Pérez de Guzmán y Gallo,
"Los emigrados de Francia, recuerdos de la Revolución," *Ilustración española y
americana*, lxxxv (1908), 74-75, 131-33, 147, 167, 169.

[16] *Moniteur*, Nov. 17, 1791.

[17] Besides the works cited in n. 15, see Llorente, *Noticia biográfica*, pp. 64-67;
Vicente Orti y Brull, *Doña María Manuela Pignatelli . . . Duquesa de Villa-
hermosa* (Madrid, 1896), ii, 71-79.

exhibited a truly catholic spirit in the efforts they made to care
for these men, whom they looked upon as martyrs for the true
faith. The monastery of Montserrat in Catalonia, to which many
were directed by the civil officials, received them "by the hundreds"
and housed five bishops.[18] Other monasteries throughout Spain
were filled with them. The Spanish episcopate especially outdid
itself: the archbishop of Valencia offered to care for seven
hundred; the very wealthy archbishop of Toledo housed, fed, and
clothed four hundred at his expense; the archbishop of Saragossa,
who was overwhelmed, was cooler in his welcome but turned
no one away; while the cathedrals of León and Sigüenza had a
hundred each and Zamora, a poor see, took in fifty. The bishops
of southern Spain, though less besought, were no less hospitable.
The most Christian welcome of all, however, was given by the
relatively poor bishop of Orense, in Galicia. He devoted all his
meager income to the task and welcomed in all some 320 French
clergymen. Among French refugees his hospitality became pro-
verbial.[19] By April 1793 over six thousand clergymen had reached
Spain, and they were distributed among all but six of the
country's fifty-eight bishoprics.[20] Considering the number of
these unexpected guests, the clergy of the two nations lived
together with surprising harmony which very few humanly
inevitable squabbles disturbed.

The clergy of course were subject to the same control as the lay
émigrés, being assigned their destinations and obligated to take
the oath not to discuss the events they had left behind. On
November 22, 1792, when they had begun to arrive in large numbers, Manuel Godoy, who had replaced Aranda as first secretary

---

[18] Dantin, p. 163; Chantreau, pp. 106-9.

[19] Arturo Vázquez Múñez, "Relación de todos los eclesiásticos franceses que
. . . han llegado a . . . Orense," *Boletín de la Comisión Provincial de Monumentos
Históricos y Artísticos de Orense,* II (1902-5), 237-44, 249-59. See Delbrel,
"Le clergé français refugié en Espagne," *loc.cit.,* pp. 26-27, 256-58. On this
bishop's reputation see Dhermand to Delacroix, July 4, 1796, quoted in Geoffroy
de Grandmaison, *L'ambassade,* p. 107, and the funeral oration of him by the
Abbé Breton cited by Pierre, *loc.cit.,* p. 492.

[20] The figures are 5,888 secular clergy, 434 regular, according to the official list of the Consejo extraordinario de Castilla, cited by Contrasty, pp. 96-97.
The figures for Catalonia are given by Ossorio y Gallardo, p. 14.

a week earlier, issued a cedula regularizing their status. Probably Aranda was its real author. The French clergymen were to live together in small numbers and only in religious houses, away from Madrid, the provincial capitals, and the French frontier. They could say mass but by no means preach. Teaching was specifically prohibited.[21] Nor did this decree become a mere dead letter; in the great majority of the cases it was rigorously enforced. Individual French priests were able to get positions as teachers, but their number was very limited.[22] The government, true to its policy of silence on the Revolution, thus complemented the natural barrier of language to prevent the émigré clergy from carrying their message of hate directly to the people. But the refractory *curés* could do what was perhaps even better: impart their message to the Spanish *curas* and *frailes*.

2

In the Spanish press the official silence on the Revolution was relaxed after June 1792 enough to permit reports in the *Gazeta de Madrid* of the Franco-Austrian war. Censorship continued to be strict on news from Paris. From reading the *Gazeta* alone, a Spaniard could have imagined that Louis XVI and Marie Antoinette were still dancing at Versailles on the day they lost their throne. This silence was brought to a violent end after the arrival on January 30, 1793, of the news of the execution of the French king.[23] On February 5 the *Gazeta* carried a brief notice that there would be three months of mourning at court for Louis XVI, "who ended his career on January 21 last with heroism

---

[21] "Fraile," Vol. 785, fols. 123-28; Aguirre, *Prontuario . . . 1792*, pp. 149-52.
[22] Contrasty, pp. 153-55; Oliver, "Catalunya en temps de la Revolució," *loc.cit.*, p. 231. Delbrel feels disobedience of the regulation was widespread, but his examples are also relatively few ("Le clergé français refugié en Espagne," *loc.cit.*, pp. 261, 274-75, 278-79). French Revolutionary observers felt both the lay and clerical émigrés were effectively painting the Revolution black, but their own exaltation and hatred of the émigrés led them to generalize from limited incidents (dispatch of Durtubise, Mar. 6, 1793, A.A.E., Esp., Vol. 635, pièce 204, which blames the émigré clergy especially; Chantreau, pp. 201-3, which is based on observation of Catalonia, where most of the lay émigrés were located).
[23] Baumgarten, p. 435.

equal to his former misfortunes and to the inhumanity of the monstrous and unheard of outrage committed upon his august person." The *Gazeta's* readers were left without further clarification. Three days later it published in full the "Testamento de Luis XVI." This also appeared on February 16 in the recently founded *Diario de Barcelona,* the first reference of this paper to events in France. The *Gazeta* returned to its diet of news from the war on France's eastern frontier until on March 29 it carried the king's message to his councils telling of his futile attempts to live in peace with France since that country gave way to impiety and anarchy, of his intercessions in favor of his cousin's life, and of the subsequent declaration of war by the Convention. Carlos IV's declaration of war on France followed. It was dated March 27, 1793.

The official commencement of hostilities did not cause the government to relax its censorship of events in France. War or no war, it still felt that it was best not to let the Spanish public become aware of the reforms made in France. On June 7, 1793 a royal order prohibited the insertion in any book or newspaper of "any reports favorable or adverse of things pertaining to the kingdom of France."[24] Within six weeks violations caused the government to repeat the order twice.[25] In February 1794 the *Correo de Murcia* was discovered to be preparing a translation of "La vida y muerte de Luis XVI" by M. Simon. The government at once stopped the project and reasserted the general rule: only official publications could report happenings in France.[26] The *Gazeta* intermittently carried news from Paris. Tales of the Terror, insults to the royal family, and the celebration of the cult of Reason in Catholic churches were considered appropriate items. The terms *guillotine* and *sans-culotte* were explained to the supposedly still ignorant public.[27] The government also permitted the

---

[24] *Nov. rec.,* viii, xviii, nota 18, quoted more fully in preamble to *real orden,* Feb. 12, 1794, "Fraile," Vol. 785, fol. 237.
[25] *Reales ordenes,* June 17, July 28, 1793, *Nov. rec.,* viii, xviii, notas 19, 20.
[26] *Real orden,* Feb. 12, 1794, *loc.cit.*
[27] *Gazeta,* Sept. 3, Dec. 17, 1793, Jan. 31, 1794.

printing in Spanish of documents covering the trial and execution of Louis XVI and Spain's intercession in his behalf.[28]

The censorship was not intended to hamper the inspiration of enthusiasm for the war. The people could be aroused against the French with very little reference to the events of the Revolution, and the government was perfectly willing to receive this kind of support for its war effort. The émigrés took advantage of the new atmosphere. The Duc d'Havré organized a funeral service for Louis XVI in Madrid during which his testament was read from the pulpits. The crowd was immense.[29] In Málaga a translation of a French priest's funeral oration for Louis was published;[30] and in Seville the Abbé Augustin Barruel's "explanation," really a condemnation, of the oath required of the French clergy.[31] This was apparently the first publication in Spanish of a work of this famous enemy of the Revolution; it was certainly not to be the last. At the same time at least five pastoral letters of émigré bishops were made public in various cities of Spain, both in the periodical press and as separate pamphlets.[32] The *Clamores*

[28] *Decretos de la Convencion Nacional para la formacion de la causa fulminada y decidida contra su inocente rey y señor natural Luis XVI* (Cadiz, [1793]). This edition is called "reimpreso," probably it was first published in Madrid. *Convencion Nacional. Defensa de Luis XVI · pronunciada . . . 26 de diciembre de 1792 . . . por el ciudadano Deseze. . . .* Traduxola para noticia del pueblo don Pedro Crisostomo Leyva . . . (Cadiz, [1793]), in "Varios," Carlos IV, leg. 20, 4°.

[29] Feb. 18, 1793 (*Moniteur*, Mar. 9, 1793, and Geoffroy de Grandmaison, *L'ambassade*, pp. 79-80.)

[30] *Oracion fúnebre de Luis XVI, rey de Francia, y de Navarra*. Por un capellan frances. . . . Traducida del idioma frances al español. Por el D. en A.D.D. Antonio Jugla y Font (Málaga, 1793), "Varios," Carlos IV, leg. 43, 4°.

[31] [Augustin Barruel], *Explicacion del juramento civico, que se prescribe á los sacerdotes que exercen cargo eclesiastico, por la Asamblea Nacional de Francia* . . . (Seville, 1793), "Fraile," Vol. 210, fol. 108 (signed "Barruel").

[32] *A la Francia por un obispo emigrante de la misma, y refugiado en Segovia, que pinta el horrendo atentado de la decapitacion del rey en la siguiente oracion* (Seville, [1793?]), "Fraile," Vol. 536, fol. 28; *Carta pastoral del ilustrísimo señor don Juan Carlos de Coucy, obispo de la Rochela dirigida a los fieles de su diocesis desde España* . . . (Seville, 1793), "Varios," Carlos IV, leg. 4, 4°; Luis Carlos Machault [*sic*], *Carta pastoral del Ill.ᵐᵒ señor obispo de Amiens, en que se explican los verdaderos e inmutables principios de la gerarquia y disciplina de la Iglesia Catolica, contra . . . la nueva constitucion civil del clero de Francia* (Cadiz, [1793?]), *ibid.*; and letters of archbishop of Tours and bishop of Castres in *Correo de Murcia*, Apr. 27, 1793 and July 21, 25, 1795.

de un Frances catolico, en la desolacion de su patria, dirigidos a la Convencion nacional were even more popular. They were produced as pamphlets in Málaga and Cadiz and inserted in the *Diario de Barcelona.*[33] All the French writers painted Spain's war as one for true religion against the excesses of a false philosophy, but this author outdid the rest in his hyperbole. Spain will be the instrument of divine wrath, he threatened his countrymen. "These are the doleful results of those perverse dogmas which your impure Voltaire prescribed to you."

The Spanish were no less enthusiastic than the émigrés. The periodical press was flooded by discourses of Spaniards on the war.[34] The ideas were always the same: "Unburden your breasts by punishing that seditious people, who tried under the beguiling echoes of Equality, Independence, and Liberty to sow the perfidious seed from which disorder, violence, furor, cruelty, injustice, deceit, ambition, and death take their origin."[35] Poetry was employed too. In both Castilian and Catalan, popular verse denounced French liberty and equality, lamented the death of Marie

[33] Both pamphlets n.d. [1793?], in "Varios," Carlos IV, leg. 36, 4⁰; *Diario de Barcelona,* May 25, 1793. The *Diario de Barcelona* also published a "Carta de un padre anciano actualmente preso en una de las cárceles de Paris a su hijo emigrante en España" of similar tone (Apr. 26, 1793).

[34] The *Correo de Murcia* published "Causas del libertinage y ateismo de nuestro siglo y su remedio," Nov. 5, 1793; "La misantropia de la Francia, anacrisis de la Falsa Filosofia," Nov. 26, 30, 1793; "Carta exhortatoria del excelentísimo señor don Joaquin de Fonsdeviela, gobernador de la ciudad de Cadiz," Dec. 28, 1793; "Exorto apologético sobre la presente guerra," May 24, 1794. The *Semanario de Salamanca* published "Discurso político, el príncipe debe dominar á todos sus vasallos por la utilidad que resulta á la sociedad, y por ser conforme á las leyes establecidas por Dios," Oct. 1, 1793; "Discurso sobre la educacion de la juventud" (the Revolution was caused by the bad education of the French, which lacked solid grounding in religion), Oct. 12, 15, 1793; "Discurso, por el que se exhorta á los Españoles sean el azote de los sedicioses Franceses, y desprecio de sus infernales constituciones," Dec. 14, 1793; "Los vasallos deben contribuir generosamente al monarca en las publicas necesidades" (signed "El amante de la religion"), Jan. 4, 1794; and "Los impios sediciosos . . . desviando el pueblo del culto . . ." (by the same author), Mar. 14, 1795. Published as a separate pamphlet was Lucas Anjel Dajarabazary, *Patetica declamacion, dirigida a la muy religiosa y muy leal nacion española, . . . en la que . . . se combate el actual gobierno frances, destruyendo y disipando las fanáticas expresiones de* igualdad y libertad *sobre que está fundado . . .* (Baeza, n.d.), "Varios," Carlos IV, leg. 36, 4⁰.

[35] *Semanario de Salamanca,* Dec. 14, 1793.

Antoinette, and urged the Spanish soldiers to defend their religion and *patria*.[36] A professor of theology at Santiago composed in verse an *Exclamacion funebre a la sangrienta y alebe muerte de Luis XVI*, devoted to showing that the head of the Bourbon family died a Catholic martyr but proving more eloquently that professing theology does not always endow one with a lyric strain.[37] Spain's leading poets, however, were silent. Only the Spanish apologist, Juan Pablo Forner, and a playwright from Cadiz, Juan González del Castillo, devoted verses to attacking the Revolution. The latter wrote a narrative poem, *La galiada ó Francia revuelta*, in which Mirabeau, maddened by reading Voltaire, is beset at night by the furies, and Religion, fleeing from France in tatters, calls for a war against sacrilege.[38] Some contemporaries, deaf certainly to the tone of the poem, apparently saw indirect praise of the Revolution in a speech its author put in the mouth of Mirabeau.[39] González del Castillo replied to their suspicions with an elegy on the death of Marie Antoinette, "aquella rosa, honor del galo suelo," and an *Oracion exhortatoria* urging Spaniards to take arms in defense of king, religion, and *patria* against "that vaunted liberty."[40]

[36] *Coleccion de varias poesias relativas al estado actual de la Francia* (Málaga, n.d.) includes "Contra la libertad francesa" and "Contra la igualdad francesa," "Varios," Carlos IV, leg. 47, 4°. The *Correo de Murcia* published a "Fabula, la palmera" drawing a moral from the Revolution (Jan. 4, 1794). For Catalan poems see Ossorio y Gallardo, pp. 78-81.

[37] Manuel Fernández, *Exclamacion funebre a la sangrienta y alebe muerte de Luis XVI . . .* (Cadiz, [1793]).

[38] Juan Ignacio González del Castillo, *Sainetes,* ed. Adolfo de Castro (Cadiz, 1846), II, 267-82. Castro gives the first edition as Puerto de Santa María, 1793 (IV, ix). Jovellanos also bewailed the Revolution incidentally in some poems. Miguel Santos Oliver, *Los Españoles en la Revolución francesa* (Madrid, 1914), pp. 117-91, "La poesía española y la Revolución," studies this poetry and remarks especially its paucity.

[39] So according to Castro (González del Castillo, IV, xxiii-xxiv).

[40] The elegy is quoted in part in Cueto, *loc.cit.,* p. clxxi. I have not seen the entire poem. Cueto does not refer to an original edition, but Oliver notes its publication was advertised in the *Diario de Barcelona* in September 1794 (*Los Españoles en la Revolución,* p. 198). Juan Ignacio González del Castillo, *Oracion exhortatoria en la qual observada la conducta de los Franceses en las actuales circunstancias, se anima a los Españoles a tomar las armas en defensa del rey, de la religion, y de la patria* (Málaga, [1794]), "Varios," Carlos IV, leg. 36, 4°.

Spain's Levée en Masse

The émigrés and laymen had perforce a limited audience, since they were confined to the press as their medium. The Spanish clergy were in a much better position. They had the pulpit. For two years after the declaration of hostilities, sermons and pastoral letters were devoted to inspiring the people to war.[41]

[41] Many of these were published as pamphlets or in the periodicals. I have seen the following:

Sermon que en la rogativa que hizo . . . la junta de . . . los empleados de la Plaza de Toros de esta corte . . . por el feliz exito de sus reales armas . . . el dia 14 de Abril del presente año dixo el R. P. Fr. Gregorio Galan . . . (Madrid, 1793), "Varios," Carlos IV, leg. 11, 4°; *Relacion de las suntuosas exequias celebradas en Sevilla el dia 8 de Junio de 1793 a expensas de varios Españoles . . . por el alma de Luis XVI . . . con la oracion fúnebre que dixo el P. D. Teodomiro Ignacio Diaz de la Vega . . .* (Seville, [1793]), *ibid.,* leg. 43, 4°; *Sermon que predico el Doctor D. Joseph Lopez de la Fuente, canonigo de la santa iglesia catedral de Mondoñedo . . . el dia 30 de Junio de 1793 en . . . dicha ciudad* (n.p., n.d.), *ibid.,* leg. 10, 4°; *Sermon que en la solemne funcion de desagravios de Jesus sacramentado, que celebraron los gefes y demas individuos de los quatro oficios de la boca de S. M. . . . el 9 de Julio dixo el M. R. P. Fr. Antonio Miguel Yurami . . .* (Madrid, 1793), *ibid.; Sermon que . . . el domingo primero de Agosto de 1793 . . . para . . . la victoria de sus armas, dixo el M. R. P. Fr. Vicente Cortes Merino y Marroquin . . .* ([Madrid, 1793]), *ibid.,* leg. 11, 4°; *Sermon que en la solemne rogativa, que la Hermandad de San Luis Rey de Francia, hizo el dia 27 de Octubre de . . . 1793, en . . . Toledo. Predico el R. P. Fr. Agustin Garcia Porrero . . .* (Toledo, [1793]), *ibid.; Exhortacion al pueblo que en observancia de la que de órden de S. M. expidió el Exc. Sr. Duque de la Alcudia con fecha de 15 de Noviembre de 1793 hizo, en la villa de Vallada el Dr. Frey Joachín Antonio Diez . . .* (Valencia, 1794), *ibid.,* leg. 7, 4°; *Oracion con que segun lo prevenido por el rey . . . exortó al servicio voluntario de las armas, a los jovenes de la . . . Universidad . . . de Orihuela . . . el Dr. D. Mariano de Perea . . . el dia 20 de Diciembre del año 1793* (Orihuela, [1794]), *ibid.,* leg. 36, 4°; *Carta pastoral del ilustrísimo señor D. Fr. Francisco Armañá, arzobispo . . . de Tarragona . . .* (2d ed.; Madrid, 1793), *ibid.,* leg. 4, 4°; *Medio seguro para triunfar de la Francia. Oracion deprecatoria y ascetica, que en el dia 10 de Junio de 1794 y segundo de las rogativas . . . en que algunos ilustres individuos de la . . . nobleza de . . . Valencia pidieron al Dios de los Exercitos su auxilio. . . . Dixo el . . . Fr. Nicolas Chornét y Añó . . .* (Valencia, 1794), *ibid.,* leg. 11, 4°; and *Nos don Manuel Ferrer y Figueredo . . . arzobispo obispo de Málaga . . . a todos nuestros amados diocesanos . . .* (signed Aug. 20, 1794) (n.p., n.d.), *ibid.,* leg. 4, 4°.

The following pastoral letters and addresses in the press: In the *Correo de Murcia,* Apr. 16, 1793, bishop of Gerona; Apr. 20, bishop of Cartagena; Dec. 14, bishop of Orihuela (also in *Semanario de Salamanca,* Dec. 28, 31, 1793); in the *Diario de Barcelona,* Apr. 16, 1793, bishop of Barcelona; May 29, 1794, archbishop elect of Valencia; in *Semanario de Salamanca,* suplemento Aug. 26, 1794, cardinal archbishop of Toledo; suplemento, Sept. 2, archbishop of Saragossa (also in *Correo de Murcia,* Sept. 30, 1794); Sept. 6, archbishop of Burgos; Sept. 16, bishop of Cartagena; Oct. 11, archbishop of Tarragona; Nov. 8, bishop of Calahorra; suplemento, Dec. 26, bishop of Gerona.

On November 15, 1793 and August 10, 1794, the king ordered public rogations held throughout the kingdom, and these were the occasion for many sermons. Others were given at services sponsored by private groups, such as the nobility of Valencia, the university of Orihuela, the employees of the Plaza de Toros of Madrid, and the "chiefs and other individuals of the four offices of the mouth of His Majesty."

Everywhere the common theme appeared. This was a war for "la Religion, el Rey, la Patria,"[42] a "defensa de la Religion y de la Patria,"[43] against a "Pueblo sin Rey, sin ley, y sin Dios."[44] References to happenings in France were prohibited, but the preachers could condemn its celebrated liberty, "una soñada libertad,"[45] a "libertad sin freno," which is only license.[46] It was safer and more convenient to denounce the new philosophy. France was suffering from its "filosofía criminal y falsa," was being ruined by "hombres irreligionarios."[47] "O maldita y exêcrable filosofía," with what a horrible aspect you appear.[48] They called upon France, "Arroja de ti los Roxeaus, Volteres, Helvecios, Bayles, Masones, y aun los Gasendos."[49] These expressions rolled off the tongues of the *curas* and *frailes* beautifully, but they could not fill up a whole hour; so their orations were filled out with suggestive references to Biblical cataclysms, with which the speakers were much more at home than with the new godless philosophy.

Occasionally someone would rise as high as the mediocre. A royal preacher, Fray Antonio Díez, produced a coherent, if extravagant, sermon defending the divine right of kings, whether they be tyrants or fathers of their people, to the obedience of

[42] Bishop of Cartagena in *Correo de Murcia,* Apr. 20, 1793.
[43] Bishop of Calahorra in *Semanario de Salamanca,* Nov. 8, 1794.
[44] Chornet y Añó, pp. 2-3.
[45] Fr. Pedro Pont, *La soberania francesa humillada y la humildad española exaltada* . . . (July 7, 1793 in Santa María del Mar), quoted in Ossorio y Gallardo, pp. 74-78.
[46] Díaz de la Vega.
[47] Cortes Merino y Marroquín, pp. 32-33.
[48] López de la Fuente, p. 9.
[49] Galán, p. 42.

their subjects. The origin of all France's ills he saw in the rise of Protestantism; the Revolution was largely the work of "Neker, Protestante, Banquero."[50] Francisco Armañá, archbishop of Tarragona and one of the most remarkable Spanish prelates, wrote a really respectable tract. The demand of the Revolution for liberty and equality, he said, was inherited from Rousseau's picture of man in the state of nature; it was a chimera to seduce the plebe. He saw in France during the Terror not liberty but "slavery under a thousand tyrants." Even he could not escape the platitude: "What really makes them vile slaves is the lack of religion, the violence of passions." "The true liberty of a republic, and of a kingdom, is for everyone to be able to enjoy what his talents, his work, his merits, or the sweat of his elders has acquired . . . to be able to find in the laws, in the authority of the government, sure refuge against all violence; above all not to be deprived of, rather to be provided with, the means to be eternally happy."[51] This was the kind of liberty Armañá said the Spanish enjoyed under their "Catholic king, just, pious, loving his vassals."

Very different in tone was a 229-page exhortation by the bishop of Santander to wage the war of the Lord against the French. It was such an exorbitant, redundant, and ungrammatical hodgepodge of Biblical references and anti-philosophic ranting that it is difficult to imagine that even his clergy read the whole tract.[52] Yet this bishop was much closer to the average than Armañá. Fray Diego de Cádiz, the peripatetic Capuchin missionary whose eloquence moved Spanish crowds to the heights of passion, wrote a "carta instructiva, ascetico-historico-politica," showing how a Catholic should prepare to go to war against the regicides.

[50] Díez, pp. 5-7, 26.

[51] Armañá, pp. 7-10, 18, 11-12.

[52] [Raphael Thomás Menéndez de Luarca], *El reino de Dios y su justicia, obradora de la paz de Christo . . . exhortacion . . . á todos los Españoles, sobre guerrear, fuertes en la fé, las guerras del Señor, contra sus enemigos los Franceses libres* (Santander, 1794). Menéndez Pelayo, although doing his best by Catholic apologists, has to admit that the bishop's work is practically illiterate (*Heterodoxos*, v, 416-17).

Dios, su Iglesia, su Fé, su Religion, sus Leyes, sus Ministros, sus Templos, y todo lo mas Sagrado; el derecho de gentes, el respeto debido á los Soberanos, y aun el fuero siempre inviolable de la humanidad se hallan injustamente violados, impiamente desatendidos, y sacrilegamente atropellados en ese desgraciado Reyno por una multitud de hombres cuyo proceder les acredita de hijos de Lucifer, y miembros perniciosos de tan infame cabeza.[53]

If this was Spain's best preacher, even the bishop of Santander probably seemed a stylist beside the common priest or monk.

Whatever their style was, their message was the same. After February 1793, the *frailes* and *curas* preached a crusade of vengeance against the enemies of God and the murderers of the head of the house of Bourbon. Crucifix in hand, they went through the villages urging the people to make sacrifices for the cause of religion and monarchy.[54] The Easter season of 1793, with its required communion, also gave an opportune occasion to exhort the faithful to take arms in defense of the true faith.[55]

3

The response of the Spanish people was immediate and astonishing. Everything that recalled the Revolution was at once openly despised. In Barcelona in February 1793 news of the royal execution brought forth demonstrations against the French and bitter posters.[56] In Madrid ladies who wore French coiffures in public were forced to let their hair down on the spot despite a

[53] Fr. Diego Josef de Cádiz, *El soldado católico en la guerra de religion. Carta instructiva, ascetico-historico-politica* . . . (Barcelona, 1794), p. 4.

[54] A. Alcalá Galiano, *Historia de España,* vi, 18 (Alcalá Galiano lived through this period); *Moniteur,* Mar. 4, 22, Apr. 1, 1793 (reports from Barcelona, Feb. 18, and Madrid, Feb. 22, Mar. 8). The *Moniteur* is suspect as a source, but in general the news it gives is fairly accurate although its viewpoint is markedly prejudiced. In this case it calls these preachers missionaries sent out by the Spanish court. That the court approved of their activity is doubtless true, but the direct inspiration probably came from their religious superiors and from their contact with the French refractory clergy.

[55] Auber, French consul in Barcelona, to Lucia, Mar. 16, 1793, in Archives de la Préfecture des Pyrénées orientales, liasse 355 (information given me by Miss Hyslop).

[56] *Moniteur,* Mar. 4, 1793.

feeble attempt at their protection by the police, and those that had the temerity to wear in the theater red liberty caps that a milliner had recently put on the market were hooted at by the pit until they gave them up.[57] The Madrid public was also treated to the spectacle of the vilification of a well-born Spaniard who had chosen to adopt the Revolution, Rubín de Celis, who was busy in Bayonne indoctrinating Spanish deserters. The Consejo de las Ordenes expelled him from the military order of Santiago. His effigy was publicly stripped of the cross, cloak, and other regalia of the order and then thrown to the ground to be trampled by the spectators.[58]

Hatred of the French became manifest everywhere. Carlos IV ordered all non-domiciled French who still remained in Spain to leave the country, travelling in groups of eight or less.[59] The occasion was used by the Spanish to persecute these Frenchmen. Many were mishandled and some killed despite the government protection promised them.[60] The antipathy remained evident throughout the war. There were riots in Valencia against the French colony on March 31, 1794. Its members had to be put in prison for their own safety.[61] In Barcelona on June 29, 1794, the report got about that French soldiers who had been weeded out of the regiments of émigrés on suspicion of Republican sympathies were dancing the carmagnole in their barracks and had painted a liberty tree and two guillotines on the wall. One guillotine was labelled for "Charles Capet." A crowd of Barcelonans formed outside and was incited by clergymen to avenge the insult to their king. Yelling "Visca la Religió i el Rei!" and "Morin els francesos!" the crowd stormed the barracks and

[57] Durtubise to Lebrun, Mar. 7, 1793, A.E.E., Esp., Vol. 635, pièce 211; *Moniteur,* Mar. 9, 1793.

[58] *Moniteur,* Apr. 12, 1793.

[59] *Real provisión,* Mar. 4, 1793, in *Gazeta,* Mar. 12, 1793.

[60] Alcalá Galiano, *Historia de España,* vi, 18; *Moniteur,* Apr. 1, 29, 1793 (reports from Madrid, Mar. 8, Apr. 8); Tratchevsky, *loc.cit.,* p. 38; Durtubise to Lebrun, Mar. 6, 1793, and "Bulletin des affaires étrangères," Madrid, Mar. 6, A.A.E., Esp., Vol. 635, pièces 203-5; Augustin Queneau to Directoire exécutif, 1 ventôse iv (Feb. 19, 1796), *ibid.,* Vol. 639, pièce 74.

[61] Desdevises, *L'Espagne,* i, 249-50.

massacred about a hundred French soldiers. By now the civil and military authorities had lost control of the situation. During the evening mobs attempted to break into the houses and convents in which they smelled the blood of more Frenchmen. They made no distinction between longtime residents and recent émigrés.[62]

Meanwhile, with the language of the priests ringing in their ears, the Spanish people joined the war effort. For the masses of the nation the Catholic religion was still their only guiding light and to participate in a crusade for it as well as for their king and country was a universal duty. They took up arms against the Revolutionary invaders as no other people in Europe did at this time. Volunteers for the army and contributions to the war chest began to flow in even before war was declared. The *Gazeta de Madrid* carried lists of "offerings made to His Majesty" in almost every issue from February 1793 until August 1795 after the peace. Those who could not afford money gave their personal possessions and clothing. When domestic gifts appeared to slacken, the paper could still be filled with others from the American colonies. Lists of volunteers were nearly as common, especially at the beginning of the war; and even when such lists did not appear in the *Gazeta*, the "offerings" published often included such items as "a son" or "his person." From all corners of Spain, towns, nobles, religious and military orders, all vied in their generosity. The archbishop of Saragossa even suggested raising an army of priests and monks, and smugglers and impressment dodgers came out to serve as volunteers. Foreign observers were astounded by the sight of this popular movement.[63]

By the end of 1793 much of the original enthusiasm had waned, largely because the Spanish advances into France did not seem

[62] Vigo, pp. 82-83; Delbrel, "L'Espagne et la Révolution," *loc.cit.*, pp. 80-81.

[63] All who have written on this phenomenon have taken pleasure in noting strange items contributed by rich and poor alike (e.g., Tratchevsky, *loc.cit.*, p. 38; Baumgarten, pp. 451-53; Godoy, I, 82 n. 2; Muriel, II, 96-97). The German traveller Fischer in 1797-98 noted that the clergy had aroused the hatred and fear of the French. It was in this hatred, the fidelity of the nation to its king, and the clergy that he saw the strength of the Spanish throne (*Travels in Spain*, pp. 210-13).

commensurate with the sacrifices being made.[64] But the French invasion of Spanish territory in 1794 reawakened the national ardor. In the east the people of Catalonia rose to oppose the Republican troops. The Spanish commander, La Union, published an address to the people on June 9 to encourage them to war against those who wished to dethrone God. He reminded them of the benefits of their religion: it alone could create a society rich in the virtues that bring strength and prosperity. "Yes, let us swear to die, to perish with religion, with our country and our monarchy, rather than to see our lives dragged out in the hardest slavery, under the cruel blade of the guillotine." Despite the qualms of Madrid at the sight of a spirit of initiative in this traditionally particularist province, the Catalans undertook to organize their defense. Men called appropriately by La Union "Promotores de la defensa de la Religion y de la Patria" were sent through the countryside to raise volunteers.[65] The local clergy was highly active in this effort. After French victories in November 1794 led to the shameful capitulation of the fortress of Figueras, without a shot in its defense, and the subsequent loss of Gerona, committees were set up in Barcelona to further recruiting and prepare the defense. A local militia of twenty thousand, organized in traditional groups called *somatenes*, was collected, and a reserve equally large. The Madrid government's fears of a revival of the spirit of independence in Catalonia were vain. The crusading zeal incited by the priests and press, together with the inevitable pillaging of the French army,[66] rendered completely futile all the Republican propaganda aimed at winning

---

[64] See Baumgarten, p. 486, citing Sandoz's dispatch of Oct. 1, 1793.

[65] Delbrel, "L'Espagne et la Révolution," *loc.cit.*, XLVII, 648-50, which quotes La Union.

[66] Ossorio y Gallardo, p. 140, notes that the sacking of Besalú by the French in the summer of 1794 had a strong effect on the Catalans. Baumgarten, p. 547 n., quotes a dispatch of the French deputy on mission, Delbrel: "Plundering, murders, and burning are the order of the day. . . ." The French also profaned Spanish churches, going so far as to bury horses in the cemeteries (Delbrel, "L'Espagne et la Révolution," *loc.cit.*, XLVIII, 60). Vigo, pp. 58-65, shows that while wanton plunder was condemned by the French commanders, systematic measures were taken for the army to live off the land.

friends among the Catalans by awakening their resentment against Castilian rule. The war revived here a mortal hatred for the French, not the Castilians. When the peace was signed in July 1795, it was the Catalan peasants and Spanish troops who were on the offensive in the eastern Pyrenees.[67]

On the western front the situation was practically identical. In July 1794 the French broke into Guipúzcoa and forced San Sebastián to surrender. The governing body of Guipúzcoa, abusing the extensive home rule of the Basque provinces, negotiated a separate peace with France. In Madrid these events were believed to be the result of treason by a populace won over to revolutionary ideals,[68] but actually there was no more danger of disloyalty here than in Catalonia. Although a small group of leaders were "encyclopedistas," the people, led by their priests, rose against the French here too. The arrest of priests and the looting and closing of churches by the French belied their talk of friendship and liberation. Vizcaya and Navarre armed spontaneously to protect their frontiers, and the Guipuzcoans rejected the treachery of their governors and fought loyally for Spain. Here too it was the local populace that saved the country from invasion in 1794.[69]

[67] On the Catalan rising see *Moniteur*, Feb. 10, 18, 27, Mar. 28, Apr. 24, 1795; Baumgarten, pp. 521, 526, 546-48, 559-61; Torres Amat, pp. 62-68. Ossorio y Gallardo devotes his book largely to the story of this rising, demonstrating that there was no danger of Catalan separatism during the war (see p. 214). He holds that the Catalans preferred Spanish rule to French because it was less centralized. I believe instead that the average Catalan who filled the *somatenes* was fighting for his God and home. Fischer in Oct. 1798 remarked repeatedly the glaring hatred for France among the Barcelonans (*Travels in Spain*, pp. 360-69).

[68] Muriel, II, 144, 251; Godoy, I, 187 n. I.

[69] Baumgarten, pp. 522-23; Lasala y Collado, pp. 112-36. Like Ossorio y Gallardo for Catalonia, Lasala y Collado destroys the legend of Guipúzcoa's treason, using Basque documents. Antoine Richard also establishes the loyalty of Guipuzcoans, especially the clergy and common people, using the reports of the French deputies on mission ("L'Armée des Pyrénées-occidentales et les représentants en Espagne [1794-1795]," *Annales historiques de la Révolution française*, XI [1934], 302-22). The spirit of the local priest who blessed and defended civil marriage (see Menéndez Pelayo, *Heterodoxos*, V, 267) was not widespread. Fischer notes that after the war the hatred for the French had grown to a sort of horror among unenlightened Basques (*Travels in Spain*, p. 100).

It was precisely the northern provinces of Spain that had had the greatest influx of Revolutionary papers in the years of peace from 1789 to 1792. It was to these districts too that the French propagandists in 1793 and 1794 had primarily directed their efforts. Whether the enticement to favor the Revolution was greater in 1790 and 1791 than after the fall of the monarchy, as it undoubtedly was, and whether there were some Spaniards who felt the attraction of the events in France even during the war, as it will be seen that there were, for the great majority of the Spanish people the French ideals remained incomprehensible and undesirable. To them "liberty" meant "license" and the Republic was an outrage to religion and royalty. For their God, their country, and their king they were eager to make personal sacrifices. The Spanish church had shown that it was far more effective in molding public opinion than were a few individuals, many of whom were foreigners, working outside the law.

CHAPTER XI

THE GROWTH OF POLITICAL OPPOSITION

ALTHOUGH the vigor of the Spanish rising against the Revolutionary armies was the most impressive phenomenon of the French war, not even contemporary observers were misled into thinking that the popular abhorrence of the regicide and irreligious Revolutionaries was the only significant development of these hectic years. That not all Spaniards shared the views of the clergy or supported the anti-French crusade soon became clear.

So long as the royal government was in the hands of Floridablanca, few partisans of enlightenment became dissatisfied with the domestic situation. Even when he curtailed progressive activities and institutions, Floridablanca still radiated the aura of Carlos III and commanded respect. Only isolated Spaniards like Marchena seriously thought of imitating France during these years. Aranda was equally respected as a veteran of the last reign. On November 15, 1792, however, Aranda was dismissed as first secretary, and the public soon learned to its astonishment that his successor was to be the handsome young Duque de la Alcudia, better known to history by his personal name, Manuel Godoy.

The public had become aware of Godoy only since the advent of Carlos IV. He had been born in 1767 into a family of provincial nobles in Badajoz. His parents had limited means but they provided him with a passable education in the liberal and manly arts. At the age of nineteen he entered the royal body guards and was stationed at the court, where after 1789 he began to rise rapidly in military rank and government position. Early in 1792 he was made a *grande* with the title of Duque de la Alcudia, and he soon became a member of Aranda's revived Consejo de Estado. His sole claim to such unheard of promotions was widely believed to be the protection of María Luisa. Before October 1791 the report had spread as far as France that Godoy was having relations with the queen and that Carlos IV played the willing cuckold.[1]

María Luisa was only following a practice she had observed in the aristocracy of Madrid. Many ladies of the capital felt the need for a gentleman to keep them company while their husbands were out of the house. Such a friend was known as a *cortejo*. Townsend was struck by his constant attendance: "If the lady is at home, he is at her side; when she walks out, she leans upon his arm; when she takes her seat at an assembly, an empty chair is left for him." Social equality was unnecessary; the *cortejo* of the first duchess of the kingdom could be a non-commissioned officer in the army.[2] The husbands were usually aware of the relationship and took it for granted. Carlos saw nothing wrong in his wife's companion; indeed he too soon found a friend in young Manuel.

After August 1792 Carlos was beset with worry over the fate of Louis XVI, awaiting trial before the Convention. Aranda had been called in early in the year to improve Louis' position by extending friendship to the Revolutionaries, and his attempt had failed. Perhaps young Manuel could find means to save the king of France. Such appears to have been Carlos' reasoning when he decided to replace Aranda with Godoy. But he reckoned without public opinion. The intimacy of the Duque de la Alcudia with the king and queen had scandalized the lower classes of Madrid, who had never approved of *cortejos*; and the ordinary people of the provinces, where the institution was less common, contrasted the morals of their rulers with the stern chastity of Carlos III's widowerhood. The sight had been demoralizing enough, but when the queen's *cortejo* was named first secretary, a cry of dismay arose from the Spanish people.

Carles, who was then a member of the French embassy in Madrid, later reported that the period following the appointment of Godoy was the only moment when he had felt the possibility

---

[1] Floridablanca to Iriarte, Oct. 20, 1791, in Chaumié, *loc.cit.*, xxxvii, 361.
[2] Townsend, ii, 144, 150. See also Bourgoing (1789), ii, 295, and Kany, pp. 212-14.

of a revolution in Spain. The rapid rise in violation of all *bien-séances* of "this adventurer" made all classes murmur, he said. The *grandes* and all nobles were aroused by this violation of their rights, the men of merit were stung by the injustice, and everyone was shocked by the lack of modesty of the "lubricious queen" enriching her favorite out of public funds. Had a leader been present in Madrid to make use of the hatred for Godoy, he could have carried out a revolution, in the opinion of Carles. But the leader had been missing.[3]

Their disgust led some persons in Madrid to side secretly with the French Revolution at just the moment when Spain was ready to break with France. A few entered into active relations with the French. As the Convention was meeting in September 1792, the French foreign minister, Lebrun, wrote to his ambassador, Bourgoing, to "set up a little spy machine" which would provide news from Spain under any circumstances.[4] Bourgoing and his aides, Carles and Taschereau, soon collected friends whom they could trust and to whom they distributed French papers.[5] The head of this group seems to have been Domingo de Iriarte, Spanish *chargé d'affaires* in Paris until August 1792, who was said, since his return to Madrid, to be heading a Francophile party of high officials and giving information to Bourgoing.[6] Early in 1793 Taschereau and Carles left Madrid for Bayonne, but the friends they left behind kept them informed of the situation in the Spanish capital.[7] Durtubise, the last French agent to leave Madrid, wrote to Lebrun after war between Spain and France had become a certainty, "We have here friends and warm partisans of liberty . . . who wish the good of their country and who groan under the servitude to which they are reduced,"

---

[3] Carles, "Estraits d'observations sur l'Espagne," May 1793, A.A.E., Esp., Vol. 636, pièce 102. See also Muriel's description of the reaction to Godoy's appointment (II, 48-58).

[4] Sept. 10, 1792, cited in Geoffroy de Grandmaison, *L'ambassade*, p. 82.

[5] Taschereau to Lebrun, Jan. 25, 1793, A.A.E., Esp., Vol. 635, pièce 61.

[6] Baumgarten, p. 555.

[7] "Extrait d'une lettre écrite de Madrid le 28 janvier 1793 par un agent politique près la cour d'Espagne" (in Carles's hand), Taschereau to Lebrun, Mar. 12, 28, 1793, A.A.E., Esp., Vol. 635, pièces 69, 230, 301.

but he admitted that they were not numerous.[8] He referred to them again in one of his last reports, on March 17:

> The bureau established in Bayonne has a regular correspondence with the Club of Madrid; several of these persons would like to go to that city but do not dare to take the risk. All would be lost if they were discovered. The government suspects something and the police are watching as closely as they can. It is in this club that we should place all our hopes; once the Spanish can talk, one will be amazed by the men that this nation contains.[9]

The word "club" is evidently a misapplication by Durtubise of Revolutionary jargon to impress his superiors, since it is no where else used by the French agents, but his employment of it implies that the Spaniards with whom he was dealing were a small, closely associated group.

Besides this body, "which is on a level with our revolution," Durtubise stated, there was a party of considerable numbers who desired a change in the Spanish government. The educated men of Spain and officers of the army and navy were said by the French agents to fall into this category. Such a person was reported to be Antonio Ricardos, the Spanish commander in Catalonia.[10] He had been a partisan of Aranda's in opposition to Floridablanca in 1788, and his career had suffered as a consequence until Aranda had given him his present command. His patron's replacement by Godoy had supposedly piqued him.[11]

After war was declared, both groups of dissatisfied Spaniards awaited French victories in order to come out into the open. They emphasized to their French friends the importance of the successes of the French armies. The Republicans should not enter Spain until they could do so with overwhelming blows, even

[8] "Bulletin des affaires étrangères," Madrid, Mar. 6, 1793, *ibid.*, pièce 202 (anon. but evidently by Durtubise).

[9] Durtubise to Lebrun, Mar. 17, 1793, *ibid.*, pièce 243.

[10] *Ibid.*, and Carles, "Extraits d'observations sur l'Espagne," May 1793, and Taschereau to Lebrun, Mar. 28, 1793, A.A.E., Esp., Vol. 636, pièce 102, Vol. 635, pièce 301.

[11] Ferrer del Rio, IV, 245, 247 n. 1; Baumgarten, p. 487.

if a delay were necessary. Then, they told the agents, the Spanish people would lose their war enthusiasm, the court would be discredited, and the Cortes could be convoked. All would be lost, however, if the French should suffer a defeat.[12]

Signs of this discontent and revolutionary sentiment meanwhile boiled up to the surface. In February 1793 revolutionary pasquinades were posted in prominent spots in Barcelona.[13] Posters also appeared in Madrid, reported by Durtubise to have carried such statements as "Madrid will be reduced to ashes, the king will perish, long live liberty!" and "The French are leaving, some one will pay for this with his head, long live liberty!" Many thought it was Spaniards who had put them up.[14] The discontent no doubt also accounted for the ladies of Madrid who donned liberty caps at this time.[15] Rumors circulated in the Spanish capital that groups had been discovered in Valencia and Barcelona in correspondence with France with subversive plans, which included blowing up the fortress of Montjuich outside Barcelona; and if they were not true they at least showed that such reports were not considered unlikely.[16] Within one of the Spanish regiments a group was revealed in April to be in sympathy with the enemy. Those involved were arrested.[17]

The beginning of the campaign put a stop to the effervescence. The enthusiasm of the Spanish malcontents, who had counted on a French victory, was dampened when the Spanish army, led by the supposedly friendly Ricardos, dealt the first decisive blows of the war. Iriarte, their reputed leader, was made ambassador to Poland to get him out of the way.[18] The remainder of 1793 passed without report of further unrest. The only use to which the French had been able to put the discontent was to

[12] "Bulletin des affaires étrangères," Madrid, Mar. 6, and dispatches of Durtubise, Mar. 17, and Taschereau, Mar. 26, 28, 1793, A.A.E., Esp., Vol. 635, pièces 202, 243, 297, 301.

[13] Ossorio y Gallardo, p. 17.

[14] "Bulletin des affaires étrangères," Madrid, Mar. 6, 1793, *loc.cit.*

[15] See above, p. 311.

[16] Dispatch of Durtubise, Mar. 21, 1793, A.A.E., Esp., Vol. 635, pièce 269.

[17] Ossorio y Gallardo, pp. 15-16, citing A. H. N., Estado, legajo 3944.

[18] Baumgarten, p. 555; Cotarelo y Mori, pp. 408-9.

harp on the reputedly scandalous relations of Godoy with the queen in their propaganda.[19]

The sight of the Terror in France at this same time helped to cool off many of the early partisans of the Revolution who had seen in it the achievement of constitutional monarchy. By May 1794 Jovellanos was revolted by the Jacobin regime. "The furor of the French republicans . . . I fear will accomplish nothing except to worsen the human race: cruelty erected as a system and glossed over with the color and forms of justice turned against the defenders of liberty," he jotted in his diary.[20] Antonio Alcalá Galiano, an official of the royal *chancillería* of Valladolid, was known to hold republican sympathies, but he later asserted that the experience of the French Revolution turned him away from his passion for the social contract.[21] After leaving Spain, Carles admitted to Lebrun that the Spanish "patriots" (that is, friends of the Revolution) were all convinced of the need for a king and of his inviolability, believing that liberty and equality could exist in a monarchy. The proclamation of the French Republic and the execution of Louis, said Carles, largely destroyed their attachment to the Revolution.[22] As has been seen, after the end of 1792 the circulation of Revolutionary papers almost disappeared in Spain. Coinciding as it did with Spanish victories, the news of the Terror dealt almost a death blow to Revolutionary sympathies south of the Pyrenees.

2

The discontent with the Duque de la Alcudia remained, however. The public did not feel that the limited invasion of France justified the personal and monetary sacrifices they had so

[19] Condorcet, *Avis aux Espagnols*, p. 10; *Lo Catala republica*, pp. 7-9.

[20] Jovellanos, *Diarios*, p. 147, May 24, 1794.

[21] A. Alcalá Galiano, *Máximas*, "prólogo." For his identity and democratic sympathies see A. Alcalá Galiano (his nephew), *Memorias*, I, 5-6.

[22] Carles, "Extraits d'observations sur l'Espagne," May 1793, *loc.cit.* An article in the *Gazeta de Madrid*, Sept. 15, 1812, entitled "Espíritu público," said that one of the reasons for the Spanish rising against Joseph Bonaparte was that the horrors of the French Revolution had calmed "a beginning of revolutionary spirit that was spreading in Spain."

generously made.²³ Many of the enemies of Godoy grouped themselves around the figure of the Conde de Aranda, who was still dean of the Consejo de Estado.²⁴ Aranda himself does not appear to have acted disloyally, but Godoy must nonetheless have felt his presence embarrassing. On March 14, 1794 Aranda objected bitterly in the Consejo de Estado in the presence of Carlos IV to Godoy's policy of continuing the war. Godoy used the scene to get a royal order dismissing Aranda from the council and exiling him to Jaén on that very day. The aged statesman never returned to Madrid. In 1795 Carlos permitted him to go to his estates in Aragon, and here the Conde de Aranda died on January 9, 1798.²⁵ To emphasize the break with Aranda, Floridablanca was released in April 1794 from the fortress of Pamplona and permitted to retire to his native Murcia. Godoy himself announced the news to the court.²⁶

Aranda's banishment aroused the group that had seen in his advent the beginning of a resurgence of the nobility in government. An incident, insignificant in itself, showed the passion to which they had been moved. Godoy received through the mail a "Discurso sobre la autoridad de los ricoshomes sobre el rey, y como la fueron perdiendo hasta el punto de opresión en que se hallan hoy." The discourse recalled medieval occasions when the "ricoshomes" actually elected and controlled the monarch and lamented the decline in their power brought about since Fernando and Isabel. The first Spanish Bourbon was especially taken to task for making them an idle class, harmful to society. A return to the medieval Spanish monarchy controlled by the aristocracy was the implied recommendation of the paper. With it were enclosed four anonymous letters saying that its author was the Conde de Teba, the young son of the Condesa de Montijo, a lady prominent in enlightened Madrid circles, and that Teba was going to read the paper in the Academia de la Historia on

²³ Baumgarten, p. 486, citing Sandoz's dispatch, Oct. 1, 1793.

²⁴ See *Moniteur,* Nov. 29, 1792.

²⁵ Godoy, I, 135-69, and Muriel, II, 202-48, give the full story from opposing points of view.

²⁶ *Real decreto,* Apr. 4, 1794, cited by Alcazar, *loc.cit.,* p. 128.

May 6. This turned out to be an idle threat, for the Academia knew nothing of the matter. Investigation revealed that Teba himself had mailed the discourse and the letters to Godoy. Godoy consulted with the Condesa de Montijo, and they agreed upon her son's banishment to desolate Ávila, where he would be out of touch with the "bad company" in Madrid, that is, presumably, the persons who had put such ideas of a revival of aristocratic rule into Teba's head.[27]

Aranda's fall led to other developments that were more significant than this puerile outburst. During the next few months Madrid was the scene of frightening effervescence. News of French victories in the eastern Pyrenees arrived in May 1794 to add fuel to the discontent. The Spanish army apparently had no resources with which to check the French invasion.[28] Reports were again current in the court of secret clubs being discovered in Barcelona with plans to blow up the citadel. In mid-June the governor of the Consejo de Castilla laid bare a plot among the councilors and other officials, lawyers, and courtiers to overthrow Godoy, call the Cortes, and set up an independent and effective Consejo de Estado.[29] Proclamations were distributed calling upon the people to demand a convocation of the Cortes, and manuscripts circulated complaining of Godoy's way of living. Sixty men were imprisoned for spreading such writings, and four members of the Consejo de Castilla were banished from the capital for suspected sympathy for Aranda.[30] An examination of Aranda's papers in the Consejo de Estado roused suspicion of the loyalty of several of its members, and these were exiled twenty miles from Madrid.[31]

[27] Condesa de Montijo to Duque de la Alcudia, Feb. 16, 1795. The paper of Teba and all the correspondence on this affair are quoted in Juan Pérez de Guzmán, "El primer conato de rebelión precursor de la revolución en España," *España moderna*, CCL (1909), 105-24, CCLI (1909), 48-68.

[28] *Moniteur*, July 11, Aug. 18, 1794 (reports from Madrid, June 6, July 19); Baumgarten, p. 515.

[29] Baumgarten, pp. 515, 528.

[30] *Ibid.*, pp. 515-16; *Moniteur*, Aug. 18, 1794 (report from Madrid, July 19).

[31] Baumgarten, p. 517. The *Moniteur's* correspondent is probably referring to this act when he says that Godoy had replaced the whole Consejo de Estado (Sept. 6, 1794, report from Madrid, July 12).

The Revolution

By July 1794 the violent discontent led to public demonstrations of sympathy for the French.[32] Aristocrats and other persons began to wear clothing indicative of their feelings: "guillotine" waistcoats, blood red ribbons, and "revolutionary" scarfs. The Prussian ambassador wrote home:

On every street everyone is asking: "Why all this recruiting and these enormous expenditures when we have neither an army nor generals? It is time for the French to come and drive out those who are unfit to govern. They need only come; they will be received with acclamations."[33]

The government was shaken by this exhibition of sentiment. The fall of San Sebastián at this time, which was blamed on local revolutionary feelings, the propaganda campaign of the French army in Catalonia, and the discovery that there were officers in La Unión's army with Revolutionary sympathies[34] added to the fears of Godoy. An American witness wrote, "The Duke and Queen were afraid to take anything on themselves during that alarm and for the first time left the other ministers masters in their own departments and at liberty to express their sentiments."[35] Beset by these anxieties, the king ordered the clergy to lead public prayers for the success of the war,[36] while Godoy caught at other straws in the wind. All the domiciled French who still remained in Spain were ordered out of Madrid and the maritime ports on September 27. Some were even made to leave the country. Two French brothers who were among those expelled reported that, despite all these measures, in Madrid, "where there are many enlightened minds," the majority favored the Revolution and were forming a powerful party. Only personal interest and the sermons of the priests still kept some

[32] Dispatch of Sandoz, July 22, 1794, quoted in Baumgarten, p. 529.
[33] Dispatch of Sandoz, Aug. 6, 1794, quoted in *ibid.*, p. 530.
[34] *Ibid.*
[35] Dispatch of William Short, Dec. 3, 1794, quoted in Samuel Flagg Bemis, *Pinckney's Treaty, a Study of America's Advantage from Europe's Distress, 1783-1800* (Baltimore, 1926), p. 258.
[36] See above, p. 308.

attached to Godoy, they said. The court had had to organize a system of terror and imprisonment.[37]

By such means the young duke was able to conjure off the storm of the summer of 1794. After their early successes, the French had bogged down on the frontier and their propaganda effort was abandoned. In Madrid spirits were somewhat calmed,[38] but the Revolution was still on everyone's lips. "In the taverns and in the fashionable salons, . . . and in the café, all one hears is battles, revolution, convention, national representation, liberty, equality. Even the whores ask you about Robespierre and Barère." So wrote a clergyman in Madrid to Forner in Seville in 1795.[39]

3

Small numbers of Spaniards not only desired to get rid of the Duque de la Alcudia but went so far as to imagine that Spain could be made to follow the French pattern. These enthusiasts formed various conspiracies, none of which ever reached a dangerous stage. The first of these was discovered early in 1795. It was directed by Juan Picornell y Gomila, a native Mallorcan who had made a stir in 1785 by examining his three-year-old son in religion, geography of Europe, and history of Spain before the faculty of Salamanca.[40] He had written several works on the education of children—which he said should stress religious truths and submission to the sovereign—and founded a private school (*colegio*) in Madrid in 1789.[41] Helped by a teacher of humanities and a candidate for the chair of mathematics at

---

[37] Interrogation of Arnaud and Antoine Goudre, 15 brumaire, III (Nov. 6, 1794), A.A.E., Esp., Vol. 637, pièce 7.

[38] Dispatch of Short, Dec. 3, 1794, *loc.cit.*

[39] Pedro Estala to Forner, 1795, quoted in Cueto, *loc.cit.*, p. ccii.

[40] *Examen publico, catechistico, historico, y geografico, a que expone don Juan Picornell y Gomila, socio de la Real Sociedad Economica de Madrid a su hijo* . . . *de edad de tres años, seis meses, y veinte y quatro dias, en un general que franqueara la Universidad de Salamanca* . . . (Salamanca, 1785).

[41] Juan Picornell y Gomilla [*sic*], *Discurso teorico practico sobre la educacion de la infancia, dirigido a los padres de familia* (Salamanca, 1786). He had also written *El maestro de primeras letras* (Nicolás Díaz y Pérez, "Datos para escribir la historia de la orden de los caballeros francmasones en España . . . ," *Revista de España*, CXXXII [1891], 578-89).

the Reales Estudios de San Isidro, both natives of Aragon, and a French teacher, a licentiate, a lawyer, a military surgeon, and an assistant of the school of royal pages, Picornell planned a rising for the day of San Blas, February 3, 1795. Together they wrote and printed a *Manifiesto* and an *Instrucción* which showed that they hoped to make a republic of Spain. They received money from an unidentified source, collected a few arms, and posted pasquinades in the most frequented squares of Madrid. Just before the date planned for their rising, they were betrayed and arrested. Five were condemned to death. Later, after the war with France had ended, the intercession of the French ambassador got their sentence commuted to life imprisonment in the colonies. This was not the end of Picornell, who escaped from his prison to continue his revolutionary activities in Spanish America, New York, and France.[42] The interference of the French government in their favor, as well as the knowledge of the affair in France by the Republican bishop Grégoire,[43] suggests that Picornell and his accomplices may not have lacked French encouragement.

[42] Muriel, II, 155-56; Díaz y Pérez, *loc.cit.* See Nicolas Díaz y Pérez, *La francmasonería española* (Madrid, 1894), pp. 180-86. Díaz y Pérez used the documents of the trial in the Archivo de Alcalá de Henares, No. 3245, which have since been destroyed by fire. He insists that it was a plot of freemasons. His account is a part of a history of freemasonry in Spain, which, like most such histories written in the nineteenth century and even in the twentieth, sees Spain riddled with masonry in the late eighteenth century. This is a fable fostered in the nineteenth century by the Spanish freemasons and their Catholic enemies for which there is no contemporary evidence. I have seen no indication of freemasonry in Spain before Napoleon's invasion in 1808 and feel confident there was none. Georges Demerson, "Une loge maçonnique espagnole à Brest en 1801-1802 'La Reunión Española,'" *Bulletin hispanique*, LVII (1955), 375-400, discusses the records of a masonic lodge established under the Grand Orient of France by naval officers of the Spanish fleet stationed at Brest, 1799-1802. These records give no evidence of any masonic affiliation in Spain. Soon after the return of the fleet to Spain, the activities of these officers were discovered and stopped. Díaz y Pérez was reading his own ideas into the documents he saw. Muriel does not suggest freemasonry in the conspiracy of Picornell, nor does Jovellanos, who was promptly informed of what had occurred in Madrid (*Diarios*, p. 197, Mar. 4, 1795). Enrique Rodríguez-Solis' account (*Historia del partido republicano español* [Madrid, 1892-93], I, 605-8) is merely a copy of Díaz y Pérez's.

[43] Henri-Baptiste Grégoire, *Mémoires de Grégoire, ancien évêque de Blois* . . . (2 vols.; Paris, 1837), II, 67.

According to Godoy's memoirs, four months after the "Conspiracy of San Blas" was discovered, intercepted correspondence revealed the French to be successfully organizing other proselytes in many important Spanish centers. Although their adherents were few in number, several *juntas* were already active.[44] They were divided among themselves as to whether to form one republic, called Iberia, or as many as there were former provinces and kingdoms in Spain.[45] The most active *junta* met in a convent and was led by secular and especially regular clergy. In Burgos one of the *juntas*, expecting the French armies soon to arrive, named deputies to welcome it fraternally. Godoy says that the discovery of this conspiracy was one of the strongest factors in determining the Spanish government to make peace in July 1795. To have continued the war might have led, according to his memoirs, to an internal rebellion that would have given France an easy victory. At the time, however, he did not mention these plots to the Spanish peace plenipotentiary but emphasized instead the need of peace to stop "the slander of the king's vassals; there are many [slanderers] and their number is growing."[46] His memoirs conveniently forget that the republican plotters were just an extreme wing of the wide section of society that disliked Godoy. To regain favor among these elements, he felt he had to make peace.

4

The refractory spirit leading to intrigues and public expressions of sympathy for the French was mainly limited to Madrid and to a lesser extent the other large cities such as Barcelona. There was another center of opposition to the regime. This was the universities. Here the discontent was of a different nature. It had grown more slowly, it was not directed so specifically at the

[44] Godoy, I, 244 n. 1. Muriel, II, 155, says there were other conspiracies besides Picornell's but does not give details.

[45] A. Alcalá Galiano, *Historia de España*, VI, 27-28, echoes Godoy but supplies this information in addition. He was in Aranjuez in June 1795 and was the nephew of the "republican" member of the Ministerio de Hacienda, Vicente Alcalá Galiano.

[46] Godoy to Iriarte, July 2, 1795, quoted in Sarrailh, p. 607 n. 4.

figure of the Duque de la Alcudia, and it did not lead to violent outbreaks. Its permanent influence on Spanish history, however, was to exceed that of the troubles in the capital.

The university reforms carried through by Carlos III had had the effect of causing new ideas to ferment within the academic walls. The spirit of reform and progress had been felt even where conservative faculties had resisted changes in the curriculum. Such was the case at Salamanca, whose professors had been among the most recalcitrant. The presence of such a person on the faculty as Meléndez Valdés, who read modern philosophers and was known to be the protégé of Jovellanos in Madrid, was enough to stir young souls. It was out of Salamanca that had come such trouble makers as Marchena, Picornell, and Urquijo. Meléndez himself left his chair of literature in May 1789 for a career in the government courts, but he continued to show an interest in the reform of education and society in poems dedicated to leaders of the government.[47]

The philosophical rebellion of the university students was intensified by news of the Revolution. Valencia, Granada, the Seminario de San Fulgencio at Murcia, and especially Salamanca were the scene of this revolt, according to José María Blanco y Crespo, who was a student at the university of Seville at this time.[48] He later described the ferment of these and succeeding years as he remembered it:

> In all the universities groups of young men were formed that educated themselves at their own expense and peril and greatly to the dislike of the faculties. Among the latter there were already men of good taste and learning who, although on the lecture platform they followed the routine required by the conditions of general oppression, encouraged the private studies of their students as much as they could.[49]

Juan Antonio Llorente, the contemporary official of the Inquisición, corroborates this picture. Besides watching the frontiers,

[47] Quintana, *loc.cit.*, p. 113.
[48] Blanco y Crespo, *Letters from Spain*, pp. 114-16.
[49] *El Español*, II (1811), 461.

the Inquisición searched out the spread of new philosophic ideas among the people.

> It is not easy to know [Llorente says] how many accusations this activity produced. The largest number of persons delated were youths of the universities of Salamanca and Valladolid, although there were others from all the universities, as well as from other cities and towns.[50]

A report sent in March 1793 by one of the secret friends whom the French diplomatic agents left behind in Madrid was evidently not devoid of truth: "The government is very frightened by the public spirit that is being shown in several cities such as Valladolid, Saragossa, and especially in Salamanca, where the students are, so to speak, in insurrection."[51]

The reading of French works was not the limit of the clandestine activity of the students. They were also engaged in the more appealing and significant diversion of circulating manuscripts specifically criticizing the situation in Spain. On August 5, 1794 the local official or *familiar* of the Inquisición in Villamiel, an insignificant town in northern Extremadura near the Portuguese border, submitted to the Inquisición de Llerena a manuscript entitled "Exortacion al pueblo español para que deponiendo la cobardia se anime a cobrar sus derechos." He had got it from the local priest, who had been given it to read by the town surgeon, Francisco Muñiz. Muñiz testified that he had received it from a youth who was a student of law at Salamanca, Vicente Xerez. Xerez had told him that several other copies existed and promised to send him other papers that were "worse." When called before the Santo Oficio on September 1, Xerez stated that another law student at Salamanca had copied the manuscript for him and revealed that he knew of three other local people who had copies. He knew that there were many copies in Salamanca. He said its contents revealed its author to be Ramón de

---

[50] Llorente, *Historia*, IX, 23-24.
[51] Taschereau to Lebrun, Mar. 28, 1793, *loc.cit.*

Salas. Salas was a professor of jurisprudence in the university, one of whose close students had been Marchena.[52]

Proceeding from this information, the investigations of the Inquisición, which soon were taken up in Salamanca, led it into a veritable maze. At least fifteen other students, both of law and of theology, youths mainly in their late teens or early twenties, were in the end questioned, most of whom admitted knowledge of this or some similar manuscript. Many of the students had made personal copies of them. The Inquisición was interested in discovering not so much who was reading these papers as who had written them. The name of Salas was repeated, but one student said the "Exortacion al pueblo español" was attributed to José Marchena, "said to be in France."[53] Was this indeed a copy of Marchena's *A la nacion española*? No copy of the manuscript is preserved with the records of the case. The Inquisición reached no satisfactory conclusion as to the identity of the author by means of questioning the students, some of whose statements give the impression of hiding information from the Santo Oficio.

One witness, while denying knowledge of the "Exortacion," admitted that he had heard one night in Salamanca a manuscript read in the house of the professor Juan Márquez Duro entitled "Diálogos del A.B.C." He had heard that its author was Doctor Salas. He had, he said, a paper called "Oracion apologética dicha en la Plaza de Toros de Madrid."[54] This evidence led the Inquisición off on another track. Many of the same students, when questioned, revealed that they had this last manuscript too, which upon being confiscated turned out to have the full title, "Oracion apologética que en defensa del estado floreciente de España pronunció en la Plaza de Toros de Madrid D.ⁿ &ra." Again the author was said to be Salas.[55] The testimony of the various students showed that it had been circulated and widely copied by

---

[52] Alarcos, *loc.cit.*, pp. 462 n. 1, 463.
[53] Testimony of Francisco Bueso, June 10, 1795, A.H.N., Inq., leg. 4473, No. 8. The documents on the case are all here.
[54] Testimony of Manuel Cleuterio Navarro, Sept. 9, 1794, *ibid*.
[55] Testimony of Francisco Pérez Durán, Oct. 1794, *ibid.*, No. 12.

the students at Salamanca since 1793. Many had taken copies with them when they had gone home. Another paper which was mentioned, although not so frequently, was "La Convenzion" or "La Combencion." This was the only one turned up whose title indicates that it dealt primarily with current events in France.[56]

Had the case stopped within the university of Salamanca, its significance, while large, would not be overly impressive. On the contrary, however, the "Oracion apologética" was turned up all over Spain. The Inquisición de Llerena sent in its report on it to the Consejo de la Inquisición in January 1795. In June the tribunal of Valladolid submitted a report on it; in December a copy was submitted from the university of Alcalá, and in April 1796 the Inquisición de Granada sent in a report concerning it. They all involved manuscript copies.[57] Such a paper could hardly escape notice in Madrid, and indeed there is evidence that it was circulating there in the winter of 1794-95.[58] In January 1795 the Inquisición determined to prohibit the "Oracion apologética," and it was put on the Index in November 1796.[59]

Although the Inquisición had been unable to establish definitely the authorship of the papers it had discovered, the name of the Salamanca professor Ramón de Salas had been suggested often enough to arouse its suspicions. As a student who disliked Salas recalled later, the university awoke one morning to find that this "friend of Marchena" had fled from the agents of the Inquisición de Valladolid during the night on a borrowed horse.[60] Suffering from hemorrhoids, he hid for a day in a small town, then rode

[56] Testimony of Francisco Bueso, June 10, 1795, and of Sebastián Gil Gordo, Feb. 9, 1795, *ibid.*, Nos. 8, 12.

[57] *Ibid.*, leg. 4482, No. 33.

[58] Hermann Baumgarten, *Geschichte Spaniens vom Ausbruch der französischen Revolution bis auf unsere Tage* (Leipzig, 1865), i, 89-91.

[59] A.H.N., Inq., leg. 4482, No. 33. Several MS copies of the "Oracion" exist here. In the early nineteenth century it was frequently reprinted with the title *Pan y toros* and attributed to Jovellanos. His authorship has been properly refuted by Cándido Nocedal, "Discurso preliminar," *Obras publicadas é inéditas de D. Gaspar Melchor de Jovellanos*, B.A.E., xlvi, xxii, and Julio Somoza de Montsoriú, *Las amarguras de Jovellanos* (Gijón, 1889), pp. 33-37.

[60] *Censor general* (Cadiz), Apr. 21, 24, 1812.

painfully on to Segovia and finally to Madrid, where the Inquisición found him prostrate in an inn and arrested him.

Salas was brought to trial accused of writing the "Diálogos del A.B.C." and the "Oracion apologética." Llorente and the *Moniteur* give reports of the trial that vary in details, but they agree that the *calificadores* of the Inquisición found no clear proof that Salas was guilty of heresy. The case came up twice for consideration. The second time personal influence was brought to bear against Salas by Felipe Fernández Vallejo, bishop of Salamanca and governor of the Consejo de Castilla, with whom Salas had once quarreled.[61] On November 25, 1796 the Consejo de la Inquisición condemned Salas to abjure *de levi* before twelve distinguished witnesses, to study sound doctrines in a monastery for a year, and to be banished from Madrid and Salamanca for three more years.[62] The case was not so easily disposed of, however, for two members of the Consejo de Castilla who had been delegated to observe the trial denounced the high-handedness of the verdict to Godoy, and Salas appealed to Carlos IV to have the case reviewed. As will be seen in a later chapter, the fate of Salas became tied up with a campaign being waged within the government to weaken the Inquisición.[63]

It is a significant comment on the thinking of enlightened Spaniards that the papers that led to the arrest of Salas and had such success as clandestine reading in Spain at the time of the war with France contained no direct reference to the Revolution. The "Diálogos del A.B.C.," thirteen in number, dealt with typical subjects of the Enlightenment—"Hobbes, Grotius, and Montesquieu," "the soul," "natural law and curiosity," and others like these.[64] The more popular "Oracion apologética" was an echo of the Masson *affaire*, which had stirred the Spanish world

[61] *Moniteur*, Jan. 21, 1797; Llorente, *Historia*, v, 217-19. See Villanueva, I, 84-85. The case of Salas is undoubtedly the central incident referred to by Quintana's biography of Meléndez Valdés in a cryptic allusion to terrorism in the 1790's that Menéndez Pelayo was unable to understand (Quintana, *loc.cit.*, pp. 116-17; Menéndez Pelayo, *Heterodoxos*, v, 299).

[62] Sentence of the Inquisición quoted in Pinta Llorente, *loc.cit.*, p. 105, who gives an account of the case drawn from A.H.N., Inq., leg. 3730.

[63] See below, p. 409.

[64] Pinta Llorente, *loc.cit.*, p. 100. [The "Diálogos del A.B.C." were a translation of part of Voltaire's *L'A, B, C, dialogue curieux traduit de l'anglais de M. Huet*. See the Spanish translation of this book, *España y la revolución del*

of letters in the last years of Carlos III. It was a mock "apologetic oration" to silence all apologies for Spain.

The oration starts with a typically "philosophic" generalization: "All nations of the world, following the steps of nature, have been weak in their infancy, ignorant in their puberty, warlike in their youth, philosophic in their manhood, legists in their old age, and superstitious and tyrannical in their decrepitude." The author has observed in Spain, however, "the most wondrous spectacle which has appeared in the universe, that is, all the periods of rational life at the same time in the highest state of perfection." Spain can be seen as a weak baby, without population, industry, wealth, patriotic spirit, or government. She can be seen a young, uneducated girl, with a noble class parading its ignorance and "universities, faithful guardians of the prejudices of barbaric ages." She can be seen in the bloom of youth, full of martial spirit, with enough officers for all the armies of the world and soldiers tried in the military experience of curling their hair. She appears in full womanhood, religious and studious of all the sciences. "The capital city has more temples than houses, more clergymen than laymen, more altars than kitchens." "Philosophy has been simplified with the artificial abstractions of Aristotle, and, freed from the tiresome observation of nature, it has been made the slave of scholastic sophisms." "Natural law is reputed to be useless and even harmful," and "physics is a science that has always worn a semblance of witchcraft and devilry," but beardless youths after six or seven years of shouting in idle disputes call themselves theologians. Spain is also old and querulous, sprouting more laws than there are human activities to control. "Why could not wine, olive oil, water, and even the air the citizens breathe also become state monopolies?" Finally, at one and the same time, Spain can be seen decrepit and superstitious. Here the Holy Scriptures have been kept from the people as mortal poison, while "the monkish influence has caused to pass for revealed truths the visions and ravings of some simple women and crack-brained men." "We are Christians

---

siglo XVIII (Madrid, 1964), pp. 275-77.—Author's note, 1969.]

in name and worse than gentiles in our customs; in fine, we fear more the obscure dungeon of the Inquisición than the tremendous judgment of Jesus Christ."

It was this acid picture of the backwardness and irrationality of their country that appealed to the enlightened youth of Spain. In the previous decade the reaction of their like-minded elders to Masson had been to protest that Spanish *luces* under Carlos III were the equal of those elsewhere. The change in spirit could not have been more glaring. Now the students were ready to hear to the last bitter note an adverse comparison of Spain, the Spain they wished to discard, with the rest of Europe.

"What is this?" cries the author. "Have I converted my job as panegyrist into that of a strict censor?" Not at all, Spain has what no other nation has; its bull fights are the ties of its society, the forges of its political habits. From them Spain derives its martial spirit, in them it learns the wisdom of its government.

If the circus of Rome produced such delicacy in the people that they noted if a wounded gladiator fell with decorum and breathed out his life with pleasant gestures, the circus of Madrid teaches how to observe if he flies gracefully over the horns and spills forth his guts with decorum. If Rome lived happy with *bread and arms*, Madrid lives happy with *bread and bulls*. The sullen English, the giddy French, spend days and nights between painful study and dangerous disputes over political matters, and only after many months of disagreement issue a law; the gay Spaniards spend their days and nights between pleasant idleness and delightful parties and in an instant find themselves with a thousand laws approved without the opposition of anyone. . . . Those peoples are like bees who are aroused and sting if their honey is taken from them; this one like the sheep who patiently suffer being shorn and slaughtered. . . . Those idolaters of liberty hold to be a sin a single link of slavery; these, dragging the chains of slavery, do not even know the idol liberty. . . . Happy Spain! My happy country, who thus achieves distinction among the nations of the world! . . . Follow, follow this enlightenment and prosperity to be, as thou art, the *non plus ultra* of fanaticism of the ages. Scorn as heretofore the skills of the jealous foreigners, abominate their turbulent maxims, condemn their free opinions, prohibit the books that have not got by the Holy Index, and sleep restfully in the pleasant warbling of the pipings with which they mock you. Let there be bread and let there be bulls and let there be nothing else. Enlightened government, bread and bulls are what the people call for, bread and bulls are the diet of Spain, bread and bulls thou shouldst give them that thou mayst then do with them what thou wouldst, *in saecula saeculorum*, Amen.

5

Peace was welcomed with joy and satisfaction by the people in August 1795.[65] The sweet news soon turned to alum in their mouths as they learned that the Duque de la Alcudia, for his achievement in ending the war, was given the title of Príncipe de la Paz (Prince of the Peace) and a large property to maintain his new status. Rarely had anyone in Spain except the direct heir to the throne, the Principe de Asturias, held the title of *principe*. Now it was given to an upstart in his twenties, the *cortejo* of the queen, placing him above all the nobility of Spain.[66] The suspicion that Godoy might not have been unworthy of his position, that he could have a "sane mind, an honest and good heart," as Bourgoing remarked,[67] hardly crossed most minds. Not only Godoy's popularity suffered; royalty too was losing its prestige because of the implied frivolity and excesses of María Luisa.

[65] There is general agreement on this. See e.g., *Moniteur*, Sept. 28, Oct. 21, 1795; dispatch of William Short, Madrid, Aug. 9, 1795, cited by Bemis, pp. 312-13.

[66] See A. Alcalá Galiano, *Memorias*, I, 24, and Muriel, III, 72-75. After the conclusion of the Peace of the Pyrenees in 1659 the *valido* Conde de Haro was made "Prince of the Peace" (M. A. S. Hume, *Spain, Its Greatness and Decay, 1479-1788* [Cambridge, 1931], p. 280). Muriel notes another case of the title *principe*.

[67] Bourgoing (1797), I, 187-88.

During the war with France, definite groups of Spaniards had turned against the government. On the one hand, some aristocrats, long unhappy over the policies of Carlos III, had become more open in their opposition to the crown than they had dared be during the ascendancy of Floridablanca. They affected Revolutionary airs only to annoy Godoy. At the other extreme were those persons who had been won over by the ideas of the Revolution strongly enough to enter into secret correspondence with the French, but their numbers were small. This means of gaining supporters proved little more successful for the French than their unprofitable attempts at propagandizing Spain after the outbreak of hostilities. The most significant part of the new opposition to the government consisted of persons who desired to see realized in Spain the scientific and economic advances achieved in Europe before 1789, not the political revolution of France since that date. Even the university students in general fell into this class. Most of these persons still believed their ideal to be enlightened despotism. Where this ideal was being replaced in their minds, it was, as will be seen, by a desire for a revival of early Spanish institutions. The conscious discontent of the progressives was with a court and government which they thought had abandoned enlightened despotism in favor of rule by a royal favorite. In the Principe de la Paz they saw another *valido* like the ones who had strutted through the worst Habsburg reigns. The desire they repeatedly expressed for a French victory was a symptom rather of their exasperation with Godoy and María Luisa than of true sympathy for the French Republic.

CHAPTER XII

THE BIRTH OF THE LIBERAL TRADITION

GODOY blamed two sources for the ideas that had aroused the hot-heads plotting revolution in 1795. One was the Republican propaganda spread by the French armies. The other was the history of Spain:

> Our own annals, from the time of the Goths, offered dangerous examples, some not so long past. The deposing of Enrique IV, the Comunidades of Castile and the Germanías of Valencia in the days of Carlos V, the prestige of the former constitution of Aragon, the disorders of that kingdom under Felipe II, and the sad recollections of the *fueros* destroyed in that reign— such memories fermented in some heads and became projects.[1]

Interest in Spanish history was not newborn in 1795. The eighteenth century had seen it emerge thanks partly to royal encouragement. In 1738 Felipe V had given formal organization and the title of Real Academia de la Historia to a committee which was meeting in the royal library to draw up a "diccionario histórico-crítico" of Spain. Its task was to be to complete an index of Spanish history and to eliminate fables from it.[2] Four years later in Valencia an Academia Valenciana was founded, devoted to historical studies. It published the *Obras cronológicas* of the Marqués de Mondéjar.[3] Under this prompting, Spanish scholars turned their attention to their national history. The beginning was hardly propitious. In 1738 Francisco Xavier Manuel de la Huerta y Vega, a member of the new royal academy, published the first volume of a long study, *España primitiva: historia de sus reyes y monarcas, desde su poblacion hasta Christo*, full of the most absurd fables of the supposed greatness of Spain in the heroic classical age. A little later a certain Juan de Flores exploited the discovery of Roman remains in Granada to pass

[1] Godoy, I, 244 n. I.
[2] *Real decreto*, Apr. 18, 1738, *Nov. rec.*, VIII, xx, 2.
[3] Cueto, *loc.cit.*, p. lxxxviii.

337

off apocryphal chronicles and titles of nobility. Soon, however, the critical spirit that Feyjóo was then so strongly encouraging led to more profitable works. No doubt the most valuable as well as the most famous were *España sagrada,* an immense collection of chronicles and documents on the ecclesiastical history of Spain, begun by the Augustinian Fray Enrique Flórez in 1747, and the *Historia crítica de España y de la civilizacion española,* written by the ex-Jesuit in exile in Italy, Juan Francisco Masdeu, on such an extensive plan that the twentieth volume was still lingering in the eleventh century. Despite his exile, the history was published in Madrid between 1784 and 1805. These monks attempted with their writing to destroy the legends that infested Spanish history. Other excellent works were written on specialized subjects, such as the *Apéndice* in four volumes with which Campomanes followed his *Discurso sobre el fomento de la educacion popular,* a collection of decrees and writings illustrating the history of industry in Spain; and Antonio de Capmany's skillful contribution to economic history, *Memorias historicas sobre la marina, comercio y artes de la antigua Ciudad de Barcelona.* In 1770 two jurists, Ignacio Jordán de Asso y del Rio and Miguel de Manuel y Rodríguez, published a study of the principles of Castilian law. They preceded it with an extensive analysis of the different authorities that had enacted legislation in Castile. In the process the medieval Cortes were described.[4] Over two hundred and fifty less outstanding pieces of historical writing were produced under Carlos III alone, the great majority being local histories or biographies of saints and annals of religious institutions.[5]

At the same time, many famous works written in the sixteenth and seventeenth centuries or earlier were republished for the new public; while others that had remained in manuscript were

[4] Ignacio Jordán Asso y del Rio and Miguel de Manuel y Rodríguez, *Instituciones del derecho civil de Castilla* (7th ed.; Madrid, 1806). See Sempere, *Biblioteca,* I, 148.

[5] Danvila y Collado, VI, 413-34, gives a list of the works written and published under Carlos III. On this historiography see also Desdevises, *L'Espagne,* III, 239-47, and Altamira, IV, 370-79.

now first brought to light. *Los claros varones de España* of Hernando del Pulgar, the secretary of Fernando and Isabel, was republished in Madrid in 1747, and his *Historia de los Reyes católicos* in Valencia in 1780 by the editor Benito Montfort. Montfort also brought forth in 1779 the *Crónica de Don Juan II*, its second edition since the sixteenth century. The Academia de la Historia gave light to the *Opera tum edita tum inedita* of the sixteenth-century historian Juan Ginés Sepúlveda and also began to publish the chronicles of Castile edited by three of its leading members.[6] The years of the French Revolution saw heightened activity. The *Crónica general de España*, begun in the sixteenth century by Florian de Ocampo and continued by Ambrosio de Morales, was reissued in fifteen volumes in 1791-92.[7] The latter's *Las antiguedades de las ciudades de España* and *Opúsculos castellanos y latinos* were also printed in these years.[8] So too was the *Historia de los reyes de Castilla* of his contemporary Prudencio de Sandoval.[9] Meanwhile a Madrid editor thought it timely and patriotic to republish the third volume of the history of Bernardo Desclot under the title *Relacion historica de la famosa invasion del exercito y armada de Francia en Cataluña en 1285, y de la valerosa resistencia que los Catalanes, Aragoneses, y Valencianos ... hicieron a los enemigos. ...*[10]

The most popular Spanish historian in these years was without doubt the Jesuit Juan de Mariana, who had flourished at the turn of the seventeenth century and had achieved international fame for advocating tyrannicide in his *De rege et regis institutione*. It was not this work but his *Historia general de España* which

---

[6] Pedro López de Ayala, *Crónicas de los reyes de Castilla, D. Pedro, D. Enrique II, D. Juan I y D. Enrique III . . . con las enmiendas de Zurita*, ed. Eugenio de Llaguno Amirola (Madrid, 1779); Gutierre Díez de Gámez, *Crónica de D. Pedro niño conde de Buelna*, ed. Eugenio de Llaguno Amirola (Madrid, 1782); Marqués de Mondéxar, *Memorias históricas de la vida y acciones del rey D. Alonso el Noble, octavo del nombre*, ed. Francisco Cerdá y Rico (Madrid, 1783); Diego Enríquez del Castillo, *Crónica del rey D. Enrique IV de este nombre*, ed. José Miguel de Flores (Madrid, 1787). See Danvila y Collado, vi, 428-33, and Bourgoing (1797), i, 280-81.

[7] Madrid.   [8] Madrid, 1792 and 1793.   [9] Madrid, 1792.
[10] Madrid, 1793. In "Varios," Carlos IV, leg. 52, 4°.

endeared him to Spaniards of the eighteenth century. Its excellent literary style and the breadth of its concept of history were no doubt factors in its popularity. It was reprinted in Madrid between 1713 and 1741. In 1780 new editions were undertaken in Madrid and by Montfort in Valencia. Another edition was published in Madrid in 1794.[11] "The incomparable Mariana," as Valladares called him,[12] became reading with which even educated ladies of the provinces were familiar.[13]

The interest in history was nation-wide. Historical works were published in twenty different cities under Carlos III, and the trend was reflected in the periodical press. One of the most important journals of the 1780's, Valladares' *Semanario erudito*, was devoted primarily to publishing little known sources and secondary accounts dealing with Spanish history from the early Middle Ages to the eighteenth century. It found a ready public. It lasted for four years with over three hundred subscribers until it was killed by Floridablanca's decree of February 1791 stopping periodical publications. *La espigadera*, which began in 1790 and lasted a bare six months, also catered to the new interest, giving light to the work of Hernán Sánchez del Tobar on the history of the thirteenth century from an unpublished manuscript in the Biblioteca Real and to an anonymous history of the military order of Calatrava. The *Correo de Murcia*, the first paper to appear in 1792 when the ban was lifted, promptly followed suit. For almost the entire first year of its publication space was regularly devoted to a "Compendio histórico de Murcia y su reyno," from pre-Roman times to 1315.

The popularity of national history also invaded the theater. A partial list of the plays that appeared between 1751 and 1800 with themes drawn from medieval Spanish history shows seventeen before 1780, thirteen in the next decade, and twelve from

[11] These are the editions of Mariana and the other historians in the Biblioteca Nacional. See advertisements of Mariana's history in *Gazeta*, Nov. 23, 1792, June 12, 1795, Nov. 11, 1796, Nov. 27, 1804.

[12] *Semanario erudito*, "prospecto."

[13] A. Alcalá Galiano notes that both his mother and grandmother, who lived in Cadiz, knew it (*Memorias*, I, 13-14).

1791 to 1800. Nine others that belong to this half century cannot be accurately dated. They were produced mainly in Madrid and Valencia, which were the major centers of historical activity. Jovellanos, Nicolás Fernández de Moratín, Cadalso, Vincente Antonio García de la Huerta, and Valladares de Sotomayor were among their authors—that is to say, leading writers of the period, dramatic or otherwise.[14]

This concern with their past in part reflected the growing nationalism of enlightened Spaniards. Jovellanos was convinced of the value of popularizing history. Besides writing the play *Pelayo*, in 1776 he urged Meléndez Valdés, in order to put his pen to profitable use, that he "intone illustrious deeds" instead of the delights of nature to which his pastoral poems were devoted. "Let your object be the Spanish heroes" from the siege of Saguntum to the victories of Felipe V.[15]

2

Gradually out of this interest in their country's past, enlightened Spanish thinkers developed an interpretation of their history which was peculiarly their own. According to this interpretation, the Spanish nation had been greatest in the Middle Ages. Its decline began in the sixteenth century after the death of the Catholic Monarchs, Fernando and Isabel. The cause for the fall was also supplied by the new view of history—in the Middle Ages Spain had enjoyed her proper form of government, her "constitution"; in the sixteenth century this had been destroyed.

As for many other facets of enlightened contemporary thought, Jovellanos provides excellent examples of the development of the new concept of Spanish history. His address at his reception into the Real Academia de la Historia in 1780 is an early one. It was a plea for the study of the legal and constitutional history of Spain as a help to the magistrates and lawyers in properly interpreting the laws of the nation. According to this speech,

[14] E. Allison Peers, *A History of the Romantic Movement in Spain* (Cambridge, 1940), I, 46-47, II, 382-84, gives a list with the full titles of the plays.
[15] "Jovino á sus amigos de Salamanca," B.A.E., XLVI, 38-39.

the constitution of Spain was established under the Visigoths between the fifth and eighth centuries. Its source was the laws of the Germanic tribes described by Tacitus and Caesar. "The fundamental principles of this constitution" were codified in the *Fuero viejo* of Castile during the Reconquista. The granting of feudal charters and privileges tended to break up the unity of Castile. "This system of government, in which the various parts into which the nation was divided were practically isolated, would have made our constitution variable and vacillating, if the Cortes, established since primitive times, had not reunited the parts that composed it for the settlement of affairs that interested the general good." On the other hand, Jovellanos' critical mind saw that the medieval constitution was not perfect:

> But above all, in this constitution I seek a free people and I do not find it. Caught between powerless princes and independent lords, what were the people but a herd of slaves, destined to satiate the ambition of their lords? . . . The only spring that could move the constitution to remove its defects was the Cortes. But in the Cortes the power of the first classes was preponderant: the nobility and the ecclesiastics were interested equally in their independence and in the oppression of the people.[16]

Jovellanos wanted the constitution to be studied, not to be imitated blindly.

The maturing effects of Jovellanos' exile and the sight of the Revolution only strengthened his belief in the need to ponder Spain's early constitution. In a letter written in 1795 to a professor at the university of Oviedo giving his view of the proper way to study law, he complained:

> Is it not shameful that there are scarcely a dozen jurists among us who can give an exact idea of our constitution? The questions that this study embraces are too important to be forgotten. Are the legislative, executive, and judicial powers all contained

[16] Jovellanos, "Discurso leido . . . en su recepcion á la Real Academia de la Historia," *loc.cit.*, quotations from pp. 293, 294, 295.

in one single person without modifications or limits? Or does some part of them reside in the nation or in its political bodies? What, in what, and how? What are the rights of the Cortes, of the tribunals, of the magistrates high and low that form our constitutional heirarchy? . . . Can one doubt that the ignorance of these articles is the true source of all usurpation, of all confusion, of all oppression and disorder?

Jovellanos, suffering banishment from the royal court, now had a higher opinion than in 1780 of the vanished constitution. It had been upset, he said, by "the brilliant and sad epoch that began with the death of the Catholic Monarchs and whose end is hard to foresee."[17]

Jovellanos was not alone among the leading thinkers of his time. The author of the anonymous letters on political and economic questions written to the Conde de Lerena between 1787 and 1790 likewise approved of the medieval constitution. "A king who rules, nobles who advise, and a people which assembles to set forth its views or accept what it must obey, here we have the admirable body of our primitive Cortes." The *grandes*, bishops, and learned men examined new laws, the deputies of the people judged which were suitable, and then the king promulgated them. Under this constitution it was clear that "the legislative power resides in the king together with his kingdom" and that "the power of the king cannot go beyond that of the laws."[18] Fernando and Isabel revived the prosperity of Spain because they maintained its civil liberty. Cardinal Cisneros, however, in his brief period of control after Fernando's death, established in Spain the theory that the royal will is law, and henceforth Spain faced disaster. The rebellion of the Comunidades against Carlos V's personal rule in 1520-21 was the "last sigh of Castilian liberty." With Felipe II, who crushed the rebellion of the Moriscos, destroyed the *fueros* of Aragon, and augmented the power of the Inquisición, tyranny triumphed in Spain.[19]

[17] Jovellanos to Doctor Prado, Dec. 17, 1795, B.A.E., L, 147.
[18] *Cartas político-económicas escritas . . . al Conde de Lerena*, pp. 27-28 (1787).
[19] *Ibid.*, pp. 46-69.

None other than Juan Pablo Forner, the leading apologist of Spain and its religion against the godless French *philosophes*, when he considered history, reached surprisingly similar conclusions. He thought enough on the subject to write a "Discurso sobre el modo de escribir y mejorar la historia de España," which he left unpublished. Spain needed a history that would teach its national constitution, the various alterations of this constitution, and the reasons for them, he said. "One can doubt whether the reign of Carlos V was so prosperous for his kingdom as favorable to the personal glory of the prince." Forner did indeed doubt it, for he asserted that the revolutions of Carlos V's day were the "origin of our decadence." He called for the writing of histories that would give the truth on the period of Habsburg rule, during which Felipe II had furthered the decline by squandering Spain's wealth throughout Europe and the growth of the clergy had quickened the depopulation of the country. According to Forner one must also study the expulsion of the Jews and Moriscos. He asked: Was the exile of four million Spaniards in whose hands lay the nation's commerce and agriculture just and necessary or senseless?[20]

In some ways the view of history of these enlightened men was not new in Spain. For two hundred years there had been Spaniards who condemned the house of Austria and looked back upon the reign of Fernando and Isabel as Spain's golden age.[21] It was no novelty either to think that there were laws which even the king could not violate. This had been a principle of European political theory in the Middle Ages. Mariana had written in 1609, "Since the power of the king is only legitimate when it has been set up by the consent of the citizens, his authority must be limited by laws and statutes."[22] This he stated in his *De rege*, a book which was less familiar to enlightened Spaniards

---

[20] In Forner, *Obras*, I, 1-143 (quotation from p. 91). Ferrer del Rio, IV, 417, says it was written about 1787.

[21] See Castro, pp. 298-99.

[22] *Del rey*, Book I, chap. viii, quoted in Salvador de Madariaga, *The Rise of the Spanish-American Empire* (London, 1947), p. 213. See Madariaga's n. 4, p. 366 on the subject.

than his history of Spain. The latter was more cautiously royalist, but it and other historical works that were finding a lively market could inspire in their readers an admiration for the various Cortes of Spain, which had been among the most vigorous parliamentary bodies of the Middle Ages.

The new interpretation of Spanish history had this domestic background to draw on. At the same time it is evident that the enlightened writers had imbibed a good dose of foreign thought. Jovellanos and the author of the anonymous letters both were looking at medieval Spain through the glasses of contemporary political philosophy. *Derecho natural y de gentes*, a subject of study popular among progressive students inside and outside the universities since the 1770's, taught much as Mariana's *De rege* that every monarchy had its "fundamental law," which it was unjust or even illegal for kings to violate.[23] Montesquieu imparted a similar lesson in his *De l'esprit des lois*. According to him, a king must rule through intermediary powers, such as the nobility, clergy, and towns, whose prerogatives are based on the "fundamental laws" of the monarchy. Destroy these intermediary powers, which check the momentary caprices of the king and force observance of the fundamental laws, and monarchy is converted into despotism. Montesquieu and the French aristocrats who took up his theory had in mind the medieval constitution of France, which they thought had been vitiated by the development of absolute monarchy, but this view of the proper form of monarchic government agreed closely with the picture that Spaniards were forming of their medieval institutions. Despite its prohibition by the Inquisición, *De l'esprit des lois* was known to enlightened Spaniards under Carlos III.[24] Both it and *derecho natural* familiarized Spanish readers with the concept of a "fundamental law" or "constitution" (as the French Revolutionaries called it). Spaniards had only to marry this concept to their knowledge of Spain's past in order to produce the new liberal interpretation of their history.

[23] See above, pp. 177-80.
[24] See above, pp. 57-59.

3

It was reserved to José Marchena, writing for Spanish consumption from the free soil of Revolutionary France, to draw in sharpest and crudest lines the emerging liberal tradition. His *A la nacion española* blamed one single episode, the defeat of the Comuneros by Carlos V, for the death of medieval Spanish liberty. Marchena hoped to excite his audience by apostrophizing the hero and heroine of the revolt and the scene of the royal victory of 1521:

> Fields of Villalar, did you perchance bury the generous heroes, defenders of the liberty, the energy, and patriotism of Hesperia? Shades of Padilla, and you, great soul of Doña María Coronel, who bewail in your tomb the cowardice of your descendants, inspire in Spaniards that valor with which you defended within Toledo the last remnants of our dying liberty.[25]

It was to regain their lost liberty that Marchena told the Spanish, "Let *Cortes, Cortes* be the universal cry." The Cortes were no danger to the just privileges of the clergy, nobility, and king, he said; for, unlike the case of the French Estates General, the rules for their organization were clearly established. "France needed a regeneration, Spain needs no more than a renovation."

Marchena's opinion was not unique. The Spaniards who were in exile with him held similar ideas,[26] and so did some in Spain. In 1797 a young poet, Manuel José Quintana, who like Marchena had been received at the university of Salamanca by Meléndez Valdés, composed an ode to Juan de Padilla. In it Padilla became the "gloria de Castilla":

> Tú el único ya fuiste
> que osó arrostrar con generoso pecho

---

[25] María Coronel was a medieval lady. Marchena meant to use the name of Padilla's wife, María Pacheco, who directed the defense of Toledo after Padilla had been captured at Villalar and executed.

[26] See "Reflexiones imparciales de un Español a su nacion" (by Santiváñez?), p. 6, and J. Hevia, "A la nacion española," A.A.E., Esp., Vol. 635, pièces 311, 310.

al huracán deshecho
del despotismo en nuestra playa triste.[27]

Within two years an economist, concerned like Forner with explaining Spain's economic decline, picked out the war of the Comuneros as its starting point. The strife ended the prosperity of the late fifteenth century by destroying the factories and "capitalists" of Castile, he explained. American gold and Spain's later foreign wars only finished the process.[28]

Marchena's plea to Spaniards to revive their Cortes was not simply the conceit of a man infatuated with the French Revolution. His tract was aimed skillfully at stirring up the thoughts he had seen fermenting in his native land. The challenge to revive Spain's ancient liberty could only be stated in private within the nation's borders—except for Jovellanos' cautious speech to the Academia de la Historia in 1780 and the passing phrase of the economist in 1799, no example that has been cited was made public at the time. Yet dissatisfied Spanish tongues were repeating Marchena's injunction. Their eager words died away unrecorded in student rooms or Madrid salons, but the subversive proclamations in 1794 calling for the Cortes and Godoy's statement about those who plotted in 1795 are evidence that they were in fact uttered. The new liberal tradition was to echo in the ears of progressive Spaniards after the turn of the century. This tradition held that Spain had had a constitution and a legislative body, that under this body the nation had seen its greatest days, and that the house of Habsburg, to establish despotism, had destroyed the constitution and brought the ruin of Spain. According to this interpretation of their history, Spaniards had no need to seek examples abroad in order to revive their liberty and greatness; they needed only to reestablish the medieval institutions of Spain.

[27] "You alone, with noble breast, dared to affront on our sad shores the hurricane unleashed by despotism." Manuel José Quintana, *Poesías,* ed. Narciso Alonso Cortés ("Clásicos castellanos," Vol. LXXVIII) (Madrid, 1944), p. 18. See pp. viii-ix.

[28] Joaquín María Acevedo y Pola, *Memoria económico-política sobre el fomento de España* (Madrid, 1799), p. 96.

CHAPTER XIII

GODOY AND THE REVIVAL OF
ENLIGHTENMENT

IN HIS memoirs, written in exile in the 1830's with the evident desire to curry popularity among Spanish liberals, Godoy looked back at his ascension to power and prided himself upon having brought back into favor the *luces*, which his predecessors, scared by the Revolution, had suppressed. Instead of fearing the "lights," he claims he took it upon himself, in the face of opposition, to spread them farther as the only way to save Spain from the dangers threatening Europe. "One could have said that my country was their refuge in those terrible days."[1] Godoy's claim ill accords with the opinion of him held at the time by those enlightened minds who circulated manuscripts in the universities, hatched plots in Madrid, and developed the liberal tradition. Only a look at the *luces* during the Revolution can determine who was mistaken, Godoy or his enlightened opponents.

Floridablanca was certainly responsible for the sanitary cordon that the Spanish government established against news from France even before the meeting of the Estates General. One will recall that his anxiety also led him gradually to repress the enlightened institutions of the previous reign, but that Aranda brought a change of spirit as soon as he replaced Floridablanca in February 1792. Aranda temporarily reopened the doors to French papers and promptly saved the young translator of Voltaire's *Mort de César*, Urquijo, from the prison of the Inquisición.

Further examples of the new first secretary's opposition to the Santo Oficio occurred in succeeding months. Bernardo María de Calzada, the translator of French works recently convicted by the Inquisición and banished from Madrid, was again allowed

---

[1] Godoy, II, 203-4.

to publish a book, although this time on a safe topic.[2] Since 1788, when the first two volumes of the Spanish edition of the *Encyclopédie méthodique* had appeared, the Inquisición had been delaying the rest of it in censorship.[3] In September 1792 the third volume was delivered to its subscribers.[4] Bourgoing, whose activity as French ambassador almost coincided with Aranda's ministry, noted that during this time he heard of no new story of inquisitorial horrors. The Santo Oficio was too busy with the spread of Revolutionary ideas, he said,[5] but a large part of the explanation was that it had suddenly found an unsympathetic man at the head of the government.

Aranda just as resolutely set aside Floridablanca's recent ban of the periodical press. On September 1, 1792 the first issue of the *Correo de Murcia* appeared. Published twice a week in small eight-page numbers, it was modelled directly on the literary periodicals of the past decade. A month later began the *Diario de Barcelona*. This was copied on the *Diario de Madrid*, whose continuance Floridablanca had tolerated, but it also contained poems and brief articles. The *Correo mercantil de España y sus Indias*, devoted to shipping news, was started at the same time. The *Gazeta de Madrid* also carried the prospectus of a *Continuacion del Semanario erudito*, "by special grace of the king . . . conceded to its editor Don Antonio Valladares de Sotomayor." This new journal was to print texts of medieval history, but it does not appear ever to have been published.[6]

Aranda's replacement by Godoy in November 1792 made no change in the favor being bestowed on the periodical press. In July 1793 the *Memorial literario* was revived, carrying news of

[2] *Genealogia de Gil Blas de Santillana* ([Madrid?], 1792).

[3] A.H.N., Inq., leg. 4481, No. 15.

[4] *Encyclopedia metodica*, Vol. III, *Geografia moderna*, traducida del frances por los señores don Juan Arribas y Soria, y don Julian de Velasco (Madrid, 1792). It contains letters M to R, thus avoiding Masson's article "Espagne." It was announced in *Gazeta,* Sept. 15, 1792.

[5] Bourgoing (1797), I, 370.

[6] *Gazeta,* Aug. 17, 1792. I have not found this continuation, and Hartzenbusch does not list it.

current publications.[7] Finally on October 1, 1793 Spain's main center of learning opened its first paper, the *Semanario erudito y curioso de Salamanca*. Like the *Correo de Murcia*, it recalled the journals suppressed by Floridablanca. Both of their circulations, too, were not unworthy of their predecessors'. The *Semanario de Salamanca* soon had nearly three hundred subscribers, of which a quarter were clergy and a sixth local faculty and students.[8] The *Correo de Murcia* reached close to two hundred and fifty, mainly circulating in Seville and the east coast cities of Spain.[9]

The beginnings of the new journals were very circumspect. They opened their columns to the anti-Revolutionary sermons and discourses of the day and otherwise limited themselves to printing mediocre articles. Gradually, although they never were able to replace those which had been killed, they began to display the interests of the earlier periodicals. The *Correo de Murcia* soon devoted space to popular science. On May 25, 1793 it published a defense, poorly written it is true, of modern science against ancient; and other articles followed stressing the progress of recent scientists[10] and the practical applications of science.[11] The *Diario de Barcelona* and the *Semanario de Salamanca* followed with similar articles.[12] In March 1797 the *Memorial literario* sang the praises of Bacon, Descartes, Newton, and Locke as in the good days of Carlos III.

The editors of the *Semanario de Salamanca*, probably because of their location, showed more interest in the problems of education. On May 6, 1794 a contributor, objecting to the dream of many a Spanish father of seeing his son become a "Don" or at least a *cura*, referred to the example of the education of the hero

[7] Hartzenbusch, p. 12. Of the new series I have seen only the issues of Oct.-Dec. 1793 prior to 1797.

[8] Lists of subscribers in issues of Oct. 22, 26, 29, Nov. 30, Dec. 31, 1793, Feb. 1, 1794.

[9] Lists of subscribers published Feb. 5 to Mar. 23, 1793.

[10] *Correo de Murcia*, Aug. 23, 26, 1794, Jan. 24, May 19, 1795.

[11] *Ibid.*, July 8, 15, 19, 1794.

[12] *Diario de Barcelona*, Nov. 23, 24, 1793; *Semanario de Salamanca*, Nov. 9, 1793, Jan. 7, 1794.

in Montengón's *Eusebio,* whose popularity was still great, to support the Rousseauan contention that all children should be taught a trade.[13] Soon articles on education, not all progressive, became frequent, with the influence of Montengón evident, and containing references to Bernardin de Saint-Pierre, Locke, and "un sabio Autor" who was none other than Jean-Jacques.[14] At Murcia and Barcelona, too, interest in the rearing of Spain's youth was reflected in the periodicals.[15]

Even more remarkable is that, in the midst of Spain's crusade against the Revolution, when denunciations of modern false philosophy were being hurled from the pulpits, pens were taken up in defense of the philosophy, and the journals lent them support. On June 18, 1793 the *Correo de Murcia* mildly quoted the once notorious praise of "nueva filosofía" pronounced in the middle of the century before the hide-bound faculty of Salamanca by the then famous scientific amateur Diego Torres Villarroel.[16] The next sally was less guarded. The *Correo* published in November, under the heading "La misantropia de la Francia," a favorable review of Zevallos' Catholic apology, *La falsa filosofia,* which was being reprinted at this time.[17] The review called forth a biting reply, "Censura apologetica de la filosofia moderna para desengaño del vulgo."[18] No more than the most reactionary patriot did its author care for the "Libertino Voltaire, Alembert, Rouseau, el Autor del *Sistema de la Naturaleza,* el du Bel'Sprit [*sic*] y otros Modernos Escritores y Enciclopedistas irreligiosos." But from the generalized attack he wished to except the true wise men who were not responsible for the horrors of the philosophic century: Newton, Wolf, Buffon, the Dutch physicists, Molière [!], and those professors who followed the new methods, the

---

[13] The article is signed "Roxas"; is this the liberal Salamancan *fraile* and poet Juan Fernández de Roxas?

[14] *Semanario de Salamanca,* Apr. 28, July 14, 30, 1795 (Montengón); June 18, 1795 (Bernardin de Saint Pierre); May 16, 1795 (Locke); July 11, 1795 (Rousseau).

[15] *Correo de Murcia,* Apr. 4, 7, June 2, 1795; *Diario de Barcelona,* Nov. 21, 1793, Jan. 15, 16, Feb. 5, 6, 1794, Jan. 10, 11, 12, Mar. 11, 12, 13, 1795, and others.

[16] On this famous speech see Cueto, *loc.cit.,* pp. xxvi-xxvii.

[17] *Correo de Murcia,* Nov. 26, 30, 1793.   [18] *Ibid.,* Jan. 11, 14, 1794.

"Catholic investigators of truth." This "Nueva Filosofía," this "Filosofía natural y experimental," he said, was helping all branches of learning, among which he included "Theología natural de Dios y su Providencia." Meanwhile the *Semanario de Salamanca* had carried an article on November 13, 1793 distinguishing between the "new Christian philosophy and the new philosophy which the impious men of our century formed on the corrupt maxims of their rotten hearts." The former seeks truth through experiment. "Disappear, then, once for all, partisans of the Peripatetic. I am, to be sure, a lover of truth, and if this is to be a modern philosopher, I find the highest pleasure in the glory of such a distinguished title." The *Semanario* continued to play up this theme, there is a good as well as a bad modern philosophy. Descartes and Newton are good.[19] So are Leibnitz and Locke, and Condillac and Jacquier (the author of the new philosophy text adopted by the universities). Their philosophy seeks new discoveries by contemplating the works of the Creator; "far from combatting true religion, it admits and approves its principles."[20]

Under the pressure of events and the universal opprobrium being heaped upon modern philosophy, the defenders of the new science had been forced to redefine their position. In 1788 they had favored "modern philosophy," and it was evident that what they had in mind was experimental science; for the anti-religious aspect of French *philosophie* had not penetrated Spain. The Spanish friends of enlightenment had hardly been aware of the dichotomy of their term. Now, in order to defend experimental science, which to them was still "modern philosophy"— after all its only place in the university curricula was in the reformed philosophy courses—they had to draw a line between this, the "new Christian philosophy," and the "false philosophy" of Voltaire and *Le système de la nature*. In so doing, they felt no less patriotic than the religious speechmakers.

[19] Manuel Sevald, "Discurso histórico del establecimiento de las ciencias en la Europa," *Semanario de Salamanca*, Jan. 17, 1795.
[20] *Ibid.*, Oct. 18, 1794, and Sevald, "La filosofia," *ibid.*, Oct. 29, 1795.

Of course, there were partisans of the religious crusade who refused to recognize such a distinction, and their discourses attacking false philosophy were published side by side with those above.[21] By printing both viewpoints, the papers were, in fact, reflecting a revival of public discussion on all topics. The articles they published support Godoy's claim that he had ordered the censors to give the periodicals a wide field except on matters affecting religion and monarchic government.[22]

The new favor shown to the *luces* that did not reflect anarchy and irreligion was not limited to the periodical press. In 1794 appeared the *Reflexiones sobre la naturaleza, o consideracion de las obras de Dios en el orden natural* by C. C. Sturm.[23] This was a German imitation of the Abbé Pluche's *Spectacle de la nature*, like which it desired the study of nature to be a glorification of God. In spirit it was very close to the Spanish defenders of "filosofía moderna." Godoy says it was translated at his order, for he made it his spiritual nourishment.[24] In the same year Valentín de Foronda published, in dialogue form for the easier understanding of youthful students, a work now becoming common knowledge among Spain's lettered classes, Condillac's *La logique*, which summed up the sensationalist philosophy of the eighteenth century.[25] Foronda also drew on the "moral arithmetic" of Buffon, the *Encyclopédie méthodique*, "Loke," and Malebranche.

The official support of science and education was even better exemplified by two acts not connected with the press. When war with France broke out in 1793, the French astronomer Pierre Méchain was in Barcelona measuring the earth's arc from Dunkirk to that city. The Spanish government immediately assured him

---

[21] E.g., *Semanario de Salamanca*, July 8, 1794, June 4, 1795, as well as the anti-French sermons (see above, p. 307).

[22] Godoy, II, 149.

[23] Advertised in *Gazeta*, Oct. 7, 1794. The first edition I have seen is the third revised edition: *Reflexiones sobre la naturaleza escritas en aleman para todos los dias del año* por M. C. C. Sturm, aumentadas . . . en frances . . . por Mr. Luis Cousin Despréaux, y traducidas al castellano (3d ed.; 6 vols.; Madrid, 1806).

[24] Godoy, II, 192.

[25] Valentín de Foronda, *Logica de Condillac puesta en diálogo* . . . (Madrid, 1794).

of its continued cooperation.[26] A year later, during the excitement caused by the French invasion of Catalonia, he was arrested. Although the Spanish commander, La Union, was the violent enemy of Republican propaganda, upon the complaint of the French commanding general, he ordered the officials of Barcelona to release Méchain, treat him with honor, and give him protection and even financial aid if he needed it.[27]

The other event was the founding of the Real Instituto Asturiano in Gijón. In 1782 Jovellanos had proposed to the society of Amigos del País of Oviedo the creation of a school of navigation and mineralogy to help develop the two main local resources. Intrigues held up the project, however, and in 1790 Jovellanos was sent to his native Asturias, primarily to remove him from Madrid, although he was given the task of studying the possibilities of the coal deposits known to exist in the province. In 1792, noting the change in official policy—the rigors of the imprisonment of his friend Cabarrús were being gradually eased and in December he was freed[28]—and seeking to remove the stigma of his own banishment from court, Jovellanos submitted his project to the government. On December 12, 1792 a royal order approved it, expressing the hope that the proposed institute would contribute to the national economy. The Real Instituto Asturiano was to have chairs of mathematics, navigation, and mineralogy. Godoy did not yet grant Jovellanos' request to be allowed to return to the capital, but he permitted the new institution to hold a gala opening that lasted four days in January 1794 and was reported at great length, with all due honor to the founder, in the *Gazeta de Madrid*.[29]

Jovellanos' speech at the opening was a noteworthy document.

[26] *Moniteur*, May 1, 1793 (report from Barcelona, Apr. 13).

[27] Arthur Chuquet, "Négotiations de Dugommier avec l'Espagne en 1794," *Séances et travaux de l'Académie des Sciences morales et politiques (Institut de France)*, N.S. LXIV (1905), 455; Delbrel, "L'Espagne et la Révolution," *loc.cit.*, XLVIII, 287.

[28] *Moniteur*, May 14, 21, 1793, Jan. 18, 1794.

[29] Vicente de la Fuente, *Historia de las universidades, colegios y demas establecimientos de enseñanza en España* (Madrid, 1884-89), IV, 202; Somoza de Montsoriú, pp. 291-93, 295; *Gazeta*, Feb. 11, 1794; Godoy, II, 208. For the history of the Instituto see Canella Secades, pp. 345-57.

He called the Instituto the gift of a good king to the people of Asturias. Kings have learned that their prosperity depends on that of their peoples, and public prosperity on the spread of enlightenment, he said. The knowledge best able to produce private and public wealth is the practical knowledge derived from the study of nature, Jovellanos continued. For too long the name of Aristotle alone has established the dogmas of physics as of metaphysics. "And if Descartes and Newton, shaking off these shackles, had not submitted their doctrine to the criterion of experiment, how far from the threshold of nature would not our reason still be erring?" But do not be led astray in uniting experiment and reason, he insisted. Observe nature, but remember it is directed by the hand of God; it is "the book that Providence laid open to men for their study."[30] Jovellanos' oration epitomized the enlightened utopia of Carlos III's day, reverence of God, progress through modern scientific studies, and enlightened despotism. The ideal was still alive in 1794.

The economic societies of Amigos del País were another institution that had declined in the last years of Floridablanca's power. Again the change in ministers brought a quick revival. The society of Madrid promptly awarded prizes that it had offered in 1790 for memoirs on agriculture and achievements in weaving. During and after the war, it regularly proposed contests in farming and the crafts and rewarded the winners. It continued to maintain and encourage with prizes for students and teachers its four elementary "patriotic schools" and its schools of embroidery and drawing. After 1792 the societies of Seville (of which Forner was the enthusiastic director[31]), Jaén, Oviedo, Vera, and Saragossa gave similar prizes. The Basque society and those of Segovia, Madrid, Saragossa, and Valladolid continued to publish memoirs. The founding fathers of the movement,

[30] Gaspar Melchor de Jovellanos, "Oración inaugural á la apertura del Real Instituto Asturiano," B.A.E., xlvi, 318-24 (quotations from pp. 321 and 320).
[31] See *Amor de la patria. Discurso que en la junta general publica que celebró la Real Sociedad de Sevilla el dia 23 de Noviembre de 1794 leyó D. Juan Pablo Forner, fiscal del crímen de la Real Audiencia y director de la sociedad* (Seville, n.d.), "Fraile," Vol. 641, fol. 79.

the Sociedad Bascongada de Amigos del País, had continued their functions unabated in 1790 and 1791, despite Floridablanca's attitude, and were the most active in all fields in 1793; but they were dealt a crippling blow by the French invasion of 1794. Not until 1798 were their yearly public functions revived, and by then the old glory was gone. Their place as the most flourishing provincial Amigos del País fell to the Sociedad Aragonesa of Saragossa. In 1797 and 1798 this society established schools of chemistry, botany, and agriculture. Its professor of economics, Normante y Carcavilla, was meanwhile teaching larger classes than under Carlos III.[32]

What the economic societies were accomplishing can be inferred from the case of the society of Murcia. It had been the eleventh founded, in 1778. The bishop of Murcia, Manuel Rubín de Celis, had been its soul and chief benefactor. He endowed it with an annual income of fifteen thousand reales. His successor had also supported it financially, and the present bishop, Victoriano López Gonzalo, besides bearing the expenses of all the prizes it offered, established factories for linen and silk ribbons and for woolen and linen cloth to give useful employment to indigent men and women. The society maintained elementary schools for boys and girls, in which learning the catechism was encouraged by the award of prizes. It had another free school for arithmetic, geometry, and drawing. The society held an annual

[32] The *Gazeta* carries reports of these activities: of Madrid in issues of May 4, 1792, Feb. 26, Apr. 2, 1793, Aug. 26, 1794, Feb. 17, 1795, July 8, Sept. 23, 1796, Aug. 29, 1797, June 1, Oct. 16, 1798, Dec. 3, 1799; Málaga, Oct. 2, 1792, Oct. 29, 1793, Oct. 24, 28, 1794; Jaén, Nov. 30, 1792, Dec. 2, 1796, Dec. 15, 1797, Sept. 28, 1798; Oviedo, Dec. 2, 4, 1794; Vera, Mar. 18, 1794, Jan. 18, 1797; Seville, Mar. 7, 1794, Dec. 22, 1795, Dec. 22, 1797, Nov. 23, 1798; Basque, Oct. 1, 4, 1793, Feb. 16, Aug. 21, 1798, Aug. 13, 1799 (see Soráluce, pp. 60-62, and Urquijo, *Menéndez y Pelayo y los caballeritos*, p. 117); Saragossa, Oct. 16, 1792, Mar. 19, 1793, Feb. 16, 19, Apr. 29, Dec. 13, 1796, May 30, 1797, May 15, Sept. 11, 1798, June 28, July 5, 9, 1799. The *Gazeta* advertised the following memoirs: Segovia, Vol. IV, Oct. 25, 1793; Madrid, four memoirs, Jan. 27, 1795, Vol. V, Nov. 13, 1795; Saragossa, Sept. 28, 1798; Valladolid, Jan. 27, 1795. The Basque society published Pedro Díaz de Valdés, *El padre de su pueblo, ó medios para hacer temporalmente felices á los pueblos con el auxilio de los señores curas párrocos. Memoria premiada por la Real Sociedad Bascongada, é impresa de su orden en Vitoria en 1793* (2d ed.; Barcelona, 1806).

meeting on the king's saint's day, at which the main event was a speech by a leading member. One time the speaker was an editor of the local *Correo de Murcia*. The discourses given on these occasions showed a full awareness of recent developments throughout Spain. They recognized and accepted the leadership of the Basque society, and they took pride in the advances made by other Amigos del País and equally in their own achievements. These men had come to look beyond provincial borders to the good of the nation and were still seeking this by the most progressive ideas of Europe without ever wavering in their love of king and religion.[33]

The society of Murcia was not exceptional. It was not even among those whose activity was reported in the *Gazeta*. Since the disappearance of Floridablanca, all over Spain the Amigos del País were again prosperous, a change for which Godoy, not without justification, assumes responsibility.[34]

As could be expected from the new activity of the economic societies, economic thought was again encouraged in Spain. The contrast with the first years of the Revolution was even more striking than in other fields. On March 17, 1790 the Inquisición prohibited, even for those with licenses to read forbidden books, both the original and the recent Spanish translation of Filangieri's *La scienza della legislazione*.[35] On March 4, 1792 it did the same to the *Recherches sur la nature et les causes de la richesse des nations, traduit de l'anglois de M. Smith* "because beneath a captious and obscure style, it favors toleration in point of religion and is conducive to naturalism"![36] Aranda, who had just assumed the reins of government, did not agree with the Inquisición in shutting out a work that Spain needed to complete its familiarity with modern economic thought. Before the year was out the Imprenta Real had published "de orden superior" the *Compendio*

[33] Speeches of "one of the editors of this *correo*," Nov. 4, 1794, and Eugenio Pérez Cortés, Nov. 4, 1795, quoted in *Correo de Murcia,* Jan. 3, 6, and Nov. 17, 21, 1795. All the above information is drawn from these speeches.

[34] Godoy, II, 128-29, 145, 157.

[35] *Suplemento al Indice,* p. 21.

[36] Edict in "Fraile," Vol. 863, fol. 152.

de la obra inglesa intitulada Riqueza de las naciones, hecho por el Marques de Condorcet.[37] Adam Smith's masterpiece was announced in the *Gazeta de Madrid* as "the best work of its class that has been written . . . very useful for public leaders and especially for propagating in the economic societies true principles which should direct their operations toward the general good of the monarchy."[38] After Godoy's advent a translation of the *Wealth of Nations* was made directly from the English by a lawyer in the royal administration of Valladolid, Josef Alonso Ortiz. He omitted various passages in the original which had offended by criticizing the expense of religious institutions, Catholic included, and he added illustrative material relative to Spain. The Inquisición, after five *calificadores* found that it had avoided the errors of the French translation, and the Consejo de Castilla granted permission for its publication. Godoy accepted the dedication of it, and it appeared in Valladolid toward the end of 1794.[39]

The enthusiasm in Spain for economics, so marked before the Revolution, was again in full flower, thanks to the new official attitude. "When I finished my legal training about 1793, the ideas of political economy were spreading in Spain with fury," testified the future Argentine patriot Manuel Belgrano. The most important contribution to Spanish economic writing was the published memoirs of the economic societies, already mentioned. The interest was reflected in the periodicals, especially the *Semanario de Salamanca*. A series of articles on practical agronomy[40] was interspersed with others exposing the physiocratic theory that it is its agriculture that a nation should first encourage, not

[37] y traducida al castellano con varias adiciones del original por don Cárlos Martinez de Irujo . . . (Madrid, 1792).

[38] *Gazeta*, Sept. 4, 1792.

[39] A.H.N., Inq., leg. 4484, No. 13. Adam Smith, *Investigacion de la naturaleza y causas de la riqueza de las naciones.* Obra escrita en inglés por Adam Smith, . . . La traduce al castellano el Lic. D. Josef Alonso Ortiz . . . (4 vols.; Valladolid, 1794). Advertised in *Gazeta*, Sept. 12, 1794. See R. S. Smith, *loc.cit.*, pp. 108-17.

[40] *Semanario de Salamanca*, Oct. 28, 1794, May 21 to 28, June 4, 6, Aug. 1, 13, 26, Sept. 8, 10, Dec. 17, 24, 1795; Belgrano, p. 13.

crafts and manufactures, which depend on the soil for their prosperity. The author, Pablo Zamalloa, who appears to have been one of the editors of the paper, however, saw in the flourishing of the arts and crafts the true basis for individual liberty, for they end economic inequality.[41] Similar articles, both progressive and reactionary, studded the *Semanario*.[42]

Editors of periodicals, Amigos del País, writers on science and economics, were all encouraged in their activities between 1792 and 1795. In the same years that the war against the Revolution produced a crusade in Spain and made hatred of French liberty and philosophy a patriotic duty, Aranda and Godoy abandoned Floridablanca's persecution of the Spanish institutions of enlightenment. Godoy could claim with some justice that his country had become the refuge of the lights that were elsewhere feared.

2

The Treaty of Basle of July 1795 between France and Spain was followed by a rapid rapprochement of the two countries. Carlos IV and the Príncipe de la Paz had not forgotten the execution of Louis XVI, but the Spanish government did not feel strong enough, especially at sea, to remain neutral in the continuing war between Britain and France. The recent alliance of Spain and Britain had been a marriage of convenience which had not calmed Spanish suspicions of their traditional colonial rival. Before 1792 the Franco-Spanish Family Pact had been one answer to the threat of British inroads in Spain's American empire; now hostile British acts made Godoy decide to reestablish the pact even in the absence of one branch of the family. An offensive and defensive alliance with the French Republic against Great Britain was signed at San Ildefonso on August 18, 1796. As soon as Spanish officials in the New World were notified of their government's intentions, Spain declared war on England on October 7, 1796.

---

[41] *Ibid.*, May 19, June 2, 1795. The author signs "Z," but signs his full name elsewhere frequently enough to be identified.

[42] *Ibid.*, Jan. 4, Mar. 18, 1794, June 25, 1795, and a series of articles proposing an economic society for Salamanca and replies to them, June 11, July 7, 21, Oct. 3, 1795.

The new official relations with France entailed a relaxation of measures taken against French papers. In the years following the Treaty of Basle the Inquisición found fans and playing cards decorated with goddesses of liberty and revolutionary or anti-clerical inscriptions in French and Spanish being sold to the public at fairs in San Sebastián, Valladolid, Ávila, Segovia, and Toledo.[43] In Barcelona the Inquisición discovered on sale a book entitled *Constitution de la République française*;[44] and it received a distressing report that a violently anticlerical *Tocsin des prêtres*, by the Abbé Bouvet, had been spread in Málaga and Cadiz.[45] French newspapers like the *Moniteur* had the run of the country. A German traveller in 1798 found that periodicals from abroad could be consulted in all major foreign commercial houses. In Cadiz the French Casa de la Camorra again had "the best and most interesting foreign newspapers . . . and there is a similar establishment at the Apollo coffee-house, where the best French newspapers may be read at any time after the arrival of the post."[46]

The rigors against persons suspected of Revolutionary intent were also mitigated. At the request of the Directory, the executive body of the French Republic established late in 1795, Carlos pardoned the Guipuzcoan officials who had surrendered their province to the French in 1794, and commuted the death sentences of Juan Picornell and his accomplices in the "Conspiracy of San Blas."[47] By the terms of the Treaty of Basle, Frenchmen were able to return to Spain and conduct their businesses as before the war. Many Spaniards could not shift their feelings as readily as Godoy shifted alliances and refused to approve all the consequences of their country's diplomatic revolution. Certain bishops in partic-

---

[43] A.H.N., Inq., leg. 4484, No. 27 (1796), and leg. 4514, Nos. 10, 11 (1798).

[44] *Ibid.*, leg. 4430, No. 11 (1797).

[45] Sarrailh, p. 299 (1796).

[46] Fischer, *Travels in Spain*, pp. 93, 308. The *Moniteur* worried the Inquisición (see A.H.N., Inq., leg. 4429, No. 30 [1797]).

[47] A. Alcalá Galiano, *Representaciones que hizo á su majestad el augusto Congreso Nacional* . . . (Madrid, 1812), pp. 32-33, in "Fraile," Vol. 350, p. 1. On Picornell see above, pp. 325-26.

ular refused to stop their priests from speaking ill of the Revolutionaries.[48] Local Spanish officials too not infrequently gave evidence of their antipathy toward returning French merchants, despite the welcome promised in the treaty.[49]

Nevertheless there was a marked change in atmosphere since the conclusion of peace with France. Tensions had relaxed, and the maritime war with England, when it came, entailed little excitement and passion. A relative calm settled over the country that was to last until 1798. Godoy was able during this period to carry on with a minimum of resistance his support of the *luces*. The Spanish press again encouraged admiration of the classic figures of the Enlightenment. Biographies in Spanish of Buffon and Franklin appeared as well as an *Espiritu del Conde de Buffon*.[50] The *Gazeta de Madrid* advertised the *Decadencia y ruina del sistema de hacienda de Gran Bretaña escrito en ingles por Tomás Paine*, the first known Spanish translation of a work by John Locke—the *Educacion de niños*—, and many of the translations published before 1791 of works of the Enlightenment.[51]

The crown gave special support to advances in higher education. New schools of cosmography, medicine, and other sciences were established, and promising students were sent abroad, as they had been by Carlos III.[52] Godoy's memoirs point to the case of a young professor at the university of Granada to show the advances that philosophy was also making under his tutelage. Narciso de Heredia y Bejines had been made professor of philosophy and mathematics in 1793 at the age of eighteen. Three years later the university sponsored a public examination of his students

[48] *Moniteur*, 10 messidor VI (June 28, 1798).

[49] See French note to Príncipe de la Paz, 30 floréal IV (May 19, 1796), A.A.E., Esp., Vol. 640, pièce 105 (noted in Desdevises, *L'Espagne*, I, 258-59).

[50] *Vida del Conde de Buffon*, advertised in *Gazeta*, Nov. 24, 1797, see Sarrailh, p. 715. *Vida del Dr. Benjamin Franklin* advertised in *Gazeta*, Mar. 27, 1798. *Espiritu del Conde de Buffon* escrito en frances por M . . . [sic] y traducido al castellano por Tiburcio Maquieyra Serrador (Valladolid, 1798).

[51] Paine and Locke both advertised in *Gazeta*, Jan. 24, 1797.

[52] *Moniteur*, Nov. 27, 1796 (new scientific chairs at the royal observatory); Godoy, III, 126 n.; Lafuente, XV, 296-97.

to display the talents of this teacher. Heredia's speech on the occasion and a description of the subjects covered by the examination were published in Málaga. Like the best enlightened Spaniards of a decade earlier, Heredia praised the spirit of modern philosophy and its accomplishments. He claimed to have taught ancient and modern systems of philosophy, including those of Vives, Montaigne, Galileo, Descartes, Newton, and Leibnitz, and issued the common warning against accepting any single system. Although he pointed out the dangers of slipping into impiety, he used the terms "Ser Supremo" and "Autor de nuestra existencia" instead of the more Christian "Dios." Specifically his students were examined in modern science, an epistemology drawn plainly from Locke and Condillac, and the "deberes del hombre."[53]

Meanwhile the recent subversive effervescense within the universities appears to have subsided. The most notable student activity recorded during these years was the flowering of an unofficial "Academia de Letras Humanas" organized in 1793 by students and teachers of the university of Seville. It included enlightened young men who were soon to become leading literary figures—Manuel Arjona, Alberto Lista, Jose María Blanco y Crespo (Blanco White), and Felix Reinoso—but their main object in joining together was to perfect their literary and poetic style.[54] Perhaps the notorious fate of Salamanca's Professor Salas intimidated the more dissatisfied students; but, judging from the case of Meléndez Valdés, who wrote at this time two epistles in verse praising Godoy's support of the *luces*, a rise of "el Principe" in the esteem of some enlightened circles may well

[53] Narciso de Heredia y Bejines, *Discurso que recitó á el claustro de la Universidad de Granada el Dr. Dn. Narciso de Heredia y Bejines . . . para dar principio al examen público de sus discípulos . . .* (Málaga, 1796); *Examen publico que han de tener los bachilleres . . . baxo la direccion del Dr. en A. D. D. Narciso de Heredia y Bejines . . .* (Málaga, 1796). See the biography of Heredia in Narciso de Heredia y Begines [*sic*] de los Rios, Conde de Ofalia, *Escritos del Conde de Ofalia*, ed. Marqués de Heredia (Bilbao, 1894), and Godoy, II, 127.

[54] See their publication [F. J. Reinoso, A. Lista y Aragón, J. M. Blanco], *Poesias de una academia de letras humanas de Sevilla* (Seville, 1797); Blanco y Crespo, *Life*, pp. 20-23; Cueto, *loc.cit.*, clxxxvi-clxxxviii.

account for the lack of evidence of the composition of seditious writings in the universities after 1795.[55]

Nevertheless, it proved impossible for the government to limit the spread of the *luces* to those of which it approved. The future historian Andrés Muriel, who was teaching theology during these years, remembered Voltaire and Rousseau as being more popular than ever with the clergy.[56] Rousseau was probably still the most widely read author on the Index, but scattered bits of evidence indicate that the Abbé Gabriel Bonnot de Mably was becoming a strong rival for the favor of enlightened Spaniards. One of his works had appeared in Spanish in 1788.[57] Godoy states that he permitted the publication of Mably's *Elementos de historia*, which had been held up; but, since no trace of such a work has been found, he may have been thinking of the *Elementos de moral escritos en frances por el Abate de Mabli*, which appeared about 1798.[58] At the same time more dangerous works by this author—whom one admirer called "the most Christian political philosopher, the most virtuous historian, and the sweetest moralist one can desire"—were circulating undercover in French or in Spanish manuscript.[59]

About the year 1795 Spanish book dealers discovered that selling prohibited foreign books could be extremely profitable. According to Blanco White, who was then a student, Madrid was the center of the trade, and from there the books spread throughout the provinces. University students were especially willing to pay well for such reading matter.[60] Muriel adds that travelling salesmen carried the literature to the smallest *pueblos*.[61]

[55] Juan Meléndez Valdés, "Epístola al . . . Príncipe de la Paz, exhortando . . . á que . . . continúe su proteccion á las ciencias y las artes" (1795) and "Epístola . . . al . . . Príncipe de la Paz con motivo de su carta patriótica á los obispos de España, recomendandoles el nuevo *Semanario de agricultura*" (1797), B.A.E., LXIII, 199, 207.

[56] Muriel, III, 113.   [57] See above, p. 72.

[58] y traducidos al castellano por D. Tiburcio Maquieyra Serrador (Valladolid, n.d.), advertised in *Gazeta*, July 30, 1799; Godoy, II, 207.

[59] Quotation from Posse, *loc.cit.*, XVI[1], 357, see XVI[2], 153; A.H.N., Inq., leg. 4450, No. 7 (1794), leg. 4493, No. 1 (1802).

[60] *El Español*, II (1811), 461.

[61] Muriel, III, 112.

For a while, in order not to upset the new alliance with France, the government winked at the development,[62] but eventually Godoy was forced to halt it. In mid-summer 1797 a Madrid printer named Quiroga was discovered putting out (presumably in Spanish, the sources are not clear) an edition of Constantin de Volney's *Les ruines, ou méditation sur les révolutions des empires*, an interpretation of history written in 1791 by a member of the French National Assembly which deeply incensed religious readers everywhere. Quiroga and other persons believed to be his accomplices were arrested by the government early in August 1797.[63] The Inquisición hastened to reissue its decree of December 1789 against Revolutionary literature and to add a special warning against *Les ruines*, "which has surpassed all other Revolutionary writings in scandal and iniquity" and "pretends to found liberty on the ruins of Religion and Monarchies."[64] In January 1798 a royal circular warned printers against publishing books that lacked a royal license and ordered bookstores to surrender any prohibited books in their possession and "not to permit in their shops arguments or conversations that are subversive to our political constitution." The cause given for the order was "the ease with which some booksellers of Madrid and the kingdom, through an excessive desire for gain, sell all kinds of prohibited books, which often fall into the hands of unwary persons who drink in the poison and later, out of an eagerness to show off, spew it forth in public or in private conversations or perhaps even in the formal acts of universities, colleges, and other educational institutions."[65]

To such a pass had Spain come in the two and a half years since the Treaty of Basle. University students might no longer be circulating libels of Godoy and the government, but their

[62] *Ibid.*, p. 116.

[63] *Moniteur*, Aug. 22, 1797 (report from Madrid, Aug. 7).

[64] Edict of Sept. 3, 1797, in "Fraile," Vol. 855, fol. 29. This incident further clarifies the mysterious passage in Quintana that puzzled Menéndez Pelayo (see above, p. 332 n. 61).

[65] *Circular*, Jan. 1798, in Josef Garriga, *Continuacion y suplemento del prontuario de don Severo Aguirre, que comprehende las cedulas, resoluciones &c. expedidas en . . . 1798* (2d. ed.; Madrid, 1804), p. 91; *Nov. rec.*, VIII, xviii, 16.

reading of prohibited books had become more common than ever. The official reaction to the trade in forbidden literature had been tardy and could hardly be effective. In 1799 the Inquisición caught two booksellers in Valladolid *flagrante delicto* and punished them with sentences that meant the ruin of their businesses.[66] The government and the Santo Oficio might instead have learned the lesson of the early years of the Revolution—so long as a sizable number of people in Spain wanted to read French writings or enjoy other lights than those sanctioned by the government, royal and inquisitorial edicts would not stop them from doing so.

3

The revival of Spanish intellectual activities under Godoy was not restricted to those favoring the Enlightenment. In the first years of Carlos IV even Catholic apologists seemed to declare a truce. Apparently the only attack on the *philosophes* published between 1788 and 1792 was the third volume of Fernández Valcarce's *Desengaños filosoficos*, directed primarily at modern "usurious" economic theories and at lay morality.[67] Not until after Floridablanca's fall did religious apologetics reappear. In 1792 the Imprenta Real published the *Reflexiones de un filosofo christiano, sobre la humanidad del siglo ilustrado, dedicadas a sus decantadores. Por D. J. C.*, which insists that "humanity," when separated from the principles of the Evangile known as "charity," is hardly more than a pretty name to cover over "a condescension to our immoderate passions," an oft-repeated theme in slightly different dress.[68] The author, like so many of his ilk, knew his classical writers far better than his antagonists, whom he scarcely cited. The *Correo de Murcia* included in its first issue a "Rasgo moral," also dedicated to the principle that the "impios de nuestro siglo" gave a "puerta franca á las desordenadas pasiones," whereas a true philosopher exposes his life "en defensa de la Religion y del Estado."[69]

[66] Llorente, *Historia*, IX, 49-50. [67] Madrid, 1790. Vol. IV appeared in 1797.
[68] *Reflexiones de un filosofo christiano*, pp. v, 17-19.
[69] *Correo de Murcia*, Sept. 1, 1792.

A few issues later this periodical began to publish "La existencia de Dios y su providencia deducidas da las maravillas de la naturaleza, traduccion."[70] The article was continued in later issues under the thoroughly orthodox heading, "Sigue la existencia de Dios." Translations of religious apologies from the French like this one were more common in 1792 than original works. Some *Reflexiones sobre las ordenes religiosas* denied the evil effects which had been attributed to the monastic orders.[71] *El éxito de la muerte correspondiente á la vida de los tres supuestos heroes del siglo XVIII, Voltaire, D'Alembert, y Diderot* tried to frighten its readers by depicting what death is like to an apostate. Editions of this gruesome work came out in Madrid, Cadiz, and Barcelona.[72] Possibly even more popular was the Spanish version of Philippe-Louis Gérard's epistolary novel, *Le comte de Valmont, ou les égaremens de la raison*, in which a young nobleman who has taken the primrose path to incredulity, women, and materialism, is led back to the straight and narrow one by the superior reasons of religion. The Spanish translator wanted the theme to be even more evident from the title page, so he called it *Triunfos de la verdadera religion, contra los extravios de la razon, en el Conde de Valmont*.[73] He devoted an introduction to combatting the "espíritus fuertes." Its publication began in Murcia in 1792. A prospectus was issued with the *Gazeta de Madrid*,[74] and the

---

[70] *Ibid.*, Sept. 29, 1792. The author of the original is not named, but it may be B. Nieuwentyt, who wrote *L'existence de Dieu démontrée par les merveilles de la nature* (Paris, 1725).

[71] *Reflexiones sobre las ordenes religiosas, ó consejos de conciencia a un personage que los ha perdido*. Traducidas del frances por D. Cristoval Talens de la Riva (Madrid, 1792).

[72] . . . traducido del idioma frances al italiano, y de éste al castellano. Por don Joseph Domenichini . . . (Madrid, 1792). The Cadiz edition had the title *Retrato histórico de la horrible muerte de aquel monstruo de la iniquidad Mr. Voltaire, cuyas perversas doctrinas pueden haber tenido mucha parte en los desordenes que afligen la Francia* (Cadiz, n.d.) (cited in Moldenhauer, *loc.cit.*, p. 130 n. 31). The Barcelona edition is cited in *Nov. rec.*, VIII, xviii, nota 19.

[73] [Philippe-Louis Gerard], *Triunfos de la verdadera religion, contra los extravios de la razon, en el Conde de Valmont. Cartas recogidas y publicadas por el Sr. N.* Traducidas del frances por el R. P. Fr. Clemente Millana, predicador . . . (5 vols.; Murcia and Madrid, 1792-93).

[74] The prospectus is bound with the issue of July 6, 1792 in the Biblioteca Nacional copy of the *Gazeta*, but it is not dated.

book was subscribed for in all the coastal cities from Barcelona to Cadiz and fairly heavily in Madrid: 568 copies in all of which 320 in the capital. Only a fifth of the subscribers were clergy; the rest almost all commoners, while one of the few nobles to buy it was the Conde de Almodóvar, Raynal's translator. This was the same type of public that the periodicals of the 1780's had had, another indication that the spirit of enlightenment in Spain had not conflicted with religious sentiment. By 1793 the venture had proved such a success that Volumes IV and V were published by one of Madrid's most respectable firms.[75]

Godoy claims credit for having encouraged the writing of Spanish defenses of Catholicism and monarchy, which now began to reappear.[76] Their revival, however, began during the brief ministry of Aranda with a request from Hervás y Panduro for a new official examination of his *Historia de la vida del hombre*, whose first two volumes Floridablanca had ordered confiscated in 1789 because the prologue outlined social theories that seemed too advanced. Circulation of the volumes without the offending prologue was now approved.[77] Volume III was published by the Imprenta Real in 1794, and after some more difficulties with the censors, the work was finally completed in seven volumes in 1799. It was by far the most interesting apology of Catholicism to be written by a Spaniard at this time and revealed a debt to the intellectual climate of Italy, where Hervás, and ex-Jesuit, was living in exile. The burden of the work is that the best ideas of the Enlightenment on political and social institutions can be reconciled with Catholic beliefs, for, according to Hervás, the attacks of the *philosophes* on religion were irrelevant to the real goals of their philosophy. Only occasional inconsistencies in

---

[75] Viuda de Joaquín Ibarra. Vols. I-III give the list of subscribers. Worth mention, too, although of a later date is an intelligent and enlightened refutation of Rousseau's *Contrat social*, translated according to the title page from an Italian original: *Discurso sobre la verdadera libertad natural y civil del hombre*. Escrito en italiano traducido al castellano por don Ventura Salzas (Madrid, 1798).

[76] Godoy, II, 192-93.

[77] González Palencia, "Nuevas noticias del abate Hervás," *Eruditos y libreros*, p. 197. Many extant copies of Vol. I lack the prologue and begin abruptly with p. xxv.

Hervás' arguments mar the general effect of the *Historia de la vida del hombre.*

Other writers trod a better known path in their counter-attacks on the doctrines of the Enlightenment and the Revolution. One of these was by a professor of oriental languages, Juan Joseph Heydeck. The first two volumes of his *Defensa de la religion christiana* were published by the Imprenta Real in 1792 and 1793. Heydeck's work was an exegesis of the Bible in support of the verity of the Catholic faith. Only in the footnotes, especially those of the second volume, did he attack his adversaries, the *philosophes* and the Protestants. Judging from the frequency he is referred to, Rousseau was Heydeck's prime bogie and *Émile* Rousseau's most dangerous book.[78] More to the point, the Imprenta Real put out in 1793 a *Catecismo del estado segun los principios de la religion,* a tract for revolutionary times written by a *calificador* of the Inquisición and royal chaplain, Joaquín Lorenzo Villanueva. It wished to establish the orthodox contention that religion is the only force capable of upholding society. Religion alone can make the subjects respect their king, as they should, whether he be good or bad, by showing that through him they are obeying the will of God. The divine right theory of Bossuet was directly cited.[79] Juan Pablo Forner, already famous as an apologist of Spain, was much more likely than Villanueva to be read when he defended the same theory in a book called optimistically *Preservativo contra el ateismo.*[80] It was little more than a forceful echo of his *Discursos filosóficos sobre el hombre.* The *philosophes,* he contended, by attacking religion, had led directly to the horror of the French Revolution. Forner's book, which was but a development of this accusation, showed that if he had lost none of his polemic powers since the Masson *affaire,* neither had he increased his philosophic capacity.

[78] Juan Joseph Heydeck, *Defensa de la religion christiana* (4 vols.; Madrid, 1792-98) ("Fraile," Vols. 589-92), notes on II, 31-33, 39, 44, 75-76, 87-89, 166-70, 214-15. Voltaire, Helvétius, and Grotius are attacked in notes on II, 40, 59, 90-91.

[79] Joaquín Lorenzo Villanueva, *Catecismo del estado segun los principios de la religion* (Madrid, 1793). Bossuet cited in title of chap. xxv, p. 243.

[80] Seville, 1795.

The climax of Spanish religious apologetics of the Revolutionary years was written in the home of the Revolution. After his
famous escape from the Inquisición to France in 1780, Pablo
Olavide had lived quietly outside Paris under an assumed name.
Exile and advancing age worked a change in his ideas, and the
French Revolution found him "entirely given over to devotion."[81]
His new point of view, coupled with a sojourn in prison during
the Terror, caused him to detest the Revolution and desire to
return to Spain. As a means to achieve this end he evidently took
his cue from the current success in Spain of the *Triunfos de la
verdadera religión . . . en el Conde de Valmont* and composed
a four-volume work on a similar theme. He entitled it *El
Evangelio en triunfo, ó historia de un filósofo desengañado.*

The story itself is third rate. Employing the fashionable, and
long-winded, epistolary style—Spanish translations of French
and English epistolary novels of the century were being advertised with increasing frequency in the *Gazeta*—*El Evangelio en
triunfo* purported to be the letters of a "false philosopher" who
is won back to religion by the sound arguments of a good *padre*
and then proselytes his former philosophic friends. The moral
is the timeworn commonplace: the new philosophy consists of
nothing but abandonment to atheism, license, and vile passions.
In describing the revolting life of the protagonist before his regeneration, Olavide was catering to the prejudices of the audience
he was writing for and hardly, as many readers have thought,
attempting to give an honest account of his own early life and
friends. Only the few truly autobiographical details in the prologue
provide any lasting interest. Here Olavide recounts how he
"found" this heaven-sent manuscript while in a Revolutionary
prison. One senses the revulsion he felt at witnessing Christian
churches turned into temples of Reason where "Marat and Pel-
letier occupied the niches from which Saint Peter and Saint Paul
had been removed in disgrace." Even in the prologue, however,
the exiled author betrayed a conscious attempt to appeal to the
recent Spanish fury against the Revolution.

[81] Fernán-Núñez, I, 226.

El Evangelio en triunfo has frequently been likened to Chateaubriand's *Génie du Christianisme,* which it anticipated by a few years. Like the French author, Olavide judged accurately the temper of his market. *El Evangelio en triunfo* was published anonymously in Valencia in 1797-98 and was immediately reprinted in Madrid. It reached a fourth edition in 1799 and an eighth in 1803. It was the Spanish best seller of the turn of century, taking the place previously held by Montengón's Rousseauistic *Eusebio.*[82]

In his anxiety to leave the land of the Revolution, Olavide tried early in 1798 to enter England by posing as a secret agent for South American revolutionaries.[83] When he failed, on May 1, 1798 he sent a formal request to Carlos IV to be allowed back to Spain. This time Olavide's wish was fulfilled. The inquisitor-general, when consulted, was cool to him, but Carlos granted Olavide's petition and bestowed upon him his former honors and a munificent pension. Oddly, no mention was ever officially made of Olavide's authorship of the book that had brought about his rehabilitation. After a royal welcome at the Escorial, the once-famous intendant of Seville retired quietly to the small Andalusian town of Baeza, wrote bad religious verses, and spent his pension on local acts of charity. One of the most agitated lives of the century finally ended in 1804, when he died at the age of seventy-five.[84]

4

A line would sometimes be difficult to draw at which Catholic apologetics ended and anti-progressive intrigues around the government began. If Godoy favored the apologetics, he did not

[82] [Pablo Olavide], *El Evangelio en triunfo, ó historia de un filósofo desengañado* (4 vols.; Valencia, 1797-98). The book was always published anonymously, but Olavide's authorship was recognized by contemporaries. See Llorente, *Historia,* v, 312-13; A. Alcalá Galiano, *Historia de España,* v, 294 n.; Puigblanch, pp. 193-95.

[83] William Spence Robertson, *The Life of Miranda* (Chapel Hill, 1929), I, 167-68.

[84] Olavide to Carlos IV, May 1, 1798, quoted in Cotarelo y Mori, p. 188; *real orden,* Nov. 14, 1798, quoted in Lafuente, xv, 294; *Moniteur,* 16 nivôse VII (Jan. 5, 1799); Puigblanch, p. 195; Danvila y Collado, IV, 60-61.

the intrigues; but one of the significant features of the reign of Carlos IV was that the royal favorite never enjoyed enough authority to control the enemies of enlightenment as Carlos III's ministers had done. Religious conservatives, moreover, had been reinvigorated by Floridablanca's recent attitude, and the crusade against the Revolution further strengthened their position. They were able to exert their new influence in devious ways. In November 1794 Jovellanos wrote to the inquisitor-general requesting permission for the Instituto Asturiano to own prohibited books on science for use by its professors.[85] Almost a year later he received the reply that there was no need to recur to foreign works for there were good enough ones by Spanish authors.[86] Within a month he found the local *comisario* of the Inquisición in the library of the Instituto reading its copy of Locke, and he began to fear silent machinations against his school.[87]

All incidents were not so trifling. In the terrible summer of 1794, when the Spanish army was on the defensive in the east and retreating in the west and La Union was reporting the invasion of French propaganda, Godoy's authority was at its lowest ebb. He was forced to replace an open-minded inquisitor-general, Manuel Abad y la Sierra, guilty of projecting a reform of the procedure of the Santo Oficio in censoring books and judging suspects, by the reactionary Francisco Lorenzana, archbishop of Toledo.[88] Then, on July 31, 1794, a royal order closed all chairs of public law and of *derecho natural y de gentes* wherever they had been established and prohibited instruction in them "where, without there being a chair, they have been taught from that of another subject."[89] This sudden measure must be grouped with

---

[85] Jovellanos, *Diarios*, p. 181, Nov. 12, 1794; see Jovellanos [to Jardine, May 24, 1794], B.A.E., xlvi, 366-67.

[86] Aug. 6, 1795, quoted in Somoza de Montsoriú, p. 46.

[87] *Ibid.*, pp. 47-48; Jovellanos, *Diarios*, pp. 265-66, Sept. 5, 1795.

[88] *Moniteur*, Sept. 6, 1794 (report from Madrid, July 12); Llorente, *Historia*, vi, 116-18; Villanueva, *Vida literaria*, i, 94-95. Godoy claims he dismissed Abad y la Sierra because he had been too strict (ii, 117-18), but evidently Godoy's eagerness to appear liberal overinfluenced his pen.

[89] *Nov. rec.*, viii, iv, 5; Aguirre, *Segunda continuacion . . . al prontuario . . . 1794*, p. 7.

Floridablanca's suppression of the periodical press in 1791 as the two major blows of the Revolutionary years to the agencies of enlightenment created under Carlos III. It ill accords with Godoy's policy since 1792. The young first secretary, shaken by the dangerous political and military situation, was evidently submitting to the conservative elements that had been aroused by the French Revolution.[90]

The feelings of the churchmen who desired this measure were expressed by one of their number, Pedro Luis Blanco, the royal librarian. The study of natural law, he claims, is not feared by the Spanish rulers, because they know that nature and religion, both coming from the hand of the "sovereign artificer," are in admirable harmony. The source of true natural law, he says, is the Bible, which teaches the proper subordination of society. Modern writers—Blanco cites Hobbes, Rousseau, Raynal, Voltaire, and the Revolutionary pamphleteers—ignoring this source, have forgotten that the state cannot be independent of religion.

> According to them man degraded himself by passing voluntarily into society from his primitive state of liberty and absolute independence, in which they put him wandering in the woods. . . . This state, so unworthy of the nobility of man, appeared so happy to a great unbeliever of this century that he confessed he had seen himself tempted to go on all fours through the hills to enjoy it and to reestablish it.

Blanco is referring to a well known comment of Voltaire, but he is felicitously oblivious of the patriarch's irony. Spain, he continues, desires that religion be not attacked by its professors of natural law (the implication is that some had forgotten Carlos III's injunction on this point). "It would be a great shame that . . . our youth, enamoured like Voltaire of the delights and joy of the wandering life, should escape to the woods on four feet

[90] Llorente attributes the measure to Floridablanca (*Historia,* IX, 22-23), and Villanueva dates it 1791 (*Vida literaria,* I, 43), but their memory failed them, for there is no error in the date of the order (see also the *real orden,* Oct. 25, 1794, *Nov. rec.,* VIII, iv, 6, assigning the chair of public law in the university of Valencia to moral philosophy).

to recover in the society of the beasts the brilliant prerogative they lost when they united with their fellow creatures."[91]

The suppression of instruction in natural law scarcely hurt the esteem in which the subject was held. The periodicals continued to publish articles referring to it.[92] Jovellanos still approved its study, and Forner exempted it from his attack on modern philosophy.[93] The approved texts were not put on the Index, and a contemporary says that *derecho natural y de gentes* was now studied more avidly than before its chairs were abolished.[94] The measure was an opportune exception to Godoy's general policy. His ministry on the whole betrayed little fear that the Spanish youth would take to the sylvan life.

In 1795 the library of a lady lover of literature in Madrid was described as containing, besides novels and classical French and Spanish works, the works of Franklin, the *Logica* of Condillac, works of Malebranche, the treatise on education of girls by Fénelon, Forner's *Discursos filosóficos sobre el hombre,* "the Buffon translated," and *El censor.*[95] In his home in Asturias Jovellanos was freely reading and discussing with his friends the works of Bernardin de Saint-Pierre, Buffon, Bossuet, Gibbon, Condillac's course of studies, Condorcet's life of Turgot, Rousseau's confessions, and Tom Paine's *Rights of Man,* as well as books of Locke, Burke, Adam Smith, and Barruel.[96] Forner alongside of *El censor* and Condillac—Locke, Smith, and Buffon alongside of Barruel— these two instances were typical of the broadminded climate of opinion in educated circles of Spain in the first years of Godoy's rule. Frightened by the Revolution, Floridablanca had attempted to check the course of enlightenment inherited from Carlos III, but his replacement by Aranda put an end to this oppression.

---

[91] [Pedro Luis Blanco], *Respuesta pacífica de un Español á la carta sediciosa del Frances Grégoire, que se dice obispo de Blois* (Madrid, 1798), pp. 49-62, quotations from pp. 51, 54-56. Blanco is identified in Grégoire, II, 66.

[92] *Correo de Murcia,* July 19, 1794; *Semanario de Salamanca,* Feb. 14, 1795.

[93] Jovellanos to Doctor Prado, Dec. 17, 1795, B.A.E., L, 145-48; Forner, *Preservativo contra el ateismo,* pp. 35-37.

[94] Llorente, *Historia,* IX, 24.

[95] *Semanario de Salamanca,* July 4, 1795.

[96] Jovellanos, *Diarios,* pp. 120-82, Jan. 1794 to Dec. 1795, *passim.*

It was the veteran of the expulsion of the Jesuits who revived the pre-Revolutionary attitude of the government. Godoy assumes credit for reopening Spain to the intellectual currents of Europe, but in this he is denying Aranda his due.[97] What Godoy did do was to continue and to further the policy of his immediate predecessor. This is no mean claim to the gratitude of his nation and one that has been recognized by leading Spanish historians.[98] At the very time of the religious war on France Spain seemed to have returned to the main stream of the Enlightenment of Carlos III.

These same years were marked by the growth of an enlightened opposition in the major cities and universities, directed primarily at Godoy. After peace with France calmed the Spanish atmosphere this opposition became less virulent, but Carlos IV, María Luisa, and their favorite never recovered the prestige once held by Carlos III and his leading secretaries. No clearer proof can be adduced to show that the French Revolution was having its effect on the friends of enlightenment. The large majority of

[97] According to the Prussian minister, Sandoz, after April 1792 the hand in control of the Spanish government was Godoy's (Baumgarten, pp. 374-76); and in his memoirs Godoy assumes credit for the liberal measures taken in 1792 (as for instance the revival of the press [II, 147-49]). Not all witnesses agree on his great influence at this time. The dispatches of the Russian ambassador indicate that Aranda was in control of the government (Tratchevsky, *loc.cit.*, p. 35), and so do the reports in the *Moniteur* (Apr. 15, May 11, June 19, 28, July 10, Oct. 20, 1792). Muriel, admittedly a partisan of Aranda, while describing the rise in favor of Godoy during Aranda's ministry, does not suggest that Godoy controlled the reins of government (I, 235-38, II, 42-51). He quotes a petition of Aranda to the king in 1794 in which Aranda says that during his ministry, while he presented his business to the royal couple in the presence of Godoy, whom they kept at hand, "I treated him with all imaginable attention and complacency, but I never discussed details of the ministry with him nor did I put myself in equivocal submission to his rubber stamp (*ni me puse en cierta sumisa dependencia equivoca con su estampilla*)" (Muriel, II, 51-52). This statement may refer, however, only to the ministry of foreign affairs, of which Sandoz admitted Aranda kept control. None of these authors recognize the fact that the abolition of the Junta de Estado on Aranda's advent deprived any one person except the king of the authority Floridablanca had had. Further study is required to show whose influence was highest in the internal regime of Spain in 1792, but until such study is made, one can logically agree with the majority of observers that it was Aranda's. An end to domestic restrictions complemented his foreign policy of placating the leaders of the Revolution.

[98] Lafuente, xv, 294-95, 306; Altamira, IV, 314.

those who rejected the leadership of "el Príncipe" did so, in part because of his reputation as the queen's lover, but more because they believed him incompetent to continue the policy of Carlos III's ministers of opening up Spain to the *luces*. Yet Godoy is justified in denying his incompetence in his memoirs. What was really happening was that the seductive principles voiced in France were stealthily stirring the progressives out of their belief that all improvement must come from above. In 1788 the government had been enlightened and had had the support of the progressives. In 1793, 1795, or 1797 it was hardly less enlightened, but it had lost much of their support. The Revolution had brought the dawn of a new age to Catholic Spain.

CHAPTER XIV

ECONOMIC POLICIES AND THE
PRICE OF WAR

O F ALL the works published under Godoy's ministry, one outshone all others in the importance of its subject, the prestige of the author, and the influence it was destined to exercise. In the 1780's Carlos III's government had commissioned the Sociedad Económica de Madrid to study various projects for agricultural reform that had been drawn up by royal officials and the reports of the intendants on the agricultural situation, and to recommend a general plan for agrarian legislation. Late in 1787 or early in 1788 the society appointed Jovellanos to carry out the task, but the labor involved was great and Jovellanos' vicissitudes disturbed his progress. After Aranda replaced Floridablanca as first secretary, the society wrote Jovellanos urging him to complete his report.[1] Aware of the new spirit in the government, Jovellanos devoted all available time to putting into words the plan he had conceived. He gave the final touches to it in the spring of 1794.[2] Later in the year it was read in a plenary session of the society of Madrid and was adopted by that body for presentation to the Consejo de Castilla.[3] The *Informe de la Sociedad Económica de esta Corte al Consejo de Castilla en el expediente de ley agraria extendido por su individuo de numero el S.ʳ D. Gaspar Melchor de Jovellanos* was published in 1795, both separately and in the fifth volume of the society's memoirs.

Jovellanos, who had already shown in his writings his passion for economics, now brought the weight of all the modern economic thought he had absorbed to bear on the Spanish agri-

---

[1] July 10, 1792, cited in Edith F. Helman, "Some Consequences of the Publication of the *Informe de ley agraria* by Jovellanos," *Estudios hispánicos: homenaje a Archer M. Huntington* (Wellesley, 1952), pp. 256-57.

[2] Jovellanos, *Diarios*, pp. 129, 133, 140, Feb. 20, Mar. 10, Apr. 14, 1794.

[3] Godoy, II, 207-8; Policarpo Sáenz de Tejada Hermosa, secretary of the society, to Jovellanos, Nov. 4, 1794, quoted in Somoza García Sala, pp. 170-71.

cultural situation. He blazoned in the beginning of the treatise the bases on which his arguments rested, for he admitted they were directly opposed to those of the solutions that had been submitted to the economic society for consideration. His principle is that laws should not attempt to protect agriculture but only to remove the obstacles to its development. He called it one of the eternal laws of nature, prescribed to man by God when he gave him dominion of the earth. It is also derived directly from the right of property, which arose when men united in society and divided the land. When men began to employ others to help till their land, another right arose, that of keeping the product of one's labor. Henceforth the fruits of the land belonged not only to the owner, but jointly to the owner and his tenants. Whenever laws protected the rights of property and of labor, agriculture would reach its perfection. Besides this, Jovellanos said, laws should only further the free play of private interest, an axiom true for all legislation but especially for agrarian legislation. He attacked the mercantilist theory whereby governments sought to protect commerce and industry at the expense of agriculture; for agriculture was the major source of a nation's wealth, and the failure of public opinion to recognize its primacy was one of the chief hindrances to its progress in Spain.

It is evident that Jovellanos' doctrines were mainly those of the physiocratic school. Like the French economists he believed in political economy as a science of immutable natural laws, laws that guarantee the right of property and condemn government interference and control. The natural agent of prosperity, according to these laws, is private initiative, especially in the raising and marketing of agricultural products, the source of national wealth. This philosophy was essentially the hedonism of Condillac and Helvétius applied to economics.

While Jovellanos so closely echoed the French physiocrats, he had also drunk deeply from the work of Adam Smith. He had read the *Wealth of Nations* in French and in the English original, which he owned, and had made a translation of it into Spanish. "How admirable when he analyses!" he exclaimed of

The Revolution

Smith.[4] In the *Informe de ley agraria* he cites the *Wealth of Nations* specifically in support of a policy of emphyteusis of entailed land,[5] and his proposition that the right of property includes the right of product of one's labor indicates Smith's influence. There was, after all, enough similarity between Smith and the physiocrats, both of whom drew heavily on Locke, for Jovellanos to lean toward both at the same time.

Jovellanos' insistence on liberty and private property as the bases of a sound agriculture led him directly to propose changes in many of Spain's institutions, even the most privileged. Common lands, now largely untilled, should be allotted to private cultivators on long term leases or by direct sale. He maintained also that the right of enclosure was a corollary of the right of property. The existing privilege of the Mesta to drive its herds during their seasonal migrations across León and Extremadura over the holdings of the hapless peasants forced by law to leave their lands open to the sheep he called "a barbarous custom born in barbarous times." "A principle of natural justice and of social right, prior to all law and to all custom and superior to both, cries out against such a shameful violation of individual property."[6] The privilege of entail, both by noble families and the church, Jovellanos insisted was a disastrous practice that has been the cause of the destruction of Spain's former prosperity. Neither the church nor private families should be permitted to receive any more land in entail, and they should be encouraged to let out their present holdings in emphyteusis. Also on the basis of the right of property, he asserted that the circulation of the products of the land should not be hindered or taxed in any way by the government. He excepted from this rule only the export of grain, which he would allow the government to prohibit until Spain should have an excess. What the government should

[4] Jovellanos, *Diarios*, pp. 277, 304-5, Nov. 21, 1795, May 25, June 1, 1796. On May 25, he began reading it for the third time. Quotation from June 1. On his translation, see Julio Somoza y Montsoriú, *Inventario de un Jovellanista* (Madrid, 1901), p. 96.

[5] Jovellanos, *Informe de ley agraria*, p. 75, citing Bk. III, chap. ii of the *Wealth of Nations*.

[6] *Ibid.*, pp. 12-19.

do was to promote the elementary education of the peasants and to spread knowledge of economics and agricultural science among large landowners, from whose example the lower classes would learn. To do this it should call on the help of the priests and the Amigos del País. And it was also the duty of the government to create irrigation projects and good means of road and water transport to facilitate the marketing of farm products.

Despite Jovellanos' belief in a natural law of economic relations which works best when left alone, his recommendations differed little from those of Campomanes and the other mercantilists who believed in state supervision of the economy. The transition of ideas was gradual—Jovellanos' prime contribution to Spanish thought was to justify on the basis of new laissez-faire theories the agrarian policies of Carlos III of limiting the rights of *mayorazgos, manos muertas,* and the Mesta and leasing town and entail land to peasants. Spanish reformers of the next century, indoctrinated in economic liberalism, took Jovellanos' *Informe de ley agraria* as their economic bible and through it inherited much of the program of Carlos III. The major difference was to be their insistence on turning entailed land into private property, a revolutionary undertaking which Jovellanos recommended with great hesitation, although his arguments led logically to such a solution for Spain's agricultural problems.[7]

No legislation of Carlos III had met greater opposition than his attempt to reform the control of the land in arid Spain. For the Sociedad Económica de Madrid to recommend the same program during the war against the Revolution and to publish it a year later with government support was a daring challenge to the conservative landowning classes. Godoy asserts that desperate resistance was offered to the publication of the *Informe de ley agraria,*[8] and Jovellanos later noticed the cool reception given him at a monastery whose *frailes* had read it.[9] The *Informe* was denounced to the Inquisición early in 1796. The *calificadores*

---

[7] On the *Informe de ley agraria* and its influence see Costa, pp. 152-60. Costa overemphasizes the difference between Jovellanos and earlier reformers.

[8] Godoy, II, 130.   [9] Jovellanos, *Diarios,* p. 389, Oct. 9, 1797.

who read it condemned its most important conclusion—that church and noble entail was an evil. They declared Jovellanos' ideas to be the same ones that had destroyed the Catholic Church in England, and they recommended that the *Informe* be prohibited not only as "antiecclesiastical but also as destructive of *mayorazgos* and therefore conducive to ideas of equality in the ownership of goods and lands." The Consejo de la Inquisición in July 1797 decided to suspend the case, but the inquisitors were not to forget the impression that Jovellanos' plan had made on them.[10]

2

More than mere love of the *luces* was behind Godoy's approval of the *Informe de ley agraria*. Its publication came at a time when the government was facing an increasingly difficult financial situation caused by the war against France, and it offered theoretical justification for some of the solutions being attempted.

Carlos IV had begun his reign on a high tide of prosperity inherited from his father. In 1788-89 the shortage of grain in western Europe, which helped arouse the people of France and led to riots in Barcelona, cost the Spanish treasury heavily; for the government decided to absorb much of the increased price of grain imported from abroad.[11] In 1790, furthermore, a threat of war with England over rival claims in Nootka Sound on the Pacific coast of North America hurt Spanish foreign trade.[12] Except for these two relatively minor setbacks, however, the period of well-being that began in 1783 continued until the war with France in March 1793. Even Floridablanca's legislation against French residents did not hurt trade between the two countries, which appears to have been especially high between September 1791 and September 1792.[13]

Spain thus entered the war with France in a strong financial position, but war soon made itself felt on the economy. Many

[10] Helman, *loc.cit.*, pp. 258-67, quoting and citing A.H.N., Inq., leg. 1478, No. 11.
[11] Hamilton, *War and Prices*, pp. 162-63.
[12] Sée, "Notas sobre el comercio francés en Cádiz," *loc.cit.*, p. 193.
[13] *Ibid.*, p. 194.

French entrepreneurs and laborers were now expelled or left the country to avoid rigorous supervision; and, because of the demands of the army, the number of available Spanish laborers also declined.[14] In Valencia about a quarter of the silk looms fell idle for lack of weavers.[15] Spain's export trade also suffered, both from the total cessation of commerce with France[16] and from the departure of French merchants. Cadiz, where French trade played an especially large role, is said to have lost 452 million reales during the war. Santander was blockaded by French privateers, and its ships had to unload their goods at La Coruña and Cadiz.[17] Presumably Bilbao and San Sebastián also suffered. In northern Catalonia the French army systematically seized food stores and the harvest of 1794 and destroyed the foundries and arms factories of Ripoll and San Lorenzo de la Muga. In August 1794 the Committee of Public Safety ordered the Army of the Western Pyrenees likewise to destroy Spanish arsenals, but how much the Basque provinces suffered as a result is not known.[18] In any case some Basque farmers and industrialists must have suffered from the French invasion. On the other hand, trade with America was not cut off—insurance rates on Spanish ocean traffic rose only 5 to 10 per cent[19]—and the other parts of the economy appear not to have been hurt. The war worked hardship on certain sections of Spanish society, but it was not a calamity for the nation's economy.

With the assistance of the volutionary financial gifts that poured in from individuals at home and in the colonies, the government was able to pay for the campaign of 1793 without additional means of income. At the end of the year, however, it had a deficit of 106 million reales,[20] and it was forced to face the fact that war

[14] Dispatch of William Short, Jan. 17, 1794, quoted in Hamilton, *War and Prices*, pp. 164-65.

[15] Carrera Pujal, v, 516, citing Cabanilles.

[16] Sée, "Notas sobre el comercio francés en Cádiz," *loc.cit.*, p. 194.

[17] Desdevises, *L'Espagne*, iii, 165 (for Cadiz); report of Consulado of Santander, 1799, cited by Carrera Pujal, v, 201.

[18] Vigo, pp. 58-62.

[19] Report of Cayetano Soler, secretario de hacienda, 1799, cited by Carrera Pujal, v, 579.

[20] Memoir of Pedro Varela, secretario de hacienda, 1796, cited by Lafuente, xv, 228 n. 2.

could not be financed by contributions alone. The ministers, the Consejo de Estado, and the Consejo de Castilla all deliberated on measures to raise more money.

Partly because mercantilist beliefs favored protecting the productive classes, and partly because a revolt in Galicia in 1790 had shown the dangers in levying new taxes on the peasants, the royal councilors sought to avoid taxing "the poorer classes of the nation, [which already] support heavy charges with their persons and possessions."[21] Although the salt and tobacco taxes were raised, most new levies hit privileged persons and institutions. During the three years of war, 4 per cent was deducted from the salaries of royal officials earning over eight thousand reales. The Inquisición and other church courts were required to use official stamped paper, and in October 1793 a levy of 30 million reales was decreed on the income of the church.[22]

For the most part the government chose to resort to borrowing to finance the war. The crown took over as a forced loan at 3 per cent certain entailed family capitals for which government agencies acted as trustees,[23] and it issued 240 million reales' worth of twelve-year 5 per cent bonds,[24] but mainly it made use once again of *vales reales*, the interest-bearing government notes that could circulate as legal tender first issued during the War of American Independence. Three new issues of *vales* were made, on January 16 and September 8, 1794 and February 25, 1795, with a total face value of 64.2 million pesos (about 967 million reales)— almost twice the value of the *vales* in circulation just before the French war.[25]

Royal officials were aware of the threat to the national credit presented by so much paper money, even though the *vales* had denominations too large for most daily transactions. The crown undertook to guarantee payment of the interest of the *vales* and their eventual redemption with a special fund, called the Caja de

---

[21] Decree of Sept. 8, 1794, quoted in Godoy, II, 68.
[22] *Ibid.*, p. 65; Lafuente, xv, 229.
[23] *Cédula*, Oct. 9, 1793, *Nov. rec.*, x, xv, 27.
[24] July 3, 1795, Godoy, II, 74-75.
[25] Hamilton, *War and Prices*, p. 83.

Amortización, entrusted to the Consejo de Castilla. In making the first issue of *vales*, the government ordered 10 per cent of the municipal incomes (the *propios y arbitrios*) paid into the Caja de Amortización. For the second issue, the crown obtained papal sanction for an annual increase of 7 million reales in the grant of the church to the crown, and it levied a tax on those who received income from renting real estate, 6 per cent on income from lands and 4 per cent on income from buildings. The third issue was met by another levy on the church (with papal approval) and by placing in the Caja de Amortización the income from vacant church offices and benefices.[26] Although no new *vales* were created at this time, shortly after the end of the war a royal decree required that 15 per cent of the value of *mayorazgos* that would be established in the future be paid to the Caja.[27]

The last measure taken to pay the interest and principal of the *vales* hit those who wished to found *mayorazgos* as the earlier ones had hit the church and the owners of real property let out to rent. By discouraging the creation of new *mayorazgos*, it complemented an early decree of Carlos IV, of May 14, 1789, aimed at hindering further entail of real property by prohibiting the founding of new *mayorazgos* without a license from the Consejo de Castilla while recommending to the Consejo that it give preference to family-owned capital invested in royal or municipal bonds or shares of the Banco de San Carlos instead of landed estates.[28]

The increased circulation of paper *vales* combined with a wartime shortage of commodities to bring about a sharp rise in prices. The rise varied from about 10 to 20 per cent in different regions of Spain. The purchasing power of the *vales* declined even more, for after April 1794 they could no longer be exchanged on the open market for an equal value of hard money. At their lowest point, just before the peace, they were being quoted at 22 per cent below par.[29]

26 See Godoy, ii, 65-74.
27 *Real decreto*, Aug. 24, 1795, *Nov. rec.*, x, xvii, 14.
28 *Ibid.*, ley 12.
29 Hamilton, *War and Prices*, pp. 84, 165, and table, p. 155.

In view of the seriousness of the war, which involved maintaining large armies in defense of the country and saw the occupation of economically valuable parts of the peninsula, the royal finances fared well. Spain did not borrow abroad or receive a foreign subsidy, whereas Prussia, as Godoy points out, had to rely on British money to put a smaller force in the field against France.[30] But what the government saved in credit, it lost in favor with influential and conservative groups by forcing the church and large landowners to provide the means to guarantee the *vales reales* and pay interest on them. "A large part of the enmities I made," Godoy says, "dated from that time."[31] These circumstances make clear why Godoy supported the publication of Jovellanos' *Informe de ley agraria* in the face of opposition from the same groups. The name of Jovellanos recalled the days of Carlos III, and his *Informe* was the strongest possible propaganda for the royal policy of imposing the cost of the war on the rural oligarchy.

3

The period of little more than a year between the peace with France and war with Britain gave the government a profitable breathing spell. During 1796, according to the *Moniteur*, four major shipments of specie reached Cadiz totaling nearly 22 million pesos fuertes (440 million reales).[32] With these shipments came many colonial products—sugar, cacao, coffee, indigo, and others—and the prices of these products fell in Spain.[33] The crown was able to redeem *vales* worth 702,000 pesos in 1795 and 1,699,-200 in January 1797. Late in 1796 *vales* were being quoted at 6 per cent below par, a recovery from their wartime depreciation.[34]

[30] Godoy, II, 93.

[31] *Ibid.*, p. 73.

[32] *Moniteur*, Mar. 6, 1796, reports 643,000 pesos fuertes from La Guaira and Montevideo; June 27, 10,000,000 from Vera Cruz and Cartagena; Oct. 4, 5,786,348 from Havana and Vera Cruz; Dec. 19, 5,538,168 from Havana and Vera Cruz.

[33] *Ibid.*, July 11, 1796.

[34] Hamilton, *War and Prices*, pp. 83-84.

Peace also helped the government to carry out economic legislation that was in line with the reforms of the previous reign. Little had been accomplished since the death of Carlos III, but two decrees of 1793 showed that the policies of Godoy's ministry were as enlightened in economics as in other fields. On January 29, 1793 all guilds of silk winders were abolished, and the king declared that any person could engage in the craft, "including especially *fabricantes*, their families, and their employees, whether [working] inside or outside their houses or shops."[35] The decree was one more step in encouraging the putting-out system in the silk industry. The second decree, of May 24, 1793, ordered that the town common lands of the province of Extremadura be divided by the town councils and distributed to private individuals to enclose and farm as seemed most fitting to each recipient. After ten years the lots that had actually been cleared and tilled were to be assigned permanently to their occupants in return for a modest yearly rent (*canon*).[36] The decree specifically referred to the edict of 1770 urging distribution of town *tierras concejiles* to peasants. Enacted under the stress of the wartime rise in grain prices, it represented a new attempt to execute the plan of Carlos III to put more land under cultivation, which the rural oligarchy had vitiated. This act provides a further explanation for Godoy's support of Jovellanos' *Ley agraria*.

A few months after the end of the French war, the government took other steps to diminish the privileges of the few. It felt strong enough financially to abolish the tax that separated commoners from nobles—the *servicio ordinario y extraordinario y su quince al millar* collected in the provinces of Castile from non-noble farmers. The decision was taken, the king's decree stated, to encourage agriculture and to reward the poorest and most numerous class of his subjects for their loyal service in the war.[37] At almost the same time, Carlos IV obtained from the pope a breve putting an end to the privilege of not paying tithes enjoyed by certain individuals, military orders, monasteries, and other

---

[35] *Decreto*, Jan. 29 1793, *Nov. rec.*, VIII, xxiii, 12.
[36] *Real decreto*, May 24, 1793, *ibid.*, VII, xxv, 19.
[37] *Real decreto*, Nov. 20, 1795, *ibid.*, VI, xvii, 12. See Godoy, II, 80-82.

religious institutions. The purpose stated by the breve was to support the indigent priests of Spain, but Godoy points out that another purpose was to increase royal revenue, since the crown received two-ninths of the tithes of the church. "Few actions as just as this one," he says, "met greater opposition or caused more displeasure to the high privileged classes."[38]

In the following years the royal policies followed the two main lines marked out by Godoy as they had been by Campomanes—to aid capitalistic manufacturers and small farmers. On December 20, 1796 a royal resolution ended price regulation on all cloths and other manufactures produced in the kingdom. Prices would depend on the mutual agreement of buyers and sellers, with the government stepping in only to punish cases of fraud.[39] In 1797 the secretary of finance (hacienda), Pedro Varela, urged the king to permit Jewish merchants to return to Spain and give them charge of liquidating the *vales*, now that "ancient prejudices have passed away."[40] The proposal was not adopted, but a royal resolution of September 8, 1797 instructed the Junta de Comercio to permit foreign non-Jewish craftsmen to establish shops or factories in Spain and admonished the Inquisición not to bother those who were not Catholic, provided they "respected the public customs."[41] Six months later guilds were ordered to authorize any person to practice their crafts who could pass the required examination, whether or not he had undergone apprenticeship in a guild.[42] Bit by bit, as under Carlos III, the government was rendering the gremios obsolete.

In the eyes of the ministers, one of the greatest needs of Spanish craftsmen and farmers was knowledge of advances being achieved abroad. The Amigos del País had long been encouraging such

[38] Breve of Jan. 8, 1796 and *cédula*, June 8, 1796, *Nov. rec.*, I, vi, 14; Godoy, II, 90; Desdevises, *L'Espagne*, II, 369. For examples of opposition by religious institutions see *Nov. rec.*, I, vi, notas 10, 11.

[39] *Resolución*, Dec. 20, 1796, *Nov. rec.*, x, xii, 9.

[40] Quoted in Lafuente, xv, 230. Godoy says the Inquisición opposed the measure (II, 226); Villanueva says it did not (*Vida literaria*, I, 47-48).

[41] *Real resolución*, Sept. 8, 1797, *Nov. rec.*, VIII, xxiii, nota 4. On it see Domínguez Ortiz, pp. 250-51.

[42] *Resolución*, Mar. 1, 1798, *Nov. rec.*, VIII, xxiii, 11.

knowledge, but they were located in cities and their memoirs did not reach the peasants or artisans. In the isolated villages of rural Spain the only persons with education and outside contacts were often the local priests. For some time leaders of economic thought—Campomanes, Jovellanos, the Basque Amigos del País—had urged the cooperation of priests in the economic revival of their country.[43] A letter of Godoy to the bishops of Spain on November 28, 1796 marked the beginning of an official undertaking to obtain this cooperation. Godoy announced the forthcoming publication of a weekly periodical for parish priests that would describe new methods of farming and manufacture. He urged the bishops to have their priests subscribe and make known the contents to their parishioners, and he pointed out that examples of such activity could be found among the Protestant clergy of northern Europe. The king, he said, felt that only by this means could the *luces* be spread from the cities to the countryside so long as "in Spain those who till do not read and those who read do not till." The first number of the proposed periodical, the *Semanario de agricultura y artes dirigido a los párrocos*, appeared on January 5, 1797.[44] Although some churchmen did not hide their disapproval of the idea behind the *Semanario de agricultura*, it was published without interruption until the Napoleonic invasion of 1808, carrying translations from contemporary foreign writers, including Arthur Young, Count Rumford, and Jeremy Bentham, as well as articles by Spaniards.

4

After 1796 economic reform again had to give way to the problems of war. The first months of hostilities against Britain, which began in October 1796, were encouraging to Spain. Gold

---

[43] Rodríguez de Campomanes, *Fomento de la industria popular*, pp. xxxii-xxxv; Jovellanos, *Informe de ley agraria*, p. 123; Díaz de Valdés. The same lesson was the burden of Miguel Ignacio Pérez Quintero, *Pensamientos políticos y económicos, dirigidos a promover en España la agricultura y demas ramos de industria* (Madrid, 1798), whose author was a member of the economic society of Madrid.

[44] Godoy's letter was published in the first issue. See Godoy, II, 146. For an example of clerical opposition, see Jovellanos, *Diarios*, p. 339, Mar. 16, 1797.

and colonial products continued to reach Spanish ports from America, and Spanish ships seized a few English fishing boats.[45] But the war soon turned to Spain's disadvantage, for, despite the efforts of a century, the Spanish navy was still unequal to the British.[46] Early in 1797 Cadiz learned of the capture of seven richly-laden ships, including one belonging to the Compañía de Filipinas said to be worth a million pesos.[47] On February 14 near Cape Saint Vincent a well-manned British fleet attacked a larger Spanish fleet under an inexperienced commander and captured four of Spain's best ships of the line.[48]

The hero of this battle, Horatio Nelson, informed Cadiz on April 11 that it was henceforth in a state of complete blockade.[49] Nelson decided a few months later to attack Cadiz and the fleet at anchor in its port, but stubborn fighting by Spanish sailors and the garrison of the city on July 3, 4, and 5, 1797 defeated his attempt.[50] Nevertheless, the blockade remained in force; in September a report from Cadiz stated that even small Moorish boats skirting the coast had difficulty in escaping the British ships, which did not hesitate to come within range of the guns of the port.[51] Local merchants, with little else to do, could stroll daily along the ramparts of the city and observe the enemy fleet in the distance cutting off their means of livelihood. By September 1798 the *Moniteur* reported them to be in distress. Some, forced to live off their capital, had left the city for less expensive nearby towns. Others were able to do some business in captured goods landed at Málaga, Sanlúcar, or Algeciras by French privateers or in Spanish American products bought from the British at Lisbon or Gibraltar—a practice the crown forbade in October 1797[52]—but for several months the commerce of Cadiz had been "reduced to

[45] *Moniteur*, Nov. 25, Dec. 19, 1796, Jan. 7, Feb. 14, 1797.
[46] Desdevises, *L'Espagne*, II, 283-87.
[47] *Moniteur*, Feb. 28, 1797, dispatch from Madrid, Feb. 1.
[48] Lafuente, xv, 255-56.
[49] *Moniteur*, May 5, 1797.
[50] *Ibid.*, July 24, 1797; Lafuente, xv, 256-57.
[51] *Moniteur*, Oct. 4, 1797. The *Moniteur* continued to report the blockade, Dec. 9, 1797, Feb. 14, Mar. 14, Mar. 29, 1798, 25 prairial VI (June 13, 1798).
[52] *Ibid.*, 3 frimaire VII (Nov. 23, 1798), dated Cadiz 5 brumaire (Oct. 26).

complete stagnation."⁵³ Not until 1800 did foreign and Spanish ships run the blockade with much success, although in that year the Spanish navy still proved unable to escort a convoy from America into the port.⁵⁴ Cadiz is said to have lost over one billion reales in trade from 1796 to 1798, double the amount it lost during the French war.⁵⁵

Although no other Spanish port was blockaded as closely as Cadiz, Barcelona and the ports of northern Spain hardly suffered less. Barcelona's trade and manufacture were both hit. In December 1796 the city's Junta de Comercio complained to the government that many ships loaded with goods for America had been caught in the port by the declaration of war and were afraid to sail.⁵⁶ Reports of March 1799 from Barcelona in the *Moniteur* stated that a British fleet made a raid on the coast of southern Catalonia, sailed frequently within sight of Barcelona, "and paralyzes the little commerce we could still carry on."⁵⁷ Cut off from sources of cotton and from their American markets, the factories of Catalonia were forced to reduce their production. To meet the resulting unemployment, the captain-general and audiencia organized public works and soup kitchens for the poor in Barcelona and nearby cities. The crisis finally passed in 1801 and the Junta de Comercio expressed the hope that trade and manufacture would revive, but the soup lines did not disappear until 1802.⁵⁸

The northern coastal ports fared little better. The British carefully permitted Bilbao to continue the export of merino wool to England,⁵⁹ but ships loaded in Santander with grain for delivery in Galicia, where there was a threat of famine, were tied up helpless as British men-of-war cruised along the coast.⁶⁰ Occa-

---

⁵³ *Ibid.*, 30 vendémiaire VII (Oct. 21, 1798).

⁵⁴ *Ibid.*, 14, 29 prairial VIII (May 4, 19, 1800); Desdevises, *L'Espagne*, II, 287.

⁵⁵ Desdevises, *L'Espagne*, III, 165.   ⁵⁶ Cited by Carrera Pujal, V, 196.

⁵⁷ *Moniteur*, 3, 28 germinal VII (Mar. 23, Apr. 17, 1799), quotation from the latter issue.

⁵⁸ Carrera Pujal, V, 103, 205.   ⁵⁹ *Ibid.*, p. 81.

⁶⁰ Consulado of Santander to Consulado of Barcelona, 1799, cited by *ibid.*, p. 201; *Moniteur*, Apr. 16, 1797.

sionally ships from the Indies slipped through to these ports. In March 1798 three warships reached La Coruña, reportedly bringing three and one half million pesos, and in July a frigate entered Santander from Vera Cruz with cochineal and half a million pesos fuertes. The *Moniteur* reported that two other ships with gold and other products from Mexico had reached Spain a few weeks earlier, but it did not state at which port they docked. Not all blockade runners got through; in November 1799 the British captured two frigates from Vera Cruz with cargoes said to be worth four and one half million pesos.[61]

The large share of the trade of Spanish America which Spanish merchants and manufacturers had succeeded after three reigns in taking away from the exporters of northern Europe rapidly slipped out of Spain's grasp. Because of the impossibility of supplying Spanish goods for the colonies, Carlos IV decided to legalize the inevitable contraband. A royal order of November 18, 1797 temporarily suspended the *reglamento* of 1778 by permitting neutral ships to carry all manner of goods to Spanish American ports except non-Spanish ribbons, silk stockings, and other foreign articles prohibited in 1778. Neutrals were allowed to load all colonial products except specie, a restriction that proved impossible to enforce. The United States, the largest neutral maritime power, derived most advantage from the decree. Clandestine contacts of its shipowners with the Spanish colonies were now multiplied openly.[62] Although the new situation permitted Spanish officials to collect duties on trade that had formerly got through as contraband, after little more than a year the government came to regret its decree. The correspondent of the *Moniteur* described the ill effects of the legalized neutral trade as they were felt in Madrid:

This trade paralyzed our industry, hurt even that of our allies the French, weakened imperceptibly the ties that unite the

---

[61] *Moniteur*, 1 floréal, 4, 27 thermidor VI, 15 frimaire VIII (Apr. 20, July 22, Aug. 11, 1798, Dec. 6, 1799).

[62] *Ibid.*, Feb. 6, 1798; A. P. Whitaker, *The United States and the Independence of Latin America, 1800-1830* (Baltimore, 1941), pp. 5-8.

home country with our colonies, and could end by making us lose the colonies completely. Moreover, it aided marvelously the mercantile greed of the English, who made shipments to Vera Cruz under the American flag with the same ease as they would to Jamaica. Protests have been raised against this abuse, especially by the merchants of Cadiz and Barcelona.[63]

On April 18, 1799 the order of November 18, 1797 suspending the Spanish trade monopoly was revoked, but many colonial officials refused to enforce the revocation because of the impossible situation that would result. In 1801 Madrid began to sell official licenses to neutral shippers to trade with Spanish American ports.[64] An end to the war provided the only hope of reestablishing Spain's economic hold over its colonies.

5

The government meanwhile had to cope with the difficulty not only of covering its regular expenses (and the royal household took much more now than it had under Carlos III) but also of supplying its navy and arming soldiers to protect the coasts without the normal income from America or from export and import duties. No satisfactory solution could be found, and in the end the credit of the state was shaken and the government had antagonized the wealthy sections of society: clergy, landowners, and to a lesser extent bourgeoisie.

As in the French war, the government attempted to meet its expenses without increasing taxes. In 1797 two issues of twelve-year 5 per cent bonds were floated for a total value of 160 million reales.[65] Although Godoy claims that these two loans were fully subscribed, by the beginning of 1798 the government was looking for more money. On February 21, 1798 Carlos decreed that all buildings belonging to municipalities that were rented to add to the municipal income (*propios*) were to be auctioned off to private individuals. The proceeds of the sales would go to the

---

[63] *Moniteur*, 23 floréal VII (May 12, 1799).
[64] Whitaker, p. 8.   [65] July 15, Nov. 29, 1787, Godoy, II, 85-87.

crown, which in return would pay 3 per cent of the amount per annum to the municipalities.[66] The decree set a pregnant precedent, for the crown thereby resorted to the sale of property in entail as a way to solve its financial problems. Income from such sales could not be available immediately, however, and the government had to fall back on loans. In May 1798 it attempted to borrow three million florins in Amsterdam, but the bankers whom it approached turned a deaf ear to the suggestion.[67] On June 17 Carlos called for a voluntary gift of money, jewels, and precious metals from all his subjects and for a voluntary loan without interest to be repaid within twelve years of the end of the war. The *Moniteur* remarked that the terms in which Carlos informed the nobles of this voluntary loan gave it the earmarks of a forced levy.[68] Nevertheless, on October 17, 1798 the government issued new bonds for 400 million reales, this issue to be paid off as soon as royal funds accumulating in America became available. At the end of the year the new bonds had not all been sold.[69]

Until the end of 1798 the ministers of finance studiously avoided new taxes or new issues of *vales reales*, whose credit they did not wish to impair, but in 1799 they were forced to have recourse to both means. On April 6, 1799, with much reluctance, the government created more *vales* as the only way to meet its current obligations. The issue had a face value of over 53 million pesos (about 800 million reales), the largest ever emitted.[70] Carlos further decreed that for the time being he would make no appointments to ecclesiastical benefices falling vacant and that their income would be applied to paying off the *vales*.[71] But the end was not yet. The minister of finance anticipated a deficit of 300 million reales for 1800, and on November 12, 1799 the crown ordered this sum paid in by the cities of Spain, each being allotted its share accord-

---

[66] *Real decreto*, Feb. 21, 1798, *Nov. rec.*, x, xv, 28.

[67] *Moniteur*, 22, 28 prairial vi (June 10, 16, 1798).

[68] *Ibid.*, 10 messidor vi (June 28, 1798); Godoy, ii, 290.

[69] *Moniteur*, 19 brumaire, 10 nivôse vii (Nov. 9, Dec. 30, 1798); Godoy, ii, 293.

[70] *Moniteur*, 12 floréal vii (May 1, 1799); Lafuente, xv, 350; Hamilton, *War and Prices*, p. 83.

[71] *Decreto*, Apr. 27, 1799, *Nov. rec.*, i, xxiv, nota 8.

ing to its estimated ability to pay, with instructions not to add new burdens to the lower classes.[72] The reaction of Barcelona suggests the public reception of this capital levy. The Junta de Comercio of the city objected that in view of the local economic crisis the city could not possibly raise the 15 million reales assigned to it. Although the secretary of finance threatened to embargo the goods of the merchants of Barcelona, the Junta had raised only three and one half million reales by 1801.[73]

All the time that the government was trying to meet its mounting expenses, it was worried over the sagging credit of the *vales*. Although no *vales* were issued between February 1795 and April 1799 and interest on them was paid punctually, their exchange value in terms of specie fell soon after the war with Britain was announced. In 1797 they circulated at 15 to 20 per cent below par and in 1798 at 17 to 25 per cent below.[74] In May 1798 a junta of financial experts was named to study solutions to their depreciation. Its leading figures were Carlos III's fiscal adviser, the Conde de Cabarrús, and representatives of the Banco de San Carlos and the Cinco Gremios Mayores.[75] Four months later, presumably on the advice of the junta and possibly with an eye on the example of the confiscation of French church lands by the National Assembly to pay off the French national debt, the crown decided on a liquidation of property in entail which made its recent decision to sell municipal buildings seem picayune. A decree of September 24, 1798 permitted the owners of *mayorazgos* to sell their lands at public auction provided the proceeds be given to the Caja de Amortización in return for 3 per cent interest in perpetuity. The *mayorazgo* would remain, only in the form of state obligations instead of real estate.[76] When it became clear that few landowners were rushing to exchange real property for royal promises, the added incentive was offered of letting them keep one eighth of the selling price "to pay off their debts."[77]

[72] Godoy, II, 300; Lafuente, xv, 352.

[73] Carrera Pujal, v, 205.   [74] Hamilton, *War and Prices*, p. 84.

[75] *Moniteur*, 13 prairial vi (May 31, 1798), dated Madrid 26 floréal (May 15); Carrera Pujal, IV, 577.

[76] *Nov. rec.*, x, xvii, 16.   [77] *Real decreto*, Jan. 13, 1799, *ibid.*, ley 17.

Meanwhile, on September 25 a series of royal decrees ordered the sale of most real property belonging to hospitals, poor houses, and other charitable religious institutions; the sale of all property formerly belonging to the Jesuits and not yet disposed of; and the confiscation of the funds of the six colegios mayores and the sale of their property. Those institutions deprived of their lands (except the Jesuits) would be given 3 per cent per annum of the selling price of the lands. The property was to be put on sale at auction in small lots, with *vales* acceptable in payment although offers of hard currency would be given preference.[78] In the end only a few *mayorazgo* owners in debt appear to have sold their estates, and few buyers came forward to take church lands before 1800.[79] Nevertheless, under the pressure of financing the war, Carlos had adopted a practice that Jovellanos had not dared recommend openly in the *Informe de ley agraria*, the transfer of farm land from entail to free private property. Although from the Middle Ages to the reign of Felipe V the crown had occasionally used this expedient to raise money,[80] the example of Carlos IV was to be felt most strongly by later Spanish governments also faced with the problem of guaranteeing a national debt. One can imagine the reaction to Carlos' decrees of those conservative churchmen who had wished to see the *Informe de ley agraria* banned for condemning entail.

For the moment, however, the decrees of September 1798 failed to improve the standing of the *vales*, which by April 1799 were being discounted 43 per cent.[81] The arrival of ships with specie from Mexico in May 1799 raised their market value by 12 per cent in one day, more than all the royal measures had been able to do,[82] but this stroke of luck was not repeated. Early in July Carlos dismissed the junta of financial experts and placed the Consejo de Castilla once more in charge of the *vales*.[83] The Con-

[78] *Ibid.*, I, v, 22, 24, VIII, iii, 9; Godoy, II, 294.

[79] Godoy, II, 309; Cárdenas, II, 155. [Later investigation shows that starting in 1799 and continuing to 1808 much property of religious institutions was sold under this legislation.—Author's note, 1969.]

[80] See above, pp. 90-91, 112.

[81] *Moniteur*, 3 pluviôse, 21 floréal VII (Jan. 22, May 10, 1799); Hamilton, *War and Prices*, p. 84.

[82] *Moniteur*, 16 prairial VII (June 4, 1799).

[83] Godoy, II, 296.

sejo took a desperate step on July 17. It pegged the *vales* at 6 per cent below hard currency, ordered the courts to enforce their acceptance at this rate in payment of all debts, and opened thirteen Cajas de Reducción or change offices in major cities to exchange *vales* for small coins in cases where their owners would otherwise suffer hardship (the smallest denomination of the *vales* was 150 reales). To provide funds for the change offices, interest payments on the *vales* were temporarily suspended, and a forced contribution of 20 million reales in hard currency was levied on landowners. The results of the step were fatal. The money to back the change offices could not be fully collected, for even *grandes* refused to pay their share. There was a run on the offices, which could only exchange a few of the *vales* presented and most of these not for coins, for these were unavailable, but for paper notes in small denominations called *cédulas de caja*. In practice the *vales* remained unredeemable, and the end of their interest payments caused a further fall in their value. Speculation in *vales* was widely reported; while tenants and debtors took advantage of the fact that *vales* had to be accepted in payment of debts to force them on their creditors.[84]

Carlos IV, who was unnerved by the fiscal crisis, considered for a moment a plan proposed by a committee of churchmen to give the clergy of Spain the administration of the *vales* and the taxes that backed them in return for a guarantee of their value. Godoy and other advisers dissuaded Carlos from a step that would have given the clergy virtual control of the state.[85] Instead, on November 10, 1799 a tax was declared on those who had servants, horses, mules, and carriages. The tax increased progressively with the number of servants or equipages—a blow aimed at nobles with large households. The same decree required shops and inns of all kinds to pay a yearly tax which varied with the type of business conducted.[86] The proceeds of these levies on aristocrats and merchants were to provide working capital for the change

84 *Moniteur*, 4 thermidor VII, 12 vendémiaire, 3 nivôse VIII (July 22, Oct. 4, Dec. 24, 1799); Godoy, II, 298-305.

85 Llorente, *Noticia biografica*, p. 97; Lafuente, XV, 253-54.

86 *Moniteur*, 7 frimaire VIII (Nov. 28, 1799); Lafuente, XV, 351-52.

offices, but they proved insufficient to raise the value of the *vales*, which sank lower and lower.

On April 7, 1800 a royal circular admitted officially that creditors were being defrauded by being forced to accept *vales*, which, it said, were now worth less than half their face value. The circular declared that debts should henceforth be paid in the medium agreed upon by the contracting parties,[87] but the crown continued to pay the salaries of its officials in *vales*, much to their anguish.[88] Four months later *vales* were 75 per cent off par, and many people were refusing to give currency for them at any price. The *vales* remained at this low rate until peace in 1802.[89]

The war with Britain thus brought hardship to most sections of society. Besides the general uncertainty caused by Spain's first bad experience with paper money, prices rose rapidly even in terms of hard currency. In 1797 and 1798 prices advanced nearly twice as much as during the French war. Plentiful crops in 1799 and 1800 reversed the price trend but wiped out only half the rise of the previous two years.[90] Perhaps peasants profited from the price inflation; the urban lower classes did not. Wages fell in central Spain during the war,[91] and in Catalonia unemployment was widespread. Popular risings occurred in Guadalajara in January 1797 and in Seville and Asturias in the spring of 1798.[92]

The upper classes, on whose shoulders the government had attempted to place the burden of maintaining the standing of the rapidly increasing royal debt, had even less cause to like the royal policies or a war that lacked emotional appeal. *Grandes* did not relish being threatened with confiscation of their lands for failure to contribute to the state deficit, clergymen disliked

---

[87] Circular quoted in Godoy, II, 303-8.

[88] See Jovellanos to bishop of Lugo, Dec. 6, 1799, quoted in Somoza de Montsoriú, *Las amarguras de Jovellanos*, pp. 308-11.

[89] Godoy, II, 309; Hamilton, *War and Prices*, p. 85.

[90] Hamilton, *War and Prices*, p. 165.

[91] *Ibid.*, pp. 208-9.

[92] *Moniteur*, Feb. 28, 1797, 12 prairial VI (May 31, 1798).

increased church grants to the crown and the decision of Carlos to withhold appointments to vacant benefices, merchants and manufacturers saw hard won markets slip away from them while they had to live off their capital and resist government levies. All moneyed classes lost confidence in the solvency of the crown, as the history of the *vales* reveals.

Many contemporaries and later historians have seen in the war with Britain the cardinal error of Godoy, which brought ruin to Spain. Britain, however, needed every available resource for the vital struggle with France in which it was engaged. Able to control the sea, it was unlikely to watch peacefully while Spanish manufacturers continued to elbow its exporters out of the Spanish American market, the richest source of bullion in the world. If Spain would not let in British trade by an alliance, other ways had to be found. One of the most serious causes cited by Carlos IV for his declaration of war was the recent British seizure on the high seas of Spanish ships loaded with American goods. A less impulsive first secretary than Godoy might have postponed open hostilities, but the Anglo-Spanish struggle was basically a product of Spain's industrial renaissance and the French Revolutionary wars, not of the levity of an untried statesman.

On the other hand the measures used to finance this war and the French War of 1793-95, while not all conceived by Godoy— indeed Godoy disclaims responsibility for the worst years, 1798 to 1800—grew naturally out of his policy of restricting the wealth of the church and landed aristocracy. Time and again solutions of long term significance seemed to be drawn from Jovellanos' *Informe de ley agraria* to solve immediate wartime fiscal crises. Antagonism toward the ministers of Carlos IV not unnaturally became bitter in conservative circles, although the special causes of this antagonism were disguised from the public by the economic hardship and insecurity being felt by other groups as well.

CHAPTER XV

JOVELLANOS, URQUIJO, AND THE JANSENIST OFFENSIVE

LATE in 1797 Manuel Godoy, Príncipe de la Paz, first secretary and royal favorite, made significant changes in the government. He decided on one more attempt to win genuine support among the followers of the *luces* and brought into his circle leading figures of Carlos III's day whom Floridablanca had banished. In November 1797 the Conde de Cabarrús was named ambassador to France, where it was hoped that he would be able to smooth rough waters in which the Franco-Spanish alliance then found itself.[1] On Cabarrús' advice, Godoy recalled Jovellanos from Asturias to become secretary of grace and justice, with control of religious affairs. Jovellanos had never before been a minister, and he was averse to becoming a partner in the government of Godoy, but Cabarrús convinced him that there was no way to escape the appointment.[2] Cabarrús also recommended a young man with a reputation for knowledge of the royal finances, Francisco de Saavedra. Saavedra was made secretary of finance.[3] Juan Meléndez Valdés, one-time protégé of Jovellanos in the faculty of Salamanca, who was currently serving in the superior court (chancillería) of Valladolid, became *fiscal* of the royal court of Madrid, the Sala de Alcaldes de Casa y Corte.[4] Finally Godoy raised to second place in his own ministry of foreign affairs Mariano Luis de Urquijo, the young translator of Voltaire whom Aranda had saved from the Inquisición in 1792. For the past two years Urquijo had been secretary of the embassy in London.[5] Not since the days of Carlos III had such a

---

[1] *Moniteur*, Nov. 30, 1797; Muriel, IV, 91-95.

[2] Jovellanos, *Diarios*, p. 391, Oct. 16, Nov. 22, 1797.

[3] Muriel, IV, 101; Henry Richard, Lord Holland, "Souvenirs des cours de France, d'Espagne, de Prusse et de Russie . . . ," *Bibliothèque des mémoires relatifs à l'histoire de France pendant le 18ᵉ siècle*, ed. F. Barrière, Vol. XXVII (Paris, 1862), p. 67.

[4] Quintana, "Noticia de Meléndez," *loc.cit.*, p. 114.

[5] Beraza, pp. 14-16.

galaxy of enlightened men been given charge of the destinies of the country.

Four months later Godoy himself withdrew from the ministry. The *Gazeta* of March 30, 1798 carried the text of a royal decree "in the king's own handwriting" accepting the request of the Príncipe de la Paz to be relieved of his duties as secretary of state. Saavedra was named first secretary in his place and was also maintained as secretary of finance. The immediate cause for Godoy's retirement, as for the previous changes in the leadership of Carlos IV's government, was provided by Spain's relations with France. The coup d'état of 18 fructidor (September 4, 1797) had given control of the Directory and government of France to strong-willed men of advanced ideas, who were determined to crush the domestic and foreign threats to the Revolution. These Directors became suspicious of Godoy's loyalty to the alliance of the two countries. His final crime in their eyes had been a continual refusal to expel the French émigrés from Spain.[6] Early in 1798 the Directors declared Cabarrús unacceptable as Spanish ambassador to France, giving as their reason that he had been born a French citizen;[7] and they worked through their ambassador in Madrid to bring about the dismissal of Godoy.[8]

Rumors also circulated to the far corners of Spain that "el Príncipe" had fallen out with the queen.[9] The rumors contained some truth, for Godoy's correspondence with the royal couple shows that for the next two years his advice on matters of government was not asked.[10] On the other hand, Godoy did not suffer the imprisonment meted out to Floridablanca and Aranda when they were dismissed. Carlos left him all his honors and emoluments and never closed to him the doors of the royal residences.[11]

---

[6] Godoy, II, 242 n. 1; Geoffroy de Grandmaison, "Le clergé français en Espagne," *loc.cit.*, pp. 947-55; Geoffroy de Grandmaison, *L'ambassade*, pp. 107, 154-55.

[7] *Moniteur*, Feb. 18, 1798; Muriel, IV, 94-95.

[8] Muriel, IV, 103-13; Godoy, II, 239-43; Lafuente, XV, 282-83.

[9] Fischer, *Travels in Spain*, pp. 245-46; Muriel, IV, 84-85.

[10] Lafuente, XVI, 4-7, quoting various letters of Godoy and Carlos IV.

[11] See *Moniteur*, 10 nivôse VII (Dec. 30, 1798).

Godoy's retirement left Jovellanos the best known figure in the government. The advent of Jovellanos to the ministry of grace and justice brought an end to the relative calm in domestic affairs that had succeeded the peace with France. The economic difficulties caused by the British war were in their most acute stage, and the financial burdens levied on the wealthy embittered the atmosphere. Not the war, however, but a fight between Jansenists and ultramontanes over the organization of the church of Spain was the overt reason for the new tensions. A ghost that had apparently been laid in the days of Carlos III suddenly reappeared more troublesome than ever.

2

Despite appearances, the ghost that now strutted onto the Spanish stage had never ceased to lurk in the wings. Although Carlos III enforced public silence on the debate between Jansenists and ultramontanes after the expulsion of the Jesuits, the antagonism was kept alive by the movements to reform education and to simplify religious practices. During the first years of Carlos IV, the expectations of Spanish Jansenists were kindled by two events outside the country.

The first event had occurred in Italy in 1786. The grand duke of Tuscany, Leopold, was engaged in enforcing a reform of the Catholic Church in his lands similar to that being enforced by Carlos III. His guiding spirit was the "Jansenist" bishop of Pistoia, Scipione de' Ricci. In 1786 Leopold ordered the bishops of Tuscany to hold diocesan synods of their priests to learn of abuses within the church and to discuss reforms. To the Synod of Pistoia Ricci invited a group of friendly theologians led by Pietro Tamburini, and together they drew up a series of proposals. With some encouragement from their bishop, the priests of the diocese voted favorably on the proposals, which were then issued as decrees of the synod. They recommended a simplification of the church service and the enforcement of a stricter morality on laity, priests, and monks, echoing the demands of the French Jansenists. In the realm of church organization, the synod accepted specifically the "Gallican articles" adopted by the church of France in 1682, and declared that only a general church council was infallible and not the pope, that bishops had final authority over their dioceses, having received their rights directly from Christ, and that the authority of the church was limited to spiritual matters. For all these various recommendations, the justification given was a return to the original practices of the church. Leopold was unsuccessful in promulgating the decrees throughout his realm, for his other bishops overwhelmingly refused to accept them. Nevertheless the acts of the Synod of Pistoia were printed and given wide publicity within the Catholic Church.[12]

The second event to affect Spanish Jansenism was the passage of the Civil Constitution of the Clergy by the French National Assembly in 1790. This piece of legislation embodied an extreme concept of regalism, this time wielded by a sovereign legislative assembly. Religious orders were abolished and the secular clergy were converted into elected civil servants. The Civil Constitution was mainly the work of French Gallicans within the Assembly and not of Jansenists properly so-called or of *philosophes*. It was enacted and put into force despite condemnation by the pope.

In Spain the question of the organization of the church was a live issue as Carlos IV's reign began. The Academia de Derecho Español y Público de Santa Bárbara, composed of lawyers of Madrid, in successive years heard discourses in favor of restricting papal authority. In 1789 a speaker defended the royal *exequatur* for publication of papal and conciliar dispositions. He cited the *Encyclopédie méthodique*, Febronius, and the example of Felipe II's reign.[13] The approach of next year's speaker was somewhat different. He lamented the passing of the simple church of early Christian days, brought about, he maintained, by the accumulation

---

[12] See Nielsen, I, 125-30; *Dictionnaire de théologie catholique*, s.v., "Pistoie, Synode de."
[13] *Espíritu de los mejores diarios*, Oct. 19, 26, 1789.

of wealth by the monastic orders. He cited medieval examples of royal legislation limiting the growth of church property in entail, to prove, as he said, that all spirit of reform did not come from across the Pyrenees (this was the year of the Civil Constitution of the Clergy). "Since we became inoculated with ultramontane doctrines, we have gone steadily from bad to worse; and, if we do not succeed in stopping their fatal effects by reducing our codes to the primitive state of the former Castilian constitution, we shall soon reach the final point of degradation and ruin."[14]

This reference to the constitution of Castile calls to mind the liberal tradition now beginning to appear. One of the persons to express a desire to return to the medieval Spanish constitution was the anonymous author of the letters to the Conde de Lerena. Interestingly, he too lamented the passing of the early church. "Jesus Christ founded his church on a rock and not on gold," he said; but now Rome had become so interested in sucking money out of Catholic countries that the church would soon collapse under the weight of its own wealth. He recommended that the king reform the religious orders, equalize the income of the clergy, and reduce the tithes, all without the consent of Rome if necessary. Joseph II had done this. "The German church should account him the restorer of pure discipline. . . . Every way that will bring us closer to the first centuries of Christianity is praiseworthy, no matter what the road be."[15] This had been the theme of the Synod of Pistoia.

In the universities under-cover reading of works associated with Pistoia was becoming fairly common. A twenty-one-year-old student at Alcalá de Henares bought Tamburini's *De ethice christiana*, and his act was discovered when a friend to whom he had lent a volume of the work was caught by the Inquisición.[16] Nowhere was the favor of the Synod of Pistoia and its authors higher than at Salamanca. A friend informed Jovellanos in 1795:

[14] Speech of Manuel de Santurio García Sala delivered June 8, 1790, published as "Sobre los frayles," *Tribuno del pueblo español* (Cadiz), Feb. 19, 1813.
[15] July 13, 1789, *Cartas político-económicas escritas al Conde de Lerena*, pp. 173-99, quotations from pp. 175-76, 179.
[16] A.H.N., Inquisición de Toledo, leg. 190, No. 20.

"All the Salamantine youth is Port Royalist [Jansenist] of the Pistoian sect." Several Jansenist writers, especially Tamburini, he said were "in everyone's hands." The news gladdened the austere heart of Jovellanos, who himself was reading Tamburini's *Vera idea della Santa Sede*. "There is hope that studies will improve when the chairs and government of the university are held by the new generation," he wrote in his diary. "Any other reform would be useless. Like that of the *frailes*."[17]

Already in some universities the partisans of Jansenism were inspired by the Synod of Pistoia to take a more extreme position than their predecessors had taken. A case which the Inquisición investigated revealed that at the university of Toledo one Antonio Rivas, acting as a substitute for the professor of canon law about 1793, cited the Bible to prove that Peter was not given preeminence over the other apostles, the conclusion being that the pope had no claim to authority over the bishops. Rivas and his friends at the university, of whom several were ordained, were partisans of Tamburini and the Synod of Pistoia, a copy of whose acts they owned. One of this group proposed at a meeting of doctors and masters of the university in November 1793 that the classic Spanish theology text of Melchor Cano be given up in favor of that of the Flemish theologian, Jean Opstraët, recommended by the Synod of Pistoia. The discussion grew so hot that the meeting had to be suspended.[18] At the university of Seville a group of students who admired the Gallican church historian Claude Fleury established an informal academy of ecclesiastical history. In 1794 this group was reading church Fathers and accounts of early councils, to the dismay of some of the faculty.[19] The popular "Oracion

---

[17] Jovellanos, *Diarios*, pp. 201, 205, Mar. 20, 30, 1795. Quoted more fully in Helman, *loc.cit.*, p. 259 n. 14. Miss Helman points out that the text of Jovellanos' diaries was tampered with by the editors, who cut out passages critical of Spanish religious institutions. Juan Antonio Posse, who was a student at Salamanca at this time, took home to a town in León copies of works of Tamburini, Fleuri, Opstraët, and the acts of Pistoia (Posse, *loc.cit.*, XVI[1], 356-58). I have not seen the new edition of Jovellanos' *Diarios* (ed. J. Somoza [Oviedo, 1956]).

[18] A.H.N., Inquisición de Toledo, leg. 190, No. 29.

[19] J. M. Sotelo to M. Fernández Navarrete, Mar. 22, 1794, quoted in Cueto, *loc.cit.*, p. cxci n. 1.

apologética," which was circulating clandestinely in manuscript among university students, supports the picture of growing Jansenist views. It complained that in Spain the study of the Scriptures had been abandoned. "The ecclesiastical antiquities have been buried beneath the decretals and abuses furtively introduced. The decisions of the curia and private opinions have gone hand in hand with dogmatic and uncontrovertible truths."[20]

The Jansenists in Madrid were busy during these years trying to get published the works they liked. As in other matters, Godoy imitated the policy of Carlos III by supporting the Jansenists, although the strength of his support varied according to circumstances. In 1793 the Jansenists succeeded in publishing a compendium of the writings of Van Espen, the Dutch partisan of episcopal authority within the church,[21] and the so-called "Naples catechism," whose use had been recommended by the Synod of Pistoia.[22] A contemporary ultramontane writer reports that the Jansenists went so far as to have the acts of Pistoia translated into Spanish and to request a license for their publication. The first censors to whom the acts were submitted found them Jansenistic. The decision was appealed to the bishop of Madrid, who sent the work to a religious community favorable to reform (presumably the canons of San Isidro), which after hesitation rejected it. The translators then asked for it to be sent to the university of Salamanca, where they were sure of friends among the faculty; but a letter of the pope to Carlos IV, this contemporary writer says, put a stop to the project.[23] On the other hand, the pope failed to get the government of Spain to come out openly against the Synod of Pistoia. On August 28, 1794, Pius VI issued an important bull, *Auctorem fidei*, condemning the errors of the synod.

---

[20] See above, p. 331 n. 59.

[21] Godoy, II, 193, 209.

[22] Francisco Alvarado, *Carta undecima del filósofo rancio* (Cadiz, 1812), p. 40. For identification of the catechism see *Dictionnaire de théologie catholique,* Vol. XII², col. 2161.

[23] Alvarado, pp. 37-39. Alvarado was a strongly controversial writer, but his letters were subject to continued attacks by the liberal press of the time. Had his story not been true, it most likely would have been denied by his enemies; but I have found no denial in the press of the period.

The inquisitor-general, Cardinal Francisco Lorenzana, joined Pius in asking for publication of this bull in Spain; but the Consejo de Castilla denied them permission after consulting the association of lawyers of Madrid and a committee of canonists and theologians.[24] All these events, including the attempt to publish the acts of Pistoia, demonstrate a remarkable growth in the temerity of Jansenists around the court.

Although the Civil Constitution of the Clergy was produced four years after the Synod of Pistoia, its impact was being felt in Spain simultaneously with the latest phase of Italian Jansenism. Prominent among the pieces of Revolutionary propaganda circulating in Spain before 1793 were justifications of the Civil Constitution. Between 1791 and 1793 the Inquisición collected three copies of a manuscript in Spanish entitled "Analysis y refutacion de la bula de S. S." It was an ironical reply to the papal condemnation of the Civil Constitution, asserting that the elements which the pope found in it were there but that they were merits and not faults. The church of France *is* persecuted, it said. But why? Because it is forced to return to its original virtues. The faith *is* lost. Why? Because the pope has lost his annates, the king his benefices, the priests their tithes. The piece was almost certainly translated from the French.[25] Another manuscript, four pages long, sent to the Inquisición from Galicia, was headed "Memoria del Illmo. Señor Scipion de Ricci en respuesta a los quesitos [*sic*] que se le han hecho relativos a las presentes diferencias de la iglesia de Francia." In it the bishop who had organized the Synod of Pistoia defended the oath to the Civil Constitution required of the French clergy.[26] Still a third manuscript in circulation was a translation of pastoral letter of the French bishop of Oléron assuring his flock that no harm would come to religion from the changes in the French church being made by the National Assembly.[27] All of these writings, unlike the majority of Revolu-

---

[24] *Ibid.*, p. 40; Muriel, VI, 119-20. On the bull see *Dictionnaire de théologie catholique*, Vol. XII[2], cols. 2204-23.

[25] A.H.N., Inq., leg. 4429, No. 35

[26] *Ibid.*, leg. 4430, No. 21.

[27] See above, p. 253.

tionary papers found by the Inquisición, had been translated and were circulating in manuscript. The fact indicates a wider interest in Spain in the developments in the church of France than in other phases of the Revolution. The correspondent of the *Moniteur* reported in May 1791: "You would be surprised in Paris to learn that in Madrid of all your major political acts it is your Civil Constitution of the Clergy that has had the most success. You did not know that we southern people, adorers of Madonnas and burners of unbelievers, are not at all courtesans of the pope."[28]

Influential members of the Spanish clergy approved of the Civil Constitution. The bishops of Ávila and Barbastro were among their number. The latter, Agustín Abad y la Sierra, whose diocese was near the Pyrenees, wrote his approval to the French Constitutional clergy, and his letter was published in France. As a result he was delated to the Inquisición in 1792 as a Jansenist. Before the year was out, his brother Manuel Abad y la Sierra was named inquisitor-general, and the case was dropped.

Other Spanish churchmen who sympathized with the French ecclesiastical revolution were intimidated by the prosecution of Bishop Abad from making their sentiments known openly, but they communicated their support to the leader of the constitutional clergy, Henri Grégoire, through friends or by private letters.[29] One of those who did so was the priest Josef de Yeregui, who had been a tutor of two royal *infantes*. In 1792 he was accused of Jansenism by the Inquisición, but the advent of Abad y la Sierra as inquisitor-general brought his absolution, and he was made an honorary inquisitor by the king. He then entered into correspondence with Grégoire, revealing to the French bishop the procedures of the Inquisición, one of the most serious offenses possible against this body, which still strongly insisted upon the secrecy of its proceedings.[30]

Another who communicated with Grégoire at this time was the Condesa de Montijo. She congratulated the French bishop

[28] *Moniteur*, May 30, 1791.
[29] Grégoire, II, 62-63; Llorente, *Historia*, VI, 115-16, IX, 39-40.
[30] Grégoire, II, 239-40; Llorente, *Historia*, V, 231-32; Pinta Llorente, *loc.cit.*, pp. 87-91.

on the emigration of the non-juring clergy, most of whom she had found to be either ignorant or fanatical.[31] The Condesa was the secretary of the Junta de Damas attached to the Sociedad Económica de Madrid[32] and a leading figure in Madrid society. Her house was among the first in Madrid where Jovellanos had been seen as a young man, fresh from the university of Alcalá, with his flowing hair and black garb strangely out of place among the gay clothes and powdered wigs of the court. Twenty years later, during his exile in Asturias, Jovellanos still corresponded with this lady.[33] More and more in the 1790's the *tertulias* of the Condesa de Montijo became gatherings of Jansenist sympathizers. Yeregui was one of these; others included canons of San Isidro and Bishop Antonio Palafox of Cuenca, brother of the Conde de Montijo.[34]

3

When Spaniards who admired Pistoia and the Civil Constitution turned their thoughts to the domestic scene, the first object of their attention was the Inquisición. The Inquisición had never lost its ultramontane spirit, and in the first years of Carlos IV it had been reinvigorated with Floridablanca's blessings to meet the dangers posed by the Revolution. The Santo Oficio maintained a suspicious eye on the Jansenists, and every increase in its authority whetted Jansenist hatred of that body. Jovellanos described the tribunal of Logroño, which he visited in 1795, as "a magnificent palace to house three clergymen and oppress a few unhappy wretches." "Each inquisitor has a magnificent and spacious room with a large and lovely garden," he observed bitterly.[35] To an English friend he wrote confidentially:

You express yourself very openly as to the Inquisición. I am

---

31 Grégoire, II, 239. Grégoire does not name the lady, but her identity is evident (see Villanueva, *Vida literaria*, I, 88-89).

32 *Kalendario manual y guia de forasteros . . . 1795* (Madrid, 1795), p. 102.

33 Muriel, IV, 136 and n. 24; Jovellanos, *Diarios*, pp. 147, 265, May 31, 1794, Sept. 2, 1795.

34 Llorente, *Historia*, V, 205-8; Villanueva, *Vida literaria*, I, 88-89.

35 Jovellanos, *Diarios*, p. 219, May 3, 1795.

of the same opinion about it, and I believe many, very many, agree with us. But how far the opinion is from being general! So long as it is not, this abuse cannot be attacked directly. The result would be as in other attempts, to strengthen its foundations and render the system more cruel and insidious. What is the answer? I see only one: begin by tearing from it the authority to prohibit books, give that authority to the Consejo [de Castilla] in general subjects and in dogmatic questions to the bishops.[36]

One who agreed with Jovellanos was his friend Meléndez Valdés. In a poem dedicated to Godoy in 1795 he urged him cryptically to overthrow the monster who was oppressing genius and holy truth:

> Mas hoy misero yace [el ingenio], y oprimido
> Del error gime y tiembla, que orgulloso
> Mofándole camina el cuello erguido.
> No lo sufrais, señor; mas poderoso,
> El monstruo derrocad que guerra impía
> A la santa verdad mueve invidioso.[37]

José Marchena, author of *A la nacion española* published by the Bayonne Jacobins, was another who had close knowledge of the enlightened public in Spain. Of the Spanish institutions which he denounced as tyrannical the Inquisición most aroused his anger:

Jesus did not come armed with the power to inculcate his religion by the force of the sword. . . . Yet the frightful caverns of the Inquisición open up to swallow the poor wretch who has incurred the indignation of the *frailes* and hypocrites. Spain is a thousand leagues from Europe and ten centuries from the

[36] Jovellanos [to Alexander Jardine, British consul in La Coruña, May 24, 1794], B.A.E., L, 366-67. Jardine is identified in Helman, *loc.cit.*, p. 263.

[37] "But today genius, lying desolate, sighs and trembles, oppressed and mocked by error, which proudly struts with uplifted neck. Do not permit it, Sire, but with your power overthrow the jealous monster that wages impious war on holy truth" (Meléndez Valdés, "Epístola . . . al . . . Príncipe de la Paz . . . ," B.A.E., LXIII, 200).

eighteenth. . . . Is it not time for the nation to shake off the intolerable yoke of the oppression of thought? Is it not time for the government to suppress a tribunal of darkness that dishonors even despotism?[38]

If Marchena felt that he could arouse Spaniards with this tirade while Jovellanos, who was no friend of revolution, believed that "many, very many, agree with us," there seems no question that an important minority in Spain hated the Inquisición.

During the ministry of Godoy, several half-hearted attempts were made to pare the newly sharpened claws of the Santo Oficio. Inquisitor-General Manuel Abad y la Sierra, who was sympathetic to Jansenism, was the author of the first attempt. In 1792 he asked an enlightened clergyman, Juan Antonio Llorente, to draw up a plan for getting intelligent men to review books and for revising the legal procedure of the Inquisición. Abad was dismissed during the stress of the French invasion of Catalonia in the terrible summer of 1794. His advanced spirit helped his downfall, and with him went temporarily all talk of reform of the Santo Oficio. After his fall, Abad was naturally accused of Jansenism.[39] The moment, as Jovellanos saw, was hardly propitious.

The next threat to the Inquisición arose out of the case of Ramón de Salas, the Salamanca professor convicted in November 1796 of writing seditious manuscripts. Salas appealed to Carlos IV to have his case reviewed. According to the usually well-informed *Moniteur*, despite a plea of the new inquisitor-general, Cardinal Francisco Lorenzana, to both the king and queen not to violate the secrecy of the tribunal, Carlos ordered the records of the case studied by his secretary of grace and justice, Eugenio de Llaguno, a friend of Jovellanos. Llaguno concluded that Salas had been convicted without sufficient evidence, and Carlos ordered Salas set free at the end of December 1796.[40]

---

[38] See above, pp. 275-76.

[39] Llorente, *Historia*, v, 116-18, ix, 66.

[40] *Moniteur*, Jan. 21, 1797 (report from Madrid, Dec. 30, 1796); Llorente, *Histoire*, ii, 469.

Meanwhile, several reactionary clergymen, led by the archbishop of Seville and the confessor of the queen, had conceived of a way to discredit the too liberal Godoy by having the Inquisición convict him of atheism and immorality. When the two prelates found Inquisitor-General Lorenzana not unnaturally hesitant to undertake an investigation of the Príncipe, they wrote to Rome asking the pope to encourage his prosecution. By chance the French commander in Italy, Napoleon Bonaparte, intercepted the pope's reply and was able to reveal the plot to the intended victim. Godoy took ironic revenge by having Carlos appoint Lorenzana and the two hostile prelates as special envoys to Rome to express the regrets of Carlos over Bonaparte's entry into the papal states and to soothe the pope's anger at Spain's alliance with France.[41] Ramón Jose de Arce, the reputedly enlightened archbishop of Saragossa, became the next inquisitor-general.

Godoy also drew up a decree ordering the Inquisición to arrest no one without first notifying the king. The miscarriage of justice in the case of Salas was the reason alleged. Whether the decree was ever signed is not clear;[42] but when Godoy was dismissed, the Inquisición was still the bastion of conservatism in ecclesiastical affairs.

4

Although opponents of the authority of Rome and the Santo Oficio had become aggressive in church, university, and government circles by 1797, the average literate person had little way to know of these developments. The issues involved were becoming public knowledge, however, through the press. The tight censorship of Carlos III on the ultramontane-Jansenist controversy broke down under the shifting governments of Carlos IV, thanks in part to the preoccupation of the authorities with

---

[41] Llorente, *Historia*, ix, 46-48; Muriel, iii, 190-95; Villanueva, *Vida literaria*, i, 71-72.

[42] Godoy (ii, 118) claims the order was issued, but, according to Llorente (*Histoire*, ii, 469), who seems correct, Godoy was dissuaded from issuing it by Bishop Fernández Vallejo, president of the Consejo de Castilla and a personal enemy of Salas.

Revolutionary papers. Two works, both widely known, broke the dam of censorship.

The first was the *Historia de la vida del hombre*, written by the ex-Jesuit in exile in Italy, Lorenzo Hervás y Panduro. Its introduction, which had caused Floridablanca to confiscate what copies he could find of the first two volumes of this work in 1789, contains an outline of the entire work. In dealing with philosophical science, Hervás said he would reject the "errors with which ignorance has monstrously obscured it in favor of the modern experimental method." He felt the same way about political science. It too had suffered from "the puerile respect attributed to unknown antiquity." Science, including legislation, is reason, and the best reasoner, not the most just man, is the wisest. Theological sciences, Hervás similarly asserted, although here he claimed to be more cautious, are subject not only to errors of ignorance but also of false devotion and superstition. Although he had been educated a Jesuit, Hervás appeared to be joining forces with the Spanish reform group. He went on to show how he interpreted reform, and here is the rub. The growth of false devotion and superstition destroyed the spirit of the sacred sciences and brought on the rise of heresy, he said. The Catholics then awoke and, fighting for their dogma, learned to be true scholars. What Hervás was really saying was that he rejected medieval theology in favor of that of the Counter-Reformation, that is, of the Jesuits. The source of theological error, he continued, is in considering the church Fathers as oracles of doctrine. They are to be accepted only when they speak as depositories of church tradition and not when they appear as philosophers, for here they are not infallible. It is in considering Saint Augustine as the sole authority that the Jansenists erred, he said.[43]

These seemingly harmless statements raked glowing embers in Spain. The fire burst forth in 1793 in the *Catecismo del estado*, ostensibly directed at the French Revolution, by the royal chaplain and *calificador* of the Inquisición, Joaquín Lorenzo Villanueva.[44]

[43] Hervás y Panduro, I, x-xvii. See above, pp. 260-61, 367-68.
[44] See above, p. 368.

Villanueva had become a leading figure among the reforming clergy. He had studied under an anti-scholastic professor at the university of Valencia and had himself later taught as philosophy the new experimental method at the nearby university of Orihuela. In 1781 he had gone to Madrid and become a protégé of the inquisitor-general. There he published an attack on the slapdash way in which many priests said mass and another work defending the recently granted permission to read the scriptures in the vernacular because, he said, such had been the early Christian usage. He began what was to become a nineteen-volume work on the saints' days celebrated in Spain, in which he made use of modern critical studies of saints' legends, including Flórez's *España sagrada* and the works of Fleury.[45]

Although the *Catecismo del estado* was primarily a defense of monarchy, its prologue was a reply to Hervás, whose beliefs Villanueva pointed to as an example of those of the Jesuits as a whole. He argued that one of the beliefs that the new irreligious thinkers had tried to establish is the existence of a distinction between moral and political, or natural, man and supernatural man, concepts which are in reality inseparable. From such a distinction they concluded that one side of man can act independently of the other, in other words that in questions of the natural and political organization of man, revealed religion is irrelevant. Many of the faithful had been seduced by this reasoning, Villanueva said. Why? Because the way was prepared by the modern theologians, who "forgetting the language of truth, which is the Scriptures and Holy Fathers, try to cure the ills of the human race not with the medicine of Jesus Christ but with others of the human spirit, which are the new doctrines seasoned to the taste of the passions."[46] The evil was based on the false distinction between natural and supernatural man and could be seen in a thousand books, he claimed. Villanueva cited as examples the famous *Histoire du peuple de Dieu* by the French Jesuit Isaac Berruyer, which had been placed on the Spanish and Roman

[45] Villanueva, *Vida literaria*, 1, 2-6, 35-37, 73-75.
[46] Villanueva, *Catecismo del estado*, pp. ii-iii.

Indexes,[47] and Hervás' *Historia de la vida del hombre*. Hervás especially scandalized him for saying that public felicity can be achieved with reason alone, neglecting, as Villanueva pointed out, antiquity, virtue, and holiness. Moreover Hervás said that man is constituted part of heaven and part of earth, his spirit of heaven, his body of earth;[48] and this in Villanueva's eyes was the dangerous distinction he opposed. The Jansenists whom Hervás attacked were "in the dictionary of this author the public enemies of lax morality."[49] In sum Villanueva blamed Hervás in particular and the Jesuits in general for having prepared with their arguments the minds of unwary Catholics to assimilate the teachings of the *philosophes*. In so doing he repeated more clearly than anyone else had yet in Spain an accusation long directed at the Jesuits by French Jansenists.[50]

The reply was promptly forthcoming. The third volume of Hervás' work, which appeared in 1794, contained a passage that cast the blame for the French Revolution largely on Jansenist plotting. According to the Spanish ex-Jesuit, who cited a mid-eighteenth-century French author, in their first days in the seventeenth century the French Jansenists had laid plans to overthrow the Christian religion. They had later formed a league with the *philosophes* to destroy both religion and the throne, and out of this alliance had come the Revolution. Hervás' reply to Villanueva was that not the Jesuits but the Jansenists prepared the way for the *philosophes* and were in league with them.[51]

Less well known works were helping to publicize the ultramontane-Jansenist controversy in Spain during the Revolution. Two sermons of the bishop of Parma, which accused Italian Jansenists of the Pistoia school of attempting to destroy all religious authority beginning with the pope, were published in Spanish in 1790.[52]

---

[47] Palmer, p. 68; *Indice ultimo*, p. 26.
[48] Hervás y Panduro, I, 4-5.
[49] Villanueva, *Catecismo del estado*, pp. viii, ix n.
[50] See Palmer, pp. 28-29, 34-35.
[51] Hervás y Panduro, III, 130-39.
[52] Carlo Maria Domenico Adeodato Turchi, *Homilia dicha al pueblo por Monseñor F. Adeodato Turchi, . . . obispo y conde* [sic] *de Parma el dia V. de Noviembre de MDCCLXXXVIII. . . .* Traducida del italiano (Valencia,

At the same time a satire on Jansenism was found circulating in northern Spain. It claimed to be translated from the French and published in Avignon.[53] On the other hand Jansenist sentiment was evident in a paper published in the Andalusian town of Écija without license. It accused the Dominicans, the heirs of Jesuit ultramontanism in Spain, of teaching the doctrines of probabilism, tyrannicide, and regicide—doctrines long imputed to the Jesuits.[54]

Further indication of the growing interest in the dispute is given by the *Correo de Murcia* in 1795. It published a long article directed at those who read French books and the acts of the Synod of Pistoia. Its author expounded the league between the Jansenists and *philosophes* and recommended the passage in Hervás' third volume. He gave a list of 119 "Jansenist" authors, including Noris, Opstraët, "Port Rayale," Bossuet, and Condillac.[55] In subsequent issues of the *Correo* a contributor replied to this article by asserting that the Jansenists were only a bogey invented by those, such as Hervás and the Jesuits, who wished to flatter the human passions.[56]

5

When Jovellanos became secretary of grace and justice, with authority in matters of religion, the ground had been prepared for a mortal fight between the opposing camps of Jansenists and ultramontanes. Jovellanos had accepted his appointment unwillingly, but once in office he did not hesitate to support the Jansenist cause, of which he was one of the most determined partisans. He found his first opportunity in a complaint made to him in December 1797 by the dean of the cathedral of Granada that the Inquisi-

---

1790) in "Varios," Carlos IV, leg 7, 4º; and *Carta pastoral del Il.mo y R.mo señor D. Fr. Adeodato Turchi . . . al pueblo, y clero de su diocesi* (Valencia, 1790) in "Varios," Carlos IV, leg. 4, 4º.

[53] A.H.N., Inq., leg. 4484, No. 12. It was found in Pamplona in 1790.

[54] *Disertacion crítico-teológica*, prohibited by *real orden*, Feb. 10, 1795, *Nov. rec.*, VIII, xviii, 15.

[55] *Correo de Murcia*, Sept. 1-15, 1795.

[56] *Ibid.*, Dec. 22, 26, 1795.

ción had closed a confessional in a local nun's convent, thereby infringing on the bishop's ordinary jurisdiction. Jovellanos asked an old friend, Antonio Tavira y Almazán, bishop of Osma, to investigate the complaint.[57]

Tavira could be counted on not to coddle the Inquisición. Now sixty years old, he had once been a professor of philosophy at Salamanca in the days before Carlos III's reforms in education. Although sympathetic with these reforms, he had taken a post at Madrid, where his lights came to the attention of the king and he was made a royal chaplain. In this position he had won the friendship of Villanueva and the respect of the future Carlos IV. He kept out of the public eye, but his influence was high. As one of the major figures in the circle of the Condesa de Montijo, he had helped introduce Jovellanos to Madrid society. About the end of 1791 Tavira was made bishop of the Canary Islands, and in 1797 he was transferred to the poor see of Osma in Old Castile.[58]

After investigating the complaint of the dean of Granada, Tavira found that there was a basis for the act of the Inquisición in an edict of the inquisitor-general of 1781, against which no bishop had then complained. But he took the occasion to object to the gradual extension of the authority of the Inquisición, which, he pointed out, was used to defend ultramontane doctrines.[59] Jovellanos brought the matter to the king's attention in a memorial that also stated his own objections to the Inquisición. Jovellanos blamed the circulation of irreligious foreign books and papers on the inefficiency of the tribunal, whose officials lacked knowledge of foreign languages, since, he said, "its positions fall to *frailes* who take them only to get an extra serving at meals and exemption from choir duty." He urged that the bishops be given back the authority to prohibit books and other jurisdictional rights

---

[57] Francisco Pérez de Quiñones to Jovellanos, Dec. 2, 1797, Jovellanos to Tavira, Feb. 15, 1798, both quoted in Antonio Tavira y Almazán, *Informe . . . sobre el procedimiento del tribunal de Inquisicion de Granada* (Seville, [1812]), in "Varios," Fernando VII, leg. 63, 4°.

[58] Muriel, IV, 131-47, gives an enthusiastic biography of Tavira. See Villanueva, *Vida literaria*, I, 85; Lafuente, XV, 345-46.

[59] Tavira to Jovellanos, Mar. 2, 1798, quoted in Tavira y Almazán.

usurped by the Inquisición. Although Jovellanos did not say so, the next step would obviously be the abolition of the thenceforth useless Santo Oficio.[60]

While the question of the Inquisición was pending, Jovellanos got a chance to attack ultramontanism in education. The reactionary bishop of Salamanca, Felipe Fernández Vallejo, had recently been promoted to the archbishopric of Santiago,[61] and Jovellanos had the official duty of nominating his successor. On May 20, 1798 he addressed a letter to the king, calling attention to the rivalry of theological parties within the university of Salamanca, where, he said, the "aristotélicos" were calling their enemies "filósofos" and blaming them for the impieties of the age, and the friends of enlightenment were accusing the "aristotélicos" of disliking "the sovereign authority and its regalias" and supporting the "usurpations of the Roman curia." He asked Carlos to appoint a distinguished prelate to the see of Salamanca, who would undertake to end the religious disputes within the university and enforce the teaching of modern philosophy and science. Bishop Tavira was the person he suggested. Although wary of the dangers of the undertaking thrust upon him, Tavira had no choice but to accept Carlos' decree of July 6, 1798, making him bishop of Salamanca.[62]

Early in 1798 Tavira and Jovellanos received support for their attack on ultramontanism from an unexpected and embarrassing source. Bishop Grégoire, of the French Constitutional Church, wrote an open letter to the new inquisitor-general, Ramón de Arce. The letter was a stirring plea for religious toleration in Spain against the practices of the Inquisición, which Grégoire called a "standing calumny against the Catholic Church." Most of his arguments were familiar to Spanish Jansenists. "Foreign to the beautiful centuries of the church, the Inquisición could

---

[60] "Representación a S. M. sobre lo que era el Tribunal de la Inquisición," quoted in Somoza de Montsoriú, *Las amarguras de Jovellanos*, pp. 301-5 (date not given). See Llorente, *Historia*, IX, 66-68; Muriel, IV, 155-56; Helman, *loc.cit.*, pp. 267-68.

[61] *Moniteur*, Nov. 27, 1797.

[62] Jovellanos to Carlos IV, May 20, 1798, quoted in Jovellanos, *Diarios*, p. 397; Muriel, IV, 130-31, 147.

arise only out of the ignorance and mire of the Middle Ages."
The Catholic religion should be restored to its pristine purity and
the bishops of Spain should be given the powers of the Inquisición.

> The cry of liberty sounds in both hemispheres. The revolutions
> begin now in Europe. . . . The Ebro and the Tajo will see
> their banks tilled by free hands; the awakening of a generous
> nation will mark its solemn entry into the universe. . . . The
> suppression of the Santo Oficio will be a preliminary measure
> for this great event. Elsewhere I have stated that it will fall
> before the most formidable power there is on the face of the
> earth, public opinion.

Such statements seemed more fitting to the revolutionary tract
of Marchena than to the letter of one Catholic bishop to another.

Grégoire's letter to Arce was published in Paris early in 1798,
both in French and Spanish.[63] The Spanish version began with
a letter by the translator to the Príncipe de la Paz urging him,
"the target of an atrocious tribunal," to make his glory eternal
by annihilating that tribunal. In the middle of March 1798 leading figures in Spain, including Godoy and a professor at Toledo,
began to turn in to the Inquisición copies of Grégoire's letter. The
copies had arrived in plain wrappers mailed anonymously in
Paris—the well known propaganda expedient was still in use.[64]

Grégoire's memoirs state that thousands of copies of the Spanish translation were sent across the Pyrenees and to the Spanish
colonies,[65] but the memoirs do not explain the purpose of this
move. His letter to Arce mentions a recent protest against the
Inquisición by a council of the French constitutional clergy
and asserts that the Inquisición's prohibition of Revolutionary
literature was harmful to the alliance of the two countries; but
profounder motives for publishing the letter doubtless existed.

---

[63] Henri-Baptiste Grégoire, *Carta del ciudadano Grégoire, obispo de Blois
representante del pueblo francés, a D. Ramon Joséf de Arce, arzobispo de Burgos,
inquisidor general de España* (Paris, 1798), and *Lettre du citoyen Grégoire . . .
a Don Ramon-Joseph de Arce . . .* (Paris, n.d.), both in Bibliothèque Nationale,
Paris.
[64] A.H.N., Inq., leg. 4463, No. 6.
[65] Grégoire, *Mémoires*, II, 65.

The correspondence of leading Spanish Jansenists with Grégoire may have convinced him that abolition of the Santo Oficio was feasible, and abolition would mean the defeat of Spanish ultramontanes. The Revolutionary clergy badly needed a boost to its waning prestige. Grégoire's letter suggests an attempt to get such a boost from a friendly Jansenist church in Spain. Why should not the Franco-Spanish political alliance against England be seconded by a religious alliance against Rome?

The Inquisición promptly prohibited Grégoire's letter, but for once Spanish officials did not consider a simple prohibition enough. So many copies in both French and Spanish had entered the country that the decision was taken to issue formal replies in print and from the pulpit—replies that did not hesitate to give detailed accounts of Grégoire's arguments. The royal librarian, Pedro Blanco, and the Jansenistic *calificador* of the Inquisición, Villanueva, wrote and published refutations of Grégoire's letter.[66] Both writers said Grégoire's real intention was not to see the Inquisición suppressed but to provoke a rebellion against the king of Spain. They accused the French bishop of getting his doctrines from Calvin and Rousseau and pointed out that religious intolerance was a correct Catholic practice. Blanco credited the Inquisición with saving Spain from religious wars like those of France, while Villanueva saw a blessing in the absence of heretics, Jews, and deists from his country.

Villanueva did not, however, carry his arguments so far as to defend specifically the existence of the Inquisición. In fact, certain regalist statements caused his book to be denounced to that body in 1799 as Jansenistic. Many opinions were solicited, and not until 1803 did the *fiscal* of the Inquisición decide to drop the case against Villanueva. "[The work] is worthy of the gratitude of the Inquisición," the *fiscal* said; "moreover, its prohibition would make the common people think that Grégoire was right in his

---

[66] Blanco (see above, p. 373 n. 91); Joaquín Lorenzo Villanueva [pseud. Lorenzo Astengo], *Cartas de un presbitero español sobre la carta del ciudadano Grégoire obispo de Blois al señor arzobispo de Burgos . . .* (Madrid, 1798). The latter, p. 1 n., admits widespread circulation of Grégoire's letter. See Grégoire, *Mémoires*, I, 120.

invectives against the Santo Oficio."[67] The failure of either Villanueva or Blanco to praise the Inquisición sufficiently probably
explains the appearance of a third answer to Grégoire in 1802,
a three-hundred-page book whose purpose was to show "the
origin, progress, and utility [of the Santo Oficio] in Spain."[68]

The letter of Grégoire was a godsend to the cause of ultramontanism in Spain. When the Inquisición was under attack
from such upright figures as Jovellanos and Tavira, its defenders
could suddenly hold it up as the target of the irreligious French
Revolutionaries, especially since Grégoire had had the lack of
foresight to describe it as a bastion against revolution.

The partisans of the Inquisición in grouping their forces
against the threats from the government were by no means
helpless. They included such prominent clergymen as Fernández
Vallejo, archbishop of Santiago and until recently president of
the Consejo de Castilla; Bishop Rafael de Muzquiz, confessor
of the queen; and Inquisitor-General Ramón de Arce, addressee
of Grégoire's letter. The leading royal official in their party was
José Antonio Caballero, a short, half-blind member of the council
of war, who was married to a lady-in-waiting of María Luisa and
had an able hand for intrigue. According to Godoy, Caballero
had helped discredit him with the king and was working to
overthrow the new liberal ministers.[69] A third element in the
ultramontane coalition was a group, largely of aristocrats, whom
the *Moniteur* called the "English party." They wished to overthrow the French alliance and the ministers who supported it[70]
—one may guess, in part because of the high levies occasioned
by the war.

Just before Godoy left office he had inadvertently furnished
the ultramontane party with a fourth ally. The French invasion of
the Papal States had threatened the peace of the Spanish ex-

[67] A.H.N., Inq., leg. 4460, No. 16, quotations from the *fiscal* of the Inquisición de Corte, Dec. 19, 1803.

[68] Riesco de Llerena (see above, p. 255 n. 61).

[69] Godoy, II, 245, 262-67; Baumgarten, *Geschichte Spaniens vom Ausbruch*,
I, 97-98.

[70] *Moniteur*, 2, 26 fructidor VI (Aug. 19, Sept. 12, 1798).

Jesuits still alive, and they had appealed to Carlos for help. A royal order of October 29, 1797 allowed them to return to Spain to live in convents that were far from the centers of population or (by a subsequent order) with their relatives if they had any. More than seven hundred came back, including Hervás y Panduro, author of the *Historia de la vida del hombre*.[71]

As soon as the ex-Jesuits returned, they and other ultramontanes began a concerted attack on their enemies. To the Inquisición they denounced Jovellanos, Tavira, the Condesa de Montijo, and members of the Condesa's circle.[72] Juan Antonio Llorente, one of the group of Jansenists, publishes in his history of the Inquisición the text of a cryptic letter in Latin addressed to the angel of Calahorra which he claims the ultramontanes sent to all Spanish bishops at this time. The letter lamented the failure of the Spanish clergy to defend Catholicism and suggested that the bishops should make the king see the error of his ways and "offer up a victim."[73]

The obvious victim whom the enemies of church reform desired to see Carlos sacrifice was Jovellanos. Rumors of Jovellanos' impending fall began to circulate in July 1798,[74] but his character did not let him fight intrigue with intrigue. In August he suffered severe stomach disorders (many suspected poisoning), and his illness was given as the reason for his dismissal on August 24 and return to Asturias.[75] Jovellanos' banishment from Madrid was accompanied by that of various nobles, army officers, and government officials, including Meléndez Valdés, recently promoted to *fiscal* of the court of Madrid, who was sent to Medina

---

[71] Severo Aguirre, *Quaderno de continuacion y suplemento . . . del prontuario . . . 1797* (Madrid, 1798), pp. 22-24; Garriga, p. 184; Hervás y Panduro, Vol. vii, "Aviso."

[72] Llorente, *Historia*, ix, 39-43, 48-49.

[73] *Ibid.*, pp. 69-71.

[74] *Moniteur*, 19 thermidor vi (Aug. 6, 1798), report from Madrid, 1 thermidor (July 19).

[75] Muriel (iv, 117-20) accuses Godoy and María Luisa of poisoning Jovellanos; Godoy (ii, 264-65) of course denies the charge and blames Caballero for Jovellanos' fall; Llorente (*Historia*, ix, 48-49) sees Jovellanos' departure as the result of his attack on the Inquisición; and the *Moniteur*, 19 fructidor vi (Sept. 5, 1798), blames the inquisitor-general.

del Campo.[76] Carlos invested his leading ultramontane councilor, José Antonio Caballero, with the secretaryship of grace and justice.

During these days Godoy's successor as first secretary, Francisco de Saavedra, retired from the scene. Saavedra was also secretary of finance, and worry over Spain's economy had weakened his health. In August 1798 he too suffered a severe attack of colic (more rumors of poison). Carlos relieved him temporarily of his duties about August 10 and entrusted responsibility for foreign affairs and the office of first secretary to the next highest official, Mariano Luis de Urquijo. Saavedra's health failed to improve, and Urquijo remained acting first secretary for over two years. Those who lamented the departure of Jovellanos turned their hopes on this young, brash man, known to detest Rome and the Inquisición.[77] Overnight Caballero and Urquijo, both new to authority, became rivals for control of royal policy.

6

Before excitement over the ministerial revolution died down, the publication of partisan works brought the religious controversy in the press to a head. On the ultramontane side an aristocrat arranged for the printing of a translation of an Italian attack on the Synod of Pistoia by a certain Rocco Bonola. The Spanish title was *La liga de la teologia moderna con la filosofía en daño de la iglesia de Jesucristo.*[78] The central part of this 118-page tract depicted a personified "modern theology" (Jansenism) urging his plans on a concourse of *philosophes*. Together, he said, they must cater to the delicate passions of man, glorify the early days of the church, and offer to help kings and bishops recover the authority usurped by the Holy See. The people will discover

[76] *Moniteur*, 19, 22, 26 fructidor VI (Sept. 5, 8, 12, 1798); Quintana, "Noticia de Meléndez," *loc.cit.*, p. 117; Godoy, II, 265.

[77] *Moniteur*, 2, 11 fructidor VI, 6 vendémiaire VII (Aug. 19, 28, Sept. 27, 1798); Holland, *loc.cit.*, pp. 74-77.

[78] Rocco Bonola, *La liga de la teologia moderna con la filosofía en daño de la iglesia de Jesucristo. . . .* Escrita en idioma italiano por el Abate Bonola . . . en 1789 (Madrid, 1798). On its publication by the Marqués de Mérito see Mier, pp. 281-82.

too late that they have been led not to Jerusalem but to Geneva, that the Catholic Church has been engulfed in a natural religion which mixes its faithful indiscriminately with philosophers and Protestants.

The Jansenists were not intimidated. An elderly Augustinian monk of Salamanca, a friend of Jovellanos and Meléndez Valdés, Fray Juan Fernández de Roxas, promptly wrote a reply to *La liga de la teologia moderna con la filosofía*. He entitled it *El páxaro en la liga* and signed it with the pseudonymn Cornelio Suárez de Molina, compounded of the names of famous Spanish Jesuits. It was dated November 25, 1798 and was published by a leading printer of Madrid.[79]

The tract purports to be a letter of the "Molinist" (the term Jesuit never appears) Suárez de Molina written to congratulate Bonola's translator on his accomplishment. Suárez de Molina was aware that various doctrines did produce materialism and atheism —he recites those moral and philosophical teachings that the Jesuits had been accused of spreading—but not until reading Bonola did he realize that upholding their exact opposite—the pure doctrines of the Scriptures and Fathers—would have the same effect. Wonderful! Perhaps Bonola and his translator have done more than they imagined. Perhaps they will awaken those who are asleep to the fact that the church cannot live without "us." Perhaps thanks to them "our institution" will be reestablished, with its kingdoms, its banks, its navy, its missions, and its university chairs, where "we" can once again teach young men to dance, ride horses, and worship "us."[80]

Since the outbreak of the French Revolution voices had been heard in Spain, especially of émigrés, that called the abolition of the Jesuits a mistake.[81] The Augustinian author of *El páxaro en*

---

[79] [Juan Fernández de Roxas], *El páxaro en la liga. Epistola gratulatoria al traductor de la Liga de la teología moderna con la filosofía, por don Cornelio Suarez de Molina* (Madrid, 1798), published by Benito Cano. Mier, pp. 281-82, is the only contemporary source to identify the author; but the work is also attributed to Roxas by Muriel, v, 172; Torres Amat, p. 86; Fraile y Miguélez, p. 373; and Menéndez Pelayo, *Heterodoxos*, v, 218 n.

[80] Fernández de Roxas, p. 14.

[81] Delbrel, "Le clergé français réfugié en Espagne," *loc.cit.*, p. 474. Fernán-

la liga now charged in print that all the worry of conservative clergymen over the impending ruin of the church was merely a pretense to urge the revival of the Company of Jesus. He was evidently hoping to arouse Carlos IV's inherited aversion to the Jesuits in order to assure royal support for the Jansenist party.

The two rival pamphlets became the talk of informed circles. One witness, who probably exaggerates, says that three thousand copies of *El páxaro en la liga* were sold in one day.[82] Urquijo was forced to issue a royal order in January 1799 to collect all copies of both works. An accompanying explanation to the Consejo de Castilla charged that the object of Bonola's tract was "to bring on a religious war by attacking sovereign authorities, whose powers are established by God himself," and that the theologians whom Bonola calls "modern authors" "are only simple teachers of the truths of the Evangile and repeaters of what the Holy Fathers have written." Urquijo left no question of where he stood. "This work was impugned by another entitled *El páxaro en la liga*, . . . which is written opportunely and attacks the other in the way it deserves." But to avoid religious disputes, he said, both must be prohibited. He ended with instructions to the Consejo to inform the *juez de imprentas* who authorized these works that it was a pity he had not proceeded with more circumspection, and in the future to submit works on theology to the first secretary (whose place Urquijo was filling) prior to giving them licenses.[83]

In Paris, meanwhile, the meddlesome if upright Bishop Grégoire seemed determined not to let the Spaniards fight out their family squabbles by themselves. In February 1799 he and three other constitutional bishops published their views on the rights of the church of Spain. Again they urged the Spanish bishops to demand a return of the authority stolen from them by

---

Núñez, the Spanish ambassador to France during the early Revolution, also suggested about 1791 that their expulsion had helped cause the Revolution (Fernán-Núñez, I, 209).

[82] Mier, pp. 281-82.

[83] *Real orden*, Jan. 17, 1799, published Jan. 26, Josef Garriga, *Continuacion y suplemento del prontuario . . . 1799* (2d ed.; Madrid, 1805), pp. 293-97.

Rome and the Inquisición. This time Grégoire's writing misfired, for his new pamphlet went unnoticed in the heat of domestic disputes. The Inquisición did not take the trouble to prohibit it until 1801.[84]

Although for the sake of appearances Urquijo ordered *El páxaro en la liga* confiscated, he favored the publication of more classic regalist and Jansenist works. Among these were the *Tentativa theologica* of Antonio Pereira, the Portuguese regalist of the middle of the century, and a Jansenistic work by the Italian Gennaro Cestari. Urquijo did not succeed in his project, for the Consejo de Castilla requested opinions on the two books from various religious institutions in Madrid, and only the canons of San Isidro returned a favorable verdict. After many weeks of discussion the king and Consejo decided against publication.[85] More success was had by a long dead member of Port Royal, Pierre Nicole, all of whose writings had been placed provisionally on the Spanish Index before 1747, pending a final examination of them.[86] Under the direction of Inquisitor-General Arce, a committee of theologians, which included Villanueva, his friend the court preacher Josef Espiga, a canon of San Isidro, and others of Jansenist sympathies, at last carried out the examination and declared that Nicole's writings contained sound doctrine. His name was taken off the Index, but his works were not published in Spanish.[87]

The first year of Urquijo's ministry thus passed without significant achievements for the Jansenist cause. A major opportunity finally came with the death of Pope Pius VI. For over a year be-

[84] [J.-S. Saurine, E.-M. Desbois, H. Grégoire, N. Jacquemin], *Observaciones sobre las reservas de la Iglesia de España, por los obispos de Dax, Amiens, Blois, y Cayenne reunidos en Paris*. Traducidas por el ciudadano Lasteyrie (Paris, 1799), in Bibliothèque Nationale. See *Suplemento al Indice*, p. 41.

[85] Torres Amat, p. 86; [Pedro Inguanzo], *Discurso sobre la confirmacion de los obispos* (Cadiz, 1813), p. v; Mier, pp. 201-2. Godoy (III, 13) says Llorente translated Pereira, but Llorente never admits this.

[86] *Indice ultimo*, p. 191.

[87] Villanueva, *Vida literaria*, 1, 70. The incident is dated by the reference to Arce, who took office early in 1798, and Espiga, who was exiled from Madrid at the end of 1800. See Alvarado, pp. 36-37, who mistakenly blames Godoy for the decision.

fore his death Pius had suffered ignominious treatment at the hands of the French. The French army had occupied Rome in February 1798 and established a Roman Republic, and Pius, although ill, was taken north by slow stages to southern France. Carlos IV gave the pope moral support and offered him unlimited financial help and a refuge in Mallorca, although in return, it is true, the king asked and received papal sanction for new imposts on the Spanish clergy. Urquijo had added the extravagant request that the pope give back to the bishops of Spain their primitive authority, but Pius, even in his present straits, refused to consider such a proposition.[88] Pius died on August 29, 1799 before he could be moved to Mallorca.

Pius's long anticipated death left the future of the papacy a subject of speculation. Would the French permit the prompt election of a new pope? Might a schism develop in the church with one pope recognized by France and another by the countries allied against France? In Spain these eventualities had been considered as early as Jovellanos' ministry,[89] and Urquijo had made preparations for them. On September 10, 1799 the *Gazeta* announced the death of Pius VI and carried the text of a royal decree. "Since in the present situation and disturbances of Europe it is not to be expected that the election of a successor to the papacy will be held with the deserved peace and calm or perhaps as soon as the church needs," the decree established the practices that the church of Spain should follow until the king recognized a new pope. The ecclesiastical courts were to continue their functions. The principal innovation announced was for the bishops to grant the matrimonial dispensations that customarily had come from Rome. What would happen if a serious matter like the consecration of a new bishop arose was left to be decided by a tribunal to be named by the king.[90]

---

[88] Muriel, v, 160-61; Lafuente, xv, 275-77, 355-56.

[89] Jovellanos to Carlos IV, n.d., quoted in Somoza de Montsoriú, *Amarguras de Jovellanos*, p. 304.

[90] *Real decreto*, Sept. 5, 1799, in *Gazeta*, Sept. 10, 1799, and Josef Garriga, *Continuacion . . . del prontuario . . . 1800* (2d ed., Madrid, 1806), pp. 265-69.

Under the circumstances in which it was issued, the decree hardly appears controversial. The only immediate innovation, that of marriage dispensations, was made on sound grounds. In many villages nearly everyone was related, so that marriages often required dispensations, which even in normal times took so long to come through from Rome that the case was not uncommon of impatient couples being disgraced by a child born out of wedlock. The question of granting dispensations in Spain, as was done in the Indies, had been examined for several years under Carlos III, partly with the object of avoiding the payments to Rome that were involved, but no action had been taken.[91] To authorize bishops to dispense permission for marriages on a temporary basis in 1799 was almost a necessity. Nevertheless, the text of the decree was known to have been written by the Jansenist court preacher Josef Espiga, and the decree was generally viewed as a Jansenist victory.[92]

The decree asked the bishops not to let their inferiors "worry the consciences of his majesty's subjects" by discussing the death of the pope or the terms of the decree. The reactions of the bishops show how divided the clergy was.[93] Known Jansenists made use of the occasion to publicize their points of view. Bishop Tavira at Salamanca directed an edict to his priests stating that the right to give marriage dispensations had always belonged to the bishops and had been exercised by the pope through "voluntary though tacit cession by the bishops." Tavira's edict was published and aroused wide interest.[94] Professors at the Reales Estudios de San Isidro at Madrid and at the university of Valencia wrote in support of his point of view, citing the authority of Bossuet, Van Espen, Febronius, Pereira, and like authors. Agustín Abad y la Sierra, bishop of Barbastro and one-time correspondent of Grégoire, issued a pastoral letter justifying the royal measure on the

[91] [Juan Antonio Llorente (ed.)], *Coleccion diplomática de varios papeles antiguos y modernos sobre dispensas matrimoniales* . . . (Madrid, 1809), pp. 48-52.

[92] Villanueva, *Vida literaria*, I, 62.

[93] Llorente later published the replies of twenty bishops and the opinions of other interested persons (*Coleccion diplomática*).

[94] See *Moniteur*, 21 vendémiaire VIII (Oct. 13, 1799).

basis of the primitive rights of Christian bishops, and at least eight other bishops wrote the king praising the decree either because they felt it was necessary and the king was acting within his rights or because they were glad to see the privileges of Rome limited.[95]

On the other hand, while no bishop dared to oppose the decree openly, many made their opposition felt indirectly. Felipe Fernández Vallejo, archbishop of Santiago, and Ramón de Arce, inquisitor-general, wrote the king perfunctory letters promising compliance, and other bishops showed their disapproval by not using the authority of dispensation given them.[96] Not a few clergymen refused to take sides, feeling, as one of them put it, that the two rival parties were ruining the church of Spain.[97]

Two months after the decree Urquijo struck at the Inquisición. A Dutch consul at Alicante had recently committed suicide, and his papers had been sealed by the local royal governor. A few nights later agents of the Inquisición had broken the royal seals, searched the consul's house, and taken books and prints valued at fifty thousand reales. Diplomatic protests from the Netherlands and France led Carlos to reprimand the Inquisición and order it to give satisfaction to the widow of the Dutch consul. The governor of Alicante was instructed never again to admit such contumacy from the Santo Oficio. The *Moniteur* reported from Madrid: "This exceptional atonement causes the greatest sensation in this city and in all Spain."[98]

7

This order was Urquijo's last success. Ultramontanes were working tirelessly to discredit him and his supporters as they

---

[95] The bishops of Saragossa, San Marco de León, Guadix, Albarracín, Calahorra, Mallorca, and Barcelona (Llorente, *Coleccion diplomática*). Felix Amat, an influental churchman but not a bishop, wrote that the decree was necessary but only as a temporary measure (Torres Amat, pp. 135-45).

[96] Llorente, *Coleccion diplomática*, pp. 67, 156; Muriel, v, 169.

[97] Torres Amat, pp. 88-89.

[98] *Moniteur*, 30 brumaire VIII (Nov. 21, 1799), which says the books and prints were worth 13,000 livres; Carlos IV to inquisitor-general, Nov. 11, 1799, quoted in Llorente, *Historia*, IX, 62-64.

had Jovellanos eighteen months earlier. In Madrid two preachers harangued the public on the dangers of Jansenist heretics meeting in the house of the Condesa de Montijo.[99] The papal nuncio had exchanged heated words with Urquijo and was now among the foremost of those urging Carlos to turn against the Jansenists. The ultramontane secretary of grace and justice, Caballero, more and more had the ear of Carlos. Urquijo, meanwhile, by an arrogant and cocksure bearing, was antagonizing even those who had favored his promotion, including Godoy and María Luisa.[100] He was treading the same path as Jovellanos.

Early in 1800 the cardinals of the church met peacefully in Venice and on March 14 elected a new pontiff, who took the name Pius VII. In France Napoleon Bonaparte had overthrown the Directory a few months earlier and set himself up as first consul of the French Republic. He asked Carlos IV to withhold recognition of the new pope until their two powers should agree on a common policy. Bonaparte had Urquijo's support for such a move,[101] but, to the annoyance of Bonaparte and the discomfort of Urquijo, immediately upon receipt of news of the papal election, Carlos publicly recognized Pius VII as legitimate pope and ordered ecclesiastical affairs in Spain restored to their status before the death of Pius VI.[102]

Urquijo made a last attempt to gain some concession from Rome. At his instigation Carlos wrote the new pope asking him to authorize a further grant of money to the crown by the Spanish church and, above all, to accept the decree of September 5, 1799 on a permanent basis.[103] Urquijo's hope was vain. After a long delay, on October 3, 1800 Pius acceded graciously to the request for a new church levy, but in an affectionate letter to Carlos he

[99] Mier, pp. 201-2; Muriel, v, 171; Llorente, *Historia*, v, 205-8.

[100] Holland, *loc.cit.*, pp. 78-79; Godoy, III, 14, 52-53; Muriel, v, 88, 105; dispatch of Ch. J. M. Alquier, French ambassador to Spain, 14 ventôse VIII (Mar. 5, 1800), quoted in Roger Peyre, *La cour d'Espagne au commencement du XIXᵉ siècle* (Paris, 1909), p. 42.

[101] Muriel, v, 173-75.

[102] *Real decreto*, Mar. 29, 1800, in *Gazeta*, Apr. 1, 1800.

[103] Dispatch of Alquier, 9 germinal VIII (Apr. 1, 1800), quoted in Geoffroy de Grandmaison, *L'ambassade*, p. 182; Godoy, III, 50-51.

complained of the spirit of innovation found in some Spanish ministers and bishops, who were encouraging doctrines prejudicial to the Holy See. In the words of Godoy, "This letter marked the ruin of the minister Urquijo."[104]

Other factors contributed to Urquijo's fall. By 1800 the wartime fiscal problems and discredit of the *vales* had reached a critical point, and good king Carlos was genuinely upset by the financial crisis.[105] Although Urquijo was not directly responsible for Spain's finances, the deplorable situation helped shake the king's faith in his leading secretary.

As in the cases of Floridablanca and Godoy, the final blow at the acting first secretary came from France. In August 1799 an important Spanish fleet had been placed under French command at Brest. The English had since been raiding the coast of Spain, while Bonaparte refused the requests of the Spanish commander at Brest for permission to return to Cadiz. On November 18, 1800 Carlos ordered the Spanish fleet to sail immediately for Cadiz, with or without French approval. Bonaparte thought he saw the hand of Urquijo behind this sudden show of independence and promptly sent his brother Lucien to Madrid to procure Urquijo's fall. The task was not difficult, for Carlos had already turned against his first secretary, and he was anxious not to anger Bonaparte lest Bourbon family interests in Italy suffer. The decision came early in December 1800. Urquijo was dismissed and packed off to prison at the citadel of Pamplona, where Floridablanca had preceded him almost nine years previously.[106]

Carlos added to the dismissal of Urquijo official notice of the victory of the ultramontane cause. According to Godoy's memoirs, Caballero had used the papal letter of October 3, 1800 to incite Carlos to vengeance on the leading Jansenists. Godoy claims credit for reaching an agreement with the nuncio to publicize the king's solidarity with the pope by a less violent act—official recognition of Pius VI's bull *Auctorem fidei* of 1794 condemning the Synod of Pistoia, which Godoy's government had refused to

---

[104] Godoy, III, 52.   [105] *Ibid.*, pp. 15, 47-48.
[106] Muriel, VI, 87-110; Altamira, IV, 84-85.

admit to Spain at the time of its publication. A royal order of December 10, 1800 gave approval to *Auctorem fidei*. In this way Carlos officially denounced the dearest beliefs of the Jansenist party and ordered them henceforth not to be taught, defended, or believed in his realms. The decree, drafted, according to Godoy, by Caballero, threatened bishops, university faculties, judges, and other authorities with severe and pitiless punishment for any infraction of its terms. The Inquisición was ordered to collect all books and papers that upheld the condemned doctrines and to punish anyone who dared oppose the bull. Although the Consejo de Castilla, in publishing the royal order, inserted the customary proviso that nothing in the bull was to be understood as violating the regalian rights of the king, the doctrine of ultramontanism had suddenly triumphed in Spain by royal command.[107]

The Inquisición at last was free to pursue its enemies. It investigated charges that had been levied against the Condesa de Montijo and her circle, her brother-in-law Bishop Palafox of Cuenca, Bishop Tavira of Salamanca, Bishop Abad y la Sierra of Barbastro, the enlightened agent of the Inquisición, Llorente, Espiga, who was author of the decree of September 1799, and the Jansenistic canons of San Isidro. The Inquisición was unable to prove any of these guilty of heresy, and several of the accused fought back valiantly. Tavira refused to disavow the validity of the marriage dispensations he had granted during the papal interregnum, and Palafox wrote a letter to the king claiming that the denunciations against his group had been instigated by the recently returned ex-Jesuits. The cases were dropped, but Espiga was ordered to the cathedral of Lerida, of which he was an official, Meléndez Valdés was sent farther away to Zamora and deprived of his position as *fiscal*, and Carlos banished the Condesa de Montijo to Logroño. The Condesa, for almost three decades an outstanding figure in enlightened circles of Madrid,

---

[107] *Real orden*, Dec. 10, 1800, published Jan. 9, 1801, *Nov. rec.*, i, i, 22; Godoy, iii, 53-61. The edict of the inquisitor-general Jan. 12, 1801, condemning the acts of Pistoia, is in "Fraile," Vol. 855, fol. 28.

was forced to pass the remaining seven years of her life in exile from the court.[108] Llorente's history and the extant papers of the Inquisición show that this tribunal had for some time been filing away for an opportune moment accusations of Jansenist sympathies made against persons of lesser rank and that it now also brought forth these records. The Inquisición dismissed some cases, but it condemned a professor at Valladolid to recant in an *autillo* and imprisoned a canon of Ávila for five years. The canon's brother escaped a similar fate by fleeing to Paris.[109]

The harshest persecution was reserved for Gaspar Jovellanos. Since his dismissal in 1798, Jovellanos had been living in Gijón, promoting his beloved Instituto Asturiano. His life had not been easy, for the Instituto lacked money and it had run into the opposition of the conservative local bishop.[110] Early in 1800 Jovellanos had been troubled by the knowledge that the anonymous translator of a Spanish edition of Rousseau's *Contrat social* published in London in 1799 had chosen to praise him and Urquijo in a foot-note. At the time, Urquijo wrote him not to worry over the incident.[111] Behind Urquijo's back, however, the anger of Carlos against his former minister was being whetted by Caballero and the others who were working on the king's religious conscience. An official memoir was drawn up, apparently by Caballero with the cooperation of the Inquisición, accusing Jovellanos of desiring to destroy the head of the church, of bragging that he was the only king in Asturias, and of spreading the vices of liberty in the Instituto.[112] Carlos became filled with an implacable hatred for

---

[108] Llorente, *Historia*, v, 208, vi, 115-16 124, ix, 39-41, 44-45; Llorente, *Noticia biografica*, pp. 103-8; Quintana, "Noticia de Meléndez," *loc.cit.*, p. 117.

[109] A.H.N., Inquisición de Toledo, leg. 190, Nos. 20, 25, 28; Llorente, *Histoire*, ii, 479 (Gregorio Vicente); Llorente, *Historia*, v, 186-89 (Cuesta brothers), ix, 40-41 (López Gonzalo).

[110] See Jovellanos to bishop of Lugo, Dec. 6, 1799, quoted in Somoza de Montsoriú, *Amarguras de Jovellanos*, pp. 308-11.

[111] Jovellanos to Carlos IV, Mar. 26, 1800, and Urquijo to Jovellanos, Apr. 2, 3, 1800, *ibid.*, pp. 318-20. On the unsolved question of who made the translation see Spell, pp. 166-68.

[112] Quoted in Somoza de Montsoriú, *Amarguras de Jovellanos*, pp. 312-17. According to the *Moniteur*, 12 fructidor vi (Aug. 29, 1798) a similar memoir had been drawn up by Inquisitor-General Arce at the time of Jovellanos' fall.

this man. Early on March 10, 1801 Jovellanos was arrested in his house, his papers were seized, and he was transported like a common criminal across northern Spain to be put in prison in Mallorca. He was kept in confinement on that island until Fernando VII ascended the throne in 1808. Even Urquijo's fate was less severe; he remained in prison only one year.

Five days after the arrest of Jovellanos, Carlos ordered all the ex-Jesuits deported who had returned to Spain. They too, he felt, deserved blame for the recent religious strife; and their sacrifice was an easy sop to a conscience troubled by the betrayal of those men who had given him and his father strongest support in their church policies.[113]

Elsewhere in Europe the accession of Pius VII brought other victories for the cause of papal supremacy. While Carlos was again expelling the former Jesuits, the new pope gave formal permission for the Company of Jesus to be reconstituted in Russia, whose tsars had never recognized the papal abolition of the company. In the same year Bonaparte and Pius signed a concordat settling the schism in the church of France. Bonaparte abolished Grégoire's moribund Revolutionary church, and in return Pius agreed to obtain the resignation of the unwanted émigré bishops. The pope's apparent concession to the French government involved a significant triumph for the papacy; for the concordat ended the immemorial tradition that duly consecrated bishops had life tenure. In the home of Gallicanism, the concordat turned bishops into representatives of the pope, removable by him when necessary. A crippling blow was dealt to the concept, so dear to Spanish Jansenists, of the episcopacy as the ultimate authority in the church.

In the period of enlightened despotism, the authority of the Holy See, under attack by an alliance of jealous monarchs and churchmen, had reached its lowest ebb in centuries. The French Revolutionaries, who pushed ecclesiastical regalism to its logical end while denying the ultimate authority of kings, occasioned a

---

[113] Lesmes Frías, *Historia de la Compañía de Jesús en su asistencia moderna de España*, Vol. I, *(1815-1835)* (Madrid, 1923), p. 51; Mier, pp. 281-82; Llorente, *Histoire*, IV, 138.

reaction that was to lead ultimately to the declaration of papal infallibility in 1870. The first significant victories of ultramontanism came at the turn of the century; and of these victories, not least important was the discrediting of regalist ministers and Jansenist churchmen in the eyes of the rulers of Spain.

8

Godoy tells his readers that Carlos offered to reappoint him first secretary, but that he refused to return to the position lest the public conclude that his resignation in 1798 had been a mark of royal disapproval.[114] The public had indeed so concluded, with more reason than Godoy would have one believe, but Godoy's intimacy with the royal pair soon revived, and before the end of 1799 the public was again convinced of his influence at court.[115] He did not take a hand in royal policy, however, until late in 1800, when he stepped in to help pacify the Jansenist-ultramontane controversy. The years out of office had tempered his political outlook. His enlightened policies had failed to win the plaudits of most enlightened Spaniards, who did not hide their antipathy for him. Godoy was sure that his enemies among the partisans of enlightenment looked to Jovellanos and Urquijo as their natural leaders,[116] and he did nothing to prevent the imprisonment of these two men to whom he had given authority in 1797. In the future Godoy's aim would be to keep domestic peace by following the middle of the road.

Although Godoy did not become first secretary—the place went to his cousin-in-law Pedro Cevallos—he was again the leading figure in the Spanish government. In 1801 Spain, still cooperating with France against Britain, waged a brief and victorious war against Portugal. The Spanish forces were commanded by "el Príncipe," whom Carlos had invested with the additional title of Generalísimo of the armies. The Portuguese

---

[114] Godoy, III, 62.

[115] *Moniteur*, 10 nivôse, 24 messidor VII, 2, 11 brumaire VIII (Dec. 30, 1798, July 12, Oct. 24, Nov. 2, 1799); Lafuente, XVI, 6-7.

[116] See Godoy to María Luisa, Feb. 5, 1801, quoted in Lafuente, XV, 347 n. 3.

war—baptized derisively by Spaniards "the War of the Oranges"
—was the last act of the war with Britain. Peace between Britain and France and Spain was concluded at Amiens on March
27, 1802. Spain lost Trinidad to Britain, but it had won the district
of Olivenza from Portugal. The end of the war enabled Carlos IV
to reestablish the *reglamento* of 1778, which gave Spanish ships a
monopoly of trade in Spanish America.[117] Peace abroad had
succeeded peace at home, and peace in both spheres was what
Spain most needed to heal the material and spiritual wounds of
the 1790's. In the end the Príncipe de la Paz could give Spain no
more than a truce in either sphere. He was to find the middle of
the road in a country of excited passions a more dangerous place
to be than either side; and in a Europe overshadowed by the am-
bitions of Bonaparte, no nation could successfully claim half of
America without fighting for the privilege of enjoying this claim.

[117] Whitaker, pp. 8-9.

CONCLUSION:

NEW UNITY AND NEW DISUNITY

WHILE Spaniards who had been born in the middle of the century—men like Gaspar Jovellanos, Juan Meléndez Valdés, and Carlos IV—were living their best years, they were unknowingly witnessing a major turning point in the history of their country. They had grown from youth to manhood when Carlos III was expelling the Jesuits and taming ultramontanism, and in their early maturity they had enjoyed the era of prosperity, hope, and good feeling of the seventies and eighties. They lacked the retrospect needed to see that Spain was meanwhile reaching the end of a thousand years' process of national unification. A few years later, middle aged men upset by the domestic conflicts of the Revolutionary years, they had no way of knowing that these new conflicts were to broaden and deepen into the dominant feature of subsequent Spanish history.

Although the celebrated marriage of Fernando and Isabel and their conquest of Granada had led to the personal union of all the lands of Spain, the loyalty of Spaniards to the new country was fashioned much more slowly. For two centuries the peoples of Castile and Aragon remained at odds—Aragon rebelled against Felipe II, Catalans fought against Castilians from 1640 to 1652, and Catalonia, Valencia, and Aragon resisted Felipe V and Castile from 1701 to 1714. In the eighteenth century these regional antagonisms were at last lulled, as the war against the Revolution dramatically demonstrated. In 1794 French propagandists searched in vain in the northern provinces of Spain for the sentiment of separatism that had once been a boon to the foreign enemies of Madrid.

During the eighteenth century the importation of enlightened ideas and the growth of a capitalist class provided bones for a contention of a different sort—between those who urged intellectual and economic change and those who clung to the past. Until the death of Carlos III, however, the two parties remained united

435

Conclusion

by more basic motivations. Conservatives and progressives differed in their points of view, but they both reacted with patriotic
fury when Masson de Morvilliers published scornful strictures of
their country in 1783 in the second French encyclopedia.

This national unity was the achievement of the Bourbon rulers
and the religious faith of Spaniards. The kings of the new house
worked steadily to unify the political and economic institutions
of Spain, distributing as evenly as they could to all regions the
burdens of government and the benefits of an expanding economy.
Because royal mercantilism favored Catalan, Valencian, and
Basque producers and shippers and opposed the landed oligarchy
of Castile, the peripheral areas of Spain felt for once that Madrid
had their interest at heart and responded with a new loyalty
to their throne and country.

Their attachment to the Catholic religion also bound Spaniards
together. By keeping progressives from hearkening to anti-Christian extremists in France, their religious faith prevented the
entry of enlightenment into Spain from destroying the spiritual
unity of educated Spaniards; while the ingrained, almost superstitious, reverence for the Catholic religion of the vast majority
who could not read caused them to respond as in bygone ages
when their priests and monks preached a religious crusade against
the Revolution. Because in the war against the French Republic
virtually no clergyman, not even the enlightened Augustinian
archbishop Francisco Armañá of Catalonia, could sympathize
with the foreign cause, the church helped knit the new bonds
between the realms of the crown of Spain. The nationalism that
imbued Spaniards from all over the peninsula at the end of the
century had as its rallying cry "Religion, King, and Country!"

Underneath its united surface, however, Spanish society was
rapidly disintegrating during the war against France. Godoy's
intelligent efforts to recreate the atmosphere of Carlos III's day
failed, and instead a bitter split opened in the ranks of the upper
classes, polarizing them between rival political and ecclesiastical
philosophies, neither of which was prepared to pay the crown its
accustomed veneration. The era of enlightened despotism in

Spain, introduced by the early Bourbons and climaxed by Carlos III, was over.

The advent of enlightened despotism had accompanied the end of Spain's seventeenth-century isolation from major European intellectual and economic currents, and the passing of enlightened despotism in Spain was also part of a general trend. In most countries enlightened despotism rested on an alliance of absolute monarchs, progressive thinkers, and those who profited from industry and commerce, bound together by a feeling of mutual advantage. The combined experience of the western world, highlighted by the events of 1776 and 1789, was destroying this feeling in monarchs and in enlightened subjects throughout Europe.

In France, at the center of the Enlightenment, the ideal of enlightened despotism lost its hold over middle class persons and intellectuals in the decade after 1776. Several factors help explain its failure. The *philosophes* and their readers, disappointed by the reign of Louis XV, welcomed hopefully the advent of his grandson in 1774; but within two years Louis XVI dismayed this public by dismissing the leading minister on whom they counted for reform. In the same year rebels in America declared their freedom from their king in England, basing their stand on the inalienable rights of men and the sovereignty of the people. France soon entered the conflict, and many Frenchmen who embarked on what seemed another colonial war against Britain returned home enthusiastic over their role in a war of independence. The new American nation became the ideal of a young generation of *philosophes*, while the generation that had admired enlightened despots—Voltaire, D'Alembert, Diderot—was dying off. With these young *philosophes* and with the middle class in general, the throne of France was fast losing both moral and financial credit. The War of American Independence had added unbearable burdens to the royal debt; and the real and imagined escapades of the queen, whom the public was ready to believe capable of deceiving Louis for a string of diamonds, were making royalty look ridiculous. By the late 1780's the magic tie of confidence on which enlightened despotism rested had been broken in France, and America had shown French minds an alternative form of good government.

In Spain the magic tie was never stronger than in the years when it was being severed in France. Although Spain also entered the War of American Independence, the imagination of Spaniards could not, even unconsciously, be affected by the ideological significance of the conflict because their imagination was engrossed by the accomplishments of their own regime. For Spain, 1776 was the year in which Carlos III dismissed his last Italian adviser and placed an enlightened Spaniard, the Conde de Floridablanca, at the head of the government. Carlos became the leader of a national revival that carried the country to heights of prestige and prosperity unknown for centuries. A widower, he had no queen to discredit the throne, and he was a model of private virtue and religious devotion. Landowners and conservative churchmen felt the lash of his policies, but they had no case to present to the public against so popular a king.

The French Revolution accomplished in Spain what the American had failed to do. It provided the irritants that transformed into cancerous growths the hitherto innocuous discords brought on by the Enlightenment and economic expansion.

No Spaniard was stirred by events in France more deeply than Floridablanca, who was frightened by the challenge of the Revolution to the doctrine of royal absolutism into checking the institutions of enlightenment that his ministry had encouraged under Carlos III. Floridablanca's reaction was similar to that of other enlightened authorities. Catherine II closed Russian frontiers to French publications and required local French residents to abjure allegiance to the Revolutionary regime; Joseph II on his deathbed in 1790 condemned the pusillanimity of Louis XVI and abolished freedom of the press in Austria; and his successor, Leopold II (recent patron of the Synod of Pistoia), pacified the nobility and clergy of the Austrian lands by abolishing enlightened reforms. In the face of the French experience, many a king suddenly welcomed support from privileged groups—the same groups against whom his ancestors had struggled for generations to establish the present position of the throne.

Floridablanca's tightening of royal and ecclesiastical censorship failed to keep French papers and tracts from slipping into all parts of Spain from 1789 to 1792. The country to which Spaniards had looked for enlightenment had now proclaimed a new political philosophy, and Spanish minds could not but be affected. Before minds could translate Revolutionary examples into projects for domestic change, however, they needed the motivation of dissatisfaction with their own regime. Despite Floridablanca's reactionary moves, the continuing prosperity of the country and the prestige that his name and that of Aranda carried over from the previous reign prevented dissatisfaction from becoming conscious before the end of 1792.

The satisfaction of Spaniards evaporated widely and suddenly when Carlos IV put at the head of the ministry a young officer of the guards, Manuel Godoy, known to most only as the queen's protégé. The idea that Spain was being governed by an empty-headed lover, a lascivious queen, and a cuckold king broke the spell that Carlos III had cast over his people. Conservatives and progressives both found a new moral duty to criticize authority, but the real importance of their righteous indignation was that it rapidly induced them to reconsider other grievances in the light of developments in France.

Conservatives had never been enthusiastic over enlightened despotism, but under Carlos III Catholic apologists remained Cassandras warning of the threat to throne and altar by the new false philosophy and the spirit of church reform. The Revolution showed how right they had been, they said. It showed that philosophers and modern theologians were actually in league to destroy kings and popes. The only defense they saw for the Spanish crown against these dangerous groups at home was for it to concede control of the Spanish church to Rome and to entrust the Inquisición with rooting out subversive ideas.

The conservative solution to the problem of the times had little novelty. Progressives were harder put to replace their political ideal of the previous age. To some, France's Civil Constitution of the Clergy suggested ways to overcome the familiar resistance of ultramontanes to ecclesiastical and educational reform, and a smaller number of progressives admired the limited monarchical constitution which France adopted in 1791. But the sting of Masson's article still smarted, and the events of the Terror made all save a few Spaniards ready to take up arms against the French Republic. After 1792 only extremists—and disgruntled aristocrats who did not mean what they said—urged the French to come and set up a new government in Spain.

Unprepared to imitate French examples blindly, most progressive minds in Spain found materials for the answers to their problems already present in their larder of ideas. They had only to mix the ingredients in new ways. Out of their interest in national history, their study of the law of nature and of nations, and their familiarity with the general theme of Montesquieu's writing, they concocted the liberal tradition. Spain, they discovered (as some had already suspected), had an ancient constitution that provided for popular control of the king through representative Cortes. They agreed with the leading figure of their group to pass over to the French camp, José Marchena: "France needed a regeneration, Spain needs no more than a renovation." After Floridablanca's resuscitation of the Inquisición, these minds were invaded by a distrust of the ecclesiastical regalism of the previous reign. Full popular control of the clergy as instituted in France did not appeal to them either; instead they added to the recipe of the new liberal tradition an old Gallican flavor recently put on the market at Pistoia and arrived at the belief that the church too had a true constitution according to which the bishops were sovereign and had authority over heretics. To these minds absolute monarchy, the Inquisición, and the supremacy of the pope now stood revealed in their true form as cankers of recent growth. However fantastic the stories were of a league of Jansenists and *philosophes* to precipitate the French Revolution, the Revolution had cemented an alliance in Spain between partisans of enlightenment and those churchmen whom their enemies with little justification had labelled "Jansenists."

Despite enlightened Spaniards' distrust of France, the liberal tradition and the new episcopal Jansenism more than slightly recalled certain of the institutions erected by the French Revolutionaries. The impact of the Revolution on Spain was more evident, however, in the reception given to the policies of Godoy. Far from being the incompetent paramour many saw in him, Godoy shunned the reaction of Floridablanca and navigated resolutely along the paths charted earlier by Carlos III and Campomanes and more recently by Aranda. He was hampered by the wars against France and Britain, which gave most Spaniards real financial injuries to add to the imagined insult of his advent. He tried to solve part of the problems of war by taxing the same groups that Campomanes had worked to weaken, but he had no way to make up for losses in trade and the forced abandonment of the roads and canals that had been projected to bring industry to the interior. Nevertheless, for over five years Godoy was able to steer the state on a generally enlightened course. Conservatives naturally hated him, but most men of enlightenment also continued to see in his rule a bitter yoke, not progressive leadership. Far more than his ambiguous position at court, it was the spell cast by contemporary French examples upon Spanish thought that kept Godoy from overcoming disfavor among the generation that had admired the enlightened rule of Carlos III and the younger one now upholding radical positions in university disputes.

If Godoy's course was at times erratic, the blame lay partly with his monarch. Carlos IV devoted much energy to problems of state, but his father's insight and steadfastness were wanting in him. During his initial years the Inquisición recovered the position it had once held under Habsburg kings as a valued defender of the crown, and when war came with France, Carlos had to thank his clergy for arousing the people. In time of need the altar turned out to be the indispensable partner of the throne, and all Carlos' admiration for young Manuel could not erase this impression from his devout mind. When conflict over religious reform threatened the peace of his land, conservatives were able to persuade him that reform and religion did not mix. For his difficulties he took vengeance on the leading proponent of both the liberal tradition and episcopal Jansenism, Gaspar Jovellanos. Louis XVI had found himself increasingly beset by bourgeois demands in the last year before the French Revolution, and he fell back on his nobility and upper clergy for aid; similarly twelve years later Carlos IV, frightened by the importunities of Jansenists and progressives, turned toward ultramontane conservatives.

The dozen years after 1789 affected Spain much as the dozen years after 1776 had affected France. Few in Spain in 1801 could be aware of the profound chasm that was opening in their society, but few in France in 1788 had sensed the coming divisions there. Although Spain seemed to be troubled only by a struggle over reform of the church, this struggle epitomized the waxing conflict between partisans of old and new ideas. Furthermore, the ecclesiastical struggle could not have arisen without a general loss of prestige by the crown, and the prestige of the crown had been an important factor in preventing the materialization of another likely struggle—that between landowning oligarchy and capitalistic middle class.

Unfortunately for Spain, its position was being weakened by more than civil division. During the recent wars English merchants had again feasted on trade with the Spanish colonies, and a taste for this trade had also been awakened among United States shippers and many Spanish colonists. Spanish colonists at the same time were finding in the American and French Revolutions philosophic justification for long-standing resentments against rule by men born across the ocean. Spain had achieved its eighteenth-century rebirth in a spirit of unity—its house could not now be divided and hope to stand against these growing challenges from outside.

The penalty for Spain's civil discord became apparent when Napoleon invaded the country in 1808. The first impulse of most

Spaniards was to unite as enthusiastically as in 1793 to fight for religion, country, and king; but in the end the fruit of the war years ripened into national disaster rather than national unity. Since the Spanish royal family had fallen into the hands of Napoleon, national Cortes, convoked at Cadiz in 1810 without royal sanction, met to give direction to the war. The liberals and Jansenists, who had a majority in the Cortes, seized the occasion to abolish *señoríos* and the Inquisición and to enact a limited monarchical constitution in 1812. Thereupon the conservative churchmen, particularly strong in the lower ranks of the clergy, turned the fire they had been directing at the French invaders upon the legislators of the Cortes. The masses of Spaniards were prepared by their priests and monks to welcome back absolutism and ultramontanism in 1814, the alliance of throne and altar that had been foreshadowed in 1801. The war years had succeeded in embittering the antagonism between upper class Spaniards and in driving the wedge of controversy down into the lower layers of society.

If Spain had recovered rapidly from the ravages of war, the domestic bitterness might have been soothed with time. But Spain's eighteenth-century economic revival had been based on colonial trade; and, abetted by interested persons in England and the United States, the Spanish colonists had been led by the absence of legitimate government in Spain after 1808 to take hesitant but irrevocable steps toward independence. No balm of prosperity came to heal the scission in Spanish society. Instead the scission between progressive-anti-clerical and Catholic-conservative Spaniards—the "two Spains" of recent history—has remained the fundamental problem of Spain. Even the troublesome nineteenth-century revival of Catalan and Basque particularism was a product more of the new disunity of Spain than of memories of the old provincial grievances that had been appeased in the eighteenth century.

Since Marcelino Menéndez Pelayo wrote his *Historia de los heterodoxos españoles* late in the nineteenth century, Spanish historians have tended to see the origin of the "two Spains" in the advent of the Enlightenment and the policies of Carlos III. It is true that some later points of dispute did make their appearance at this time—what changing society does not have internal tensions?—but so long as Carlos III and his associates directed the government these tensions could not match the cohesive forces of traditional royal prestige and religious faith and long maturing patriotism. This ideal of enlightened absolutism was shattered in the first decade of Carlos IV's reign by the impact of the Revolution in France and its accompanying wars. Together these disturbed the even course of royal policy, stirred existing domestic conflicts, deepened the contrast between Carlos IV's court and his father's, and infused new ideas in Spain. Only then did tensions in Spanish society begin to outpull cohesive forces. History has no way of telling in which direction the balance of social forces would have moved without the French Revolution, but it can say that the balance showed no signs of favoring the divisive forces before the Revolution and that divisive forces then began to predominate over cohesive forces and have since been so repeatedly predominant that today there exist "two Spains."

The critical turn in recent Spanish history therefore revolved around the loss of faith in enlightened despotism—in the ideal of a disabused absolute monarch directing his people toward justice, prosperity, and happiness. The destruction of the state of mind necessary for the continuation of the old order—which occurred in France before 1789 and in Spain between 1792 and 1801—was the real revolution of the late eighteenth century, in Spain and France and Europe in general. In Spain this eighteenth-century revolution was the product, not of the reign of Carlos III and the advent of the Enlightenment, but primarily of the conflicts of ideas and nations brought on by the French Revolution.

BIBLIOGRAPHICAL NOTE

THOSE who wish to investigate the history of Spain are fortunate in the bibliographical aids they have available. Foremost among these is the painstaking bibliography by B. Sánchez Alonso of sources and secondary studies of the history of Spain and its empire, now in its third edition: *Fuentes de la historia española e hispanoamericana* (3d ed., 3 vols.; Madrid, 1952). Since 1953 the Centro de Estudios Internacionales, Universidad de Barcelona, has been publishing the *Índice histórico español*, a quarterly which aims to give prompt critical notices of books and articles on Spanish history. Beginning with Volume LX (1954-55) the listing of current articles on history in the *American Historical Review* has a section on Spain and Portugal compiled by Professor C. J. Bishko. Bishko has conveniently commented on other sources of current bibliography of Spanish history in "The Iberian Background of Latin American History: Recent Progress and Continuing Problems," *Hispanic American Historical Review*, XXXVI (1956), 55-56. No bibliography can be counted on to be complete, but those that are available enable one to embark with ease on research in Spanish history.

I have also had reason to appreciate certain special bibliographical studies, in particular the following four:

Arturo Farinelli, *Viajes por España y Portugal desde la edad media hasta el siglo XX* (Madrid, 1920);

R. Foulché-Delbosc and L. Barrau-Dihigo, *Manuel de l'hispanisant* (2 vols.; New York, 1920-25), very useful for orienting oneself in Hispanic studies;

Eugenio Hartzenbusch [e Hiriart], *Apuntes para un catálogo de periódicos madrileños desde el año 1661 al 1870* (Madrid, 1894);

Paul Mérimée, *L'influence française en Espagne au XVIIIe siècle* (Paris, 1936);

Bibliographical Note

Since bibliographical data has been given in the first reference to each work cited in this study (and these references include almost all works that have been of use), little would be gained by listing them in full in a bibliography. The Bibliographical Index gives the names of authors and the titles of periodicals and other anonymous works cited in the text and indicates in what note full bibliographical information is given for each. After the first citation of a work, subsequent footnote references identify it only by the name of its author, unless more than one work by the author has *already* been cited.

In the eighteenth century, Spanish orthography had not yet developed its present hard and fast rules. I have attempted to follow the original spelling of personal names of contemporaries (whether authors or other persons) and of the titles of published works. Accent marks have been inserted in personal names according to present day usage, but in the case of titles I have tried to give only those accents used in the originals. (Most titles were printed in capitals, and fewer accents were shown than would be normal even according to eighteenth-century usage.) Errors will inevitably turn up, since I was not able to check back to many of the original works after I began writing. Furthermore, I have made no attempt to get back to the original spelling when my information came from a secondary work that had modernized the spelling.

The scope of this study is too broad for me to have attempted to see all the relevant primary material available, since everything written or published in Spain in the last third of the eighteenth century and still preserved could be grist for the mill. I have drawn on two sources of unpublished manuscripts. In Madrid I used the records of the Inquisición in the Archivo Histórico Nacional. Those that belong to the Consejo de la Inquisición are catalogued in A. Paz y Melia, *Papeles de Inquisición, catálogo y extractos*, 2d ed. by Ramón Paz (Madrid, 1947). Unfortunately this catalogue gives its own numbering to the cases it lists and not the *legajo* and number under which each case is filed in the Archivo Histórico Nacional. Only the Archivo has the key to correlate the number in Paz y Melia's catalogue with the Archivo reference. As a result, it is difficult from a citation of records of the Inquisición by a secondary study to identify the case in Paz y Melia.

I have used the following sets of records of the Inquisición (numbers 473 to 516 in Paz y Melia concern French Revolutionary papers and propaganda):

Archivo Histórico Nacional, Inquisición (cited in notes as "A.H.N., Inq.")		Paz y Melia catalogue Numero	A.H.N., Inq.		Paz y Melia Numero
Legajo	Numero		Leg.	Num.	
4429	1	490	4430	7	510
	2	484		8	479
	4	485		9	493
	5	487		10	494
	6	477		11	516
	8	512		12	495
	9	488		13	503
	12	504		14	501
	13	506		15	480
	14	473		16	507
	15	500		17	475
	17	497		20	499
	26	505		21	502
	27			22–31	476
	28			33	484
	29	486	4450	7	1328
	30	515	4460	7	166
	32			16	1039
	34	496	4463	6	1334
	35	508	4464	8	171
4430	1–4	481	4465	25	
	5	482		27	1033

Bibliographical Note

Archivo Histórico Nacional, Inquisición (cited in notes as "A.H.N., Inq.") Legajo	Numero	Paz y Melia catalogue Numero	A.H.N., Inq. Leg.	Num.	Paz y Melia Numero
4473	8	610	4484	10	1326
	12			12	
4474	4	446		13	1327
4481	15			27	380
4482	33	957	4493	1	552
4483	11	583	4514	10–11	548

and *legajo* 15, No. 2, *legajo* 190, Nos. 5, 11, 20-22, 25, 28, 29, 35, 39, from the Inquisición de Toledo not catalogued in Paz y Melia.

Records of the Inquisición that are important to my subject that I have not seen have been studied by Jean Sarrailh, *L'Espagne éclairée de la seconde moitié du XVIIIᵉ siècle* (Paris, 1954); Edith F. Helman, "Some Consequences of the Publication of the *Informe de ley agraria* by Jovellanos," *Estudios hispanicos: homenaje a Archer M. Huntington* (Wellesley, 1952), pp. 253-73; and Miguel de la Pinta Llorente, "El sentido de la cultura española en el siglo XVIII e intelectuales de la época," *Revista de estudios políticos*, No. 68 (Mar.-Apr. 1953), pp. 79-114.

In conjunction with the papers of the Inquisición I have used the history of that institution by Juan Antonio Llorente, *Historia crítica de la Inquisicion de España* (10 vols.; Madrid, 1822), which originally came out in French (4 vols.; Paris, 1818). Llorente was made secretary of the Inquisición de Corte (Madrid) in 1789 and remained associated with the Inquisición off and on until Napoleon abolished it in 1808. Joseph Bonaparte then gave him authority over the records of the Inquisición, and for five years Llorente was able to draw on them for his history. Most of the papers he used appear to have since been lost or destroyed. Since Llorente denounced the Inquisición, some historians have questioned his veracity, but in the parts of his history that deal with the period I have covered, I have found no case of obvious misrepresentation. Much that Llorente says is confirmed by other sources, notably the contemporary reports in the Paris *Moniteur* and the subsequent autobiography of Joaquín Lorenzo Villanueva, who was a court preacher and *calificador* of the Inquisición under Carlos IV (*Vida literaria* [2 vols.; London, 1825]). Villanueva was an enemy of the Inquisición and seems to have refreshed his memory by reading Llorente's history, but it is unlikely that he consciously repeated falsehoods from Llorente. Many of Llorente's and Villanueva's political opponents were alive when they wrote and would have jumped on any glaring untruths in their accounts.

The other collection of documents that I used was the Archives des Affaires étrangères, Paris. Its Correspondance diplomatique, Espagne (cited in footnotes as "A.A.E., Esp."), Vols. 634-36 (1792-93), provide the records of the official attempt to propagandize Spain; and I also consulted papers in other volumes of this series to which my attention had been called by secondary works. M. Geoffroy de Grandmaison, *L'ambassade française en Espagne pendant la Révolution (1789-1804)* (Paris, 1892), has made extensive use of the Archives des Affaires étrangères for the whole period of the Revolution.

More information could be gained by an investigation of the existing records of the various Spanish ministries and councils and of local archives, but I do not believe that research in these documents would have made me change more than details of the picture I have given.

For most of my story I relied on printed sources, making an attempt to cover as thoroughly as available time permitted the Spanish publications of the last two decades of the eighteenth century. I used the contemporary periodicals now in the Biblioteca Nacional, Madrid, and the Hemeroteca Municipal de Madrid (which is devoted to collecting all journals and newspapers ever published in Madrid). The *Gazeta de Madrid*, although largely given over to foreign news, furnished accounts of official functions and advertisements of contemporary publications. I examined it for the years 1789 to 1814 (beyond the end of this study). I tried to see the other important Spanish journals for the years 1780 to 1814 and the *Gazette nationale ou le Moniteur universel* of Paris from its beginning in November 1789 down to 1800. The *Moniteur* carried excellent reports on Spain, being free to print news that Spanish papers could not.

These periodicals and other sources furnished titles of books and pamphlets published in Spain in these decades. I searched for those that seemed of interest in the catalogues of the Biblioteca Nacional, the library of the Ateneo of Madrid, the library of the Academia de la Historia, the Biblioteca Municipal de Madrid, the Bibliothèque Nationale, Paris, and the Library of Congress, Washington.

Another source for many contemporary pieces was the "Colección documental del fraile" in the library of the Servicio Histórico Militar, Madrid. This collection consists of over one thousand bound volumes containing books, pamphlets, periodicals, and posters published from 1738 to 1824 and assembled at random by a Capucin monk, Fray Joaquín de Sevilla (1766-1830), into whose hands they came. A catalogue of this curious and totally disorganized mass of material has happily been published: Estado Mayor Central del Ejército, Servicio Histórico Militar, *Colección documental del fraile* (4 vols., Madrid, 1947-50). My footnotes indicate which sources are to be found in this collection, referring to it as "Fraile."

Finally, thanks to the permission and help of the officials of the Biblioteca Nacional, I was able to consult the uncatalogued pamphlets stored in its Sala de Varios. I went through the pamphlets in-quarto (the most common size—the Spanish quarto corresponds to the French octavo) published in the reign of Carlos IV, fifty-six bundles or *legajos*. Material found here has been identified in the footnotes by the word "Varios" followed by the *legajo* number.

For the period before 1780 and for the chapters on the economy of Spain my research has been less extensive, but I have endeavored to give an accurate and original picture, using the available secondary studies and the most important primary sources.

Bibliographical Note

The main sources for the information on the production and trade of Spain about 1785 given on maps II, III, and IV are the works of Bourgoing, Townsend, Sarrailh, Desdevises du Dezert, and Carrera Pujal (all described below), and Alexandre de Laborde, *Itinéraire descriptif de l'Espagne, et tableau élémentaire des différentes branches de l'administration et de l'industrie de ce royaume* (5 vols.; Paris, 1808). The highways shown on Map IV are largely based on Gonzalo Menéndez Pidal, *Los caminos en la historia de España* (Madrid, 1951).

* * *

Those who wish to read further on this period of Spanish history will find the following works of particular interest:

[Jean François Bourgoing], *Nouveau voyage en Espagne, ou tableau de l'état actuel de cette monarchie* (3 vols.; Paris, 1789), and Joseph Townsend, *A Journey Through Spain in the Years 1786 and 1787* (3 vols.; London, 1791), both study the society, economy, and political institutions of Spain as well as the natural and architectural features of interest to the average traveller. They provide readable descriptions of Spain on a par with the famous one of France on the eve of the Revolution by Arthur Young. Bourgoing brought his work up to date several times in the next fifteen years, and there is an English translation of it.

The most valuable accounts of the reign of Carlos IV are Manuel Godoy's memoirs, written in Paris in the 1830's as an *apologia* (*Memorias de don Manuel Godoy, Príncipe de la Paz, ó sea cuenta dada de su vida política* [6 vols.; Paris, 1839]), and Andrés Muriel, *Historia de Carlos IV* ("Memorial histórico español," Vols. xxix-xxxiv) (6 vols.; Madrid, 1893-94). Muriel was a contemporary of Godoy who had also gone into exile in France, in his case for having supported Joseph Bonaparte after 1808. He conceived his history largely as a refutation of Godoy's memoirs and a defense of the policies of the Conde de Aranda, some of whose official papers he appears to have possessed. His manuscript was not published until the end of the nineteenth century, but before then it was in the Real Academia de la Historia and was used by various historians.

Scholarly historical writing on the period began with Antonio Ferrer del Rio, *Historia del reinado de Carlos III en España* (4 vols.; Madrid, 1856). Although this is a frank defense of Carlos III and several extensive histories of that king have since appeared, I find Ferrer del Rio more readable and informative than the later historians of this reign.

Modesto Lafuente, *Historia general de España* (30 vols.; Madrid, 1840-67, and several later editions), contains to my mind the best history of Spain under Carlos IV. Among his sources Lafuente used official decrees, the memoirs of Godoy, and the then still unpublished history of Muriel.

Hermann Baumgarten, *Geschichte Spanien's zur Zeit der französischen Revolution* (Berlin, 1861), is the most thorough work on the years 1789-95. Baumgarten's major source was the dispatches of the Prussian minister to Spain, Sandoz-Rollin. Sandoz admired Floridablanca and disliked Godoy intensely, and Baumgarten adopted his prejudices somewhat uncritically, but otherwise the work is admirable.

The original third volume of Marcelino Menéndez Pelayo, *Historia de los heterodoxos españoles* (3 vols.; Madrid, 1880-81, reprinted in 8 vols.; Santander, 1947-48), included the first extensive study of the Spanish Enlightenment, blaming those who supported it for the later ills of Spain. Although this account was written with more verve than judgment and is now largely out of date, it deserves reading as a classic work of Spanish historiography by a young man who later became an outstanding student of Spanish letters.

A similar point of view is held by Luis Sánchez Agesta in *El pensamiento político del despotismo ilustrado* (Madrid, 1953), which contains good discussions of some of the major topics ventilated by enlightened Spaniards. Much of it is devoted to Feyjóo and Jovellanos, whom the author contrasts favorably with other partisans of enlightenment.

Bibliographical Note

A convincing reply to Menéndez Pelayo and his disciples is furnished by Jean Sarrailh, *L'Espagne éclairée* (see above, p. 448). Sarrailh studies in detail the ideas of enlightened Spaniards and concludes that they were a sincerely religious, patriotic, and idealistic élite, but that the forces they struggled against were too strong for them. The leading figure of his élite is Jovellanos, who, interestingly, is also viewed with approval by Menéndez Pelayo and Sánchez Agesta. Sarrailh gives an extensive bibliography.

Besides being a biography of the standard bearer of the Spanish Enlightenment, G. Delpy, *L'Espagne et l'esprit européen, l'oeuvre de Feijóo* (*1725-1760*) (Paris, 1936), provides a penetrating look at the intellectual atmosphere in Spain in the days before Carlos III.

Jefferson Rea Spell, *Rousseau in the Spanish World Before 1833* (Austin, 1938), deals with the influence of one author on thought in the Spanish empire. It is particularly well documented for Spain under Carlos III.

The most complete study of society and institutions is G. Desdevises du Dezert, *L'Espagne de l'Ancien Régime*, Vol. I, *La société*, Vol. II, *Les institutions*, Vol. III, *La richesse et la civilisation* (Paris, 1897-1904). It does not attempt to present a narrative history and offers difficult reading, but it is still unexcelled as a work of reference. Its volumes have good bibliographies. They were reprinted with some modifications in *Revue hispanique*, LXIV (1925), 225-656, LXX (1927), 1-556, LXXIII (1928), 1-488.

To Desdevises's volume on society must be added the recent authoritative and more readable study of Antonio Domínquez Ortiz, *La sociedad española en el siglo XVIII* (Madrid, 1955). Domínguez deals very well with the lesser cities and towns and the countryside of Castile and Aragon, but less adequately with the larger cities and the prosperous areas of northern and eastern Spain.

Further information on the agricultural situation is given by Joaquín Costa, *Colectivismo agrario en España* (Madrid, 1898), and Rudolf Leonhard, *Agrarpolitik und Agrarreform in Spanien unter Carl III.* (Munich, 1909). Both use the published reports of the intendants and the deliberations of the Consejo de Castilla and other bodies. Costa is concerned with the theory and practice of communal landholding in Spain throughout history and does not study the eighteenth century by itself. Leonhard covers the attempts of Carlos III's government to improve agriculture but does little more than paraphrase his sources.

The last three volumes of Jaime Carrera Pujal, *Historia de la economía española* (5 vols.; Barcelona, 1943-47), cover the eighteenth century. The work draws on many sources but often fails to organize clearly this wealth of material and to draw conclusions from it.

Earl J. Hamilton, *War and Prices in Spain, 1651-1800* (Cambridge, Mass., 1947), is a study of monetary policy, prices, and wages, but it is also informative on general economic conditions and policies. It should be supplemented by the articles by Hamilton and Pierre Vilar cited in the footnotes.

BIBLIOGRAPHICAL INDEX

Note: References are to first citations, which give full name of author, title, and publication data, and in some instances to later citations giving additional information. When footnotes cite a work only by the author's name and more than one work of the author is listed in this bibliography, an asterisk (*) indicates which work is intended (see p. 446). Works mentioned in the footnotes that are not part of this bibliography are listed in the general Index (see p. 465).

455

Bibliographical Index

456

Bibliographical Index

Bibliographical Index

Bibliographical Index

López de la Fuente, *Sermon*, 307 n.
41

Mably, *Elementos de moral*, 363
———, *Entretenimientos de Phocion*,
72 n. 105
Macanaz, *Defensa critica de la Inquisicion*, 192 n. 131
Machault, *Carta pastoral*, 304 n. 32
[Marchena], *A la nacion española*,
275 n. 19
———, *In-promptu*, 275 n. 17
———, *Obras literarias*, 274 n. 14
Marín, *La sabiduria del siglo convencida de necedad*, 218 n. 54
Marín [y Mendoza], *Historia del derecho natural y de gentes*, 173 n.
73
Marqués y Espejo, *Diccionario Feyjoniano*, 40 n. 9
Masson, *Le département des affaires étrangères pendant la Révolution*,
272 n. 10
Masson de Morvilliers, "Espagne," 220
n. 59
Mathiez, *La Révolution française*, 278
n. 26
Maupertuis, *Ensayo de filosofía moral*,
69 n. 98
Meléndez Valdés, "Cartas inéditas a Jovellanos," 27 n. 38
———, "Epístola[s] al Príncipe de la Paz," 363 n. 55
Memorial literario, 53 n. 44
[Menéndez de Luarca], *El reino de Dios y su justicia*, 309 n. 52
Menéndez Pelayo, *El Abate Marchena*,
274 n. 13
———, *Historia de la ideas estéticas*,
80 n. 138
*———, *Historia de los heterodoxos españoles*, 14 n. 3, 332 n. 61, 364
n. 64, 452
Menéndez Pidal, *Los caminos en la historia de España*, 131 n. 40, 451
Merimée, E., "Études sur Meléndez Valdés," 167 n. 50
Merimée, P., *L'influence française en Espagne au XVIIIe siècle*, 445
Mier, *Memorias*, 172 n. 71
Miguélez, M. F. *See* [Fraile y] Miguélez

Milhaud and Soubrany, *Proclamacion*,
290 n. 70
Moldenhauer, "Voltaire und die spanische Bühne," 67 n. 91
Moniteur. See *Gazette nationale*
Montengón, *Eusebio*, 65 n. 84
Morales, *Discurso sobre la educacion*,
55 n. 50
Moreau de Jonnès, *Statistique de l'Espagne*, 30 n. 48
Morel-Fatio, *Études sur l'Espagne*, 74
n. 112
———, "José Marchena," 273 n. 12
———, "Andrés María de Guzmán,"
279 n. 28
———, *La satire de Jovellanos*, 73 n.
109
Moret y Prendergast, *El Conde de Aranda*, 29 n. 46
Mousset, *Un témoin ignoré de la Révolution, Fernán Núñez*, 234 n. 91
Mugica, "Un caso curioso de viruelas,"
44 n. 22
Muiñoz Sáenz, "La Orden Agustiniana en la Guerra de la Independencia,"
171 n. 64
Muriel, *Historia de Carlos IV*, 239 n.
1, 270 n. 2, 451-52

Narganes de Posada, *Tres cartas sobre la instruccion publica*, 170 n. 62
Nielsen, *The History of the Papacy*,
18 n. 11
Nocedal, "Discurso preliminar," *Obras de Jovellanos*, 331 n. 59
Nonnotte, *Defensa de la religion*, 213
n. 35
———, *Los errores de Voltaire*, 213
Normante y Carcavilla, *Discurso sobre los conocimientos economico-politicos*, 57 n. 56
———, *Espiritu del señor Melon*, 51
n. 41
Novísima recopilacion de las leyes de España (*Nov. rec.*), 19 n. 14
Núñez de Arenas, "Don Vicente María Santiváñez," 281 n. 38

Observaciones sobre las Cortes de España, 242 n. 10
Ocampo, *Cronica general de España*,
339 n. 7

460

Bibliographical Index

Bibliographical Index

INDEX

465

Index

Index

Index

Index

Declaration of the rights of man and the citizen (French), known in Spain, 243, 245, 246, 251, 288

Defoe, Daniel: *Robinson Crusoe*, 77, 205

Deforgues, François, 285, 286

Delbrel, Pierre, 293-94

Denina, Carlo, 223, 224

Derecho natural y de gentes, 173-80, 345, 371-73, 440

Descartes, René: details, 4, 5; cited, 38, 45, 70, 82, 164, 165, 170, 186, 225-26, 350, 352, 355, 362; cited unfavorably, 215-16, 224; in work of Piquer, 41; influence in Spain, 169; biography of published in Spain, 190

Desclot, Bernardo, 339

Despoblados, 87, 115

"Diálogos del A.B.C.," 330, 332

Diario curioso, erudito, economico y comercial, 193

Diario curioso, histórico, erudito (Barcelona), 194

Diario de Barcelona, 303, 305, 349, 350, 351

Diario de Madrid, 44-45, 193, 260, 262, 349

Diario Pinciano (Valladolid), 194

Diderot, Denis: edits *Encyclopédie*, 5; reception in Spain, 72, 78, 83, 366; and Olavide, 74; and Aranda, 75; mentioned, 66, 437; *Le fils naturel*, 263

Diego Josef de Cádiz, Fray, 160-61, 309-10

Díez, Fray Antonio, 309

Diputados del común, 113

Directory (French), 360, 399, 428

Discurso que comprehende . . . las pruebas naturales . . . de Dios, 214

Discursos mercuriales, 63

Dominican order, 16, 19, 172, 203, 414

Duende de Madrid, El, 188, 263

Dugommier, Jacques Coquille-, 287, 290

Durtubise (French agent in Madrid), 318-19, 320

Ebro valley, 132, 133

Echo des Pyrénées, 285, 286

Écija, 414

Economics, interest in, 48-57, 84-85, 358-59

Eguia, P.: *Los Jesuitas y el Motín de Esquilache*, 22n

Elche, 95

Émigrés, 298-99, 300-2, 399

Encyclopédie, 5, 43, 72, 161

Encyclopédie méthodique: reception in Spain, 43, 161, 220-22; translation of, 222, 349; cited, 353, 401; mentioned, 201, 227, 259, 436

"Encyclopedistas," 221, 314

Enfiteusis, 99-100

England, cited as example of govt., 179, 181, 182

English language, knowledge of in Spain, 77

English merchants in Spain, 140, 149, 257

Enlightened despotism in Spain, 235, 436, 439, 444

Enlightenment, 5, 6, 36. *See also Filosofía; Luces*

Enrique IV, 337

Enríquez del Castillo, Diego: *Crónica del rey D. Enrique IV*, 339n

Ensenada, Marqués de la, 192n

Entail, 31, 378, 392. *See also Manos muertas, Mayorazgos*

Equivalente, 129

España triunfante en el actual siglo filosófico, 218

Espiga, Josef, 424, 426, 430

Espigadera, La, 259, 340

Espiritu de los mejores diarios literatos que se publican en Europa: details, 45, 190-91; on economics, 56; on Filangieri, 61; on torture, 62; cites Rousseau, 64; on Voltaire, 69; on *philosophes*, 83; cites Raynal, 71-72; *derecho natural* in, 181; subscribers, 195-98; publication stopped, 262; mentioned, 163, 258

Esprit, De l'. *See* Helvétius

Esquilache, Marqués de. *See* Squillace

"Esquilache, Mutiny of," 21

Estates General (French), 346

Estudios de gramática, 119

Estudios de San Isidro, Reales, 163-64, 173, 176, 198, 273, 326, 426

Exequatur, 19, 401

471

Index

Index

Index

Index

Index

Index

Index

Index

Index

Index

Index